Law and Philosophy Library

Volume 110

The Law and Philosophy Library, which has been in existence since 1985, aims to publish cutting edge works in the philosophy of law, and has a special history of publishing books that focus on legal reasoning and argumentation, including those that may involve somewhat formal methodologies. The series has published numerous important books on law and logic, law and artificial intelligence, law and language, and law and rhetoric. While continuing to stress these areas, the series has more recently expanded to include books on the intersection between law and the Continental philosophical tradition, consistent with the traditional openness of the series to books in the Continental jurisprudential tradition. The series is proud of the geographic diversity of its authors, and many have come from Latin America, Spain, Italy, the Netherlands, Germany, and Eastern Europe, as well, more obviously for an English-language series, from the United Kingdom, the United States, Australia, and Canada.

More information about this series at http://www.springer.com/series/6210

Maksymilian Del Mar • William Twining
Editors

Legal Fictions in Theory and Practice

Springer

Editors
Maksymilian Del Mar
Department of Law
Queen Mary University of London
London
United Kingdom

William Twining
Faculty of Laws
University College London
London
United Kingdom

ISSN 1572-4395 ISSN 2215-0315 (electronic)
ISBN 978-3-319-09231-7 ISBN 978-3-319-09232-4 (eBook)
DOI 10.1007/978-3-319-09232-4
Springer Cham Heidelberg New York Dordrecht London

Library of Congress Control Number: 2014951719

Printed on acid-free paper

Springer is part of Springer Science+Business Media (www.springer.com)

Preface

It is legendary that Karl Llewellyn and Soia Mentschikoff fell in love over a shared passion for the beauty of the letter of credit. Whether this legend is fact or fiction or somewhere in-between is unclear. But it is clear that both were fascinated by the crafts and technology of law and emphasised the importance of imagination and invention in legal practice (Twining 2012, pp. 197–199, 2002, pp. 167–171).

This book explores in depth the history, theory and debates surrounding fiction(s) in law. Many writers treat legal fictions of all kinds as artefacts, a species of legal invention. Typically, such fictions have been responses to practical problems about jurisdiction or mitigating the results of formal rules or bringing about more or less covert legal change. However, some abstract or 'theoretical fictions', such as the social contract, the veil of ignorance or the mantra that judges 'apply law, but do not make it' seem to be of a different kind. So too do mythical characters such as 'The Bad Man', Hercules, 'the reasonable man', or '*homo juridicus*'. These are not technical solutions to practical problems, but rather devices for resolving intellectual puzzles. These feature in this book, but the main emphasis is on technical fictions. Do all of these give rise to different kinds of questions or do they belong to a single topic of 'fictions in law'?

When I was a student in the 1950s one encountered talk of fictions in English legal history (for example, the action for ejectment), in Jurisprudence and Company Law (mainly in relation to legal personality) and in Roman Law. However, neither the books nor our teachers perceived them to be closely linked. As an undergraduate I wrote an essay on "Legal Personality" that concluded that English law did not have a theory of legal persons and did not need one. Each example of an extension of 'legal subject' needed to be explained in practical terms on a case by case basis. Similarly, exotic entities treated as subjects of rights and duties, such as Hindu idols, Caligula's horse, artefacts, funds, ancestors, ghosts and unborn children needed to be explained by the context, beliefs and perceived problems of their inventors.[1] My paper made no links to Maine; it dismissed Continental theorising as 'metaphysical'. Indeed, no hint of problems of epistemology or ontology sullied

[1] See further William Ewald's incisive analysis of the case of the rats of Autun (Ewald 1995).

its pages—I did not even know what the words meant. The so-called 'fiction theory' explained nothing.[2]

By 1960 interest in historical jurisprudence had waned and, under the influence of Hart, analytical jurisprudence was becoming more abstract, though no more tolerant of metaphysics. For example, the index to Wolfgang Friedman's excellent *Legal Theory* (4th edition, 1960) has a one page reference to 'Fictions in evolution' and under a separate heading 'Fiction Theory, see Corporate personality.' Other student books of the time either had similar perfunctory entries or else no entry at all (e.g. Lloyd (1959), Dias (1964) and Wortley (1967)). Interest in Bentham's theory of real and fictitious entities[3] and feminist writings about personality developed later (e.g. Schofield (2006), Naffine (1990) (2002)). Thus, at least in England, for about 50 years there was a fallow period of scholarly and theoretical treatment of 'fictions', except in a few specialist enclaves. It was not recognized as a single topic. Later, when I studied Bentham's frenetic attack on fictions in English Law (wilful falsehoods), this seemed to be difficult to reconcile with his epistemology, which treats 'fictitious entities' as useful, indeed necessary, constructed tools for grasping the real world. Either he was inconsistent or else he conceived the relevant passages as being concerned with two sets of only very loosely related questions—the first with pragmatic political concerns about the sinister interests and mystifications of the legal profession (Hart 1973), the latter with how we describe, explain and improve the world (see further Quinn, Chap. 4 below, pp. 67–68).

Accordingly, about 5 years ago I was surprised when Maks Del Mar asked my advice about organizing a panel on "Legal Fictions" at the World Congress of Legal and Social Philosophy in Frankfurt in 2011. I suggested that the label was unfashionable and dealt with disparate issues that should not be conflated. However, when I revisited some of the jurisprudential literature and learned more about Vaihinger and the early Kelsen, I began to see that these seemingly disparate concerns were closely related, but in quite complex ways. Moreover, this was a good time to revive interest in the area: some post-modernists had challenged the distinction between epistemology and ontology, feminists had challenged male-dominated assumptions about personhood, technical legal fictions were still very much alive (what else are the imaginative constructions of clever tax advisers?) and 'globalisation' had stimulated a wide range of new issues: e.g. do multi-national corporations exist? (Dine 2005); do MNCs have human rights? (Baxi 2006); are 'indigenous peoples' to be treated as legal persons or as politically fashioned constructs? (Kingsbury 1998);

[2] Lively debates in the United States e.g. Dewey (1926), Fuller (1930), Berle and Means (1932) appear to have faded earlier, perhaps because of Realist scepticism of abstract concepts and because it was recognized that corporate power had shifted from shareholders to managers (Twining 2009, Chap 15). Roscoe Pound's *Jurisprudence* (1959) Vol. III, Chap. 17 has a lengthy discussion of fictions, but this was largely a synthesis of his earlier work.

[3] Philip Schofield (Schofield 2006, p. 2, n 14) points out that 'The use of the phrase "theory of fictions" to refer to Bentham's thinking on ontology, logic, language and grammar is potentially confusing. Bentham did very occasionally use the term "fiction" to represent what he meant by the term "fictitious entity", but the two terms normally referred to two distinct, but related ideas.' On fictitious entities see id. Chap. 1 and Hart (1982), Chaps. 1 and 2.

and are all transnational legal actors to be treated as persons in a world of legal pluralism? (Alston 2005).

So Maks went ahead. He proved to be right. He did the work, I merely stirred. This book is the result. It brings together a wealth of contributions from legal scholars, legal theorists and historians from several countries. There is a wealth of concrete examples, some highly original analysis, cross-references that link seemingly disparate topics, and some differences in the interpretation of the ideas of 'fiction', 'truth' and 'reality'. However, I suggest that many aspects of the area are less controversial today than they were 50 years ago. Indeed, it is not clear to what extent there is a broad consensus or real disagreements among the contributors and more generally.[4] For example, few common lawyers subscribe to the view that 'judges apply law, but do not make it'. Nearly all recognize that upper courts in the common law tradition are agents of at least interstitial legal change, but in ways that differ from legislation and vary by time and place and situation. Similarly, I know of no jurist who accepts Bentham's characterisation of common law fictions as 'wicked falsehoods'—for who was deceived? Fictions constructed by judges, litigants and their advisers have usually been devices to solve practical problems and surmount obstacles. Each needs to interpreted and explained in its specific context. Few scholars, and none of the contributors, believe that fictions are a thing of the past, though some argue that employing fictions is usually a crude and unnecessary way of solving particular kinds of problem. Del Mar (Chap. 11 below) argues strongly that some kinds of fictions still have a positive role to play in legal change. The cat and mouse battles between tax collectors, tax avoiders and evaders (and their advisers) show that creating ingenious legal devices is still lucrative. Most agree that it is sometimes hard to differentiate fictions, presumptions, metaphors, models, and analogies; and that there is no avoiding fundamental philosophical issues about fact, fiction, truth and knowledge. On a more controversial note, I suggest that most contributors are committed to a constructivist view of both legal fictions as technical devices and of concepts as thinking tools. But some contributors and readers may disagree.

William Twining

References

Alston, Philip, ed. 2005. *Non-state actors and human rights*. Oxford: Oxford University Press.
Baxi, Upendra. 2006. *The future of human rights*. 2nd ed. Delhi: Oxford University Press.
Berle, A. A., and G. Means. 1932. *The modern corporation and private property*. New York: MacMillan.
Dewey, John. 1926. 'The historic background of corporate legal personality' 35. *Yale L Jo*. 655
Dine, Janet. 2005. *Companies, international trade and human rights*. New York: Cambridge University Press.

[4] See Del Mar, Introduction, below.

Ewald, William. 1995. Comparative jurisprudence I: What was it like to try a rat? 143 *U. Pennsylvania L. Rev.* 1889.
Friedmann, Wolfgang. 1960. *Legal theory*. 4th ed. London: Stevens
Gray, John Chipman. 1921. *The nature and sources of law*. 2nd ed. New York: Macmillan.
Hart, H. L. A. 1982. "The demystification of the law" in *Essays on Bentham*. Oxford: Oxford University Press.
Kingsbury, Benedict. 1998. "Indigenous peoples in international law: A constructivist approach to the Asian controversy", 92 *Am. Jo. Int.L.* 414.
Lloyd, Dennis. 1959. *Introduction to jurisprudence*. 1st ed. London: Sweet and Maxwell.
Naffine, Ngaire. 1990. *Law and the sexes*. London: Allen and Unwin
Naffine, Ngaire. ed. 2002. *Gender and justice*. Aldershot: Ashgate.
Paton, George W. 1964. *A textbook of jurisprudence*. 3rd ed. with David Derham. Oxford: Oxford University Press.
Pound, Roscoe. 1959. *Jurisprudence*. 5 vols. St Paul: West.
Salmond, Sir John W. 1966. *Jurisprudence*. 12th edn by P.J. Fitzgerald. London: Sweet and Maxwell.
Schofield, Philip. 2006. *Utility and democracy: The political thought of Jeremy Bentham*. Oxford: Oxford University Press.
Twining, William. 2002. *The great juristic bazaar: Jurists' texts and lawyers' stories*. Aldershot: Ashgate.
Twining, William. 2009. *General jurisprudence*. Cambridge: Cambridge University Press, Ch 15 (accessible at www.cambridge.org/twining).
Twining, William. 2012. *Karl Llewellyn and the Realist Movement*. 2nd edn; ist edn, 1973. New York: Cambridge University Press.
Wortley, Benjamin A. 1967. *Jurisprudence*. Manchester: Manchester University Press

Introducing Fictions: Examples, Functions, Definitions and Evaluations

Maksymilian Del Mar[1]

Faced with the obstinacy of reality, litigants and judges have sometimes, if not often, sought refuge in legal fictions. The motivation for seeking refuge has been multifarious, e.g. from the perspective of a litigant, seeking a remedy despite not meeting the requirements of the relevant form of action or rule, or minimising costs by attempting to bring his or her claim via a cheaper, more convenient route—or, from the perspective of the judge, introducing a tentative change in the law without dismantling pre-existing rules and principles, or trying to do justice to a claimant who, for want of better (or any) evidence, simply could not prove certain operative facts.

It is not only motivations that are multifarious: multiple, too, are the examples offered of so-called paradigmatic or typical fictions, and there as many definitions of fictions as there are apparent functions of them (i.e. jobs they perform or enable) and alleged benefits and disbenefits they bring. Add to this the broader epistemological and ontological context in which discussion of fictions inevitably must occur,[2] and also the issue of the place of fictions in legal history, and the entire experience of thinking about fictions becomes a seriously vertiginous business.

The epistemological and ontological context referred to above requires some unpacking. Any reader pursuing the topic will quickly discern that there is an oscillation in the literature between those who think legal fictions are an illusory category because there is no sense in which law makes claims on what is real (instead, it simply regulates conduct), and those who see legal fictions everywhere, claiming that law is awash with artificial mental constructions that contradict reality (treating

[1] Precious thanks go to David Foster for his help with the preparation of the text of this volume, and to Andrew Bell for his assistance with the translation in Chap. 1. I would like to add personal warm thanks to William Twining, whose support and enthusiasm for this project from the beginning has seen it through and made it incomparably better than it would have been. It should be noted that a smaller version of this project had an earlier life as a workshop at the IVR (International Association of Legal and Social Philosophy) Congress in Frankfurt in the summer of 2011, which resulted in four of the chapters published being published in earlier versions in the *International Journal of Law in Context* (see Nr. 4 of Volume 9, December 2013). The chapters in question are by Del Mar, Gordon, Petroski and Quinn.

[2] This is not to say that it must occur under those terms, or indeed that it must accept any distinction between ontology and epistemology.

corporations as if they were persons, kings as if they had two bodies, and other such marvels). Clearly, whether one sees fictions everywhere or nowhere is going to depend on certain intuitions (or, naturally, well worked out theories) of what we know (and how we can know it) and what exists. Part and parcel of that is going to be an attitude to language, including the status of specialised languages such as that of law, e.g. one will need to ruminate over the extent to which, if at all, legal language is to be held up to the standards (or, better, the rough ground) of ordinary discourse.

An important early decision anyone thinking about legal fictions has to make is to consider whether one is primarily interested in fictions in legal practice or fictions in legal theory. Is one going to analyse the construction of explanatory devices (possibly with normative purposes) by legal theorists seeking to understand (and, again, possibly, on normative grounds, seeking to recommend a certain understanding of) the nature (or history) of law and legal reasoning? Or is one going to focus on the use of fictions (whether flagged in that way or not) by—and here too there are decisions to make—actors within the world of legal practice: by litigators, lawyers, and/ or judges?[3] This decision as to the object of one's inquiry connects up with the above-mentioned epistemological and ontological context: for example, one can see fictions everywhere in theory, but nowhere in practice, based on different criteria one attaches to what is being claimed (or not) in one or the other domain.

This volume tackles these and other problems head on. Its focus is on legal fictions in practice, though without entirely neglecting the fictions of legal theory. Chapters were commissioned from different traditions of inquiry—though with particular focus on the major players in this field: William Blackstone, Hans Vaihinger, Jeremy Bentham, Sir Henry Maine, Hans Kelsen and Lon Fuller—as well as from a variety of different traditions of practice, including from different times and places: covering, for example, the early and contemporary common law, Roman law, Rabbinic Law, as well as fictions in such areas of law as intellectual property law, tort law, land law, criminal law and class action procedure. Of course, even this depth and breadth is inevitably very selective: many areas of practice of great relevance to legal fictions are only discussed incidentally (e.g. tax law),[4] as are many traditions of practice (e.g. Islamic law, to mention but one example). Nevertheless, it is hoped that sufficient resources are offered for future excursions into this topic in those other areas.

Particular care has been taken here to bring together both legal theorists and legal historians. This is not only because dialogue between those two disciplines is much needed—but also, and indeed primarily, because the topic of legal fictions necessitates it. Any argument about fictions—whether that is at the level of definition or evaluation—must, surely, take into account their role in the practice of law over time.[5] As is well known but too easily forgotten, legal fictions were a hot topic

[3] No doubt one can complicate this picture further and broaden out to a greater range of actors, e.g. tax consultants.

[4] But see Prebble 2011.

[5] This is in addition to anything one might learn from a comparatively historical exercise, comparing instances of reliance on legal fictions in different times and places.

in the days when historical jurisprudence was in vogue: one read Blackstone and Maine and mused over the role of fictions in the development of law, considering, for instance, whether they are best thought of as temporary scaffolding, to be discarded once their modest (but necessary) function has expired, or as a more permanent feature of the legal phantasmagoria. In part, then, returning to legal fictions as this collection has done is a reminder of that much-too neglected meeting place of theory and history.[6]

This introduction goes on to provide a glimpse into the riches of the subsequent chapters in the following way: the first part offers a smattering of examples of fictions that appear in the collection; second, some of the functions (or jobs) that fictions are said by the contributors to play are highlighted; third, the definitions of fictions offered or relied on by our contributors are mentioned; fourth, a flavour is provided of the debates in this collection over the advantages and disadvantages—the good, the bad and the ugly—of fictions; and fifth, some further themes and questions for future work are identified. The hope is that this approach is more conducive as an introduction to the volume than the usual parade of chapter summaries.

I. Examples of Legal Fictions

Before one can proceed to offer and evaluate opinions about the utility, or otherwise, of fictions, one needs to get a sense of the examples associated with the term. As noted above, the focus of this collection is on fictions in practice, and thus the examples given below focus on these. Fictions of legal theory are returned to briefly in the fifth part of this introduction, as devices deserving of greater attention than has hitherto been devoted to them. When they are mentioned in what follows, it is as but contrasts or comparisons to fictions in practice. It is important to underscore, though, that the distinction between fictions of theory and fictions of practice is an important one, and to some a fundamental one: for example, Kelsen argues that Vaihinger fails to make this distinction, and as a result, classifies as fictions (those in practice) that are not fictions at all, while not spending enough time on those that are genuine fictions (i.e. the fictions of legal theory).[7]

Putting aside, then, the issue of whether they ought to be thought of as fictions at all, these are the examples of legal fictions in practice that appear in the collection:

- A number of contributors in this collection use the example of the legal person, but there is also disagreement about classifying this as a fiction.[8] The chapter in

[6] See also Del Mar and Lobban 2014.

[7] See Chap. 1, and see also the chapters by Kletzer, Samuel and Gama.

[8] Kelsen refers to the fiction of the 'legal subject' as a fiction of legal theory, saying of it (and of the other example he gives: 'subjective right') that 'These are fictions of the attempt to know the law, fictions of the intellectual mastery of the legal order': see Kelsen, Chap. 1 below, p. 5. Kelsen does not elaborate on what he means by 'legal subject', so we are left to ponder whether it is the same as 'legal person' for our contributors. This raises the broader issue of how to determine whether

which this fiction is perhaps most prominent is Lind's, where both the alleged fiction of the corporation as a person, and that of the 'personality of the ship', receive extensive discussion. Schauer is an example of a contributor here who expresses doubt as to whether the corporation-as-person is fictional, arguing that 'at least for some purposes' it is not because 'corporation' is a term constituted by law—unlike, for instance, 'Minorca' which is not so constituted (see Schauer, Chap. 6, below, p. 123, n. 17).

- It is useful to mention examples offered by Vaihinger, which are in turn criticised by Kelsen as not being fictions at all. Thus, for example, Vaihinger offers as an example Article 347 of the *German Commercial Code* 'where it is stipulated that a good which is not in time returned to the sender has to be treated as if it had been approved and accepted by the receiver'. According to Kelsen (see Chap. 1 below, p. 9), there is nothing fictional here, for what is being done by this article is the creation of a norm of action where 'neither actuality nor anything else is intended to be comprehended'. Similarly, the example of a rule thanks to which the offspring of an adulterous wife is treated as the child of the husband is, says Kelsen, not a 'claim that under certain conditions the husband is the father … the law does not assume a matter of fact … Rather it only regulates for certain reasons and to certain ends, that under certain circumstances the husband has the same duties and rights in relation to a child which was conceived by his wife in an adulterous relation and that this child has the same duties and rights in relation to this husband as they exist between the husband and his own children which were conceived in wedlock' (Kelsen, Chap. 1 below, pp. 10–11).
- Bentham, in turn, categorises fictions into the following categories: first, 'legal/ moral fictitious entities', such as obligation and power; second, procedural or linguistic expedients used by courts, e.g. jurisdictional devices such as those treating foreigners as if they were Roman citizens under Roman law; and third, 'fallacies' or theoretical fictions, e.g. assertions that judges do not make law. For our purposes, the second is the category of most interest.[9]
- Continuing from the example given above, many contributors in this volume identify jurisdictional fictions. An oft-mentioned case is that of *Mostyn v Fabrigas* (1773) in which Lord Mansfield, 'recognising that denying jurisdiction here would leave someone who was plainly wronged without a legal remedy, concluded that Minorca was part of London for purposes of this action' (Schauer, Chap. 6 below, p. 122). As Schauer adds, 'That conclusion was plainly false and equally produced a just result', and Schauer takes this to be 'a paradigmatic example of using a fiction to achieve what might in earlier days have been done through the vehicle of equity' (Ibid). An analogous example is that of the Bill

something is a fiction of practice as distinct from a fiction of theory: it seems that for Kelsen, the nub of the distinction lies in who is using the term, for this will determine whether they can be said to be making a claim which might contravene reality (so a theorist/ scientist using the term might be said to be employing a fiction, whereas a judge would not). For further discussion, see Kletzer, Schauer and Samuel in this volume.

[9] For a detailed discussion of Bentham on these fictions, see Quinn in this volume. For the jurisdictional fiction in Roman law, see Ando in this volume.

of Middlesex and the latitat procedure (which was premised on fictitious arrest) used by the King's Bench (very successfully, its business increasing ten-fold over the period 1560–1640) to acquire jurisdiction (for a discussion, see Lobban's chapter).[10]

- Lind (see Chap. 5 below, pp. 104–5) offers two examples of what he calls 'falsification fictions' (which, as we will see below, he is not fond of): first, the fiction of the contract ideal, which is 'premised on agreements with mutuality of benefits and burdens, entered into voluntarily and at arm's length, by rational agents with knowledge and understanding of the commitments they are making' (this being something that 'clashes with everyday social experience'), and second, *terra nullius*. These fictions are returned to below.
- Two further examples from Schauer's chapter are as follows: first, from American laws of inheritance, where two people own property jointly, and one of them kills the other in order to secure full ownership, several courts have proceeded as if the killer died before the victim. As Schauer says, 'in almost every situation this conclusion will be patently false', and he classifies this as a 'false statement of fact' (see Schauer, Chap. 6 below, p. 122); second, and a very recent example, comes from *R (on the application of Robinson) v Torridge District Council* (2006), where 'in order to allow R his relief the court concluded that the blockage caused by the bridge was to be treated as having 'choked' the watercourse, even though it plainly had not done so according to any of the definitions of what it is to choke a watercourse' (see Schauer, below, 17).[11]
- Examples that one often finds in the literature on fictions often come from Fuller amongst those being: constructive notice, constructive fraud, vicarious liability, the doctrine that children lured by attractive nuisances had been invited onto the land, and implied conditions in contract as resting on agreement of the parties—and these are indeed mentioned by some contributors here (see, e.g. Schauer and Lobban).[12] On the whole, though, these are not leading examples in this volume.
- An interesting category of examples are classified under the term 'metaphysical fictions' by Lobban, where, Lobban explains, 'courts treated something which

[10] Jurisdictional fictions receive a strange twist in Gordon's chapter, where a judge employs the re-narration of the facts of the case before him in order to deny the jurisdiction that he would otherwise have acquired. The Judge did so by saying that 'the jurisdictional objection was filed first, and the entry of appearance was merely a motion for an extension of time' (whereas it was in fact the other way round): see Gordon, Chap. 18 below, p. 387). As far as I can tell, this is the only instance of a re-narration of the present facts in this volume, and one in which no generalisation (of a possible rule for future cases) is even attempted—it is a particular way to solve a particular problem.

[11] There may be an interesting distinction between these two examples: the first has developed, or is clearly developing, into a rule (or an exception to the rule), and can confidently be generalised; the second, reads more like a one-off decision, though with the (perhaps in this case, questionable) potential that other courts will see fit to extend the meaning of 'watercourse' by analogy with the way it is extended in that case. This distinction, if one accepts it, shows the importance of looking at the use of fictions over time, and not at one isolated instance (though, of course, in some cases, there may only be one use, not picked up on by future courts).

[12] Lobban adds the 'implied warranty of authority', an example provided by Pollock: see Lobban, Chap. 10 below, p. 218.

had happened at one time as having occurred at another, or where something which no longer appeared to exist was deemed to have a continued existence' (Lobban, Chap. 10 below, p. 200). Lobban's examples here come mainly from a list offered by Dodderidge J in 1625: 'abeyance, relation, representation, remitter, and presumption' (Lobban, Chap. 10 below, p. 204). For example, the treatment of a husband and wife as one person is an example of the metaphysical fiction of 'representation'. To give one more: 'The doctrine of remitter allowed a person who had both an ancient and a more recent title to property, but who had entered by the recent title which turned out defective, to be taken to hold it by virtue of the older and surer right' (Lobban, Chap. 10 below, p. 205).

- A fiction that re-appears several times in this volume, and that receives extensive attention in the chapter by Sparkes, is that of the action of ejectment (see also Lobban). Indeed, Sparkes calls this 'the ultimate legal fiction in the early nineteenth century' (Sparkes, Chap. 13 below, p. 275). What is particularly impressive about Sparkes' analysis is the attention he pays to the life-span of this fiction—showing how 'an action designed to secure the recovery of a leasehold term, *ejectione firmae*, was modified by a series of procedural innovations so as to become the primary means of recovering freehold land' (ibid)—an approach returned to below. Briefly, this is an example of a fiction because, at a certain point, the action comes to rest on a fictitious lease by a real claimant to a fictitious nominal plaintiff. In the declaration, it is claimed that the plaintiff enters onto the lands in question, and is 'therefore possessed', until another fictitious person, known as the 'casual ejector', enters 'with forces and arms' and ejects him. This may also serve as an example where introducing one fiction leads one to create others to hold it up.
- Turning from historical to contemporary examples in the common law, a number of contributors discuss the employment of fictions in tort law, as in the series of cases (beginning with *Fairchild v Glenhaven Funeral Services* (2002) and most recently arising in The 'Trigger' Litigation (2012)) dealing with negligence claims arising from asbestos exposure (see Del Mar and Lee in this volume).[13] The fiction here arises out of the unavailability, or perhaps better indeterminacy, of scientific evidence, with the result that one cannot choose between a number of possible hypotheses as to who caused the harm in question. In such circumstances, the court suspends the usual 'but for' test of causation, and instead proceeds on the basis as if the defendant caused the harm (potentially introducing a new test, requiring only that the defendant 'materially contribute to the risk of the disease'). Both Del Mar and Lee take it to be important to analyse and evaluate the use of this fiction over time.
- Fictions in Roman law have already been mentioned above, and they appear in a number of chapters, though they receive extensive and focused analysis in Ando's chapter. Ando says fictions are 'ubiquitous' in Roman law, and given

[13] Lee also discusses the relevance of counter-factual scenarios to liability in the tort of self-imprisonment, the intuition being that there is something fictive about not considering or ignoring the fact that the claimant in these cases would have been imprisoned anyway.

their importance, here are five examples from his chapter (see Ando, Chap. 14 below, pp. 297–8):

- *Actio Serviana*: a purchaser or would-be possessor of the goods of a deceased had no action in statute law against those who held the decedent's property or owed the decedent money, and so was allowed by the Praetor to sue as if he were heir to the property in question;
- *Actio Rutiliana*: such a purchaser or possessor might be allowed to sue in the name of the decedent for recovery of goods or payment of debts, but the defendants would be condemned in the name of the purchaser, and so upon victory the goods or debt would be delivered to him;
- *Actio Publiciana*: a person who had acquired possession lawfully but not yet completed the time period for usucapion could not, upon losing possession, sue for the item in statute law, and so a Praetor allowed such persons to employ the fiction that they had in fact completed the period of usucapion and might sue as owners;
- Citizenship could be fictively attributed to an alien, thereby bringing the alien's claim with jurisdiction of the court, 'provided that it is just that the action in question be extended to an alien' (here Ando is quoting Gaius); and
- If one's opponent in a lawsuit had suffered a penalty entailing a diminishment in legal rank and concomitant inability to appear in a Roman court, Praetorian law permitted the fiction that the diminution of status had not occurred.

- In Rabbinic law, analysed in Moscovitz's chapter, examples of fictions included: treating, for the purposes of determining whether a liquid could be used to sprinkle on the altar, wine as if it were water—because if blood was mixed with water and this still looked like blood, then it was acceptable to use (see Moscovitz, Chap. 15 below, p. 329; who classifies this as an 'assessive' fiction); and being asked to disregard certain facts or objects, or to treat them as non-existent, as where the general rule was that two rows of six loaves were required, where there was one row of an equivalent number of loaves, one could ignore the fact that there were not two rows, or where there was reference to 'a beam', one could treat two beams as if they were one (see Moscovitz, Chap. 15 below, pp. 330–2).
- Finally, there is a range of examples from criminal law, courtesy of the chapter by Alldridge. In fact, Alldridge asserts in his opening sentence that 'The criminal law in England arose from the fiction that particular incidents between subjects violate the King's Peace' (Alldridge, Chap. 17 below, pp. 367), thus immediately emphasising the importance of the topic of fictions for an understanding of that area of law. His examples include (see Alldridge, Chap. 17 below, pp. 378–80):

   - Jury nullification, which involves the jury finding facts in order to acquit in the face of the evidence, thereby avoiding the judge's direction to return a guilty verdict, as was the case for instance in relation to the crime of manslaughter by driving a car (here, the jury's unwillingness to convict resulted in a change in the law, changing the relevant crime to that of causing death by driving dangerously);

- various fictions designed to avoid the death penalty, as exemplified in the fictional uses made of the benefit of clergy (e.g. at one point becoming available to all first-time offenders of lesser felonies); pleading the belly (where it was clear many women who benefited from this were not pregnant) and the insanity defence;
- The 'ancient fiction underlying forfeiture', where there was said to be something 'criminal about the thing itself' (see Alldridge, Chap. 17 below, pp. 378–80)

There is, then, considerable variety in the examples relied upon in this collection. Does this mean it is fragmented and does not form a cohesive whole? Hardly—first, there is some overlap in the examples the contributors work with; but further, the richness of examples is a strength and offers excellent resources for thinking through certain fundamental questions concerning the role of law—especially concerning the extent of its autonomy from everyday social experience and discourse. Time, then, to delve into those questions, all the while keeping an eye on common themes and issues as well as disagreements amongst the contributors.

II. Jobs for Fictions

A good initial way into the thicket is to consider the functions—or jobs, both enabled and performed—by fictions.[14] As will become clear, what the contributors identify as the function(s) of fictions, and how they phrase them, already offers some insights as to how they are likely to be evaluated. Here is a selection:

- According to Lind, fictions are often used to combat evasions of responsibility (Lind, Chap. 5 below, e.g. p. 95 and p. 103)[15]—thus, for example, thanks to the use of a fiction (the personality of the ship), the 'admiralty proceeding in rem was relaxed, such that actions for condemnation and forfeiture could proceed without proving the ship-owner's involvement in a vessel's wrongdoing' (Lind, Chap. 5 below, p. 96). The point here was that ship-owners' were evading responsibility because it was virtually impossible to prove their involvement. However, Lind also recognises that fictions can sometimes work the other way, i.e. enable evasions of responsibility—thus, for example, the fiction of the contract ideal allows companies to evade responsibility because it hides from view the fact that consumers do not enter into many contracts voluntarily and at arm's

[14] In focusing on functions, we are putting aside the question of motivation (without deriding its importance)—on motivations, see Fuller (1930–1), whose list of exploratory, emotive, expository, descriptive, historical and apologetic/ merciful motivations is instructive.

[15] One can put this point in different terms, and it might be interesting to consider whether this makes a difference to how we understand the jobs fictions do—e.g. is there a difference between saying that fictions are employed to do justice to a worthy claim by a litigant, and saying that fictions are used to avoid injustice (or harm) to either that litigant or another party (or group of persons)? Might the former be, for example, more expansive than the latter?

length with knowledge and understanding of the commitments they are making (Lind, Chap. 5 below, p. 104).[16]

- Picking up on this first function, it is worth adding here that a number of the chapters in this volume consider the link between legal fictions and difficulties of proof—perhaps most robustly, Del Mar claims that legal fictions are one means of coping with problems of proof, especially concerning proof of causation and intention. Legal fictions, on his view, are ways of enabling the temporary suspension of an otherwise required operative fact—very often, precisely one requiring proof of causation or intention (see also Lee).
- Further, according to many—for instance, Lind—fictions perform the function of mitigating the harshness of a rule,[17] while still leaving the rule intact, e.g. the fiction of constructive eviction was 'fashioned to redress the often bitter results induced by the common law doctrine that lease covenants were independent obligations', and it did so by 'treating a breach of the implied covenant of quiet enjoyment as a constructive eviction, thereby relieving a tenant of the obligation to pay rent' (Lind, Chap. 5 below, p. 102).
- Other contributors also stress the capacity of fictions to retain and keep intact, or not undermine, a pre-existing rule (or body of rules),[18] but less for the sake of mitigating the harshness of a rule, and more for the sake of neutrally pragmatic concerns—enabling disputes to be decided (for example, through jurisdictional fictions: see Stern) or creating a more convenient, cost-effective route to a remedy (see Lobban, below, 6, on the *indebitatus assumpsit*).
- For some, in the context of jurisdictional fictions,[19] for example, what is crucial is not so much that fictions do not undermine pre-existing rules, but that they allow a dispute to be decided without creating a new rule. This is a point made powerfully

[16] One might argue the two are not equivalent: in the first one, there is a judicial determination to treat the ship as having a personality for purposes of resolving particular cases; in the other, there is a general rule that, over time, we discover clashes with social realities. The second seems less a strategic intervention in the law, and more a failing of the law we (scholars) discover (or claim there to be) in light of changing commercial practices.

[17] A more general way to put the point is that fictions enable the decision-maker to escape the consequences of an existing specific rule of law but without putting the entire rule into question: (as articulated by Fuller and endorsed by Gordon in this volume). Here, it is also important to recognise that it is not just harshness to the present litigants that may be in issue: as Lobban points out, fictions were sometimes used 'to prevent a third party [from] being harmed' (see Lobban, Chap. 10 below, p. 212).

[18] Of course, the line between keeping a rule intact and undermining it is blurry. In his chapter on the uses of fictions in Roman law, Ando observes that sometimes it seems that the principle is in fact being subverted: e.g. as when provincial land is being treated as if it were sacral—thus subverting the principle that that alone that is consecrated by the authority of the Roman people, either by law or by decree of the Senate, is sacred (see Ando, Chap. 14 below, p. 307). There is a very interesting question here as to the criteria we might employ to judge whether we think the principle has been disturbed or not, undermined or not.

[19] Ando refers not to 'jurisdictional fictions' but to fictions as a means of dealing with 'justiciability issues': 'the case coming before the court fell short of some threshold. What was at stake, therefore, was the transfer of an individual, action or thing across some taxonomic divide: from purchaser to heir; from possessor to owner; from alien to citizen' (see Ando, Chap. 14 below, p. 298). There is an interesting sub-function identified here: fictions as enabling travel across legal categories.

by Stern, who uses it to show the difference between employing fictions and analogy: the former's 'ability to yield consequential effects is radically limited' (see Stern, Chap. 8 below, p. 158). If, for instance, the court acquired jurisdiction by pointing out similarities between Minorca and London, it would be offering more robust resources for future courts, for future courts could use those statements on similarity to attain jurisdiction in other claims originating outside England. The fiction, in this sense, is a device that allows one to seal off the normativity-producing capacity of a decision. Stern thus emphasises the 'purpose-built role and tightly restricted application' of fictions (see Stern, Chap. 8 below, p. 169). A similar point is made by Schauer, who says that judges will often recognise that 'modifying the law to produce the right result in the case at hand will have greater effects on future cases than will mis-describing the facts in order to accomplish the same result' (see Schauer, Chap. 6 below, pp. 121–2, n. 12).[20]

- Several contributors in this volume continue the long tradition of associating (at least some)[21] fictions with enabling change and the development of law (for instance, in Maine). Thus, Lobban points to how 'procedural fictions' 'allow litigants to use an historically-established form of procedure for purposes for which it was not originally designed' (Lobban, Chap. 10 below, p. 200), and in doing so pave the way for new areas of the law to be developed. For example, 'the medieval action of *trespass vi et armis*, which was a remedy for forcible wrongs contra pacem regis could give birth over time to a general action for torts ... a contractual action ... and an action to recover property' (ibid; see also Sparkes, Lee and Del Mar). An interesting twist on this theme of change and development (especially the latter), occurs in Ando's chapter, where he points out that fictions enabled 'the reduplication of institutional structures, without the necessity for constitutional innovation', e.g. the fiction of 'prorogation', which served 'to

[20] Schauer links this both to statutory interpretation—as when one uses a fiction to 'avoid a direct judicial rewriting of a legislatively enacted statute'—and interpretation of past cases, as when a judge recognises that 'Legal rules typically exist as part of an interlocking network of other rules, and so there may well be times when changing one rule will have indirect effects on other rules in ways that simply misapplying rules will not' (see Schauer, Chap. 6 below, p. 124). The idea that employing fictions is a matter of misapplying rules appears to be a more negative way of saying the same thing that could be put more positively, e.g. temporarily suspending one or more requirement(s) of a rule. Elsewhere in his chapter, Schauer says that a fiction is a 'justificatory manoeuvre in order to avoid simply saying that they [the judges] are not following the rule' (see Schauer, Chap. 6 below, p. 114). One could here ask: what is the difference between misapplying and not following the rule?

[21] Lobban argues explicitly that not all fictions are about enabling legal change and development, e.g. 'metaphysical fictions' (see above, in part 1), are instances 'where courts treated something which had happened at one time as having occurred at another, or where something which no longer appeared to exist was deemed to have a continued existence' (Lobban, Chap. 10 below, p. 200)—none of which need be connected to any change or development of the law in general. Lobban also wisely asks us to be on our guard when seeing the term 'fictions', for sometimes the term is used simply to explain or describe legal effects, there being in those cases no distinction between fictions, analogies or metaphors (see ibid). For example, the 'conceptual fiction' of a King having two bodies, which generated the other 'fiction' that 'the King never dies' was in reality a metaphor, for there was in fact legal disruption when the King died: see Lobban, Chap. 10 below, p. 207).

create individuals with the powers of magistrates although they were not such', precisely enabled this institutional growth (see Ando, Chap. 14 blow, p. 310). Fictions, then, might allow for both doctrinal and institutional development.

- Connected to this theme of change and development is the idea that fictions may be used not so much to introduce change, as to test whether it should be introduced. This is the major point made by Del Mar: that we need to analyse the role of fictions over time, thereby seeing that some fictions are picked up on by future courts and expanded while others are left behind and further quarantined. Alldridge, too, in his chapter notes that fictions may be understood 'As means of testing out possible moves towards a better legal structure' Alldridge, Chap. 17 below, p. 368). Another way to put the point is to say that a fiction does not necessarily *make* a change—it can be seen to be something that enables a 'let's wait and see' attitude.
- There are also a number of less traditional functions identified by contributors. One is the idea that 'legal writers seem generally, and increasingly over time, to have used the "legal fiction" label to signal their sense of the futility of further justification to a non-legal audience' (Petroski, Chap. 7 below, p. 132). On this view, legal fictions are forms of communication or communicative devices for signalling the technicality (the semi-autonomous character) of legal language. Perhaps in a similar way, Ando points out that legal fictions in Roman law may have provided 'a cognitive apparatus to assess the gap between social reality as the Romans perceived it and the world the law at once described and called into being' (Ando, Chap. 14 below, p. 296).
- According to Lobban, some fictions are used more for the purpose of either explaining, justifying or making sense of the law—for example, 'historical fictions' are used to justify a rule that looked anomalous, as when one used the fiction of all lands being securely fenced (in the past) to explain why a more severe penalty is imposed on the seemingly lesser offence of stealing already cut corn (as opposed to also cutting it) (see Lobban, Chap. 10 below, pp. 10–11). Here, there is no clear connection either to doing justice, or avoiding harm, or enabling change or development—instead, there is a concern for the rational intelligibility of the law.
- Fictions need also not be seen as exclusively related to resolving disputes. Sometimes, a litigant may employ a fiction in order to enable a legal act, such as transferring property or resettling estates. Lobban provides the example of 'common recovery, a device that involved a collusive real action, in which the tenant in tail would grant the land to another in fee simple. That grantee would then bring a real action claiming title to the land against the tenant, who would vouch a third party to warrant his title' (Lobban, Chap. 10 below, p. 203). This 'vouchee … would request a delay but then not appear to defend the case … the vouchee was a man of straw' (ibid).
- Finally, in those traditions where law permeates everyday life, such as Jewish law, fictions may be used not in order to do justice or avoid injustice, but simply as a matter of practicality, or 'common sense'. Thus, Moscovitz in this volume says that 'the vast majority of legal fictions in rabbinic literature do not seek to further moral, legal or utilitarian goals or to amend unsatisfactory existing law' (see Moscovitz, Chap. 15, pp. 334–5). Thus, where there are pre-existing rules

that are phrased in very concrete terms—e.g. requiring two rows of six loaves—a fiction may be employed to allow different versions of this (e.g. one row of twelve), meeting the same substantive aim of the rule.[22]

We see, from the above analysis, some common themes developing—although, still at a level of great variety of different functions/ jobs for fictions. Further, some of the jobs may be simultaneous, e.g. a court may be seeking to acquire jurisdiction but also seeking to do justice to an otherwise worthy claim or avoiding harm to a third party.

III. Defining Fictions

A decision was made at the outset of this project that no attempt would be made to impose any one example or function, or indeed definition, on the contributors—the point being to see how they carved out the object of their inquiry. In other words, the idea was to capture the variety of phenomena referred to as 'fictions' and the complexity of the different functions they play in different contexts (including different areas of the law).

In the result, the following possible definitions of legal fictions appear in the collection:

- First, it may be beneficial to recall some of the classic definitions, made by authors who the contributors here discuss. Thus, as reported by Kelsen in this volume (Chap. 1 below, p. 20), for Vaihinger in the 'formula [of the fiction] it is stated, that some given actual entity, some particular thing was likened to something legal, the impossibility or non-reality of which is at the same time claimed ... e.g. in the juridic fiction the formula is as follows: this heir is to be treated as he would have been treated had he died before his father, the bequether, i.e. he is to be disinherited'. Further, as Kletzer spells out, for Vaihinger there were four features of fictions: '1) they include a contradiction with reality or a self-contradiction; 2) the fiction has to be fundamentally provisional, i.e. it has to disappear later on or be logically eliminated; 3) the awareness of the fictivity has to be expressly stated and 4) the fiction has to be expedient' See Kletzer, Chap. 2 below, p. 24). As noted above, for Kelsen, many of the fictions Vaihinger identifies with the above definition and features are not fictions at all—accepting, for the sake of argument, Vaihinger's criteria, Kelsen only identifies theoretical fictions (fictions of legal theory) as genuine fictions.[23]

---

[22] There is an interesting question here concerning the link between the style of expression of rules and principles (especially their degree of concreteness) and the popularity of recourse to fictions. Are fictions, for instance, more likely to be popular when the pre-existing rules and principles are highly concrete?

[23] One point one might make here is that Kelsen is working with a very small sample of fictions in practice—one wonders what he would have said about some of the fictions identified in part 1

- Fuller's definition, mentioned by many of the contributors here, was that a 'fiction is either (1) a statement propounded with a complete or partial consciousness of its falsity, or (2) a false statement recognised as having utility' (see Fuller, 1930–1931, 369). There is, however, considerable controversy in this volume over whether or not fictions are (1) false (see e.g. Lind, who argues that they are true statements);[24] and (2) require any consciousness of falsity (thus, for instance, Del Mar does not look at fictions through the prism of truth or falsity, but through the prism of what can or cannot be proved). Of course, and as noted above, much here will depend on whether one thinks, for instance, there is any sense in holding law up to the standard of reality, of thinking of law as a cognition of reality (to use Kelsen's language). A sophisticated discussion of these issues appears in Quinn's chapter, in which he shows the oscillation between realism and constructivism in Bentham[25]—on the one hand, Bentham recognises that there can be no mirroring, by language, of the external world (no correspondence in that sense), but on the other hand, for the sake of showing the superiority of utilitarianism over other moral philosophies, Bentham needs some kind of realist standard (he needs, in other words, to be able to say that the entities of pleasure and pain are real, or more real, in ways that other terms employed by other moral philosophies are not). Again, there is disagreement in this volume over whether, and the extent to which, one ought to hold legal language up to, for instance, the standard of common or everyday experience (e.g. consider Lind, Schauer, Petroski and Schafer and Cornwell). It might be possible to say that our contributors are largely constructivists, nevertheless recognising that there are cases where realism ought to come in to keep in check law's enthusiasm for its own metaphysics. In this respect, it is worth quoting Schauer:

> ...legal language cannot be understood as entirely technical ... Legal fictions are thus parasitic on a gap between legal language and all-things-considered sound results. Without this gap, we would be unable to understand the idea of a legal rule, and unable to understand the way in which law, however technical it may at times get, must remain tethered to the language in which it is written, and thus tethered to the language of the community in which the legal system exists. (See Schauer, Chap. 6 below, p. 127).[26]

---

above. Is it the case, for instance, that all of them can be seen to be but abbreviations of functional equivalences?

[24] One wonders whether there are sometimes different kinds of falsity appealed to: one possible sense of falsity is that of using a category in a way that conflicts with everyday discourse, and another that there is something false in pretending one has not changed the law. Most theorists have the first kind of falsity in mind, but clearly the second kind has played a major part in the literature on fictions. Thus, for example, Maine defines a fiction as 'any assumption that deliberately "conceals, or affects to conceal, the fact that a rule of law has undergone alteration, its letter remaining unchanged, its operation being modified" (Lind, Chap. 5 below, p. 86, and see Maine (1931) [1861], 22). Perhaps it is better to call this second kind 'pretence', restricting 'falsity' to the first sense mentioned above.

[25] If one is after a one-sentence definition from Bentham, one could quote: 'a legal fiction is an assumed fact, notoriously false, upon which one reasons as if it were true' (Bentham 1840, p. 91).

[26] If Schauer is right, this shows why we cannot just be hard-nosed constructivists—even if one disagrees that the very idea of legal fictions requires some modicum of realism to make sense, one

- For Lind, as hinted at above, the dominance in the literature of the association of fictions with 'consciously false assumptions' is 'regrettable'. Lind suggests 'instead that legal fictions be understood as true legal propositions asserted with conscious recognition that they are inconsistent in meaning or otherwise in semantic conflict with true propositions asserted within some other linguistic system (or elsewhere within the law)' (Lind, Chap. 5 below, p. 100). On this approach, 'the legal fiction is simply a form of creative lawmaking,[27] a phenomenon of legal (primarily judicial) technique employed to resolve trouble in the legal environment' (ibid). For Lind, to 'claim that legal fictions are consciously false assumptions depends on viewing legal propositions outside the linguistic jural systems within which they originate and are used. It presumes a realm of reality that services as *the* yardstick against which every legal claim can be tested for truth value' (see Lind, Chap. 5 below, p. 93; original emphasis).
- The statement of Schauer's that comes closest to a definition is that the fiction is a 're-description of the facts of some event in order to make those facts compatible with the rule while at the same time permitting what appears to be the right result' (see Schauer, Chap. 6 below, p. 115). One concern one might raise for this definition is that in some cases, courts may not be re-describing the facts of the present case but accepting those facts and treating them as temporarily equivalent to the operative fact of the rule. Whether this amounts to the same thing is a matter for further discussion.
- According to Petroski, we ought to go further in rejecting the traditional way of thinking about fictions—we need to question the various assumptions behind the traditional way of defining them, namely assumptions 'that there is a sense in which propositions can be true about the world, or "factual", as well as counterfactual ... [assumptions] about the nature of legal communication, and related assumptions about the extent to which propositions generated within a legal system can be factual in the same sense as non-legal propositions' (Petroski, Chap. 7 below, pp. 135–6). For Petroski, the idea that fictions are 'consciously counterfactual propositions is historically contingent and incomplete' (Petroski, Chap. 7 below, p. 132). As noted above, Petroski prefers to think of fiction as a communicative device, signalling the futility of further justification to a non-legal audience.
- For Del Mar, legal fictions may be defined as 'any suspension of one or more of the required operative facts leading to the imposition of an associated normative consequence, whether this suspension is introduced because of (1) the absence of proof of some previously required fact; or (2) the presence of proof to the contrary' (Del Mar, Chap. 11 below, p. 225). In a way, for Del Mar legal fictions are also (as they are to Petroski) communicative devices—though less with

might think it is useful to retain a level of realism in order to assess when the law has moved too far from everyday use. Whether, phrased this way, it is still appropriate to refer to 'realism' is a good question to raise.

[27] As flagged above, not everyone in this collection would agree that legal fictions necessarily are forms of law-making: Del Mar would insist that fictions may be a way of testing the waters, inviting future courts to consider whether a change is appropriate/ desirable.

non-legal audiences and more with future courts (inviting the courts to consider whether to make that suspension more permanent and introduce a new rule or principle). But it is also important to recognise that the fictions used are making a difference in the present case: they are, for example, allowing the claim to be made under the rubric of a particular rule.

- Gama, in his chapter, raises the interesting issue of where, if anywhere, to draw the distinction between fictions and presumptions. This is a theme that is entertained by a number of contributors (e.g. Del Mar and Moscovitz)[28], but receives systematic treatment in Gama's chapter. For Gama, fictions are 'neither statements nor assertions', and nor are they 'consciously false assertions or statements formulated with consciousness of their falsity'—and this is because 'fictions created in the application of law are not assertions that pretend to express an empirical truth' (Gama, Chap. 16 below, p. 362). Instead, fictions 'are operations at the level of rules by which, irrespective of their legitimacy or illegitimacy, a judge extends the application of an existing rule to a situation of fact that cannot be subsumed under that rule, and in so doing so he creates a new rule' (ibid).[29] Looking at fictions at the level of rules, says Gama, means that we see that there is much more overlap (if not outright identity) than we might have otherwise thought between fictions and presumptions.

There remains considerable disagreement amongst the contributors at the level of definition. For instance, there is disagreement as to whether to think of fictions as 'false', with a number of contributors (Lind, Petroski) urging we drop this so-far dominant assumption in the literature, and others suggest retaining some level of realism is needed, if only to keep law's tendency to run away with language in check (Schauer, Schafer and Cornwell). There is also disagreement as to the extent to which one thinks using legal fictions is necessarily a matter of creating a new rule or principle (e.g. Gama thinks it is, while Del Mar and Lee think it is not). No doubt evaluative considerations creep in here, e.g. the extent to which one thinks that legal language ought to be held against the standards of everyday life, which is a value judgement, will influence one's definition of fictions.[30]

[28] For Moscovitz, a fiction is 'the assertion for legal purposes of "facts" which are clearly untrue: this distinguishes them from presumptions since the facts which they presume are not clearly or necessarily untrue' (Chap. 15 below, p. 327).

[29] At the risk of repetition, let us recall that there is thus disagreement here between Gama and Del Mar: for Del Mar, a fiction does not necessarily create a new rule—it is more of an invitation (which may never be taken up) to a future court to consider whether to generalise/abstract the temporary suspension of an operative fact into a rule.

[30] According to Quinn, the 'central disagreement' between Vaihinger, Bentham and Fuller concerned 'the degree to which, and the manner in which, such falsehood can be removed from language' (see Quinn, Chap. 4 below, 62). This was in part an ontological issue, but also in part a value-based judgement as to the appropriate extent to which the law might be sealed off from everyday discourse. Of course, this is not to say this is the only disagreement between those thinkers: at another point in his chapter, for instance, Quinn points to another, arguably more fundamental disagreement (at the ontological level): namely, that although Bentham anticipates Vaihinger in regarding many of the basic categories with which thought seeks to understand the world as ficti-

IV. The Good, the Bad and the Ugly: Evaluating Fictions

It will be instructive to continue our inquiry into the themes of the volume by pointing out some of the positive and negative claims made about fictions:[31]

- As with definitions, many of the contributors in this volume look back to the evaluative statements made by classic authors on fictions. Thus, many observe that for both Vaihinger and Fuller fictions are necessary and useful elements in legal thought. Bentham is more complex, though he too, says Quinn, recognised that some fictions were inevitable, and did not need to involve any intention to deceive.[32] What this raises is something common to virtually all the contributors in this volume, namely, that some fictions are better than others—or, put differently, that there can be good and bad fictions.[33]
- Perhaps the best example of this balanced analysis of the merit of fictions appears in Lind's chapter. It is worth quoting the following passage at length:

> Questions about the merits of a legal fiction should go to whether the fiction damages established truths, meanings, or understandings in some extralegal realm or within law itself as a result of collision in meaning. Used well, legal fictions inflict no damage while producing workable and beneficial doctrines or rules. Used nefariously, they upset settled meanings or truths, work injustice, or mask underlying process of legal reasoning. As with other modes of creative legal technique, legal fictions must be evaluated case-by-case in context. The technique as such is neither sickly nor sinister. (Lind, Chap. 5, p. 84–5)

Lind goes on to provide examples of good and bad fictions. To recall, the fiction of the personality of the ship was a good fiction, not only because it 'did not unsettle everyday understandings of ships or personhood' (see Lind, Chap. 5, p. 96), but also because it enabled courts to combat evasions of responsibility. There is recognition, here, then, that it is conceivable for a fiction to cause unacceptable inconsistency with everyday parlance, at least to the extent we subscribe to the ideal of a rule of law, at least in the sense of it not being a repository of cognitive surprise—of it being too remote from common sense (e.g. imagine that, for certain purposes, judges began to treat fruit as if they were cars, or cars as if they were fruit). Lind's examples, though, of nasty or 'pernicious' fictions are ones that are bad less on the semantic level, and more on the level of justice: thus, as already noted above, the fiction of the contract ideal enables the evasion of responsibility by companies;

---

tious entities, he disagrees with Vaihinger's idea that the thing and its qualities are inseparable, preferring to think only of the bodies to which qualities are attributed as real (see Quinn, Chap. 4 below, p. 61).

[31] For an important relatively recent defence of fictions in the pre-existing literature, see Knauer 2010.

[32] For Bentham, to recall, it was the third category—theoretical fictions—that deserved the greatest disapprobation. But he also thought that procedural fictions, where they buttressed theoretical fictions, were best got rid of (for further discussion, see Quinn).

[33] I am putting aside here the issue of the comparative utility of fictions in different domains, e.g. law and science. Thus, one may be more sympathetic to fictions in natural science than in law or morality (as Bentham arguably was: see Quinn).

and the fiction of *terra nullius* leads to the dispossession of lands belonging to Aboriginal peoples in Australia and elsewhere. We might put in the same category the fiction of consent that underlies legal blindness to 'marital rape', which as Alldridge notes in his chapter, was only laid to rest in English law in 1991.

- In keeping with the jobs identified above, many contributors recognise that fictions can help avoid or at least mollify the rigidity of law—whether this be at a moral level or at a level of pure practicability (recall Moscovitz). To the extent they do so, and thus to the extent they allow us to avoid injustice, fictions are a good thing. Of course, a lot of what one thinks of fictions will depend on what one thinks counts as an appropriate justification for a legal decision: according to some, a legal decision cannot be justified in law unless it amounts to an universalisation properly tested by the requirements of coherence and consistency with existing and established rules of law.[34] Thus, it is not enough for a fiction to be good for it to avoid injustice in a particular case; its use, to be justified, must be universalised or at least universalisable. To enter into further discussion of this issue, however, would lead us into the thickets of theories of legal reasoning.[35]
- Apart from semantic and justice-based considerations in evaluating fictions, one might also consider—as does Lobban[36]—the doctrinal level. Thus, one can recognise that certain fictions may help explain doctrinal developments, but equally, one ought to see that fictions may also 'hinder the development of better models' (Lobban, Chap. 10 below, 219)—Lobban's example is that of 'the notion that the parties had implicitly agreed on what was to be done if the subject matter of the contract were destroyed', which was an useful way to explain the evolving doctrine of frustration, but was also constraining in many ways.[37] Similarly, one might also claim that some fictions—especially some of those fictions related to extended uses of certain forms of action (ejectment and the like)—were obfuscatory, for they 'hid the real nature of the dispute between parties' (see Lobban, Chap. 10 below, 216).
- Finally, there is the defence of fictions offered by Del Mar in this volume. According to Del Mar, legal fictions can be a useful instrument of careful experimentation—a way of testing the extent to which the potential introduction of a rule will be beneficial. On this view, fictions are not signs of the immaturity of a system (as they were, for instance, for Maine), but instead dynamic resources that allow courts, over time, to balance flexibility and responsiveness with stability and predictability. That balancing, of course, can be done well or badly—but

[34] See MacCormick 1978.

[35] There may, for example, be an interesting tension here between that universalised-based view of the justifiability of legal decisions and Del Mar's claim that there is value in a fictional solution that is only at best potentially universalisable (indeed, its value depends in part on the court not universalising it, at least initially).

[36] See also the sources from the eighteenth and nineteenth centuries mentioned in Lobban's chapter—as Lobban says, defences of fictions was quite common then (in contrast to today). It may be instructive to consider why that is so—to the extent it is!

[37] This was a point that was also recognised by Maine—fictions had to be got rid of at one point, for they could become the greatest obstacles to further development and understanding of the law.

the general point is that we would be much worse off if we did not have the resource of fictions.

The overall consensus here may be articulated as follows: that most, if not all, contributors recognise that there is some value in some fictions. There seems to be little enthusiasm for saying that fictions, in themselves, are either good or bad—instead, like other techniques, they are liable to be abused, but also to be put to good use. Further, there is, as everywhere, evaluative complexity here: a number of different considerations are often in play, including the level of semantics, justice, the practice of legal reasoning, and the intelligibility of doctrine. One's view of fictions will inevitably depend on the stances one takes in relation to each of those criteria.

V. Some Further Themes and Questions for Future Work

The above has but touched on the themes that appear in this collection. In this final part, some further themes are identified, together also with some questions that deserve further analysis:

- An important theme in this collection is the relationship between fictions and other devices and modes of reasoning. There are different ways in which one can pool devices, of course—one might want to put together all the different modes of argument, looking for example at fictional, exemplary, analogical, hypothetical and consequential reasoning in one pool; or, one can pool together only those that fall under the category of 'legal artifice' (see Stern), such as fictions, metaphors, exclusionary rules, and various narratological devices (such as parables); or one may have a more general—and perhaps anomalous—pool of devices such as: presumptions (conclusive and rebuttable), deemings, (false) hypotheses, lies, deceptions, errors and so on. One may wish to draw a line, for instance, between those devices and modes of reasoning related to issues of fact on the one hand, and those related to law on the other (see further Gama). Or, one may wish to focus on a particular relationship: e.g. between fictions and classification/ taxonomy (see Samuel); or between fictions and analogy (see Stern and Schauer); or between deeming and fictionalising (see Alldridge). Finally, and in a particularly creative turn, one may look at fictions through the prism of the way law treats fictional objects (such as characters in novels in intellectual property law): on this, see Schafer and Cornwell.
- In addition to comparing fictions to related devices or modes of argument, one might go on to consider how the topic of fictions fits into or clashes with some long-held views within theories of legal reasoning: what, for example, does the utility of legal fictions tell us about the idea of universalisation being the foundation of justification? Are fictions but misapplications of rules—and if not, what does this tell us about the very idea of application/ misapplication? At what point does a fiction subvert (rather than keep intact) a pre-existing rule or principle? Finally, do not legal fictions undermine the exclusive focus within legal reason-

ing on instances of decision-making—for do they not show that one must analyse and evaluate modes and devices of legal reasoning as they function over time?

- The topic of legal fictions can also offer an interesting way to analyse the role of scientific evidence in law—including how one deals with that evidence often falling short of its own requirements (recall Del Mar and Lee on evidence of causation in asbestos claims). In this volume, both Petroski and Gordon offer some valuable insights as to the role and limits of scientific evidence in the law.[38]
- Another fascinating topic—picking up from the immediately preceding last question—is the life-cycle of fictions. The most brilliant exposition of this theme in this collection comes from Sparkes, who analyses the birth, development, and finally death of the fiction of ejectment. He shows, for example, how the fiction might have been born, with it being but a small step towards a fiction from a case in which a claimant for possession sued not the master, but the servant living on the property, for fear of the master absconding and thus avoiding the proceeds (see Sparkes, Chap. 13 below, p. 280). There are the twin energies here of fictionalisation and de-fictionalisation, and all the imaginative baggage that accompanies these processes (perhaps especially the first, involving as it does flights of nomenclature fancy). There is farce here, certainly, but also serious questions concerning the use of fictions depending on the trust (or distrust) the judiciary has in the legislature. It should be added that there is room, too, for disagreement: for example, where Sparkes sees scaffolding (fictions being built on fictions), Alldridge sees but ad hoc repairs and patches (see below, 2). In summary, what Sparkes shows is that there is great promise here in more historical work on legal fictions, continuing, though not necessarily agreeing with, the tradition of Maine, Milsom[39] and others.
- Related to this is the issue of the sociological conditions that might be said to accompany the utility and/ or popularity of fictions. For example, consider Ando's claim that there were two historic changes that may have led to more fictions: 'the creation of a new source of law in the early second century BCE, to wit, the granting to the praetor of not merely the power to hear cases but to create new legal actions'; and second, the expansion of the empire, which demanded the reduplication of institutions of governance, including both magistracy and jurisdiction (see Ando, Chap. 14 below, pp. 319–20). Further work on such sociological conditions, in comparative historical vein, would surely be highly desirable.
- Finally, let us observe that a great deal more work could be done on fictions in legal theory—on the use of fictional constructs in general jurisprudence, e.g. in modelling judges, in drawing on utopias or dystopias of various kinds.[40] As noted above, the focus in this introduction (and the collection as a whole) is on fictions in practice. Nevertheless, there are some very valuable contributions in this respect in this volume. The most extensive discussion appears in Samuel's chapter

[38] For some resources in this respect, see Del Mar and Schafer 2014.

[39] See Milsom, 2003, Chap. 2.

[40] This could be as part of an overall inquiry into the literary qualities of theorising about law—both today and in the past.

(though see also Gama, Kletzer and Schauer), where the following examples of purported fictions of legal theory are given: Dworkin's Hercules; Hart's Rule of Recognition (a controversial example, as Samuel realises); Hart's (and one might also add, Fuller's) King Rex; Kelsen's Grundnorm;[41] and Holmes' Bad Man. Mention has already been made that Kelsen thought that theoretical fictions were the only genuine fictions on Vaihinger's own criteria of them, and here it is difficult to resist quoting a lovely image from Kelsen's review of Vaihinger's *As-If*, in relation to the utility of these fictions of legal theory:

> And we have to speak of a fiction as soon as cognition (and especially juridic cognition) takes a detour in knowing its object (and in juridic knowledge this object is the law, the legal order, the legal ought) a detour in which it consciously sets itself in contradiction to this object; and be it only in order to better grasp it: just like a rock-climber, in order to avoid an obstacle and reach his goal more easily, is sometimes forced to temporarily climb downwards, i.e. in a direction directly opposed to his goal, the peak. (Kelsen, Chap. 1 below, p. 5)

Conclusion

It is hoped that the list offered in the final part of this introduction shows not only the riches to be mined in this collection, but also that the topic of legal fictions is a fascinating one, deserving of further treatment. Of course, this volume has not aimed at a final word—instead, an attempt has been made to look afresh at this topic. Valuable work has been done, but so much more remains to be considered, and what is so wonderful about the topic of legal fictions is that it forces one to dip one's paintbrush into many colours: epistemological, ontological, sociological, historical, cognitive, and linguistic, to mention but the obvious. Thus, if nothing else, it is hoped that the collection has shown the fruits for and the need for more work, especially within scholarship on legal reasoning, and particularly at the intersection of the conceptual, the evaluative and the historical.

Note on the Index In preparing the index we have tried to meet the interests of scholars interested in fictions in general or in particular examples. For that reason, we have been inclusive of examples that have been candidates to be called 'fictions' even if this categorisation is disputed or rejected. We have been similarly inclusive of authors who have written about fictions in general, but parsimonious in regard to other authors and proper names. Finally, rather than a full table of cases, we have only listed those cases that we consider particularly important for the topic.

[41] See also Schauer, who observes that 'The Grundnorm may be a legal fiction, but only in the sense that any assumption or presupposition is potentially fictional' (Chap. 6 below, p. 117). As he adds, the assumption is thought here to be 'afactual', rather than 'counterfactual' in the traditional legal fiction.

References

Bentham, J. 1840. *Theory of legislation*. Vol. 1 Boston: Weeks, Jordan & Co.

Fuller, Lon. 1930–1931. 'Legal Fictions'. *Illinois Law Review* 25:363–399; 513–546, 877–910.

Del Mar, M. and M. J. Lobban, eds. 2014. *Legal theory and legal history*. Surrey: Ashgate.

Del Mar, M. and B. Schafer, eds. 2014. *Legal theory and the natural sciences*. Surrey: Ashgate.

Knauer, N. 2010. 'Legal Fictions and Juristic Truth', *St. Thomas Law Review* 23:1–51.

MacCormick, N. 1978. *Legal reasoning and legal theory*. Oxford: Clarendon Press.

Maine, Sir H. 1931 [1861]. *Ancient law*. London: Oxford University Press.

Milsom, S. F. C. 2003. *A natural history of the common law*. New York: Columbia University Press.

Prebble, J. 2011. 'Fictions of Income Tax', Victoria University of Wellington Legal Research Paper No. 29/2011. http://papers.ssrn.com/sol3/papers.cfm?abstract_id=1604978. Accessed 2 June 2014.

Acknowledgement Of Previous Publication

The following chapters have been previously published in earlier versions:

Chapter 4
Fuller on Legal Fictions: A Benthamic Perspective
Michael Quinn
Previously published as:
'Fuller on Legal Fictions: A Benthamic Perspective' (2013) 4 *International Journal of Law in Context* 466–484

Chapter 7
Legal Fictions and the Limits of Legal Language
Karen Petroski
Previously published as:
'Legal Fictions and the Limits of Legal Language' (2013) 4 *International Journal of Law in Context* 485–505

Chapter 11
Legal Fictions and Legal Change in the Common Law Tradition
Maksymilian Del Mar
Previously published as:
'Legal Fictions and Legal Change' (2013) 4 *International Journal of Law in Context* 442–465

Chapter 18
Fictitious Fraud: Economics and the Presumption of Reliance
Randy D. Gordon
Previously published as:
'Fictitious Fraud: Economics and the Presumption of Reliance' (2013) 4 *International Journal of Law in Context* 506–519

Contents

About the Authors

Peter Alldridge is Drapers' Professor of Law at the Department of Law, Queen Mary, University of London, and author of *Relocating Criminal Law* (2000) and *Money Laundering Law* (2003).

Clifford Ando is Professor of Classics, History and Law in the Department of Classics at the University of Chicago, as well as Research Fellow in the Department of Classics and World Languages at the University of South Africa.

Hans Kelsen (1881-1973) was one of the twentieth's centuries most important legal theorists.

Jane Cornwell is Lecturer in Intellectual Property Law at the School of Law, University of Edinburgh.

Maksymilian Del Mar is Senior Lecturer in Law and Philosophy at the Department of Law, Queen Mary University of London, and Academic Fellow of the Honourable Society of the Inner Temple.

Raymundo Gama is Professor of Law at the Instituto Tecnológico Autónomo de México (ITAM).

Randy D. Gordon is an adjunct professor in the Dedman School of Law and a lecturer in English at Southern Methodist University. He is also a partner in the Complex Litigation Group of Gardere Wynne Sewell LLP.

Christoph Kletzer is Senior Lecturer in Legal Philosophy at the Dickson Poon School of Law, King's College London.

James Lee is a Senior Lecturer in Law at the Dickson Poon School of Law, King's College London and an Associate Academic Fellow of the Honourable Society of the Inner Temple.

Douglas Lind is Professor of Philosophy in the Department of Philosophy, University of Idaho.

Michael Lobban is Professor of English Legal History at the London School of Economics.

Leib Moscovitz is Professor and Chair of the Talmud Department in Bar-Ilan University, Israel. He specializes in the study of the Palestinian Talmud and jurisprudential aspects of rabbinic literature.

Karen Petroski is Associate Professor of Law at the Saint Louis University School of Law.

Michael Quinn is Research Associate at the Bentham Project, based in the Department of Laws, University College London.

Geoffrey Samuel is Professor of Law at the School of Law, University of Kent, and Professor *affilié*, Law School, Sciences-Po, Paris.

Burkhard Schafer is Professor of Computational Legal Theory at the School of Law, University of Edinburgh.

Frederick Schauer is David and Mary Harrison Distinguished Professor of Law at the School of Law, University of Virginia.

Peter Sparkes is Professor of Property Law at the School of Law, University of Southampton.

Simon Stern is Associate Professor in the Faculty of Law and the Department of English, University of Toronto.

William Twining is Emeritus Quain Professor of Jurisprudence at the Department of Laws, University College London.

Part I
Theories of Fiction, Fictions of Theory

Chapter 1
On the Theory of Juridic Fictions. With Special Consideration of Vaihinger's Philosophy of the As-If

Hans Kelsen
(Translated by Christoph Kletzer)

Abstract This is a translation into English of Kelsen, Hans. 1919. Zur Theorie der Juristischen Fiktonen: Mit besonders Berücksichtigung von Vaihingers Philosophie des Als Ob, *Annalen der Philosophie* 1: 630–658.

1.1 Content

I. The notion of a fiction and the object of cognition in legal science. The opposition to "reality". The actuality of nature and the actuality of the law. The extension of Vaihinger's concept of a fiction. True fictions of legal *theory*. The legal subject.

II. The so-called "fictions" of legal *practice*. The pseudo-fictions of the legislator. Their fundamental difference from epistemological fictions; the absence of a cognitive aim and the absence of an opposition to the actuality of nature or the actuality of the law. Article 347 of the German Commercial Code. The praesumptio iuris. The praetorian fictions.

III. "Fictions" in the application of the law. The analogy. Its uncorrectable conflict with the actuality of the law and its juristic inadmissibility. The legally required analogy.

IV. Legal theory and legal practice. The moral fiction of "freedom". Its dispensability in the case of a dissolution of the faulty syncretism of the perspectives of is and ought. The fiction of the "social contract" establishing the state. Its dispensability for legal positivism.

V. The sovereignty of the legal order. The independence of law from morality. The allegedly fictitious character of this separation. Vaihinger's "practical" fictions. The legal norm and legal duty are not fictions.

C. Kletzer (✉) · H. Kelsen
The Dickson Poon School of Law, King's College London, Strand,
London WC2R2LS, UK
e-mail: christoph.kletzer@kcl.ac.uk

M. Del Mar, W. Twining (eds.), *Legal Fictions in Theory and Practice*,
Law and Philosophy Library 110, DOI 10.1007/978-3-319-09232-4_1

1.2 I

A considerable part of Vaihinger's notable theory of fictions has been developed by reference to the so called "juridic" fictions. As a matter of fact, Vaihinger understood juridic fictions to be a paradigmatic case of fictions. For him, apart from mathematics, there was hardly another field better suited to the deduction of logical laws, to the illustration or development of logical methods in general, and of the method of the fiction in particular, than the law. He further expressed his regret about the fact that logicians have so far neglected the juridic fiction since they did not see that logic has to take its subject material from an actually living science.[1] For Vaihinger the juridic fictions are "scientific" fictions[2] and they do not in principle differ from epistemological fictions.[3] He explicitly stresses "the formal identity of the actions of understanding and of the whole intellectual state in juridic fictions with all the other scientific fictions".[4]

However, the notion of a "juridic fiction" captures quite a broad variety of phenomena: only a relatively small part of them can be seen as fictions in the actual sense of this term, i.e. as fictions according to Vaihinger's own definition. After all, most of the phenomena which Vaihinger himself treated as "juridic fictions" and which he uses to lay the foundations of his meritorious theory, are no fictions at all; at least they do not serve as examples of the intellectual constructs, to which the very qualities apply which he so fittingly describes. Thus, even though we have to unreservedly agree with the main results of Vaihinger's philosophy of the As-If, it is especially in relation to the juridic fictions, i.e. in relation to the kind of fictions Vaihinger prefers to use, that the arguments have to be seen to be unconvincing.

According to Vaihinger a fiction is characterised both by its end and by the means through which this end is reached. The end is the cognition of the actual world; the means, however, is a fabrication, a contradiction, a sleight of hand, a detour and passage of thought. It might be a somewhat odd means, the fiction is nevertheless a means that logic uses; it has epistemological character and has its relevance as an instrument of cognition.[5]

It is the cognition of *actual reality* which the fiction serves. "The conscious turning away from actual reality is meant to prepare the cognition of the latter."[6] And the opposition to actual reality is one of the principal characteristics of the fiction.[7]

Now, it has to appear doubtful from the very beginning whether in the natural sciences we could ever come across fictions which do not in their essence aim at the cognition of actual reality. If we take a fiction to be an—admittedly somewhat

---

[1] Vaihinger (1913, p. 46).

[2] Ibid 257.

[3] Ibid 447.

[4] Ibid 250.

[5] Ibid 175 ff and passim.

[6] Ibid. 27.

[7] Ibid 171 ff.

odd—means to grasp actual reality, then only a view of legal science which has completely strayed off its usual ways could make use of a fiction in this sense, and accordingly a fiction in this sense could never yield legal scientific cognition, not even in an indirect sense, via a detour. If by means of a fiction we claim the actuality of something (and be that in contradiction to actuality itself), then in a scientific endeavour which does not even attempt the cognition of something existing in actual reality, a fiction can only ever be an illegitimate and completely useless, viz. only harmful error.

As a matter of fact, Vaihinger was himself well aware of the true nature of legal science! He repeatedly stresses that the task of legal science is not to gather knowledge of something that exists in actual reality. "So far the only truly scientific fiction we talked about was the juridic fiction; however, it needs to be stressed that legal science is not actually an empirical science, a science that deals with what actually exists, but a science that deals with human, arbitrary institutions."[8] Legal science aims at the knowledge of an *ought*; calling this object "human arbitrary institutions" is not entirely correct, since human arbitrary institutions, too, are something actual and can be objects of an empirical science, e.g. of sociology.

However, no grave objection to Vaihinger's theory of fictions emerges from all of this. What emerges is only a significant modification. After all, legal science does indeed make use of fictions. We will demonstrate below, what kind of fictions these are and that most of Vaihinger's "juridic fictions" are not true fictions at all. All that needs to be said here is that Vaihinger's concept of a fiction becomes too narrow, as soon as one allows only empirical reality to be the object, the only target or product of cognition. And insofar as one wants to accept as sciences also those sciences which are not natural sciences, such as, for instance, ethics and, in particular, legal science, then such a restrictive understanding of fictions cannot be accepted. A thus appropriately expanded concept of a fiction emerges, as soon as we replace "actual reality" as the specific object of cognition with this "object of cognition" itself, understood in general terms. And we have to speak of a fiction as soon as cognition (and especially juridic cognition) takes a detour in knowing its object (and in juridic knowledge this object is the law, the legal order, the legal ought), a detour in which it consciously sets itself in contradiction to this object; and be it only in order to better grasp it: just like a rock-climber, in order to avoid an obstacle and reach his goal more easily, is sometimes forced to temporarily climb downwards, i.e. in a direction directly opposed to his goal, the peak.

It is in this sense that there are true, i.e. epistemological fictions in legal science. They are fictions of the attempt to know the law, fictions of the intellectual mastery of the legal order. They are fictions of *legal theory*. Such a fiction, an auxiliary concept, an auxiliary construct, is, for instance, the concept of a legal subject or the concept of a subjective right.

In this context we do not need to fully investigate the concept of a legal subject or a person in all its facets. What should suffice is to show how fruitful the application of Vaihinger's philosophy of the As-If to the fictions of *legal theory* can be.

[8] Ibid 257.

In the common juristic understanding a person—and be it the physical person or the legal person—exists as an object distinct and independent from the legal order. We usually call this object the "bearer" of duties and rights and attribute to it more or less actual existence in the real world. Whether one wants to limit this kind of independent existence to the physical person or wants to extend it also to the so called legal person (like the organic theory wants to do) does not matter here. What suffices is to note the marked tendency to posit the person as something that exists in actual reality.

Now, if the physical as well as the legal subject can be shown to be nothing but the *personification of a complex of norms*[9] for the purposes of simplification and illustration—something which cannot be comprehensively demonstrated in this article—then the idea of a person, which is commonplace in legal theory, would be a typical example of a fiction; and Vaihinger has to be credited with making the interesting and complex thought-mechanism of the latter transparent. It is an intellectual construct which aims at capturing the object of legal science, i.e. the legal order, yet is nevertheless itself merely a product of imagination and is in thought *added to the object of cognition.* It is thus somehow a duplication of the object and a distortion of cognition. By that, this mere aid-to-thinking sets itself in direct opposition to the object, i.e. to the specific legal reality, and becomes in itself contradictory, just like any analysis of the concept of the person would reveal. Now, if the person (which was originally only set up as a specific aid-to-thinking, as a mere framework aimed at grasping the legal order) is posited to be an actually existing thing, i.e. as a kind of natural object, then a thus enhanced fiction does indeed involve an opposition to actual reality, which can only be possible in the transgression of a legal theory, thus in a theory that claims to have natural facts as its objects.

The concept of a legal subject is primarily a kind of fiction which Vaihinger calls a "personifying fiction". They emerge from our tendency to anthropomorphically personify intellectual constructs, a tendency which has forever dominated our intellectual capacities, and which forms this "undying inclination of man"[10] to hypostasise everything which is purely intellectual into the shape of a person or subject and to thus make it intelligible. "The common principle is the hypostasis of phenomena in some respect, irrespective of how far the hypostasis aligns itself with this image of the person. This image of the person is also the truly determining factor in the category of the thing."[11] "The basic scheme of substantiality is, after all, personality."[12] This does indeed apply to the personifications of the law (i.e. of the legal norm), and it is in this way that we have to understand the legal subject. The legal norm, i.e. the fact that certain human behaviour ought to be a certain way, presents itself as the hypostasis of this purely intellectual object. And the insight that the concept

---

[9] In the case of the personification of the legal order as a whole we arrive at the so-called person of the state and in the case of the personification of individual legal order we arrive at the physical or legal person.

[10] Ibid 391.

[11] Ibid 50.

[12] Ibid 391.

of a thing is also a personifying fiction lets the legal subject and the subjective right, which are somehow understood as “things” appear to be quite similar, if not identical hypostases of the “objective” legal norm. It cannot be stressed enough that the concept of the legal subject has the same logical structure as the most characteristic form of personifying fiction, i.e. of the concept of the soul, or the concept of force,[13] the logical untenability of which does not militate against its actual practicability. It would certainly be a worthwhile endeavour to try to understand the legal person as a kind of *legal soul*. And it is by no means moot to clarify that the concepts of ethical personhood and of the “conscience”, too, are illustration-serving personifications of a norm, namely the moral norm. Vaihinger very appropriately characterises this *duplication* of the object of cognition which is effected in the fiction in general, and in the personification in particular, and one could not describe this strange duplication of the law, this tautology, which can be found in the legal subject, better than with the words of Vaihinger, who in this passage did not intend to capture the legal concept of the person, but the concept of a force: “It was especially the seventeenth century which has created many of these concepts in its sciences;[14] it was believed that by means of these concepts one has actually understood something; however, such words are but shells, which are supposed to hold together and contain a material nucleus. And just as the shell in all its forms traces the nucleus and in duplicating the latter simply represents it externally, so these words or concepts are but tautologies, which simply repeat the actual thing in external clothing.”[15]

The contradictions, which are posited in the notion of a legal subject, which claims to be a thing distinct from the legal norm (of the “objective law”), but which is just the latter’s repetition, these contradictions may not be resolved, but they at least become transparent to us as soon as we accept (after Vaihinger has told us), that it lies within the nature of fictions to entangle us in contradictions. “By its very own doing thought leads us onto certain pseudo-concepts just as seeing leads us into unavoidable optical illusions. As soon as we recognise this optical semblance as being necessary, as soon as we consciously accept the fictions created by it (e.g. God, freedom etc.) and also see through them we can bear the ensuing logical contradictions as necessary products of our thought and reach the insight that they are the necessary consequences of the inner mechanism of the thinking organ itself.”[16]

This is why the fiction of the legal subject, which is in itself contradictory, can nevertheless be accepted without harm to legal science, since it has the advantages of *illustration* and *simplification*. This, however, is true only as long as and insofar as one remains aware of its fictitious character and of the duplication which is effected by means of the concept of the person. Until then we can dispense of what Vaihinger calls the *correction* of the fiction. “Insofar as the fiction presents an opposition to actual reality, it can only have value if it is employed *provisionally*. This is why

[13] Ibid 50.

[14] It has to be noted here, that Schloßmann (1906) also traces the concept of the legal person back to the systematic of the seventeenth century.

[15] Ibid 52.

[16] Ibid 223.

… it needs to be corrected."[17] "The mistake has to be reversed by simply discharging of the construct which was fictitiously introduced."[18] Vaihinger expressly states: "Such a correction does not seem to be necessary for juridic fictions; and it indeed is not necessary. Since here we are not dealing with an exact estimation of something actual, but with a subsumption under an arbitrary law, a man-made construct, not a natural law, not a natural relation.a"[19] However, Vaihinger thereby does not really refer to the kind of fictions which are found in the legal concept of a person. The latter concept is created by legal science, by legal theory or the cognition of law. This is not the case with thewith the "juridic" fictions employed by the legislator or someone applying the law. However, it is to these that Vaihinger mainly refers even though they are intellectual constructs which do not serve cognition and are thus not fictions in the *logical* sense. Still, Vaihinger's comments pertain precisely to the fiction of the legal subject employed by *legal theory*. However, by claiming that in legal science we do not intend to capture an actual reality he has characterised the essence of legal science as opposed to natural science only in a negative sense. Put positively, legal science intends to comprehend an ought, it intends the cognition of norms.

The concept of the legal person can be employed with benefit as long as it is understood in accordance to its own logical structure, i.e. as a mirror image. However, this concept has not been able to avoid the danger that comes with any personification: its hypostatisation into an actual object of nature. Insofar as theory takes a mere mirror image as an actual thing, it stretches the contradiction—one by which the law as subject (i.e. the legal subject) already stands, in and of itself and before any position of actuality exists, against the law as object (i.e. the objective law)—to a contradiction against actuality. In the concept of a legal person a natural thing is claimed to exist, which never and nowhere exists in actual reality. This is true both for the "physical" and for the so-called "legal" person. Vaihinger aptly compares the fictitious constructs of thought with "knots and nodes" which thought ties into the threads presented to it, "knots and nodes … which provide ancillary service to thought, which, however, become pitfalls for thought, as soon as the knot is taken as something that is contained in experience itself."[20] It is precisely this illicit positing of the person as being something actual which leads—as Vaihinger has shown in relation to the other fictions—to all the"pseudo problems", the "artificially created difficulties", the "self created contradictions" which abound in the doctrine of the "legal" person just as they abound in all philosophical and scientific theories that gather around a fictitious concept.[21]

At least here, however, a "correction" has to step in, and this correction can happen in no way other than by a reduction of the concept of the person to its natural boundaries, by means of a self-reflection of legal science, by means of a

[17] Ibid 173.

[18] Ibid 297.

[19] Ibid 197.

[20] Ibid 230.

[21] 'A solution of the so-called ultimate puzzle of the world will never be found, since that which seems puzzling to us, is the contradictions created by us, which emerge from the playful engagement with the mere forms and shells of cognition': Ibid 52.

clarification of its logical structure. If one had not demanded from the legal concept of the person more than it can in its essence provide, then one could have been spared the entirely fruitless discussion which has developed around the person, and in particular around the concept of the "legal" person; then the downright naive and paradox blunders of juridic theory and the excesses of an organic theory could have been avoided, blunders and excesses which can only be explained by reference to the delusive power of fictions, which also mislead scientific thought, and which lost itself in juristic mysticism.

1.3 II

What needs to be clearly distinguished from the fictions of legal theory are the so-called "fictiones juris", the fictions of legal *practice*, i.e. of the *legislator* and of the *application of the law*. Now, as firstly concerns the "fictions" employed by the legislator, the fictions *within* the legal order, it must be stressed that these do not constitute "fictions" in Vaihinger's sense. After all, the positing of a norm, the legislative activity, is not a process of thought, and does not have *cognition* as its goal. It is rather an act of will, if indeed we want to see it as a process or a procedure at all. The legal order is expressed in words and these words undoubtedly often display the grammatical form which normally is found behind *epistemological* fictions: the "As-If". However, due to the lack of any aim of cognition within the legal order—which as such is the object of cognition, and not itself cognition or an expression of cognition—the words of a legal norm can never contain a "fiction" in Vaihinger's sense.

Let us immediately have a look at the example Vaihinger uses in his chapter on "juridic fictions": Article 347 of the German Commercial Code "where it is stipulated that a good which is not in time returned to the sender has to be treated *as if* it had been approved and accepted by the receiver."[22] In this example we are supposed to immediately see the identity in principle between the analogous fictions, e.g. the categories, and the juridical fictions. However, in the categories, just as in all true fictions, the human intellect aims to comprehend actuality or some other object. In the fiction of Article 347, however, neither actuality nor anything else is intended to be *comprehended*, it should rather be *regulated*, a norm of *action* is given, i.e. an actuality is supposed to be *created*. Of course, there is a deep connection between the intellect which *orders* the world by employing categories and which thus creates the world as ordered unity, on the hand, and the law that regulates and thus creates the legal world, on the other. However, the difference of principle between the epistemological and juridic fiction of the legislator shows in the fact that in the latter case there can never be found an opposition to actuality, be it to the actuality of nature, or be it to the actuality of law (i.e. of the law as an object of cognition). Such a contradiction could only be found in a statement about what is (and if one

[22] Ibid 46 ff.

wants to accept the extended concept of a fiction here proposed: about that what ought to be). However, the law cannot include such a statement. In a law no *cognition* is expressed. The statements in which the law expresses itself are not statements in this sense. Article 347 by no means states that the goods not returned in time to the sender are actually approved and accepted. It simply states that in case goods are not returned in time the same norm applies as in the case the goods are accepted; it states that in this case the sender and the receiver have the same duties and the same rights as in the case of actual acceptance. Article 347 stipulates that goods not returned in time have to be treated *just as* goods which are accepted. The grammatical form of the "As-If" thus is not in any way essential, it can be replaced by a mere "just as". If the law subsumes two cases under the same norm, it by no means claims that both cases are alike—in the sense of *naturally* alike. Or otherwise every general norm would be "fiction" since there are no two men, two facts which are alike. However, "legally" they are effectively, actually and truly alike, since they are made alike by the legal order. Article 347 is, just like any so-called "fiction" of the legislator, nothing but an abbreviating expression. The law simply wants to attach the same legal consequences to one case as it does to another. To phrase this in a separate norm would be too cumbersome, too laboured; or maybe the second case was not even considered in the first place. It would be superfluous to repeat all the rules which have already been set down for the first case. The legislator can rest content with declaring that in the second case the same rules apply as in the first case. It is a misunderstanding to suppose that this effect would be achieved by forcing the person applying the law to accept the idea that both cases are alike, i.e. that they do not differ as a matter of fact. That they are "legally" the same simply means that despite a natural *difference* in fact the *same* legal consequence is supposed to follow. And this difference of fact can by no means be ignored in applying the law. The judge first has to *establish* the facts; he has to establish whether the goods were accepted *or whether* they were not returned in time. If the recipient claims: I have not accepted the goods, then it has to be established that he did not return them in time. Where do we here find the opposition to reality?

In the context of distinguishing between the fictio juris (the fiction of the legislator) from the praesumptio, Vaihinger defines the juridic fiction as follows: "In the praesumptio a presumption is made *until the opposite is established.* By contrast, the fiction is the assumption of a statement, of *a fact, even though the opposite is certain.*" He uses the following example: "If a man, whose wife commits adultery, nevertheless is treated as the father of the child born from this adulterous relation when in fact he was actually in the country at the time of the conception, then he is treated *as if* he were the father, even though he is not the father and even though everyone knows he is not. This last sentence distinguishes the praesumptio from the fictio."[23] However, even though it is quite correct to insist on a distinction between the fictio and praesumptio, the fictio is not accurately captured here. The law does not claim that under certain conditions the husband is the *father*, i.e.

---

[23] Ibid 258.

the natural father, the *progenitor* of a child which has been conceived in an adulterous relation. The law does not make any such claim; it does not assume a matter of fact, even though the opposite is certain. Rather it only regulates for certain reasons and to certain ends, that under certain circumstances the husband has *the same* duties and rights in relation to a child which was conceived by his wife in an adulterous relation and that this child has *the same* duties and rights in relation to this husband as they exist between the husband and his own children which were conceived in wedlock. Now if the law uses the phrase, that the husband under given circumstances is treated "as father" of the illegitimate child, that he is to be treated "as if" he was the legitimate father, then this is nothing but the abbreviated formulation of a legal norm. No opposition to actuality is therein in any way posited. After all, one can, without committing such a contradiction to reality, even claim in terms of legal theory that the husband *is* the father in a legal sense, that he is the "legal" "father" of the illegitimate child, as long as by means of the term "father" one constructs a specific legal concept, i.e. the subject of particular duties and rights, *personification of a particular complex of norms*. A fiction in the sense of a contradiction to actuality would only emerge if one identified this legal notion of a "father" with the *natural object* of the male *progenitor* who bears the same name. Such a fiction, however, would be *plainly* mistaken, harmful and completely unnecessary. It would be the same fiction as the one characterised above in the hypostatisation of the legal person into the natural fact of *man*, or the "real" organism. And in this case it would be a fiction of legal theory, i.e. of an activity directed at the *cognition* of the law, and not of the legislators, whose activity is directed at the *creation* of the law.

One of the greatest achievements of Vaihinger's analysis is the insight into the deep relation between the mathematical method and the conceptual technique of legal science.[24] However, the complete identification of in particular the *legislative* fiction with the fictions of mathematics surely is mistaken. "The similarity of method of both sciences is not limited to their basic concepts, which in both fields are of purely fictitious nature, but equally shows in their entire methodological procedures. As concerns the latter, what we have to deal with in both fields most of the time is to subsume a singular case under a universal, the determinations of which should only be applied to this singular. However, the singular resists this subsumption. For the universal is not comprehensive enough to comprehend the singular under itself. In mathematics we have to deal, for instance, with the case of having to subsume warped lines under the straight ones; after all, this has the great advantage of allowing us to make computations with them. In legal science we want to bring the single case under a law in order to apply the benefits and criminal sanctions of the latter to the former. Now, in both cases a *relation, which in actually does not pertain* is seen to pertain: thus, for instance, the warped line is taken to be straight and the adoptive son is taken to be the actual son. A warped line never is straight and an adoptive son never is an actual son; or, to take another example: the circle should be conceived of as an ellipse; in legal science the defendant who does not

[24] Ibid 80, 251, 69 ff, 187.

show up in court, is treated *as if* he submitted to the charge, and in case of demerit the appointed heir is treated *as if* he had died before the deceased testator." [25] However, Vaihinger seems to overlook the fundamental difference between the thought processes of mathematics and the formulations of the legislator: it is true, in both cases we want to subsume a single case under a universal norm or concept, where, however, the norm or concept is not universal, not broad enough to capture the single case in question. But what does the legislator do? He simply *broadens* the norm, he extends it to the new case—and he does so without any fiction, without any contradiction to actuality. The new case relates to the extended norm in no way differently than any other case relates to the norm regulating it. The intended relation *is* established; within the field of law this relation it is *not* a relation which "*cannot in actual reality* be established", but it is effectively established in the "actuality" of the law. In contrast, mathematics claims that the circle is an ellipse and that the warped line is straight and thereby sets an opposition to reality. However, the law does *not* claim—after all it does not claim anything—that the adoptive son is an actual son, that the defendant who does not show up has actually submitted to the charge, or that the unworthy heir died before the testator. It only "claims", i.e. it posits—and this positing stands in opposition *to nothing*—that the same norms apply to the adoptive son as apply to the actual son—just as it posits that certain norms apply to men and women alike irrespective of their gender difference—and it posits, that the failure of the defendant to appear in front of a court has the same legal consequences as the acceptance of the claim, etc.

Similarly, no true fiction can be found in the principle of English law, which Vaihinger uses as an example of a fiction: the king can do no wrong.[26] The king "truly" can do no wrong insofar as the legal norm withdraws its validity in relation to him. After all, "wrong" is no natural fact. A "wrong" is a matter of fact only in its relation to a legal norm, only by means of the fact that it is included as content in a prescriptive norm, or as a condition in a legal norm that prescribes punishment or a sanction. Insofar as the legal order does not forbid acts or omissions of the king, insofar as it does not make them conditions of punishment or a sanction, *there is* no wrong of the king. The principle of Austrian and German law, which is analogous to the English principle, i.e. the monarch is immune, simply creates the legal fact, to which alone a legal fiction could stand in opposition. The *mistaken view*, that a wrong would be a natural fact, that murder was a legal wrong, even when it were not forbidden by law or threatened by a sanction, creates the opinion that the mentioned legal principles, which only limit the applicability of the legal order in certain ways, are fictions because they could come into contradiction with actuality.

It seems that Vaihinger did actually have a sense of the difference between the "fictions" of the legislator and the mathematical fictions. He obfuscated this difference for himself by first correctly juxtaposing legal *science* and mathematical cognition, then, however, by dealing with constructs of the *legislator* and not of legal science. He states: "It is, however, much easier for legal science to deal with its

[25] Ibid 70.

[26] Ibid 697.

fictions than it is for mathematics: in the case of legal science actual facts stand in opposition to arbitrary legal rules; thus, a transformation is quite easy. One simply has to think that the matter were as such." However, here we do not have to deal with a "transformation" at all; the legislator—and with him everyone applying the law—does not "think" that the matter were as such, he rather *decrees* whatever he wishes. This is how the "matters" become actually, i.e. legally, as they are. Within his realm, the legislator is almighty, since his function rests in nothing but his ability to tie certain legal consequences to legal conditions. A fiction of the legislator would thus be as impossible as a fiction of nature itself. After all, the law could only be opposed to itself—i.e. to its own reality. This, however, would be nonsensical.

The opposition which is posited in the fictions of legal science (which have to be distinguished from "fictions" which are mere abbreviations within legal parlance) can occur only in relation to the legal order, to the law as the object and thus to what counts as the "actuality" of legal science. As soon as it is translated into an actual statement, the construct created by legal science, i.e. the ancillary concept, has to imply a claim which stands in opposition to the legal order, which cannot be deduced from the legal order. Such a case has been exemplified above in the concept of the person. Such a contradiction to the legal order is, of course, impossible in the case of the fictions of the legislator, it is only a superficial semblance created by mere use of certain words.

We can see from the following example of the praetorian fiction of Roman Law that Vaihinger himself actually had the opposition to the legal order in mind when he spoke of juridic fictions. He quotes Pauly's *Realenzyklopädie des klassischen Altertumswissenschaft,* III, p. 473: "The Romans called fictio a *facilitation of the circumvention of the law* allowed by praetorian law, which consisted in the license that under certain circumstances some condition demanded by strict law can be considered to be fulfilled, even though it has not actually been fulfilled. Thereby certain legal consequences ensue, even though the conditioning facts have not occurred in the way demanded by the law".Vaihinger comments as follows: "This explanation mutatis mutandis *neatly* fits the *scientific* fiction in the narrower sense; here, too, a facilitation and circumvention of difficulties takes place, which here, too, is a consequence of the very complex state of affairs: here, too, the demands of the *strict laws* of logic are circumvented, here, too, consequences and practical conclusions occur, which are *correct*, despite that which is presupposed is itself *incorrect*." However, neither Pauly's description of the "fictio", nor Vaihinger's conclusions drawn from it are entirely correct. The conclusions drawn depend on the claim that the Praetorian fiction is a "circumvention of law", and that it posits an opposition to what the law demands. However, this is not the case, as the Praetor himself is a legislative organ, since he—by means of *constitutional* law—does not only apply the law, but he creates it. Now, if the Praetor allows a peregrinus to institute legal proceedings which according to the ius strictum only a civis can do *as if* he were a civis, this means nothing but the following: a *legal* norm has been posited, in which certain rights and duties of the civis are extended to the peregrinus and this legal norm can be formulated without any reference to an 'As-If' and without any fiction: the peregrinus is allowed to levy the claim just as the civis is.

The "consequences and practical conclusions" which here occur, are not "correct", *despite* the conditions being incorrect, but only *because* the conditions, too, are "correct", i.e. lawful, and are in line with the new legal rule created by the Praetor. The mistake made here is to take the strict ius civile as the only element of the legal order, just as if the Praetorian law—as fully valid, objective law—were not part of it. The right to institute an action by the peregrinus cannot contradict the legal order, since it itself rests on one of its rules! However, at least one fiction can be uncovered here: the fiction that the Praetor does not *make* law, but that he only *applies* the law. As someone merely applying the jus civile the Praetor, in granting the peregrinus the right to institute an action which only the civis has, would set a contradiction to the legal order which consisted entirely in the jus civile. And this contradiction which occurs in the *application of law* would have to hide beneath a fiction. This fiction, however, does not consist in the claim that the peregrinus actually is a civis, but in the claim that the legal order also grants the right to institute an action to the peregrinus. The Praetor in no way denies the difference between the civis and the peregrinus in general. He only denies it—insofar as he presents himself as someone applying the law—in terms of standing, i.e. he claims: the peregrinus, too, has standing. However, this fiction becomes superfluous, nay, impossible, in the very moment that the other fiction falls away, the fiction that treats the Praetor as someone merely applying the law and not as a delegated legislator.

1.4 III

From what has been said so far it should emerge that as concerns the possibility of a fiction—which depends on the possibility of a contradiction to the legal order—the application of the law differs from legislation. In relation to the legal norms someone applying the law actually does face a situation very much like the one mathematics faces in relation to concepts like circles, ellipses, the warped or straight line, etc. The judge, the businessman, cannot arbitrarily extend and restrict the legal norms, in other words: they cannot tie arbitrary legal consequences to arbitrary legal conditions. If one wishes to subsume a certain case under a norm, which does not capture this case, then a fiction may seem expedient: to treat the case *as if* it fell under the legal norm. The law threatens a sanction for the damaging of a public telegraph, but leaves a similar damaging of a public telephone without threat of sanction, or if it threatens the delict with—in the view of the person or organ applying the law—too mild a sanction, then it is a fiction if the judge applies to someone who damages a public telephone a sanction, which the law had intended only for someone damaging a public telegraph, in that he uses the norm intended to protect the telegraph to protect the telephone; the judge here does not proceed *as if* the telegraph were a telephone, this is not what the judge claims and wants to claim, but he proceeds as if the law threatened the same sanction to a damaging of a telephone as it does to the damaging of a telegraph. The juridic fiction can only involve a fictitious *legal* claim, and not a fictitious *actual* claim. After all, the judge has to explicitly determine the facts and must not ignore that a *telephone* and not a telegraph was damaged. His claim, which stands in opposition to the *legal* order and not to actual reality, is: the public telephone, too, *must* not be damaged. Claiming the validity of an—invalid—general norm is the means by which he reaches the correct judgement, at least the one intended by him. It is not the claim that a telephone is a telegraph.

The fact that the application of the law can include legal fictions, derives from the fact, that it itself presupposes legal *cognition*, or, put more correctly, that the compound act of legal application includes an element of legal *cognition*. However, it has to remain doubtful whether these fictions of the application of the law—which are identical with the cases of interpretation by means of *analogy*—are similar to the epistemological fictions in the sense that the latter reach a *correct* conclusion—and be it by means of an explicitly incorrect idea. After all, the "correctness" of legal application can only mean *legality*, and not utility. The fiction that the warped line is a straight line is a mathematically correct result. It would have to be a legally correct, i.e. a lawful result which is reached by means of the analogous-fictitious interpretation. Now, the legality of this result can only be measured against the legal order itself; however, the *contradiction* to the legal order in the case of a fictitious-analogous application of law is not merely a provisional, correctible one, but a definite one, one which cannot be corrected in due course. Now, Vaihinger claims as a central feature of the fiction, "that these (fictitious) concepts either historically become obsolete or logically fall away." "Insofar as we deal with an opposition to actual reality, a fiction can only be of value as long as it is employed provisionally …" And he says particularly about semi-fictions: "That is why … a *correction* has to step in; since without such a correction they would not be applicable to the actual world.[27] Of the juridic fictions, however, he claims that such a correction is not necessary. After all, in this case we do not deal with the exact estimation of actual reality, but with the subsumption under an arbitrary law, a human artifact, not a natural law, not a natural relation.[28] However, it is thereby by no means established that the correction of juridic fictions in case of the *application of the law* is superfluous! For the intellectual activity that makes use of the juridic fiction (fictions of legislation as well as the fictions of the application of law) cannot be seen to be an estimation of *actual reality*. This, however, can only have the consequence that there is no need for an opposition to actual reality and for an epistemological fiction in Vaihinger's sense. Insofar as epistemological fictions are possible as "juridic" fictions, they can only be fictions of the cognition of the law. And for them the contradiction, which constitutes the essence of a fiction, relates to the legal order, which is the "actual reality", the object of cognition of legal science. *This kind* of contradiction, however, is just as much and just for the same reasons in need of correction, as the *analogous* contradiction in the case of physical, mathematical or otherwise (in the broader sense) scientific fictions, since without such a correction the juridic fiction would be just as inapplicable to the legal order, i.e. to the actuality of juridic

[27] Ibid 172/73.

[28] Ibid 197.

cognition, as the other fictions would be inapplicable to nature. The fictions of the *application of law*—i.e. the analogical interpretation—, conversely, sets an *irresolvable* opposition to the legal order. It is not a detour, which in the end leads us to the "actuality" of the law, but an error, which might lead to what the feigning actor thinks helpful and expedient, but which never leads to the object of legal science: *the law*. For this very reason, the *justification* of this kind of juridic fiction, i.e. the fiction of the application of law, has to be seen to be theoretically impossible. This needs to be expressly stressed since Vaihinger wants to include in particular these juridic fictions as *equal* and *equivalent* phenomena into his system and his theory of fictions, which, after all, by and large intends to be an apology of fictions.

However, what needs to be considered is that in fact such an inadmissible fiction *only* occurs, as soon as an undeniable and irresolvable opposition to the legal order is posited. This is *not* the case in all of those instances of analogical applications of law where the legal order allows for, indeed under certain circumstances requires, an analogy. Now, whether this is expressly stipulated in a legal norm, like, for instance, in Article 7 of the Austrian Civil Code, or whether one relies only on a norm of customary law or—in the cases in which one does not rest one's claim on positive law—on a natural principle of law, does not matter, since an opposition to the legal order—and thus a fiction—is impossible as soon as the legal order itself allows for the application of the analogy and thus also demands the decision reached by means of the analogy. One should not forget that no jurist, who declares the analogy to be admissible, will ever decline to let the decision reached by analogous interpretation be called *law*. This, however, means: the statement, which demands the analogy, has to be claimed to be a *legal norm*. The establishment of the existence of such a legal norm is, of course, an entirely different matter. In the light of legal theory a fiction of the legislator is thus impossible, a fiction of someone applying the law is completely inadmissible, since it is *in violation of the purpose of the law*.

1.5 IV

In order to demonstrate that the fictions of the application of the law do not belong within Vaihinger's system of fictions, it needs to be stated, that *cognition* of law—which alone can lead to a fiction in the true sense of the term—only plays a subordinate role in the application of law. It is not the essence, the actual purpose of this activity, but only the means by which it reaches its goal. The application of law, just as the creation of law, does not really intend the cognition of law, but its realisation, it is about *acts of the will*. The cognition of law, the *theory* of law, only prepares the practice of the law, it creates the tools for the latter.

Now, Vaihinger may himself have made a distinction between legal *theory* and legal *practice*.[29] However, he overlooked the principled difference between the truly epistemological fictions of legal *science* and the pseudo-fictions of legal practice. What is more, Vaihinger nearly exclusively concerned himself with the so-called

[29] Ibid 257.

"fictions" of legal practice. Still, at least some fictions of legal theory can be found in his work. Unfortunately, they are most of the time only sketched out by a catch-word and presented without further analysis. He especially missed out on an analysis of the legal person in general and of the legal person of the state in particular.[30] The fictions of "freedom" and of the "social contract" establishing the state, which Vaihinger also deems necessary for the establishment of public criminal law, are not fictions of legal theory, but ethical fictions. The "right" of the state, to punish, demands a moral, and not a juridic justification; and the freedom of the will as a foundation of this right is by no means a *necessary* ethical fiction. Since the principle of general prevention or deterrence, too, which Vaihinger mentions, is a justification of punishment, which rightfully exists without any fiction of freedom. The "fiction" of freedom only emerges when one mistakenly applies a normative category to the—causally determined—natural reality, when one illicitly and syncretistically combines an is with an ought, a syncretism which, at least for the sake of juridic cognition, is certainly superfluous. One acts or is going to act in a certain way (consideration of is), only if one *can* act in this way, or if one *must* act in this way. The statement which declares that a certain act actually *will happen* (in the future), even though this act has been seen to be impossible, posits a contradiction to the object it tries to capture in the statement: to actual reality; it is thus inadmissible and worthless. However, the statement: someone *ought* to act in a certain way, never posits a contradiction—be it to actual reality, or to any other object of cognition—not even in the case in which the action, which ought to be performed, appears to be impossible. Only if one ignores the difference between is and ought (as two distinct forms of cognitions) and takes the *possibility of being actual* as a conditions of an ought-statement, only then the illusion is created that there existed a contradiction between the statement, which posits that something *ought to be*, and the statement, which claims as a *matter of fact* that this something is actually impossible; only then the following error emerges: that a certain content (the action which ought to occur) has to be *actually* possible, the actor thus has to be *feigned to be free*, in order to make possible the statement of ought, and thereby to simultaneously make possible the duty to act and maybe even the duty to act differently than one actually acts, differently than one actually must or can act. A methodological error leads to the fiction of freedom, which becomes superfluous as soon as one acknowledges this error. This is the only way to explain the curious fact that a strict opposition between the freedom within ethics and jurisprudence, on the one hand, and the un-freedom within natural science, on the other, could emerge, yet could at the same time be ignored by both sides. The ethical fiction of freedom thus is useful and necessary only as long as the adequate methodological insight is absent. And it is in this way that Vaihinger's second main characteristic of the fiction must seem so very fitting: "If there is a contradiction to actual reality, the fiction can only be of value if it is used provisionally. Until experience is enriched, or until the methods of thought are sufficiently sharpened, to be able to replace these provisional methods with definite ones."[31]

[30] Ibid 259.

[31] Ibid 17.

Vaihinger does not capture the fiction of the social contract establishing the state correctly, when he claims: "The state does not want to base its coercive law on mere might, not even on purely utilitarian grounds, but it wants to establish it as true right: this, however, is possible only by means of the fiction of a contract: after all, the jurist knows of no other rights than those emerging from contracts." However, the fiction of the social contract establishing the state, just as the fiction of freedom, does not actually serve the *juridic* justification of the coercive functions of the state. After all, such a juridic justification contains nothing but the fact that something is derived from a juridic norm. However, what is demanded here is the justification of the legal norm, i.e. of the norm which orders the infliction of coercion itself. This justification is effected by means of a higher, extra-legal norm: the moral or "natural" fundamental principle: pacta sunt servanda. *This is the reason why* the contract has to be feigned, and not because the jurist allegedly knows no other law than that which emerges from contract. Moreover, the latter statement is factually mistaken. The contract is but one of many matters of facts, to which the legal order attaches rights and duties.

The social contract establishing the state thus is in fact no fiction of legal theory, but an ethical fiction, a fiction of a moral world-view. A jurisprudential perspective has to drop precisely such a fiction and the imagination of an ethical justification of the law.

1.6 V

After all, legal science—as cognition of a particular object—can only be possible if one assumes the *sovereignty of the law* (or, which is the same, of the state), i.e. if one takes the legal order as an independent system of norms which is not dependent on any higher order. Otherwise only a moral science (ethics) or theology would be possible, depending on whether one takes the law to be a result of morality or religion. (As long as we consider the law to be an order, a complex of norms, we do not need to consider here a possible natural science or sociology of law, which clearly would also have to be considered a science of law). Now, Vaihinger thinks that a fiction lies precisely in this separation of law from morals. The "fictitious isolation", that occurs in the positivistic view (i.e. in a view which presumes the law to be an independent, sovereign order), was "the provisional departure from an integrated part of reality."[32] Vaihinger thinks that for the legislator and jurist the separation of law and morality as two distinct realms might be of high value, however, one should not forget, that here the "in fact" had to be replaced by an "as-if". "Since, however one wants to determine the relation of these two very important areas of life, one can hardly reach the conclusion that these two, as a matter of fact, have no relation to each other whatsoever. This comment is of particular importance, as due to a lack of methodological insight jurists regularly take this fiction to be an actual

[32] Ibid 375.

relation, which is a disastrous error. The one-sided approach can do many a good service to legal science and the practical life of the law, however, at a certain point the abstraction, which has been provisionally made, always needs to be replaced with full actual reality being reinstated."[33] However, this view cannot—especially not from the point of view of Vaihinger's own theory of fictions—be agreed with. After all, the claim that the law was a system of norms which is independent from morality, which in its normative validity is not reducible to an ethical order, can for the very reason not be a "provisional" departure from an integrated part of reality, as neither law nor morality—both being considered as complexes of norms—are part of the realm of that actuality, which for Vaihinger is the benchmark from which the fiction departs, and which is identical with nature, with the world of the senses, and as neither legal science nor ethics try to capture this actuality in their objects. The relation of law and morality is in no sense a relation between two "realms of life" as two parts of *natural* reality. Their "actual" relation is no relation in actuality, i.e. in reality which can be captured by natural science understood in the broadest sense and also including social sciences. The juridic perspective which Vaihinger accuses of committing a fictitious isolation, cannot depart from an integrated part of actuality, not even in determining the relation of its object to morality, since it does not even have actuality in view. However, insofar as law and morality are considered as—social—facts, as "actual" going-ons in nature (and it remains an open question whether this is at all possible), they are not objects of specific juridic cognition, or of normative ethics. And in this sense the related fictitious isolation cannot take place at all. There is no need for it at all. For an inquiry of the actuality of the so-called experience of law, of the factual moral ideas and the "moral" actions effected by them—its methodological possibility simply assumed—law and morality are something completely different than what these two same words denote as objects of normative legal science and ethics. And for an act of cognition aiming at actual psychological facts and actions there can be no fundamental difference between an actuality called "law" and an actuality called "morality", and certainly no expediency of a fictitious isolation of both, and be it only a provisional one. Vis-a-vis a juridic perspective such a "full actual reality" can never be "given back its rights".

Now, for Vaihinger the representation of a legal order—as a complex of norms of ought—just as the representation of a moral order appears as a fiction. According to him concepts like norm, duty, the ideal etc. have to be subsumed under the class of practical fictions.[34] Now, even though Vaihinger does not extensively engage with the concept of a legal norm, of the legal ought and of the legal duty, etc. it should be assumed that we can say the same about them as we can say about the ethical concepts, which Vaihinger all expresses as fictions. Thus, one could say with Vaihinger: the jurist treats the law, *as if* it were a sum of ought-norms. However, *if* this is a fiction, if the law *in actuality* is not an ought-norm, what *is* the law "in actuality"? And moreover: What *is* an ought-norm? Put differently: if the assumption that the law as an ought-norm is a fiction, then the law needs to be able to be something

[33] Ibid 375.

[34] Ibid 59 ff.

else, something "actual", and then the "ought-norm" has to be something "actual"; however, it has to be something else than the law "actually is" and the ought-norm must not itself in turn be a fiction. Since the fiction obviously consists in a likening, i.e. in the erroneous identification of something actual with something else which is actual. To put it in the formula of a fiction: X is treated, *as if* it were Y (even though X is not Y); this means, however, that both X and Y have to be actual, or they have to be claimed to be actual. It is not their existence but only the identification which is fictitious. In Vaihinger the formula of fiction is the following: "In this formula it is stated, that some given actual entity, some particular thing was *likened* to something else, the impossibility or non-reality of which is at the same time claimed … e.g. in the juridic fiction the formula is as follows: this heir is is to be treated as he would have been treated had he died before his father, the bequeather, i.e. he is to be disinherited"What is relevant in this context is only the insight that both elements, the "heir" and "the one having died before the bequeather" in and for themselves, i.e. irrespective of their position in the relationship of the fiction, are something *actual*. Vaihinger continues: "What is expressed here is, first and foremost, a *likening*, i.e. the invitation to perform a likening or a subsumption; such a statement initially claims nothing else but the following: man is to be considered as a gorilla. But why should he be considered as such? Simply because he is like a gorilla. All other cases are like this one: we are invited to liken something to something else, however, together with this invitation we are also made aware that the likening rests on an *impossible condition*; however, instead of declining to undertake the likening, it is nevertheless still performed, albeit for other reasons."[35] The fiction consists in the likening of two actualities, despite the impossibility of this likening.

However, the law from the very beginning is nothing actual. There is no part of natural reality which can be called law. And even if one wanted to disregard this fact, and wanted to still consider the law, *as if* it were an ought-norm, the question emerges, what an ought-norm actually *is*? Well, nothing actual, but itself a fiction. And the fiction here does not only consist in the 'as-if' formula, but also in that, to which the law is likened by means of a fiction. The fiction, the fictitious statement, claims—in the statement which starts with the as if—the actuality of something (and be it in opposition to the latter). The analysis of every fiction has to lead to certain elements of actual reality, which may be erroneously connected, but still exist; the fiction has to be resolvable, or otherwise it hovers in mid air.

Thus it has to appear as if the characteristics of the concepts of a fiction, which Vaihinger himself established, do not really fit his "practical fictions". Basically, Vaihinger had to declare *all* ethical concepts to be fictions. He does so explicitly as concerns the concepts of the ethical world order, of duty, the ideal and some others. However, in the case of all these concepts precisely that element, which according to Vaihinger is essential to the fictions, is missing: the contradiction to actual reality. After all, a contradiction to actual reality can only exist, when something actual is claimed, when something actual is at all to be known. Vaihinger states: "The ideal is a conceptual construct which is both inherently contradictory and stands in con-

[35] Ibid 164/65.

tradiction with actual reality, which, however, has tremendous, world-transcending value. The ideal is a practical fiction."[36] This could be said of any ethical or juridic concept, since it can be said of the concept of the *ought*, which is identical with the *formal* concept of the ideal. However, where can we find the contradiction with actual reality in any ought-statement, even in one which has something actually impossible as its content? The statement which expresses an ideal, a duty, an ethical demand: e.g. X ought to be charitable, and the statement describing actual reality: e.g. X is not charitable, are not contradicting each other in any way. Even if one concedes—and one has to concede this—that everything which happens, *has to* happen as it happens, and *cannot* happen otherwise, so that any ought which has a different content than the is would demand something *impossible*, no contradiction between is and ought would be present. The fact of *a* is only contradicted by the fact of *non-a* and not by the ought of *non-a*. Unless one wanted to resolve the ought-statement into an as-if-statement and claimed that in saying that *a* ought to be, I act as if *a* were the case; and if I claim: X ought to be charitable, I feign X (in thought) as actually being charitable, even though in reality he is not charitable. Ought would then be a feigned is. However, this view is obviously incorrect. In the representation of ought we make use of a form completely different from the representation of an is, a form which can take any arbitrary content without getting into logical opposition to any representation of an is, which has an opposing content. Rather than calling the ought a feigned is, I could, with the same legitimacy, call the is a feigned ought. This is why a normative concept can be inherently contradictory, however it cannot possibly contradict reality. After all, normative cognition is not directed at actual reality at all. Of course, within normative cognition fictions can very well exist, i.e. concepts can exist that are opposed to the specific object of cognition. However, this object of cognition itself and the entire activity of cognition cannot be called fictions. The concepts "god and conscience" may be fictions. The "ought", the "duty" and the "norm" certainly cannot. This is clearly shown, as soon as one tries to present the "fiction" of a duty in an "as if" statement: we ought to act as if it were our duty to act in a certain way. However, already in the first clause: we ought to act, we find included the assertion of a duty. The statement would thus be: we are *under a duty* to act as if we were under a duty. Duty and ought are identical. However, does the statement: we ought to act in a certain way, have the meaning of a fiction? It would indeed have such a meaning if we were to claim: we act in such a way, even though we do *not* act in such a way. However, precisely this assertion is not involved, but rather the following: we *ought to* act in such a way, even though maybe we do not act in such a way.

It is an entirely different question, whether and how the claims expressed in ought-statements can be demonstrated or proven, whether not every system of norms was ultimately based on a basic ought statement which is not provable. This can be conceded without thereby conceding the character of a *fiction*, i.e. of a contradiction to actuality (as natural reality).

---

[36] Ibid 67.

The concept of the ought—and with it the concepts of a duty, of a norm, of the ideal, of (objective) value—could be called fictions, would we not by a fiction understand a construct which serves the cognition of actual reality, and at the same time posits a *contradiction* to precisely this actual reality. And ought statements—the ethical just as the legal—are "fictions" only if by a fiction we understand everything which is not the expression, and particularly a consistent expression, of *natural* reality. So, even if we can concede to Vaihinger that legal norms—just as the entire world of the ought—are imaginative products of the human mind, phantasy constructs which have to be contrasted from the empirical world of the natural being,[37] a contradiction to this actuality, which is the first of his "basic features", by which one can "immediately detect every fiction",[38] by no means becomes necessary. It is precisely in the category of the ought that a form is being created, in which the phantasy can unfold without any contradiction to actual reality. On the other hand the world of the ought has to count as an object of (ethical and juridic) cognition, as its own variety of actual reality, which, albeit different from, must nevertheless be seen as equal with, natural reality, if there is to be a *true* fiction.

Vaihinger has thus illustrated his brilliant theory by precisely those juridic fictions (i.e. those of legislation and application of the law), the discovery of the nature and cognitive value of which on closer inspection cannot be seen to be his greatest merit. On the other hand, legal science knows of other, by all means analogous auxiliary concepts. However, it is not legal science which sheds a light on those fictions—as Vaihinger thinks—but vice versa: the true, theoretical fictions of legal science become more comprehensible only through the fictions of mathematic and other sciences. The fictions of legal theory have nothing specifically juridical to them at all, they do not constitute a method characteristic to legal science.

References

Schloßmann, S. 1906. *Persona und προσωπον im Recht und im christlichen Dogma*. Kiel: Lipsius & Tischer.

Vaihinger, H. 1913. *Die Philosophie des Als-ob*. 2nd ed. Berlin: Reuther & Reichard.

[37] Ibid 70.

[38] Ibid 171 ff.

Chapter 2
Kelsen on Vaihinger

Christoph Kletzer

Abstract This is a comment by the translator on the translation of Hans Kelsen's 'On the Theory of Juridic Fictions. With special consideration of Vaihinger's Philosophy of the As-If' (Chap. 1).

Vaihinger's philosophy of the As-If is a work which is almost as famous as it is unread and the strong intuitive appeal of its programme—so very neatly expressed in its title—has not been appealing enough to generate a lasting debate or something of a heritage in the English-speaking world.[1] However, Kelsen's early engagement with this work is still relevant and should attract our attention. This is so not only because of Kelsen's comments on the concept of juridic fiction, but also because in this work Kelsen sketches out, and be it en passant, early ideas on freedom, normativity and the relation of law and morality. In this early discussion of his ideas we can see themes evolve which are central to the Pure Theory albeit not yet overburdened by the discourse of the basic norm.[2]

Apart from a respectful but largely critical analysis of Vaihinger's use of juridic fictions, to which I will turn in a moment, Kelsen also makes two important points not trivially related to the question of juridic fictions. Kelsen claims, firstly, that the concept of the freedom of the will with all its metaphysical confusions is an unnecessary consequence of an insufficient separation of the realm of the is and the

[1] Being a commentary on Kelsen's essay, this is not the place to discuss Vaihinger's work in any detail. It has to suffice to say that it is a surprisingly erudite work, rich in detail which mainly suffers from a repetitive urge to subsume everything under the construct of the fiction and to claim that all problems of philosophy can be solved thereby. Vaihinger is convinced the fiction is the key to a mediation between the actual and the ideal, a mediation which he calls "idealistic positivism" and which turns out to be a thoroughly un-dialectical assemblage of disparate and incompatible elements. He is drawn to the fiction because in it he believes to have found a construct that allows us to continue to talk about the phantasies and dreamt up concepts we hold so dearly, yet still remain devoted to cognition of the actual world. It is thus a theory which promises to allow us to eat the cake, yet at the same time have it. Philosophically Vaihinger's work is a combination of voluntarism, naturalism, Nietzscheanism, pragmatism and a reading of Kant along the lines of pragmatism.

[2] On the misunderstood role of the Basic Norm, see Jestaedt 2013.

C. Kletzer (✉)
The Dickson Poon School of Law, King's College London, Strand, London WC2R2LS, UK
e-mail: christoph.kletzer@kcl.ac.uk

M. Del Mar, W. Twining (eds.), *Legal Fictions in Theory and Practice*,
Law and Philosophy Library 110, DOI 10.1007/978-3-319-09232-4_2

realm of the ought and that as soon as one accepts this separation, the concept of freedom becomes superfluous; he claims, secondly, that the law can only ever be an object of cognition if it is understood as a sovereign normative order not derived from morality or religion and that, accordingly, law and morality cannot stand in any relation to each other, because they are not realms of actuality.

But let us start with the fictions themselves. According to Kelsen, Vaihinger is right in his general characterization of them. They are very peculiar intellectual constructs: they help us gain a better understanding of the world, but they do that by making claims about the world which are in clear opposition to facts or are plainly self-contradictory. For instance, in mathematics we make regular and expedient use of the concept of the "infinitely small", despite it being clear that there is nothing in the world which is actually infinitely small and that the concept of something being infinitely small yet not being nothing, is self-contradictory; the same holds true for imaginary numbers (the square root of negatives); ditto for concepts like "matter", "force", and so on.[3] In a fiction we treat X as if it were a Y in order to better understand the world, even though we very well know that X actually is not Y or cannot be Y.

From this Vaihinger develops the four main characteristics of fictions: (1) they include a contradiction with reality or a self-contradiction, (2) the fiction has to be fundamentally provisional, i.e. it has to disappear later on or be logically eliminated, (3) the awareness of the fictivity has to be expressly stated, and (4) the fiction has to be expedient.[4]

So far so good. However, Vaihinger states that it was only in mathematics and in the law that fictions have so far been systematically discussed,[5] and goes on to elaborate his understanding of the use of fictions in the law. And it is precisely this to which Kelsen takes exception. He claims that on close inspection nearly all the examples Vaihinger uses to illustrate juridic fictions cannot count as fictions in Vaihinger's own sense. After all, Vaihinger quite naively talks about the "fictions of the law" and does not distinguish between the various possible authors of fictions, i.e. between who exactly makes the fictitious statement. According to Kelsen, Vaihinger refers to at least three possible authors: the legislature, the judiciary (and other agents applying the law) and legal science. Now, of these three, only the latter can be said to satisfy all four of Vaihinger's own characteristics of fictions.

(A) Fictions of the legislator, e.g. cases where the legislator decrees "that goods not returned to the sender within the proper time are regarded *as if* the recipient had definitely authorised and accepted them"[6] cannot count as proper fictions as by

---

[3] Vaihinger actually ends up arguing that nearly every concept is a fiction. In the 800 pages of his work there seems to be no linguistic construct which he thinks would not benefit from being understood as a fiction. After all he says that every abstract and every general term is a fiction. Now, since every term, even an indexical, has an element of generality, according to Vaihinger every term must have a fictional element. This, however, is clearly proving too much as this generality robs fictions of any explanatory power.

[4] Vaihinger (1924, p. 97).

[5] Vaihinger (1924, p. 33).

[6] Vaihinger (1924, p. 35).

means of them the legislator does not attempt to facilitate knowledge of the actual world and they do not set up an explicit contradiction to the actual world. Legislative acts are acts of will, and as such they do not intend to represent knowledge of anything. What is more, a legislative act cannot set itself in contradiction to actuality (which it does not even intend to represent). All it does is create a normative reality. So when the legislator says that A is to be treated as if it were a B, then by that he is not asking us to treat A as B in order to better know A, even though we know A not to be B. Rather, the legislative act normatively *makes* A a B. This means that the same normative consequences which are attached to B are by means of this "fiction" also attached to A. The legislator does not ask us to treat A "as if" it was a B, but he asks us to treat A "just as" B. Rather than being "fictions" in Vaihinger's sense these constructs are only a convenient way of legislating, they are mere regulative shortcuts.

There can be little doubt that Kelsen is correct here. Whether he has made more than a terminological point, and whether he ever intended more, remains, however, doubtful. What nevertheless warrants comment is the fact that since Kelsen has not yet incorporated Merkl's doctrine of the "double-headedness of the legal act",[7] he did not yet seem to appreciate the fact that there can be no difference in principle between legislation and adjudication, since both apply existing law and create new law.

(B) In contrast, the fictions of the application of the law, e.g. fictions used by a judge to treat a case which is explicitly not covered by a statute as if it were covered by a statute, might satisfy the "cognition requirement" in that as a subaltern element the application of law involves a cognitive element in relation to the law which is applied; however, what this supposed "fiction" lacks is expediency, since, according to Kelsen, these "fictions" cannot reach a *correct* conclusion. They cannot reach a correct conclusion, Kelsen claims, since as concerns the cognition of the law, only the law itself can be the standard of correctness. Now, adjudicative "fictions" do not simply provisionally treat cases as if they were different, but they permanently alter the legal material, thus violating criterion (2) and (4) of Vaihinger's above stated characteristics of fictions.

Kelsen is correct, as long as we presuppose the truth of positivism, i.e. as long as we accept that the law includes only positive norms and not some interpretative elements. However, Kelsen himself seems aware of the limitation of his position as he concedes that since juridic fictions are ultimately indistinguishable from analogical interpretations, they have to be accepted as legitimate insofar as the legislator himself allows for the latter or insofar as they are warranted by means of customary law or a "natural principle of law".[8] If that is the case, however, then it is doubtful how much Kelsen has actually shown in his discussion of the fictions of the application of law. It is generally unclear if the big problems of interpretation and the filling of legal gaps can be adequately discussed under the heading of juridic fictions.

[7] Merkl (1918).

[8] See Kelsen, Chap. 1 above, p. 16.

However, Kelsen's treatment of the fictions of the application of the law faces another challenge, one similar to the one faced by the legislative fiction: after all, just as legislation has also an element of the application of (constitutional) law, so adjudication has an element of creation of law. In that sense the "fictions" of adjudication cannot be true fictions at all, since the judge in his judgment not only applies law, but also creates new law and the same logic of legislative "fiction" applies. Now, whereas Kelsen is aware of this legislative function of judges when he talks about the Roman Praetor being a legislative organ,[9] he does not take this into consideration when dealing with fictions of the application of law.

(C) So the only legitimate fictions are the fictions of legal theory itself, i.e. the fictions used by legal science to better understand the law. So, for instance, Kelsen takes the legal subject and the legal person (including the legal person of the state)[10] to be but a personification or hypostatisation of a complex of norms which is effected by legal theory in order to better understand and handle this complex of norms. According to Kelsen there is no actual bearer of legal rights and duties out there in the world. Rather the legal subject is a construct. The fiction is created for the purpose of simplification and illustration and it becomes an error only when we mistake it to not be a mere (provisional and counterfactual) fiction, but a hypothesis or even dogma about the actual world.

(D) Let us now turn to Kelsen's discussion of freedom. Here Kelsen presents an argument he will take up again in his *Allgemeine Staatslehre* and according to which the concept of the freedom of the will is mainly the result of a profound confusion. Freedom is certainly not a fiction in Kelsen's view. It is a mistaken solution to a pseudo-problem that emerges from the insufficient distinction of the realms of the is and the ought. As soon as we sufficiently distinguish between the realms of the is and the ought, the need for freedom of will withers away:

> Only if one ignores the difference between is and ought (as two distinct forms of cognitions) and takes the possibility of being actual as a condition of an ought-statement, only then the illusion is created that there existed a contradiction between the statement, which posits that something ought to be, and the statement, which claims as a matter of fact that this something is actually impossible; only then the following error emerges: that a certain content (the action which ought to occur) has to be actually possible, the actor thus has to be feigned to be free, in order to make possible the statement of ought, and thereby to simultaneously make possible the duty to act and maybe even the duty to act differently than one actually acts, differently than one actually must or can act. A methodological error leads to the fiction of freedom, which becomes superfluous as soon as one acknowledges this error. This is the only way to explain the curious fact that a strict opposition between the freedom within ethics and jurisprudence, on the one hand, and the un-freedom within natural science, on the other, could emerge, yet could at the same time be ignored by both sides. The ethical fiction of freedom thus is useful and necessary only as long as the adequate methodological insight is absent.[11]

[9] See Kelsen, Chap. 1 above, p. 13.

[10] For a discussion of Kelsen's treatment of legal persons see Paulson (1998). It is unfortunate that Paulson does not refer to Kelsen's fiction paper.

[11] See Kelsen, Chap. 1 above, p. 17.

Freedom seems necessary only if we claim that the statement

1. A ought to φ

can be true only if[12] the statement

2. A actually can φ

is true. Now, Kelsen's argument simply is that an ought statement cannot be conditioned by an is statement. For Kelsen (1) cannot have as its necessary condition (2), as normative and factual statements cannot stand in any logical relation to each other whatsoever. They can not contradict each other and they cannot condition each other. The absence of the relation of implication can be seen from the fact that (1) does not contradict

3. A actually cannot φ

Now, to claim that (1) implies (2) means that (1) cannot be true without (2) being true. But this, according to Kelsen, can only be the case if (3) conflicted with (1), which, according to Kelsen, it does not. "Peter ought to be nice" does not conflict with "Peter is not nice". Nor does it conflict with "Peter cannot ever be nice" or "Peter is not free to be nice". But if "Peter ought to be nice" does not conflict with "Peter is not free to be nice" then it is hard to see how "Peter ought to be nice" could ever presuppose "Peter is free to be nice".

The point Kelsen is making is simply that the existence of freedom, which would be a fact, cannot ever be derived from the statement of a norm.

However, Kelsen thinks that even if we make the Kantian assumption that the natural world is fully determined causally, and that there is no place for freedom, there is still a point of talking about the ought. The normative realm can do well without freedom the concept of freedom is the result of a misunderstanding of the normative realm as having a logical relation to the actual realm.

According to Kelsen the statement "Peter ought to be nice" makes sense even when we do not attribute a magical quality of being able to suspend causation to Peter, just as it makes sense to state "The coffee ought to be hotter" without attributing any such quality to the coffee. Of course, one might argue that "The coffee ought to be hotter" only makes sense if understood as "Someone ought to have made the coffee hotter". But, this begs the question as then again we could ask whether this someone, who supposedly ought to have made the coffee hotter, was actually in a position to have been able to make the coffee hotter.

The point Kelsen is making is that we do not need freedom to make sense of ought statements. Ought cannot and does not need to be analysed in terms of freedom, it is rather itself fundamental. We know what we mean by "Peter ought to be nice", "The coffee ought to be hotter", "Brutus ought not have killed Caesar" and this understanding does not presuppose freedom of will. This Kelsenian view, of course, sits much more comfortably with a non-cognitivist, expressivist or emotivist

[12] The relation here is the relation of simple implication: (1) → (2) making (2) a necessary but not a sufficient condition of (1).

meta-ethical commitment, which takes the above statements to mean: "Peter is not nice, but I'd prefer if he was", "The coffee is not hot, but I'd prefer if it was", and "Brutus did kill Caesar, but I'd prefer if he had not" and thus takes ought-statements as expressions of desires and not of beliefs. This again shows that despite claims to the contrary Kelsen in his fundamental normative convictions might be much closer to Hume than to Kant.

(E) The second theme that Kelsen discusses en passant his debate of juridical fictions is the epistemological constitution of the object of legal science, i.e. the understanding that the sovereignty of the law is a necessary epistemological presupposition of legal science. This theme will later move more to the centre of Kelsen's legal theory and turn out to be one of the foundations of the Pure Theory of Law. Here, in contrast to the above discussion, we can find strong Kantian allusions:

> After all, legal science—as cognition of a particular object—can only be possible if one assumes the sovereignty of the law (or, which is the same, of the state), i.e. if one takes the legal order as an independent system of norms which is not dependent on any higher order. Otherwise only a moral science (ethics) or theology would be possible, depending on whether one takes the law to be a result of morality or religion. (As long as we consider the law to be an order, a complex of norms, we do not need to consider here a possible natural science or sociology of law, which clearly would also have to be considered a science of law).[13]

In this statement we can find neatly encapsulated many themes Kelsen will develop further later on: the separation of law and morality as a condition of legal science, the distinction of the legal order as a normative order from other possible objects of empirical sciences, and the sovereignty of the law as an overspill of an epistemological requirement into the quality of the law itself.

What follows from this is that opposed to what Vaihinger claims, the separation of law and morality cannot be fictitious. Or, as Kelsen himself put it in exceptional clarity:

> The relation of law and morality is in no sense a relation between two "realms of life" as two parts of natural reality. Their "actual" relation is no relation in actuality, i.e. in reality which can be captured by natural science understood in the broadest sense and also including social sciences. The juridic perspective which Vaihinger accuses of committing a fictitious isolation, cannot depart from an integrated part of actuality, not even in determining the relation of its object to morality, since it does not even have actuality in view. However, insofar as law and morality are considered as—social—facts, as "actual" goings-on in nature (and it remains an open question whether this is at all possible), they are not objects of specific juridic cognition, or of normative ethics. And in this sense the related fictitious isolation cannot take place at all. There is no need for it at all. For an inquiry of the actuality of the so-called experience of law, of the factual moral ideas and the "moral" actions effected by them—its methodological possibility simply assumed—law and morality are something completely different than what these two same words denote as objects of normative legal science and ethics.[14]

Kelsen's engagement with Vaihinger's theory of fictions is an early text which despite suffering from some defects, like the language in places being laboured and

[13] See Kelsen, Chap. 1 above, p. 18.

[14] See Kelsen, Chap. 1 above, p. 19.

stilted, or Kelsen not yet having fully found his elegant voice and intellectual vocabulary, surprises in many passages with deep insights and fresh formulations still unburdened by his later systematic endeavours.

References

Hans Kelsen. 2014. On the theory of juridic fictions. With special consideration of Vaihinger's Philosophy of the as-if. In *Legal fictions in theory and practice,* ed. Maksymilian Del Mar and William Twining. Dordrecht: Springer.

Jestaedt, Matthias. 2013. Geltung des systems und Geltung im system. Wozu man die Grundnorm benötigt—und wozu nicht. *Juristen Zeitung* 21:1009–1021.

Merkl, Adolf. 1918. Das doppelte Rechtsantlitz. *Juristische Blätter* 57:425–427.

Paulson, Stanley L. 1998. Two problems in Hans Kelsen's legal philosophy. In *Pragmatism, reason and norms. A realistic assessment,* ed. Kenneth R. Westphal, 219–242. New York: Fordham University Press.

Vaihinger, Hans. 1924. *The philosophy of 'As-If'. A system of the theoretical, practical and religious fictions of mankind.* Trans. C. K. Ogden. London: Routledge and Kegan Paul.

Chapter 3
Is Law a Fiction?

Geoffrey Samuel

Abstract Taking its cue from Walter Jones' 1940 monograph on the history of legal theory—one of whose chapters is entitled The Fiction Theory—this present chapter examines the credibility of such a theory. Much of course depends upon how one defines fiction. However if one adopts Hans Vaihinger's philosophy of 'as if' as an 'epistemic attitude' and applies it, not so much to law as an object in itself, but to the constituent parts of legal knowledge (individual theories, concepts, categories, rules and reasoning methods) the philosophy can begin to seem one that should be taken seriously by jurists. Vaihinger is not without his critics, it must be said, and if care is not taken the whole notion of a legal fiction can lose its meaning. Yet the philosophy of 'as if' can survive these criticisms and force jurists to think, if not about fictions themselves, then at least about its opposite, namely reality. What is law as a 'reality'? If it is a 'thing' made up of its constituent 'properties', then these properties, on closer examination, incorporate many fictional elements and notions. Then, again, perhaps one might think of law 'as if' it is a fiction.

To pose the question whether or not law is a fiction is, equally, to pose a question about the relationship between legal theory and legal history.[1] For the idea of fictions in law is one associated with a past stage of legal development from which, so modern lawyers like to assert, legal thinking has largely, if not completely, escaped.[2] Yet this relationship between theory and the history of theory has not been subject, at least in more recent times, to intense scrutiny in the English language literature, perhaps because a synchronic approach has been so dominant since the rise of positivism (itself an idea that is very much older than many might think). The conception of law as a system of rules or norms has underpinned legal theory—jurisprudence in the common law world—with the result that, until recently, there has been little attempt to distinguish between a theory, a philosophy and an epistemology of

[1] Cf Lobban (this volume, Chap. 1).

[2] Jones (1940, pp. 164–165).

G. Samuel (✉)
Kent Law School, University of Kent, Canterbury, Kent CT27NS, UK
e-mail: g.h.samuel@kent.ac.uk

M. Del Mar, W. Twining (eds.), *Legal Fictions in Theory and Practice*,
Law and Philosophy Library 110, DOI 10.1007/978-3-319-09232-4_3

law.[3] What might be called the rule model has dominated legal thought.[4] One exception, however, to this lack of scrutiny is Walter Jones' monograph on the history of legal theory in which the chapter headings are, perhaps, not quite what a modern specialist on jurisprudence might expect.[5] Certainly there is a chapter devoted to the law of nature, but other schools of legal thought are distributed among headings such as sovereignty theory, psychological theories, and the metaphysicians. There is also a chapter entitled the fiction theory. And it is to this chapter in Jones' book that this present chapter returns.

3.1 Introduction: Problems of Definition

The fundamental question of course that underpins any attempt to examine fiction theory is one of definition. What does one actually mean by the expression 'legal fiction'?[6] If one adopts a narrow definition the term could be said to apply only to situations where a statement asserts something to be true that is patently untrue. In fact what a narrow definition entails is the distinguishing of 'fiction' from a range of other terms like 'presumption',[7] 'concept', 'classificatory device', 'name', 'juristic creation' and so on. In this situation the notion of a legal fiction becomes little more than an island in what might be called a conceptual landscape of legal thought with the result that it is rendered incapable of acting as the basis of a theory about law itself. Perhaps, then, the history of legal fictions is not just one of escape from this seemingly primitive device but also of the isolation and confinement of the very term 'fiction'.[8]

Yet even if the notion of a legal fiction is isolated and confined by definition it still has the capacity to provoke fundamental epistemological questions as Jones indicates.[9] The debate around the question of whether a corporation is a fictional legal person (*persona ficta*) or a thing that actually exists (*res*) relates directly to the nominalist revolution of the late Middle Ages.[10] Do forests exist or are there only trees? In the eyes of the nominalist a generic expression such as forest exists only in the mind and not outside of it and thus is only a name (*nomen*) or sign (*signum*) and not an actual thing (*res*).[11] This debate had, and has, profound implications for legal theory in that nominalism challenged the idea that the mere existence of

[3] See eg Lloyd and Freeman (2008, p. 1).

[4] See in particular Susskind (1987, pp. 78–79).

[5] Jones, *op.cit.* However see also Jolowicz (1963).

[6] On this question see generally Fuller (1967). On Fuller and legal fictions Quinn (this volume, Chap. 4).

[7] *Ibid,* pp. 40–48.

[8] On which see Riles (2010).

[9] And see also Del Mar (this volume, Chap. 11).

[10] Jones (1940, pp. 166–170).

[11] Hoenen (2007, p. 975).

society implied the existence, and need for, law: *ubi societas ibi ius*.[12] If 'society' is merely a name—a fiction?—and what exist are only individual men and women[13] (although Margaret Thatcher added families as well)[14] then the question arises as to why one should be obliged politically and legally. This led to another fiction, that of social contract theory.[15] "If there was in truth no contract", notes Jolowicz, "then it is merely useless fiction to base state and law upon it."[16]

It is not difficult, then, to move from a specific debate about fiction theory—namely the one surrounding the nature of a legal corporation—to the more general idea that the institutional system of legal thought as devised by Gaius is itself a fictional structure.[17] Just as the development of the legal person (*persona*) is a fiction (*persona ficta*) so the extension of a 'thing' (*res*) to encompass intangible property is equally a fiction.[18] Gaius says that such property—namely the *res incorporalis*—is a creation of the law (*ius*), but as Jones explains the Post-Glossators tended to merge the idea of law and fiction through expressions such as *fictio iuris*.[19] Is not therefore the whole institutional system of *persona*, *res* and *actio* nothing but a *fictio iuris*?[20] Certainly Michel Villey saw the system as *un vaste théâtre qui est le monde du droit* in which there are actors (*personae*), props (*res*) and acting (*actiones*).[21] And Jones notes that there "are indeed not a few writers who frankly accept the conclusion that if, as they hold, the legal personality of the corporation is a fiction, so is also the notion of a legal right, a legal duty, and of obligation generally".[22] Yet such a conclusion does have some serious epistemological implications not just for law but also for epistemology in general. Are all conceptual structures—including those employed in the natural sciences—nothing but fictional creations?

One response to this question is to focus on the function and the validation of the conceptual model in issue. In the natural sciences the conceptual constructions for the most part are developed to model the behaviour of an external object which in its turn can act as the means of validating the model itself. If the model both explains and predicts the behaviour of the object, then the functional efficacy of the conceptual construction can be verified through correspondence between model and object. Scientists for the most part are applying a causal scheme of intelligibility to an inert object and the credibility—some would say 'truth' value—of the scheme is achieved through rigorous testing. In short, the function of a scientific model is to *explain* a phenomenon. Social science models are different because the object of

[12] See Heith-Stade (2012).

[13] Jolowicz (1963, p. 88).

[14] Thatcher (1987, p. 8).

[15] Jones (1940, pp. 109–110).

[16] Jolowicz (1963, p. 93).

[17] Samuel (1997).

[18] Sometimes envisaged as a 'person' (*hereditas repræsentat personam*): Thomas (2011, p. 229).

[19] Jones (1940, p. 169).

[20] *Ibid*, p. 171.

[21] Villey (1979, p. 44).

[22] Jones (1940, p.173).

the conceptual scheme are humans whose free will behaviour makes causal analysis extremely difficult and controversial. Causation becomes entangled with interpretation resulting in a scheme of intelligibility that emphasises *comprehension* or understanding of a phenomenon rather than an explanation of it.[23] Thus the historian who analyses an event and its effects as a 'revolution' is interposing between the event and its analysis a concept that is as much interpretative as causal. What qualifies an event as being a 'revolution'? Just as important is the level of observation. As Desjeux observes, "social reality cannot be reduced to a single equation" and so when "the level of operation changes the reality being observed changes".[24] Accordingly the historian who works on a history *de longue durée* is not denying that there are no individual heroes or great men. For if one focuses on the individual it is normal not to see social classes or institutions but this does not mean that they do not exist.[25]

Between the natural and the social sciences there is, then, a difference of epistemological representation. The schemes of intelligibility employed by the social sciences are not, it might be said, direct representations of the object under examination nor are they based on logical relations. They are an argumentative process founded on "imaginative forms of inference".[26] The model is thus a "figurative" representation of an object "which cannot be represented in its properties in directly reducing them to a conceptual determination".[27] This is what endows the regime with its fictional character.[28] The model can never bring together representation and reality; it can only provide a linguistic or textual treatment necessitating a hermeneutical, and not a causal, scheme of intelligibility. Thus the reasoning method associated with this 'fictional' model is neither deductive nor inductive. It is abductive in that concepts are regarded 'as if' they were 'true' so as to provide a means of comprehension of an object that could not otherwise be comprehended.[29]

Does this mean that social science concepts are inferior to those employed in the natural sciences? Certainly Granger asserts that a theory dealing with human facts is constantly threatened, unless one is careful, with turning into an ideology whereby myths are substituted for concepts and prescriptions for descriptions.[30] But one response is to say that social science facts do not permit themselves to be conceptualised within specific contextualised constructions capable of predicting the behaviour of the phenomenon through the manipulation of logical (often mathematical) relations. In other words there is not some objective 'reality' waiting out there to be seized by an accurate model of concepts. There are only realities existing within the models themselves and thus the 'reality' or the 'truth' is located as much in the model as in some objective reality of social facts. Another response is to say

[23] Makkreel (2006, p. 441).

[24] Desjeux (2004, p. 116).

[25] *Ibid*, p. 95.

[26] Borutti (2006, p. 461).

[27] *Ibid.*

[28] *Ibid.*

[29] Jones (1940, pp. 165–166); Borutti (2006, p. 462).

[30] Granger (1995, p. 99).

that this is just as true of models in the hard sciences as in the social sciences. In other words that all concepts are *fictiones rationis* and that once this is admitted all that matters is the "practical value in facilitating the play and speed of our mental processes."[31]

The leading exponent of this theory that all concepts, including those employed in the natural sciences, are *fictiones rationis* is Hans Vaihinger.[32] Jones regarded this theory as "somewhat gratifying to the self-esteem of lawyers [in] that in the hands of Vaihinger the legal fiction has become the starting point of a new system of philosophy." The human mind, according to this philosophy of 'as if' "is so constituted that it cannot dispense with fictions."[33] In fact Vaihinger's research question was much more sophisticated than perhaps Jones' description might suggest. How is it, to borrow Fuller's translation, that with consciously false ideas we are nevertheless able to reach conclusions which are 'right' or 'true'?[34] Or, as Christophe Bouriau, puts it: how can one reach truth through falsity?[35] In mathematics for example one can deduce from apparently absurd notions such as infinity and negative numbers results that are anything but absurd.[36] In the other sciences, on closer examination, the fundamental concepts such as energy and matter turn out to be tautological,[37] if not metaphorical.[38] Yet these models seem not only to explain a natural phenomenon or object but to predict its behaviour. Indeed, as we have seen, the validity of the scientific model lies in its refutability (or potential refutability), that is to say in its relation to the actual behaviour or existence of the object or phenomenon. But what is this reality—these objects and phenomena? The problem, as Fuller notes, is to be found in the notion of a 'thing' which is defined only in terms of its properties.[39] One defines sugar in terms of its sweetness and other properties thus making a distinction between a thing (sugar) and its properties (sweetness etc); yet the "properties *are* the thing".[40] Even reality becomes fictional, as if 'things' exist independently of their 'properties'. As Fuller goes on to say, the difficulty is not answering Vaihinger's question; the difficulty lies in "the assumptions that were made in *asking* the question."[41]

---

[31] Jones (1940, p. 166).

[32] On which see Fuller (1967, p. 94 ff.). There is an English translation (*The Philosophy of "As If"*, 1924, Routledge. Trans C. K. Ogden) but Fuller said that it is very unsatisfactory: Fuller (1967) at 94 (footnote). There is now a French translation by Christophe Bouriau: H Vaihinger, *La phiosophie du comme si* (Éditions Kimé, 2nd ed, 2013). See also Kelsen (this volume, Chap. 1).

[33] Jones (1940, p. 166).

[34] Fuller (1967, p. 97).

[35] Bouriau (2013a, p. 13).

[36] Fuller (1967, p. 98).

[37] *Ibid*, pp. 99–100.

[38] *Ibid*, p. 115 (a "metaphorical element taints all our concepts").

[39] On Fuller and fictions see Quinn (this volume, Chap. 4).

[40] Fuller (1967, p. 101).

[41] *Ibid*, p. 103 (emphasis in the original).

3.2 Legal Science and Legal Theory: Fact or Fiction?

When one moves from social science theorising in general to theorising about law a number of particular problems emerge that are perhaps less of an issue in other social science disciplines. What actually is the object of a legal theory? Is it 'law' or is it 'social reality'? Or, again, is it the actors within the legal world? This issue has emerged with regard to the notion of a legal 'science' which, thanks to the expression *scientia iuris* to be found in the Roman sources, has something of a long history.[42] Is one talking of law as a science or is one talking of a science of law? The issue is one both of meta-language and of epistemology.[43] If one is talking of a science of law then the object of the science (or theory) is 'law'. What is law as a 'fact', or at least as an object of scientific inquiry? If, however, one is talking of law as a science the object is different: how does law conceptualise social reality? These two different levels are evident when, for example, one compares the writings of Ronald Dworkin with those of Peter Birks. Dworkin's enquiries were aimed at explaining the notion of 'law' itself while Birks was concerned with how legal systematics relates to social practices.[44]

As has been mentioned, another object of investigation is what might be called legal actors, for example judges, lawyers, legal academics, policemen, bailiffs and so on. The meta-language to be employed here depends upon the nature of the enquiry: is one looking at what these officials do or is one theorising about how they think—or indeed about how they ought to think? These different levels of operation are not always clearly discernible in the literature on legal theory—in courses on 'jurisprudence'—because the emphasis tends to be on describing, analysing and contrasting the theories of different theorists or schools of theorists. Thus for example Dworkin is often presented as the antagonist of Herbert Hart and while Dworkin did indeed build his theories on a critique of an aspect of Hart's positivism it does have to be remembered that the two authors had two rather different objects in mind. Hart was primarily concerned with fashioning a theory of law in which his object was a model of rules. Dworkin, in contrast, had as his object one of the key actors in the legal world, namely the judge and judicial decision-making. For the most part were they really talking about the same thing?

These distinctions are important when looking at legal theories in the context of fictions. Hart, in claiming that his theory was sociological in its orientation ("an essay in descriptive sociology"),[45] would no doubt have been disturbed by the idea that his thesis was a work of fiction, although as we have seen fiction theory has a respectable place in social science epistemology.[46] Moreover Hart actually uses a

---

[42] Troper (2003, p. 26 ff.).

[43] *Ibid*, p. 33.

[44] See Samuel (2013, pp. 99–104).

[45] Hart (1994, p. vi).

[46] Borutti (2006).

fictional character to help explain his concept of law.[47] Dworkin, however, openly made use of fiction in two principal ways: he created a fictional superhuman judge and he compared the writing of judgments with the production of a chain novel. Had, then, Jones been updating his book today it would be interesting to see under which chapter headings these two legal theorists would have been discussed. In fact this issue is more interesting than it might first appear given that Jones did not employ the kind of headings with which legal theorists are today familiar. Positivism is located primarily, although not exclusively, in the chapter on metaphysical theories and while this is understandable in respect of a positivist such as Hans Kelsen—actually given his own chapter by Jones under the heading of Pure Theory—it might at first sight seem that such a label would be inappropriate for the Hart's 'sociological' version of positivism.

However Hart's key notion underpinning his thesis—the notion that provides a system of rules with its legal authority—is the 'rule of recognition'. As he says, this may take a variety of forms,[48] but "unlike other rules of the system" the assertion that the rule of recognition exists "can only be an external statement of fact." It exists as the "practice of the courts, officials, and private persons in identifying the law by reference to certain criteria."[49] In insisting on its "existence as a matter of fact"[50] is not Hart actually asserting that the courts, officials and private persons act 'as if' there is a rule of recognition? And even if the rule were to be reduced to a tangible text of some sort would this actually alter its 'as if'—its fictional—quality? The point that needs stressing is that to say that the rule 'exists' because one can observe legal actors apparently observing it is to provide a constructive model that is not actually directly representing the object in question. The empirical object in question is the totality of practices of the actors which means that the rule of recognition is unobservable as an empirical reality. The rule of recognition can only be envisaged; it can only be presented 'as if' it is there in the practices.[51] Dworkin's 'as if' construction—his analogy between judging and writing chain novels—might be further removed as a schematic model from the actual object (judging) being described than is the case with respect to the rule of recognition and the practices of legal actors. But this does not make the Hart model any less of a fictional ('as if') construction. Just as the practices to be observed in churches and monasteries are of religious actors acting 'as if' there is a God, so legal actors act 'as if' there is a rule of recognition.

Another way of approaching this rule of recognition issue is to compare Hart's model of primary and secondary rules with Hans Kelsen's theory of norms.[52] In order to avoid infinite regression and to provide a foundation for his pyramid of norms Kelsen proposed the fundamental norm (*Grundnorm*) as a 'necessary supposition'

[47] Hart (1994, pp. 51–78).

[48] *Ibid*, pp. 94–95.

[49] *Ibid*, p. 110.

[50] *Ibid*.

[51] Borutti (2006, p. 461).

[52] On which see Kelsen (this volume, Chap. 1) and Kletzer (this volume, Chap. 2).

or hypothesis. Later, however, and influenced by Vaihinger, he abandons hypothesis for the word fiction on the basis that hypothesis is a notion that applies only to something that has existed.[53] A hypothesis claims to correspond with facts.[54] The *Grundnorm*, in contrast, not only does not correspond with any fact but also contains an internal contradiction which renders it an 'authentic fiction'.[55] It is contradictory, notes Christophe Bouriau in his work on Hans Vaihinger, because it conflicts with the definition of a legal norm which asserts that such a norm has as its source an effective and identifiable will. The fundamental norm has no such source. Moreover it sets itself up as being above any original constitution and is thus a fiction in as much as it functions only 'as if' it is valid.[56] Hart's rule of recognition appears to avoid this 'as if' function in as much as it is a hypothesis and not a supposition; the rule of recognition is a term that applies to existing fact. The rule is there, within Hart's hierarchy of rules, as an endlessly living fact which continually validates, from the viewpoint of descriptive epistemology, the concept of law. Hart would no doubt have argued that there is nothing 'as if' about the rule of recognition since it is not a supposition.

Moreover this continuity of the rule of recognition would prevent it, following Vaihinger, from being a pure or authentic fiction. An authentic fiction is one which is annulled the moment that it has served its purpose, that is to say the moment it has achieved the correct result through its use.[57] Bouriau gives an example. A father decides to leave his camels to his three sons. The oldest is to get at least half of them; the middle son is to inherit at least one third; and the youngest is to be left at least one ninth. The problem is that the father leaves them only seventeen camels. The problem can be solved, notes Bouriau, by acting *as if* there are 18 camels: nine can be left to the oldest son; six to the middle son; and two to the youngest. The total, of course, comes to 17, but the problem of the inheritance is solved by the fiction that there are 18, a fiction that is immediately annulled the moment that the distribution figures are determined.[58] One difficulty, then, with Kelsen's use of the term fiction is that it does not fit the Vaihinger test since the *Grundnorm* is not annulled the moment that Kelsen's pyramid is established. In answer to this problem, Bouriau suggests that a distinction needs to be made between fictions employed for knowledge of reality—in which the Vaihinger test applies—and fictions used in transcendental constructions where the test is not vital.[59] The Vaihinger requirement "does not apply to the fundamental norm since it does not attach to the thing itself, but to the very process of thinking (*pensabilité*) about a coherent legal practice."[60]

[53] Bouriau (2013a, pp. 160–162). And see generally Bouriau (2013b).

[54] Bouriau (2013a, p. 161).

[55] *Ibid.*

[56] *Ibid.*

[57] *Ibid*, p. 74.

[58] *Ibid*, pp. 76–77.

[59] *Ibid*, p. 163.

[60] *Ibid.*

According to this logic, Hart's rule of recognition cannot be an authentic fiction because it attaches to reality and is not annulled the moment the model of rules is constructed. Yet, when one compares the rule of recognition with the *Grundnorm*, the question arises as to whether it is sufficient for Hart simply to declare that it attaches to reality. Hart certainly offers no serious empirical research to support his assertion and seems, subsequently, to admit that it is something of a presupposition.[61] Hart would no doubt point to his claim that 'assuming the validity' (Kelsen) is to be distinguished from 'presupposing the existence' (of the rule of recognition). But simply to say that a given notion exists empirically is, as already suggested, not enough to lift it out of the 'as if' category. What Hart seems to be saying is that one should proceed on the basis as if there is a rule of recognition existing as a social fact and that it is enough that those acting within the legal model act as if (that is presuppose) its existence. If challenged, then one would have to establish its existence "by appeal to facts, i.e. to the actual practice of the courts and officials of the system when identifying the law which they are to apply."[62] Yet can this 'thing' be found to exist as a reality in the same way that black-holes in space, once presupposed, can be found to exist? Might not the facts reveal only a group of actors acting 'as if' there is a rule of recognition? What if the empirical research indicates that the actors—say French or German public lawyers—are acting 'as if' they are operating within a Kelsenian pyramid of norms whose validity is founded on some basic constitutional norm? Does the *Grundnorm* then become transformed into a rule of recognition? It seems arguable that the moment a legal theorist appeals to the idea of presupposition, he or she is entering the world of 'as if'—of fiction theory.

Kelsen, Hart and Dworkin are not the only legal theorists of course. What of the legal realists: can their theories be viewed in terms of fiction theory? At first glance American Realism appears as a clear reaction against 'transcendental nonsense'—that is to say against transcendental formalism in law.[63] Yet the whole realist movement was to an extent triggered by a fictional creation, namely Holmes' Bad Man, who does not care about conceptual and transcendental constructions but wishes only to know what the courts are likely to do as a matter of fact.[64] Of course Holmes was not asserting this fictional figure as some kind of validating supposition for a theoretical construct. In fact the figure is employed as a means of deconstruction—a revolt against formalism, as has been noted. But in order to be effective the Realist school, and those schools that followed it such as Critical Legal Studies, need to create a formalist image of law in order that they have an object that can be criticised. For example Duncan Kennedy's essay on the ideological content of legal education devotes much space to describing what he feels is the typical activity in an American law school.[65] Can this description, undoubtedly set out in good faith and arguably creating an image that many law graduates would describe

[61] Hart (1994, pp. 292–293).

[62] *Ibid*, p. 293.

[63] See eg Cohen (1935).

[64] Holmes (1897).

[65] Kennedy (1982, p. 595 ff.).

as completely accurate or true, nevertheless be described as fiction? Is Kennedy proceeding on an 'as if' basis? The point to be made here is not whether Kennedy's model of the law school is inaccurate; indeed it may be the model that most closely corresponds to the typical American law school. The point is that Kennedy's model is just one amongst several possible constructions.[66] Kennedy is creating a fictional (as if) construction of a typical law school in order to achieve a particular practical purpose, namely a critique of law schools. All discourse on legal theory, in short, is about trading in fictions in the sense that to be critical it is necessary to create an object—an intellectual construction—that can act as the thing to be criticised. Movement within any school of jurisprudence is, it might be said, entirely dependent on an 'as if' *point de départ*.

3.3 Law as a Science: Science or 'As If' Science?

One of the principal contributions made by the realist and critical schools is the way in which they deconstruct traditional legal discourse in turn provoking questions about the nature and reliability of legal knowledge. Nevertheless at the abstract level of legal theory itself such schools tend to be presented as being independent of the other jurisprudential schools such as positivism, natural law, sociological jurisprudence and so on. Realism is just one school of thought amongst many, each, perhaps, having equal validity in its own right. At lower levels of abstraction the position becomes more complex because such schools of thought are often eclipsed behind the concepts and categories employed both by practitioners and by many academics. Of course there are critical contract courses, philosophy of tort or property modules and the like. But a glance at standard textbooks suggests that a largely positivistic approach—often called a 'black-letter' approach—to legal knowledge remains dominant.[67] In fairness, on closer inspection, the position may prove to be more complex. A seemingly black letter work on contract may actually reveal influences from the law and economics theorists while a work on tort might display much realist learning. After all, as William Twining once observed, "we are all realists now".[68]

Given what might be called this lower level of legal thought—the level of concepts, categories and principles—the question arises as to whether, and if so how, fiction theory is relevant. Again, of course, one is forced to ask what one means by fiction, but if an 'as if' approach is adopted as an 'epistemic attitude'[69] it will at least permit one to think about legal concepts and categories and the extent to which they accord with socially real objects such as humans and physical things. Rather than ask, then, whether conceptual constructions and categorisations are fictions in

---

[66] Bouriau (2013a, p. 79).

[67] See Cownie (2004, p. 49–50).

[68] Twining (1985, p. 382).

[69] Bouriau (2013a, p. 119).

themselves—a question admittedly not to be avoided—one can ask instead the extent to which fictions intervene in the legal perception of social reality. Two seemingly obvious fictions are of course the legal person and the intangible thing, the former certainly attracting the label from the late medieval jurist Baldus (*persona ficta*)[70] and from the modern English judiciary.[71] They intervene in what has been labelled the institutional system of legal thought[72] by way of extending the notion of a person and a thing to intangible forms. They are 'as if' institutions which, unlike the human person or the item of physical property, have no tangible counterpart in the real world.[73]

The idea that corporations and intangible property were fictions does not seem to find direct expression in Roman law itself. However the Romans made great use of an 'as if' attitude.[74] Gaius appears to suggest that towns are sometimes treated as if they are a private person,[75] while another jurist states that an inheritance is an 'as if' (*fungitur*) person in the same way as (*sicuti*) a *municipium* is treated as if a human.[76] Acts and deeds by an imperial procurator are treated as if they were the emperor's own acts;[77] adoption is based on the notion that the child is 'as if' (*quasi*) it was a natural born son;[78] a person who is not an heir might be treated 'as if' (*quasi*) he was an heir in certain circumstances;[79] and so on and so forth.[80] This 'as if' (*quasi*) attitude is also found at a more formal level in the two *quasi* categories that act as sources of obligations, namely quasi-contracts and quasi-delicts. The quasi-contracts were based on situations 'as if' a contract had been transacted and so, for example, one who receives a mistaken payment will be liable 'as if' the money was received under a contract for a loan.[81] Similarly quasi-delicts occurred in situations where there was no delict as such but the facts dictated that an obligation ought to be imposed as if there had been an actionable wrong. Thus a judge who made a case his own, while not having committed any actual wrong, was to be treated 'as if' he had acted wrongfully.[82]

Can these 'as if' situations be regarded as fictions? Peter Birks thought that the quasi categories were "a response to the challenge of the residual miscellany" and that the "elegant symmetry" of the fourfold classification of obligations into

[70] Canning (1987, p. 190).

[71] See eg Lord Reid in *Tesco Supermarkets Ltd* v *Nattrass* [1972] AC 153, at 170.

[72] Stein (1984, pp. 125–129).

[73] Canning (1987, p. 190).

[74] Thomas (2011, pp. 137–154, 169–186). And see in particular Ando (this volume, Chap. 14).

[75] D.50.16.16.

[76] D.46.1.22.

[77] D.1.19.1pr.

[78] D.1.7.6.

[79] See eg D.4.4.3.9.

[80] See further Thomas (2011, pp. 169–186).

[81] D.44.7.5.3.

[82] D.44.7.5.4.

contract, delict, quasi-contract and quasi-delict "deceives".[83] His argument was based on the assertion that legal rights have "causative events" which bring them into being.[84] The categories of contract and delict were directly based upon the causative events of contractual agreements and wrongs but the two 'as if' categories had no such underpinning. Thus, said Peter Birks, they were "only a variation upon the theme that all birds must be either pigeons or sparrows" and "that all those which are neither pigeons nor sparrows must be counted either as though they were pigeons or as though they were sparrows."[85] Professor Birks no doubt thought that he was asserting an epistemological truth, but his analogy between causative events and bird species displays as much of an 'as if' attitude as the quasi categories themselves. Causative events are being treated as if they are an external reality like birds which in fact they are not. Causation, as Christophe Bouriau points out, was not a reality at all but an "analogical fiction" based on our experience of a voluntary act in which we ourselves appear as the author (that is to say cause) of our actions on the world (effect). What we have done is to extend this relation to things outside of us in conceiving certain of these as the 'cause' of certain events.[86] The idea that cause is to be found in things themselves and that these things have a "mysterious power" to produce such and such effect is an error. For in reality an indefinite number of factors contribute to the production of the smallest event. In short, in isolating just one cause for an event we are abusively simplifying the complexity of reality.[87]

Even if one were to take issue with this general assertion about cause, there is no denying that it certainly applies to the notion of a 'causative event'. As one critic of Birks' thesis says, classification "by causative event presupposes … that we can identify from [a] list of necessary factual elements one, or perhaps some combination, which can be regarded as *the* causative event, with the other facts to be considered in some sense ancillary, or as forming the background to, the 'true' causative event."[88] And of course in reality events "do not come neatly packaged into pre-established categories."[89] The 'quasi' categories of Roman law might well, then, be 'as if' notions but as classificatory devices they are no more and no less of a fiction than Professor Birks' idea of a causative event. Indeed to claim that a causative event in law is an object to be compared with a specific bird displays a misunderstanding of classification in law as compared to classification in zoological science. The latter is founded on the identification of specific and identifiable traits in an existing tangible object while the former is a scheme that largely comprises of objects created by the classificatory scheme itself. Now whether or not fiction theory applies to scientific classification is a question, interesting as it is, that cannot

[83] Birks (1997, pp. 18–19).

[84] *Ibid*, p. 17.

[85] *Ibid*, p. 19.

[86] Bouriau (2013a, p. 110).

[87] *Ibid*.

[88] Webb (2009), 215, pp. 225–226.

[89] *Ibid*, p. 228.

be determined here.[90] However with respect to the correlation between causative event and legal category it is difficult to escape from the conclusion that both these notions are the result of a powerful imagination rather than of an accurate depiction of social reality. Indeed another commentator has recounted how Professor Birks was very fond of using storytelling—fiction—in his legal writings and how these stories have helped construct a law of restitution.[91]

It is arguable that all discourse about taxonomy in law is little more than a form of storytelling if one includes within the idea of storytelling the notion of 'as if'. Take the category of 'tort' or 'delict' founded in turn on the idea of a wrong. Such a wrong has been defined "as the *violation of a right*, and therefore a breach of duty."[92] Now the author who asserts this definition goes on to define each of these three terms, as one might expect, and produces a model in which the three terms are interdependent. Thus a right is defined entirely in relation to a duty and a wrong is defined entirely in relation to a right.[93] Rights and duties are, of course, purely normative concepts and thus relate to no external empirical object, but the concept of a wrong is, one might at first think, different in that it seemingly relates to some socially real event. Yet it is defined only in relation to a fully normative concept (right). Now, let it be said at once, this is not to suggest for one moment that this model is of no value; it might be fundamental to sound legal reasoning which in turn no doubt has a vital social role in European society.[94] But it is of course completely fictional in the sense that rights, duties and (legal) wrongs are not attempting in any way whatsoever to justify themselves through correspondence with some empirical object. The assertions cannot be tested or falsified in the way that a scientific thesis can be falsified ('the dinosaurs were wiped out by a meteorite'). Indeed, instead of an act which might constitute a 'wrong' being tested empirically, it is 'tested' (to see if it 'exists') against a concept that is wholly 'fictional'. In other words one is dealing with a model—rights, duties and wrongs—which is a pure 'as if' construction. This construction in turn is encapsulated within a category, tort or delict, which thus has as its contents nothing but fictional objects. The other categories of law—for example contract—can be viewed in a similar way. Thus the formation of a contract is often assessed in terms of an 'offer' that is 'accepted' by another party; yet what amounts to an 'offer', for example, is determined not, in the end, by reference to some empirical act but in relation to other notions such as an 'invitation to treat (to make an offer)', the 'giving of information' or a 'mere puff'.[95]

So what is the status of taxonomy in law? The answer would appear to be to provide 'a map' of the law so as to "understand how its different parts relate to one

[90] But cf Bouriau (2013a, pp. 114–119).

[91] Wu (2009) at 457.

[92] Descheemaeker (2009, p. 17) (emphasis in the original).

[93] *Ibid*, pp. 19–23.

[94] Thus for example Hohfeld fashioned his conceptual model of rights and other notions with the object of bringing more clarity into judicial reasoning: Hohfeld (1966).

[95] See eg *Pharmaceutical Society of G.B. v. Boots* [1953] 1 QB 401; *Carlill v. Carbolic Smoke Ball Co* [1893] 1 QB 256.

another."[96] Indeed it would seem that taxonomy "matters in law possibly more than in any other field of knowledge because 'pigeon-holing' of a factual situation into a particular box typically comes with a string of legal consequences."[97] This is a large claim and one wonders if the author is moving from an 'as if' construction into some more wild fictional fantasy: surely taxonomy in medicine is more important? But be that as it may, the point to be made here is that taxonomy and fiction are in a close relationship at the level not just of metaphor (classification as maps) but also of an 'as if' construction that is justified, not by reference to some empirical object, but to the notion of justice. Like cases being treated alike and predictability are the reference points.

In a revealing essay on the relation between theology and mathematics, John Puddefoot says that in a system of axioms posed by the human mind, rather than one being discovered in nature, all the various properties are deduced from the system and it is no longer necessary to ask if these properties are real.[98] One can therefore proceed intellectually without reference to the real world. This is surely just as true of legal concepts and categorisations. In constructing 'maps' or 'systems' of legal concepts that are completely isolated from any (or much) reference to the real world, the jurist is creating his or her own world; the jurist is in this sense like the novelist whose creations may receive a certain stimulus from empirical reality but are independent fictional creations.

3.4 Legal Reasoning and the Employment of Fiction

So why should the jurist wish to produce such fictional constructions? One answer, as we have seen, is to provide a reasoning model that will ensure, first, that like cases are treated alike and, secondly, that the outcome of cases (or more importantly potential cases) are predictable. Any model that ensures these two outcomes could be said to be valid irrespective of whether the model itself is a fiction. Fiction theory must not, then, be regarded as pejorative; it is simply an issue of epistemology.[99] Nevertheless, the moment that one does adopt fiction as an epistemological attitude the processes of legal reasoning begin to exhibit a complexity that simply cannot be explained by reference to some 'map' or taxonomical structure.[100]

Anyone familiar with the civil law will know that its history has been in many ways a movement from casuistic reasoning to inferential models.[101] Up until the last century, a *juge automate* was once expected to be little more than a calculating

[96] Descheemaeker (2009, p. 216).

[97] *Ibid*, p. 217.

[98] J Puddefoot (2007, p. 861).

[99] Cf Lind (this volume, Chap. 5).

[100] Although not founded on fiction theory as such, an excellent analysis of the gap between legal mapping and actual reasoning in cases can be found in Waddams (2003).

[101] See further Samuel (2009).

machine applying the axioms of a code by way of a syllogism.[102] The role of doctrine was therefore to fashion an ever more coherent model of law.[103] This epistemic attitude has by no means completely disappeared—as the legal taxonomists so vividly illustrate—nor has it been without influence on common lawyers.[104] Thus a Law Lord once observed that a "judicial decision will often be reached by a process of reasoning which can be reduced into a sort of complex syllogism, with the major premise consisting of a pre-existing rule of law (either statutory or judge-made) and with the minor premise consisting of the material facts of the case under immediate consideration." And the "conclusion is the decision of the case, which may or may not establish new law".[105] As for the written law, there is the assumption that a statute (or any other written document) can be clear and unambiguous. "[I]n a society living under the rule of law", said the same Law Lord, "citizens are entitled to regulate their conduct according to what a statute has said, rather than by what it was meant to say or by what it would otherwise have said if a newly considered situation had been envisaged."[106]

It would of course be unfair to claim that what is being asserted here is a mathematical approach to legal reasoning. The Law Lord was being more nuanced in his attitude. Yet the application of a written text, even one seemingly clear in its meaning, can present problems simply because language is not like numbers. What happens when the syllogism breaks down?

Take the following case. A married couple, before going on a world trip, drew up a will that made a particular provision if the deaths of the couple were to 'coincide'. A small ship on which they were travelling disappeared without explanation and the question arose as to whether their deaths coincided. Lord Denning MR, in a dissenting judgment, approached the problem in the following manner:

> I decline … to ask myself: what do the words mean to a grammarian? I prefer to ask: What did Dr Rowland and his wife mean by the word 'coincide' in their wills? When they came to make their wills it is not difficult to piece together the thoughts that ran through their minds.

The judge then continued:

> The doctor might well say: 'We are going off for three years to these far off places and in case anything happens to either of us we ought to make our wills. If I die before you, I would like everything to go to you, but if you die before me, I should like it to go to my brother and his boy.' She might reply: 'Yes, but what if we both die together? After all, one of those little ships might run on the rocks or something … ' 'To meet that,' he would say, 'I will put in that if your death coincides with mine, it is to go to my brother and his boy just the same'. He would use the words 'coinciding with', not in the narrow meaning of 'simultaneous', but in the wider meaning … It would not cross Dr Rowland's mind that anyone would think of such niceties as counsel for the first defendant has presented to us.[107]

[102] Carbasse (1998, pp. 293–294, 304–305).

[103] Jestaz and Jamin (2004, pp. 158–161); Jouanjan (2005, pp. 219–230).

[104] On which see Gray and Gray (2003, p. 204).

[105] Lord Simon in *Lupton v. FA & AB* [1972] AC 634, pp. 658–659.

[106] Lord Simon in *Stock v. Frank Jones* [1978] 1 WLR 231, p. 237.

[107] *Re Rowland* [1963] 1 Ch 1, p. 11.

Anyone adopting fiction theory as an epistemic attitude cannot but be struck by the fictional nature of the reasoning. Lord Denning as Terence Rattigan. Moreover in response to this argument, Russell LJ was equally vivid in his recourse to a fictional approach:

> If the evidence was that the testator and his wife were below decks in their cabin and the vessel plunged abruptly to the bottom of the sea, the view might be taken that their deaths were, metaphysics apart, coincident in point of time. But we simply do not know what happened to them. Counsel for the appellants could not suggest, in the case of either spouse, whether the correct inference was death by drowning, trapped in the ship, or death by drowning, sucked down by the sinking ship after going overboard, or death by shark or similar fish, or by thirst, or by drowning after swimming about or floating for a greater or less period with or without a lifebelt. This makes it plain that there is no evidence at all that the deaths were coincident in point of time (in the natural sense of simultaneous) in the mind of the ordinary man.[108]

This is not in the spirit of *The Deep Blue Sea* it must be said. It is perhaps closer to *Jaws*. Yet the fictional construction is equally evident; what the two judges were trying to assert is that the application of a text requires not just an interpretation of a word (coincide) but a vision or image of a factual situation. Yet factual descriptions are themselves dependent upon what might be termed an epistemological attitude, namely whether a holistic or an individualistic paradigm is to be brought to bear on the accident at sea. Fiction provides the ideal vehicle in which these different paradigms can be exposed since one is not talking facts but creating *une construction philosophique*.[109]

This interpretation of a will case is perhaps particularly vivid. Nevertheless the use of imaginary factual situations is frequent in common law legal reasoning;[110] one starts with one factual situation (perhaps an actual case) and then moves to another, fictional one, through the use of expressions such as 'what if?'[111] For example in a case concerning a tender that was carelessly not considered by a local authority, despite the fact that the tenderer had fulfilled all the stipulated tendering conditions as laid down by the authority, the Court of Appeal held the local authority liable to the tenderer for breach of a collateral contract.[112] The holding is perhaps surprising in some ways given both the nature of a tendering procedure, which normally (by its nature) puts the pre-contractual risk on the tendering party, and the principle that a contract to contract is not a contract.[113] However Bingham LJ justified his decision through the posing of 'what if' questions:

> During the hearing the questions were raised: what if, in a situation such as the present, the council had opened and thereupon accepted the first tender received, even though the

---

[108] *Ibid*, p. 17.

[109] Valade (2001 p. 401).

[110] See in particular Lee (this volume, Chap. 12).

[111] See Salter (1992).

[112] *Blackpool & Fylde Aero Club Ltd v. Blackpool BC* [1990] 1 WLR 1195.

[113] *Courtney & Fairbairn v. Tolani Brother (Hotels) Ltd* [1975] 1 WLR 297.

> deadline had not expired and other invitees had not yet responded? Or if the council had considered and accepted a tender admittedly received well after the deadline?[114]

The judge went on to hold that if the tenderer "submits a conforming tender before the deadline he is entitled, not as a matter of mere expectation but of contractual right, to be sure that his tender will after the deadline be opened and considered in conjunction with all other conforming tenders or at least that his tender will be considered if others are." And he supported this decision by saying:

> Had the club, before tendering, inquired of the council whether it could rely on any timely and conforming tender being considered along with others, I feel quite sure that the answer would have been "of course." The law would, I think, be defective if it did not give effect to that.[115]

In addition to imagined fact situations, judicial reasoning often has recourse to fictional characters such as the 'reasonable person' and the 'reasonable businessman'. Such a person has been described as "no more than the anthropomorphic conception of justice" of which the court is the "spokesman".[116] And, of course, the 'reasonable man' character himself has been the subject of a fictional case which highlighted the gap between this 'spokesman' and social reality.[117] This gap between what a court thinks and social reality can equally manifest itself when judges have recourse to policy arguments. For example the courts have made it difficult for a person damaged by certain kinds of police carelessness to sue the police for damages in the tort of negligence. This has been justified on the ground that "the imposition of the liability principle upon the police would induce in them a detrimentally defensive frame of mind" which would make them "inclined to err on the side of over-reaction."[118] Perhaps it would, but no empirical evidence whatsoever is offered to justify this assertion;[119] and given that the police are often held liable in other legal jurisdictions without, seemingly, these side-effects manifesting themselves[120] one can only conclude that these images of police work are more fictional than real. One is not reflecting a social reality but imagining one.[121]

Ronald Dworkin famously attacked policy reasoning by judges arguing that it was their role to decide cases on the basis of rights not social goals.[122] Rights, he said, are derived from principles while policies describe goals.[123] Dworkin goes on to invent his fictional judge, Hercules, who must "construct a scheme of abstract

[114] [1990] 1 WLR 1195, p. 1201.

[115] *Ibid*, p. 1202

[116] Lord Radcliffe in *Davis Contractors Ltd v. Fareham UDC* [1956] AC 696, p. 728.

[117] Herbert (1997, pp. 1–6).

[118] Lord Brown in *Van Colle v Chief Constable of the Hertfordshire Police* [2009] 1 AC 225, at para 132.

[119] All that the Law Lord said was: "So far from doubting whether this would in fact be so, it seems to me inevitable" (para 132).

[120] Markesinis (2001, p. 304).

[121] And see further in Lee (this volume, Chap. 12).

[122] Dworkin (1977, pp. 82–84).

[123] *Ibid*, p. 90.

and concrete principles that provides a coherent justification for all common law precedents and, so far as these are to be justified on principle, constitutional and statutory provisions as well."[124] The judge is clearly a fiction in the sense that he is an invention and has superhuman skills.[125] Yet it is arguable that creating a distinction between 'rights' and 'social goals' is equally inventive, at least when one approaches the issue from the point of view of historical jurisprudence. As Stephen Waddams concludes, after his historical analysis, there is a paradox in that "the concept of principle has prevailed only by appearing to be what it is not".[126] Principle and policy have, in (historical) truth, been "mutually interdependent" and that the history of a central area of case law reasoning like contract "has not been reducible to any single explanatory concept, internal or external: considerations in opposition to any proposed principle, dependent in part on the general exercise of judgment, can themselves be formulated as countervailing principles."[127] Professor Waddams is not suggesting that Dworkin was indulging in imaginative fiction when he asserted a sharp divide between principle and policy; but Dworkin can still be regarded as constructing an 'as if' model. Judges should proceed on the basis 'as if' there is such a distinction.

Hercules was not the only element of fiction created by Ronald Dworkin to underpin his hermeneutical thesis. The whole judicial reasoning process could, he said, be compared with the writing of a chain novel. "In this enterprise", he explained, "a group of novelists writes a novel *seriatim*; each novelist in the chain interprets the chapters he has been given in order to write a new chapter, which is then added to what the next novelist receives, and so on." Each chapter writer is under an obligation to make the novel being constructed the best it can be and this adds a further complexity to the task. But, he concludes, it is "the complexity of this task [that] models the complexity of deciding a hard case under law".[128] It is tempting to think that this 'as if' enterprise—that is to say judges acting 'as if' they are chain novelists—is the closest that speculation about legal reasoning gets to fiction theory. However if one turns to the civil law, it could be argued that another, if different, fictional analogy has underpinned the work and methods of the judiciary. This image is, as we have seen, the judge as computer applying the law as if it was a mathematical system; instead of the judge as chain novelist, there is the image of the *juge automate* mechanically applying the statutory text.[129] Yet, as Jean-Louis Bergel points out, this image is nothing but a myth. "One can dream", he says, "of a legal rule which would be deduced through strictly logical reasoning thanks to a rigorous terminology, to a hierarchy of rules enshrined in the positive law and to the possibility of extracting particular solutions from a certain number of incontestable axioms." But "this method is irreconcilable with legal method" in that the "law is

[124] *Ibid*, pp. 116–117

[125] *Ibid*, p. 105.

[126] Waddams (2011, p. 230).

[127] *Ibid*, p. 21.

[128] Dworkin (1986, p. 229).

[129] Depambour-Tarride (2003, p. 871).

teeming with departures from logical solutions deduced from an axiom" and that these "exceptions result from other preoccupations, other principles and other axioms whose sheer number, confusion and differing intensity render impossible an expression of positive law in mathematical form."[130] Explanations of how judges ought to reason seem plagued by myth and fictitious analogies.

3.5 Can Law be Reduced to a Fiction?

Yet if one returns to the fundamental question of whether law is a fiction one is equally plagued by doubt. Walter Jones, in his innovative chapter, finally concluded that "the notion of legal reality is as vague and subtle as that of legal fiction"; and that when "applied to the law, reality means something of which we approve, and 'legal fiction' is always at hand to supply a convenient term of denigration."[131] However it is important to recall that fiction theory need not be pejorative in its orientation, especially if it is defined in terms of an 'as if' construction.[132] What matters is its function or utility.[133] "Theories don't have to be right", said the fictional character Hunter in one of the old television series of *Callan*, "they just have to work." In the end much depends on how one defines fiction in relation to reality. If one takes a narrow view of the former and a wide view of the latter, then to say that law is a fiction seems unconvincing, as in fact Jones indicated. And, indeed, this has largely been the approach of judges and jurists, for when "facts are admitted to have certain well recognized legal consequences, there is a fiction until the concept used to express these results appears so much a matter of course, that the purely intellectual or conventional element in it never occurs to anyone."[134] Thus fictions gradually become realities.[135] Or, as one French jurist put it, the "law becomes a kind of reality imposed on social fact, putting it into form, and finally ending up in becoming more 'true' than the facts."[136]

It is accordingly not difficult to be sceptical. To describe law as a fiction seems at first sight somewhat simplistic and, perhaps, too convenient a tool for those who distain the whole Western concept of law. Law is nothing but a series of 'bourgeois

[130] Bergel (2012, pp. 307–308).

[131] Jones (1940, p. 186).

[132] See generally Bouriau (2013a). And see Lind (this volume, Chap. 5) and Del Mar (this volume, Chap. 11).

[133] Cf Lind (this volume, Chap. 5).

[134] Jones (1940, p. 185).

[135] Writing about the natural sciences, Robert Blanché observed: "Already Whewell remarked that the ideas through which we interpret the facts little by little get incorporated into the facts themselves as we perceive them, so much so that we no longer distinguish them as such and believe that we can read them directly in experience; the ideas of one generation thus become the facts for the generation which follows": Blanché (1983, p. 83).

[136] Ellul (1982, p. 28).

fictions'.[137] Yet what emerges from this present, if admittedly somewhat superficial, study is a much more complex situation. Certainly the idea of law itself, as a whole, is so omnipresent, and its institutions, both physical and intangible, so solid that it is a social construct or model which is as 'real' as any fully operational natural science theory or construct. The pragmatic function of the model defines its ontological and epistemological status. However the moment one enters into this construct and examines each level—namely theory, concepts and reasoning—the harder it becomes to dismiss fiction theory taken in the Hans Vaihinger sense of an 'as if' construct. In other words if one adopts the notion of 'as if' as an epistemic attitude the scepticism towards fiction theory begins to evaporate. At the level of theory a notion such as the *Grundnorm* is, even for Kelsen himself, a fiction[138] while the Rule of Recognition seems, in the end, to be no more real despite its supposedly empirical foundation. It is difficult to escape from the view that Hart's model rests not on the existence of the Rule as some empirical object but on the existence of the Rule as if it is such an object. At the opposite end of the spectrum, realist theories might seem determined attempts to ground law in social reality. Yet mythical notions such as the Reasonable Man, seemingly expelled through the door, creep back as the Bad Man through the window.

At the level of legal concepts and categories there are obvious fictions such as the legal corporation and the intangible thing. Or at least they are fictions in the 'as if' sense: the corporation is treated as if it is a human person and the intangible thing as if it is physical property. Yet an 'as if' epistemic attitude also permits one to see, as Annelise Riles notes, how "legal fictions, far from just helping to order social, political or economic phenomena, actually constitute those phenomena by providing the frames through which social actors apprehend social realities."[139] The legal concepts, categories and relations function within the facts themselves with the result that issues such as whether the claimant has an 'interest' or has suffered 'damage' or, again, is in 'possession' of a thing (which itself might be fashioned by the legal concepts) is as much determined by the 'as if' model as by factual 'reality' itself. Categories, equally, are fictional in the 'as if' sense. And so, for example, while the distinction between public and private law might be of considerable use to legal thought and perhaps even to problem-solving, few would claim that the distinction reflects any kind of empirical reality. The distinction depends entirely upon the institutional and definitional 'as if' criteria used to give expression to social reality.[140]

Another layer of fiction is added by those who reason in law. Here, however, there are two sub-layers; there are, as has been seen, the fictional creations employed by practitioners and judges to justify a particular interpretation, or the fashioning of a particular rule or exception, and there are fictional creations used by those who are external to such legal reasoners, that is to say the theorists who theorise

137 Jones (1940, p. 285).

138 On which see Bouriau (2013b).

139 Riles (2010, p. 4).

140 See generally Bonnet and Deunier (eds) (2010).

about how judges reason or should reason. The theorist provides a fictional ('as if') model for the judges within which the judges employ fictional ('as if') images to relate law to social fact, this social fact itself resulting from an 'as if' construction operating both within and without the facts. One might, then, have to distinguish further sub sub-layers. Judges are operating not just with one 'as if' construction but two or, perhaps, more; and the same is true of theorists. Dworkin has provided an openly fictional judge who is made to reason in an 'as if' way ("Hercules must construct …"); yet at a more detached level the whole process of interpretation is likened to the writing of a chain novel.

Is therefore fiction theory convincing? Vaihinger's 'as if' thesis is a seemingly powerful epistemological tool, but it is not without its critics, perhaps the most relevant in respect of legal fictions being the accusation that if all legal thought is a fiction then the word fiction loses any meaning within legal thought.[141] Such a criticism leads one back to the problem outlined at the beginning of this investigation: much will depend upon how fiction is defined. Nevertheless the traditional notion of a legal fiction is founded on the idea of a sharp division between fictional concept—the fiction—and reality and this in itself is now seen as problematic. The distinction between law and fact is not just epistemologically elusive, as Annelise Riles has noted,[142] but one that certainly cannot be employed any longer to determine how 'fiction' ought to be defined (unless of course as an 'as if' proposition).

Annelise Riles has also turned her attention to another criticism of the Vaihinger thesis: the criticism that the 'as if' theory deprives law of its authority.[143] Once the metaphysical illusion is gone this deprives the law of its power. In other words the 'as if' thesis destroys what might be called the authority paradigm.[144] One immediate response to this criticism is to say that it is not necessarily the job of theorists—especially epistemologists—to bolster up the authority paradigm. That is a mission to be left either to politico-legal philosophers or to judges and practitioners whose role depends upon the paradigm. Moreover the criticism profoundly misunderstands Vaihinger's own philosophy.[145] However Riles goes further and argues that the 'as if' thesis does not in fact destroy the authority of the law; indeed it can actually enhance it. New fictional legal doctrines like the implied term—fictional because it is not a term agreed by the parties to a contract—can have profound effects in positive law and can also act as an agent of replication in legal education enhancing its authoritative power.[146] This defence is very much within the spirit of Vaihinger in that he always insisted that his thesis was not to be understood in any pejorative sense; his point only was that reality cannot be directly perceived.[147]

[141] Fuller (1967, p. 123).

[142] Riles (2010, pp. 4–5). And see generally Samuel (2003).

[143] Riles (2010, p. 17).

[144] On which see Samuel (2008).

[145] See generally Bouriau, *op.cit.*

[146] Riles (2010, pp. 18–21).

[147] This important point is regularly emphasised by Bouriau: see generally Bouriau (2013a, b).

3.6 Concluding Remark

Fiction theory can, accordingly, survive its critics, at least with respect to the discipline of law. However another means of approach is the one adopted in this present investigation, namely to identify the role of 'as if' thinking at the various levels—or individual aspects—of legal thought (theory, concepts and categories and reasoning). Fiction seems to emerge as an undeniable element at all of these levels with the result that one is faced with a question. Do these different levels or aspects add up to more than the sum of their parts? In other words, is law itself a fiction? As we have seen, there is something of a paradox here the moment one thinks of these various aspects or levels as 'properties' attaching to the 'object' law. Such a distinction between an object and its properties is itself a fiction. Logically therefore one can conclude that law itself is a fiction, but such a conclusion must be seen, probably, as an 'as if' construction.

References

Bergel, J.-L. 2012. *Théorie générale du droit.* 5th ed. Dalloz: Paris

Birks, P. 1997. Definition and division: A meditation on institutes 3.13. In *The classification of obligations,* ed. P. Birks. Oxford University press: Oxford

Blackpool & Fylde Aero Club Ltd v Blackpool BC. 1990. 1 WLR 1195.

Blanché, R. 1983. *L'épistémologie*. 3rd ed. Presses Universitaires de France: Paris

Bonnet, B., and P. Deunier, eds. 2010. *De l'intérêt de la summa divisio droit public-droit privé.* Dalloz: Paris

Borutti, S. 2006. Fiction. In *Le dictionnaire des sciences humaines,* eds. S. Mesure and P. Savidan. Presses Universitaires de France: Paris

Bouriau, C. 2013a. *Le 'comme si': Kant, Vaihinger et le fictionalisme*. Les Éditions du Cerf: Paris

Bouriau, C. 2013b. *Les fictions du droit: Kelsen, lecteur de Vaihinger*. ENS Éditions: Lyon

Canning, J. 1987. *The political thought of Baldus de Ubaldis*. Cambridge University Press: Cambridge

Carbasse, J. -M. 1998. *Introduction historique au droit*. Presses Universitaires de France: Paris

Carlill v Carbolic Smoke Ball Co. 1893. 1 QB 256.

Cohen, F. 1935. Transcendental nonsense and the functional approach, *Columbia Law Review* 35:809.

Courtney & Fairbairn v Tolani Brother (Hotels) Ltd. 1975. 1 WLR 297.

Cownie, F. 2004. *Legal academics*. Hart: Oxford

Davis Contractors Ltd v Fareham UDC. 1956. AC 696.

Del Mar, Maksymilian. 2014. Legal fictions and legal change in the common law tradition. In *Legal fictions in theory and practice,* ed. Maksymilian Del Mar and William Twining. Dordrecht: Springer.

Depambour-Tarride, L. 2003. Juge (Longue durée). In *Dictionnaire de la culture juridique,* eds. D. Alland and S. Rials. Presses Universitaires de France: Paris

Descheemaeker, E. 2009. *The division of wrongs: A historical comparative study*. Oxford University Press: Oxford

Desjeux, D. 2004. *Les sciences sociales*. Presses Universitaires de France: Paris

Dworkin, R. 1977. *Taking rights seriously*. Duckworth: London

Dworkin, R. 1986. *Law's Empire*. Fontana: London

Ellul, J. 1982. *Histoire des institutions: 3—Le Moyen Age*. 9th ed. Presses Universitaires de France: Paris
Fuller, L. 1967. *Legal fictions*. Stanford University Press: Stanford
Granger, G.-G.1995. *La science et les sciences*. 2nd ed. Presses Universitaires de France: Paris
Gray, K., and S. Gray. 2003. The rhetoric of reality. In *Rationalizing property, equity and trusts,* ed. J. Getzler. Butterworths: London
Hart, H. L. A. 1994. *The concept of law*. 2nd ed. Oxford University Press: Oxford
Hans Kelsen. 2014. On the theory of juridic fictions. With special consideration of Vaihinger's Philosophy of the as-if. In *Legal fictions in theory and practice,* ed. Maksymilian Del Mar and William Twining. Dordrecht: Springer.
Heith-Stade, D. 2012. http://davidheithstade.wordpress.com/2012/06/02/ubi-societas-ibi-ius/.
Herbert, A. P. 1977 [1935]. *Uncommon law*. Methuen: London
Hoenen, J. F. M. 2007. Nominalisme. In *Dictionnaire critique de théologie,* ed. J.-Y. Lacoste. 2nd ed. Presses Universitaires de France: Paris
Hohfeld, W. 1966 [1919]. *Fundamental legal conceptions*. Yale University Press: Yale
Holmes, O. W. 1897. The path of the law. *Harvard Law Review* 10:457
Jestaz P, and Jamin C. 2004. *La doctrine*. Dalloz: Paris
Jolowicz, H. F. 1963. *Lectures on jurisprudence*. Athlone: London
Jones, John W. 1940. *A historical introduction to the theory of law.* Oxford: Clarendon Press.
Jouanjan, O. 2005. *Une histoire de la pensée juridique en Allemagne (1800–1918)*. Presses Universitaires de France: Paris
Kennedy, D. 1982. Legal education and the reproduction of hierarchy. *Journal of Legal Education* 32:591.
Kletzer, Christoph. 2014. Kelsen on Vaihinger. In *Legal fictions in theory and practice,* ed. Maksymilian Del Mar and William Twining. Dordrecht: Springer.
Lee, James. 2014. Fictions in tort. In *Legal fictions in theory and practice,* ed. Maksymilian Del Mar and William Twining. Dordrecht: Springer.
Lind, Douglas. 2014. The pragmatic value of legal fictions. In *Legal fictions in theory and practice,* ed. Maksymilian Del Mar and William Twining. Dordrecht: Springer.
Lloyd, D. and M. Freeman 2008. *Lloyd's introduction to jurisprudence*. 8th ed. Sweet & Maxwell: London
Lobban, Michael. 2014. Legal fictions before the age of reform. In *Legal fictions in theory and practice,* ed. Maksymilian Del Mar and William Twining. Dordrecht: Springer.
Lupton v FA & AB. 1972. AC 634.
Makkreel, R. 2006. Expliquer et comprendre. In *Le dictionnaire des sciences humaines,* eds. S. Mesure and P. Savidan. Presses Universitaires de France: Paris
Markesinis, B. 2001. *Always on the same path: Essays on foreign law and comparative methodology Volume II*. Hart: Oxford
Pharmaceutical Society of G.B. v Boots. 1953. 1 QB 401.
Puddefoot, J. 2007. Mathématiques. In *Dictionnaire critique de théologie,* ed. J.-Y. Lacoste. 2nd ed. Presses Universitaires de France: Paris
Quinn, Michael. 2014. Fuller on legal fictions: A benthamic perspective. In *Legal fictions in theory and practice,* ed. Maksymilian Del Mar and William Twining. Dordrecht: Springer.
Riles, A. 2010. Is the law hopeful? *Cornell law faculty working papers*. Paper 68. http://scholarship.law.cornell.edu/clsops_papers/68.
Rowland, Re. 1963. Ch 1.
Salter, M. 1992. Towards a phenomenology of legal thinking. *Journal of the British Society for Phenomenology* 23:167.
Samuel, G. 1997. Classification of obligations and the impact of constructivist epistemologies. *Legal Studies* 17:448.
Samuel, G. 2003. *Epistemology and method in law*. Ashgate: Aldershot
Samuel, G. 2008. Is law really a social science? A view from comparative law. *Cambridge Law Journal* 288.

Samuel, G. 2009. Interdisciplinarity and the authority paradigm: Should law be taken seriously by scientists and social scientists? *Journal of Law and Society* 36:431.
Samuel, G. 2013. *A short introduction to the common law*. Edward Elgar: Cheltenham
Stein, P. 1984. *Legal institutions: The development of dispute settlement*. Butterworths: London
Stock v Frank Jones. 1978. 1 WLR 231.
Susskind, R. 1987. *Expert systems in law*. Oxford: Oxford University Press: Oxford
Tesco Supermarkets Ltd v Nattrass. 1972. AC 153.
Thatcher, M. 1987. Aids, education and the year 2000, *Woman's Own* (3 Oct.).
Thomas, Y. 2011. *Les opérations du droit*. Seuil/Gallimard: Paris
Troper, M. 2003. *La philosophie du droit*. Presses Universitaires de France: Paris
Twining, W. 1985. *Karl Llewellyn and the realist movement* (Weidenfeld & Nicolson: London 1973; reprint 1985).
Vaihinger, H. 1924. *The philosophy of "As If"* (Trans: C. K. Ogden). Routledge: London
Vaihinger, H. 2013. *La phiosophie du comme si*. (Trans: Christophe Bouriau). 2nd ed. Éditions Kimé: Paris
Valade, B. 2001. De l'explication dans les sciences sociales: holisme et individualisme. In *Épistémologie des sciences sociales,* ed. J.-M. Berthelot. Presses Universitaires de France: Paris
Van Colle v Chief Constable of the Hertfordshire Police. 2009. 1 AC 225.
Villey, M. 1979. *Le droit romain*. 7th ed. Presses Universitaires de France: Paris
Waddams, S. 2003. *Dimensions of private law: Categories and concepts in anglo-american legal reasoning*. Cambridge University Press: Cambridge
Waddams, S. 2011. *Principle and policy in contract law: Competing or complementary concepts*? Cambridge University Press: Cambridge
Webb, C. 2009. Treating like cases alike: Principle and classification in private law. In *The goals of private law,* eds. A. Robertson and T. H. Wu. Hart: Oxford
Wu, T. H. 2009. Storytelling in the law of unjust enrichment. In *The goals of private law,* eds. A. Robertson and T. H. Wu. Hart: Oxford

Chapter 4
Fuller on Legal Fictions: A Benthamic Perspective

Michael Quinn

Abstract This paper attempts first to explain Bentham's distinction between a fiction and the name of a fictitious entity, and to relate that distinction to his rationale for the critique of legal fictions. A second goal of the paper is to investigate the tensions involved in Bentham's ontology and epistemology, and more specifically the tension between the objectivist and subjectivist Bentham. It is argued that Bentham's objections to legal fictions were traceable to their use in deceptive or fallacious argument, whilst his logic provided a means of rehabilitating the use of the names of those fictitious entities which could be explicated through his technique of paraphrasis (that is, explained in terms of real entities), in relation to which both meaning and truth might be exchanged. In passing, Bentham's realist and naturalistic conception of truth is contrasted with that of Kelsen, whose own critique of Vaihinger reveals a commitment to a disjunction between fact and value which Bentham could not share, since he sought to ground value in what he took to be natural facts about human beings. It is also argued that Bentham's discussion of the basis of well-grounded belief anticipates the treatment of the same issue by Peirce. Bentham's apparent naturalist and realist perspective differs markedly from that of Fuller, who, following Vaihinger, rejects the attempt to replace fiction with truth. There are significant areas of agreement between Bentham and Fuller, on the figurative nature of much language, and even, in certain contexts, on the utility of the self-conscious deployment of fictions. However, in the context of law and morality, it appears that his development of a route to truth through paraphrasis makes Bentham the enemy of fictions, since, in this field at least, truth and utility stand or fall together.

A version of this chapter was previously published as 'Fuller on Legal Fictions: A Benthamic Perspective' (2013) 4 *International Journal of Law in Context* 466–484.

M. Quinn (✉)
UCL Faculty of Laws, Bentham House, Endsleigh Gardens,
London WC1H 0EG, UK
e-mail: m.quinn@ucl.ac.uk

M. Del Mar, W. Twining (eds.), *Legal Fictions in Theory and Practice*,
Law and Philosophy Library 110, DOI 10.1007/978-3-319-09232-4_4

4.1 Fictions and Fictitious Entities

4.1.1 Fuller's Definition of a Fiction

For Lon Fuller, 'A fiction is either (1) a statement propounded with a complete or partial consciousness of its falsity, or (2) a false statement recognized as having utility' (Fuller 1930–1931, p. 369), while a fiction differs from a lie by its freedom from the intention to deceive. Fuller seeks not only to analyze legal fictions, but, informed by the philosophy of Hans Vaihinger, to rehabilitate fictions as necessary and useful elements in human thought. For Vaihinger, it is the fundamental contradiction between the physical world—the chaotic flux of reality as detected by sensation—and the conceptual world—the product of the active thought processes by which the human intellect seeks to grasp, understand and manipulate that world—which renders the use of concepts we know to be false essential to thought (Vaihinger 1925, pp. xiii–xvii).[1] In addition, Fuller seeks to provide some answer to the question 'Are there good and bad fictions, and if so, how do we tell the difference?' (1930–1931, p. 365) and, again following Vaihinger, indicates that the legitimacy of a fiction depends not on its truth—an incoherent standard when interpreted as correspondence with reality—but on its usefulness, in simplifying and organizing data, and in converting new experiences into familiar terms (1930–1931, pp. 887–895; Vaihinger 1925, pp. 3–4). On this fictionalist account, the central virtues of any theory are explanatory power, capacity to unify observational data, and predictive accuracy (Rosen 2005, p. 14).

4.1.2 Bentham on Fictions and Fictitious Entities

Bentham's attitude to fictions is somewhat obscured by inconsistencies of expression, and, sometimes, of argument. Thus his references to fictions (especially legal fictions) are mostly harshly critical. However, he too believed that the employment of 'names of fictitious entities' is an inevitable feature of every remotely complex language, and he too sought to elaborate rules for their proper use. Bentham contributed to the confusion by occasionally using the noun substantive 'fiction' to refer to other specific noun substantives, for instance 'natural law' or 'natural right' (Bentham 1977, pp. 17, 20, 439–31; 1838–1843, iii. 218–219), but more usually to refer to propositions, consisting at a minimum of a noun substantive, a copula and a predicate. Resolutions of this apparently contradictory attitude to fictions/fictitious entities have been offered by several commentators. For instance, it has been argued that Bentham anticipated the central elements of Vaihinger's 'philosophy of the as if' (Ogden 1932, pp. xxxi–xxxii; Stolzenberg 1999), and that his excoriation of legal fictions was not, therefore, a rejection of fictions per se, since his own logic

[1] For a discussion which appreciates Fuller's reliance on Vaihinger see Karen Petroski's chapter in this volume (Chap. 7).

consisted of a 'theory of fictions' in which he is just as dismissive of truth as the goal of theory as Vaihinger is in the 'philosophy of the as if'. Conversely, Philip Schofield has recently sought to resolve the contradiction by arguing that Bentham's standard usage of the term fiction applies not to noun substantives, which name entities—whether real, fictitious or fabulous—but to propositions (2006, p. 20). Applied to propositions, the term fiction is closely related in Bentham's lexicon to the term 'fallacy', which he defines as: 'any arguments that are considered as having been employed or considerations suggested, for the purpose, or with a probability of producing the effect of deception' (UC ciii. 1 (1838–1843, ii. 379)). Now Bentham certainly attacks legal fictions as deceptious, that is, as supplying the grounds for fallacious reasoning, but he is also clear that 'fiction—the mode of representation by which the fictitious entities ... are dressed up in the garb, and placed upon the level, of real ones' (UC cii. 23 (1997, p. 84; 1838–1843, viii. 198)), was inevitable in language, and did not necessarily involve the intention to deceive, while there were methods by which fictitious entities might be expounded in ways which eliminated the fiction, and allowed truth and meaning to be exchanged. It will be argued that Bentham's final position does appear to contain unresolved tensions between a realist and a fictionalist perspective, between, that is, the view that the use of propositions containing fictitious entities might only be legitimized insofar as they could be replaced with propositions containing only real entities, and the view that the sole criterion of legitimacy for the use of fictional constructs was a pragmatic one, namely the degree to which that use generated accurate predictions.

Bentham explicates 'fictitious entities' as follows:

> By this term is here meant to be designated one of those sorts of objects which, in every language, must for the purposes of discourse be spoken of as existing—be spoken of in the same manner as those objects which really have existence, and to which existence is seriously meant to be ascribed, are spoken of ... *but without any such design as that of producing any such persuasion as that of their possessing each for itself any separate, or strictly speaking any real existence.* (UC cii. 24 (1997, p. 86; 1838–1843, viii. 198) emphasis added)

Bentham contrasts fictitious entities with real entities, which, unsurprisingly, he defines as 'an entity to which, on the occasion and for the purpose of discourse, existence is really meant to be ascribed' (UC cii. 16 (1997, p. 164; 1838–1843, viii. 196)).

Bentham is also less than clear in his treatment of the category of real entities. Sometimes, he states that the only real entities are substances:

> The only objects that really exist are *substances*. They are the only real entities. To convey any notion by words which are the names of any objects [other] than substances, we are obliged to attribute to such objects what in truth is attributable only to substances: in a word we are obliged to feign them to be substances. These others, in short, are only fictitious entities. (UC clix. 241)[2]

[2] Alternatively: 'Names of *real* entities are, if proper names, names of so many individual masses of matter: if *common* names, names respectively of all such individual masses of matter as are of such or such a particular description, which by these names are indicated or endeavoured to be indicated' (UC ci. 341 (1838–1843, viii. 262)).

Elsewhere, he states that the only entities whose reality we perceive directly are the mental phenomena to which our experience of the external world gives rise, that is sensations and impressions. Bentham never seems to have resolved the tensions between these two views, between an objectivist and a subjectivist perspective. Thus, on the one hand, he wastes no time in accepting the reality of the external world, on the basis that no bad consequences could follow from such acceptance, in contrast to the pain quickly imposed by the physical sanction if we act, for instance, on a philosophical denial that the wall in front of us exists (UC cii. 15 (1997, p. 182; 1838–1843, viii. 197)). On the other hand, the subjectivist Bentham asserts that all knowledge of the external universe comes to human beings through the mediation of their sensory experience, while the only entities they perceive directly are the mental events detected by sensation and perception, so that the existence of material objects is properly speaking inferential (UC cii. 15 (1997, p. 180 (1838–1843, viii. 196)); see also 1983a, p. 271n): we conclude that the wall exists because we make highly plausible, but by no means indefeasible inferences from the sensory data delivered by sight and touch. On this view, given that no-one has direct access to any perceptions or sensations which are not internal to their own mind, each of us lives in an irreducibly private reality.

Schofield argues that Bentham's final position is that it is 'more straightforward' to view corporeal substances as the only perceptible real entities (2006, p. 16), but the passage he relies on explicitly limits itself to the category of 'substances', within which only corporeal substances are perceptible, while alleged incorporeal substances, such as souls and God, are at best inferential (UC cii. 15 (1997, pp. 180; 1838–1843, viii. 196)). Indeed, if sensations like pleasure and pain were to fail to qualify as real entities, the entire utilitarian project would fail to get off the ground. For her part, Stolzenberg argues that Bentham introduced the distinction between real and fictitious entities only to subvert it immediately: 'the category of the fictitious effectively swallows up the domain of the real by the time Bentham finishes his analysis' (1999, p. 239). She dismisses Bentham's statements that real entities exist, and that we can exchange truth in relation to them, on the basis that such passages are 'more than offset' by the combination of his assertion that the reality of substances is, strictly speaking, inferential, and her own assertion (which Bentham explicitly contradicts) that he regarded perceptions and ideas as 'the paradigmatic fictions' (1999, pp. 241–242). Further discussion of the difficulties with this interpretation will be undertaken in due course, but, even given Bentham's inconsistencies on this topic, it would surely be quite remarkable for a writer as pre-occupied with clarity as he to state his position in such an esoteric fashion, that is by insisting on the importance of 'the comprehensive and instructive distinction—between *real* entities and *fictitious* entities: or rather between their respective *names*' (UC ci. pp. 341; 1838–1843, viii. 262), which he actually regards as no distinction at all.

It is true that the division between real and fictitious entities occurs entirely within language, but the fundamental linguistic distinction between names which have referents in the world, and names which have no such referents, nevertheless reflects, for Bentham, an ontological distinction between things which exist, and things which do not. 'What I assume then, is that of the objects, the things, we are in use to speak of, some do, others do not exist. Those which do exist may be said to have their archetypes in nature: those which do not exist may be said *not* to have their archetypes in nature' (UC lxix. 52). Jackson is quite correct in asserting that for Bentham the reality attributed to real entities 'is a *discursive* construction: a *claim to reality* made *within* discourse' (1998, p. 498), but that simply reflects the fact that language is the only instrument by which humans can communicate any assertions, and that that instrument very often misdescribes the world.[3] Whilst the world really exists, the names 'reality' and 'existence' are, for Bentham, names of fictitious entities (UC cii. p. 74 (1997, p. 150; 1838–1843, viii. 210)), substantified linguistic labels, which do not refer to actually existing phenomena.

One solution to the paradox is to accept the reality of both substances and sensations, and to hope that, for the most part, there will be a correspondence between the reality of the external world and our perception of it, and this appears to be Bentham's preferred solution: 'Entities are either physical or psychical. *Physical* are either real or fictitious. *Psychical* again are either real or fictitious: real psychical are either present to perception, i.e. impressions, or present to memory, i.e. ideas' (UC ci. p. 347 (1838–1843, viii. 267)). If this is correct, Bentham is in fact anxious to retain both objective and subjective elements in his epistemology and ontology. The only resources available to us in discovering the objectively existing world are sense experience and reflection on it (UC ci. 183 (1838–1843, viii. 238)). Substances (real entities) deposit impressions (real entities) on human sense organs (real entities), which impressions we can recall with a reasonable degree of accuracy. If our sense perceptions do indeed deliver reliable information about the world, we can know reality when it comes to real entities.

Bentham is, however, careful to add a caveat that the correspondence between reality and perception will not be entire, since it is possible for us to be mistaken in our interpretation of sensory data, while that possibility reveals once more the inferential nature of our knowledge of the external world, which depends not simply on passive perception, but active judgement:

> When perception has place, the source or perceptible object from whence it is derived being an individual portion of matter—a real, corporeal entity … *impressions* are at the time in question made on *sense*: on some one or more or all of the senses, to the cognizance of which the object stands exposed: of the perception thereupon obtained these *impressions* are the immediate object and subject: the body itself—i.e. the existence of it, is but, in a *secondary* and comparatively *remote* way, the object or subject of perception: of this supposed source of the perceptions that are experienced, the existence is, strictly speaking, rather a subject of *inference* than of perception: of inference, judgment, ratiocination, which is liable to be erroneous, and in experience is very frequently found to be so.
>
> Scarce does a perception take place, but it is accompanied … with a corresponding *judgment* or *act* of the judicial faculty. (UC ci. 118 (1838–1843, viii. 224)).

[3] Bentham is quite explicit that the distinction between real and fictitious entities is a different, though corresponding distinction to that between their respective names. See UC cii. 462 (1838–1843, viii. 331): 'Coæval with the very first steps that can be taken in the endeavour to give a clear explanation of the true nature of language must be the intimation given of the distinction between real and fictitious entities, and the correspondent distinction between names of real and names of fictitious entities.'

The subjectivist nature of our engagement with the world, combined with the need to communicate with our fellows, explains the inevitable deployment of fictitious entities in language, the tool of both communication and thought itself. The subject of the earliest communications for Bentham were really existing objects, while in referring to such objects we were aided by the unambiguous link between the object, the name by which we designated it, and its idea, that is its mental image. If we were standing together and could both see, we could disambiguate our referents simply by pointing at them. If we no longer have sight of the referent, I must rely on the ability of its name to call forth its idea in your mind. 'A proper substantive, the name of a real entity, is understood immediately and of itself, it offers a certain image to the conception. An improper substantive offers no such image. Of itself it has no meaning' (UC lxix. 229). Such designation, the beginning of both language and logic, became embedded in the structure of language and thought, so that 'a material image is the only instrument by which, the only medium through which, conceptions can be conveyed from mind to mind' (UC cii. 463). Because of this connection, encountering a name gives rise to the expectation of a corresponding thing:

> Words, viz. words employed to serve as names, being the only instruments by which, in the absence of the *things*, viz. the *substances*, themselves, the ideas of them can be presented to the mind, hence, wheresoever a word is seen which to appearance is employed in the character of a *name*, a natural and abundantly extensive consequence is—a disposition and propensity to suppose the existence, the real existence, … of a correspondent thing—of a thing to which it ministers in the character of a name (UC ci. 341 (1838–1843, viii. 262)).

Such an expectation, however, is founded on a fundamental error, since in every language the majority of noun substantives do not name existing things (UC ci. 340 (1838–1843, viii. 262)). The symbol system that is language is a construction of the human mind, and the moment it evolves beyond the declaration of desire or aversion towards particular real objects, it necessarily ascribes existence to things which have none.

4.1.3 Similarities and Differences Between Bentham and Fuller (and Vaihinger)

Bentham, Fuller and Vaihinger would all agree that it is indeed impossible for language strictly to mirror the world, while to demand that it should is to demand the reduction of human capacity to communicate verbally to the level of animals unable to form abstract concepts (UC cii. 23 (1997, p. 84; 1838–1843, viii. 198)). Bentham asserts that all language which deploys the names of anything other than real entities is figurative, or metaphorical (UC cii. 466 (1838–1843, viii. 331)). As such, the propositions it contains are fictions (UC cii. 23 (1997, p. 84; 1838–1843, viii. 198)), that is, they are strictly speaking falsehoods, which seem to assert the existence of things which do not exist. Thus far, Bentham appears to anticipate the insights of

Vaihinger, and thence of Fuller: 'All the language of abstract thought is metaphorical' (Fuller 1930–1931, p. 374).

If we want to exchange meaning about fictitious entities, that is, broadly, about abstract terms, the easiest way is to speak as if they were physical objects, even though this is a misdescription. It is this metaphorical substantification of the immaterial which gives rise to confusion, since it is seen everywhere in language, whether in the constructions 'in motion', 'at rest', or in the naming of properties or qualities: apples exist, many apples are ripe, but ripeness is a fictitious entity which we locate *in* ripe apples (Bentham, UC cii. 461–465 (1838–1843, viii. 330–331)).[4] The logical analysis by which 'ripeness' is first abstracted from the real apple, then designated as a noun substantive in its own right, and then attributed to other similarly coloured objects itself abounds in fictions, false propositions about the world, since ripeness relies on the existence of real objects in which it might inhere, and has no independent existence. Bentham certainly anticipates Vaihinger in regarding many of the basic categories with which thought seeks to understand the world as fictitious entities (Bentham, UC cii. 35–56 (1997, pp. 88–120 (1838–1843, viii. 199–206)); Vaihinger 1925, pp. 157–166). However, while they both regard qualities as fictitious, for Bentham, the particular bodies to which qualities are attributed are impeccably real (UC cii. 461 (1838–1843, viii. 330); 1983a, p. 262). For Vaihinger and for Fuller, conversely, there is nothing apart from its qualities, while both are equally fictions: 'By adding a Thing to which sensations are supposed to adhere as attributes, thought commits a very serious error' (Vaihinger 1925, p. 167; see also Fuller 1930–1931, 883).

For all three thinkers, fictitious entities are useful, they permit the exchange of complex and subtle information relating to the exterior world, even though they do not, in themselves, designate actually existing objects. No project which sought to cleanse language of fictitious entities could succeed, since fictitious entities are essential not only to all except the most basic communication, but also, since language is the medium for thought, and constrains thought, to all except the most basic thought. Thus no discussion of qualities can occur without the false assertion of the existence of the quality, no discussion of mental acts can occur without the substantification of the mind and its faculties, that is the pretence that motive, disposition and a host of other fictitious entities are really existing objects.

> To say that, in discourse, fictitious language ought never, on any occasion, to be employed, would be as much as to say that no discourse in the subject of which operations, or affections, or other phenomena of the mind are included, ought ever to be held: for no ideas being ever to be found in it which have not their origin in sense, matter is the only direct subject of any portion of verbal discourse; on the occasion and for the purpose of the discourse, the mind is all along considered and spoken of as if it were a mass of matter: and it is only in the way of fiction that when applied to any operation, or affection of the mind, anything that is said is either true or false. (1983a, pp. 371–372)

[4] Rosen notes Bentham's assertion of the ubiquity of this spatial metaphor, but questions whether it represents Bentham's considered position, since it is 'obviously a *mad, mad* view' (2005, p. 53).

4.1.4 *The Central Disagreement: Bentham's Rehabilitation of Fictitious Propositions by Their Exposition in Terms of Real Entities*

Language may indeed be 'an instrument for the communication of thought from one mind to another' (UC cii. 456 (1838–1843, viii. 329)), but language, because of the unavoidable employment of names of fictitious entities as if they were real entities, is necessarily littered with falsehoods: 'Pure from all moral turpitude, deception, though so frequently … not being, unless by accident, the object of it, this falshood … notwithstanding all of those inconveniences of which in respect of clearness of conception it is so apt to be productive, is interwoven with the very essence of language' (UC cii. 463). Again, Vaihinger and Fuller would agree, but here emerges the crucial difference between Bentham's view and theirs, which concerns the degree to which, and the manner in which, such falsehood can be removed from language.

Because fictitious entities are not associated with images which correspond to substances, they possess no obvious shared meaning. Insofar as propositions including such entities can have any meaning, it is only a connection with real entities which can bestow it. Fortunately, such connections are available for the set of words (right, obligation, power, title) which constitute the currency of law, and Bentham's method for explicating those entities, the combination of the processes of phraseoplerosis and paraphrasis, consists precisely in making those connections explicit. Taken singly, the name obligation has no referents in the external world, and means nothing. It is true that, as for all fictitious entities, any images associated with propositions employing its name derive from images of real entities in the external world, whilst those images are sometimes discoverable through a third process of archetypation, which in this case reveals the original referent of obligation in the image of a man tied up (Bentham 1983a, p. 272n).[5] However, in order to make sense of the term, it is necessary first to include it in a proposition (phraseoplerosis), and then to substitute for that proposition another which replaces the fictitious entity with a real one (paraphrasis) (UC cii. 217 (1838–1843, viii. 246); UC lxix. 221; 1983a, p. 272n.). In the paraphrasis of normative abstractions, the real entities which do the heavy lifting are the sensations of pleasure and pain. Harrison notes that the difficulty involved here concerns the criteria according to which we are to conclude that the substituted proposition possesses the same meaning as the original (1983, p. 68), and concludes, quite correctly, that for Bentham it is simply impossible to compare the import of the two, since the first proposition, like the term itself, has no cognoscible meaning, but is simply nonsense. 'The options are either nonsense or taking it to mean what the analysis says: there is no separate way of understanding it' (Harrison 1983, p. 72). Or, with Bentham:

[5] In fact, Bentham offers more than one archetype for obligation (UC ci. 223 (1838–1843, viii. 247)). Jackson criticizes modern commentators for overlooking archetypation as 'an etymological fifth wheel on the coach' (1998, pp. 507–509). Bentham's treatment of this subsidiary process is, once again, not entirely consistent. For an attempt to reconcile some of the inconsistencies, see Quinn (2012a).

> Nothing has no properties. A fictitious entity, being as this its name imports—being, by the very supposition, a mere nothing, can not of itself have any properties: no proposition by which any property is ascribed to it can therefore be in itself and of itself a true one, nor therefore an instructive one: whatsoever of truth is capable of belonging to it can not belong to it in any other character than that of the representative of—the intended and supposed equivalent and adequate succedaneum of—some proposition having for its subject some real entity (UC cii. 217 (1838–1843, viii. 246)).[6]

Paraphrasis provides Bentham's standard answer to Fuller's question concerning the difference between good and bad fictions. All propositions concerning fictitious entities are, in Bentham's terms, fictions—they appear to assert the existence of something which has no existence. However, paraphrasis offers the means to rehabilitate fictitious entities, by their exposition in terms of real entities. As will be discussed in § III, there are occasions on which Bentham allows for the utility of fictitious entities, and the fictions asserted in propositions containing them, which are not resolvable by paraphrasis, but on most occasions he insists that paraphrasis is the only route to making sense of fictitious entities (UC lxix. 221; UC ci. 217 (1838–1843, viii. 246); 1977, p. 495n; 1983b, pp. 74–75; 1838–1843, iii. 286, 594n), so that a good or useful fictitious entity is either one which can be explicated by paraphrasis, or a species of a generic fictitious entity which is itself capable of such exposition.

Fuller once more follows Vaihinger in recommending the deployment of fictions in the form of metaphorical representations, in full awareness that 'the fiction must drop out of the final reckoning' (Fuller 1930–1931, p. 895; see also Vaihinger 1925, p. 68, 69, 98, 104, 109, 177). This recommendation bears comparison with Bentham's solution to the semantic problems arising from the fact that fictitious entities have no physical existence. For Bentham, if the fictitious entity has been successfully subjected to paraphrasis, there is in fact no need to eliminate it, as long as the speaker can supply on demand an exposition in terms of real entities (Bentham 1983a, p. 373). Paraphrasis rehabilitates fictitious entities precisely by eliminating the fiction—the assertion that the fictitious entity has real, independent existence—involved in propositions which contain them. One of Bentham's early projects was to develop a lexicon of legal and political terms (Bentham, UC lxix. 134), the availability of which would save legislators from the requirement to replace all fictitious terms with their paraphrastic exposition every time they were used in law.

A significant disagreement between Fuller and Bentham appears when the former approvingly cites Holmes' reference to the 'metaphor' by which '"legal duty" becomes simply "a prediction that if a man does or omits certain things he will be made to suffer in this or that way by the judgment of the court"' (Fuller 1930–1931, pp. 894–895). For Bentham, this is precisely *not* metaphor, but a less than perfect

[6] Similarly, 'A proposition having for its subject the name of a fictitious entity is not clearly understood any further than as it can be translated into a correspondent proposition having for its subject the name of some real entity. Falsehood, then, or nonsense, is the only import, of which, abstractedly from all relations to any proposition having for its subject the name of some real entity, a proposition having for its subject the name of a fictitious entity is susceptible' (1983b, p. 75).

example of paraphrasis, that is, the explication of the term legal duty by the provision of a phrase which refers—albeit only implicitly—to the real entity pain. Insofar as the notion of legal duty can possess any meaning at all, Holmes' 'metaphor' has expressed it well enough. What Fuller takes to be a neglective fiction, a simplifying theoretical operation serving to focus investigation by ignoring all but one aspect of a phenomenon, Bentham views as delivering the truth—the observable, empirically testable truth—via the substitution of discussion of real entities for that of fictitious ones. For the most part, then, Bentham asserts that paraphrasis alone permits access to both meaning and truth in relation to fictitious entities, whereas for Fuller and Vaihinger, to believe that truth can be spoken in relation to fictions is to be committed to a fool's errand. Neither Fuller nor Vaihinger discuss Bentham's logic in any depth, or recognize the importance he attached to paraphrasis as the key to exposition of fictitious entities. Vaihinger omits all mention of Bentham's logic, and his discussion of Bentham is limited to a brief consideration of whether he viewed the assumption that all human motivation was self-interested as a fiction—a self-consciously false but theoretically useful simplification—or as an hypothesis—an empirically testable assertion—which concludes that Bentham failed to appreciate the difference between the two (Vaihinger 1925, pp. 187–188).

It is a similar failure to take the slightest cognizance of paraphrasis (the utter failure, that is, to address Bentham's apparatus for speaking truly or comprehensibly about fictitious entities) which undermines Stolzenberg's interpretation (1999). As noted above, Stolzenberg wastes no time in dismissing Bentham's statements that real entities do exist, and that truth can be spoken about them, on the basis that such statements are contained in passages which do not fit with Bentham's core understanding. However, these statements by Bentham, and his assertion that the key to the legitimate use of fictitious entities lies in their explication in terms of real entities, are emphatically not contained in one or two isolated passages, but constitute the bulk of the textual evidence. If Bentham thinks that there is no possibility of exchanging truth, why does he insist repeatedly that there is, straightforwardly in relation to real entities (1983b, p. 74; UC ci. 217 (1838–1843, viii. 246); UC cii. 302 (1838–1843, viii. 300); UC lxix. 241; 1838–1843, iii. 189; 1838–1843, vii. 81), and, in relation to fictitious entities, via their analysis in terms of real ones (1983a, pp. 271–272n; 1983b, pp. 74–75; UC ci. 217 (1838–1843, viii. 246); UC lxix. 221)? What is it that he thinks is gained by the process? Most tellingly perhaps, if Bentham were to accept that there were no ontological distinction between real and fictitious entities, he would be denying to utilitarianism its most effective weapon in the struggle with competing moral theories. Thus the superiority of the principle of utility over its major competitor, the principle of sympathy and antipathy, or ipse-dixitism, consisted precisely in the reliance of its conclusions on matters of fact, that is, on the real entities constituted by pleasure and pain.[7] To abolish the distinction between real and fictitious entities is to reduce Bentham, in his own terms, to just one more ipse-dixitist.

[7] Of course, Bentham also recognizes the principle of Asceticism as a competitor, and one that also allows the exchange of sense. However, in Bentham's view, a proper understanding of the principle can only result in its rejection (Bentham 1996, p. 21).

4.1.5 A Crude Taxonomy, and the Foundation of Bentham's Hostility to Legal Fictions

If fictitious entities are capable of rehabilitation through their connection with really existing entities, why does Bentham become so exercised about the use of fictions in law and politics? Fuller poses the question of how a lie, which even its purveyors admitted to be a lie, could deceive anyone, and thereby lead to the consequences which Bentham asserts to issue from its use (Fuller 1930–1931, p. 519). Isn't Bentham simply being carried away by his animus against the legal profession, and investing fiction with a magical power which in fact it lacks?

In attempting to clarify the object and origin of his hostility, three different types of fiction will be distinguished, all of which Bentham would recognize, though for the most part he would avoid referring to the first type as 'fictions'. First come the legal/moral fictitious entities, such as obligation and power, which Bentham and Fuller both believe to be utterly essential to discourse about law or morals. For Bentham, the meaningful use of this type of fictitious names is conditional on their capacity to be successfully paraphrased. For Fuller, they are useful neglective fictions, the result of simplifying mental operations which actually make no claim to describe the totality of a particular phenomenon.[8] Second come the procedural or linguistic expedients used by courts, for instance to bring particular cases within their remit. The rule of Roman Law which treated foreigners 'as if' they were Roman citizens, or the decision of a London court that Minorca was in London (Fuller 1930–1931, p. 376, 390), are classic examples of this type of sleight of hand. Finally, come what we might call theoretical fictions, and what Bentham would call fallacies, for instance the assertions that Common Law judges do not make law, but merely apply law which has always existed, or that a body of (divinely prescribed) natural law both underlies and limits all systems of human law. Bentham's critique of legal fictions leaves every 'fiction' of the first type which is capable of successful paraphrasis wholly unimpugned; but finds no more than, at best, a temporary justification for the second type.[9] Indeed, his chief interest in fictions of the second type is related to his persuasion that they often arise from, and usually serve to buttress, intellectual and linguistic practices which facilitate the deployment of the third type. It is against this third type, the theoretical fallacies, that he directs his most bitter criticism, and he does so because he believes them to be a serious danger to general well-being.

---

[8] For Kelsen, these are not fictions at all, since the autonomous spheres of law and morality make no attempt at the cognition of reality, and therefore cannot contradict reality: 'After all, normative cognition is not directed at actual reality at all. Of course, within normative cognition fictions can very well exist, i.e. concepts can exist that are opposed to the specific object of cognition. However, this object of cognition itself and the entire activity of cognition cannot be called fictions. The concepts "god and conscience" may be fictions. The "ought", the "duty" and the "norm" certainly cannot (this volume, Chap. 1, p. 21, and see the discussion in section 1.6).

[9] For a sophisticated defence of legal fictions of this second type, over a much more extended timescale than Bentham might allow, but founded on the utilitarian benefits of flexibility and adaptability which he would recognize, see Maks Del Mar's article in this volume (Chap. 11).

Thus, Bentham might point out that many legal fictions of the second type were in fact wholly unnecessary: what is the point of deliberately misdescribing reality when an accurate *description* is easily available? Such a critique might prove effective against many of the procedural fictions found in the common law practice of Eighteenth century England: why not simply change the law, where the law needed changing, without resort to the linguistic gymnastics which underlay 'ejectment' or *latitat*?[10] Such a strategem might conceivably be justified on utilitarian grounds once, in an urgent case which required speedy adjudication, but its repetition simply encourages lawyers and judges to lie with a straight face. For Fuller too, 'it seems exceedingly questionable whether it is ever truly convenient to employ a fiction where the judge introducing the reform can state the new rule in non-fictitious terms' (1930–1931, p. 524). As Bentham would argue, if the reasons for the decision are given, we can all make an assessment as to their quality, and therefore come to a judgment as to whether we are witnessing a justified extension of judicial competence or merely a power grab.

Fuller argues that many legal fictions arise from intellectual conservatism, from the judge's attempt to fit new realities into a limited existing set of conceptual resources: 'we find ourselves compelled to force new situations, which bob up out of the eternal flux of reality, into the confining framework of an existing intellectual apparatus' (1930–1931, p. 525). Bentham would agree that analogy was absolutely central to the development of human thought, and that our existing frame of reference determines the manner in which we assimilate new facts. Indeed, Bentham and Fuller use the same illustration, that of a first encounter with a horse by persons whose previous knowledge of large quadrupeds extended only as far as dogs, who initially assimilate the unfamiliar phenomenon to the existing category 'dog' (Bentham, UC ci. 335 (1838–1843, viii. 266); Fuller 1930–1931, p. 892).[11] However, while Bentham would also agree with Fuller on the need to attend to the motives operative upon the instigators and perpetrators of legal fictions, he would differ markedly in assigning the salient motives in the development of legal fictions of the second and third types detailed above.

For Bentham, the problem with fictions of these types arose from their use as a tool of misrule. The most plausible explanation for their prevalence lay in the commitment of common lawyers to the overarching fiction that the common law had existed unchanging since time immemorial, and that judges did not make law, but merely applied existing law. As Postema notes, Bentham's core objection to common law was that it was a fictitious entity masquerading as law: a set of customary rules alterable at the will of judges, which did not satisfy the essential criteria for law, that is clarity, determinacy, authority and content (1986, pp. 295–299).[12] The

[10] In ejectment, a civil action to recover title to land, two imaginary tenants to actually existing parties to the case were simply invented, one being alleged to have evicted the other from rightful possession. A *latitat*, a writ of summons to appear and answer in the court of King's Bench, declared the person summoned to be in hiding.

[11] Whereas Fuller imagines his hypothetical pattern-matcher as a small boy, Bentham relies on a reported classification by the inhabitants of Tahiti.

[12] Note the considerable overlap between Bentham's criteria for law and Fuller's account of the inner morality of law (Fuller 1964, pp. 33–94).

fiction that the normative justification of government and law rested upon an original contract which established political society was another dangerous, because obscurantist and investigation-stifling, fallacy, which diverted attention from that which mattered, namely the impact of any decision or any law on the experience of pains and pleasures: 'the only firm foundations that Law can have must be a set of accurate speculations concerning pain and pleasure' (UC lxix. 125; see also Bentham 1977, pp. 439–449). In exactly the same way, propositions about natural law were meaningless assertions about a non-entity, but the consequence of their deployment was to stifle investigation and debate. 'The great mischief of the expression is that, by furnishing men with the semblance of a reason ready made, it prevents them from looking after a real one' (Bentham UC lxix. 126). Fuller notes that a 'fiction taken seriously, i.e. "believed", becomes dangerous and loses its utility' (Fuller 1930–1931, p. 370), while Bentham would argue that the overarching fictions about the status of common law, natural law, and original contract are often swallowed whole by the mass of the people, since lawyers and politicians use them as if they were true.

'By fiction, in the sense in which it is used by lawyers, understand a false assertion of the privileged kind, and which, *though acknowledged to be false, is at the same time argued from, and acted upon, as if true*' (1838–1843, ix. 77). How can I expect compliance in acting on an assertion which I admit to be false? Bentham's answer lies in the manner in which the faculty of judgment is subject to the influence of will: 'Judgment, opinion, persuasion, is in a very considerable degree under the dominion of the will; discourse, declared opinion, altogether' (1838–1843, vii. 107). The powerful know that to determine the terms of discussion is to rule. The point of legal fictions, especially the grand substantive personifications of natural law and common law, is to divert attention and sow confusion, and thereby to stifle investigation. Fuller compares fictions to temporary scaffolding supporting new developments in thought, and notes both that scaffolding gets removed once building work is complete, and that legal fictions, precisely because of their transparent falsity, are easily removable, so that their persistence can only be justified by 'considerations of social and economic policy' (1930–1931, p. 529), that is, in Bentham's terms, by their utility. For Bentham, the need for such scaffolding is at an end as soon as the option of following a Benthamic path becomes available, that is as soon as it is possible to deploy fictitious entities only where they can be connected to real entities, so that sense can be effectively exchanged. Further, there can be no lasting utilitarian justification for the fictions deployed by natural or common lawyers, since, in policy terms, they served only the sinister interest of the political and legal establishment. Instead, paraphrasis sets limits to the legitimate exercise of analogy:

> At the age at which the world is now arrived, the mine of extraordinary cases ought to have been worked out: whatsoever cases have not yet happened to present themselves to the Judge, analogy, if diligently consulted, is ready to point out to the Legislator. Jurisprudence, the science of the blind, ought long ago to have been consigned to oblivion: it is a disgrace to the architect that rubbish and scaffolding should continue in any part to deform the building. (UC xx. 91)

Thus judges and politicians can choose clarity over obfuscation should they be so inclined. They are not so inclined because constraining discussion within the realm of fiction buttresses existing structures of power, and prevents the application of attention to the reality of the situation (1838–1843, vii. 107). Perhaps the most significant power wielded by judges and politicians is an epistemological power, a power precisely to supply the analogies by which the rest of us make sense of legal and political events. The immutable common law and the law of nature are pernicious fictions because neither is capable of paraphrastic exposition, while both serve to divert attention away from facts: 'he who is completely master of men's discourses, is little less than completely master of men's opinions' (1838–1843, vii. 108). Dominant discourses make everything which contradicts them unthinkable, while the fictional underpinnings of law and political theory render rational exchange concerning reality much more difficult: 'Of moral science, the only true and useful foundations are propositions enunciative … of facts; viz. of the existence of human feelings, pains or pleasures, as the effects of this or that disposition of law' (1838–1843, vii. 81n).

All our judgments are liable to be influenced by our perceived interest, while the ambiguity of language offers a means not only to conceal this influence from others (as in the case of sinister interest), or indeed from ourselves (as in the case of interest begotten prejudice), but to mislead others concerning the nature of their interests (as in the case of adoptive prejudice). Note that the evils of reliance on fictions are not limited to the deliberate deception of one set of people by another, but extend to self-deception on the part both of those who benefit from the fiction, and on the part of those who suffer from it, so that Bentham's argument is more subtle than is usually allowed (see, for example, Jackson, 1998, p. 528). Since accuracy in judgment varies directly with attention (1838–1843, vi. 226), it is the failure to examine the fiction, the failure to attend to the fallacious assumptions on which it is grounded, which explains these phenomena. Fictions which become embedded in our mental furniture prevent salient questions from occurring to us, so that we think under the direction of an unconscious self-denying ordinance. Malcolm Quinn argues that the central distinction for Bentham was not that between the real and the fictitious, but that between fact and fallacy (Quinn 2011). There is abundant evidence, however, that for Bentham the latter distinction is derived from the former, since the appeal to 'facts' directs attention to evidence, and evidence consists in empirically verifiable propositions about the condition of real entities. The reason facts are facts is that they are in principle verifiable, and that observation provides evidence of their existence. If I wanted to make assertions capable of truth as well as falsehood, I needed to refer to facts: 'Truth can operate only by supporting evidence' (Bentham 1838–1843, x. 146).

4.1.6 Kelsen Versus Bentham on Legal (and Ethical) Fictions

The constraints of time, space and competence rule out the attempt to engage systematically in this chapter with Kelsen's discussion of Vaihinger, which is subtle, sophisticated and challenging.[13] For present purposes, however, the salient issue is the way in which Bentham's insistence on founding moral science on the facts constituted by the experience (actual or predicted) of pains and pleasures, sheds light on the contrast between his understanding and Kelsen's understanding of the relations between law and reality on the one hand, and between law and morality on the other. Kelsen argues that Vaihinger misconceives the nature of legal fictions, since a variety of concepts and constructs which the latter identifies as legal fictions are not characterized by that opposition to reality which he himself had identified as the hallmark of fictions. As noted above, for Kelsen the normative spheres of law and morality are concerned not with the world of the 'is', but with that of the 'ought'. Law, as a normative order, simply cannot contradict reality, since statements of law in no sense aim at cognition and description of reality, but simply at the accurate cognition, description and declaration of legislative will: 'the positing of a norm, the legislative activity, is not a process of thought, and does not have *cognition* as its goal. It is rather an act of will' (Chap. 1, pp. ???). As for normative justification, Kelsen is, in effect, completely agnostic: the legitimacy of the *grundnorm*—the 'basic norm' which underpins a legal system—is simply presumed. Thus he notes of the social contract:

> The social contract establishing the state thus is in fact no fiction of legal theory, but an ethical fiction, a fiction of a moral world-view. *A jurisprudential perspective has to drop precisely such a fiction and the imagination of an ethical justification of the law*. Chap. 1, p. 18; (emphasis added)

If legal theory must simply presume the legitimacy of the basic norm, the question of the validity of the basic norm can only be answered by an empirical or sociological analysis of the 'efficacy' of the legal system to which it gives unity and coherence, that is the extent therein of compliance with legal norms.

There are echoes in all this of central elements in Bentham's theory of law. Thus the understanding of law as a statement of will is pure Bentham, for whom law was 'an assemblage of signs declarative of a volition' (Bentham 2010, p. 17); and the explanation of the normativity of law in terms an appeal to existing social practices—that is in terms of the observation that human beings operating in particular legal systems do in fact treat the dictates of law as normatively binding—might easily be rendered as an analysis of their disposition to obey, or their 'habit of obedience' to, prescriptions originating from what they regard as a legitimate authority (Bentham 1977, pp. 429–430). Yet further, Kelsen's determination to divorce positive assertions about reality from normative considerations might as easily be rendered in terms of Bentham's distinction between the tasks of the censor and the expositor, the former being concerned to 'explain to us what … the Law is', and the latter to 'observe to us what he thinks it ought to be' (Bentham 1977, pp. 397–398). As Schofield has recently argued, however, Bentham introduces the censor–expositor distinction to attack Blackstone 'not for linking law to a particular substantive content, but for linking it to the wrong substantive content' (Schofield 2010, p. 157). This insight has been developed by Zhai, who articulates the way in which the

[13] For such an analysis see Christoph Kletzer's chapter 2 in this volume.

expositor's central tool, natural arrangement, relies precisely on the 'interesting properties'—that is consequences for the creation and distribution of pleasures and pains—of certain actions, in explicating the connection between offences on the one hand, and real entities on the other, or, in other words, in explicating the connection between (penal) law and reality: 'A really meaningful account of the nature of law as it is abstracts and describes the interesting properties of really existing laws' (Zhai 2014, p. 176). On Bentham's view, the implicit justificatory assumption underlying laws in general, and penal laws most obviously, is that they produce a balance of good over evil. Natural arrangement makes this assumption explicit, and thus constitutes at one and the same moment a test of the truth of that assumption in relation to existing laws, and, by the same means, a test of the utility of those laws:

> The mischievousness of a bad law would be detected, at least the utility of it would be rendered suspicious, by the difficulty of finding a place for it in such an arrangement: while, on the other hand, a technical arrangement is a sink that with equal facility will swallow any garbage that is thrown into it. (Bentham 1977, p. 416)

Whilst Kelsen's discussion of legal fictions thus resonates at several points with Bentham's, their understandings of the role of fictions in general, and in law in particular, end up in direct opposition on two related issues. First, Bentham (but presumably not Kelsen), would assert that it *is* possible to provide a true account of law, where true means correspondent to reality. Second, Bentham would ultimately reject Kelsen's attempt to assert the 'sovereignty of law', that is to insulate the sphere of law from that of morality. Thus when Kelsen dismisses the notion that obligation is a fiction by arguing that 'ought statements—the ethical just as the legal—are "fictions" only if by a fiction we understand everything which is not the expression, and particularly a consistent expression, of *natural* reality' (this volume, Chap. 1, p. 18), he dismisses precisely Bentham's understanding of a fiction. When Kelsen proceeds to proclaim the independence of law from morals, he reveals the full extent of the gulf between their views: 'Legal science … can only be possible if one assumes the *sovereignty of the law* … i.e. if one takes the legal order as a system of norms which is not dependent on any higher order. Otherwise only a moral science (ethics) or theology would be possible' (this volume, Chap. 1, p. 18). For Bentham, it might equally well be asserted that legal science is a branch of moral science, or that moral science is a branch of legal science, since both, as Kelsen correctly notes, equally deal in the currency of obligation. The central point, for Bentham, is not about the primacy or foundational nature of either law or morality, since both depend for whatever truth they express on a science of pleasures and pains, and both depend for their normative justification on the single fountainhead of any and all such justification, the principle of utility.

For Kelsen, the need to insulate law from morals, and to insulate both from natural reality, arises from his determination to avoid a naturalistic fallacy (Moore 1993/1903, pp. 91–93). By contrast, for Bentham normative statements are precisely a particular sort of factual statement: 'When established on the basis of sensation, however, morality is as strictly and properly a science founded upon experiment, as any branch of Natural Philosophy' (UC lxx. 22).[14] Now Bentham has often been accused of falling into a naturalistic fallacy. However, as Schofield argues, Bentham would have rejected the idea that deriving prescription from description was an error, since there was simply no where else whence to derive it (Schofield 2003, pp. 4, 11–28). It does seem, however, that to endorse utilitarianism as against its competitors—asceticism and the principle of sympathy and antipathy—requires two further moves which do not themselves depend on facts, but upon premises of value. The first move, which consists in accepting what Bentham thinks is the foundational principle of rationality, namely that pleasure is preferable to pain, serves to see off asceticism. The second, which consists in accepting an egalitarian premise that the moral agent has no reason for preferring the happiness of one individual to that of another, debars the sympathist/antipathist from prioritizing the welfare of those to whom he is well-disposed as against that of those to whom he is ill-disposed. Bentham makes both moves, though the second is never expounded at length.[15] He would assert, I think, that the sympathist/antipathist will simply not be able to adduce any facts from which to derive his substantive moral premises, whilst any attempt so to do will perforce oblige him to engage in what is, in effect, utilitarian reasoning.

4.2 Facts and Opinions: Objectivity and Subjectivity in Bentham

4.2.1 Morality and Law as Science: A Big Bold Claim and a Great Many Caveats

It has been argued so far that Bentham appears committed to an ontological distinction between real and fictitious entities, which in turn commits him broadly to some kind of philosophical realism. His justification for seeking to purge legal and political discourse of those fictitious entities which were incapable of explication with reference to real entities, depended on the possibility of such explication with reference to many fictitious entities. It is time to note Bentham's awareness of the difficulties involved in exchanging meaning through discussion of facts.

Bentham confidently identified the tools for the progressive unveiling of the world around us: 'Experience—Observation—Experiment—Reflection on the results of each and of all together: these are the means, these are the instruments,

[14] A scientific morality depends upon the discovery of a common metric for the quantification of pleasures and pains, and Bentham discovers his metric in the measurement of sensation, the value of which is either negative (pain) or positive (pleasure), and is the product of its intensity and its duration, discounted by its uncertainty and temporal distance, multiplied by its extent (1996, pp. 38–41).

[15] Bentham did however assert (1838–1843, vii. 475) that his 'system of arithmetic … on all political occasions' was 'every individual in the country tells for one; no individual for more than one'.

by which knowledge, such as is within the power of man, is collected' (UC ci. 183 (1838–1843, viii. 238)). Bacon's inductive method offered a means through which assertions and hypotheses could be tested, and thus offered the prospect of objectivity in the physical sciences: their empirical methods of verification generated knowledge. For Bentham, the same methods are capable of rendering morality equally a science. He viewed the binary opposition between pleasure and pain as *the* route to objective knowledge about human beings and the interactions between them. It was only by relating moral and political discourse to these real entities that it was possible to exchange meaning instead of nonsense, and it is by this route that morality is reduced to a matter of fact, which is to say, becomes a science. For Bentham, all knowledge (of law and morality just as much as of physics) is 'matter of fact', while a facts is: 'The existence of any expressible state of *things*, or of persons, or of both, whether it be *quiescent* or *motional* or both, at any given point or portion of time' (UC cii. 301 (1838–1843, viii. 300)).

Bentham early on detailed the morally relevant facts: 'Now this matter of fact is no other than this: viz. the state of sensations, upon the commission of an act, of the persons within the circle of its influence: viz. of sensations, partly present, partly future in certainty, partly future in contingency, œstimated all together at their present value' (UC lxx. 22). Rules require reasons, while 'a maxim, to be intelligible, must openly refer to, and … be … justifiable by, a balance of utilities' (UC lxx. 22). Without such comparison, morality and law are neither defensible nor comprehensible. With such comparison, as noted in § 1.6, both morality and law are capable to dealing in natural facts in the same way as natural philosophy.

The conclusions of any science are only as valid as the data, or with Bentham the facts, from which they are derived. Does moral reasoning permit certainty? '[T]he answer is plain, the same that those facts are in each case susceptible of, and none other' (UC lxx. 23). Now the facts in question in moral reasoning are sensations, while 'sensation is the highest evidence' (UC lxx. 23). This looks like a promising start, but the disjunction between external reality and our perception of it gives rise to a series of potential pitfalls.[16] First, as previously noted, perception itself usually depends on judgment. 'A judgment-involving perception is the perception of a relation: i.e. of the existence of a relation between some two objects' (UC ci. 407 (1838–1843, viii. 279)). The moment we do more than simply report the existence of a sensation, the moment, for instance, we endeavour to assert a relation of cause and effect between the sensation and some other object, the probability of error increases, because causation, like all relations, is a fictitious entity (UC cii. 460 (1838–1843, viii. 330); and see 1838–1843, vii. 83n.). The attribution of cause and effect is 'a soil in which the greatest understandings have toiled with great labour and no fruit' (1838–1843, vi. 237). I have direct access to my own sensations, but in explaining them I make choices from a limitless range of potential candidates for my list of influencing circumstances.

[16] For a discussion of the irresistibly seductive appeal of scientific discourse in law, and of the dangers involved in it, see Randy D. Gordon's article in this volume (Chap. 18).

> Every *body*, it is plain, is a circumjacent body with respect to every other body; every event is a circumstance to every other event. The thread that links them together may, for aught we know, be the same for all. Every one may influence every other. If the fly that 2 min ago was perched upon the left hand page of the paper I am writing on had perched upon the right hand page, the Turkish empire might have been to have a different sovereign this day 500 years from him it will have (UC lxix. 174).

Second, if the inferences I draw from my own sensations can only be provisional, the caveat applies much more to the inferences I draw from what I assume to be the sensations of others (UC cii. 460 (1838–1843, viii. 330)). In moral reasoning, the relevant sensations are not discoverable by straightforward introspection on the part of the reasoner, for the simple reason that they are not *his* sensations, but those of other people (UC lxx. 23). Since all legal and moral reasoning beyond the purely prudential concerns the sensations of others, to which I have no introspective access, I should be cautious in attributing sensations, and doubly so in attributing their causes (Bentham UC cii. 71 (1997, p. 146; 1838–1843, viii. 210)).

Third, in any project of rule-making, the sensations in question do not simply exist outside the direct introspective experience of the rule-maker, but do not exist at all: they are '*no more than a presumption of what would be the sensations, in a case which is not present, of other men*' (UC lxx. 23; emphasis added). Rule making operates in the subjunctive rather than the indicative mood. The pains and pleasures which form the basis of calculation are putative, constituted by predictions of sensations which do not yet exist, and are not present to me, but are the product of my beliefs about the probable future, and thus literally figments of imagination. On what does the decision-maker base his predictions of sensation? '[U]pon recollection, observation and analogy—recollection of one's own sensations upon past occasions—observation of the conduct of others—analogy according to which such conduct … is presumed to originate from like sensations as those which give birth to the same conduct in ourselves' (UC lxx. 23). To aid him in his efforts, he has first his lived experience, mediated by memory; second, the observed behaviour of others; and third, the pattern-matching faculty of analogy.

Although recollection, observation and analogy 'are the very grounds (and the only ones we have) of conduct which are universally received as sufficient for the most … important concerns of common life' (UC lxx. 23), when we undertake the process of estimating the value of 'sensations, partly present, partly future in certainty, partly future in contingency', we are all too likely to get it wrong:

> These observations of experience may be erroneous, [they] may be incomplete, though just: the analogy binding together the experiences and observations, according to which the sensations of others are presumed to be what we remember our own to have been in cases similar, though true as to the kind of those sensations, may be erroneous as to their degree. (UC lxx. 23)

Thus we rely on our memories and on second hand data, both of which may be inaccurate; we are prone to leave out of the account some sensations without which our calculation is incomplete; we become confused in making analogies and attributing causes, so that we mistake irrelevant circumstances, and even obstacles, for causes

(Bentham, UC cii. 71 (1997, p. 146; 1838–1843, viii. 209)); finally, we choose appropriate analogies, but we err in estimating 'degree', that is, we assess the intensity of the relevant sensations incorrectly.

Concern about the accuracy of such judgments is strengthened by Bentham's recognition that moral and legal reasoning has a serious disadvantage as against natural philosophy, which is that in this field fundamental and conflicting interests are at stake, so that 'the judgment is in a peculiar degree liable to be disturbed and led astray by the several sources of illusion:—by original intellectual weakness—by sinister interest—by interest-begotten prejudice—by adoptive prejudice' (Bentham, UC cii. 71 (1997, p. 146; 1838–1843, viii. 210)). Human beings develop their ideas within a network of power relations which limit choices and ground thought. They are historically and concretely situated in particular positions within overlapping networks of influence and power. They are empiricists—experiencing sensations, developing hypotheses of cause and effect, and modifying them once falsified—but they interpret the world with the tools made available to them by their particular language, and by the habitual ways in which they put that language together, in an arena where the accurate construction of meaning through the assertion of significant relations between real entities is vitiated by the weight of prevailing conceptual presumptions and prescriptions, themselves fictitious and fallacious constructs, which often falsely assert the reality or salience of non-entities, and deny the reality or salience of real sensations, and of the connections between them.

4.2.2 Assessing Judgments, Beliefs, and Opinions: The Demand for Evidence

In exchanging meaning through discourse, what we actually exchange is information about the state of our opinions, our judgments, and, centrally, the degree of confidence with which we assert those opinions and judgments: 'when *information* is professed to be given, *judgment*, vis. the judgment existing or declared to exist concerning the matter in question in the mind of the alledged informant, is the utmost that in truth is communicated' (UC cii. 203). As Schofield puts it: 'A statement about what existed in the physical world could not be separated from a statement about what was believed to exist' (2006, p. 18; see also Postema 1983, p. 53). While human beings could believe things about the world and communicate that belief to others, absolute knowledge was incompatible with human experience. 'Certainty, absolute certainty, is a satisfaction which on every ground of enquiry we are continually grasping at, but which the inexorable nature of things has placed for ever out of our reach' (1838–1843, vii. 105). The statement 'I am certain that … ', communicated the highest degree of subjective conviction, but the predicate, being derived from the doubly fictitious entity 'certainty',[17] asserted a falsehood, which was corrected by reframing the statement in terms of belief: 'I believe as strongly

[17] Whilst all qualities are fictitious entities, that is, have no existence outside the particular entities in which we speak of them as being 'lodged', the concepts of, for instance, certainty, impossibility,

as it is possible for me to believe that ... '. Similarly, the assertion that something was impossible could only be sensibly interpreted as an assertion that the speaker considered that thing to be unlikely in the highest degree (1838–1843, vi. 46).

Instead of the reductionist Gradgrind insisting on nothing but facts, lacerated by Dickens in *Hard Times* Surely (1995 [1854]), we seem close to a subjectivist and constructivist Bentham for whom facts, whilst existing, are never completely knowable, and for whom belief seems the irreducible and inaccessible product of esoteric psychological processes. However, whilst it is true that Bentham relied on a subjectivist epistemological model, he also asserted that opinions, and the judgments which underlay them, were capable of rational assessment. For instance, individual assessments of the probability of an event's having occurred are, for Bentham, simply statements of the individual's persuasion or belief that the event did occur. As reports of the internal state of the individual mind, they are infallible, at least so long as the individual is being honest, and his faculty of introspection is functional. However, this emphatically does not imply that every individual's assessment of probability is equally valid, because assessments of probability depend upon evidence, and evidence is 'any matter of fact, the effect tendency, or design of which, when presented to the mind, is to produce a persuasion concerning the existence of some other matter of fact' (1838–1843, vi. 208). Once more, the introduction of facts—'the existence of any expressible state of *things*, or of persons ... at any given point or portion of time'—provides an escape route from terminal relativism. We cannot simply choose to believe whatever we like, since, given full attention, the faculty of understanding is governed by evidence.

> Now, what is in man's power to do, in order to believe a proposition, and *all* that is so, is to keep back and stifle the evidences that are opposed to it. *For, when all the evidences are equally present to his observation, and equally attended to, to believe or disbelieve is no longer in his power. It is the necessary result of the preponderance of the evidence on one side over that on the other.* (1838–1843, x. 146 (emphasis added); see also 1838–1843, vi. 18n.)

For Bentham, 'A Belief is an act of the Judgment' (Bentham, UC lxix. 133), while judgments about facts do admit of meaningful and rational assessment. Whilst absolute certainty is incompatible with human existence, what Bentham calls 'Practical certainty, a degree of assurance sufficient for practice' (1838–1843, vii. 105), is not. How can humanity approach toward practical certainty? We fall back on the basis of all knowledge: experience, observation, experiment and reflection.

As noted at the end of § I.5, Bentham recognized that human judgments are all too liable to be influenced by our perceived interest, which is to say that judgment is subject to the pervasive influence of the faculty of will—the fictitious substantification of the utterly basic desire to eschew pain and pursue pleasure. Indeed, it has been argued that the dangers of the perversion of common judgment by habitual errors of omission and uncritical acceptance of fallacious premises and modes of reasoning lie at the root of the anathema he pronounced on legal fictions. Now

---

probability and necessity are doubly fictitious in that they are not properly ascribed to any really existing entities (Bentham, UC cii. 75–76 (1997, pp. 152–154; 1838–1843, viii. 210–211)).

he also investigated the range of strategies available to the will in its attempt to cloud, confuse and manipulate the understanding, which boil down to the decision to look the other way, that is, to ignore or disregard inconvenient evidence. Whilst the pragmatist Charles Peirce apparently regarded Bentham as ‘a shallow logician’ (Peirce 1931–1958, v. Para. 158),[18] Bentham’s discussions of the range of methods available to someone anxious to look the other way constitute a truly remarkable anticipation of the Peirce’s later analysis of flawed methods for attaining the fixation of belief, that is, for rendering beliefs unassailable by doubt (Peirce 1931–1958, v. Paras. 377–383). Peirce’s ‘tenacity’ (simple refusal to consider evidence to the contrary), ‘authority’ (refusal to think on the ground that someone else has done it for us), and ‘the *a priori* method’ (that is, begging the question by assuming the truth of the contested premise in the construction of the enquiry) would all look very familiar to Bentham, with the latter two especially receiving extended discussion in his discussion of political fallacies (1838–1843, ii. 387–395, and 436–438).

Since not all assertions which relate to real entities, directly or indirectly, are true, the central problem for human beings who wish to exchange meaningful and accurate information about the world is the nature of the criterion by which we differentiate between truth and falsehood. Now since sense experience is the only source of knowledge, that criterion itself reduces to consistency with such experience, with observation and experiment. For Peirce, as for Bentham, the definition of truth remains correspondence or agreement with reality:

> There are Real things, whose characters are entirely independent of our opinions about them: these Reals affect our senses according to regular laws, and, though our sensations are as different as are our relations to the objects, yet, by taking advantage of the laws of perception, we can ascertain by reasoning how things really and truly are; and any man, if he have sufficient experience and he reason enough about it, will be led to the one True conclusion. (Peirce 1931–1958, v. Para. 384)

Bentham would, I think, have been happy to endorse Peirce’s comment that ‘The opinion which is fated to be ultimately agreed to by all who investigate, is what we mean by the truth, and the object represented in this opinion is the real.’ (Peirce 1931–1958, v. Para. 407). The point is that this approach shifts the focus from the problem of truth to the problem of knowledge: the interesting question concerns the criterion by which human beings can tell truth from falsity. On what basis do we accept a proposition as true, as an accurate reflection of reality? Bentham and Peirce would agree that the world exists independently of human actions or language, and that truth is a human construct, a fictitious entity which human beings ascribe to propositions. Both men rely for verification on the observed regularities of experience, and the way in which predictions based on those regularities are verifiable by further experience.

[18] No extended discussion of Bentham’s logic appears in Peirce’s *Collected Papers*, though he seems to have been familiar at least with *Chrestomathia* (Bentham 1983a; Peirce 1931–1958, vii. Para. 199). For a fuller discussion of the relation between Bentham’s logic and pragmatism see Quinn (2012b).

In essence, we make progress towards truth by undertaking an ongoing process of mutual checking, and we learn from our mistakes. We can be fairly confident, for instance, in regarding as improbable the existence of reported 'facts' which appear 'contrary to the order of nature' (1838–1843, vii. 83). 'The better acquainted we are with the course, the ordinary course, of nature, the better qualified we are, of course, for judging whether a given fact be conformable or unconformable to it' (1838–1843, vii. 94). We may not all be skilled natural philosophers, but we can all purchase publications dealing in the subject and adopt their opinions, subject to our persuasion of the validity of that opinion. Centrally, human wisdom grows with experience. As far as the natural world is concerned, Bentham's close to absolute persuasion of the correctness of Newtonian physics looks a little optimistic to twenty-first century eyes—no quantum uncertainties for him—but his general point, that human knowledge increases as human experience—and access to reports of, and reflections on, that experience—increases (1838–1843, vii. 92), is surely more that just an enlightenment prejudice.

Since, given adequate attention and a desire to uncover the actual state of things, judgment depends on evidence, Bentham is also committed to the view that the presentation of identical evidence to a plurality of persons with broadly similar levels of knowledge and probity should give rise to a tendency to agreement between those persons. As Postema puts it, Bentham's account of probability is not radically relativist because 'given the same store of background beliefs regarding the ordinary course of nature, people would make the same assignments of probability' (1983, p. 60). Postema argues, quite correctly, that nothing in Bentham's subjectivist epistemology supports such a conclusion, which requires a separate premise akin to what Cohen calls 'universal cognitive competence' (1983, pp. 1–21). There is ample evidence in Bentham's writings that he, in company with many Enlightenment thinkers, did subscribe to such a premise:

> In point of political discernment, the universal spread of learning has raised mankind in a manner to a level with each other, in comparison of what they have been in any former time: nor is any man now so far elevated above his fellows, as that he should be indulged in the dangerous licence of cheating them for their good. (Bentham 1977, p. 441)

Indeed, without such an egalitarian premise, Bentham's entire rationale for representative democracy collapses.[19]

---

[19] Note that Bentham's qualification for the franchise was in large part a cognitive one: literacy. Access to written language is access to both statements of government and the opinions of others. For Bentham the premise represents a valid empirical generalization, to which there will be exceptions. Thus general cognitive competence underpins Bentham's political economy, which is driven by individual perception of individual interest: I can only know my interest if I can make reasonably accurate assessments of the probable consequences of the options before me. As he notes in comparing the indigent man with his more affluent fellows: 'He knows what is his interest as well as they do, and is as well disposed and able to pursue it as they are' (1787, p. 33 (1838–1843, iii. 7)). In his poor law writings, Bentham asserts that a minority of the indigent have an erroneous conception of their interests, but this assertion is always accompanied by the attribution of the error to a lack of education (2001, p. 85, 100).

4.3 The Useful or the True?

4.3.1 Fuller After Vaihinger: There is Only the Useful

Fuller echoes Vaihinger in noting the way in which human minds, and human languages, cannot simply mirror the external world, since such a mirroring would be simply chaotic: 'If we dealt with reality as it is, in its crude, unorganized form, we should be helpless' (1930–1931, p. 886). If truth is equivalent to exact correspondence with reality, then the expectation that human beings can deal in truth is simply a false one, since in the very act of describing reality we alter it (1930–1931, p. 885). As noted above, Bentham too is acutely aware that in its efforts to describe the physical world, human thought, and its instrument language, actively construct a purely mental model of the world. He recognizes that basic categories of human thought (matter, form, quality, quantity) are indeed fictitious entities. He gives an extended parable of the way in which thought deconstructs (analyses) external reality in creating logical, but fictitious qualities, and then reconstructs (synthesises) it, in accordance with concepts and the organization thereof, which are its own, fictitious, invention (1983a, pp. 261–273), thus recognizing that, even in the description of real entities, thought alters reality by imposing classificatory schemes and concepts which are the product of human artifice. The question, however, remains, do these constructivist elements render Bentham a fictionalist?

Fuller applies a thoroughly pragmatic criterion in assessing the worth of scientific fictions. He adopts Vaihinger's description of the two tasks of science: '1. to determine the actual sequences and co-existences; 2. to give the ideas with which we invest reality a more concise, more adequate, more useful and more harmless form' (Vaihinger 1925, p. 67; Fuller 1930–1931, p. 886). The first task is impeccably realist, since Vaihinger, like Bentham, asserted the reality of the external world: 'The only thing that is real and will remain real is the observable unchangeability of phenomena' (Vaihinger 1925, p. 124). However, the second task is wholly pragmatic, and human creativity is central to its successful completion, by developing theoretical concepts which link observed phenomena together in fruitful ways.

4.3.2 Bentham: Useful Truths and Useful Fictions?

Postema notes that Bentham's logic too is entirely pragmatic in origin (1983, p. 50), and without doubt Bentham was committed to evaluating everything according to its consequences. For him, the confusion in language arising from the necessary use of names of fictitious entities in law has had appalling consequences, while his method for the ascription of meaning is capable of preventing such consequences in future. The pragmatic necessity to impose order on the potential chaos of reality demands the invention of a host of fictitious entities which are essential to interpret reality in all areas of life. Logic provides a method for 'giving, to the best advantage, direction to the human mind, in its pursuit of any object or purpose' (UC ci.

92 (1838–1843, viii. 219)), while the end of logic, as of all rational action, is well-being. Bentham then, explicitly subjects all knowledge to utilitarian evaluation (UC ci. 153 (1838–1843, viii. 233)), but clearly differentiates between truth and utility, and identifies truth with 'the knowledge of what facts really did exist' (1983b, p. 354). As he expressed his project in his writings on sex: 'Of the present enquiry the sole objects are general utility—or the maximum of human happiness—and in so far as conduces to that object, the truth of things or, in one word, useful truth' (UC lxxiv. 39 (2014, p. 50)).

Fuller comments that the 'lack of a physical counterpart for our intellectual processes is the thing which has led us to call our ideas "false". But whence comes this notion that our ideas must have physical counterparts in nature?' (1930–1931, p. 885). The first part of this quotation in fact summarises a main premise of Bentham's logic, while he would be puzzled by the question, since the lack of counterpart in nature constitutes precisely the characteristic which differentiates fictitious entities from real ones: things 'which do exist may be said to have their archetypes in nature: those which do not exist may be said *not* to have their archetypes in nature.' He would however, agree that the non-existence of fictitious entities by no means implied the necessity to remove them from language. The central fruit of his own logic was precisely a method for eliminating the falsity, indeed the incomprehensibility, involved in the use of central legal concepts which do not correspond to things. For this reason, Bentham could not endorse Fuller's dismissal of the distinction between 'fact' and 'theory' as superficial: '"Facts" are only those thought constructs which are useful for so many purposes and are so commonly accepted that no one doubts their "existence" or "reality"' (1930–1931, p. 908). This definition of facts, or in effect, the wholly constructivist denial of their existence, might seem to Bentham either vacuous or vicious, exactly, in fact, like a fiction.

For Lee, Bentham's inductivist commitment to the reliability of sense experience as a guide to reality constitutes the central difference between his thought and that of Vaihinger. On this account, Bentham simply refuses to abandon the search for facts: 'What is true has its basis in reality or may be said in some way to be a reflection of it' (Lee 1990, p. 108). Vaihinger and Fuller, then, err in jettisoning the idea of truth understood as correspondence to external reality. For Vaihinger, as for Bentham, we find ourselves surrounded by a world that is real, and to which our access is mediated by sensory data which provide which both starting point and terminus for all logical activity (1925, pp. 4–5), while even Vaihinger accepts the reality of empirically verifiable experimental and observational data (1925, p. 68). Good theoretical models produce accurate predictions of such data, so that the criterion of a good model is entirely pragmatic: good models are good guides to action (Vaihinger 1925, p. viii; Fuller 1967, p. xi). If such fictionalism does deliver such useful predictions, it is legitimate to ask on what basis Bentham could possibly reject it, especially given his recognition of the inescapably figurative nature of much language. Nevertheless, as the bulk of the above discussion bears witness, he seems to do just that, in his insistence that only through paraphrasis is the route opened to truth and meaning in relation to fictitious entities. Rosen recognizes the tensions in Bentham's views, and declines to endorse either a fictionalist or a realist reading, noting however, that insofar as he belives paraphrasis uniquely capable of delivering truth in relation to fictitious entities, Bentham sounds very like a reductionist realist (2005, p. 55).

In essence, it all depends on what Bentham means by translating 'figurative language into language without figure', or by the fictitious having its 'necessary root' in the real (1838–1843, iii. 181; 1983b, p. 75). If it means simply that the employment of the fictitious entity in a theoretical model gives rise to predictions about the condition of real entities, which can be corroborated by observational data, Bentham might plausibly be read as a proto-fictionalist. However, if Bentham's repeated claims for paraphrasis are taken at face value, and fictitious entities incapable of successful paraphrasis are thereby illegitimate, he is no fictionalist, but cleaves to truth understood as the accurate description of reality. Considerable textual evidence for the realist interpretation has been adduced above, but there is some textual support for the alternative, since there are occasions on which Bentham does seem directly to anticipate key elements of Vaihinger's account of fictions. Thus, he consistently recognizes that the concepts used in geometry (line, point, circle) are fictitious, that is, lacking referents in the world (1983a, pp. 346–348), and that mathematics while thus not 'true', remains extraordinarily useful, thanks simply to resemblance of those concepts to real phenomena. More tellingly, in discussion of Newtonian fluxions, he explicitly recognizes that the self-conscious employment of a fiction can lead to the acquisition of new knowledge (1983a, pp. 370–371; and compare Vaihinger 1925, pp. 60–61). His insistence in such cases is 'not that no such fictions ought to be employed, but that to the purpose and on the occasion of instruction, whenever they are employed, the necessity or use of them should be made known.' (1983a, p. 371) Finally, in his universal grammar, Bentham defines non-figurative language not as language without figure, since almost all language is figurative, but as language 'in which, for the conveyance of the immaterial part of the stock of ideas conveyed, no other fictions—no other figures—are employed than what are absolutely necessary to, and which consequently are universally employed in, the conveyance of the import intended to be conveyed' (UC cii. 466 (1838–1843, viii. 331)). These examples do appear to open methods other than paraphrasis for the rehabilitation of fictitious entities: they can be justified by necessity (we simply cannot speak without them), and by utility (they allow us to calculate right answers to problems which were previously insoluble).

There is no obvious reconciliation between these two views, both of which Bentham expresses. It is possible, however, that Bentham believed different attitudes to fictions to be appropriate in different contexts. Thus, paradoxically, but on impeccable utilitarian grounds, he might well endorse Vaihinger's fictionalism in natural, but not in legal science. If fictional theoretical constructs like gravity, atoms, and the rest generate models, and thereby predictions, which are testable by the observational data, and which are flexible enough to be revised when the observational data contradict them, what does it matter that the concepts which make up the model do not actually exist as real entities? However, in the area of Bentham's primary interest, morality and law, he believes that the investigation-stymieing consequences of deference to unparaphrasable fictions has been a disaster, and that, therefore, a thorough revision of language is urgently necessary. That revision takes the form of interpreting the fictitious entities in which legal discourse abounds in terms of real entities, and specifically the entities of pleasure and pain. Such a revision would at once produce significant progress toward truth (understood as accurate reference to that which exists), and an equally significant gain in utility, since, in this sphere at least, truth and utility stand or fall together. Ultimately, it is the rooting of utility in the real entities of pleasure and pain, that is to say the exposition of the fictitious entity utility[20] in terms of alleged facts which are themselves capable of empirical verification or falsification, which bestows all the utility on the term 'utility'. In morals at least, then, it is probable that he would endorse Lee's reading that there can be no conflict between truth and utility, because only the true can in fact be useful: 'Any construct, which itself does not refer to a real entity and is not reducible to others which do, is bound to lead to disutility' (Lee 1990, p. 204).

References

Bentham, Jeremy. (UC). UCL collection of Bentham manuscripts, boxes i–clxxvi.

Bentham, Jeremy. 1787. *Defence of Usury; shewing the impolicy of the present legal restraints on the terms of pecuniary bargains*. London: Payne.

Bentham, Jeremy. 1838–1843. *The works of Jeremy Bentham, now first collected; under the superintendence of his Executor, John Bowring*. 11 vols. Edinburgh: Tait.

Bentham, Jeremy. 1977. *A Comment on the Commentaries and a Fragment on Government,* eds. J. H. Burns and H. L. A. Hart. London: Athlone.

Bentham, Jeremy. 1983a. *Chrestomathia,* eds. M. J. Smith and W. H. Burston. Oxford: Clarendon Press.

Bentham, Jeremy. 1983b. *Deontology Together with a Table of the Springs of Action, and the Article on Utilitarianism,* ed. A. Goldworth. Oxford: Clarendon Press.

Bentham, Jeremy. 1996. *An Introduction to the Principles of Morals and Legislation,* ed. J. H. Burns and H. L. A. Hart. Oxford: Clarendon Press.

Bentham, Jeremy. 1997. *De l'ontologie et autres Textes sur les Fictions,* ed. P. Schofield (trans. J.-P. Cléro and C. Laval). Paris: Seuil.

Bentham, Jeremy. 2001. *Writings on the Poor Laws: I,* ed. M. Quinn. Oxford: Clarendon Press.

Bentham, Jeremy. 2010. *Of the Limits of the Penal Branch of Jurisprudence,* ed. P. Schofield. Oxford: Clarendon Press.

Bentham, Jeremy. 2014. *Of Sexual Irregularities, and Other Writings on Sexual Morality,* ed. P. Schofield, C. Pease-Watkin, and M. Quinn. Oxford: Clarendon Press.

Cohen, L. Jonathan. 1983. Freedom of proof. In *Facts in law*, 1–21. Wiesbaden: Steiner.

Del Mar, Maksymilian. 2014. Legal fictions and legal change in the common law tradition. In *Legal fictions in theory and practice,* ed. Maksymilian Del Mar and William Twining. Dordrecht: Springer.

Dickens, Charles. 1995. *Hard times, (first published 1854)*. Harmondsworth: Penguin.

Fuller, Lon. 1930–1931. Legal fictions. *Illinois Law Review* 25:363–399, 513–546, 877–910.

Fuller, Lon. 1964. *The morality of law*. New Haven: Yale University Press.

Fuller, Lon. 1967. 'Introduction'. In *Legal fictions*, vii–xiii. Stanford: Stanford University Press.

[20] 'By utility is meant that property in any object, whereby it tends to produce … pleasure … or … to prevent the happening of … pain … to the party whose interest is considered' (Bentham 1996, p. 12).

Gordon, Randy D. 2014. Fictitious Fraud: Economics and the presumption of reliance. In *Legal fictions in theory and practice,* ed. Maksymilian Del Mar and William Twining. Dordrecht: Springer.

Hans Kelsen. 2014. On the theory of juridic fictions. With special consideration of Vaihinger's Philosophy of the as-if. In *Legal fictions in theory and practice,* ed. Maksymilian Del Mar and William Twining. Dordrecht: Springer.

Harrison, Ross. 1983. *Bentham*. London: Routledge & Kegan Paul.

Jackson, Bernard S. 1998. Bentham, truth and the semiotics of law. *Current Legal Problems* 51:493–531.

Lee, Kukok. 1990. *The legal-rational state: A comparison of Hobbes, Bentham and Kelsen*. Aldershot: Avebury.

Moore, G. E. 1993/1903. In *Principia ethica* (revised edition), ed. T. Baldwin. Cambridge: Cambridge University Press.

Ogden, Charles K. 1932. *Bentham's theory of fictions*. London: Kegan Paul, Trench & Trubner.

Peirce, Charles Sanders. 1931–1958. *Collected papers of Charles Sanders Peirce,* ed. C. Hartshome, P. Weiss, and A. W. Burks, 8 vols. Cambridge: Harvard University Press.

Petroski, Karen. 2014. Legal fictions and the limits of legal language. In *Legal fictions in theory and practice,* ed. Maksymilian Del Mar and William Twining. Dordrecht: Springer.

Postema, Gerald J. 1983. Fact, fictions and law: Bentham on the foundations of evidence. In *Facts in law,* ed. W. L. Twining, 37–64. Wiesbaden: Steiner.

Postema, Gerald J. 1986. *Bentham and the common law tradition*. Oxford: Clarendon Press.

Quinn, Malcolm. 2011. The invention of facts: Bentham's ethics and the education of public taste. *Revue d'études benthamiennes* 9.

Quinn, Michael. 2012a. L'archétypation et la recherche d'images signifiantes: signifiant et signifié dans la logique de Bentham. *Essaim* 28:170–181.

Quinn, Michael. 2012b. Which comes first, Bentham's chicken of utility or his egg of truth?. *Journal of Bentham Studies* 14.

Rosen, Gideon. 2005. Problems in the history of fictionalism. In *Fictionalism in metaphysics,* ed. M. E. Kalderon, 14–64. Oxford: Clarendon Press.

Schofield, Philip. 2003. Jeremy Bentham, the principle of utility, and legal positivism. *Current Legal Problems* 56:1–39.

Schofield, Philip. 2006. *Utility and democracy: The political thought of Jeremy Bentham*. Oxford: Clarendon Press.

Schofield, Philip. 2010. Jeremy Bentham and H. L. A. Hart's "Utilitarian tradition in Jurisprudence". *Jurisprudence* 1:147–167.

Stolzenberg, Nomi M. 1999. Bentham's theory of fictions—"a curious double language". *Cardozo Studies in Law & Literature* 11:223–261.

Vaihinger, Hans. 1925/1911. *The philosophy of 'As if': A system of the theoretical, practical and religious fictions of mankind* (Trans.: C. K. Ogden). London: Kegan Paul.

Zhai, Xiaobo. 2014. Bentham's natural arrangement and the collapse of the censor–expositor distinction in the general theory of law. In *Bentham's theory of law and public opinion,* eds. X. Zhai and M. Quinn, 143–182. Cambridge: Cambridge University Press.

Chapter 5
The Pragmatic Value of Legal Fictions

Douglas Lind

What shall we call a thing anyhow? It seems quite arbitrary, for we carve out everything, just as we carve out constellations, to suit our human purposes
– William James, *Pragmatism* [122]

Abstract Using a jurisprudence grounded in pragmatist philosophy, this chapter proposes a reconceiving of the concept of legal fictions. By tradition, fictions are treated in legal theory as consciously false assertions. This is unfortunate, for it engulfs law in logical contradiction, marginalizes all fictions as metaphysically suspect regardless of social value, and compromises the integrity of law and judicial decision-making. I argue instead that legal fictions be understood as propositional legal truths—doctrines, rules, principles—asserted in conscious recognition that they are inconsistent in meaning or otherwise in semantic conflict with true propositional claims made outside (or elsewhere within) the law. If the conflict produces no damage outside law or within—i.e. no confusion, incoherence, or functional destabilization—and if the fiction works some efficiency or functional improvement within the system of law, then the fiction has value and utility. But to the extent a legal fiction wreaks intersystemic havoc—generates confusion or incoherence, frustrates ability to function—or does not work some genuine utility within law, it is not useful, but problematic. Harmless and workable legal fictions hold pragmatic value and are law-worthy, while problematic, pernicious fictions should be removed from the law.

D. Lind (✉)
Philosophy Department, University of Idaho, P.O. Box 443173,
Moscow, ID 83844-3173, USA
e-mail: dlind@uidaho.edu

M. Del Mar, W. Twining (eds.), *Legal Fictions in Theory and Practice*,
Law and Philosophy Library 110, DOI 10.1007/978-3-319-09232-4_5

5.1 Introduction

Legal fictions present the law with an enigma. Law exists as a mechanism of social organization and control. It creates institutions and procedures to structure the social order toward the ends of securing life and liberty, distributing benefits and burdens, and resolving disputes without recourse to private force. In ideal form, the law fulfills these functions in a harmonic unity of fact, truth, and justice. Legal fictions ill-fit this ideal aspirational vision. For legal fictions seemingly fashion legal truths out of factual falsehoods.

Accounting for legal fictions has proven difficult for legal theory. For it is hard to craft a jurisprudential standard that appears to countenance deliberate falsehood on the part of legal officials. The very idea famously drew a volley of criticism from Jeremy Bentham, who characterized legal fictions metaphorically as a pestilence of judicial depravity, a systemic rottenness that reduces the administration of justice to the "most pernicious and basest sort of lying" (Bentham 1843, I 235). Still, fictions pervade the law. To account for them—or to argue convincingly against their worth as instruments of legal thought and expression—is thus an imperative of any systematic study of law.

This chapter attempts such a systematic accounting of legal fictions using a jurisprudence grounded in pragmatist philosophy. I employ a classical/analytic sense of pragmatism, influenced most by the early American pragmatists William James, John Dewey, and Alain Locke, along with their European contemporaries F.C.S. Schiller and Ludwig Wittgenstein.[1] My sense of pragmatist jurisprudence is further indebted to certain analytic philosophers in the pragmatist tradition, notably C.I. Lewis, W.V.O. Quine, and Hilary Putnam, and to Hon. Benjamin Cardozo, who disclosed the pragmatist nature of common law adjudication nearly a century ago.

Though tentative and preliminary, I propose a reconceiving of the concept of legal fictions. Standardly, fictions are treated in legal theory as consciously false assumptions. This is regrettable. For it creates logical confusion, renders fictions unnecessarily confounding, and compromises the integrity of law and judicial decision-making. I suggest instead that legal fictions be understood as *true* legal propositions asserted with conscious recognition that they are inconsistent in meaning or otherwise in semantic conflict with true propositions asserted within some other linguistic system (or elsewhere within law). Understood this way, fictions need not present legal theory with an intractable enigma. For the legal fiction is simply a form of creative lawmaking, a phenomenon of legal (primarily judicial) technique employed to resolve trouble in the legal environment. Questions about the merits of a legal fiction should go to whether the fiction damages established truths, meanings, or understandings in some extralegal realm or within law itself as a result of a collision in meaning. Used well, legal fictions inflict no damage while producing workable and beneficial doctrines or rules. Used nefariously, they upset settled meanings or truths, work injustice, or mask underlying processes of legal reasoning.

[1] Like several others today I consider it appropriate to associate Wittgenstein, in his later philosophy, with the pragmatist tradition (see, e.g. Brandom 2011; Putnam 1995).

As with other methods of creative legal technique, legal fictions must be evaluated case-by-case in context. The technique *as such* is neither sickly nor sinister.

My argument rests on the pragmatist meaning of truth. Before turning to that theory and developing this pragmatist sense of understanding legal fictions I will consider briefly the current status of the legal fiction. I ask, to begin, what are legal fictions and how have they been defined or characterized within jurisprudential tradition.

5.2 Characterizing Legal Fictions

The paradox of legal fictions begins in a puzzle of definition. Just what is a legal fiction? This simple question yields no easy answer.

From the final third of the eighteenth century through the first third of the twentieth, the legal fiction was a common topic among writers in legal philosophy and history. The discussion in this era went primarily to what the concept denotes and how fictions function in law, not to what the term 'legal fiction' intensionally means. Bentham characterized the legal fiction quite generously before denouncing the entire category as the product of either wishful theoretical fancy or illicit judicial lawmaking. Most jurists treated fictions less critically, often describing them as commonplace and relatively unexceptional features of law. The broadest and most favorable characterization came from Pierre de Tourtoulon who conceived of the legal fiction as the source of law's most significant progress and practical growth. To Tourtoulon, all legal institutions begin and evolve through fictions, such that "if one would try to strip the Law of every fiction of the past as well as of the present, not much would be left" (Tourtoulon 1922, p. 388). Roscoe Pound considered construction of legal fictions to be a central form of creative adjudication. Focusing on procedural fictions and what he regarded as the bolder, more general fictions of equity, natural law, and judicial interpretation, Pound saw fiction-making as an inventive technique that allows growth in law through creation of new institutions, principles, and precepts. Savigny similarly saw the fiction as a critical factor in the development of law, a form of legal thinking that permits the joining of new rules and doctrines with existing legal institutions in a way that preserves certainty and minimizes disturbance. Jhering, and following him John Chipman Gray, classified fictions as historical or dogmatic. Their historical category includes fictions fashioned to introduce new law or extend remedies. Dogmatic fictions arrange and classify existing law, often in creative ways. To Jhering, the primary function of all fictions is the analogical extension and classification of legal concepts. Toward that end he saw them holding high value, for they make growth and adaptation of law more efficient by unburdening lawmakers from modifying the form of the law while saving jurists the trouble of adjusting the concept. Blackstone too perceived fictions as "highly beneficial and useful" in furthering growth in legal doctrine and avoiding mischief in the application of general rules, though he was troubled by what he considered the strange logic on which they depend (Blackstone 1979, III 43). Sir Henry

Sumner Maine defined the legal fiction broadly as any assumption that deliberately "conceals, or affects to conceal, the fact that a rule of law has undergone alteration, its letter remaining unchanged, its operation being modified" (Maine 1861, p. 22). While he extolled fictions as "invaluable expedients for overcoming the rigidity of law" so essential in certain formative stages of social progress, Maine cautioned that as legal systems mature, fictions work against coherent understanding of legal rules, becoming instead "the greatest of obstacles to symmetrical classification" (Ibid., pp. 22, 23).

The most notable jurisprudential effort to intensionally define the legal fiction came from Lon Fuller in the early 1930s. In what has become the classic definition of the legal fiction, Fuller opined: "A fiction is either (1) a statement propounded with a complete or partial consciousness of its falsity, or (2) a false statement recognized as having utility" (Fuller 1967, p. 9). Certain points here deserve emphasis. To Fuller, a legal fiction is neither a lie nor a statement made in error; it is a knowingly false assertion "adopted by its author with knowledge of its falsity. A fiction is an 'expedient, but *consciously false*, assumption'" (Ibid. p. 7, quoting Vaihinger 1984). The author must not intend to deceive nor offer the fiction "with the intention of producing belief in *its* truth" (Fuller 1967, p. 7). Further, the fiction must be known to be false and disbelieved by others. To Fuller, fictions are only safe and beneficial when used with complete consciousness of their falsity: "A fiction taken seriously, i.e., 'believed,' becomes dangerous and loses its utility" (Ibid., pp. 9–10).

After Fuller, the legal fiction fell for several decades into relative jurisprudential obscurity. Jerome Frank in 1936 appended some notes on fictions to his *Law and the Modern Mind.* Edwin Patterson briefly broached the topic in his comprehensive mid-century treatise, *Jurisprudence: Men and Ideas of the Law*. Alf Ross, in a thoughtful essay published in 1969, challenged the traditional treatment of legal fictions as involving consciously false assumptions. A handful of law journal articles addressed the topic in the 1970s and 1980s (e.g. Campbell 1983; Schane 1987; Soifer 1986). Otherwise the fiction received for many years just occasional hurried references. H.L.A. Hart twice commented in passing on Bentham's treatment of obligation, right, and duty as fictitious entities (see Hart 1982a, pp. 42–43; Hart 1982b, pp. 128–131). Lord Devlin spoke only once of fictions, cautioning that historical fictions, used commonly by judges "to reform the law without obvious innovation," can be "dangerous because they have a tendency to spread" (Devlin 1979, p. 162). By 1990 Louise Harmon could rightly observe that the legal fiction had become a nearly forgotten topic in legal theory.

This changed with the new century. The legal fiction recently has risen from its jurisprudential dormancy. Some legal scholars have reignited the traditional inquiry into understanding the concept of legal fictions. Others take a new, critical tack, cataloging several "new legal fictions"—e.g. the institution of slavery, the entire field of tax law, certain evidentiary and interpretive presumptions, and the doctrine of discovery that figures so prominently in American Indian law. This new line of scholarship differs in two respects from the traditional approach. First, it does not aim to understand philosophically the concept of legal fictions. Instead it is doctrinal and normative, a critical examination of certain substantive legal regimes or doctrines said to be fictitious. Second, it tends to use 'legal fiction' as a term of rebuke. In the new scholarship the legal fiction has become, for the most part, an inflammatory concept marking a legal doctrine or regime as manifestly unjust, needlessly complex, or intentionally deceptive. Unlike the Benthamite worry that the process of fiction-making is inherently flawed, much of the new scholarship assumes, without discussion, that any legal fiction *as such* is substantively clandestine.

In one respect, however, the new scholarship resembles the old. Falsehood. Across time nearly all legal theorists have presumed that every legal fiction makes a consciously false assumption. Bentham thundered against legal fictions because they perpetrate "wilful falsehood" (Bentham 1977, p. 509). Tourtoulon admitted "the fiction does falsify reality" (Tourtoulon 1922, p. 385). Among today's theorists, Frederick Schauer affirms: "Fictions are, by definition, false, and thus a legal fiction is a legal falsehood" (this volume, Chap. 6, p. 126). John Prebble argues that tax law fictionalizes a duplicitous and incoherent tax base that has no complement in reality but instead offends the "real business profits ... [that] exist in the natural world" (Prebble 2002, p. 310). Prebble sees the fictions of tax law as importantly different from classical legal fictions, though they share the necessary condition that "a pure legal fiction is a statement that is truly false" (Prebble 2011, p. 19). In portraying the doctrine of discovery as a fiction, Jen Camden and Kathryn Fort define a legal fiction as "a statement that the judge knows is false and uses it as such" (Camden and Fort 2008, p. 85). Nancy Knauer takes issue with Prebble and Camden and Fort, maintaining that so-called new legal fictions such as theirs are miscast as fictions. For to Knauer none of the new fictions are "demonstrably false," a criterion she considers necessary for a legal proposition to qualify as a fiction (Knauer 2010, pp. 40, 49). Knauer draws this requirement from Fuller whose classic definition captures the sentiment, common to the earlier era and the new scholarship, that a legal fiction involves a consciously false assertion: "A statement must be false before it can be a fiction. Its falsity depends upon whether the words used are inaccurate as an expression of reality" (Fuller 1967, p. 11).

This emphasis on falsehood is unfortunate. Certainly it is useful in referring to the Roman *fictio*, the ancient practice of allowing false averments in pleadings that a defendant could not contest. But to say today, following Fuller, that any "statement must be false before it can be a fiction," or, with Schauer, that "a legal fiction is a legal falsehood" creates logical confusion. For utterances in the form of legal fictions are not, generally speaking, false *within law*—e.g. corporations *are* jural persons. That is a true proposition of law. Yet if, as Fuller and tradition would have it, every legal fiction makes a consciously false assertion, then that true proposition is also false. The practice of fiction-making thus not only, on the traditional account, fills the law with falsehood, it also ensnares it in logical contradiction.

Few who have written on legal fictions have apprehended this logical dilemma. John Dewey did in the specific context of the fiction of corporate personality. Alf Ross did too, noting more generally that "the prevalent definition of fiction as consciously false assumption is contradictory and therefore has no reference" (Ross 1969, p. 224). Ross sought to remedy this dilemma by reconstructing the concept of legal fictions. His reconstruction was by way of circumvention. He argued that, as to fictions, truth value is irrelevant. Certain fictions do assert openly untrue assumptions—e.g. fictions that mutate geography to accommodate suit within a certain jurisdiction or venue. Ross denied that such creative fictions suffer from illogic. Rather, he saw them as linguistic devices employing odd manners of speech wherein the falsity of their pronouncements do not matter. Other fictions, those more theoretical in nature (e.g. that courts do not legislate), Ross characterized as "posed," not asserted propositions, thereby also making their truth value irrelevant (Ibid., p. 229). Such theoretical fictions are best understood, he argued, as analogous to myths, the stuff of legends and ideals that function independently of truth value.

Ross, I argue, was correct in seeing that the concept of legal fictions needs reconstruction. And he was right to identify the traditional treatment of fictions as consciously false assumptions as the reason why they have for so long confounded and troubled legal theory. Yet he was incorrect in maintaining that truth and falsity are irrelevant. Truth value matters critically in law. To suggest that legal fictions render truth irrelevant provides fodder to a Bentham-like fury against all jural fiction-making as a renegade activity. The way truth matters in the context of legal fictions, however, is very different than the traditional debasement of every legal fiction as a consciously false assumption. That standard approach to fictions rests on a set of implicit assumptions about the nature of reality and truth. It assumes there is a reality external to law about which there are knowable, objective truths—'facts of reality'—against which a legal fiction can be measured or compared. The comparison always shows a mismatch, a logical inconsistency between the fiction and some known (or supposed as known) factual content found in reality. Further, that extra-legal reality is treated as privileged. That is, when a logical inconsistency appears between a legal fiction and a 'fact of reality', the fiction must give way—the fact is appraised as true, while the fiction is devalued as false.

I want to question these assumptions about truth and reality. Is there a realm of objectively knowable reality? If so, why is it privileged, in terms of epistemic truth, over the legal realm, such that its factual truths provide the rule and measure for exposing legal fictions as falsehoods? These assumptions, which metaphysically undergird the traditional approach to legal fictions, at the very least call for justification. For perhaps it is the case, as Alain Locke once observed, that all of our cognitive processes are value-laden, such that even "'pure' thought and 'absolute' truth" are "fictitious" (Locke 1989, p. 115). Perhaps even what we take and formally regard as "'fact'… may turn out to be only a methodologically convenient 'fiction'" (Ibid., p. 119). To give consideration to such possibilities, and perhaps thereby gain reason to question the traditional conception of legal fictions, requires a foray into the pragmatic meaning of truth.

5.3 Pragmatic Meaning of Truth

Pragmatism disavows belief in absolute truths. Rather truth, pragmatically considered, is an attribute of belief. It marks a relation between idea and object. We live in a phenomenological world of sensible experience. There we encounter, in a primordial sense, what William James called the "perceptual flux" of concrete existent particulars (James 1911, p. 49). This flux of immediate, unfiltered present perception—of "plain unqualified actuality, a simple *that*, as yet undifferentiated into thing and thought" (James 1912, p. 74)—is punctuated with unity and continuous percepts, though characterized largely by chaos and discontinuity. Through reflection and thought we sift through the chaos of experience, separating 'real' objects (those from which consequences follow—e.g. those fires that burn sticks) from the fanciful (the inconsequential—mental fires that ignite no sticks), and identifying a core of individually consistent experiences that we share in common with each other.

Consequences, consistency, and commonality thus provide the basis for differentiating and naming 'things' out of the flux, for postulating relations that connect and separate them, and for constructing more or less orderly world-structures out of the original chaos of raw experience. Through the collective of cognitive processes that Hilary Putnam called "our criteria of rational acceptability," we evaluate consequences, mark off points of consistency and commonality, and thereby "build up a theoretical picture of the 'empirical' world" (Putnam 1981, p. 134). That picture—reality, as we conceive it, is largely a product of our own creation. In Quine's terms, it depicts a "man-made fabric" (Quine 1953, pp. 20, 42). James put it more emphatically: the form and order we package under the name 'reality' is "flagrantly man-made" (James 1907, p. 119), no more than "an accumulation of our own intellectual inventions" (James 1909a, p. 209).

Not only is the world of raw experience without inherent form or order, it is also devoid of value. That which we perceive in the primordial flux is neither good nor bad, true nor false. The facts we perceive there merely are. Only through active cognitive processing of perceptual experiences, followed by inferences of rational acceptability and the crafting of general rules and concepts do the data of immediate experience come to possess any value. Rational reflection and conceptual thinking, that is, allow us to not only sort through the helter skelter of the phenomenal world, but to give meaning and value to the inherently undifferentiated and nameless.

Foremost among the values we assign to those objects, relations, and general concepts that we extract from the experiential realm is *truth value*. For rational construction of belief-sets of coherent, consistent 'truths' is a practical activity of preeminent value. Our everyday excursions into the external world expose us to objects not of our making, so-called 'laws of nature' that we cannot elude, and social situations of inscrutable complexity and dubious benefit. Possessing ideas that reliably distinguish the useful from the baleful, and that foretell which to expect is of great practical importance. Developing a stockpile of coherent, consistent truths, a meaningful conceptual structure for encasing 'reality' as we conceive it is fundamental to attaining a degree of control over the sometimes comforting, yet often menacing environment. 'Truth', quite literally, is thus an incredibly useful possession. As James put it, true ideas have "cash-value;" they are "profitable to our lives" (James 1907, pp. 32, 41, 42). Still, as Dewey emphasized, "truth is valuable not *per se*, but because, when given, it leads to desirable consequences" (Dewey 1916, p. 318). That is, truth is valuable only in relation to us. We value it because it helps us secure safe passage through life's practical struggles. True ideas are just those ideas that "*work satisfactorily*" in leading us gainfully from trouble and uncertainty to beneficial outcomes, thereby providing "that specific *truth*-satisfaction, compared with which all other satisfactions are the hollowest humbug" (James 1907, p. 120, 1909a, p. 271).

Truth accordingly is 'practical' insofar as how we perceive the outside world, take it in, classify, order, and reorder it, depends upon the problems, interests, and purposes we have in mind. Truth 'satisfies' to the degree it *works* toward meeting those purposes and interests. As James famously put it: "*'The true,' to put it very briefly, is only the expedient in the way of our thinking*" (James 1907, p. 106). We are neither indifferent nor disinterested, nor even fully objective, when it comes to truth. We search for truth, undertake rational, thoughtful inquiry for the most part to resolve questions that bear practically upon our lives and future conduct. "If we had no desires and no purposes," Dewey reasoned, "then … one state of things would be as good as any other" (Dewey 1929, p. 39). In Schiller's words, the truth of a proposition depends on its "consequences *to* someone engaged on a real problem *for* some purpose" (Schiller 1903, p. 59). James agreed: "Human motives sharpen all our questions, human satisfactions lurk in all our answers, all our formulas have a human twist" (James 1907, p. 117). We never seek truth with spectator-like indifference. Rather, "we carve out everything, just as we carve out constellations, to suit our human purposes" (Ibid., p. 122).

Nonetheless, though the pursuit of truth is a practical activity driven by our distinctly human purposes and interests, pragmatism demands fidelity to the primal 'facts' that we experientially encounter. As Quine put it, our systems of belief "must be kept squared with experience" (Quine 1953, p. 45). The belief-convictions, conceptions of reality, and truths we fashion must originate in and remain steadfast to what we assume to be a reality independent of us. The 'satisfaction' that accompanies truth directly grows out of that assumption of a supposed independent reality. For truth-satisfaction begins in the intellectual comfort we take in salutary, harmonious interaction with the phenomenal data of experiential life. Propositions only work toward meeting our purposes and interests when they fit together in coherent, efficacious, and logically consistent configurations that help us pick our way through the brambles of practical life. The satisfaction truth provides thus depends both on how coherently our ideas fit together and how harmoniously they relate to the supposed reality. More than anything, consistency among our beliefs gives satisfaction. As James expressed it: "Above all we find *consistency* satisfactory, consistency between the present idea and the entire rest of our mental equipment, including the whole order of our sensations, and that of our intuitions of likeness and difference, and our whole stock of previously acquired truths" (James 1909a, pp. 104–105).

Reflective inquiry in pursuit of truth is thus a practical and satisfying undertaking. It is never, however, a finished process. We delude ourselves to think we have attained truth absolute—fixed, static, and certain for all time. For reality is continually under construction. "What really *exists*," James wrote, "is not things made but things in the making" (James 1909b, p. 263). The experiential world is literally a flux, an objective environment of ready change and fluctuation. Since all we experience is unstable and in a process of change, "no point of view can ever be *the* last one. Every one is insufficient and off its balance, and responsible to later points of view than itself" (James 1909a, p. 221). The truths we posit about reality are thus, of necessity, provisional. They are working hypotheses ever subject to reconsideration, correction, and revision. The double influence of experience and inquiry ensures that truth grows, reality evolves. Experience allots us a continual flow of information—concrete facts, new and renewed, unforseen social circumstances, once unimaginable technologies—that must be digested and incorporated into the general stock of truths that populate reality as we know it. So too we encounter agitation in the conceptual realm. Through inquiry we rationally confront matters over which we harbor doubt. We frame new concepts and adjust, amend, and sometimes abandon the old to accommodate our perceptual experiences and attain more workable conceptual structures. Throughout, our stocks of previous truths undergo review and revision, all the time leading toward the practical end of attaining more refined, workable, and satisfying views of reality.

The provisional nature of truth does not mean, however, that we lightly discard hypotheses previously filed away in our storehouses of belief. We do not welcome change. Challenges to our stocks of previously accepted beliefs take several forms: encountering facts incompatible with them; meeting someone who disagrees with them; realizing through reflection a contradiction; or finding they no longer work to satisfy our intellectual desires. These challenges trigger inward trouble. From such trouble we seek escape using the only means possible—resistance, reconsideration, and, if unavoidable, rearrangement of our previous stock of preconceptions, ideas, and opinions. In this process of conceptual *re*-formulation, James rightly observed "we are all extreme conservatives" (James 1907, p. 35). *Loyalty* to the older truths is the first principle in this process; most often it wins out. So committed are we to our conceptual *status quo* that by far the most common approach to phenomena so novel that they demand serious modification of our previous beliefs "is to ignore them altogether, or to abuse those who bear witness for them" (Ibid.). When neither avoidance nor abuse is possible, rearrangement becomes necessary. We strive then to find or fashion a new idea that we can splice into our existing stock of beliefs with a minimum of disturbance. Conceptually we gear the new idea into a workable notion that reconciles satisfactorily the new truth and the old stock. The new idea *becomes* true, "makes itself true," James insisted, "by the way it works; grafting itself then upon the ancient body of truth, which thus grows" (Ibid., p. 36). Throughout, the operative principle is *minimum disturbance/maximum continuity*. James writes:

> [The] new idea … adopted as the true one … preserves the older stock of truths with a minimum of modification…. New truth is always a go-between, a smoother-over of transitions. It marries old opinion to new fact so as ever to show a minimum of jolt, a maximum of continuity. We hold a theory true just in proportion to its success in solving this 'problem of maxima and minima.' But success in solving this problem is eminently a matter of approximation. We say this theory solves it on the whole more satisfactorily than that theory; but that means more satisfactorily to ourselves. (Ibid., p. 35)

A new idea thus comes to be accepted as 'true' insofar as it satisfactorily assimilates fresh experience or refined thinking into the general stock of our previous beliefs. Throughout this process of truth-making, fidelity and the least possible disruption to the general stock remains the guiding principle. For we cling to our established truths with an unflagging proprietary interest. Yet we do not cling to them as isolated tokens in a disorganized conceptual space nor even as members of a single grand 'reality'. Rather, the composites of truths, meanings, and concepts that comprise the realities we conceive inhabit *systematic* storehouses of belief. Everything we experience, every fact we encounter, every concept we inquire into, discuss, and deliberate comes to us situated contextually within some more or less systematic field or situation of ongoing conditions. Given that, as Dewey put it, "[f]ields and/or situations possess spatial and temporal *togetherness* of the existences and events which constitute them" (Dewey 2012, pp. 334–335), the truths we create are dependent upon and inseparable from the contextual field or system of their birth and application. Truth, that is, not only reflects a relation between idea and object, but a relation between idea and context—field, situation, system, surrounding. The truths we fashion from experience and reflection accordingly are "effective in just the degree in which [they have] been worked into a system—a comprehensive and orderly arrangement" (Dewey 1916, p. 54). Only such a systematic arrangement allows us to move freely and beneficially among the general stock of our truths as well as across our conceptual structures. While any single idea or concept is true insofar as belief in it '*works satisfactorily*', it is nonsensical to think of a proposition 'working' in isolation. As Wittgenstein advised, we only "understand a proposition as *a* member of a system of propositions" (Wittgenstein 1975, p. 59). For no proposition can "sit in solitary glory and refuse to mix with other[s]" (Wittgenstein 1978, p. 376). Only when situated in a context where it mixes in linguistic togetherness with the whole nest of propositions and techniques of usage that constitute a system can any belief be said to be 'workable'. Likewise, evaluating a propositional belief as unworkable, incoherent, or otherwise ineffective requires giving consideration to its functioning within a system of propositions. Even a mistake, a blunder, is only "a blunder in a particular system" (Wittgenstein 1966, p. 59). Hence, to speak of propositions or beliefs as 'working satisfactorily' or not—as *true* or *false*—is of necessity to speak with contextual reference to some specific system of belief.

5.4 Pragmatic Characterization of Legal Fictions

The pragmatic meaning of truth, as just sketched, offers a way of reconceiving the concept of legal fictions that avoids the problems of logical contradiction, metaphysical confusion, and compromised justice that accompany the traditional approach. As discussed above, that approach treats falsehood as a necessary condition for a legal proposition to be understood as a fiction. This emphasis on falsehood engulfs the law in logical contradiction. It also marginalizes as metaphysically suspect all legal fictions, no matter their social value, and demeans lawmaking, especially judicial decision-making, as a disingenuous practice where truth is manipulated at will and frequently in opposition to justice.

A pragmatist understanding of legal fictions avoids these problems that result from the falsehood characterization. For on the pragmatist account, legal fictions are not, at least by definition, knowingly false assertions. No legal fiction can be presumed to assert a legal falsehood. I am not convinced that there may not be some legal fictions that do make false assertions, and I consider that possibility later. But in terms of characterizing or defining the concept of legal fictions, falsehood is an unhelpful consideration. This is because the claim, on the traditional approach, that legal fictions are consciously false assertions depends on viewing legal propositions outside the linguistic jural systems within which they originate and are used. It presumes a realm of reality that serves as *the* yardstick against which every legal claim can be tested for truth value. Legal propositions that fail that test of truth are those that come to be called legal fictions. Hence the necessary connection, on the traditional account, between fiction and falsehood. Yet if it is correct, as pragmatism contends, that no proposition can be understood except in the context of its functioning within a system of propositions, then the truth value of a legal proposition can only be evaluated by viewing it together with the whole nest of propositions and according to the practices and techniques of usage that surround its use within the highly specialized linguistic system of law. Hence the irrelevance, on the pragmatist account, of falsehood on fiction.

By the pragmatist understanding, an utterance in the form of a legal fiction, such as 'A corporation is a person', must be investigated for meaning and evaluated for truth strictly *within law*. By all accounts, in that context it is a true proposition. Corporations *are* legal persons. They have been treated as such in the Western world for centuries. To say they are not legal persons is to state a falsehood. For corporations bear legal rights; they suffer legal duties. From their actions legal consequences flow. As to most legal transactions, referring to corporations as persons generates no confusion. Only when the reference goes outside law to some other context of linguistic usage—e.g. the context of so-called everyday reality—does confusion potentially arise. For in the realm of everyday reality—a realm comprised in part by facts drawn from sensible physical experience and in part by social conditions and influences—the word 'person' generally includes only human beings. Hence, in that context, the statement 'A corporation is a person' is false. By tradition, the falsity of the statement as an expression of everyday reality provides the singular evidential criterion that makes corporate personality a legal fiction. On the pragmatist account of legal fictions, such judgments of falsehood drawn from an extralegal reality are irrelevant and beside-the-point.

The fact that a legal proposition, true within law, would be a false proposition if asserted under different techniques of usage in a belief system or realm of reality other than law (e.g. everyday reality) has no bearing on the proposition's truth value within law. Nor does it produce a logical contradiction. For the propositions are different. Though the simple statement 'A corporation is a person' may be uttered in both linguistic systems, its meaning must be understood relative to its use in each system. That is, the idea expressed in the simple statement is incomplete. Before its meaning (and truth) can be determined, it must be placed in context. More completely, the simple statement 'A corporation is a person' divides contextually into the separate utterances 'A corporation is a person *within law*' and 'A corporation is a person *in everyday reality*'. These are entirely distinct propositions. As such, the fact that one is true and the other false creates no logical contradiction. Yet while not logically contradictory, the two statements do employ different meanings of the term 'person'. As used in law, the term 'person' includes corporations within its extension; the use the term receives in the context of everyday reality does not. To that extent the two statements are inconsistent. The question then becomes of what significance, for understanding legal fictions, is this inconsistency in denotation.

I suggest that such inconsistency in denotative meaning is central to the concept of legal fictions. Indeed, it is just such collisions in the extension of words, phrases, and concepts that mark certain legal propositions as fictions. A legal fiction, that is, could be defined as a legal proposition that is inconsistent in denotative meaning or otherwise in semantic conflict with some proposition(s) asserted as true within some extralegal linguistic system. Generally, though not always, a legal fiction is asserted as a claim of legal truth in conscious recognition (or disregard) of the inconsistency or conflict. Whether used in knowing awareness of intersystemic inconsistency or not, legal fictions have value to the extent they function beneficially within law and work no havoc on any general stock of beliefs outside law (or within). Inconsistency in denotative meaning is harmless if it involves a collision between belief systems that inflicts no damage to established truths, meanings, or understandings in the extralegal realm or within law itself. If a legal fiction produces only harmless inconsistency while working some functional utility or effectiveness within law, then the fiction has value as a legal truth. That is, legal fictions have pragmatic value insofar as they work satisfactorily as propositional claims of legal truth without harming or upsetting any accepted meanings or truths with which they collide.

Now this suggestion that it is intersystemic inconsistency in extensional meaning, not falsehood, that marks a legal proposition as a legal fiction is likely to encounter some objections. For one, since pragmatism regards consistency across the full range of our beliefs as the most important determining factor in a proposition working satisfactorily, does not intersystemic inconsistency in extensional meaning render legal fictions unsatisfying *per se*? No, for collisions of meaning between belief systems only disrupt our intellectual comfort when they upset settled truths, meanings, or ways of understanding. Everyday life routinely presents us with intersystemic conflicts of meaning. We are well accustomed to deciphering words that carry multiple meanings. Experience makes us quite adept at parsing senses of use to avoid equivocation. So long as we understand each conflicting use as craft-bound to a belief system and have at least some sense of each system's techniques of usage, the conflicts usually cause no consternation. The centuries-long fictional status of corporations as jural persons likely has never thrown anyone into intellectual distress other than students of law. Even there the anxiety is not over discommoded conceptions of extralegal reality but as to the law's rational coherence. Still, any genuine anxiety that the idea of corporate personality may once have caused is long passed. As Pollock and Maitland noted, "we have become so familiar with the idea of 'a corporation aggregate of many' that we have ceased to wonder at it. When we are told by statute that the word 'person' is to include [corporations], that seems to us a very natural rule" (Pollock and Maitland 1959, p. 486). Familiarity begets normalcy. Once just a "blank form of legal thought" (ibid.), corporate personhood has become a commonplace legal truth. Given how effectively it legitimizes conceptually the corporate form in Western law and provides the basis for allotting to each business entity its legal status as "a right-and-duty-bearing unit" (Dewey 1926, p. 25), the fiction can only be said to work remarkably satisfactorily, despite its superficial oddity.

The same can be said of the more fantastic fiction of the personality of the ship. Early in the nineteenth century federal courts in the United States began to assign will and personality to sailing ships. This came in response to a troubling jurisdictional weakness in the country's nascent admiralty law. Shipowners were routinely evading responsibility for violating embargo laws and for carrying outlawed cargo, including slaves. Such piracy was going unanswered because when vessels were seized and condemned, the captains and shipmates would pass legal responsibility on to the shipowners who, in turn, would present innocent manifests while maintaining they had no knowledge of the renegade activity carried out by captain and crew. In 1818, a frustrated John Marshall, sitting by designation as a trial judge in a case involving alleged violation of a federal embargo statute, took control over the troubled legal seas, declaring:

> [T]his is not a proceeding against the owner; it is a proceeding against the vessel for an offence committed by the vessel, which is not less an offence, and does not the less subject her to forfeiture, because it was committed without the authority, and against the will of the owner. (*United States v. The Little Charles* 1818, p. 982)

As the nineteenth century progressed, this fiction of vessel personification grew to become the preeminent American theory of the ship. Justice Joseph Story formally put the Supreme Court's imprimatur upon it in the 1844 case *United States v. Brig Malek Adhel*. By century's end the Court considered it well-settled, not only as to matters of piratical commerce but also in cases involving collisions and allisions, that the "offending ship is considered as herself the wrongdoer, and as herself bound to make compensation for the wrong done" (*The John G. Stevens* 1898, p. 122). The boldness of the metaphysic the Supreme Court came to entertain with the ship fiction comes across most vividly in the case *Tucker v. Alexandroff*. There the Court described as follows the transformation of a mere thing of personal property into a ship in the legal sense:

> A ship is born when she is launched, and lives so long as her identity is preserved. Prior to her launching she is a mere congeries of wood and iron—an ordinary piece of personal property—as distinctly a land structure as a house.... In the baptism of launching she receives her name, and from the moment her keel touches the water she is transformed, and becomes a subject of admiralty jurisdiction. She acquires a personality of her own; becomes competent to contract, and is individually liable for her obligations, upon which she may sue in the name of her owner, and be sued in her own name. Her owner's agents may not be her agents, and her agents may not be her owner's agents. She is capable, too, of committing a tort, and is responsible in damages therefor. She may also become a *quasi* bankrupt; may be sold for the payment of her debts, and thereby receive a complete discharge from

all prior liens, with liberty to begin a new life, contract further obligations, and perhaps be subjected to a second sale. (*Tucker v. Alexandroff* 1902, pp. 437–438)

This ship personification doctrine is as ontologically wild a fiction as any the law has ever known. John Chipman Gray belittled it as a "barbarous notion" (Gray 1909, p. 47). During his entire tenure on the Supreme Court, Oliver Wendell Holmes, Jr., sought to run it aground. He claimed it fostered "metaphysical confusion" (Holmes 1881, p. 33) and perpetuated the ancient and no longer worthy legal notion of deodand. Clearly the fiction of the personality of the ship creates intersystemic conflict. It collides head-on with both everyday and nautical reality. Yet droll as the idea of anthropomorphized vessels may seem, it is difficult to imagine the ship fiction begetting metaphysical bewilderment. It noway unsettled everyday understanding of ships or personhood. Though seafarers and poets had before John Marshall fancied sailing ships as more than mere assemblages of wood and iron, nothing in the realm of nautical reality was affected by law's fictional personification of the ship. There were no reports of seafarers responding to the fiction by setting ships adrift to navigate the seas according to their own volition. Shipmates remained responsible to fix rigging and fasten jibs. Storms at sea still presented danger to vessel, crew, and cargo. Whether to weather a storm by heaving to or lying ahull still required human deliberation.

The fanciful vitalism contrived by the fiction of the personality of the ship thus engendered only harmless intersystemic conflict. The fiction did not disrupt any beliefs or practices in either everyday or seafaring life. There is little reason to think it would. John Marshall did not fancy the chimerical. He acknowledged in *The Little Charles* that, "It is true that inanimate matter can commit no offence" (*United States v. The Little Charles* 1818, p. 982). In *Tucker*, the Supreme Court was clear that the ontological justification it offered for the ship fiction went only to when an artifact "became a ship in its legal sense" (*Tucker v. Alexandroff* 1902, p. 437). The Court, that is, fully understood that the vital principle it assigned vessels was a legal construct with only legal relevance and application. In that realm of law its influence was profound. Because of it, the admiralty proceeding *in rem* was relaxed, such that actions for condemnation and forfeiture could proceed without proving the shipowner's involvement in a vessel's wrongdoing. The ship fiction brought about this beneficial adaptation in the law with but a minimum of disturbance to the existing procedures of admiralty practice. It thus achieved the desirable consequence of a more just, coherent, and workable admiralty jurisprudence while maintaining, for the most part, continuity and consistency in the law. Though it carries far less significance today than in the nineteenth century, the fiction remains an operative doctrine in maritime law. As I have argued elsewhere, it lives on because it works effectively and fits the law harmoniously (Lind 2010). For nearly two centuries it has served admiralty law well as a highly expedient way of thinking. By virtue of that expediency and given the harmlessness of the intersystemic conflict it effects, the fiction of ship personification remains an intellectually satisfying, true and vital doctrine of admiralty.

Another challenge to the view here advanced could be to suggest that pragmatism exaggerates the degree to which meaning and truth are socially constructed and contextually relative. Advocates of the traditional falsehood approach to legal fictions arguably could agree that meaning and truth are, in part, socially constructed, yet still cling to the position that there is one singular realm of reality, an *uber-reality*, that provides *the yardstick* for measuring truth and hence deserving a privileged status whenever intersystemic inconsistencies arise. Since pragmatism, so the argument would go, puts forth an unrealistic view of the system or context-relativity of truth and meaning, it fails to appreciate this singular reality and the underlying falsity of legal fictions.

This singular reality argument is unavailing for at least two reasons. First, we fashion *all* of our realities. Presumably, the realm of reality that is privileged on the traditional account of legal fictions is some form of everyday reality, likely a composite of physical, social, and historical 'facts'. Yet as James argued, the world we experience is to a great extent a flux of undifferentiated and unnamed phenomena until we give it shape, form, and order. What we fashion through our criteria of rational acceptability is not a single world-structure, but a multiplex of realities. This is not to suggest that reality as we conceive it is a manufactured product of mere whim and fantasy. To say, with James, that we "carve out everything, just as we carve out constellations, to suit our human purposes" (James 1907, p. 122), is not to say that we sculpt reality with unlimited discretion. Rather, our conceptions of reality become purposeful and beneficial only insofar as they grow out of our finite experiences. Strict fidelity to the "originally chaotic pure experiences" is the first principle in reality-making (James 1912, p. 35). We do not carve the phenomenal world randomly, but, to borrow from Plato, we "carve nature at its joints" (Plato 1995, p. 265e). The form and order we give reality reflects things found, not stuff fancied. Hence, reality as we present it through say, our scientific systems, e.g. biological classification or natural astronomy, depicts patterns and content painstakingly drawn from the phenomenal flux. Yet it is still we who carve those systems. The classifications of taxonomy, the names of celestial objects and the constellatory patterns represent how we rationally have processed the facts of our experience. The truths of biology and astronomy serve our purposes and represent our intellectual and practical needs for order, not nature's. The red panda did not alter its habits of behavior in response to biology's flip-flopping over whether to classify it as a raccoon, a bear, or in a taxonomic family all its own. The star pattern known in the West as Orion has captured the imagination of human cultures across time. Yet only in our wildest anthropocentric fantasies do we imagine the hyenas and leopards of the Sub-Saharan savannahs taking special care in their nocturnal hunts to evade the watchful eye of a belted human warrior in the starlit sky. When we speak of 'reality' we are speaking not of a single and singular realm of objectively knowable facts, but of criss-crossing realities—nature, the sciences, economics, psychology, history, etc.—each with its own ways of investigating, interpreting, classifying, speaking, and judging truth. Each provides a yardstick to measure the truths arrived at by its practitioners according to its techniques of practice. Yet none can boast a universal yardstick to measure truth as such. Hence, none can claim the status of reality extraordinaire.

Second, even if there is a singular reality worthy of privileging, it does not itself provide a yardstick for measuring *conceptual* truths, such as populate the law. Take the tomato. Is it a vegetable or a fruit? The phenomenal world gives us tomatoes. Yet it does not give us the categories 'vegetable' and 'fruit'. We carved those classifications. Thus, when the U.S. Supreme Court in the case *Nix v. Hedden* was called upon to decide, for purposes of the Tariff Act of 1883, whether a tomato is a fruit or a vegetable, 'reality' offered no yardstick. Moreover, the Court found inconsistent meanings in different propositional systems. Commercial trade, the most relevant field of activity, offered no definition; botany listed the tomato unequivocally as a fruit; everyday social practice, "the common language of the people," in the words of Justice Gray, classed the tomato as a vegetable (*Nix v. Hedden* 1893, p. 307). Since the tomato's "principal use" is most analogous to things classified as vegetables, Gray opted for the common usage (Ibid.).

Legal fictions likewise frequently give rise to intersystemic conflicts involving conceptual terms unknown to the phenomenal world and defined inconsistently across social realities. Human beings exist in natural reality. Yet the classifications 'Roman citizen', 'foreigner', 'heir', and 'debtor to the king', so central to many early legal historical fictions, do not. Even the basic classification 'person' does not come from the phenomenal world. It is a social construct, and a highly contentious one at that. As today's controversies over abortion and euthanasia show, defining 'person' flummoxes not just law but religion and politics. The term's familiarity and ostensible clarity conceals a woefully perplexing and controversial social concept. Is there a realm of everyday or social reality that can be said to contain a privileged definition of 'person' such as to provide *the* measure of reality against which the law's fictional extension of the concept to include corporations stands juxtaposed as an unquestioned *falsehood*?

It would appear there is not such a singular reality with a yardstick-worthy definition of 'person'. For as John Dewey once argued, the definition of 'person' confounds even more in other social realities than it does in law. The everyday, religious, and philosophical notions of 'person', 'personality', and 'personhood' have long included various and inconsistent factors. Indeed, to Dewey, the principal source of confusion in law over the meaning of the term 'person' has been the often unconscious "merging of popular and philosophical notions of the person with the legal notion" (Dewey 1926, p. 25). From everyday reality and philosophy have come "the conception that before anything can be a jural person it must intrinsically possess certain properties, the existence of which is necessary to constitute anything a person" (Ibid.). The properties are fully anthropocentric: physical existence as a living organism, ability to act intentionally, possession of a will of its own, being a subject of moral rights and duties. The fictions of corporate personality and ship personification have strained to incorporate these properties. Each has done so only in part. Yet any uneasiness that may come from law's defining 'person' to include corporations and ships pales in comparison to the anxieties and injustices that have accompanied the law's (and society's) efforts to define person in other contexts. Historically, no society has ever unambiguously treated all human beings as fully equal persons. The category 'natural person' has changed recurrently across time, generally to reflect social conceptions of normalcy. In the nineteenth century, while courts in the United States were coming to bestow legal personality on sailing ships, they were simultaneously denying full status as persons to certain human beings on account of race. Today, the divisive social issues of abortion and euthanasia reflect Western society's ambivalence in defining the beginning and end-points of a human being's personhood. In the near future, law, society, and philosophy may well be wrestling with snarly new questions of artificial personhood—the status of robots as legal persons or the independent tort responsibility of autonomous cars. Judges may well be asked whether computers with human-level intelligence as envisioned by the singularity theorists should be treated fictitiously as subjects of legal rights and duties. Compared to these nettlesome social and technological questions, the notions of corporate and ship personality are trivial and uncontroversial. It would help greatly if the advocates of a singular reality would step forward now to clarify the meaning of 'person' before the courts become clogged with issues that compel them to fictionalize anew.

Yet another objection to the instant intersystemic conflict thesis is that it rests on an unrealistic view of the language of law as insular and technical. Frederick Schauer raises this challenge, arguing that "the very idea of a legal fiction presupposes that *not* all legal language is technical language. Legal fictions exist by virtue of legal terms having non-legal meanings, such that a non-standard application of that meaning is false" (this volume, Chap. 6, p. 126). The pragmatist point, though, is not that legal language is technical *per se*. Nor does pragmatism deny that legal fictions exist by virtue of terms having both legal and non-legal meanings. That they do is presupposed by the idea of intersystemic conflict. The pragmatist point is that claims of legal truth are inextricably craft-bound to the practices of lawmaking, especially judicial decision-making, and that conflicts between legal meaning and extralegal meaning do not render true legal propositions false. Law does employ a highly specialized linguistic system. In this respect it resembles science, music, engineering, art, religion. All these are central human cognitive activities where meaning, judgment, and truth are craft-bound to system-specific methods, practices, and techniques of language usage. The pragmatist theory of legal fictions set forth herein says nothing about the technicality of legal language beyond its system-specificity in a way equally applicable to any of our central cognitive practices. As Wittgenstein noted in another context, "In a religious discourse we use such expressions as: 'I believe that so and so will happen,' and use them differently to the way in which we use them in science" (Wittgenstein 1966, p. 57). The "great temptation" Wittgenstein warned against is that of thinking that similarity in language usage and even in methods of evidential investigation makes the truths of science and religion susceptible to intercomparison (Ibid.). The same holds for legal fictions. What matters is not that the language of law is technical, but that the truth and meaning of legal propositions can only be assessed in context, i.e. by looking within the language of law to the processes of use, the doing and the saying, that surround the practices of carving legal truths. That legal fictions assert legal truths that are inconsistent in extensional meaning with propositional truths found in extralegal contexts is what makes them fictions. But it does not make them false.

5.5 Assessing the Pragmatic Value of Legal Fictions

A final objection, potentially more troubling for the pragmatist position here advanced, is that pragmatism serves as an apologetic for legal fictions. This objection is understandable given that pragmatism disavows that legal fictions make false assertions. Further, it is fair to say that pragmatism celebrates legal fictions. For fictions provide the law, particularly judicial decision-making, with an expedient method of creative lawmaking. They are, in the words of Roscoe Pound, a judicious form of "inventive activity to devise new institutions, provide new precepts and find new principles" (Pound 1932, p. 130). To pragmatism, beliefs and concepts, no matter how inventive and fictional, that can facilitate practical control over trouble in an environment while structuring and portraying the world in a coherent, comprehensive, and consistent way are highly valuable as "mental modes of *adaptation* to reality" (James 1907, p. 94). Legal concepts that can perform this adaptive function to remove trouble in the legal environment are thus highly valuable, fictional or not.

Nonetheless, the apologist objection misconstrues the pragmatist argument for legal fictions. For pragmatism does not celebrate legal fictions categorically. It only fastens value to them insofar as they work effectively to remove or regulate some trouble in the law while inflicting no harm on settled truths, meanings, or understandings in any extralegal realms with which they conflict in extensional meaning. Assessing the value of legal fictions thus requires, as Maksymilian Del Mar argues in this volume, viewing them in "the practical context in which they are used" (Chap. 11, p. 243). Pragmatism is fully committed to contextual, systemic understandings. It well-recognizes that, when viewed in practical context, some legal fictions are workable, beneficial, and harmless, while others can be metaphysically confounding, pernicious, or even stoke the flames of injustice. Rather than serving as an apologetic for legal fictions, pragmatism offers a method for assessing their value.

Central to the pragmatist approach taken here is the claim that a legal fiction is a propositional legal truth—doctrine, rule, principle—that conflicts or is in some respect inconsistent with a propositional claim or claims made outside (or elsewhere within) the law. If the conflict produces no damage outside law or within—no confusion, no incoherence, no inability to function—and if the fiction works some efficiency or functional improvement within the system of law, then the fiction has (to that extent) value and utility. But to the extent it wreaks intersystemic havoc—generates confusion or incoherence, frustrates ability to function—or does not work some genuine utility within law, it is not useful and is a problematic fiction. Problematic fictions should be removed from the law.

Pragmatism thus not only tends to view the legal fiction more charitably as a method of creative lawmaking than do most analyses grounded in the traditional falsehood approach, but it also offers a more perspicacious method to evaluate them. For the falsehood approach unavoidably depreciates the practice of fiction-making in law. Tourtoulon gave acclaim to legal fictions in general, but the weight to accord his approval must be tempered by his overall sentiments that "at bottom all law is reduced to a series of fictions heaped one upon another in successive layers," that some fictions are motivated not by interest in achieving justice, but to ensure that "judicial decision is able to preserve a respectable and dignified attitude," and that judges are "concerned with [truth] fundamentally to only a very moderate extent" (Tourtoulon 1922, pp. 387, 395, 396). Fuller spoke favorably of most historical and dogmatic fictions, but diminished them as founded principally on pretense. Maine praised fiction-making as a worthy technique of creative lawmaking for legal systems in their formative stages where rigidity in legal doctrine can thwart development. Yet he warned against reliance on fictions in mature systems where they undermine harmony and coherence in the legal order. Fictions have that effect, he argued, because every fiction is fundamentally clandestine, nothing more than an "assumption which conceals, or affects to conceal, the fact that a rule of law has undergone alteration, its letter remaining unchanged, its operation being modified" (Maine 1986, pp. 21–22). Others, such as Gray, followed Maine in viewing fictions as "scaffolding,—useful, almost necessary, in construction,—but, after the building is erected, serving only to obscure it" (Gray 1909, p. 35). Standardly, legal theorists agree with Maine that fiction-making is no more than judicial chicanery: e.g. "fiction is frequently resorted to in the attempt to conceal the fact that the law is undergoing alteration in the hands of the judges" (Smith 1917, p. 150); "The only use and purpose ... of any legal fiction is to nominally conceal this fact that the law has undergone a change at the hands of the judges" (Mitchell 1893, p. 262); "Courts resort to a legal fiction ... to avoid open confession that they are pouring new wine into old bottles" (Hogue 1966, p. 11).

By so tarnishing the legitimacy of legal fictions, the falsehood tradition cannot account for even the most salutary fictions without tainting them as spoils of compromised justice. Pragmatism, to the contrary, does not view fiction-making in law as a knavish practice. Accordingly, it can assess the value of individual fictions without the taint of illegitimacy. On the pragmatist account, the general categories of fictions labeled historical and dogmatic by Jhering and Gray are, for the most part, quite worthy. Historical fictions, such as those in early Roman and English law that permitted fictional pleading of venue, were modes of legal adaptation that effectively rectified unjust application of rigid rules. Lord Mansfield's ruling in *Mostyn v. Fabrigas* that the Mediterranean island of Minorca was part of London is geographically ludicrous. But he did not offer it as a rebuff to cartographers. Fabrigas had suffered a genuine wrong that no court could hear. Mansfield turned to fiction to permit venue in the Court of Common Pleas in London. The outrageousness of the fiction, combined with its limited effect, ensured that it inflicted no damage outside law or on the general stock of legal truths within. Given its beneficial effect in working justice in Fabrigas' case, the fiction carries much pragmatic value.

The fictions of corporate and ship personality warrant similar approval as pragmatically beneficial legal fictions. The virtue of those fictions is underscored by their long-standing influence. Yet permanence is not a necessary condition for a fiction to be worthy of acclaim. As has often been observed, there are many fictions that served justice admirably for a time only to fade away when conditions in the legal environment no longer required them (e.g. Maine 1861, pp. 22–23; Pound

1959, pp. 449–461). The fiction of constructive eviction provides an apt example. State courts in the United States fashioned the fiction to redress the often bitter results induced by the common law doctrine that lease covenants were independent obligations. The fiction mitigated the harshness of the common law rule by treating a breach of the implied covenant of quiet enjoyment that underlies all leases as a 'constructive eviction', thereby relieving a tenant of the obligation to pay rent. To make the fiction operable, the lessee had to abandon the entire leased premises. Only then could rent be withheld. Over time, the fiction was modified to allow partial abandonment followed by withholding a proportional share of rent. But even then the rule of independent covenants continued to produce severe results. States considered ways to achieve more substantial fairness than the fiction of constructive eviction could effectuate. Some states adopted the more flexible concept of the implied warranty of habitability; others chose the principle of mutually dependent lease covenants. With these developments, the doctrine of constructive eviction no longer served a beneficial purpose and it faded away. One court described its fading: "Although the fiction of constructive eviction served the useful purpose of ameliorating the harshness of the rule of independent covenants while continuing to use recognized common law vocabulary and concepts, even the doctrine of constructive eviction had limited capacity to achieve fairness" (*Richard Barton Enterprises, Inc. v. Tsern* 1996, p. 375).

The growth and decline of constructive eviction illustrates well the pragmatic nature of the practice of fiction-making in law. Trouble in the law—the grim reality that an existent rule of law produced harsh, unfair results—led courts in search of a remedial mode of adaption. The fiction of constructive eviction offered a concept that fit harmoniously with the existent stock of legal truths, using recognized common law language and concepts, with a minimum of disturbance to settled truths and expectations. Given that the concept of 'eviction' comes from law itself, any conflict the fiction imposed on truths and meanings outside law was modest and harmless. For years the fiction worked to effect some relaxation of the independent covenants doctrine. But as Benjamin Cardozo observed, legal rules and principles do not originate as "final truths" needing only to be plucked by judges "full-blossomed from the trees" (Cardozo 1921, pp. 23, 103). Rather, the practice of common law adjudication is primarily empirical and largely experimental. New doctrines emerge organically as "working hypotheses" in the paradigmatically pragmatic process of case-by-case decision-making (Ibid., p. 23). Every new case presents a new experiment where the hypotheses are tested and reconsidered in light of a new set of facts and circumstances. Rules and principles that prove to be expedient by contributing beneficially and efficiently to social justice are affirmed and reinforced. Those that do not work beneficially or even work injustice are reconsidered, modified, or abandoned. Constructive eviction worked beneficially to lessen the harshness of the rule of independent covenants. But the rule was resilient. To soften it further, courts extended the fiction's reach to allow lessees to withhold rent after vacating only part of a leasehold. Even then new cases arose that further exposed the fiction as an hypothesis that could work justice only partially. So new working hypotheses were fashioned, the implied warranty of habitability and the principle of mutually dependent covenants. These proved more socially expedient and beneficial under the experimental testing of new cases than the fiction of constructive eviction. Hence, the fiction fell into disuse. Its decline does not sully its virtue as a once-valuable legal fiction, though. It merely confirms that in the vital, evolving context of the law's growth and development, some legal rules and principles, including some of fictional form, do not live forever.

5.6 Fictions of Nullification and Falsification

Earlier I reserved the question whether there may not be some fictions that do make knowingly false assertions. I think there are. Some are beneficial; others are worrisome.

I have argued that legal fictions are not, by definition, knowingly false assertions. It is intersystemic inconsistency in extensional meaning, not falsehood, that marks a legal proposition as a fiction. When a legal fiction produces only harmless inconsistency while working some functional utility within law, it has value as a propositional claim of legal truth. Some legal fictions, however, are not harmless. I will briefly sketch two categories of such fictions: fictions of nullification and falsifying fictions. The first boasts substantial pragmatic social value. The second is pernicious.

Fictions of nullification are fictions created by law to respond to and nullify actions taken or truths formed outside law in a deliberate effort to avoid legal responsibility. The fiction of ship personification somewhat fits this category of fiction, though imperfectly. A better example is another maritime fiction, the doctrine of continuous voyage. Like the fiction of the personality of the ship, the continuous voyage fiction is a product of an earlier age, the seventeenth through nineteenth centuries, when sailing ships enjoyed their apex of importance in the Western world's trade and commerce. When nations were at war, trade between them suffered. Ships of belligerent nations were subject to seizure and condemnation, even when carrying wholly innocent cargo. Entrepreneurs from warring countries would try to carry on trade by contracting with ships bearing neutral flags which could claim immunity. The English courts refused to countenance such practice, treating the neutral vessels as engaged in the enemy's commerce and, as such, subject to condemnation. The business and shipping interests responded with a fictional visit to a neutral port that supposedly broke a voyage into two separate trips, each between one belligerent port and a neutral. The ships would call at the neutral port but not unload or pay duties. Again the English courts disapproved, ruling the voyage continuous notwithstanding the stop. Undeterred, the neutral vessels then adopted the practice of unloading their cargo, paying duties, and reloading at the neutral port before continuing the voyage. Such calls at neutral ports were 'real', yet obviously designed to evade the restrictions of English law. At first the courts of England wavered. Then beginning with *The William* in 1806, the English courts fashioned the fiction that "a cargo shipped from a hostile port to a neutral port, then unloaded with payment of duties but shortly reloaded, and, as part of the original design, shipped to a hostile port, is in one continuous voyage throughout" (Gregory 1911, p. 168). This legal fiction was anything but harmless in its conflict with the economic fiction fashioned by the shipping interests. By design it was meant to render the business fiction of importation a nullity.

Another example of a nullification fiction comes from tax law. John Prebble recently has urged that the entire regime of tax law be understood as a fiction. Prebble grounds his analysis in the falsehood tradition, arguing that tax law is discontinuous with economic reality, hence false and fictitious. Yet he astutely notes that the fictions of tax law are of a distinctly different character from most legal fictions. Instead of being based on pretense, as Fuller and others argue is characteristic of most legal fictions, Prebble argues that tax fictions are based on "duplicity," by which he means that tax fictions do not serve only as vehicles to reach a just result, but instead "the duplicity of a taxation fiction is part of the result itself" (Prebble 2011, pp. 11–12). This is to say that "the fictions of income tax law are an integral part of the law's modus operandi" (Prebble 2002, p. 311). That seems right. Tax law cannot function without fictions, for it is inherently separated from and operates in a parallel reality to its subject matter, i.e. economic activity, much of which is conducted using accounting methods and devices aimed at circumventing the payment of taxes. The analogy to the doctrine of continuous voyage is plain. Only by using fictions that pretend to unite the separation between economic 'reality' and the rules of tax law can the law nullify the effects of economic measures taken in avoidance of taxation. As Prebble puts it, "Tax law can operate *only* by using fictions; and these fictions are based not in policy but in the pragmatic need to make income tax work" (Prebble 2011, p. 19).

Falsification fictions, like the fictions of nullification, produce harmful intersystemic conflicts of truth, meaning, or understanding. The similarities between the two categories of fictions ends there however. For the nullification fictions are pragmatically beneficial. The extralegal upset they effect is meant to achieve social justice by nullifying actions taken to avoid legal responsibility or otherwise evade the law's reach. Falsification fictions, by contrast, involve intersystemic conflicts that produce adverse social consequences, from reducing responsibility and respect for law to working injustice outright.

There are, I believe, many falsification fictions. I can here only give brief mention to two. First, the law of contract is premised on agreements with mutuality of benefits and burdens, entered into voluntarily and at arm's length, by rational agents with knowledge and understanding of the commitments they are making. Increasingly, this contract ideal is a fiction with no purchase in everyday reality. Consumer contracts are becoming unilateral form agreements that few individuals read and even fewer understand. The once-maligned paper sale-and-purchase agreement dotted with 'fine-print' has given way to the point-and-click internet contract with terms the corporate creator reserves the right to alter in perpetuity. Some website user agreements run to nearly twice the length of *Hamlet*, Shakespeare's longest play. Informed consent agreements that patients must sign before receiving medical care have come to be little more than "an empty ritual in which patients are presented with complex information that they cannot understand and that has little impact on their decision making" (Lidz et al. 1988, p. 1385). Disclosure statutes that mandate the sharing of vital contractual information are well-intended, but their primary effect, like the informed consent agreements themselves, has become indemnification of corporate actors under the pretense that the disclosed information was understood and precipitated a free, informed choice. Modern contract law, as Danielle Kie Hart correctly observes, is a system "deeply flawed in theory and practice" that relies on "perpetual myth" and "legal fictions" to pretend that contracts are voluntary, informed, and the result of rational deliberation when in fact many are not (Hart 2011, pp. 79–80).

These contract examples illustrate how falsifying fictions do not address but rather create trouble in legal and extralegal environments. The intersystemic conflicts the fictions of modern contract law create exert a falsifying effect on the realm of everyday social reality. When contract law sanctions, as legitimate and legally binding, informed consent forms or other contracts that nearly no one reads or understands, the general respect for law diminishes. As individuals come to routinely click 'agree' so as to bypass internet terms of use agreements, the moral force of individual commitment and responsibility declines. These pernicious consequences are the product of legal fictions fashioned not to adapt law toward more substantial justice but to serve the self-interested ends of a certain class of social actors.

Another example of a falsifying fiction is the now widely condemned doctrine of *terra nullius*. One of the so-called 'new legal fictions' discussed in legal scholarship today is the doctrine of discovery that John Marshall relied upon in the 1823 case *Johnson v. M'Intosh* to justify the European settlement of what became the United States. This doctrine, however, was not a fiction. Formulated by the natural law philosopher Francisco de Vitoria in 1539, the right of discovery provided philosophical justification for the parceling of the Americas by European nations. The doctrine advanced a principle of first discovery. But it limited the European dominions by recognizing the presence of indigenous peoples, acknowledging their prior occupancy, and admitting the just force of their land claims. The doctrine was widely discussed among writers on the law of nations and influenced European exploration and settlement in the Americas for nearly three hundred years before Marshall entertained it. His importation of it into early American law came not by fictive invention but by embracing a philosophical, natural law doctrine that had become a mainstay in the law of nations. Its content was not inconsistent with the extralegal socio-political reality in the early American republic at the time of the *Johnson* decision. While its justice is debatable, it cannot be said to be a legal fiction.

The doctrine of *terra nullius*, however, was a legal fiction. *Terra nullius*—land belonging to no one—became the operable concept in certain lands of European colonialization as an alternative to the right of discovery. Australia is most notable. England began settling Australia in 1788. Indigenous peoples already inhabited the continent and its surrounding islands. These populations did not live under forms of political organization understandable to the British, nor could European-style political leaders be identified. Hence, unlike North America, the British settled and appropriated the Australian continent without the formal process of treaty agreements.

By the early nineteenth century, the Crown began to claim full beneficial ownership of all the lands in the then-Colony of New South Wales and prohibited any land transfer by indigenous inhabitants. The fiction of *terra nullius* was born. Under it, the territory of New South Wales came to be treated as unoccupied or uninhabited for legal purposes as of 1788, allowing the Crown's claims to full beneficial ownership to have vested unaffected by any claims made by the indigenous inhabitants. The doctrine's effect over time was to dispossess those indigenous peoples of most of their traditional lands.

Terra nullius remained a controlling concept in Australian law until the 1992 *Mabo* case. There the High Court of Australia expressly overruled it, declaring that, "The fiction by which the rights and interests of indigenous inhabitants in land were treated as non-existent was justified by a policy which has no place in the contemporary law of this country"(*Mabo v Queensland* 1992 [Brennan J. ¶42]). *Terra nullius* was a fiction in the falsifying sense. It juxtaposed *retroactively* the legal proposition that the Colony of New South Wales was practically unoccupied in 1788 against the extralegal fact that the Colony had hundreds of thousands of inhabitants. The fiction's falsifying effect was in the dispossession. Since, as stated by the High Court, "[t]he lands of [the] continent were not terra nullius or 'practically unoccupied' in 1788," under the common law the Crown's acquisition of lands should have been "reduced or qualified by the burden of the common law native title of the Aboriginal tribes and clans to the particular areas of land on which they lived or which they used for traditional purposes" (*Mabo v Queensland* 1992 [Deane and Gaudron JJ. ¶56]). The fiction of *terra nullius* thus rang a discordant tone wholly out of harmony with other common law principles, resulting in dispossession on fictional grounds directly in opposition to the common law principle of native law. When a legal fiction is carried out to such effect as to override other propositions in the general stock of legal truths and counterbalance fundamental notions of justice, it diminishes the moral authority of law, forces need for rectification and reconciliation, and can leave in its wake "a national legacy of unutterable shame" (Ibid. [Deane and Gaudron JJ. ¶50]).

Conclusion

In this pragmatist inquiry I have suggested that it is misleading to characterize legal fictions around falsehood. Legal fictions are not, by definition, consciously false assertions. Rather, they are true propositions of law that conflict in extensional meaning or are otherwise inconsistent with other truths found elsewhere within law or in some realm of reality outside law. Legal officials create legal fictions to resolve trouble in the law that requires creative lawmaking. A legal fiction is valuable if it is intellectually satisfying, i.e. to the extent it does no damage to any general stock of beliefs outside law or within, and insofar as it makes law more effective and efficient while maintaining harmony and consistency across the full range of legal beliefs.

Legal concepts such as personality have been forged into highly valuable legal fictions through being extended to entities like corporations or artifacts like ships. Though it collides with statements of truth outside law, the concept of legal personality wreaks no havoc, does no damage to our everyday understandings of corporations, ships, or personhood. Within law, it facilitates many beneficial legal actions. Other fictions, such *terra nullius*, do inflict damage. By falsely fictionalizing non-existence, *terra nullius* facilitated theft. Such pernicious legal fictions carry no pragmatic value and have no justified place in the law.

References

Bentham, Jeremy. 1843. *Works*. Edinburgh: William Tait.

Bentham, Jeremy. 1977. *A fragment on government*. In *A comment on the commentaries and a fragment on government,* eds. J. H. Burns and H. L. A. Hart. Oxford: Clarendon Press.

Blackstone, William. [1765–1769] 1979. *Commentaries on the laws of England*. 4 vols. Chicago: University Chicago Press.

Brandom, Robert B. 2011. *Perspectives on pragmatism: Classical, recent, and contemporary*. Cambridge: Harvard University Press.

Camden, Jen, and Kathryn E. Fort. 2008. 'Channeling Thought'—The legacy of legal fictions from 1823. *American Indian Law Review* 33:77–109.

Campbell, Kenneth. 1983. Fuller on legal fictions. *Law & Philosophy* 2:339–370.

Cardozo, Benjamin. 1921. *The nature of the judicial process*. Yale: Yale University Press.

Del Mar, Maksymilian. 2014. Legal fictions and legal change in the common law tradition. In *Legal fictions in theory and practice*, ed. Maksymilian Del Mar and William Twining. Dordrecht: Springer.

Devlin, Patrick. 1979. *The judge*. Oxford: Oxford University Press.

Dewey, John. [1916] 1954. *Essays in experimental logic*. New York: Dover Publications.

Dewey, John. 1926. Corporate personality. *Yale Law Journal* 35:655–673.

Dewey, John. [1929] 1984. *The quest for certainty*. In *The later works 1925–1953,* ed. Jo Ann Boydston. Carbondale: Southern Illinois University Press.

Dewey, John. 2012. *Unmodern philosophy and modern philosophy*. Carbondale: Southern Illinois University Press.

Frank, Jerome. 1936. *Law and the modern mind*. New York: Tudor Publishing Co.

Fuller, Lon L. 1967. *Legal fictions*. Stanford: Stanford University Press.

Gray, John Chipman. 1909. *The nature and sources of the law*. New York: Columbia University Press.

Gregory, Charles Noble. 1911. The doctrine of continuous voyage. Harvard Law Review 24:167–181.

Harmon, Louise. 1990. Falling off the vine: Legal fictions and the doctrine of substituted judgment. *Yale Law Journal* 100:1–71.

Hart, H. L. A. 1982a. Bentham and Beccaria. In *Essays on bentham: Studies in jurisprudence and political theory*. Oxford: Clarendon Press.

Hart, H. L. A. 1982b. Legal Duty and Obligation. In *Essays on bentham: Studies in jurisprudence and political theory*. Oxford: Clarendon Press.

Hart, Danielle Kie. 2011. Contract law now—Reality meets legal fictions. *Baltimore Law Review* 41:1–81.

Hogue, Arthur R. [1966] 1985. *Origins of the common law*. Indianapolis: Liberty Press.

Holmes, Oliver Wendell Jr. [1881] 1938. *The common law*. Boston: Little, Brown & Co.

James, William. [1907] 1975. *Pragmatism*. Cambridge: Harvard University Press.

James, William. [1909a] 1975. *The meaning of truth*. Cambridge: Harvard University Press.

James, William. [1909b] 1996. *A pluralistic universe*. Lincoln: University Nebraska Press.
James, William. [1911] 1996. *Some problems of philosophy*. Lincoln: University Nebraska Press.
James, William. [1912] 1996. *Essays in radical empiricism*. Lincoln: University Nebraska Press.
Jhering, Rudolf von. 1913. *Law as a means to an end* (Trans.: Isaac Husik). Boston: Boston Book Co.
Jhering, Rudolf von. 1924. *Geist des römischen Rechts auf den verschiedenen Stufen seiner Entwicklung*. 6th ed. Leipzig: Breitkopf and Hartel.
Johnson v. M'Intosh. 1823. 21 U.S. (8 Wheat.) 543 (1923).
Knauer, Nancy. 2010. Legal fictions and juristic truth. *St. Thomas Law Review* 23:1–49.
Lidz, C. W., P. S. Appelbaum, and A. Meisel. 1988. Two models of implementing informed consent. *Archives of Internal Medicine* 148:1385–1389.
Lind, Douglas. 2010. Pragmatism and anthropomorphism: Reconceiving the doctrine of the personality of the ship. *University of San Francisco Maritime Law Journal* 22:39–121.
Locke, Alain. 1989. Value. In *The philosophy of Alain Locke: Harlem renaissance and beyond*, ed. Leonard Harris. Philadelphia: Temple University Press.
Mabo v Queensland [1992] HCA 23; (1992) 175 CLR 1
Maine, Sir Henry Sumner. [1861] 1986. *Ancient law*. New York: Dorset Press.
Mitchell, Oliver R. 1893. The fictions of the law: Have they proved useful or detrimental to its growth? *Harvard Law Review* 7:249–265.
Mostyn v. Fabrigas 1 Cowp. 161, 98 Eng. Rep. 1021 (K.B. 1774) (Mansfield, L.J.)
Nix v. Hedden 149 U.S. 304 (1893)
Patterson, Edwin W. 1953. *Jurisprudence: Men and ideas of the law*. Brooklyn: Foundation Press.
Plato. 1995. *Phaedrus* (Trans.: Alexander Nehamas and Paul Woodruff). Indianapolis: Hackett.
Pollock, Sir Frederick, and Frederic William Maitland. 1959. *The history of english law*. 2nd ed., 2 vols. Washington, D.C.: Lawyers' Literary Club.
Pound, Roscoe. 1932. *Interpretations of legal history*. Cambridge: Cambridge University Press.
Pound, Roscoe. 1959. *Jurisprudence*. St. Paul, Minn.: West Pub. Co.
Prebble, John. 2002. Income taxation: A structure built on sand. *Sydney Law Review* 24:301–318.
Prebble, John. 2011. Fictions of income tax. Victoria University of Wellington Legal Research Paper No. 29/2011. http://papers.ssrn.com/abstract=1604978. Accessed 16 Dec 2013.
Putnam, Hilary. 1981. *Reason, truth and history*. Cambridge: Cambridge University Press.
Putnam, Hilary. 1995. *Pragmatism: An open question*. Oxford: Blackwell.
Quine, Willard van Orman. 1953. Two dogmas of empiricism. In *From a logical point of view*, 20–46. Cambridge: Harvard University Press.
Richard Barton Enterprises, Inc. v. Tsern. 1996. 928 P.2d 368 (Utah 1996).
Ross, Alf. 1969. Legal fictions. In *Law, reason, and justice: Essays in legal philosophy*, ed. Graham Hughes, 217–234. New York: New York University Press.
Savigny, Frederick Charles von. 1831. *Of the vocation of our age for legislation and jurisprudence* (Trans.: Abraham Hayward). London: Littlewood.
Schane, Sanford A. 1987. The corporation is a person: The language of a legal fiction. *Tulane Law Review* 61:563–609.
Schauer, Frederick. 2014. Legal fictions revisited. In *Legal fictions in theory and practice*, ed. Maksymilian Del Mar and William Twining. Dordrecht: Springer.
Schiller, F. C. S. 1903. *Humanism: Philosophical essays*. London: Macmillan.
Smith, Jeremiah. 1917. Surviving fictions. *Yale Law Journal* 27:147–166.
Smith, Peter J. 2007. New legal fictions. *Georgetown Law Journal* 95:1435–1495.
Soifer, Aviam. 1986. Reviewing legal fictions. *Georgia Law Review* 20:871–915.
The John G. Stevens 170 U.S. 113 (1898)
The William 5 C. Robinson, 385 (1806)
Tourtoulon, Pierre de. 1922. *Philosophy in the development of law* (Trans.: Martha McC. Read). New York: Macmillan.
Tucker v. Alexandroff 183 U.S. 424 (1902)
United States v. Brig Malek Adhel 43 U.S. (2 How.) 210 (1844)
United States v. The Little Charles 26 F.Cas. 979 (C.C. Va. 1818) (No. 15,612)

Vaihinger, Hans. [1924] 1984. *The philosophy of 'As If': A system of the theoretical, practical and religious fictions of mankind* (Trans.: C. K. Ogden). London: Routledge & Kegan Paul.
Vitoria, Francisco de. [1539] 1991. On the American Indians. In *Political writings*. Cambridge: Cambridge University Press.
Wittgenstein, Ludwig. 1966. Lectures on religious belief I. In *Lectures and conversations on aesthetics, psychology and religious belief*, ed. Cyril Barrett. Berkeley: University of California Press.
Wittgenstein, Ludwig. 1975. *Philosophical remarks*, ed. Rush Rhees (Trans.: Raymond Hargreaves and Roger white). Chicago: University Chicago Press.
Wittgenstein, Ludwig. 1978. *Philosophical grammar*, ed. Rush Rhees (Trans.: Anthony Kenny). Berkeley: University of California Press.

Part II
Community, Language and Literature

Chapter 6
Legal Fictions Revisited

Frederick Schauer

Abstract A rarely noticed feature of legal fictions is their dependence on a certain understanding of the nature of legal language. If the language of the law is understood as a largely technical language internal to law and its goals, then that language can be applied without need for recourse to fictions. But if, instead, law's language is in important ways related to and dependent on ordinary language, then the language of the law may at times frustrate law's goals. When this happens, there will be a need for legal fictions, and thus the very use of a legal fiction presupposes a controversial view about legal language as being, at least in part, ordinary language.

It is no compliment nowadays to accuse a judge, court, or theorist of employing a "legal fiction." But it was not always so,[1] and the literature on legal fictions is replete with claims that legal fictions are occasionally or often necessary to carry out the various goals of a legal system.[2] Such defenses of legal fictions are increasingly rare, however, and the accusation of using a "legal fiction" may have overtaken "formalist" as the most ubiquitous and ill-defined of jurisprudential condemnations.[3] But while it is clear that a charge of relying on a legal fiction is overwhelmingly pejorative these days, it is less clear just what is being condemned, and why what is being condemned justifies the condemnation.

[1] An important survey of the use of legal fictions going back to Roman Law is Olivier (1975). Also comprehensive is Harmon (2002).

[2] The classic (albeit qualified) defense of legal fictions remains Fuller (1967). Earlier efforts include Blackstone (1768, p. 43) ("And these fictions of law, although at first they may startle the student, he will find upon farther consideration to be highly beneficial and useful …"), von Jhering (1914, 1923) and de Tourtolon (1922). Even more qualified are Frank (1930), Maine (1861), and Ross (1969).

[3] An example of the modern pejorative use is Smith (2007). And a commendable effort to rescue the traditional and more precise understanding of a legal fiction from the modern broad, pejorative, and often ill-defined usage is Knauer (2010). And of course this very volume (see especially Del Mar, Chap. 11) represents an effort both to clarify the idea of a legal fiction and to show how legal fictions may often be of value.

F. Schauer (✉)
School of Law, University of Virginia, 580 Massie Road, Charlottesville, VA 22903, USA
e-mail: schauer@virginia.edu

M. Del Mar, W. Twining (eds.), *Legal Fictions in Theory and Practice*,
Law and Philosophy Library 110, DOI 10.1007/978-3-319-09232-4_6

The basic problem is that a fiction is, by definition, untrue. And although telling untruths is expected of novelists, playwrights, and poker players, in most domains intentionally saying something that is false is at least prima facie unacceptable. A legal fiction, an intentional untruth in the law, thus seems an especially odd thing for an institution allegedly committed to truth-finding to tolerate. In analyzing the various uses of legal fictions, however, and the diverse deployment of the term "legal fiction," we will see why not every legal fiction is to be condemned, and why legal fictions have had their defenders over the years. Understanding the occasional virtues of legal fictions, however, takes us into the realm of legal truth itself, and into a confrontation with the complex relationship between legal truth and truth *simpliciter*, a relationship that in turn exposes important complexities surrounding the connection between legal truth and legal language.

The principal structure of this paper (which brackets entirely the technically fictional aspects of metaphor and other figurative uses of language) is in three parts, seeing legal fictions, in perhaps a strained effort to be alliterative, as *presuppositions*, as *presumptions*, and as *prevarications*. The first part is the least important and least original. But because the notion of a legal fiction plays such a major role in Kelsenian legal philosophy, it is necessary to say something about Kelsen and the *Grundnorm* as a fiction in order to distinguish this conception of a fiction from the ones I examine more closely here.

The heart of this essay begins in Section II, exploring legal presumptions such as the traditional common law presumption that the husband of a child's mother is the child's father. Obviously this is not literally (or biologically) true in some of the cases to which the presumptions apply, and thus it is not surprising that such presumptions are often described as legal fictions, and almost as often criticized for their deceptiveness, even if not for their substantive import. As we shall see, however, not only is this variety of legal fiction common, but it is also a fiction only in the sense that any rule is a fiction, precisely because it is a characteristic feature of any rule that it will treat what is ordinarily the case as if it were always the case. Presumptions that are sometimes false in particular cases may be an easy target of critics, but they are little more than the occasional vivid embodiment of the way in which any enterprise that trades in generality—which law most certainly does—will wind up drawing conclusions that may not always be literally correct.

Yet the connection between legal fictions and legal rules is even closer than this, as discussed in Section III, examining legal fictions as common devices for effectuating the (contingent) defeasibility of legal rules. Because rules are, necessarily, actually or at least potentially both under- and over-inclusive with respect to their background justifications, or with respect to broader notions of fairness, justice, efficiency, or utility, rules will frequently generate what appear to be, and what often are, suboptimal or simply erroneous outcomes. In such circumstances, and following a lead going back as far as Aristotle's discussion of equity as a remedy for the inevitable coarseness of rules, legal systems will often permit their decision-makers to treat the system's rules as defeasible, subject to being set aside in order to produce a good rule-independent outcome rather than a bad rule-generated one. But because judges, especially, are required to justify such departures from rules, they resort to some number of justificatory maneuvers in order to avoid simply saying that they are not following the rule. One of those maneuvers, although hardly the only one, is one kind of legal fiction, the re-description of the facts of some event in order to make those facts compatible with the rule while at the same time permitting what appears to be the right result.

In examining this last type of legal fiction—the re-description of an *X* (or the class of *X*'s) as a *Y* in order to avoid an embarrassing outcome—we confront the largest issues of legal language and legal truth, and thus of law itself. When we say that what appears by all accounts to be an *X* is really a *Y* for purposes of the law, are we lying? Are we engaged in a fiction? Or are we recognizing, as some would have it, that legal language exists in an uncomfortable relationship with ordinary language? Part IV begins an exploration of this issue, opening up an inquiry into so-called terms of art and into the question of whether legal language is ordinary language, technical language, or some combination of both.

6.1 I

In a work appropriately recognized by many of the contributions to this volume, but still unfortunately neglected in mainstream analytic philosophy, the German philosopher Hans Vaihinger offered the perspective of, in German, *als ob,*[4] which, in its most common English translation, means "as if." Vaihinger's philosophy of "as if" was for some years highly influential,[5] and for our purposes noteworthy for the influence that it had on Hans Kelsen (Bindreiter 2002; Paulson 1992a), and, at more or less the same time, Fuller (1967, pp. 94–137). Vaihinger's basic idea has both logical and psychological dimensions. With respect to the former, the idea is straightforward: the premise of an argument can typically be presented in hypothetical form, and we are highly familiar with the idea of assuming something for the sake of argument, or with presupposing the truth of one proposition in order that we can make sense of some other proposition. To take the standard example from Bertrand Russell (1905), the statement "The King of France is bald" presupposes that there is a king of France, and we can accordingly make sense of the statement on the assumption that there is a king of France, even though, in fact, there actually is no king of France. Thus, the presupposed factual proposition that there is a king of France is a fiction insofar as it allows the sentence in which it is contained to make sense even if and when the proposition is false. But it is a fiction only contingently, because the logically equivalent statement, "The Queen of England is not bald," similarly presupposes that there is a Queen of England. But because there actually is a Queen of England, the presupposition in this case, contingently but not necessarily, is not false and consequently not a fiction at all.

Sometimes, however, we assume some fact for the sake of argument, or hypothesize some fact, under circumstances in which it simply does not matter whether the

---

[4] Vaihinger (1911, 1924).

[5] References to Vaihinger pervade Frank (1930), for example. And see Seidel (1932) and Handy (1967).

assumed fact is true or false. Yet although the actual fact of the matter is irrelevant, we nevertheless assume the existence of some fact because the assumption makes some other point understandable, or clearer. So consider the following: "Assume that 70 % of some population favors a particular policy. Then, in a democracy, that is the policy that should be adopted." Here it does not matter whether in this or that instance the 70 % assumption is true or false. Rather, the 70 % majority is an assumption that enables us to understand the idea of democracy, an understanding which is independent of the actual truth or falsity of the factual assumption. In discussing "fictions" as important elements of thought, therefore, Vaihinger was less concerned with the facticity of the "as if" than with the way in which "as if" thinking often facilitated human understanding and comprehension. That Vaihinger was an important Kant scholar and the founder of the journal *Kant-Studien* underscores the similarities between Vaihinger's philosophy of "as if" and the Kantian transcendental understandings which are related to but not quite the same as the factual presuppositions in Russell's example and in the subsequent philosophical literature (Strawson 1952, pp. 174–179).

Vaihinger's perspective links closely with Kelsen's *Grundnorm*.[6] The *Grundnorm* under Kelsen's system is not a factual presupposition as much as it is a Kantian transcendental understanding (Paulson 1992b; Raz 1979), but such a transcendental understanding, or at least the factual components of it, might still turn out to be either factually true or factually false. If factually true—if making sense of a legal system requires that we adopt an understanding that turns out, contingently, to mirror reality, then it would be odd to describe that understanding as a fiction. But if the understanding is not true, or if, more precisely, it simply does not matter whether it is true or not, then we can understand why Kelsen would describe the understanding that is the *Grundnorm as* a fiction. It is thus the contingent falsity and, even more, the irrelevance of the factual truth or falsity of the *Grundnorm* that explains why it is commonly thought of as a legal fiction in Kelsenian legal theory.[7] But although the assumed existence of something that may not exist perhaps justifies (but only barely) the term "fiction," and although it is the very assumption rather than the factual existence of the truth of the *Grundnorm* that distinguishes it from Hart's (derivative) ultimate rule of recognition (Hart 2012),[8] the use of the term "fiction" in this context seems substantially metaphorical. If we understand a fiction not so much as an assumption (whether a transcendental understanding or not) whose factual truth is not relevant but as a statement that is both literally false

[6] Kelsen refers to Vaihinger in Kelsen (1960, p. 99), albeit primarily in the context of a discussion of free will. Kelsen does not mention Vaihinger in the first (1924) edition (Kelsen, 1992), but he does conceive of the *Grundnorm* in terms of a Vaihinger-fiction in Kelsen (1986). For Kelsen's thoughts about legal fictions more broadly, and in ways that also draw on Vaihinger and which connect with the subsequent sections of this paper, see Kelsen (1919); Chap. 1.

[7] Kelsen (1991, p. 256) explicitly says that the *Grundnorm* differs from a hypothesis in Vaihinger's scheme because a fiction is uttered with the knowledge that reality does not agree with it (Paulson 1992a, pp. 269–270). See also the differing views in Gustafsson (2010), Stewart (1980), and Tur (1986).

[8] On the similarities and differences between Kelsen's *Grundnorm* and Hart's ultimate rule of recognition, see Alexander and Schauer (2009) and Green (2009).

and known by the maker of the statement to be literally false—were it otherwise we would call it a "mistake" and not a "fiction"—then the common usage of "legal fiction" to refer to Kelsen's idea of the *Grundnorm* is itself at least slightly fictional with reference to the term "fiction" itself.

Both Kelsen and Vaihinger recognized that it is sometimes important to act and speak as if something were true, and that we do so not necessarily only when what we assume to be true is false, but also when we do not want the truth or falsity of the assumption to matter. Vaihinger's and Kelsen's ideas were thus not primarily about counterfactual assumptions, but instead about "afactual" assumptions in which the factual truth or falsity of the assumption is largely irrelevant. The connection between Vaihinger and Kelsen thus seems apparent, but what appears as well is the conclusion that to describe the ideas of "as if" or the *Grundnorm* itself as "fictions" is a usage that, while not plainly wrong, is at least somewhat non-standard. Normally we understand a fiction as being closer to a lie—the intentional statement of a falsity—but lacking the deceptive component of actual lying. Unlike lies, fictions are known by their recipients to be false, and that is why we do not normally think of novelists and screenwriters as liars, even though they are saying things that are literally untrue and known by the novelists and screenwriters to be untrue. Despite the intentional falsity, however, we do not understand playwrights and novelists as liars because the audience is aware of the untruth and thus the element of deception necessary for a proposition to count as a lie is missing. The audience or the readers may be expected to suspend their disbelief in the truth of the fictional narrative while they are reading or listening, and this may be a variant on the kind of transcendental understanding that is the key to the idea of the *Grundnorm,* but the fictional aspect of the *Grundnorm* is no more problematic than is fiction in general. The *Grundnorm* may be a legal fiction, but only in the sense that any assumption or presupposition is potentially fictional, and fictions of this variety are such a large part of our conceptual machinery as scarcely to deserve notice at all, let alone even the mildest of condemnation. More importantly, the use of "fiction" to describe the *Grundnorm* is sufficiently distant from the traditional way in which "fiction" has been used in "legal fiction" in common law discourse as to suggest that discussions of the fictional aspect of the *Grundnorm*, while important in themselves, are largely peripheral to the topic of legal fictions itself.

6.2 II

Once we turn from presuppositions to presumptions, the tendency to condemn legal fictions accelerates. Thus it is often said that legal presumptions, or at least many legal presumptions, are legal fictions because such presumptions require judges or juries to accept as true things that are false, and that this is highly undesirable.[9] Yet

[9] Much of Bentham's famous excoriation of the fictions of the law (Ogden 1932) has this flavor. Among Bentham's stronger statements, although still entirely representative, were "the pestilential breath of Fiction poisons the sense of every instrument it comes near" (Bentham 1962, vol. 1, p. 235) and "[I]n English law, fiction is a syphilis, which runs in every vein, and carries into every

although phrasing a presumption as the mandatory acceptance of that which is not true does suggest some degree of falsity or fictionality in the typical presumption, the initial impression—and Bentham's impression—that a presumption is a fiction, or even that it allows fictions, turns out, as Raymundo Gama explores in greater depth in this volume (Chap. 16), to be more misleading than helpful.

Consider a typical generalization in a non-legal context. "Swiss cheese has holes," for example. Or "Volvos are reliable." Such statements are not true of all members of the described class. There is Swiss cheese without holes that is still Swiss cheese, and there are unreliable Volvos. But if that is so, then what is it to make a statement about a class? And what makes a statement about a class true? Or false? Consider, for example, the class of Yugos, a notoriously unreliable automobile manufactured in the former Yugoslavia in the 1970s and 1980s. Assuming (possibly counterfactually) that there were at least two reliable Yugos, it would be true to say that "some Yugos are reliable," yet the statement "Yugos are reliable" seems false. But if there are some unreliable Volvos and some reliable Yugos, then why is the statement "Volvos are reliable" true and the statement "Yugos are reliable" false? And the answer is that according to the standard pragmatics of standard English, a statement about a class which attributes a property to the class is true if and only if the property is present within the class to a greater extent than the property is present within another class with which the class under discussion is being explicitly or implicitly compared. Note that there is thus no requirement that the property appear within a majority of the members of a class for the statement about that property within the class to be true. It would be accurate to say that "Yugos are unreliable" even if only 45 % of Yugos were unreliable, because 45 % is a rate of unreliability far higher than the rate for cars in general or other models of car. Similarly, it is correct to say that "pit bull dogs are aggressive" even though only a minority of them are, and that is because the rate of aggression for the class of pit bulls is higher than the rate of aggression for most other breeds and higher than the rate for all other dogs. Thus, statements attributing a property to a class—generics (Cheng 2011; Leslie 2008; Schauer 2003)—may be true if the property appears in all members of the class, if the property appears in a majority of members of the class, or if the property appears within the class to a greater degree than the property appears within some implicit comparison class.

The point of the foregoing is to establish that probabilistic statements about a class may indeed be true (or false) without being universally true (or false) for all members of the class. And this analysis can be transferred from descriptive generalizations to the prescriptive generalizations we call rules (Schauer 1991). Prescriptive rules are designed to serve background justifications, as with a "no driving in excess of 100 km/h" rule that is designed to foster the background justification of highway safety. As in this example, rules are also probabilistic generalizations, because rules are generalizations about the forms of conduct that will serve those background justifications. So if we prohibit vehicles in the park because we wish to secure peace and quiet in the park (Hart 1958, 2012, p. 129; ; Schauer 2008), we

part of the system the principle of rottenness." (*Ibid.*, vol. 5, p. 92). And see also Quinn, this volume, Chap. 4; Schofield (2006), Chap. 1.

have made the assessment that prohibiting vehicles, in general, will advance peace and quiet, again in general and not necessarily in every case. The prohibition is embodied in a rule with the full and necessary acceptance of the fact that the rule can be the right rule even though some vehicles might not be detrimental to peace and quiet (over-inclusion) and even though some non-vehicles might turn out to be detrimental in just the way that vehicles ordinarily are (under-inclusion).

Legal presumptions typically, even if not always or necessarily, operate to precisely the same effect, even if not in exactly the same way. So let us consider the classic historical common law presumption of paternity—the presumption that the husband of the mother is the father of any child born to the mother during the marriage (Glennon 2000). Assuming for the moment—but only for the moment, as we shall see in Section III below—that fatherhood is a physiological state requiring some biological connection between the father and the child and requiring that the father have had sexual relations (or a modern scientific or technological equivalent) with the mother in order to produce the child, then some number of people presumed by the law to be fathers will not in fact *be* fathers. It is, after all, quite possible to be the biological father of a married woman's child without being the person to whom the mother was married at the time of conception or the time of birth. But the law, partly because it reflected a traditional social aversion to illegitimacy, and partly to create and enforce obligations of support, presumed that all men married to women at the time the women gave birth were the fathers of the child so born, even though, in fact, only most of them were.[10]

The connection between rules and presumptions is now exposed. Most legal rules treat the typical as universal, as when they treat ordinarily peace-and-quiet-hampering vehicles as if they necessarily hampered peace and quiet. And so too with, for example, the ordinary speed limit, which is based on an assessment of the maximum safe speed for average drivers in average vehicles under average road, weather, and traffic conditions, but which is nevertheless the speed limit for all drivers in all vehicles under all conditions. Thus, instrumental legal rules *presume* that all vehicles will detract from peace and quiet even if only most of them will, and presume that all drivers can drive safely only up to a certain speed, even if in fact some drivers can drive safely at a higher speed. Accordingly, the similarity between the typical rule and the typical presumption is not merely the parallel between the two in treating what is typically or ordinarily the case as if it were always the case. Rather, rules in many cases, and always when rules serve instrumental purposes vis-à-vis their background justifications, just *are* presumptions, although this feature of rules is sometimes obscured by the way in which presumptions are normally expressed. But the presumption that the husband of the mother of a child born during wedlock could also be expressed in terms of a rule requiring the husband of the mother of a child born during wedlock to support the child, treat the child as

[10] Many of the common law's presumptions, including this one, were rebuttable (Swadling 2008). But because even a rebuttable presumption shifts the burden of proof, a rebuttable presumption can be expected to produce some outcomes in which the presumed fact is not actually a fact at all. And thus we should not be surprised that Bentham, Fuller, and most of the writers on legal fictions have spent some time on the fictions produced by even rebuttable presumptions.

legitimate, etc. In that case, the very same consequences flowing from the presumption would be articulated in the form of a rule rather than a presumption, but the legal import of the two would be identical.

We can now see why the common talk of presumptions as fictions is in many important respects the product of confusion. Asking legal decision-makers to assume for the purpose of decision that that which is false is true does indeed often look like a fiction, but no more or less so than asking legal decision-makers to apply rules in the area of their under- and over-inclusiveness. When a police officer stops an experienced and safe driver for exceeding the speed limit under ideally safe traffic and weather conditions, the officer is assuming that the driver and the conditions are average even though they are not (Schauer 2009, Chap. 1). When the park official keeps out a non-peace-and-quiet-hampering vehicle he is assuming (or effectuating the rule-maker's assumption) that the vehicle will hamper peace and quiet even though it will not. In these and countless other cases, the application of a rule in the area of its under- and over-inclusiveness can be seen to be a fiction in just the same way that the typical factual presumption is a fiction in the area of its factual falsity. Perhaps rigid rule-following is itself a problem, and this possibility will be the subject of the next section. But if rigid (or even non-conclusive) rule-following itself has its place and has its uses, then there is no reason to believe that there is anything alarming about achieving the same end through the use of a presumption, a presumption that we can see as doing pretty much exactly the same thing in pretty much exactly the same way.

6.3 III

In the previous section we assumed that rigid rule-following might in some contexts be desirable (Schauer 1988, 2009, Chap. 2), but such an assumption is by no means universally held. And thus we must return to Aristotle, who in his discussion of equity recognized that rigid rules might generate the "false" results that we examined in the previous section. Aristotle described rules as "law," and then went on to say that:

> … all law is universal, and there are some things about which it is not possible to pronounce rightly in general terms; therefore in cases where it is necessary to make a general pronouncement, but impossible to do so rightly, the law takes account of the majority of cases, although not unaware that in this way errors are made. And the law is none the less right; because the error lies not in the law nor in the legislator, but in the nature of the case; for the raw material of human behavior is essentially of this kind. So when the law states a general rule, and a case arises under this that is exceptional, then it is right, where the legislator owing to the generality of his language has erred in not covering the case, to correct the omission by a ruling such as the legislator himself would have given if he had been present there, and as he would have enacted if he had been aware of the circumstances … This is why equity, although just, and better than a kind of justice, is not better than absolute justice—only than the error due to generalization. (Aristotle 1977, § 1137a–b).

Aristotle's basic idea had been expressed earlier by Plato in the *Statesman* (1952, p. 294a–b) and was then subsequently developed by Cicero and other Roman philosophers and jurists (Cicero 2001, 1.57; Frier 1985), and thereafter by the English in creating the formal institutions of equity in English law (Schauer 2003, pp. 27–54). But the important point here is not the history of the idea, but rather the idea itself. And that idea is that any rule, and thus any legal rule, might produce a wrong answer in a particular case by virtue of the generality of a rule. Equity, broadly understood, is consequently the contingent mechanism by which such errors are corrected (Solum 1994). But I say "contingent" because it would be open to any rule-governed domain to deny the equitable power, and thus to take the position that the errors of under- and over-inclusion of any rule are better tolerated than empowering any group of judges or other officials to determine when such an error has occurred. Rule-governed domains such as law are formal insofar as such powers are not granted, and might be considered equitable to the extent that somewhere in the system there is a remedy for the mistakes generated by the under- and over-inclusiveness of written-down rules.

But what then might those remedies be? One remedy would be some sort of separate system to correct the errors necessarily wrought by under- and over-inclusive rules, and indeed this was the remedy that was embodied in the earliest appearance of equity in English law. Judges of law, in the narrow sense of "law," were not empowered to ameliorate the mistakes generated by general rules, but someone aggrieved by such mistakes could go the Chancellor, and later to an elaborate series of Chancellor's courts known as courts of equity, in order to gain equitable relief from the rigidity of law (Guy 1985). More recently, many common law countries, perhaps most prominently and substantially in the United States, have often empowered ordinary judges to exercise such powers, and thus the ordinary judge might legitimately conclude that the application of the rule would be unjust or inconsistent with the purposes behind the rule, and proceed to treat the rule as inapplicable to the case at hand, or subject to a previously unexpressed exception, in much the way that Aristotle first envisaged (Atiyah and Summers 1987; Calabresi 1982; Laycock 1993).

Although resorting to equity in order to produce an all-things-considered just result is therefore increasingly acceptable in many jurisdictions, doing so in direct contravention of explicit and precise legal rules appears to retain much of the bad odor of earlier eras. It is difficult, for reasons that are as much psychological and political as they are jurisprudential, for judges to appear to rewrite what seem to be the clear words of a clear statute.[11] Accordingly, it has long been considered more acceptable in the pursuit of justice in the individual case to re-describe the facts in order to achieve the right result than to rewrite a law in order to do the same thing, even though, in reality, re-describing (and thus mis-describing) the facts to make them fit the law is little different from re-describing the law in order to make it fit the actual facts.[12]

---

[11] "[Legal] authorities … admit that fiction is frequently resorted to in the attempt to conceal the fact that the law is undergoing alteration in the hands of judges" (Smith 1917, p. 150).

[12] The consequences in the particular case may be virtually identical, but, depending on issues of precedent and judicial power within a given jurisdiction, it may be that modifying the law to

Despite this similarity between the two approaches, for a long time, and perhaps precisely because of the psychological and political reasons just noted, the re-description of facts in order to produce a just result has seemed preferable to the more overt re-writing of a legal rule, and from this preference—a preference for judicial prevarication over judicial activism—there emerges an important version of the legal fiction. Thus we see the classic example of *Mostyn v. Fabrigas*, decided by the King's Bench court in 1774. Fabrigas, a resident of the Mediterranean island of Minorca then occupied and controlled by England, was imprisoned by Mostyn,[13] at the time the governor of the island. Because no suit could be brought against Mostyn in Minorca without the approval of the governor, and because the governor was the defendant in the very lawsuit Fabrigas wished to pursue, Fabrigas sued instead in the Court of Common Pleas in London for trespass and false imprisonment, and proceeded to win a jury verdict of 3000 £. On appeal, Mostyn claimed, correctly, that the trial court had been granted jurisdiction only in cases brought by residents of London, but Lord Mansfield, recognizing that denying jurisdiction here would leave someone who was plainly wronged without a legal remedy, concluded that Minorca was part of London for purposes of this action. That conclusion was plainly false and equally plainly produced a just result, and thus *Mostyn v. Fabrigas* represents the paradigmatic example of using a fiction to achieve what might in earlier days have been done through the vehicle of equity.[14]

More recently, American courts have done the same thing with the laws of inheritance. As is often the case, two people may own property jointly, and sometimes one joint-owner kills the other in order to secure full ownership. Under such circumstances, the killer, although obviously subject to criminal liability, would under the traditional rules about joint ownership obtain full ownership of the previously jointly-held property. But in order to avoid such an unjust outcome, several courts have deemed the killer to have died before the victim.[15] In almost every situation this conclusion will be patently false, but it is a conclusion that will achieve a just result without modifying the general terms of the laws regarding jointly held property. And thus, again, the fiction as a false statement of fact is used to achieve a just or equitable result. Accordingly, we see the maxim *in fictione juris semper aequitas*

produce the right result in the case at hand will have greater effects on future cases than will mis-describing the facts in order to accomplish the same result. If and when this is so, we can understand the preference for judicial mis-description over judicial re-writing.

[13] It is likely that Fabrigas's imprisonment was part of a political vendetta, and thus Fabrigas's substantive claim was likely a legally sound one.

[14] There is a story, probably apocryphal, that, in 1939, the renowned and beloved deer which graze on the grounds of Magdalen College, Oxford, were at risk of being requisitioned during the wartime food shortage by the Ministry of Food. In order to prevent such an occurrence, it is said, influential Magdalen graduates in the government arranged to have the deer reclassified as vegetables and thus be spared from the slaughterhouse. More recently, it is reported that Magdalen's noisy swinging door has been informally classified as a musical instrument in order to bring it within the prohibition on playing musical instruments at certain hours.

[15] *Estate of Sparks*. When the New York courts will adopt such an approach and when instead they will take the course famously exemplified by *Riggs v. Palmer* takes us deep into the interstices and intricacies of the New York law of wills and estates (Olenn 2001).

existit—in a fiction of law, equity always exists (Jowitt and Walsh 1959, vol. 1, p. 799).

For a third and final example, consider the 2007 United Kingdom case of *R(Robinson) v. Torridge District Council.*[16] Robinson's land had been flooded and damaged as a result of a bridge whose pilings had constricted the flow of water, thus producing the flooding. His action against the relevant authorities would have been sound had their actions involved failing to remedy a watercourse "so choked or silted up as to obstruct or impede the proper flow of water," and in order to allow Robinson his relief the court concluded that the blockage caused by the bridge was to be treated as having "choked" the watercourse, even though it plainly had not done so according to any of the definitions of what it is to choke a watercourse, definitions consistent with the statute's reference to "choked or silted up." But the false re-description of the problem enabled Robinson to recover, and still again a legal fiction—which is in actuality a fiction of fact and not a fiction of law is employed as the instrument for producing an equitable outcome, and an instrument seemingly preferable for many judges to the alternatives either of producing an unjust result or of appearing to rewrite a statute.

The examples in the previous section all involved particular (and more or less unique) facts in particular cases, but it is even more common for fictions of this type to be employed with reference to categories of events that a court may perceive to be mis-treated or non-treated by the relevant legal rule. It is in some sense a fiction to treat a corporation as a person, for example, by virtue of the simple fact that corporations are not people according to any standard understanding of what a person is. But because there were perceived numerous reasons to treat corporations *as if* they were people, the fiction that corporations were people developed and was allowed to flourish (Schane 1987).[17]

Such categorial, rather than particularized, legal fictions abound, in much the same form as the fiction of corporate personality, and thus we see implied contracts, which treat non-contracts as contracts (Stone 1968, pp. 260–261), the rise of the doctrine of ejectment, which allowed English courts to try the title to land even though no one had been ejected from anything by anyone (Langbein et al. 2009, p. 252), the rule declaring illiterate males to be members of the clergy in order to fall within the law granting the benefit of clergy only to literate males (Langbein et al. 2009, pp. 621–622), the legal rule declaring children who are trespassers to be invitees even under circumstances in which they have decidedly not been invited (Fuller 1967, p. 66), court decisions concluding that someone will be deemed to have notice of some event even when they did not (*Jones v. Flowers*, 2006), and the American constitutional doctrine that provides that a citizen of his own state is

[16] The litigation and its surrounding jurisprudential issues are engagingly described in Munday (2008).

[17] The example is complicated, because, as I explore in Sect. IV, the idea of a corporation and the word "corporation" may be constituted by law, having no pre-legal or extra-legal meaning. To the extent that this is so, then there is nothing fictional about treating a corporation as if it were a natural person, at least for some purposes, and in this respect the status of the word "corporation" is legally-constituted in a way that the status of the word "Minorca," for example, is not.

a citizen of "another" state, thereby extending the jurisdictional bar in the Eleventh Amendment beyond its literal meaning in order to produce an internally consistent doctrine about when citizens could use federal courts to sue state entities (*Monaco v. Mississippi* 1934).

In none of these instances is there the kind of deception that is normally associated with lying, and indeed the characteristic way of differentiating the fiction from the lie, both in law and elsewhere, is with the observation that fiction is typically known to be untrue, where the lie is in attempt to pass of falsity as truth to those who are unaware that some statement is untrue. But if legal fictions are known to be fictional, then why are they used? One answer to this question, suggested above, lies in the word "deem," which is sometimes used in this context and sometimes assumed even when it is not explicit. To say that a bird is deemed to be a "beast," even though it is not,[18] or that the husband of the mother of a child is deemed to be the father even when he is not, is simply to say that something that something that is not an *X* will be deemed to be an *X*—will be treated as if it were an *X*—because the reasons for treating *X* in manner *m* apply as well to some non-*X*s, which will consequently be treated in the same way.

Although there is nothing mysterious about such a process, and although in important ways it relates to the use of presumptions discussed above, it remains slightly mysterious, especially in common-law decision-making where judicial law-making is (more or less) accepted, why the fiction of the not-*X* being taken to be an *X* is the preferred course rather than the straightforward declaration that this non-*X*, albeit a non-*X*, will be treated in the same way as an *X* because the reasons for treating *X* in such-and-such a way apply to some non-*X*s as well. But there seem to be two justifications for such a circuitous, albeit not deceptive, approach. One is that in the case of interpreting a statute, as opposed to modifying or extending a common law rule, the circuitous approach of the legal fiction appears to avoid a direct judicial rewriting of a legislatively enacted statute and thus, as discussed above, may seem more legitimate or more politically palatable, even though the consequences are exactly the same in the particular case, and often substantially the same even for future cases. And the other justification is captured by the familiar adage that the law is a "seamless web" (Maitland 1898, p. 13; Solum 2011). Legal rules typically exist as part of an interlocking network of other rules, and so there may well be times when changing one rule will have indirect effects on other rules in ways that simply misapplying rules will not.

Yet although there may be justifications for a circuitous approach, and although there is no genuine deception in the typical use of a legal fiction, the basic theme is the same—the use of a legal fiction to produce what seems to be the right result as a matter of justice, equity, or policy when the literal or non-fictional application of an existing rule would produce injustice, inequity, or bad policy.

---

[18] See *Westley v. Fulewelle*, as described in Moglen (1990).

6.4 IV

But now matters become more complex. In order for a legal rule to have the capacity to produce a legally poor outcome that a legal actor would be legitimately empowered to correct, it must be the case that the legally poor outcome is produced by virtue of understanding in non-legal terms the language that is used within the law. That this is so becomes clear when we examine the process of extending an intrinsically legal term. Consider, for example, the process by which a court could conclude that a "trust" was created even absent an intention on the part of some agent to do so. It is true that the law may previously have treated trusts as requiring a certain kind of intent, but it is also true that a trust is itself a creature of the law. Putting aside for the moment questions about which legal actors have the power to change the law, it seems no affront to truth for the legal system to find a trust to have existed even absent intent, and that is because the truth of whether some instrument is or is not a trust is itself entirely a legal matter. "Trust" is *defined* by the law, and the truth or falsity of something being subsumed by that term is consequently similarly and necessarily a legal matter.

The point is obvious with respect to trusts and the word "trust," and perhaps even more obvious for terms that simply do not have any non-legal meanings at all—but the question is whether the same form of analysis holds true for all language that is used within and by the law (Morrison 1989). That is, is *all* language used in the law technical in just the same way that "trust" is, such that all language has a legal meaning when used in law? Does the legal use of *any* language transform that language into legal language? Consider, for example, Lon Fuller's (not entirely clear) suggestion with reference to H.L.A. Hart's famous "no vehicles in the park" example that perhaps Fuller's hypothetical military truck used as a war memorial was not a vehicle at all, at least for purposes of the law and when the word "vehicle" was used in a legal rule (Fuller 1958, pp. 655–656; Moore 1981, 1985). The man on the Clapham omnibus may think of the truck as a vehicle, but when the word "vehicle" is incorporated within a legal rule and subject to interpretation by legal officials, then it may be that *vehicle* becomes *vehicle'*, where *vehicle'*, superficial appearances to the contrary, is a legal term of art in just the way that "trust" is a legal term of art with a characteristically legal meaning. And if this is so, then saying that the military truck is not a vehicle, assuming it would be absurd to apply the "no vehicles in the park" regulation to it, is no longer false. Similarly, the conclusion that Minorca is part of London would no longer be false, because the London of a statute regulating the jurisdiction of the courts would not necessarily be the London of the cartographers.

Propositions are creatures of language, and thus for a proposition to be false there must be a way in which reality diverges from the meaning of the proposition. But if all legal propositions incorporate the full set of goals of a legal system, and if among those goals is the power of the interpreter—typically the judge—to achieve a just result, then the meaning of *vehicle'* incorporates that power, and when a judge concludes that a military truck in the park is not a *vehicle'* she is not saying anything false at all, and thus not employing a fiction. This seems to be what Fuller was claiming, and it is not entirely implausible. Indeed, when Fuller (1967, pp. 23–27) maintained that law progresses to the extent that more of its terms become technical terms and are understood as technical terms , and when the contracts scholar and legal theorist Edwin Patterson (1953) noted that much confusion could be eliminated were all legal concepts to have "pure" legal labels,[19] they recognized the way in which language in legal context might solely by virtue of the legal context take on a meaning different from the meaning that the same words would have in non-legal contexts. And if that is so, then perhaps every word in the law necessarily has a legal and not ordinary meaning, and then perhaps as well every legal meaning incorporates the norms and goals of the legal system. If, with Fuller for example, one believes that law necessarily must avoid absurd constructions of rules inconsistent with the purposes lying behind those rules, then it is only a short step to the conclusion that *vehicle'*, the legal term, incorporates the goal of avoiding the non-absurd result, and thus a truck used as a war memorial, even though clearly a *vehicle*, is simply not a *vehicle'* at all.

Yet although Fuller's view is not entirely implausible, it is inconsistent with the very idea that there *is* something that we call a legal fiction. That is, the very idea of a legal fiction presupposes that *not* all legal language is technical language. Legal fictions exist by virtue of legal terms having non-legal meanings, such that a non-standard application of that meaning is false, regardless of the justifications for the falsity. And of course if law is to serve its function of guiding ordinary folk, the meaning of some or most of its terms must be in the language that those ordinary folk use and understand. Fuller's (1949, pp 631–637) almost offhand suggestion that the military truck was not a vehicle at all was offhand and tentative for a reason, for Fuller at other times and in other places fully recognized that without some connection between legal language and ordinary language, and thus between legal truth and truth *simplicter*, law could not achieve its primary purposes at all.

6.5 V

The examination of legal fictions, therefore, is not simply an examination of an epiphenomenal and largely quaint feature of legal reasoning. Rather, it is an entry into the difficult problem of legal truth. Fictions are, by definition, false, and thus a legal fiction is a legal falsehood. But for there to be legal falsehoods there must be actual or potential divergence between what the law *says* and what the law or some legal actor should *do*. Accordingly, the very idea of a legal fiction presupposes a view of legal truth that makes legal truth not entirely discontinuous with truth *simpliciter*, and such a view about the relationship between legal truth and truth in turn presupposes a view of legal language such that legal language is not, and cannot be, entirely sui generis in all of its words, all of its sentences, and all of its meanings.

---

[19] A proposal he recognized as unrealistic.

That legal language cannot be understood as entirely technical is consistent with the view that legal language cannot be understood in such a way that the all-things-considered best outcome can be collapsed into the meaning of legal language. Legal fictions are thus parasitic on a gap between legal language and all-things-considered sound results. Without this gap, we would be unable to understand the idea of a legal rule, and unable to understand the way in which law, however technical it may at times get, must remain tethered to the language in which it is written, and thus tethered to the language of the linguistic community in which the legal system exists. Were it otherwise, there would be no need for law. More importantly, were it otherwise, there could be no legal truth, no legal falsity, and, quite simply, no possibility of law at all.[20]

References

Alexander, Larry, and Frederick Schauer. 2009. Rules of recognition, constitutional controversies, and the dizzying dependence of law on acceptance. In *The rule of recognition and the US constitution,* ed. Matthew D. Adler and Kenneth Einar Himma, 175–192. New York: Oxford University Press.

Aristotle. 1977. *Nicomachean ethics*. Trans.: J. A. K. Thomson. Harmondsworth: Penguin.

Atiyah, P. S., and R. S. Summers. 1987. *Form and substance in Anglo-American law: A comparative study in legal reasoning, legal theory and legal institutions*. Oxford: Clarendon Press.

Bentham, Jeremy. 1962. *The works of Jeremy Bentham,* ed. J. Bowring. London: Russell & Russell.

Blackstone, William. 1768. *Commentaries on the laws*. vol. 3. London.

Bindreiter, Uta. 2002. *Why Grundnorm? A treatise on the implications of Kelsen's doctrine*. The Hague: Kluwer.

Calabresi, Guido. 1982. *A common law for the age of statutes*. Cambridge: Harvard University Press.

Cheng, Kai-Yuan. 2011. A new look at the problem of rule-following: A generic perspective. *Philosophical Studies* 155:1–21.

Cicero. 2001. *De Oratore*. Trans.: J. M. May and J. Wisse. Oxford: Oxford University Press.

de Tourtolon, Pierre. 1922. *Philosophy in the development of law*. Trans.: Martha McC. Read. New York: Macmillan.

Del Mar, Maksymilian. 2014. Legal fictions and legal change in the common law tradition. In *Legal fictions in theory and practice,* ed. Maksymilian Del Mar and William Twining. Dordrecht: Springer.

Estate of Sparks 15 N.Y.S.2d 926 (Surr. Ct.) (1939)

Frank, Jerome. 1930. *Law and the modern mind.* New York: Brentano's Publishers.

Frier, Bruce W. 1985. *The rise of the Roman jurists: Studies in Cicero's Pro Caecina*. Princeton: Princeton University Press.

Fuller, Lon L. 1949. The case of the Speluncean explorers. *Harvard Law Review* 62:616–645.

[20] This paper was prepared for the Project on Truth and Law of the Instituto Tecnológico Autónomo de México (ITAM), and for the Project's colloquium in Mexico City in October, 2011. I am grateful for helpful comments from Jorge Cerdio, Raymundo Gama, German Sucar, William Swadling, and Michael Wells. I have also benefited from the discussion when earlier versions of this paper were presented at the University of Girona, the University of Virginia, and the University of Notre Dame.

Fuller, Lon L. 1958. Positivism and fidelity to law—A reply to professor Hart. *Harvard Law Review* 71:630–661.
Fuller, Lon L. 1967. *Legal fictions*. Stanford: Stanford University Press.
Glennon, Theresa. 2000. Somebody's child: Evaluating the erosion of the marital presumption of paternity. *West Virginia Law Review* 102:547–605.
Green, Michael Steven. 2009. Kelsen, quietism, and the rule of recognition. In *The rule of recognition and the US constitution,* ed. Matthew D. Adler and Kenneth Einar Himma, 351–378. New York: Oxford University Press.
Gustafsson, Hakan. 2010. Fiction of law. *Rechtstheorie* 41:319–363.
Guy, J. A. 1985. *Christopher St. German on chancery and statute*. London: Selden Society.
Handy, Rollo. 1967. Hans Vaihinger. In *Encyclopedia of philosophy*. vol. 8, 221–224. New York: Macmillan.
Harmon, Louise. 2002. Falling off the vine: Legal fictions and the doctrine of substituted judgment. *Yale Law Journal* 100:1–71.
Hart, H. L. A. 1958. Positivism and the separation of law and morals. *Harvard Law Review* 71:593–629.
Hart, H. L. A. 2012. *The concept of law,* ed. Penelope A. Bulloch, Joseph Raz, and Leslie Green. 3rd ed. Oxford: Clarendon Press.
Jones v. Flowers 547 US 220 (2006)
Jowitt, Earl, and Clifford Walsh. 1959. *The dictionary of English law*. London: Sweet & Maxwell.
Kelsen, Hans. 1919. Zur Theorie der Juristischen Fiktonen: Mit besonders Berücksichtigung von Vaihingers Philosophie des Als Ob. *Annalen der Philosophie* 1:630–658.
Kelsen, Hans. 1960. *Reine Rechtslehre*. Vienna: Franz Deuticke.
Kelsen, Hans. 1986. The function of the constitution. In *Essays On Kelsen,* ed. Richard Tur and William Twining. Oxford: Oxford University Press.
Kelsen, Hams. 1991. *General theory of norms*. Trans.: Michael Hartney. Oxford: Clarendon Press.
Kelsen, Hans. 1992. *Introduction to the problems of legal theory: A translation of the first edition of the Reine Rechtslehre or pure theory of law*. Trans. Bonnie Litschewski Paulson and Stanley L. Paulson. Oxford: Clarendon Press.
Knauer, Nancy J. 2010. Legal fictions and juristic truth. *St. Thomas Law Review* 23:1–48.
Langbein, John H., Renée Lettow Lerner, and Bruce P. Smith. 2009. *History of the common law*. New York: Aspen.
Laycock, Douglas. 1993. The triumph of equity. *Law & Contemporary Problems* 56:53–82.
Leslie, Sara-Jane. 2008. Generics: Cognition and acquisition. *Philosophical Review* 117:1–47.
Maine, Henry Sumner. 1861. *Ancient law: Its connection with the early history of society, and its relation to modern ideals.* London: John Murray.
Maitland, Frederic William. 1898. A prologue to a history of English law. *Law Quarterly Review* 14:13–33.
Moglen, Eben. 1990. Legal fictions and common law legal theory: Some historical reflections. *Tel Aviv University Studies in Law* 10:33–62.
Monaco v. Mississippi 292 US 313 (1934)
Moore, Michael. 1981. The semantics of judging. *Southern California Law Review* 54:151–294.
Moore, Michael. 1985. A natural law theory of interpretation. *Southern California Law Review* 58:277–398.
Morrison, Mary Jane. 1989. Excursions into the nature of legal language. *Cleveland State Law Review* 37:271–316.
Mostyn v. Fabrigas 1 Cowp. 161, 98 Eng. Rep. 1021 (K.B.) (Mansfield, L.J.) (1774)
Munday, Roderick. 2008. The bridge that choked a watercourse, or repetitive dictionary disorder. *Statute Law Review* 29:26–44.
Ogden, C. K. 1932. *Bentham's theory of fictions*. New York: Harcourt, Brace & Co.
Olenn, Julie J. 2001. "Til death do us part": New York's Slayer rule and in re estates of covert. *Buffalo Law Review* 49:1341–1378.
Olivier, Pierre J. J. 1975. *Legal fictions in practice and legal science*. Rotterdam: Rotterdam University Press.

Patterson, Edwin W. (c.). 1953. Manuscript of Chapter 3 of *The law of contracts* (unpublished, available in the archives of the Columbia Law School Library).

Paulson, Stanley L. 1992a. Kelsen's legal theory: The final round. *Oxford Journal of Legal Studies* 12:265–274.

Paulson, Stanley L. 1992b. The neo-Kantian dimension of Kelsen's pure theory of law. *Oxford Journal of Legal Studies* 12:311–332.

Quinn, Michael. 2014. Fuller on legal fictions: A benthamic perspective. In *Legal fictions in theory and practice,* ed. Maksymilian Del Mar and William Twining. Dordrecht: Springer.

Raz, Joseph. 1979. Kelsen's theory of the basic norm. In *The authority of law: Essays on law and morality*, 122–145. Oxford: Clarendon Press.

Riggs v. Palmer 22 N.E. 188 (N.Y.) (1889)

R(Robinson) v. Torridge District Council (2007) W.L.E. 871; [2006] 877 (Admin.)

Ross, Alf. 1969. Legal fictions. In *Law, reason and justice: Essays in legal philosophy,* ed. Graham Hughes. New York: New York University Press.

Russell, Bertrand. 1905. On denoting. *Mind* 14:479–493.

Schane, Sanford A. 1987. The corporation is a person: The language of a legal fiction. *Tulane Law Review* 61:563–614.

Schauer, Frederick. 1988. Formalism. *Yale Law Journal* 97:509–548.

Schauer, Frederick. 1991. *Playing by the rules: A philosophical examination of rule-based decision-making in law and in life*. Oxford: Clarendon Press.

Schauer, Frederick. 2003. *Profiles, probabilities, and stereotypes*. Cambridge: Harvard University Press.

Schauer, Frederick. 2008. A critical guide to vehicles in the park. *New York University Law Review* 83:1109–1134.

Schauer, Frederick. 2009. *Thinking like a lawyer: A new introduction to legal reasoning*. Cambridge: Harvard University Press.

Schofield, Philip. 2006. *Utility and democracy: The political thought of Jeremy Bentham*. Oxford: Oxford University Press.

Seidel, August., ed. 1932. *Die Philosophie des Als Ob und Das Leben*. Berlin: Reuther & Reichard.

Smith, Jeremiah. 1917. Surviving fictions. *Yale Law Journal* 27:147–166, 317–329.

Smith, Peter J. 2007. New legal fictions. *Georgetown Law Journal* 95:1435–1495.

Solum, Lawrence. 1994. Equity and the rule of law. In *The rule of law: NOMOS XXXVI,* ed. Ian Shapiro, 120–147. New York: New York University Press.

Solum, Lawrence. 2011. The law is a seamless web. Legal theory lexicon. http://lsolum.typepad.com/legaltheory/. Accessed 31 July 2011.

Stewart, Iain. 1980. The basic norm as fiction. *Juridical Review* 25:199–224.

Stone, Julius. 1968. *Legal system and lawyers' reasonings*. Sydney: Maitland.

Strawson, P. F. 1952. *Introduction to logical theory*. London: Methuen.

Swadling, William. 2008. Explaining resulting trusts. *Law Quarterly Review* 124:72–102.

Tur, Richard. 1986. The Kelsenian enterprise. In *Essays on Kelsen,* ed. Richard Tur and William Twining, 149–183. Oxford: Clarendon Press.

Vaihinger, Hans. 1911. *Die Philosophie des Als Ob*. Berlin: Reuther & Reichard.

Vaihinger, Hans. 1924. *The philosophy of "as if": A system of theoretical, practical and religious fictions in mankind*. Trans.: C. K. Ogden. London: Routledge.

von Jhering, Rudolf. 1914. *Law as a means to an end*. Trans.: Isaac Husic. Boston: Boston Book Company.

von Jhering, Rudolf. 1923. *Geist des römischen Rechts auf den verscheidenen Studen der Entwicklung*, 7th ed. Leipzig: Breitkopf & Hartel.

Westley v. Fulewelle Y.B. Mich. 3 Edw.II pl. 50, p. 149 (1309) (Selden Soc.)

Chapter 7
Legal Fictions and the Limits of Legal Language

Karen Petroski

Abstract Since Lon Fuller published his 1930 trilogy of essays on the topic, students of the legal fiction have focused on identifying additional examples of fictions or challenging Fuller's classic taxonomy. But Fuller did more in these essays than propose a definition and a classification system; he also argued that legal fictions are examples of a more general phenomenon found in many systems of specialized language usage. Drawing on work done in the intervening decades on related issues outside the law, this chapter develops this insight in new directions, seeking to understand in more detail one of Fuller's principal concerns: the points at which legal language stops communicating, points that may shift over time but will never completely disappear. The analysis indicates that the currently prevailing understanding of legal fictions as, in essence, consciously counterfactual propositions is historically contingent and incomplete; that legal writers have generally used the "legal fiction" label to signal those writers' sense of the futility of further justification to a non-legal audience (even when they are using the term in a justification likely to be read only by a legal audience); and, contrary to the assumptions of many post-Fuller theorists, that the boundaries of the legal vocabularies recognized as self-justifying may have become less distinct over the past century.

7.1 Introduction

Ever since Lon Fuller published his trilogy of essays on legal fictions in 1930 (Fuller 1930a, b, c), students of the topic have focused on identifying additional examples of fictions that match or challenge Fuller's classic definitions and taxonomy. But Fuller did more in these essays than propose a definition and examples. He also explicitly identified the legal fiction as a linguistic phenomenon and extensively discussed its relation to legal facts, on the one hand, and scientific fictions and facts,

A version of this chapter was previously published as 'Legal Fictions and the Limits of Legal Language' (2013) 4 *International Journal of Law in Context* 485–505.

K. Petroski (✉)
Saint Louis University School of Law, 100 N. Tucker Blvd.,
Saint Louis, MO 63116, USA
e-mail: kpetrosk@slu.edu

M. Del Mar, W. Twining (eds.), *Legal Fictions in Theory and Practice*,
Law and Philosophy Library 110, DOI 10.1007/978-3-319-09232-4_7

on the other. In Fuller's account, these relations are shaped by continuous processes of linguistic and conceptual conventionalization. Since Fuller's time, scholars in a variety of fields have developed new ways of studying such processes. Drawing on these advances, this paper explores some of the less-examined aspects of Fuller's account, presenting a twenty-first-century understanding of the legal fiction consistent with Fuller's but departing from the classic formulation familiar to most of his followers.

Explaining both the standard twentieth-century approach to the topic and the overlooked aspects of Fuller's account, Part 7.2 below reviews the 1930 essays and the limits of their extensions by commentators. Part 7.3 then briefly introduces some recent work in the scholarly analysis of specialized discourse systems. This work does not acknowledge Fuller as a forebear, but it does systematically examine linguistic and conceptual conventionalization in specialized communities. Part 7.4 examines what these kinds of analysis, applied to some of the issues that directly concerned Fuller, suggest about the ways lawyers, judges, and legal scholars communicate about legal fictions and facts. The analyses indicate that the currently prevailing understanding of legal fictions as, in essence, consciously counterfactual propositions is historically contingent and incomplete; that legal writers seem generally, and increasingly over time, to have used the "legal fiction" label to signal their sense of the futility of further justification to a non-legal audience (even when they are using the term in a justification likely to be read only by a legal audience); and, contrary to the assumptions of many post-Fuller theorists, that the boundaries of the legal vocabularies recognized as self-justifying may have become less distinct over the past century.

7.2 Fuller on Legal Fictions

Fuller's trilogy has been the starting point for most subsequent theoretical discussions of the legal fiction (e.g., Campbell 1983, p. 341; Soifer 1986, pp. 875–876 and n. 13; Harmon 1990, pp. 2, 14; Note 2002, p. 2229; Knauer 2010, p. 1 n. 1). Each of his three essays focuses on a different topic: the first on definition, the second on explanation and taxonomy, and the third on the philosophical work of Hans Vaihinger. Post-Fuller theorists of the legal fiction have mostly expanded on the topics and approach of the first two essays; they have not seemed to know what to do with the third. But the issues Fuller addressed in that third essay remain at least as vital as his concerns with definition and classification.

7.2.1 The Allure of Counterfactuality and Taxonomy

In his first essay, Fuller distinguishes the legal fiction, as a type of proposition, from other types of non-truthful propositions. More generally, he defines the legal fiction as a particular type of language usage. His second essay moves from definition to an exploration of the reasons fictions exist; he proceeds largely by examining the motivations for the use of fictions, and this examination becomes a taxonomy of types of legal fiction. Subsequent theorists have been drawn more to the first than to the second of Fuller's definitions (conceiving the fiction as a type of proposition), and they have focused more on his taxonomy than on his effort to explain the phenomenon. (As discussed further in the next Part, theorists have largely remained silent about Fuller's third essay.)

Fuller's differentiation of legal fictions from other types of statement, including "truthful statement[s], ... lie[s], ... [and] erroneous conclusion[s]," is perhaps the best-known aspect of all of his work on the topic (Fuller 1930a, p. 366). Positively, Fuller defines a legal fiction as "either, (1) a statement propounded with a complete or partial consciousness of its falsity, or (2) a false statement recognized as having utility" (p. 369). This definition of legal fictions as, centrally, counterfactual propositions have been the nearly universal starting point for later work on legal fictions, even when that work proposes refinements on Fuller's definition.[1]

Most of those who accept Fuller's identification of legal fictions as "statements" also accept his underlying assumption about the necessarily linguistic nature of legal fictions (usually, however, without discussing this premise in any detail):[2]

> Anyone who has thought about the legal fiction must be aware that it presents an illumination of the all-pervading power of the word ... [W]e are here in contact with the mysterious influence exercised by names and symbols. In that sense the fiction is a linguistic phenomenon ... [T]he inaccuracy of a statement must be judged with reference to the standards of language usage. Simple as this truth is, nothing has so obscured the subject of legal fictions as the persistent failure to recognize it. (p. 371)

Fuller's first essay is full of other references to legal fictions' status as "linguistic phenomen[a]" (see, e.g., pp. 373–375, 377–379, 384–386, 389). In this he follows (without citing or discussing) Bentham, who similarly regarded the legal fiction as a special form of the linguistic fiction, itself a special form of the linguistic abstraction (Ogden 1932).[3] But unlike Bentham, Fuller emphasizes the constructive function of legal fictions; according to Fuller, they exist at least partly because of "the impulse to keep the form of the law persuasive" (Fuller 1930a, p. 387).[4] Thus, according to Fuller, fictions as counterfactual propositions are rhetorical devices for persuasion or self-persuasion.

---

[1] Jeremy Bentham's criticism of fictions in law focused on a similar subcategory of counterfactual propositions, as Michael Quinn explains in his contribution to this volume (Chap. 4).

[2] Many commentators thus, explicitly or implicitly, focus on the propositional content of such statements, rather than on their status and features as statements (e.g., Campbell 1983; see also Del Mar, this volume, Chap. 11). One exception is Louise Harmon, who recognized that "Fuller was the first writer on the subject to treat the legal fiction as a linguistic phenomenon" (Harmon 1990, p. 14; see also Soifer 1986, p. 915).

[3] Arguably, this characterization oversimplifies Bentham's attitude toward the function of language (see Quinn, this volume, Chap. 4); still, Bentham explored the relation of fictions to communication in much greater detail than subsequent writers have.

[4] This impulse "is frequently the impulse to preserve a form of statement which will make the law acceptable to those who do not have the time or the capacity for understanding reasons which are not obvious—and this class sometimes includes the author of the statement himself" (Fuller 1930a, pp. 382–383; see also pp. 363–364, 380).

Fuller's second essay more systematically explores the motivations for using legal fictions (Fuller 1930b, pp. 517–524, 537–538 and n. 147, 539; see also Fuller 1930c, pp. 887, 903). As Fuller enumerates these motivations, his explanation becomes a typology: he identifies "exploratory" (Fuller 1930b, pp. 527–528), "emotive" (p. 517), "expository" (p. 518), "descriptive" (p. 537), "historical" (p. 538 n. 147), and "apologetic or merciful" (p. 539) fictions, among others. The classifying focus of this essay has also become a model for the work of later theorists.[5] Virtually every student of the legal fiction since Fuller has emphasized either Fuller's definitional formulations, his enumeration of types of fiction, or both.

The variations among later theoretical discussions of legal fictions owe more to differences in their authors' disciplinary affiliation and shifts in academic fashion than to any fundamental reconsideration of Fuller's study. Work in the 1980s and 1990s tended toward the interdisciplinary, while more recent American legal scholarship has become increasingly doctrinally focused and critical of the legal use of fictions.[6] A good example of scholarship during the earlier period is Kenneth Campbell's philosophically informed 1983 examination of Fuller's essays (Campbell 1983). Campbell acknowledges that Fuller saw legal fictions as intimately related to the legal recognition of "facts"—also a matter of legal language usage (Campbell 1983, p. 359)[7]—but explicitly disavows any desire to examine "lawyers' linguistic practices" (p. 341; see also Chap. 11). Although he does characterize the legal fiction as a type of language usage, Campbell is concerned only with the philosophical implications of this insight.[8] Campbell describes fictions as "means of changing the application of the law by relying on a tension between two classifications of fact" (Campbell 1983, p. 339)—one of the functions highlighted by Fuller—but like Fuller, he does not examine in detail how such "classifications of fact" come to exist or to differ.

Many later writers have focused on demonstrating the continued operation of legal fictions by identifying examples not considered by Fuller. Up to the mid-2000s, commentators tended to stress the analogies between legal fiction and "fiction" in a more everyday sense, often taking a humanistic approach. In a 1986 essay, for example, Aviam Soifer disavowed any desire to present a definitive taxonomy (Soifer

[5] The subject of Fuller's third essay, Hans Vaihinger, shared the taxonomizing impulse, as the discussion below explains.

[6] Citations to Fuller's essays and to the book collecting them that was published in 1967 have increased in recent decades. For instance, one or more of the essays have been cited a total of 111 times in subsequent articles indexed in Hein Online, while the book has been cited 249 times. (Searches run March 21, 2012.)

[7] Campbell writes, "Fictions are created by rules of law, but the relevant rules govern matters which the law itself regards as questions of fact. The fiction arises from the content of the rule being false when regarded as a question of fact according to non-legal classifications" (p. 359).

[8] Campbell concludes that legal fictions "are used to give any rule of law a wider, or narrower, ambit than it would have if applied non-fictitiously, while at the same time preserving the rule's original form and the meaning of its terms. The change occurs by creating a supplementary rule in which $fact_L$, which is an antecedent in the principal rule, is not equivalent to $fact_N$. It is the discrepancy between the two classifications which not only explains what fictions are, but why they are so useful … Fictions are necessarily about changes in the application of the law" (p. 365).

1986, p. 873), but followed a catalog approach anyway, presenting "a few leading fictions, both literary and legal, to suggest and assess a continuum in law and literature" (p. 873).[9] In a 1990 article, Louise Harmon likewise declared her desire to reestablish the importance of the legal fiction as a topic on the "jurisprudential agenda" (Harmon 1990, p. 1) through analysis of "the history of a particular legal fiction, the doctrine of substituted judgment" (pp. 16, 22). The author of a 2002 Harvard Law Review Note similarly argued that the "debate over the legal fiction should be reawakened"; this author aimed "to prevent the more modern conceptions of the legal fiction from being unfairly stigmatized and dismissed as were their earlier counterparts" (Note 2002, p. 2228).

Over the past decade, work on legal fictions has become more doctrinal and critical, but it continues to identify Fuller as a starting point and to stress definition and classification. In a 2007 discussion of "new legal fictions," for instance, Peter Smith emphasizes the same counterfactuality that Fuller identified: "A judge deploys a new legal fiction when he relies in crafting a legal rule on a factual premise that is false or inaccurate" (Smith 2007, p. 1437). But Smith argues that Fuller's list was incomplete; a taxonomy of "new legal fictions" (pp. 1439–1440), Smith contends, is necessary to prevent abuse of these practices of accepted departure from factually accurate statement (pp. 1441).[10] In a response to Smith, Nancy Knauer has defended the utility of at least some legal fictions. Emphasizing definition rather than taxonomy, she concludes that most of the new legal fictions Smith identifies do not merit the label under Fuller's counterfactual definition: "Empirical legal errors, discredited regimes, and complex statutory schemes [Smith's 'new legal fictions'] are not classic legal fictions" (Knauer 2010, p. 49).[11]

Resolution of the debate over the status of the devices described by Smith is impossible without analysis of the assumptions underlying Fuller's definition of legal fictions as counterfactual propositions. These assumptions include the notion that there is a sense in which propositions can be true about the world, or "factual," as well as counterfactual; they thus also include assumptions about the nature of

[9] The fictions Soifer discusses include examples from literature and opinions of United States courts (pp. 883–905). Like Campbell, Soifer acknowledges the linguistic nature of fictions only briefly: "[W]e need fictions in and about law to challenge our nation's complacent faith in American continuity and progress. We need words in law to learn the sins as well as the glories of the past, to give voice to current conflicts, and to retell and recreate our own myths" (p. 873).

[10] Smith presents six such categories: (1) fictions "based on a misunderstanding or misreading of empirical reality"; (2) fictions needed as a result of "the law's general imperviousness to social science and change"; (3) fictions that serve as "devices, conscious or not, for concealing the fact that the judges are making normative choices in fashioning legal rules"; (4) fictions that serve as "devices for operationalizing legal theories"; (5) fictions that "serve functional goals and promote administrability in judicial process"; and (6) fictions that "serve a legitimating function" (pp. 1439–1440).

[11] Knauer writes, "Wrongly valued for their veracity, empirical legal errors are mistakes—not fictions. The discredited legal regimes of slavery and discovery … were not acknowledged to be false, despite being morally wrong. The complex statutory schemes are artificial legal frameworks replete with legal fictions, but the schemes themselves are neither demonstrably false nor commonly held to be false" (p. 49).

legal communication, and related assumptions about the extent to which propositions generated within a legal system can be factual in the same sense as non-legal propositions. No post-Fuller theorist of legal fictions has directly considered these issues, although some of the contributions to this volume do (see especially Chaps. 6 and 8). Neglect of these questions is consistent with a broader tendency in legal scholarship to avoid inquiring too directly into what makes a legal "fact" and the relationship of such "facts" to other aspects of legal discourse (e.g., Twining 2006, p. 15; Allen and Pardo 2002, p. 1770). The same tendency probably explains commentators' relative inattention to the subject of Fuller's third essay: the roles of fictions in science and law.

7.2.2 Fuller and Vaihinger: Fictions in Science and Law

Fuller's third essay focuses on Hans Vaihinger's general philosophy of fictions and on the functions of fictions in science (Vaihinger's main focus) and law (Fuller's).[12] Fuller's decision to devote a third of his overall discussion to these issues suggests that he considered it necessary to look beyond legal concepts and vocabularies, including to philosophical, scientific, and everyday discourse, to understand the dynamics, function, and potential risks of specifically *legal* fictions. Yet only one post-Fuller theorist has acknowledged the space Fuller devoted to these issues in his trilogy (Samek 1981).[13] As a result, the work of Vaihinger, as well as Fuller's position on the parallels between scientific and legal fictions, is little known to contemporary English-language theorists of the legal fiction.

Vaihinger was a German neo-Kantian philosopher who wrote the work for which he is best known, *The Philosophy of "As-If,"* in the late nineteenth century; the linguistic philosopher C.K. Ogden published an English translation in 1924,[14] but apart from Fuller's treatment, the work has since its translation received little English-language discussion.[15] Typical of his generation, Vaihinger constructed a syncretic, systematic theory drawing on contemporary trends in biological science, psychology, and transcendental philosophy; he called his theory "positivist idealism" or "idealist positivism" (Vaihinger 1924, p. xli). Vaihinger's central idea, building on Bentham's theory of fictions and paralleling some of the insights of

[12] Neither Vaihinger nor Fuller's discussion of him is mentioned by Campbell, Harmon, Smith, the author of the Harvard Law Review note, or Knauer. Soifer mentions Vaihinger only in referring readers to the discussion of Vaihinger in Samek (1981) (see Soifer 1986, p. 874 n. 9).

[13] Samek separately addresses the theories of fictions advanced by Bentham, Vaihinger, and Fuller and, in the section on Fuller, begins not with Fuller's definition and taxonomies but with Fuller's consideration of Vaihinger (Samek 1981, pp. 292–314). Samek identifies Vaihinger's most important advance over Bentham in theorizing fictions as his "Law of the Preponderance of the Means over the End," which Samek relabels "the meta phenomenon" (pp. 290–291, 300).

[14] Ogden also collected Jeremy Bentham's work on legal fictions in Ogden (1932).

[15] See above, note 12; another partial exception is Iser (1993, pp. 130–151).

then-contemporary American pragmatism,[16] was that human cognitive operations originate in the biological necessity of coping with an environment but are nevertheless inevitably "emancipated" from this instrumental function to become themselves the objects of cognitive operations (p. 15).[17] This process generates both abstraction and "fiction" (pp. xxix–xxx), which Vaihinger calls "'As if,' i.e. appearance, the consciously-false, [which] plays an enormous part in science, in world-philosophies and in life" (p. xli).

Vaihinger's exploration of these ideas runs to nearly 400 pages in the English translation. Half of the book focuses on the operation of fictionalizing in various spheres of human activity, particularly mathematics and the sciences (pp. 1–177). Vaihinger explains fictions in scientific and technical fields as devices for helping us to discover facts about reality.[18] And he describes "juristic fictions" as precisely analogous to such mathematical and scientific fictions as the concepts of zero, negative numbers, and infinity.[19] Fuller summarizes much of this information in his third essay on legal fictions. In particular, Fuller reiterates Vaihinger's point regarding the parallels between scientific and legal fictions:

> The contention that Vaihinger's philosophy has no useful application to the law proceeds upon the assumption that there is a fundamental difference between the methods of the law and those of the physical sciences. The substance of the argument consists in saying that Vaihinger develops his philosophy around the fictions of those sciences which are concerned with the discovery and description of the facts of external reality, while the task of the law is not to discover the 'facts' or 'laws' of nature, but to establish a set of rules for the conduct of human beings. (Fuller 1930c, p. 902)

But, Fuller continues, at least those legal fictions that "attempt to describe the 'nature of the law in general,'" or "jurisprudential fictions," "represent a precise parallel to the methods of the physical scientist," in that "[t]hey are attempts to reduce

[16] Fuller acknowledged this parallel, identifying Vaihinger's views as "similar[to] those of American Pragmatism" (Fuller 1930c, p. 879).

[17] Vaihinger regarded this development as a kind of law of nature (p. xxx), which Vaihinger dubbed the "Law of the Preponderance of the Means over the End": "It is a universal phenomenon of nature that means which serve a purpose often undergo a more complete development than is necessary for the attainment of their purpose. In this case, the means, according to the completeness of its self-development, can emancipate itself partly or wholly and become established as an end in itself (Law of the Preponderance of the Means over the End)" (pp. xliii, xlvi).

[18] To Vaihinger, such "facts" as the mean of a population, for example, are kinds of fiction (p. 23). Hans Kelsen's 1919 essay on Vaihinger, translated in this volume, also identifies this characteristic as central to Vaihinger's understanding of fictions (Chap. 1). Kelsen also anticipated Fuller's point regarding the parallel between such clarifying scientific fictions and "jurisprudential fictions," discussed in the text.

[19] He writes, for example, "[S]ince laws cannot include within their formulae all particular instances, certain special examples of an unusual nature are treated as if they belonged to them. Or else, because of some practical interest, an individual interest is brought under a general concept to which it does not really belong. Anyone conversant with the method of jurisprudence will easily understand how important this artifice is for legal practice. It is just as essential for law as for mathematics.… Apart from mathematics there is hardly any domain more suitable than law for the deduction of logical laws and their illustration, or the discovery of logical methods" (p. 33; see also pp. 44, 51).

a complex reality to a simple formula, and thus render it tractable to calculation" (p. 903). Moreover, Fuller also describes the more workaday "fictions of legal technique," such as "[t]he notions of a legal right and duty, of legal powers and liabilities, of legal personality," as "all … in the Vaihingerian sense, fictions, and … essentially similar to the concepts of the physical sciences" (p. 905).[20]

Fuller uses Vaihinger, then, to argue for the existence of basic similarities between legal fictions and other linguistic devices developed outside the law to manage social relations and interactions with a complex non-human world. Fuller does not see fictions as unique to the law; although they might take some legally specific forms, for Fuller, any special characteristics of legal fictions indicate not legal pathologies (as Bentham had maintained) (see Samek 1981, pp. 198–199; see also Chap. 4), but just the functions of those fictions in particular social and institutional settings. Fuller adds to Vaihinger's framework as well: Fuller's account is slightly more sensitive than Vaihinger's to the importance of communities of convention and practice for the existence, maintenance, and utility of fictions, as well as to the need for those within such communities to justify their activities to others, a need Fuller presents as a matter of "persuasion" in his first essay. In Fuller's view, legal fictions differ from other fictions mainly due to their generation within a specific community, that of legal practice and commentary; scientific and technical fictions result from parallel processes within different communities.

Unfortunately, post-Fuller theorists have not made much use of these points. Instead, they have virtually without exception adopted legal-doctrinal or analytic philosophical vocabularies to discuss the topic. They have, that is, participated "internally" in processes of conventionalization that Fuller's trilogy suggested could be fully grasped only from a partly "external" perspective. This self-limitation is not necessarily vicious. Among other things, it has kept the commentary on legal fictions comprehensible to others within the same discourse communities. But it has also left important implications of Fuller's theory unexplored.

The rest of this paper pursues some of these implications. Part II turns to a survey of some post-Fuller developments in the study of communities of linguistic convention, describing the approaches and findings of major late-twentieth-century work on the analysis of academic and professional discourse. Part III applies these approaches to two bodies of relevant professional discursive practice: first, the roughly 100 Supreme Court opinions that have used the "legal fiction" label, with a focus on the normative and persuasive function of the label in these sources; and, second, the 50-plus most-cited American law review articles on the subject of the legal use of scientific evidence.[21] These discussions make available insights inaccessible

[20] Michael Quinn discusses Bentham's treatment of the same category of "currency of law" fictions in his contribution to this volume (Chap. 4). For his part, Fuller, like Bentham, does acknowledge that not all legal fictions are of this variety: "[T]he fictions of emotional conservatism and of policy and apologetic and merciful fictions proceed from stresses in the judicial mind which, although probably not wholly unknown to the scientist, are nevertheless not an important factor in his mental life" (p. 906).

[21] Detailed summaries of the materials used by the author in these studies are available upon request.

to Fuller's previous commentators, suggesting, among other things, the limits of Fuller's counterfactual definition and some of the reasons for the necessarily ever-shifting shape and location of legal fictions in legal discourse.

7.3 The Possibilities of Discourse Analysis

In the late twentieth century, academic rhetoricians developed an approach to discourse analysis that incidentally investigated a number of issues Fuller had recognized as important, namely, the patterns of linguistic and technical convention that mark particular discursive communities as distinctive and that make their products available for use by others. This work deserves to be better known to legal scholars, since it is relevant not only to matters that interested Fuller, but also to many other legal topics.

7.3.1 The Study of Discourse Patterns

Over the past several decades, rhetoricians who teach and study writing across the curriculum or for professionals-in-training began to produce a cohesive body of studies of discourse patterns in nonfiction texts (e.g., Bazerman 1988; MacDonald 1994; Halliday 1973; Swales 1990). These scholars' pedagogical and scholarly interests drew them to practical, detailed analysis of the differences in discourse patterns between different academic and professional communities. As Charles Bazerman, a pioneer in the area, put it, the driving assumption in this work is that "[r]hetoric is ultimately a practical study offering people greater control over their symbolic activity" (1988, p. 6 n. 7).

The work tends to be highly interdisciplinary. Qualitatively, it continues the traditions of close reading and analysis developed in literary criticism, hermeneutics, cultural anthropology, social and intellectual history, the philosophies of language and science, and phenomenology. But it also examines material features of bodies of texts (as opposed to the single texts that tend to be the focus of close reading); sometimes this undertaking supports more quantitative approaches drawing on bibliometrics and citation analysis (techniques originally developed in information science fields), all considered in light of more general theories about the social and material setting of such practices, drawn from the sociology of knowledge and the professions, as well as psycho- and sociolinguistics and psychology.[22]

A few legal scholars have adopted similar approaches, especially to citation analysis, but legal scholars have not paid much attention to most of this work (see

[22] The large-scale, multi-text, historically sensitive scope of some discourse analysis is based on insights consistent with those presented by Maksymilian Del Mar in his contribution to this volume; discourse-analytic approaches could be ideal tools for the kind of diachronic inquiry he urges (Chap. 11).

Petroski 2012, pp. 368, 371, 374–378). The most analogous legal scholarship seeks, rather, to assess the influence of legal scholarship on legal decisionmaking outside the academy (e.g., Petherbridge and Schwartz 2011; Harner and Cantone 2011) or to advance the legal realist project of demystifying legal discourse (the most recent work on legal fictions discussed above tends to fall into this category). But the findings of discourse analysis also yield other possible paths of inquiry. The rest of this Part outlines some of these possibilities suggested by two influential works in this area: Charles Bazerman's 1988 study of the historical development and features of the scientific "experimental article" and Susan Peck MacDonald's 1994 extension of this work to the study of academic writing in the humanities and social sciences.

Bazerman's pioneering book characterizes academic scientific discourse as the primary product of a particular inherently social activity.[23] To Bazerman, "a[ny] community constitutes itself in developing its modes of regular discourse" (p. 79); this is true of both scientific and academic communities, whose members are devoted to the generation of discourse and in turn find their communities shaped by features of that discourse.[24] Historically, Bazerman traces how the social and publication structures of mid-eighteenth-century English scientific practice coalesced around a strategy of "exclusivity" rather than "inclusivity" (p. 136); how "empiricism" then developed as "a mode of persuasion" by which the private witnessing of empirical facts began to require special training to translate into explanations of experimental results (p. 140); how scientific articles subsequently increased in length and began citing other articles at higher rates, especially as article writers started integrating citations into their arguments as a kind of shorthand reference to complex concepts (p. 167); how the conventional grammar and syntax of experimental prose likewise changed in ways "suggest[ing the] increasing intellectual complexity" of the claims being made (p. 169); and, ultimately, how writing in social-scientific fields began to "imitat[e] the forms of argument developed within the natural sciences" (p. 257). In part, Bazerman bases these conclusions on analysis of the microstructures of scientific writing, including sentence structure as well as argument structure and content; these features affect and restrict what can be said and how, even though the acknowledged purpose of scientific discourse is "just simply to record the natural facts" (p. 14). We see scientific discourse as unproblematically fulfilling that purpose, Bazerman contends, partly because these microstructures are so familiar as to be invisible to us—but they were not always so. Bazerman does not explore the implications of his approach for legal discourse, but his concerns and general conclusions are completely consistent with Fuller's.

Although Bazerman's focus is on scientific writing, he does suggest that scholarly writing in the social sciences (pp. 257–288) and humanities (pp. 39–45) might

[23] Bazerman explains, "[T]he essential social purpose of the communities examined here is to produce statements of knowledge…. [T]ext production is the goal, and the activity cannot be understood without seeing the centrality of texts…. Regularized forms of writing are social institutions, interacting with other social institutions" (p. 22).

[24] It is true as well of legal and, more specifically, judicial common-law communities of discourse over time, as Maksymilian Del Mar explains in his contribution to this volume (Chap. 11).

differ from scientific writing in meaningful ways. Susan MacDonald has further explored some of these differences (MacDonald 1994, pp. 4–5, 7). Continuing Bazerman's inquiry into microstructures of communication, MacDonald examines "sentence-level differences in disciplinary knowledge-making" (pp. 147–169). The centerpiece of her analysis is a classification of grammatical sentence subjects[25] in academic writing from three disciplinary subfields of psychology, social history, and literary criticism and theory (pp. 56–70, 75–107, 109–144). This study shows, according to MacDonald, that writing in disciplines conventionally considered scientific or quasi-scientific, like psychology, contains a relatively greater number of abstract, "epistemic" sentence subjects (p. 160), suggesting "that psychologists place greater importance on cooperative disciplinary knowledge making than historians and literary academics" (p. 160) and that disciplines of this sort tend toward "disciplinary compactness," i.e., "progressive[]" "build[ing] upon the work of … predecessors," rather than reinvention of problems and solutions anew with each scholarly effort (pp. 25, 64–65). Literature scholarship, in contrast, has a "less epistemic focus" (p. 164) than academic writing from the other two subfields; literature scholarship includes more concrete, "phenomenal" grammatical subjects (p. 159). MacDonald surmises that this difference might be related both to literature scholars' almost exclusively textual subject matter[26] and to these scholars' relative lack of disciplinary community after the erosion of an early twentieth-century "gentlemanly tradition of politeness in [literary] scholarship" (p. 121).

Bazerman and MacDonald are just two among many academics with similar interests in language usage within specialized communities dedicated to the production of written material. The professional and academic legal communities share this dedication, as Fuller recognized. Many of the core features of academic writing, such as its presumed "transparency,"[27] are also present in professional legal writing (but see Mellinkoff (1962)). And like academic writing, legal writing is a central product of a professional community largely defined by its members' relationship to a tradition of publicly disseminated texts. More generally, the legal community

[25] Sentence subjects and themes are a traditional focus of English-language discourse analysis because they allow assessment of the referents, audience, and tone of discourse. MacDonald's classification system comprises two general categories: "phenomenal" ("the material the researcher studies") and "epistemic" ("the methods, conceptual tools, and previous research that the researcher brings to that material") (p. 157). Within the phenomenal category she differentiates among (1) "particulars" (e.g., particular individuals), (2) "groups" (e.g., "estate holders"), and (3) "attributes" (e.g., "emotional responsibility") (pp. 157–158). Within the epistemic category she differentiates between (4) "reasons" (e.g., "evidence" for a conclusion), (5) "research" (e.g., names or attributed findings of prior researchers), (6) "isms" (e.g., schools of academic thought), and (7) "audience" (e.g., "we") (pp. 157–158).

[26] MacDonald notes, for example, that "the humanities tend to be rooted in phenomena, data, or texts which are potentially worth knowing about for their own sake … and … tend to involve more intermediary generalizations—such as literary texts—between raw phenomena and generalization, thereby creating their own phenomenal layers" (pp. 35–36).

[27] As MacDonald notes, at least up to the final quarter of the twentieth century, academic writing tended to be regarded as a means only, not a subject of study in itself (p. 5). One could see the work of Bazerman and MacDonald as examining Vaihinger's Law of the Preponderance of the Means in operation. See supra note 17.

shares academic communities' goals of engaging in "socially negotiated inquiry" (MacDonald 1994, p. 7) and the making of "knowledge claims" (p. 9). It therefore makes sense to use discourse analysis to study the discourse of both judicial opinions and legal scholarship. Yet the types of discourse analysis done by Bazerman and MacDonald have been little noted by legal academics to date.[28]

7.3.2 How Studying Discourse Patterns can Advance Fuller's Project

One reason for the relative scholarly inattention to the microstructures of legal discourse might be the difficulty of locating this discourse precisely along the continuum of discourse modes proposed by Bazerman and MacDonald, which runs from the natural-scientific at one extreme, through the social-scientific, to the humanistic at the other extreme. Modern judicial opinions and legal briefs involve and depend on considerable "disciplinary compactness"; parenthetical cites to precedential opinions, as well as "string cites,"[29] epitomize this discursive characteristic. This feature of opinions and briefs makes them resemble academic writing in natural-science disciplines. On the other hand, legal opinions and briefs, like humanistic work, focus largely on texts considered as texts. Legal scholarship shares both of these features of opinions and briefs, and thus also resembles both natural-scientific and humanistic scholarship. So it is not immediately obvious where legal discourse fits within the schemes developed by discourse analysis.

This difficulty, however, does not make it impossible to study the microstructures of legal discourse. On the contrary, it suggests that such study might usefully advance both our understanding of the kinds of issues that concerned Fuller and our understanding of other specialized discourse communities. For example, we can test both Fuller's understanding of legal fiction as a species of linguistic convention and the prevailing understanding of the phrase as referring to counterfactual propositions by examining how and when judicial opinions have actually referred to parties' or their own statements as legal fictions. As Part III.A below explains, over the past two hundred years or so, justices of the United States Supreme Court have changed their patterns of such reference in some surprising ways. These changes suggest that the prevailing equation of legal fictions with counterfactual propositions may be too narrow; instead, it seems that judges most commonly use the phrase when they become aware of the futility of further justification to non-legal audiences.

[28] As of August 3, 2011, Bazerman's book had been cited in five law review articles according to Hein Online, five according to Westlaw (search run on "Shaping Written Knowledge"), MacDonald's book had been cited in one law review article according to Hein Online, one according to Westlaw (search run on "Professional Academic Writing"/p MacDonald).

[29] Heavily used in United States legal briefs and judicial opinions, string cites consist of an unelaborated list of authorities supporting a proposition; their use is often criticized (e.g., Cooney 2006, pp. 44–45).

The received "counterfactual" conception of the legal fiction suggests a dichotomy between properly factual and fictional propositions. On this understanding, legal discourse that relies on fictions would seem to be the antithesis of factual scientific discourse. Notably, however, Fuller did not make this argument. Rather, like Vaihinger, and anticipating the implications of Bazerman's work, Fuller argued that in certain ways the parallels between legal fictions and scientific discourse outnumber the differences. But both Vaihinger and Fuller considered legal and scientific discourse as distinct, nonoverlapping systems of communication. They did not directly consider what might happen when members of these different communities try to communicate with members of others, or to make use of the products of other communities' efforts. In legal writing, we can see this intersection of discourses most dramatically in the treatment of scientific information for purposes of dispute resolution. To investigate the legal treatment of "fact" in this sense, Part III.B looks at features of legal scholarship on the relations between scientific and legal discourse, analyzing shifts over time in the topics addressed, the assumed knowledge of readers, charges to readers, and grammatical subjects (see Bazerman 1988, p. 25). These shifts, like the changes in use of the term "legal fiction," show that the recognized boundaries of what is communicable in legal texts—even to scholarly audiences—have not only altered but become more indefinite over time.

7.4 Defining the Limits of Legal Language through Legal Fiction and Scientific Fact

7.4.1 The Functions of "Legal Fiction" in United States Supreme Court Opinions

Writers of United States Supreme Court opinions have consistently used the "legal fiction" term to mark claims that lie on the boundaries of what the writers perceive as justifiable to those outside the legal community's conventions. Their usage of the term also suggests that the types of claims perceived as difficult to justify to the non-specialist have themselves shifted over time. These conclusions are based on a study of 120 Supreme Court opinions in which the phrase "legal fiction" has appeared (a total of 142 uses of the term).[30] The study traced shifts in the frequency with which the term has been used, as well as shifts in what it has been used to

[30] These appearances include references in reports of arguments drafted by reporters (in early opinions), but exclude references to "fictions" alone. I analyzed six features of each reference: (1) the semantic referent of each one; (2) the grammatical subject of each sentence or independent clause containing the phrase; (3) the valence attached to the concept in each reference (positive, negative, or neutral); (4) whether the author of each reference accepted the fiction (i.e., endorsed it as a ground for further conclusions) or rejected it; (5) whether each reference was quoted from an earlier text or originated with the author; and (6) the type of opinion (majority, concurrence, dissent, or argument of counsel) in which each reference occurred. For more information about the analysis, see below, note 35.

refer to—its semantic content. In addition, the study identified shifts in the term's syntactic function, that is, in the frequency with which the term or its referent has coincided with the grammatical subject of the clause in question. The purpose of focusing on the semantic and syntactic functions of the label was to examine how the term has functioned to hook legal justifications up to the semantically indicated "real world" of non-legal fact beyond legal authority.[31]

One limitation of the study is that opinions referring to "fiction" or "fictions" alone, rather than to "legal fiction" or "legal fictions," were excluded. The group of opinions studied is therefore underinclusive. But it is not necessarily unrepresentative, since it still includes a wide variety of usages of the term. Moreover, a narrower focus on references to "legal fiction" usefully singles out particularly ambivalent references to the concept. The bare noun "fiction" can connote insubstantiality or illegitimacy (especially but not only when contrasted with "fact"). The modifier "legal," however, counters that implication, asserting the effectiveness of the fiction and underlining its transformation into a kind of social fact. More directly than references to "fiction" alone, references to "legal fictions" in legal rationales mark moments of ambivalence about the task of legal justification.[32]

This ambivalence seems to have grown with time. References to "legal fictions" in Supreme Court opinions increased significantly starting in the 1970s, following an earlier, isolated high point during the 1930s.[33] The increase cannot be fully

[31] This perspective was inspired in part by Bazerman's discussion of Ludwick Fleck's theory of "active" and "passive" constraints on the activities of a "thought collective" or epistemic community (Bazerman 1988, pp. 312–313).

[32] A complementary explanation for this ambivalence is suggested by the other contributions to this volume. Some justices might well regard fictions, more or less consciously, as devices for communicating with future judges in situations where proof seems unusually, but systemically, difficult or where the reconciliation of existing norms with the apparent requirements of justice in a particular case suggests a need for modification of the rules (Chaps. 11 and 18). Justices might also, perhaps at the same time, perceive concepts or statements they label "fictions" as serving the power-consolidating, "investigation-stymieing" purposes Bentham criticized (Chap. 4). My argument is that the concepts and statements labeled "legal fictions" by Supreme Court justices often, perhaps usually, have both effects, in that they are simultaneously charitable and self-interested. They are self-interested because they do not seek to make explicit the arbitrary suspension of a proof requirement for equitable purposes, and they thus shield judges from criticism. They are charitable in that they indicate judges' awareness that this denial of arbitrariness is inconsistent with other characteristic tropes of legal discourse and the virtues those tropes affirm, such as consistency and transparency.

[33] There were two references prior to 1800 (out of approximately 99 opinions), zero between 1800 and 1809 (out of 110), 3 between 1810 and 1819 (out of 330), 1 between 1820 and 1829 (out of 350), 7 between 1830 and 1839 (out of 400), 4 between 1840 and 1849 (out of 380), 2 between 1850 and 1859 (out of 860), 3 between 1860 and 1869 (out of 890), 2 between 1870 and 1879 (out of 1770), 1 between 1880 and 1889 (out of 2160), 5 between 1890 and 1899 (out of 2340), 4 between 1900 and 1909 (out of 1900), 2 between 1910 and 1919 (out of 2240), 8 between 1920 and 1929 (out of 1900), 13 between 1930 and 1939 (out of 1520), 5 between 1940 and 1949 (out of 1340), 8 between 1950 and 1959 (out of 900), 6 between 1960 and 1969 (out of 1000), 15 between 1970 and 1979 (out of 1300), 13 between 1980 and 1989 (out of 1400), 17 between 1990 and 1999 (out of 950), 14 between 2000 and 2009, and 6 so far since 2010. Estimated numbers of Supreme Court opinions per year per decade are taken from Lupu (1998, p. 1328 n. 22).

explained by an increase in the number of opinions issued. This increase challenges the assertion made by some theorists that legal fictions are being overlooked. The Supreme Court, at least, seems to be increasingly alert to the possibility of legal fictions' existence and operation. This fact does not, of course, invalidate Smith's argument that courts, including the Supreme Court, are recognizing and relying on new legal fictions. But over time, the number of references to legal fictions in concurring and dissenting opinions, as opposed to majority opinions, has increased.[34] These separate opinions are usually less concerned with orthodox legal justification and the articulation of doctrine (Smith's focus) than with *criticism* of the authoritative justifications advanced in majority opinions.[35] The function of such separate opinions is to assert, and thereby create, a weakness in the justificatory authority supplied by the majority opinion (and this is true even when the separate opinions thereby contribute to the Court's overall institutional legitimacy). Both the increased frequency of concurrence and dissent and the increased use of the "legal fiction" term in such separate opinions indicate increased ambivalence about the defensibility of legal justification in general and certain justifications in particular.

Patterns in the semantic content of the term "legal fiction" tell a similar story. To examine these patterns, I classified the referents of the term "legal fiction" in the opinions using a scheme based on MacDonald's classification of grammatical subjects.[36] She used two general categories—"phenomenal" (referring to the real world) and "epistemic" (referring to knowledge and/or discourse)—and several subcategories within each. Many referents of the term "legal fiction" in Supreme Court opinions, however, do not seem to fall into any of MacDonald's subcategories, which she developed for the analysis of scholarly writing. I therefore created two new subcategories of epistemic-phenomenal referents: one for legal status, rights, relations, and duties (e.g., the legal personhood of a corporation,[37] legal equality,[38] the party status of an organization in litigation[39]), and the other for explicitly counterfactual propositions (e.g., the assumption that Congress is collectively aware of judicial

[34] The term first appeared in a mid-nineteenth-century dissenting opinion. *Woodruff v. Trapnall* (1850) 51 U.S. 190, 216 (Grier, J., dissenting) ("The statutory proceeding is only held a judgment, as a mere legal fiction, and cannot stand in the way of a court of equity.").

[35] There is a large legal scholarly literature on the rhetoric and implications of dissenting opinions (e.g., Guinier 2008; Note 2011; Primus 1998; Stack 1996).

[36] I departed from MacDonald's list of seven categories (see above, note 24) because certain features of the language used in judicial decisions seemed to call for further specification. The ten categories into which I sorted semantic referents and grammatical subjects were: (A) Phenomenal, consisting of (1) particulars (historical events, individuals); (2) groups, including institutions (e.g., Congress, courts); and (3) attributes, including nonlegal qualities (e.g., hesitation); (B) Epistemic, consisting of (4) reasons, bases, arguments, justifications, and positions; (5) research; (6) legal authority (e.g., precedent); (7) -isms, legal doctrines, and schools of thought; and (8) audience (e.g., the public, you); and (C) Epistemic-Phenomenal, consisting of (9) legal status, rights, relationships, and duties; and (10) counterfactual propositions (e.g., mental states of collective bodies).

[37] *Samantar v. Yousuf* (2010) 130 S. Ct. 2278, 2286 (Stevens, J.); *Citizens United v. Federal Election Comm'n* (2010) 130 S. Ct. 876, 972 (Stevens, J., conc. in part and dissenting in part).

[38] *Fisher v. Hurst* (1948) 333 U.S. 147, 152 (Rutledge, J., dissenting).

[39] *Dakin v. Bayly* (1933) 290 U.S. 143, 157 (Stone, J., dissenting).

interpretations of a statute,[40] the notion that public figures have consented to make their lives public[41]). These two categories are effectively epistemic-phenomenal hybrids; they refer to (epistemic) legal utterances, acts, or assumptions that link the extralegal (phenomenal) world of individuals and groups with the legal (epistemic) world of, among other things, rights, duties, litigation, legislation, imputed mental states, and judgments.

These two epistemic-phenomenal referent subcategories are by far the most common types of referent of the term "legal fiction" in the opinions analyzed.[42] Nearly half of the 142 occurrences of the term refer to legal rights and status, and nearly another quarter refer to counterfactual propositions. The only other referent types occurring more than a handful of times fall into MacDonald's fourth subcategory (the epistemic subcategory she calls "reasons," which I broadened to include arguments, grounds, justifications, bases, and positions, and which accounted for 14 of the 142 referents) and her seventh subcategory (the epistemic category she calls "-isms," which I broadened to include doctrines and classes of legal rules, and which accounted for 18 of the 142 referents).

This distribution—particularly the disproportionate frequency of references to legal rights and status, which outnumber references to counterfactual propositions—shows that the "legal fiction" label has been most often applied, in Supreme Court opinions, not to postulates or propositions acknowledged to be untrue or inaccurate, but rather to postulates and propositions that give some phenomenal reality a legal meaning, applying to that reality a label that users of legal discourse can work with. Interestingly, it was only in the twentieth century—shortly before Fuller published his trilogy and around the time Vaihinger was writing—that the Supreme Court began using the phrase "legal fiction" to refer to counterfactual propositions. Before the 1920s, opinions used the phrase to refer to legal rights and status far more often.[43] Despite the stress on counterfactuality in defining "legal fiction" since Fuller, then, legal writers were using the term long before this to refer merely to artificial legal designations, legal terms and concepts describing and effectuating the interface between the phenomenal world and the world of legal language.[44] And they have continued to do so.

---

[40] *Jerman v. Carlisle*, McNellie, Rini, Kramer and Ulrich LPA (2010) 130 S. Ct. 1605, 1625 (Scalia, J., conc. in part & conc. in judgment).

[41] *Gertz v. Robert Welch*, Inc. (1974) 418 U.S. 323, 363 (Brennan, J., dissenting); Rosenbloom v. Metromedia (1971) Inc., 403 U.S. 29, 48 (Brennan, J.).

[42] There are 2 examples of category 1 referents (particulars), none of category 2 referents (groups, including institutions), 1 of category 3 referents (nonlegal attributes of particulars or groups), 14 of category 4 referents (reasons, bases, arguments, justifications, positions), none of category 5 referents (research, although in the judicial opinion context this category is not easy to distinguish from category 7), 2 of category 6 referents (legal authority or precedent), 18 of category 7 referents (-isms, doctrines, schools of thought, disciplines), none of category 8 referents (audience), 67 of category 9 referents (legal status, relationship, rights, duties), and 34 of category 10 referents.

[43] The earliest references to counterfactual propositions are *Ribnik v. McBride* (1928) 277 U.S. 350, 355 (Sutherland, J.); *Tyson & Bro.-United Theatre Ticket Offices v. Banton* (1927) 273 U.S. 418, 438 (Sutherland, J.). These earliest examples could also have been classified as references to legal rights or status.

[44] See discussion supra note 19 and accompanying text.

The syntactic function of the term in Supreme Court opinions supports similar conclusions about its role in justification.[45] Rhetorical analysis often focuses on grammatical subjects because they receive the primary emphasis in English propositions; subjects are usually either the agent or recipient of the action described by the clause in question. When clauses are structured indirectly, so that the grammatical agent is not the rhetorical theme of the clause, this indirection may itself be significant; it often suggests that the writer is deemphasizing or avoiding full commitment to the rhetorical theme.[46] In almost every instance in the present study—all but 12 of the 142 referent clauses analyzed—the referent of "legal fiction" differs from the grammatical subject. If we assume that "legal fiction" is the theme of most of the clauses in which the term appears, this lack of coincidence between subject and theme in Supreme Court opinions indicates that the writers of these sentences have lacked confidence that they could persuasively describe legal fictions as affecting the world in any meaningful way—or simply did not want to do so.[47] When identifying legal fictions, that is, opinion writers have grammatically emphasized not the fictions themselves, but the grounding of the writers' propositions in phenomenal reality or in some further legal reason or evidence.[48] Sometimes this emphasis is a matter of dismissal: the writer is seeking to discredit another opinion-writer's position by arguing that the position rests on a legal fiction. But at other times, opinion writers have apparently used the term "legal fiction" to concede a point to skeptics while arguing for an admittedly fictional position.[49]

[45] To analyze this function, I examined the number of independent clauses in which the term "legal fiction" operated as the grammatical subject, the referent category of the term in each clause, and for those clauses with grammatical subjects distinct from the phrase, the referent category for that subject. I included sentences and independent clauses in which the term "legal fiction" is part of a noun phrase as grammatical subject, but not sentences in which the phrase is a subject complement or the referent of a pronoun. If complements and pronoun referents were included, the count would increase about threefold.

[46] As MacDonald notes, "When 'subject' and 'topic' do not coincide, the usual explanation is that some other strategy involving focus or emphasis has caused the nontopical word to occur in the subject position. I … argue that if the subject position is the natural place for topical focus to occur, whatever we find in the subject position should be taken very seriously as an indication of agency or epistemic accounting" (MacDonald 1994, pp. 153–154).

[47] Of the 12 examples, one is from 1836, one from 1902, one from 1905, one from 1911, one from 1928, one from 1939, one from 1948, one from 1975, one from 1980, one from 1982, and one (the most recent) from 1989.

[48] In each of the clauses in which the term coincides with the grammatical subject, the referent/subject falls into either subcategory four (reasons) or subcategory nine (legal status). But the most common subcategory for grammatical subjects in general is not subcategory nine or ten (as was the case with referents for the phrase "legal fiction"), but subcategory four (reasons or bases), an epistemic subcategory, followed by subcategories one (particulars) and two (groups), both phenomenal subcategories that the referents of the term rarely fell into. This pattern has been consistent over time. The specific counts for grammatical subjects are as follows: 21 subjects in category 1, 22 in category 2, 7 in category 3, 46 in category 5, zero in category 5, 16 in category 6, 15 in category 7, 1 in category 8, 10 in category 9, and 5 in category 10.

[49] See, e.g., *Samantar v. Yousuf* (2010) 130 S. Ct. 2278, 2286 (Stevens, J.) ("But the phrase 'separate legal person" typically refers to the legal fiction that allows an entity to hold personhood separate from the natural persons who are its shareholders or officers.").

Overall, the location, semantic content, and syntactic function of these references tell a consistent, if complex, story. Supreme Court opinion writers have consistently used the term "legal fiction" to mark assertions of specifically legal "fact": relations and powers created and recognized by humans in the legal system by means of legal language, not just counterfactual propositions in the broadest sense. When such a legal "fact" gets tagged as a "legal fiction," it is a sign that the explanation in question is coming close to the limit of what the writer perceives as justifiable to readers who are outsiders to the legal community's conventions. The term functions as a label for other legal terms, or for concepts named by legal terms, that cannot be succinctly justified in lay language, but are nevertheless accepted by judges and lawyers as ingredients of conventional forms of legal reasoning. Those who are legally trained understand these terms and concepts as meaningful, but non-lawyers generally do not. Justices' use of the term also acknowledges the public role of judicial reasoning in the United States; Supreme Court opinions are not addressed only to legal insiders, even though they are most understandable to insiders (Short 2012; Staszewski 2009). It is in part through their publicity, and their presumed acceptability by nonlegal actors (if not their actual acceptance), that these opinions claim legitimacy and declare their effects on social ordering (Cover 1986; Schauer 1995). The "legal fiction" label thus combines an assertion that legal language transforms real-world relations with a defensive concession that the non-legally trained might not understand exactly how or why.

Occasionally, opinion writers have made something like this acknowledgment explicit. In a 1948 majority opinion, for instance, Justice Frankfurter argued against "call[ing] commerce [that is] in fact interstate 'local commerce' [simply] because under a given set of circumstances" it may be regulated without violating the dormant commerce clause; this labeling, Justice Frankfurter argued, would be "to indulge in a fiction," and "[e]specially in the disposition of constitutional issues are legal fictions hazardous, because of the risk of confounding users and not merely readers."[50] In part, Justice Frankfurter is arguing against misuse of a conventional legal term, "local commerce." But in making that argument, he also more generally cautions judges to use legal fictions with care and only when necessary, and he distinguishes between the effects of fictions on "users" and "readers." In so doing, he expresses unusual self-awareness about the close and somewhat self-defeating relationship between the "legal fiction" label and the task of legal justification.

7.4.2 The Boundaries of Communication in Scholarship on Science and Law

It thus seems that the term "legal fiction" has a broader semantic compass than post-Fuller theorists have suggested in their emphasis on counterfactuality. Consistently, writers of Supreme Court opinions have applied the label to aspects of

[50] Central Greyhound Lines of *N.Y. v. Mealey* (1948) 334 U.S. 653, 659–660 (Frankfurter, J.).

their legal justifications that provoke ambivalence because further defense or explanation seems difficult. They use the term and the concept to mark some of the points at which legal language directly impinges on the extra-legal world of what MacDonald calls phenomenal fact.

Legal language is, of course, not the only specialized communication system that impinges on the phenomenal world. Bazerman's history of the experimental article focuses on another such system, that of experimental science. Bazerman describes this system as one that identifies and delineates in words—and not only for initiates—the factual world of "passive constraints" on what can be said and understood.[51] Legal writing performs an analogous function, and it also interacts with the systems analyzed by Bazerman. Scholarship on the legal treatment of scientific evidence directly addresses that interaction. From the presentation of the claims made in this scholarship, we can tell how science has been described to make sense to lawyers and where legal vocabularies have been seen to need alteration to accommodate issues considered significant by scientific and technical communities. We can assume that scholarship on these topics that has gained wide readership in the legal community—measured by the imperfect yardstick of citation counts—has been most influential in negotiating and shaping this boundary between discourse systems.

To explore how this shaping has occurred, I analyzed features of the 52 most-cited articles published in American law reviews on the legal use of scientific and technical expert evidence.[52] The historical scope of these materials is slightly narrower than that of those discussed above: publication dates range from 1901 (Hand 1901) to 2000 (Risinger 2000). Overall, the materials indicate that over this period, anxieties about the integration of scientific and legal discourse have increased. Article authors have grown less confident that their readers share a common understanding of how the phenomenal world should be perceived and described, but more confident that such a shared understanding is desired or expected. They have thus also apparently felt greater pressure to map out specific prescriptions for that understanding and to stress the capacity of legal discourse to absorb divergent vocabularies.

[51] See above, note 30.

[52] I gathered the articles through a Hein Online search for articles containing the phrase "expert evidence" and receiving more than 75 citations, on Hein Online's count, as of July 12, 2011. I discarded articles not addressing the use of scientific or technical knowledge and discourse and excerpted the first and last sentence of each article to analyze (1) whether the opening sentence stated a proposition presented as uncontroversial or identified a puzzle; (2) whether the opening sentence contained a descriptive or normative proposition; (3) whether the assertion in each closing sentence was concrete or abstract (roughly, phenomenal or epistemic in MacDonald's terms, see supra note 24); and (4) using the classification described supra note 35, the subcategory for the grammatical subject and rhetorical theme of each sentence, as well as whether the subject and theme coincided in each sentence.

There has been an increase over time in the number of highly cited articles addressing this set of topics, with twenty of the fifty-two examples in the study having been published in the 1980s. Admissibility has been the most popular subject among the highly cited articles since the beginning of the period covered; psychology and psychiatry begin to compete with this subject in prominence in the 1950s.

These articles map the boundaries of legal discourse in part through the articles' own boundaries: their opening and closing sentences. As Bazerman notes, the "attention" an academic article pays to its readers "can be seen in the knowledge and attitudes the text assumes that the readers will have, in the types of persuasion attempted …, and in the charge given by the author to the readers (i.e., what the author would like the readers to do after being convinced by the article)" (Bazerman 1988, p. 25). An article's opening sentence is the first, most basic statement of the "knowledge and attitudes" the author assumes readers have; its closing sentence gives a "charge" to readers. My analysis therefore focused on these features of the articles.

Some opening sentences are declaratory statements, asserting information that author and audience (the legal academic or practitioner reading the article) are assumed to share. The assumption may be relatively explicit. A 1939 article on blood-alcohol testing techniques, for example, opened with the following: "The great number of injuries and deaths resulting from motor vehicle accidents caused by drunken drivers is a matter of common knowledge with which the public is vitally concerned" (Ladd and Gibson 1939, p. 191). But not all articles open with such a blunt declaration. Others pose or describe a puzzle or problem, an area where consensus is acknowledged to be lacking, as in this opening sentence taken from a 1943 article: "We can think of no more vexed or vexatious law-medicine problem than the proper appraisal and just compensation of so-called 'traumatic neurosis'" (Smith and Solomon 1943, p. 87). An opening sentence of this kind states a puzzle: it registers insecurity about the area of consensus. It establishes the need for a particular contribution, identifying how the contribution will complete existing understandings. Over the period covered by this study, "puzzle" opening sentences have become more common, but not markedly so. Only during the 1980s did sentences of this kind outnumber declaratory, propositional opening sentences.[53]

Other trends in opening sentences are more pronounced. Some opening sentences describe concrete, phenomenal events or states; others describe more abstract propositions such as relations or concepts.[54] No opening sentences with concrete

[53] The number of articles opening with propositional and puzzle sentences per decade were as follows: from 1900 to 1909, 1 propositional, 0 puzzle; from 1910 to 1919, and from 1920 to 1929, no articles in the study; from 1930 to 1939, 1 propositional, 0 puzzle; from 1940 to 1949, 0 propositional, 1 puzzle; from 1950 to 1959, 2 propositional, 1 puzzle; from 1960 to 1969, 3 propositional, 2 puzzle; from 1970 to 1979, 7 propositional, 2 puzzle; from 1980 to 1989, 9 propositional, 11 puzzle; from 1990 to 1999, 6 propositional, 5 puzzle; from 2000 on, 0 propositional, 1 puzzle.

It might be that puzzle sentences are more commonly used to open articles that address topics of transient interest or unsettled conceptualization and that compete with articles addressing the same topic in different terms; that over time, the vocabulary used to discuss such topics settles into a specific pattern; and that, as a result, the articles most cited over the longer term are those addressing topics of more lasting concern or, perhaps, summarizing the vocabularies used to discuss new topics, and thus are more likely to open with propositional sentences. If so, we would expect to find that the rate of citation of articles with puzzle opening sentences would decrease once the articles reached a certain age. Further study might make it possible to draw firmer conclusions on these points.

[54] An example of an "abstract" opening sentence appears in the earliest article in the group: "No one will deny that the law should in some way effectively use expert knowledge wherever it will

referents appeared in any articles in this study published before 1970. We might explain this by noting that concrete opening sentences presuppose a shared sense of what counts as "phenomenal," so they are a feasible rhetorical approach only in the wake of a process of factualization like the one described by Bazerman in scientific communities. The increase in concrete opening sentences could therefore indicate an increase in the perceived stability and authority of scientific discourse and knowledge, both absolutely and relative to legal discourse. Together, the increased rates of puzzle and concrete opening sentences might suggest an increasing desire to draw on the stability of those extra-legal specialized vocabularies; in turn, and in combination with the patterns described below, this suggests a corresponding increase in uncertainty about the precise boundaries of shared legal vocabularies.

Closing sentences indicate similar pressures. Two types of closing sentence correspond to the proposition and the puzzle, respectively: a closing sentence may either describe a state of affairs (perhaps making a prediction)[55] or summon readers to action.[56] Over time, call-to-action closing sentences have become more common; in fact, since the 1960s, they have consistently outnumbered descriptive closing sentences (with the exception of the period since 2000, for which the study included only one article).[57] Such call-to-action closing sentences began to appear in highly cited articles around the same time, in the mid-twentieth century, as puzzle opening sentences.[58] This might not be entirely coincidental; both devices imply that the current treatment of scientific information by law is in some way dysfunctional, posing a problem and requiring changed behavior. Given the forum in which these articles have circulated—journals addressed to legal academics and professionals—it is un-

---

aid in settling disputes" (Hand 1901, p. 40). The earliest example of a "concrete" opening sentence appeared in 1970: "In *People v. Collins*, the Supreme Court of California rejected a prosecutor's effort to link the defendants to a crime by using mathematical statistics" (Finkelstein and Fairley 1970, p. 489). The number of articles with abstract and concrete opening sentences were as follows: from 1900 to 1909, 1 abstract, 0 concrete; from 1910 to 1919, and from 1920 to 1929, no articles in the study; from 1930 to 1939, 1 abstract, 0 concrete; from 1940 to 1949, 1 abstract, 0 concrete; from 1950 to 1959, 3 abstract, 0 concrete; from 1960 to 1969, 5 abstract, 0 concrete; from 1970 to 1979, 8 abstract, 1 concrete; from 1980 to 1989, 15 abstract, 5 concrete; from 1990 to 1999, 7 abstract, 4 concrete; from 2000 on, 1 abstract, 0 concrete.

[55] An example appeared in a 1939 article on blood alcohol test evidence: "Historically, the legal inhibitions could not apply to the blood test, and today the modern development of the law is moving in the direction of wider admissibility of evidence wherever new proof will aid the courts in a just determination of the causes which come before them" (Ladd and Gibson 1939, p. 267).

[56] A good example appeared in a mid-twentieth-century article on the general topic of codifying rules for expert testimony: "There is everything to be gained and nothing to be lost by the adoption of the Model Acts" (Ladd 1952, p. 431).

[57] The number of articles with descriptive and normative closing sentences were as follows: from 1900 to 1909, 1 descriptive, 0 normative; from 1910 to 1919, and from 1920 to 1929, no articles in the study; from 1930 to 1939, 1 descriptive, 0 normative; from 1940 to 1949, 1 descriptive, 0 normative; from 1950 to 1959, 2 descriptive, 1 normative; from 1960 to 1969, 2 descriptive, 3 normative; from 1970 to 1979, 2 descriptive, 7 normative; from 1980 to 1989, 7 descriptive, 13 normative; from 1990 to 1999, 2 descriptive, 9 normative; from 2000 on, 1 descriptive, 0 normative.

[58] The earliest puzzle opening sentence appeared in 1943 (Smith and Solomon 1943); the earliest normative closing sentence appeared in 1952 (Ladd 1952).

surprising that closing sentences, in contrast to opening sentences, have *not* become more frequently concrete over the past century. Virtually all of the closing sentences in the study are abstract.[59] Even if the relative authority and perceived stability of scientific, phenomenal discourse have increased, that is, and even if that authority increasingly requires accommodation by legal discourse, no analogous process of factualization seems to have occurred in this area of legal discourse. More and more, legal discourse is being asked to account for facts—whether agreed-upon or contested—without itself being able to generate anything similar.

The grammatical subjects of opening and closing sentences also support this understanding. The subjects of opening sentences are fairly evenly distributed among the ten subcategories used for analysis but fall mostly into the first, second, and seventh: phenomenal particulars; phenomenal groups; and epistemic "-isms," schools of thought, and doctrines.[60] Closing sentence subjects are also fairly evenly distributed, with a slight majority falling into the second and seventh subcategories, groups and "-isms."[61] (In the study of Supreme Court opinions discussed above, grammatical subjects also often fell into category four, reasons.) These patterns support Bazerman's claim that opening sentences indicate areas of assumed consensus and/or authorial goals: authors of scholarship on scientific evidence have consistently sought to anchor their discussions in a shared reality by using phenomenal subjects and to state their objective of shaping legal vocabularies to accommodate such reality by using "-ism" subjects (the most common type of subject for articles' opening sentences and the second most common for closing sentences). But in more than half of the opening sentences using epistemic subjects referring to schools of thought or disciplines (seven out of thirteen), those subjects refer to *non-legal* "-isms," such as general scientific advancements (McCormick 1982, p. 879), laboratory methods (Skolnick 1961, p. 694), technologies for determining truthfulness (Wicker 1953, p. 711), multiple regression analysis (Fisher 1980, p. 702), social science data (Fineman and Opie 1987, p. 107), psychology (McCord 1987, p. 19), psychiatry (Hall 1956, p. 761), and teratology (Note 1962, p. 552). In contrast, in more than three quarters of closing sentences using these types of epistemic sub-

[59] Only one article, an anomaly in that it was a book review rather than a free-standing argument, had an arguably concrete closing sentence: "Galileo would attribute the prominence of the book and its author to clever public relations, not merit, and would denigrate it as junk scholarship in search of 'junk science.' Such would be Galileo Galilei's retort to Peter Huber" (Chesebro 1993, p. 1726).

[60] There are 13 opening sentences with category-1 subjects (8 propositional and 5 puzzle), 11 with category-2 subjects (5 propositional and 7 puzzle), 4 with category-3 subjects (2 propositional and 2 puzzle), 2 with category-4 subjects (both propositional), 1 with category-5 subjects (propositional), 1 with a category-6 subject (puzzle), 15 with category-7 subjects (9 propositional and 6 puzzle), 2 with category-8 subjects (1 proposition, 1 puzzle), 2 with category-9 subjects (1 propositional and 1 puzzle), and 1 with a category-10 subject (propositional).

[61] There are five closing sentences with category-1 subjects (4 descriptive and 1 normative), 14 with category-2 subjects (3 descriptive and 11 normative), 6 with category-3 subjects (3 descriptive and 3 normative), 8 with category-4 subjects (2 descriptive and 6 normative), 1 with a category-5 subject (normative), 1 with a category-6 subject (1 descriptive and 1 normative), 10 with category-7 subjects (6 descriptive and 4 normative), 1 with a category-8 subject (normative), 2 with category-9 subjects (both normative), and 3 with category-10 subjects (all normative).

jects (seven of ten), the subjects refer to *legal* schools of thought or doctrines, such as rules of relevancy (McCormick 1982, p. 916), standards for the admission of expert testimony (Black 1988, p. 695), the legislation of such standards (Hand 1901, p. 58; Slobogin 1984, p. 174), a proposed "defendant-first" approach to evidentiary standards (Ladd and Gibson 1939, p. 267), the trial process in mass toxic-exposure litigation (Sanders 1993, p. 86), and employment discrimination law (Note 1975, p. 421). That is, when they refer to settled epistemic areas, the articles refer mostly to non-legal areas at the beginning and legal areas in closing. This pattern is not surprising, given the common goal of all of the articles to digest the "-isms" of non-legal epistemic communities for use by the legal epistemic community. Like the other opening- and closing-sentence patterns described above, patterns in subject category suggest that authors have felt greater confidence over time about the need for legal discourse to accommodate these non-legal "-isms," without correspondingly increasing confidence that it will do so successfully.

We can see these articles as records of efforts to correct for the kinds of gaps in the justificatory capacities of legal vocabulary memorialized by the uses of the term "legal fiction" discussed above. A reference to a "legal fiction" signals an opinion writer's sense that additional explanation of an appellate court's decision to a non-specialist audience is not feasible for one reason or another. Legal scholarship on scientific evidence, in contrast, proposes new resources for the decision and justification of individual issues and cases. Those proposing such resources seem to have been growing more and more confident that they are needed and that scientific discourse is an appropriate place to look for them.[62] But even as this has been occurring, many of the same writers seem to have been growing less and less confident that their legal readers share a common understanding of how the phenomenal world should be described or how legal discourse should be changed to accommodate any such understanding. Of course, the new resources these writers have proposed would not all, as such, be directly available to appellate courts like the Supreme Court, and the authors of this scholarship are not explicitly addressing those areas of justificatory weakness tagged "legal fictions" by the Supreme Court. But these materials do tell complementary stories about at least two crucial kinds of limit on the capacity of legal language to form an epistemic community consistent with its members' aims, and they indicate the continued validity and suggestiveness of Fuller's observations on the linguistic nature of fictions and their relation to scientific fact.

Conclusion

Many modern theorists of the legal fiction, concentrating on counterfactuality and the role of fictions in legal change, have assumed that fictions either are or should be becoming less prevalent in legal discourse. Fuller made no such general claim,

[62] For a complementary account of the results of a similar trend in one particular area of United States law, see Randy Gordon's contribution to this volume (Chap. 18).

and if the conclusions drawn from the studies presented here are sound, we should expect references to legal fictions, and the kinds of explanatory shortcomings these references signify, to stay frequent, if not to increase. The term and concept remain viable not necessarily because the law is driven to self-delusion or mystification of power relations, nor even just because its actors must constantly adjust legal norms to accommodate new circumstances, but, more mundanely, because legal conventions of communication will always be slightly out of step with conventions used outside the legal sphere, and many legal actors acting in good faith will likely continue to note and compensate for that disparity. Following Fuller's example now requires us to pursue more directly his points about the relationship between fictions and specialized language usage. By doing so we can develop his insights in new directions and understand in more detail one of his principal concerns: the points at which legal language stops communicating, points that may shift over time but will never completely disappear.

Acknowledgements Thanks to Jonathan Bollozos and Erin McGowan for research assistance, to the Saint Louis University School of Law Summer Faculty Scholarship Stipend Program for support, and to Maksymilian Del Mar and the participants in the Special Workshop on Legal Fictions at the XXV World Congress of the IVR in August 2011.

References

Allen, Ronald, and Michael S. Pardo. 2002. The myth of the law-fact distinction. *Northwestern University Law Review* 97:1769–1808.
Bazerman, Charles. 1988. *Shaping written knowledge: The genre and activity of the experimental article in science*. Madison: University of Wisconsin Press.
Black, Bert. 1988. A unified theory of scientific evidence. *Fordham Law Review* 56:595–696.
Campbell, Kenneth. 1983. Fuller on legal fictions. *Law & Philosophy* 2:339–370.
Chesebro, Kenneth J. 1993. Galileo's Galileo's retort: Peter Huber's junk scholarship (book review). *American University Law Review* 42:1637–1726.
Cooney, Mark. 2006. Stringing readers along. *Michigan Bar Journal* 2006:44–45.
Cover, Robert M. 1986. Violence and the word. *Yale Law Journal* 95:1601–1630.
Del Mar, Maksymilian. 2014. Legal fictions and legal change in the common law tradition. In *Legal fictions in theory and practice,* ed. Maksymilian Del Mar and William Twining. Dordrecht: Springer.
Fineman, Martha L., and Anne Opie. 1987. The uses of social science data in legal policymaking: Custody determinations at divorce. *Wisconsin Law Review* 1987:107–158.
Finkelstein, Michael O., and William B. Fairley. 1970. A Bayesian approach to identification evidence. *Harvard Law Review* 83:489–517.
Fisher, Franklin M. 1980. Multiple regression in legal proceedings. *Columbia Law Review* 80:702–736.
Fuller, Lon L. 1930a. Legal fictions. *Illinois Law Review* 25:363–399.
Fuller, Lon L. 1930b. Legal fictions. *Illinois Law Review* 25:513–546.
Fuller, Lon L. 1930c. Legal fictions. *Illinois Law Review* 25:877–910.
Gordon, Randy D. 2014. Fictitious Fraud: Economics and the presumption of reliance. In *Legal fictions in theory and practice,* ed. Maksymilian Del Mar and William Twining. Dordrecht: Springer.
Guinier, Lani. 2008. The supreme court, 2007 term—Foreword: Demosprudence through dissent. *Harvard Law Review* 122:4–138.

Hall, Jerome. 1956. Psychiatry and criminal responsibility. *Yale Law Journal* 65:761–785.

Halliday, M. A. K. 1973. *Explorations in the functions of language*. London: Edwin Arnold.

Hand, Learned. 1901. Historical and practical considerations regarding expert testimony. *Harvard Law Review* 15:40–58.

Hans Kelsen. 2014. On the theory of juridic fictions. With special consideration of Vaihinger's Philosophy of the as-if. In *Legal fictions in theory and practice*, ed. Maksymilian Del Mar and William Twining. Dordrecht: Springer.

Harmon, Louise. 1990. Falling off the vine: Legal fictions and the doctrine of substituted judgment. *Yale Law Journal* 100:1–72.

Harner, Michelle M., and Jason A. Cantone. 2011. Is legal scholarship out of touch? An empirical analysis of the use of scholarship in business law cases. *University of Miami Business Law Review* 19:1–50.

Iser, Wolfgang. 1993. *The fictive and the imaginary: Charting literary anthropology*. Baltimore: Johns Hopkins University Press.

Knauer, Nancy J. 2010. Legal fictions and juristic truth. *St. Thomas Law Review* 23:1–49.

Ladd, Mason. 1952. Expert testimony. *Vanderbilt Law Review* 5:414–431.

Ladd, Mason, and Robert B. Gibson. 1939. The medico-legal aspects of the blood test to determine intoxication. *Iowa Law Review* 24:191–267.

Lupu, Ira C. 1998. Time, the supreme court, and the federalist. *George Washington Law Review* 66:1324–1336.

McCord, David. 1987. Syndromes, profiles and other mental exotica: A new approach to the admissibility of nontraditional psychological evidence in criminal cases. *Oregon Law Review* 66:19–218.

McCormick, Mark. 1982. Scientific evidence: Defining a new approach to admissibility. *Iowa Law Review* 67:879–916.

MacDonald, Susan Peck. 1994. *Professional academic writing in the humanities and social sciences*. Edwardsville: Southern Illinois University Press.

Mellinkoff, David. 1962. *The language of the law*. Boston: Little, Brown & Company.

Note. 1962. Impact of medical knowledge on the law relating to prenatal injuries. *University of Pennsylvania Law Review* 110:554–601.

Note. 1975. Beyond the prima facie case in employment discrimination law: Statistical proof and rebuttal. *Harvard Law Review* 89:387–421.

Note. 2002. Lessons from abroad: Mathematical, poetic, and literary fictions in the law. *Harvard Law Review* 115:2228–2249.

Note. 2011. From consensus to collegiality: The origins of the "respectful" dissent. *Harvard Law Review* 124:1305–1326.

Ogden, Charles Kay. 1932. *Bentham's theory of fictions*. New York: Kegan Paul, Trench, Trubner.

Petherbridge, Lee, and David L. Schwartz. 2011. An empirical assessment of the supreme court's use of legal scholarship. *Cornell Law Review* 96:1345–1374.

Petroski, Karen. 2012. Does it matter what we say about legal interpretation? *McGeorge Law Review* 43:359–402.

Primus, Richard. 1998. Canon, anti-canon, and judicial dissent. *Duke Law Journal* 48:243–304.

Quinn, Michael. 2014. Fuller on legal fictions: A benthamic perspective. In *Legal fictions in theory and practice,* ed. Maksymilian Del Mar and William Twining. Dordrecht: Springer.

Risinger, D. Michael. 2000. Navigating expert reliability: Are criminal standards of certainty being left on the dock? *Albany Law Review* 64:99–152.

Samek, Robert. 1981. Fictions and the law. *University of Toronto Law Journal* 31:290–317.

Sanders, Joseph. 1993. From science to evidence: The testimony on causation in the Bendectin cases. *Stanford Law Review* 46:1–86.

Schauer, Frederick. 1995. Giving reasons. *Stanford Law Review* 47:633–660.

Short, Jodi L. 2012. The political turn in American administrative law: Power, rationality, and reasons. *Duke Law Journal* 61:1811–1882.

Skolnick, Jerome H. 1961. Scientific theory and scientific evidence: An analysis of lie-detection. *Yale Law Journal* 70:694–728.

Slobogin, Christopher. 1984. Dangerousness and expertise. *University of Pennsylvania Law Review* 133:97–174.
Smith, Peter J. 2007. New legal fictions. *Georgetown Law Journal* 95:1435–1496.
Smith, Hubert Winston, and Harry C. Solomon. 1943. Traumatic neuroses in court. *Virginia Law Review* 30:87–175.
Soifer, Aviam. 1986. Reviewing legal fictions. *Georgia Law Review* 20:871–915.
Stack, Kevin M. 1996. The practice of dissent in the supreme court. *Yale Law Journal* 105:2235–2260.
Staszewski, Glen. 2009. Reason-giving and accountability. *Minnesota Law Review* 93:1253–1326.
Swales, John M. 1990. *Genre analysis: English in academic and research settings*. Cambridge: Cambridge University Press.
Twining, William. 2006. Taking facts seriously. In *Rethinking evidence: Exploratory essays,* ed. William Twining, 14. Cambridge: Cambridge University Press.
Vaihinger, Hans. 1924. *The philosophy of 'As as If'if': A system of the theoretical, practical and religious fictions of mankind*. Trans.: C.K. Ogden. New York: Harcourt, Brace & Company.
Wicker, William. 1953. The polygraphic truth test and the law of evidence. *Tennessee Law Review* 22:711–727.

Chapter 8
Legal Fictions and Exclusionary Rules

Simon Stern

Abstract Although the law abounds in fabrications, the term "legal fiction" is best reserved for what Alf Ross describes as "posed propositions," which hazard a premise only to secure a particular doctrinal result. On this view, legal fictions lack the generative potential of metaphors, because fictions depend on a truncated causal chain that excludes any consequence other than the doctrinal consequence the fiction was created to license, whereas metaphors spur on the imagination to make further connections. I explore this idea by drawing on research in the psychology of reading, which distinguishes between the care that readers take in restricting their use of "artificial" information, and their willingness to integrate information they take to be factual. Legal information (facts, doctrines) might similarly be arranged according to how narrowly or broadly the information may be applied. This approach allows us to locate particular examples along a spectrum, characterizing them as more or less fictional rather than simply placing them inside or outside the category of fiction. After developing the implications of this empirical research in psychology, I suggest that legal fictions exhibit the same kind of artifice as exclusionary rules, and that given the relative ease of implementing their artificial requirements, fictions may have facilitated the development of exclusionary rules by inspiring confidence about their workability. Finally, I turn to legal and literary examples that display similar kinds of artifice, focusing on deeming provisions and Wilde's play *The Importance of Being Earnest*.

Although the law abounds in fabrications, relatively few of them are treated as exhibiting the inventive or imaginative qualities that merit the label of a legal fiction. The term itself suggests that these particular fabrications display the kind of creativity we associate with literary writings. In a companion to this essay, I argue that the fabrications that qualify as legal fictions make up an even smaller set than is usually assumed, and that they lack certain crucial features of the narrative structure that governs the movement of stories (Stern 2015). Here, I offer further reasons for distinguishing legal and literary fictions, based on research in the psychology of reading. That research shows how we might differentiate varieties of legal

---

S. Stern (✉)
Faculty of Law, University of Toronto, 84 Queens Park, Toronto, ON M5S2C5, Canada
e-mail: simon.stern@utoronto.ca

M. Del Mar, W. Twining (eds.), *Legal Fictions in Theory and Practice*,
Law and Philosophy Library 110, DOI 10.1007/978-3-319-09232-4_8

fabrications according to how broadly or narrowly their implications are allowed to extend—that is, according to whether the fabrication is purpose-built only for a single end, or is used throughout a particular area of law, or extends broadly across doctrinal domains. On this view, legal fictions display a very creative and highly artificial structure, involving a kind of fabrication rarely found in the literary realm.

This way of framing the inquiry suggests that constraints on how legal rules and concepts apply might be understood as versions of exclusionary rules, the legal device most explicitly aimed at barring certain uses of material that would otherwise be accepted as helping to resolve a dispute. The logic of the exclusionary rule has great significance for legal argumentation generally: at the analytical level, the art of legal argument is the art of manipulating more or less complicated exclusionary rules, to bar some analogies and to promote others. After showing how research on the psychology of reading bears on our understanding of legal fictions and their relation to exclusionary rules, I will close by turning briefly to two implications of the argument, first asking how deeming provisions fit into the model, and then considering what kinds of literary analogies might remain.

8.1 The Limited Uses of Legal Fictions

In a classic essay on types of legal fictions and their functions, Alf Ross observes that the variety he calls the "creative legal fiction" is "no more than a peculiar technique for the analogical extension of legal rules."[1] The peculiarity, as Ross explains, consists in the vehicle that leads to the extension—a vehicle that takes the form of an asserted equivalence or identity:

> To say that a barbarian is a Roman citizen amounts to extending for foreigners the application of the procedural rules that have hitherto been confined to Roman citizens. To say that Bordeaux is in Middlesex amounts to saying that the rules … hitherto … confined to claims originating in England, are now … extended … [to] claims originating in other countries. (Ross 2000, p. 222)

In these examples, the fiction arises because of the role of what Ross usefully calls a "proposition" that is "only posed, not affirmed" (Ross 2000, p. 231; see also pp. 228–229). The proposition may seem to make an affirmative statement, but because it is only posed (or suggested), it remains tentative, hypothetical—and as I argue below, because it remains in this limbo of the incomplete, its ability to yield any consequential effects is radically limited in a way that does not apply to doctrines.[2]

[1] Ross's other two varieties—"dogmatic" and "theoretical" legal fictions—occupy less of his attention, and would not necessarily be regarded as legal fictions at all by many commentators. For a fuller and very helpful discussion of Ross's analysis of legal fictions see Lind (2014, this volume, Chap. 5, pp. 87–8).

[2] Because these consequential effects are so limited, the suppositional or hypothetical nature of the legal fiction also differentiates it from the kinds of counterfactuality posed in literary narrative, which usually speculates about alternative paths precisely to follow out their implications. For example, Saler (2013, p. 19) argues that novels positing "alternative realities" and "virtual worlds" can habituate readers "to see narratives as complex, provisional, and pragmatic"—a process that can occur only if the readers attempt to understand where the hypothetical premise would lead.

If the proposition were affirmed, it would be converted into an ordinary doctrine, with the same potential for further extension and application that all doctrines have in common. To extend the ambit of the procedural rules by saying that non-Romans are also subject to them, or to extend the ambit of the jurisdictional rules by saying that an English court can hear claims originating outside of England, would involve no fiction at all, but would merely articulate a doctrinal conclusion. Nor is any fiction involved when a court reaches these conclusions after contemplating various rationales for and against adopting them. We encounter Ross's "peculiar technique" only when a court arrives at a legal conclusion by justifying it according to the kind of premise illustrated in his two examples, a premise that might be regarded as a factual statement, although Ross resists that view by speaking of posed propositions.

The analogical extension of rules is a pervasive feature of legal argument and analysis, usually achieved without the vehicle that Ross isolates. The process itself is too commonplace to have been treated by any commentator in this area as involving the use of a legal fiction, which is taken to pick out a more distinctive set of legal concepts and operations.[3] The distinction between legal fictions and reasoned conclusions tracks the contrast between metaphor and simile, differentiating the statement that a barbarian simply "*is* a Roman citizen," and therefore is subject to the same procedural rules, from the statement that the same rules apply because barbarians *resemble* Roman citizens—that is, that the parties should be treated the same way because they share the same features in light of the rules' purposes.[4] In literary theory, and in research on cognitive psychology, metaphors are seen as more productive than similes, because the former are less confined to a particular ground of similarity (Gentner et al. 2000, p. 200). At least implicitly, similes usually suggest a particular feature that the two terms share; thus the implications they propose also depend on that feature, whereas metaphors, lacking this implied restriction, exert a dynamic and almost unrestrainable force. As Ellen Spolsky observes, they

[3] None of the familiar definitions of legal fictions would apply to analogical rule-extensions as a general matter. For example, according to Bentham (1840, p. 91) a legal fiction is "an assumed fact, notoriously false, upon which one reasons as if it were true." Maine (1861, p. 26) defines a legal fiction as "any assumption which conceals, or affects to conceal, the fact that a rule of law has undergone alteration, its letter remaining unchanged, its operation being modified." Fuller (1967, p. 9) says that a legal fiction is "either (1) a statement propounded with a complete or partial consciousness of its falsity, or (2) a false statement recognized as having utility."

[4] Many legal fictions do not take form of a metaphor. For example, there is no asserted identity between two terms when—as with the "procedural fictions" discussed in Lobban (2014, this volume, Chap. 10) the fiction is premised on an event that did not occur (e.g., a promise, or the act of a "causal ejector"). Nevertheless, the metaphor's structure offers a useful template for understanding how these procedural fictions operate. They do not assert that the situation *resembles* one in which that event occurred, nor that policy requires the court to treat parties *as if* that event had occurred; rather, the procedural fictions simply posit the event and bypass any discussion of an asserted likeness, thereby constraining their own consequential use in precisely the fashion I explore here. Lewis (1852, p. 423) similarly hints at both the elimination of the explanatory scaffolding, and the targeted consequentiality of the fiction, when he observes that judges use fictions as a shorthand for the particular consequences they entail, rather than "saying that acts done under certain circumstances entail certain consequences, and enumerating these consequences at length," all of which might invite elaboration and justification Lobban (2014, this volume, Chap. 10, p. 215).

"breed promiscuously in the brain, producing analogies among unconnected or incommensurable ideas" (Spolsky 2003, p. 161).

In the case of the legal fiction, the generative potential operates in precisely the opposite fashion. The fiction (the legal version of the metaphor) is constrained in a way that doctrines (the similes) are not. If a jurist were to rationalize the application of identical procedural rules by first identifying the similarities between barbarians and citizens, the result would be to leave open the possibility of further doctrinal changes based on parallel reasoning: those similarities might warrant the treatment of barbarians as citizens in other contexts, where the same considerations matter. If a jurist forgoes the comparison (and its attendant rationale) and simply asserts that barbarians are citizens, the result is to foreclose any opportunity for extension.[5] By replacing the simile with a metaphor and presenting the relationship as an identity, the jurist eliminates the generative effects that the analogy would promote.

We may bring this view of legal fictions into clearer relief by considering the distinction between fact and fiction taken from research on the psychology of reading. Rather than defining fictions according to their content or their means of inciting speculation, I suggest that we can distinguish fact and fiction according to the differentiations that readers make when encountering material they associate with one or the other. This approach has the benefit of drawing on empirical research rather than giving a definition laid down by fiat and justified by the proponent's own intuitions, and it allows us to locate particular examples along a spectrum, rather than simply characterizing them as inside or outside the category of fiction. A proposition may be more or less fictional—or, to use the terminology in the psychological research, more or less artificial—according to the way the reader uses it. Even those who disagree with the following account of legal fictions, then, might find that it nevertheless offers the tools for providing an alternative account.

In recent decades, research on how readers use the material they glean from texts has distinguished in particular between material that is used just for the purpose of understanding the text that furnishes it, and material that is "incorporated into a person's existing knowledge of the world" (Potts et al. 1989, p. 304). One of the most influential contributions to this discussion, by George Potts and his colleagues, showed that "artificial information"—that is, information that readers regarded as having been created specifically for the text at hand—was tightly compartmentalized, so as not to interact with information accepted as generally true ("real information"). Readers combined real information with existing knowledge to yield further hypotheses, insights, and beliefs, while restricting artificial information to the domain in which it originated, allowing it to produce new information only through interaction with other material within that domain. Attending to the functional effects of this distinction, Potts notes that "compartmentalized information … is difficult to retrieve and use … in a context that is different from the one in which it was learned," and that while "organizing information as a unit unto itself may hinder the application of that information to new situations," this means of storage "may actually serve to facilitate the retrieval of that information in a memory task

[5] For fuller discussion, see Ando (2014, Chap. 14, pp. 303–4).

that requires one to access only that limited body of newly learned information" (Potts et al. 1989, pp. 305–306).

While there are many contexts outside of fiction that offer "artificial information," numerous studies undertaken in the wake of Potts's research have shown that readers apply precisely this distinction to material taken from literary narratives (Rapp et al. 2013; Busselle and Bilandzic 2008; Prentice et al. 1997; Gerrig and Prentice 1991). By engaging in "source monitoring," readers cabin some details absorbed from their reading, and fiction constitutes one of the main sources that prompts this response (Johnson et al. 1993). This research on how readers manage the information they absorb has the potential to clarify some points of contention in longstanding philosophical and aesthetic debates about "truth in fiction," as Stacie Friend has recently shown. Drawing on the work of Potts and other scholars in this area, Friend argues that instead of attempting to specify the "necessary and sufficient conditions for fictionality," by identifying the features of a text or statement that mark it as fictional, we should instead "look at the *practices* that underpin our *interaction* with various texts" (Friend 2008, pp. 166, 165, emphasis added). Here I take the same approach and use Potts's concept of artificial information to consider how compartmentalization is related to the management of legal fictions and legal artifice more generally.

Commentators on "truth in fiction" distinguish between details that are only "true in the story" and details that are also "real world facts" (Weisberg and Goodstein 2009).[6] This distinction explains why, even if readers consider Sherlock Holmes to be a fictional character, they might nevertheless believe that different kinds of tobacco have a distinctively colored ash (Doyle 2005 [1891], p. 126), and more generally that Holmes's deductive methods are applicable to everyday life. Law allows for a similar, but perhaps more finely calibrated, set of distinctions. While empirical research on compartmentalized and incorporated information in the legal field might reward further study, copious examples of those phenomena are already conveniently available, in forms that serve as useful counterparts to the versions that figure in the cognitive psychology literature, if we look to legal practices of argument and citation. Just as information in a literary narrative might be applicable only within the narrative, whereas information in a textbook might be applicable more broadly within the same field of inquiry, in law some kinds of compartmentalized information are limited to a particular case, and other kinds are limited to the legal arena generally. Just as textbooks speak of "frictionless planes, spherical planets, [and] … perfectly rational agents" (Frigg 2010, p. 257), courts speak of "rational basis review," "estoppels," and "consideration"—concepts that are artificial, not because they were created for a particular piece of writing, but because they were created for a particular area of inquiry. In both contexts, the value of the concept depends not on whether it accurately corresponds to something outside

[6] Scholarship in this area has also been concerned with the knowledge that readers apply to fiction unless the author expressly forbids it. As Gallagher (2011, p. 332) observes, "When we find normal novelistic characters and events probable … we fold them into the world we inhabit without inconsistency."

the field of analysis, but on how well it explains phenomena within that field.[7] (As Wolcher (2010, p. 297) nicely puts it, "Legal form exiles all that is 'extraneous' in reality." The corollary is that legal form adopts new expedients to fashion its own reality.) Finally, some kinds of legal information may be incorporated into the reader's knowledge about the world. Borrowing from the philosophers, we may say that some details are "true in the case," some are "true in law," and some are also true in the world outside of the law.[8]

For the most part, legal convention requires that facts may be applied only within the case that presents them. Once they have been proved and treated as part of the record, the facts may be combined with the other established facts in the case, to produce legal conclusions, but may not be transposed to other cases. They may even be false in other cases. For instance, a defendant might escape liability in one dispute because the plaintiff could not establish certain facts, but might find herself liable when sued by another plaintiff for a claim arising out of the same incident because the second plaintiff introduced evidence unavailable to the first one, thereby creating a factual record that contradicted the record in the previous case. To become applicable to other legal disputes, the facts usually must be freed from their case-bound moorings by a doctrine that expressly permits the move, either through the workings of res judicata or by virtue of having been subject to judicial notice.

Unlike facts, legal doctrines—even those articulated for the first time—are taken to be potentially transposable to new cases.[9] A court might decline to adopt the doctrine on any number of grounds, but not on the ground that the doctrine was by its very nature incapable of applying to other disputes. (A controversial exception involves the rule, in some jurisdictions, that treats foreign law as a question of fact.[10]) Few doctrines apply generally without qualification; the varieties of direct and analogical extension—and the constraints on them—are manifold, and hence there are endless gradations along the spectrum between restriction to a single case and complete integration across legal fields. Some doctrines can be generalized only within

---

[7] As Morgan (2011, p. 24) observes, it is by attaching the textbook's or the law's constructs to a prediction, that artificial information is made to yield the kind of fact that corresponds with phenomena outside of the system (e.g., of economic theory or of law): it is the prediction (and not the construct itself) that may "become sufficiently fact-like to enable people to act upon [it]. For example, predictions about the future economy have to become not only sufficiently stable, but also congruent in a particular framework with facts about today and about the past—that is, they have to be brought into a perspectival relation with facts—before they can be acted upon on as facts."

[8] Although the question has not, to the best of my knowledge, been taken up in the philosophical literature, arguably fiction also offers material whose "truth" extends beyond a particular work (and beyond the works of an author who writes serially about the same characters) to a broader literary realm, but not to the world outside that realm. Certain generic conventions, for example, might fall into that category.

[9] That doctrines are assumed to be transposable by their very nature is evident from the incredulity that follows when courts attempt to avoid this result—such as the response to the U.S. Supreme Court's declaration in *Bush v. Gore* that "[o]ur consideration is limited to the present circumstances." 531 U.S. 98, 109 (2000) (per curiam).

[10] That doctrine serves to make foreign law, but not domestic law, vary from one case to another. For examples, see Fentiman (1998). In the U.S., federal courts treated foreign law as a question of fact until the adoption of Fed. R. Civ. P. 44.1 in 1966.

the same area of law; others can be generalized across common-law domains but not to constitutional law; and most are subject to more intricate limitations relating to the doctrine's context, rationale, or historical origins. The techniques for justifying the extension of legal rules have generated a vast literature, and no useful purpose would be served here by attempting to enumerate or arrange them according to their tendency to make doctrines more or less transposable. Suffice it to say that whereas Potts emphasizes the cognitive burdens that make it hard to apply compartmentalized information to new situations, and the comparative ease of retrieving that information in its original context, the routine demands of legal analysis reveal a further level of complexity in light of the many contingencies that give doctrinal information an ambiguous status, making it arguable that the information may be incorporated, but not necessarily permitting it. Arguments for broader or narrower doctrinal expansion tax the ingenuity of lawyers on a daily basis, and these endless possibilities suggest that legal analysis is in large part a question of manipulating information to make it more or less artificial. Just as few doctrines are broadly "true in law," so also few are only "true in the case" that sponsors them.

Finally, just as literary narratives may supply readers with information they accept unreservedly as facts to be incorporated, legal decisions also offer information of this order. Facts that are not necessarily applicable to another case might nevertheless be accepted by readers as revealing information about the parties, or about human behavior, that can yield new insights when integrated with other beliefs. Perhaps readers also incorporate information they find in the analytical parts of legal decisions. It is unclear to what extent doctrinal information is restricted to the legal realm—and by what kinds of readers (e.g., lay or professional, parties or would-be litigants). Empirical researchers have studied readers' use of material encountered in various media—such as textbooks, biographies, novels, movies, and ads—but have not included legal decisions as possible sources of information. Because courts explain themselves by referring not only to doctrines and prior decisions, but also to details outside of the legal realm, and because legal doctrines themselves may incorporate assumptions about non-legal phenomena, judgments offer an intriguing prospect for further research. It might turn out that readers are willing to incorporate material from some of the doctrinal and analytical aspects of judgments.[11] If so, this result could contribute to our understanding of the referential qualities of legal language.

Readers' practices of compartmentalization and incorporation, with respect to literary narratives and legal decisions, show how we might consider both forms of writing to include elements that fall at the fictional end of the spectrum (or the "artificial" end, in Potts's terminology) and elements that fall at the factual (or "real") end. This distinction provides a handle for reconsidering various phenomena that are often characterized as legal fictions, including doctrines such as constructive

[11] A related and more familiar line of research examines how laypersons apply information from various sources (such as books, newspapers, television, and movies), when sitting as jurors. The "CSI effect" (successor to the "Perry Mason" effect) is among the most frequently studied forms of such information transfer, and its power has recently been cast in doubt (Cole and Diosa-Villa 2009).

possession and constructive eviction, presumptions such as that everyone is assumed to know the law, and deeming provisions such as that a federal statute is deemed to have carried, from the day of its passage, whatever meaning the highest court in the land ultimately assigns to it. At first glance, it might seem that all of these provisions are fictional in the same way that compartmentalized aspects of stories are fictional. That is, it might be said that even when the content of these provisions is such that a reader could extract information from them and apply it to non-legal phenomena, the reader's source-monitoring would prevent any such application. Hence one might conclude that these should all be characterized as legal fictions because they are treated as fictional in the same fashion as material that fiction-readers take to be "true in the story" but lacking any generalizable truth.

Closer scrutiny, however, shows that the analogy cannot be sustained. Insofar as these propositions have carrying power beyond the case in which they arise, they resemble the artificial information of the textbook, rather than the more restrictively compartmentalized information of the literary narrative. One might reply that what is "true in law," no matter how widely true in that domain, is still a legal fiction so long as it fails to correspond to our experience of the world, and that this is precisely what makes it a fiction.[12] What that answer helps to show, however, is that deeming provisions, presumptions, and constructive modes of liability are neither more nor less generalizable than ordinary legal doctrines of all sorts.[13] Doctrines such as "clean hands" and "mootness" apply across many legal domains but not outside of the legal arena. If we take compartmentalization to be a marker for the artificial, it becomes clear that law's artifice permeates all legal domains, and is no more salient in deeming provisions and the like, than in any instance of doctrinal application or expansion. If the concept of the legal fiction picks out certain phenomena as fictional, or artificial, in a fashion that is not simply characteristic of law in general, it must involve a tighter constraint than one that simply cordons the legal from the non-legal.

This observation returns us to Ross's distinction between run-of-the-mill analogical extensions and legal conclusions that result from a posed proposition. The proposition that a barbarian is a citizen, only with respect to the question of which procedure applies, involves the same kind of compartmentalization as the artificial information in a literary narrative, except that the former is even more tightly compartmentalized. A plot detail, by virtue of being "true in the story," is "true" throughout the story, with the consequence that the reader is expected to consider it in relation to the other events that follow. (I discuss exceptions in the final section.) By contrast, the proposition about the barbarian has no bearing on any other issues in the same dispute. Once proved by one of the parties, a fact is "true in the

[12] For helpful elaborations of this view, see Ando (2014, this volume, Chap. 14, pp. 312–4), Lind (2014, this volume, Chap. 5, pp. 88–92), and Samuel (2014, this volume Chap. 3, pp. 36–40). For a fuller discussion of the difficulties presented by an expansive view of legal fictions, see Knauer (2010).

[13] This is precisely what Justice Park suggests, in *Garland v. Coleridge* (1837) 4 Scott 587, 707–708, when commenting on the doctrine of "relation" and observing that "[t]his rule has not been considered as a fiction, but a just and necessary rule," in part because of the doctrine's widespread application (see Lobban 2014, this volume, Chap. 10, p. 237, n. 30).

case" and may be used to reach any number of conclusions related to the dispute (e.g., to establish liability for every claim that involves that fact, or to show that the adverse party was lying, or to vitiate one of the opponent's defenses); to that extent, it resembles an event in the plot of a literary narrative. The proposition that the barbarian is a citizen, however, is purpose-built only to make way for the conclusion about the applicable procedural rules. The proposition cannot be used to show what language the barbarian speaks or to identify any substantive rights the barbarian enjoys. The same condition applies to all stipulations of the kind that Ross singles out. The proposition that the illegitimate child has no parent, just with respect to the question of inheritance if the father dies intestate, cannot be combined with other facts to yield any other legal result (Del Mar, Chap. 11, p. 230). When the creator of an "attractive nuisance" is said to have "invited" a child onto the property, just with respect to the owner's liability for the child's harm, nothing else may be inferred from the invitation (Stern 2015). These details are compartmentalized so tightly as to be ineligible for any kind of incorporation at all. Unlike information that is "true in law," or even "true in the case," these propositions are true only for the particular doctrinal conclusion they were invented to justify. They are almost universally false, even within the legal sphere.

One implication of this contrast is that when commentators explore the parallels between literary fiction and legal fabrication by attaching the label of "legal fiction" to doctrines such as civil death, constructive possession, and marital unity, this exercise imposes a needlessly restrictive scope on the comparison. Law abounds in fabrications ("ripeness," "preemption," "notice") that are invoked precisely to generate some result, in a fashion akin to a detail in a story's plot. Frigg (2010, p. 260) pursues the same analogy when likening models (rather than legal concepts) to fictions: as he observes, in both imaginative enterprises "the 'working out' of the details usually consists in deriving conclusions from the primary assumptions" that initiate the exercise. Similarly, Green (2010, p. 360) argues that fiction often serves as a kind of thought experiment that proceeds by "supposing" certain premises so as to "determine what consequences will plausibly follow." Law's fabrications work the same way. In law, as in other areas, an interest in fiction relates broadly to questions about what it takes to incite the imagination to generate narratives, and how the mind constructs and develops them, rather than a focus on a few doctrinal instances that appear especially fanciful.[14]

While other kinds of legal propositions might happen to be similarly constrained in their application, it is not necessary to their operation, in the way that it is for Ross's propositions. That a doctrine has not gained sufficient acceptance to become widely integrated into the legal system is not, by itself, sufficient to render the doctrine fictional in the sense elaborated here. Doctrines that are controversial or that are only beginning to gain acceptance remain unintegrated simply because they have not had the opportunity to spread, whereas fictions are accompanied with a prohibition that denies them this opportunity altogether. Today's dissent

[14] Samuel (2014, this volume, Chap. 3) develops this idea with great acuity, showing how law's fabrications generally (doctrines, rights, duties, standards, concepts, etc.) may be regarded as fictions.

may become tomorrow's majority view, but the fictional proposition is not even a candidate for adoption: if the result that the fiction entails should become widely embraced, the proposition that was originally used to secure that result would simply fall away. Newly emergent doctrines may also fail to take hold, but in any case it remains open to lawyers and jurists to argue for their further development. This would be a misguided endeavor on behalf of a fiction, which is already understood to be incapable of blossoming in such a fashion.

8.2 Artifice and Exclusionary Rules

Because of its extreme artificiality, the legal fiction offers a useful means of thinking about legal artifice more generally. By virtue of being so strictly constrained, the legal fiction exemplifies a kind of artifice associated with exclusionary structures.[15] Exclusionary rules brand, as legally irrelevant, information that might otherwise figure significantly in determining a party's liability. The hearsay prohibition excludes statements that may be relevant and highly reliable, as does the prohibition on propensity evidence. The exclusionary rule in criminal procedure has the same effect, for illegally acquired evidence and its derivatives. Exclusionary rules are artificial not only because they require the adjudicator to ignore information that the parties would gladly use if their dispute were not being resolved in a legal forum, but also because these rules often serve to parse admissible and inadmissible aspects of the same evidentiary material, according to the reason for introducing it. An out-of-court utterance may be inadmissible to prove the truth of any assertion it makes, but may be admissible to prove something else about the speaker (e.g., that she did not have laryngitis on the date in question). The artifice that governs the use of exclusionary rules is therefore most evident when they are used to admit evidence for a limited purpose.

When they were first introduced, in the sixteenth and seventeenth centuries, the hearsay rules operated categorically. Once a statement was labeled hearsay, that would have been sufficient to bar the statement from the evidentiary record.[16] In the course of the nineteenth century, this area became significantly more nuanced, and courts developed rules admitting out-of-court utterances for purposes other than to

[15] Bentham (1827, p. 455), in his attack on the "absurd" principles governing the exclusionary rules in English evidence law, branded these principles with the same label he applied to legal fictions, calling them "notoriously false." See note 2.

[16] The categorical nature of the prohibitions is based largely on inference, from the examples given in Koch (2006). That a court, in a particular case, refused to admit an out-of-court statement offered as evidence of the statement's truth cannot, by itself, prove that the statement would also have been inadmissible for any other purpose. However, the jurisprudence from the era that marks the emergence of the hearsay rule does not offer examples in which such statements were admitted for a limited purpose.

establish the statement's truth.[17] The artifice, in this case, depends on controlling the ends to which the statement is put. Experimental results have cast doubt on the ability of fact-finders to monitor these uses effectively (Wistrich et al. 2005; Park 2003). Indeed, given that the trier of fact will probably be unable to separate the permissible and impermissible strands of the statement, the courts' refusal to abandon the prohibition suggests that lawyers have a basic penchant for artificial distinctions of this sort.

Legal fictions display the same kind of artifice. As we have seen, the legal fiction introduces a fact that is permitted to generate a particular conclusion, and only that conclusion. It is not allowed to interact with other facts in the record. Like the out-of-court statement, admitted to prove that a conversation took place on a certain date, but not to derive any conclusions about the truth of what the witness heard, the legal fiction cabins the train of thought that follows from its factual premise. Again, we see a contrast similar to the one involving plot details in stories: the legal fiction imposes an even tighter constraint on the use of its facts than does the hearsay rule, because the latter (like the detail that is "true in the story") permits nearly any implications except those that treat the utterance as communicating a factually correct statement, whereas the legal fiction specifies a fact precisely in order to yield a single legal conclusion and nothing else.

Indeed, it might be argued that the structural similarity between the legal fiction and other legal exclusionary rules is not merely fortuitous, but that the legal fiction models a conceptual structure that facilitated the evolution of these other rules. The legal fiction, unlike the intricate hearsay distinctions that emerged in the nineteenth century, is cognitively easy to manage, and might have encouraged a certain degree of confidence in the workability of exclusionary rules. Where a fact is stipulated in such a way as not to solicit belief, is purpose-built to yield a certain legal outcome, and is understood by all involved to have been created solely for that purpose (Klerman 2009), there is little risk of its being misunderstood or misapplied. No one, in the inheritance dispute, would imagine that the illegitimate child, having been pronounced the child of nobody, is freed of genealogical ties with respect to any other purpose for which they might be relevant (e.g., to decide whether the degree of consanguinity is an impediment to marriage). No one, in the case of the jurisdiction-creating proposition about the location of Bordeaux, would seek to combine it with other facts (e.g., to establish that the weather in London and Bordeaux was the same). The facts, in these cases, are so easily managed, their status so clearly provisional, their production so obviously motivated by a single doctrinal goal, that they can hardly be called facts in the conventional sense—hence

[17] Although scholarship on the history of hearsay has not, to the best of my knowledge, emphasized this point, this distinction is evident from the examples in Stone and Wells (1991, pp. 312–313). The history of propensity evidence follows a similar pattern, as may also be seen from the examples in Stone and Wells (1991, pp. 228–241). Rumor is another form of evidence that may not be accepted as true but may nevertheless be invoked as performing some kind of informative function; see Williams (2013, pp. 93–94).

Ross's preference for "posed proposition."[18] The tendency to describe legal fictions as involving "facts" doubtless accounts for much of the confusion in this area. Legal fictions resemble facts only because of their formal role as the ancillary step leading to a legal conclusion. They occupy the same position as facts that parties might dispute, but do not come into the argument in the same fashion.[19] Once they have been introduced, the cognitive cost of source-monitoring burden is trivial, because they have not been proved up in the usual fashion and do not track information that is even notionally subject to empirical proof. The artificial process by which they serve to license only a particular legal conclusion, then, carries no risk of misapplication, because neither their mode of production nor their content is of a kind that is susceptible to confusion.

The hearsay rule, by contrast, resembles other exclusionary rules in displaying significantly higher monitoring costs. Exclusionary rules involving evidence, of necessity, relate to the kind of evidence that is normally proved up, and that may be well known to all participants, even if it cannot form part of the record. Hence the confidence that might seem to be warranted, on the basis of the fiction's operation, is not warranted in the case of these exclusionary rules, even though they may appear to share the same structure. Legal fictions may have provided a conceptual precedent that led lawyers, even if unconsciously, to be readier to adopt exclusionary rules and to believe in their workability. Despite the superficial similarities, however, legal fictions involve a radically different relationship to provable facts and the kind of referentiality that accompanies them.

8.3 Where Can Fictions Lead?

This argument has emphasized the distinctive features of Ross's "posed propositions" that separate them from other modes of legal fabrication and from literary narratives. At the same time, the argument has sought to develop an analogy between legal and literary fabrications, suggesting that both areas furnish examples that may be located on a spectrum between the purely artificial and the entirely real. This conclusion briefly considers two analogies to the legal fiction, as analyzed here—one drawn from law, and one from literature.

Deeming provisions are often likened to legal fictions, and are sometimes treated as standard illustrations of the concept (e.g., Fuller 1967, p. 1). On the account given here, the resemblance is significant but is at most contingent, because even a highly restricted deeming provision may grow to cover new situations. This means

---

[18] Similarly, see Gama (2014, this volume, Chap. 16, p. 353), in noting that presumptions are traditionally associated with questions of fact, while fictions are traditionally associated with questions of law, may be thought implicitly to cast doubt on the "factual" nature of these propositions.

[19] This circumstance accounts for the maxim that "proof is not admitted to contradict a fiction: for what would the proof of truth avail, where fiction counterfeits truth?" ("Contra fictionem non admittitur probatio; quid enim efficeret probatio veritatis, ubi fictio adversus veritatem fingit"; Blackstone 1768, p. 43).

of producing a legal equivalence, then, falls on a spectrum between the fiction and the widely generalizable doctrine: unlike the fiction, the deeming provision is at least eligible for extension, and very few such provisions even begin in the uniquely bespoke manner of fictions. As an instance of a deeming provision, consider the Lacey Act, which provides that anyone who charges money for "guiding, outfitting, or other services … for the illegal taking of fish or wildlife" will be "deemed to [have engaged in] a sale of fish or wildlife."[20] On its face, this provision does not assert that selling services and selling fish are the same; it only states that the two will be treated the same way. Yet if it does not pose the proposition that selling services is the same as selling fish, the provision seems to be constrained in its reach, in the same fashion that characterizes legal fictions. The deeming provision takes very nearly the same metaphorical form as the fiction, in this case specifying that certain activities will be treated as instances of the prohibited conduct, rather than explaining (in the manner of a simile) that they are forbidden because they *resemble* the prohibited conduct. The deeming provision follows the structure of a legal fiction, in its apparently purpose-built role and tightly restricted application. Yet the constraint depends on how many different ways the statute conceives of illegal acts connected with the sale of protected fish. If the statute features only one such act, the deeming provision has the same function as a legal fiction. Even in that case, however, there always remains the possibility that the provision's reach will expand. Any statute may grow over time, extending to cover numerous acts or entities beyond those it originally specified (Clark 1977), and to that extent, any deeming provision in the statute may be similarly generalized. As its reach grows, the provision drifts away from its fiction-like origins and begins to share the features of a transposable doctrine. It moves towards the middle of the spectrum, rather than remaining at the end that is marked by extreme artificiality.

Moreover, deeming provisions are often created with a broader ambit from the outset. A criminal code, for example, might define "possession" as covering not only physical custody but also storage of an object anywhere "for the use and benefit of [the person charged with an offense] or of another person," and might add that if "one of two or more persons, with the knowledge and consent of the rest, has anything in his custody or possession, it shall be deemed to be in the custody and possession of each and all of them."[21] The two parts of this provision take different forms: the first part is presented in the form of an identity (stating, in effect, that "storage of an object on someone else's property is possession") while the second part takes a constructive form ("possession by any person in the group is deemed to be possession by each person in the group"). Yet both parts operate identically to extend the reach of the various possession offenses enumerated throughout the code. The same implications follow, with even greater force, for deeming provisions established in the common law, rather than by statute, because of the ineluctable pull of analogical reasoning in common-law argumentation. On this account, then, deeming provisions have an ambiguous status, in some cases aligning

[20] 16 U.S.C. § 3372(c)(1).

[21] R.S.C. 1985, c. C-46, s. 4(3)(a)–(b) (Can.).

perfectly with the place of the legal fiction but often behaving more like ordinary doctrines. It would follow that deeming provisions cannot be categorically treated as legal fictions, but must instead be studied individually to see if they operate under the same constraints.

What of literary fictions? The idea of a fantastic premise that generates an elaborate plot finds numerous literary analogies, triggering pronouncements about immersion in fictional worlds, the ease (or difficulty) of believing six impossible things before breakfast, and the relations between plausibility and probability. By contrast, an exclusionary structure that approves some consequences and prohibits others yields much less by way of literary analogy. Even fantasy and science fiction are rarely governed by plot structures with this kind of constipated consequentiality.[22] A likelier analogy might be sought in the theater of the absurd, and in certain forms of surreal fiction, but their plots tend to traffic in non sequiturs and the inexplicable rather than the limited causal structure of the legal fiction (Cohn 1965, p. 234; Fehrle 2011, p. 227; Zunshine 2006, pp. 40–41). They describe events that have no consequences, or events with unpredictable consequences, rather than events with a truncated casual chain. Stories with multiple endings, such as Godwin's *Caleb Williams* (1794) or Dickens's *Great Expectations* (1860–1861, 1863) present the structure in reverse: rather than allowing only some of the expected consequences, these novels allow for different consequences, even mutually inconsistent ones, from the same events.

However, Wilde presents his audience with something like a legal fiction in *The Importance of Being Earnest* (1895). In that play, it becomes evident that no man can be eligible for marriage unless he claims to be named Ernest. Although both of the women who exact this requirement claim to have a solid reason for it,[23] it turns out to be a mere formality, as we see when the play concludes with an impending marriage not only for Jack (who proves to be named Ernest) but also for Algernon (who is not). In a play that devotes an unusual amount of attention to the pretenses of polite society, it may not appear surprising to see an insistence of rigid conformity to convention taken so far as to require eligible bachelors to answer to a particular name. Most of the repartee, however, takes the opposite form, revolving around efforts to adhere literally to social conventions and to treat any lapse as a moral failing. In short, the play's usual solution is to attach too much consequence to every demand, not to cut off their possible consequences. Moreover, no one in the

[22] However, Gallagher (2011, pp. 324–325) notes that some texts rapidly produce numerous counterfactuals, all with an eye to asking (for example) "what a singular person's options were, what he might have known, when he might have known it, and how he might have acted on the knowledge," and she likens this pattern to the "indeterminate, multiple, and nonlinear [patterns] … of postmodern fiction." In such a case, the causal implications of each counterfactual are foreclosed as that option gives way to another; however, since those options are all produced heuristically and then abandoned, none of them actually yields any consequence in the text. Thus they are even more tentative and provisional than the legal fiction, whose premise is adopted specifically so that its consequence may be given effect.

[23] According to Gwendolyn, "There is something in that name that inspires absolute confidence" (Wilde 2008 [1895], p. 262). Cecily uses almost exactly the same phrase (ibid., p. 285).

play calls attention to Algernon's successful evasion of this nominal requirement. In its closing lines, the last act focuses entirely on the discovery of Jack's true name and his fiancée's insistence that her faith has been vindicated (born Ernest John Moncrieff, he is both Jack and Ernest after all). That Algernon can still expect to be married is simply taken for granted, when he and Jack both embrace their brides, and despite all the concern about Jack's name, nobody remarks that Algernon's name is not an impediment after all.

Several features conspire to bring off this nonconsequential effect. No one can tell in advance whether this particular requirement will prove to be optional, and given the elaborate measures that Wilde employs to make Jack's assertion true, one might imagine that Algernon will make a similar discovery. The requirement's purely formal status becomes evident only by implication at the play's close, with the result that the causal chain is cut off by the drop of the curtain. Far from presenting his audience with a causal snag to puzzle over as the play continues, Wilde airily dispenses, at the last moment, with a contrivance that motivates a significant amount of action in the course of the play. Having introduced an elaborate plot device, he withdraws it at the last possible opportunity, showing the play's inventiveness to surpass even its enabling conditions. Perhaps only in a play so intent on celebrating its own extreme artifice would we find a parallel to this highly artificial legal device.

Acknowledgment Thanks to Richard Gerrig and Daniel Williams for terrific suggestions on previous drafts.

References

Ando, Clifford. 2014. Fact, fiction, and social reality in roman law. In *Legal fictions in theory and practice*, ed. William Twining and Maksymilian Del Mar. Dordrecht: Springer.

Bentham, Jeremy. 1827. *Rationale of judicial evidence*. Vol. 5. London: Hunt & Clark.

Bentham, Jeremy. 1840. *Theory of legislation*. Vol. 1. Boston: Weeks, Jordan.

Blackstone, William. 1768. *Commentaries on the laws of England*. Vol. 3. Oxford: Clarendon.

Busselle, Rick, and Helena Bilandzic. 2008. Fictionality and perceived realism in experiencing stories. *Communication Theory* 18:255–280.

Clark, Robert Charles. 1977. The morphogenesis of subchapter C: An essay in statutory evolution and reform. *Yale Law Journal* 87:90–162.

Cohn, Ruby. 1965. The absurdly absurd: Avatars of *Godot*. *Comparative Literature Studies* 2 (3): 233–240.

Cole, Simon A., and Rachel Diosa-Villa. 2009. Investigating the "CSI effect" effect. *Stanford Law Review* 61:1335–1373.

Del Mar, Maksymilian. 2014. Legal fictions and legal change in the common law tradition. In *Legal fictions in theory and practice*, ed. Maksymilian Del Mar and William Twining. Dordrecht: Springer.

Doyle, Arthur Conan. 2005 [1892]. The Boscombe Valley mystery. In *The new annotated Sherlock Holmes,* ed. Leslie S. Klinger, vol. 1. New York: Norton.

Fehrle, Johannes. 2011. Unnatural worlds and unnatural narration in comics? In *Unnatural narratives—unnatural narratology,* ed. Jan Alber and Rüdinger Heinze, 210–245. Berlin: de Gruyter.

Fentiman, Richard. 1998. *Foreign law in English courts*. Oxford: Oxford University Press.

Friend, Stacie. 2008. Imagining fact and fiction. In *New waves in aesthetics,* ed. Kathleen Stock and Katherine Thomson-Jones, 150–169. Basingstoke: Palgrave Macmillan.
Friend, Stacie. 2014. Believing in stories. In *Aesthetics and the sciences of mind,* ed. Greg Currie, et al. Oxford: Oxford University Press. http://publications.heythrop.ac.uk/1782/. Accessed 19 Aug 2014.
Frigg, Roman. 2010. Models and fiction. *Synthese* 172 (2): 251–268.
Fuller, Lon L. 1967. *Legal fictions*. Stanford: Stanford University Press.
Gallagher, Catherine. 2011. What would Napoleon do? Historical, fictional, and counterfactual characters. *New Literary History* 42:315–336.
Gama, Raymundo. 2014. Presumptions and legal fictions: A Collingwoodian approach In *Legal fictions in theory and practice*, ed. William Twining and Maksymilian Del Mar. Dordrecht: Springer.
Gentner, Dedre, et al. 2000. Metaphor is like analogy. In *The analogical mind: Perspectives from cognitive science,* ed. Dedre Gentner, et al., 199–253. Cambridge: MIT.
Gerrig, Richard J., and Deborah A. Prentice. 1991. The representation of fictional information. *Psychological Science* 2:336–340.
Godwin, William. 1794. *Things as they are; or, The adventures of Caleb Williams*. London: Crosby.
Green, Mitchell. 2010. How and what can we learn from fiction? In *A companion to the philosophy of literature,* ed. Garry L. Hagberg and Walter Jost, 350–366. Malden: Wiley-Blackwell.
Johnson, Marcia K., et al. 1993. Source monitoring. *Psychological Bulletin* 114 (1): 3–28.
Klerman, Daniel. 2009. Legal fictions as strategic instruments. http://extranet.isnie.org/uploads/isnie2009/klerman.pdf. Accessed 19 Aug 2014.
Knauer, Nancy J. 2010. Legal fictions and juristic truth. *St. Thomas Law Review* 23:1–49.
Koch, Frederick W. J. 2006. The hearsay rule's true raison d'être. *Ottawa Law Review* 37:249–289.
Lewis, George Cornewall. 1852. *A treatise on the methods of observation and reasoning in politics*. London: Parker.
Lind, Douglas. 2014. The pragmatic value of legal fictions. In *Legal fictions in theory and practice*, ed. William Twining and Maksymilian Del Mar. Dordrecht: Springer.
Lobban, Michael. 2014. Legal fictions before the age of reform. In *Legal fictions in theory and practice*, ed. William Twining and Maksymilian Del Mar. Dordrecht: Springer.
Maine, Henry Sumner. 1861. *Ancient law*. London: Murray.
Morgan, Mary S. 2011. Travelling facts. In *How well do facts travel? The dissemination of reliable knowledge,* ed. Peter Howlett and Mary S. Morgan, 1–42. Cambridge: Cambridge University Press.
Park, Roger C. 2003. Visions of applying the scientific method to the hearsay rule. *Michigan State Law Review* 4:1149–1174.
Potts, George R., et al. 1989. Incorporating new information into existing world knowledge. *Cognitive Psychology* 21:303–333.
Prentice, Deborah A., Richard J. Gerrig, and Daniel S. Bailis. 1997. What readers bring to the processing of fictional texts. *Psychonomic Bulletin & Review* 4 (3): 416–420.
Rapp, David N., et al. 2013. Amazing stories: Acquiring and avoiding inaccurate information from fiction. *Discourse Processes*. doi:10.1080/0163853X.2013.855048. Accessed 19 Aug 2014.
Ross, Alf. 1969. Legal fictions. In *Law, reason, and justice,* ed. Graham Hughes, 217–234. New York: New York University Press.
Saler, Michael. 2013. *As if: Modern enchantment and the literary prehistory of virtual reality*. New York: Oxford University Press.
Samuel, Geoffrey. 2014. Is law a fiction? In *Legal fictions in theory and practice*, ed. William Twining and Maksymilian Del Mar. Dordrecht: Springer.
Spolsky, Ellen. 2003. Cognitive literary historicism. *Poetics Today* 24 (2): 161–183.
Stern, Simon. 2015. Legal and literary fictions. In *New directions in law and literature*, ed. Elizabeth Anker and Bernadette Meyler (forthcoming).
Stone, Julius, and W. A. N. Wells. 1991. Evidence: Its history and policies. Sydney: Butterworths.

Weisberg, Deena Skolnick, and Joshua Goodstein. 2009. What belongs in a fictional world? *Journal of Cognition and Culture* 9 (1–2): 69–78.

Wilde, Oscar. 2008 [1895]. *The importance of being earnest.* In *The importance of being earnest and other plays,* ed. Peter Raby. Oxford: Oxford University Press.

Williams, Daniel. 2013. Rumor, reputation, and sensation in *Tess of the d'Urbervilles. Novel* 46:93–115.

Wistrich, Andrew J., et al. 2005. Can judges ignore inadmissible information? The difficulty of deliberately disregarding. *University of Pennsylvania Law Review* 153:1251–1345.

Wolcher, Louis. 2010. Unreal city, unreal law. *International Journal of Law in Context* 6:295–306.

Zunshine, Lisa. 2006. *Why we read fiction: Theory of mind and the novel.* Columbus: Ohio State University Press.

Chapter 9
Law's Fictions, Legal Fictions and Copyright Law

Burkhard Schafer and Jane Cornwell

Abstract This paper analyses legal fictions—the use of certain constructs in legal reasoning—through the eyes of law's fictions—the way in which law accounts for fictional objects in copyright law. Recent developments in philosophy that saw increased interest by analytical philosophers and logicians in the Austrian tradition of ontology, provide the theoretical framework for analysing both types of occurrence of fictional objects in legal discourse. This paves the way for a future formal and computational theory of copyright law on the one hand, a 'computational metaphysics' of the jurisprudential theory of legal fictions on the other.

9.1 From Legal Fiction to Law's Fiction: Outline of a Research Programme

The aim of this paper is to lay the philosophical foundations for a computational theory of legal reasoning with and about fictions. Jurisprudential theories of legal fictions typically focus on the first question, and the way in which fictions are created by courts (and more rarely, legislators) to justify a certain legal outcome. The term "legal fiction" in this tradition is a meta-concept that is used to label and classify certain argumentative tropes, it is however not a term that is found directly in the reasoning of the courts or the texts of statutes. In contrast, we argue that this discussion can benefit also from an analysis of the way in which law reasons explicitly *about* the nature of fictional entities—a type of argument we find in particular in copyright law. In these legal texts, the term "fiction" is used directly by the courts, as part of the legal object language. Conversely, attempts to give philosophically sound and formally rigorous accounts of certain aspects of copyright law can benefit from the jurisprudential discussion of legal fictions. We aim to show that in particular, the recent interaction between

B. Schafer (✉) · J. Cornwell
School of Law, University of Edinburgh, Old College,
South Bridge, Edinburgh EH8 9YL, Scotland
e-mail: B.Schafer@ed.ac.uk

J. Cornwell
e-mail: jane.cornwell@ed.ac.uk

M. Del Mar, W. Twining (eds.), *Legal Fictions in Theory and Practice*,
Law and Philosophy Library 110, DOI 10.1007/978-3-319-09232-4_9

Anglo-American analytical philosophy and the Austrian school of ontology provides a promising theoretical framework to understand the problems that both types of legal discourse about fictions have faced. It also suggests some answers, which might eventually lead to a computational and formal theory of reasoning with and about fictions in law. While this is the ultimate aim of our research, the discussion in this paper remains informal and tries to establish, in system theoretical terms, how the law thinks about fiction. We do this by explicating and analyzing some of the underlying intuitions that inform legal reasoning about fictions in copyright law, and indicate the structural similarities to jurisprudential questions about legal fictions.

In intellectual property law, the law address what it means to be a story or a fictional object within a story, what it means to "create" a fiction, what constitutes the identity of a fictional object and, most importantly for philosophers, under which conditions two fictional objects can be said to be the same. Following Quine's famous dictum that there can be no entity without identity (Quine 1969, p. 23), when discussing fictional objects we must first ask questions such as:

Are the unicorns in Peter S. Beagle's novel *The Last Unicorn* "the same as" the unicorns as conceived by Terry Brooks' *The Black Unicorn*, and how can we know?
Is "Sherlock Holmes" the same person in all the Conan Doyle novels?
Is he the same "amateur detective" in the Doyle novel *The Lost Special,* even though he is never identified by name there?
Is he the same Holmes in *Sherlock Holmes: The Published Apocrypha*, written by Doyle but never intended by him to be published?
Is he the same person as the Holmes in *The Exploits of Sherlock Holmes*, not written by Conan Doyle but by his son Adrian?
Is he perhaps the same person as Sherlock Holmes in Sandy Ross's *Sherlock Holmes in the 22nd Century*, even though the setting in that book is no longer Victorian England?
Or is he even "the same" character as Hayao Miyazaki's *Sherlock Hound,* where all the characters are portrayed as anthropomorphic dogs?

These philosophical questions surface in different ways but in the same form in copyright law. In a US copyright infringement case, *Walt Disney Productions v Air Pirates*,[1] the alleged infringement was the depiction of various Disney characters, including Mickey Mouse and Donald Duck, in the defendant's adult counter-culture comic books. The defendant's characters had the same names but were a "a rather bawdy depiction of the Disney characters as active members of a free thinking, promiscuous, drug ingesting counterculture".[2] Were they, or were they not, in broad terms, the same as the Disney characters, and what does "the same" mean in this case? In an infringement dispute in Russia between the

[1] *Walt Disney Productions v Air Pirates* 581 F.2d 751 (9th Cir. 1978).

[2] *Walt Disney Productions v Air Pirates* 581 F.2d 751 (9th Cir. 1978), p. 753, quoting from K. Wheelwright, "Parody, Copyrights and the First Amendment" 10 U.S.F. L. Rev. 564 1975–1976, p. 582.

"Harry Potter" creator JK Rowling and the Russian writer Dmitri Yemets, author of the highly popular "Tanya Grotter" books threats of litigation by Rowling were not followed up with successful legal action. While Yemets' argument that "The characters and the stories in the book are Russian folklore based on Russian culture and traditions" was therefore not tested in court, they show the type of argument that seems to carry weight when deciding if, while inspired by Potter the differences between the characters and the stories might be so substantive that they are not any longer "about the same" fictitious person, Harry Potter. In contrast, the Dutch courts have ruled that, despite all the changes, Yemets' books did not create a new and sufficiently independent work of art (see Karjala 2006).[3] In the language of the court, this was due to the similarities between the storylines. For us, this raises the additional question of the relation between "storyline" and "character"—can we infer for instance that if two storylines involving fictional characters are the same or nearly the same, that also the fictional characters depicted in them are the same or nearly the same? The final example is a dispute over the extent to which the "Sherlock Holmes" and "Dr Watson" characters could still be entitled to copyright protection. In December 2013 the United States District Court for the Northern District of Illinois decided that copyright in these characters had expired, but only for the characters as depicted in the older Conan Doyle novels. All aspects of their characters that were only mentioned in the later novels, set after Sherlock Holmes' retirement, remain however protected.[4] But how do we distinguish these two Holmeses? And if an author now wants to write a new Holmes novel, but is prohibited from mentioning almost everything pertaining to Professor Moriarty (who only rose to prominence in the later work *Valley of Fear*), how can we say that he is still writing about "the same" Holmes, given how much his character was formed through the interaction with his nemesis? Does this not render any new Holmes necessarily "incomplete", that is lacking character traits and memories Holmes is "known to" possess, according to the canonical work? We will later see how various forms of "incompleteness" or ontological underdeterminacy are indeed diagnostic features that set fictional objects, both in copyright law and the theory of legal fictions, apart from ordinary objects.

[3] See: at first instance *Joanne Kathleen Rowling, Uitgeverij de Harmonie BV, Time Warner Entertainment Company LP v Uitgeverij Byblos BV* (Case KG 03/477 SR, District Court of Amsterdam) [2003] E.C.D.R 23; and on appeal *Uitgeverij Byblos BV v Joanne Kathleen Rowling, Uitgeverij de Harmonie BV and Time Warner Entertainment Company LP* (Cause List No. 844/03 SKG, Court of Appeal of Amsterdam) [2004] E.C.D.R 7.

[4] *Leslie S Klinger v Conan Doyle Estates Ltd* (US District Court Northern District of Illinois Eastern Division) 23 December 2013 (available at: http://freesherlock.files.wordpress.com/2013/12/klinger-order-on-motion-for-summary-judgment-c.pdf, accessed 3 April 2014). The aspects of character added in the later stories (for examples of which, see footnote 8 below) were newer 'increments of expression' of those characters which, at least on the evidence before the court at the summary judgment stage, were entitled to copyright protection and, given the rules on copyright duration, remained in copyright for some years to come.

Copyright law also helps us better to understand the difference between fictional and non-fictional objects. Assume that, living an isolated life in a Bavarian mountain hut, I had never heard about Harry Potter. There I wrote a book about a schoolboy, Heinrich Toepfer, whose parents were killed by a nameless, powerful dark wizard. He joins a school for wizards, makes friends with Ronald Wiesel and Hermione Amtmann and eventually overcomes the foe who killed his parents. In this case, I would not have violated any copyright belonging to JK Rowling, regardless of how similar the stories or characters are. Absent a causal link of copying from her creation to mine, no amount of identical characteristics between Harry Potter and Heinrich Toepfer make them "the same" person for the purposes of copyright infringement. The stories are "about" different fictional people. Physical objects are different. Assume that I had instead discovered the properties of a field that exists throughout space and breaks certain symmetry laws of the electroweak interaction. In this case, Peter Higgs and I would have described, independently of each other, the *same* field. Had our respective theories differed regarding the attributes they ascribed to that particle, one of us would have been wrong and not the discoverer of yet another different field that has just these properties.

As we have seen, questions of the identity of fictional characters feature prominently in both philosophy and copyright law. They are, however, not normally raised in the jurisprudential debate on legal fictions. We argue that, just as the philosophy of fiction takes the question of identity between fictional objects as its starting point, so too should the discussion on legal fictions. Can different jurisdictions recognise "the same" legal fiction, even when they have discovered/invented it independently? If, as some theories of fictional objects argue, the creator of a fictional entity has a unique role to play in determining its features (see e.g., Voltolini 2006; Thomasson 2003), how does this fit into the legal reality where one court may invent a legal fiction, and other courts are not just permitted but often requested to "fill in" its attributes and develop the concept over time? How many changes can we accept until we have to conclude that we are now referring to a "different" entity? Before we try to bring together the debate in analytical philosophy and copyright law, we will briefly consider the discussion on legal fictions. We identify a systemic problem in this discussion—the vanishing of its subject matter—and indicate how this problem in particular can benefit from linking together philosophical and legal doctrinal discussions on the nature of fiction more generally.

9.2 Legal Fictions: Law's Troxler Effect?

In his critical analysis of Lon Fuller's seminal work on legal fictions, Kenneth Campbell argues that Fuller's work, while particularly rich in examples, falls well short of stating a *theory* of legal fiction (Campbell 1983). In particular, it fails to establish criteria that are necessary and sufficient to distinguish legal fictions from a whole variety of other phenomena, ranging from perjury to mistakes to mere metaphorical expressions. Fuller himself accepts this difficulty when he tries to analyse the relation of legal fictions to metaphorical word use on the one hand and presumptions on the other. Ultimately, he acknowledges that fictions may turn out to be a merely stylistic, surface phenomenon.

In a particularly interesting analysis, Frederick Schauer has recently reached a similar conclusion (Schauer in this volume, Chap. 6). He openly states what Campbell only hints at—that if we follow Fuller's account, there might not be such a thing as a discreet phenomenon of "legal fiction" left. Schauer considers this outcome unsatisfactory, taking as a given the existence of legal fictions. He concludes, convincingly, that the problem of legal fictions cannot be separated from that of legal truth, and ultimately of truth simpliciter (Chap. 6). In Schauer's words, legal fictions are therefore always "parasitic" on the gap between legal language and the legal ideal. Law has to use a language tethered in everyday language. If this were not so, "legal fictions" would simply be technical terms, "true in law", but not corresponding to anything outside it. But law also has to use rules, and rules by their very nature cannot respond to the more nuanced differences that we find in the world they try to regulate. Fictions are the necessary glue that permits judges to fill the gap between a legal ideal and the inevitable limitations that the constraints on technical legal language impose. This leads to a normative account of legal fiction as a necessary part of "good interpretative practice".

While there are sound intuitions behind this analysis, a comparative approach shows how precarious this solution is. In particular, the jurisprudential discussion of fiction in Germany demonstrates that the concept cannot possibly be dependent upon the act of juridical interpretation, since the very same issues also arise in a discussion of rational law making. In 1859, Gustav Demelius' influential work on legal fiction demonstrated its importance for codified legal systems where the legislator and not the judge, avails themselves of this tool. In 1969 and 1976 respectively, Josef Esser and Dieter Meurer published extended monographs that explicitly put the discussion of legal fictions into the context of a theory of good law making (Esser 1969; Meurer 1976). Esser in particular developed an account of legal fiction that follows in many respects that of Schauer. For Esser, there cannot possibly be "true" or "epistemic" legal fictions; any attempt to claim that legal fictions involve an element of deception or error is for him a throwback to discredited nineteenth century jurisprudence that sees law as a set of abstract statements about causal relationships in a "legal world". He writes:

> The often-heard opinion that there are in addition to the "referring", non-essential or formal legal fictions also "essential" or "real" legal fiction (which, by "obscuring legal truth", force the judge to distort facts), has to be ascribed to the realm of pure fantasy. It can only be understood as the total misunderstanding of the normative character of law. To be "misled" presupposes that a descriptive judgement was intended in the first place. The proponent of this mistaken idea has therefore to assume that law is a system of descriptive statements (with truth claims). (Esser 1969, p. 28, translation by one of the authors)

Esser thus echoes Schauer's notion that legal fictions are essentially normative and not descriptive. However, contrary to Schauer, they are not the result of ordinary language use in law, nor are they conceptually dependent on the judicial interpretive practice. This makes his analysis a more explicit statement of an idea that Fuller also ponders but does not pursue to its logical conclusion: that legal fictions might be a mere stylistic quirk. Fuller discusses the legal expression "X is deemed (in law) to be Y" and concludes that it functions in close analogy to a legal fiction properly so-called. However, the openness with which the language of the law here acknowledges that X is "only deemed" to be Y means that a necessary characteristic of a legal fiction, its falsity, is lacking. "X is deemed to be Y" cannot be false for a very similar reason why Esser's "referring fictions" cannot be false—they do not even try to make a statement about the external world. Fuller concludes that "legal fictions" as developed in common law countries and "deemed to be" constructions in Roman law seem indeed to be functionally identical. This leads to the conclusion that any difference in surface expression is an issue of legal style and not ontological substance.

At this point, we can identify a common problem in jurisprudential theories about legal fictions. The very moment we try to take legal fictions seriously and focus our analytical gaze upon them, they seem to disappear into nothing. Rather than describe them as "parasitic" as Schauer does, a better metaphor might be that of an optical illusion, such as the Troxler effect, where we have difficulty focusing our gaze on a "floater" in our field of vision. For Bentham, legal fictions are very much the villain of the piece, and are "to justice exactly as swindling is to trade" (Bentham 1938, p. 235). If they are villains, though, then they are very much like the villainous *Weeping Angels* in the universe of Dr Who: terrifying, fast, dynamic and ultimately lethal, but only when not looked at. The moment we focus our eyes on them they become just an immobile part of the decoration, rendered harmless and ineffectual by the very process of observing them.

We can get an initial idea why this might be the case by looking at some proposed diagnostic criteria for legal fictions:

- a statement which is propounded with a complete or partial consciousness of its falsity
- which is, however, not a lie
- and also not an error
- yet has some utility (based on Fuller 1930).

The first three criteria all use a privative definition; they tell us more what legal fictions are *not* than what they are. Legal fictions are *not* true, they are *not* lies and they are *not* mere errors. Following Fuller's analysis, Schauer concludes that, because the concept of legal fiction is parasitic upon the concept of legal truth, we cannot determine what legal fictions actually are unless we have a theory of legal truth. We argue that the intuition behind this idea is sound, but that the way it is expressed conflates two crucially different issues that the separate philosophical debate on fictions can help us differentiate. First, "truth" and "falsity" are properties of propositions, not of objects. The literature on legal fictions, including Bentham,

Fuller and Schauer, tends to conceive of legal fictions as statements or doctrines. This leads naturally to thinking of them as something that is "not true". But this is a problematic starting point for whatever one thinks about legal fictions, it seems obvious that there are many statements using legal fictions that are literally true. "Legal personhood of companies is a legal fiction" is an obvious candidate. "Legal persons do not have a right to vote in elections in the US" is a more interesting, intuitively true statement. Since we can always make true statements about objects that, in one way or another, do not "exist" in reality, it is not therefore the true/false dichotomy that should concern us, but a question of ontology: to what, if any, part of reality do terms for legal fictions (such as "legal person") refer? A related question of metaphysics now arises: what properties do these objects need to have, if they exist, to do what they do? Legal fictions, being objects, cannot be lies, mistakes or true accounts of the law. They are of a different syntactic category altogether. Rather, the question is what terms for fictional objects contribute to the truth value of the sentences in which they appear and whether this differs systematically from the contribution other objects make.

Philosophical discussions on the nature of fictions tackle this issue head on. Bertrand Russell's highly influential work "On denoting" (1905) is a case in point: in his example sentence "The King of France is bald", the term "The King of France" behaves differently from "The Queen" in "The Queen of England is bald". Both sentences are false, but only in the second case can we infer that the monarch has hair. Russell proposes "unpacking" the fictional "King of France" as a complex statement that eliminates the need to talk about fictional entities, rendering it as: "There is one person only who is king of France and bald". Although Russell's eliminative approach remains influential in the philosophical discussion of fiction, it faces the problem that his eliminative stance means that sentences that we intuitively judge to be true turn out to be false or meaningless.

While his analysis resonates with accounts of fictions that relate them to lies or mistakes, transposing it to *legal* fictions faces problems and creates difficulties. Russell's analysis tries to understand fictional objects as the opposite of physical objects. However, it is not only legal *fictions*, but also many other pieces of our legal "deontic furniture" (Hage 2012) that are different from physical objects. Physically, money is just a piece of coloured paper, what makes it money is that it "counts as" a way of making payments. Registering a land purchase does not alter its physical properties, but henceforward it "counts as" property. Searle's "counts as" conditionals are central for the creation of the "legal world" and its institutions (see e.g. Boella and van der Torre 2006). "Counts as" fulfils the same linguistic function as the "deemed to be" construction for legal fictions discussed above. If we were to eliminate legal fictions Russell-style, we risk eliminating most of the law's institutions along with them. The implicit physicalism that underpins his analysis is unsuitable for an analysis of legal ontology.

A possible way out for the eliminist is to focus on the act by which fictions are created. For Searle, "counts as", like its cousin "deemed to be", are speech acts. We could consider the performative act by which judges create legal fictions as an "unauthorised" attempt to add objects to our ontology. Historically, this is the line that Bentham took, and it continues to influence the common law analysis of legal fiction. But in Searle's analysis, performative acts without the right authority simply fail: the judges in such a case may have *tried* to create a new object, but failed to do so. In such a case, "legal fictions" are simply errors. Here, too, legal fictions ultimately "disappear": there can be no such thing. Nor does this analysis account for the creation of legal fictions by the legislature, which by definition has all the authority needed. However, as our comparative analysis has shown, legal fictions can be created through statute.

By blurring the distinction between mistakes and legal fictions, we also fail to account for the understanding of fiction within the legal community. For example, lawyers understand intuitively that there is a difference between someone claiming that legal persons in Scots law must have only female partners (a mistake) and a judge granting a company the right to file charges against a debtor (a "correct" use of the legal fiction that employs the concept). If "legal person" had no referent, both sentences would be equally wrong.

Finally, Russellian eliminativism also makes it impossible to distinguish different legal fictions from each other. If I fail to build a house, and also fail to plant a tree, then I do not create two new and distinct objects—"my failed-to-be built house" and my "failed-to-be-planted tree"—that have properties distinguishing them from each other. In both cases, I created the same thing, that is a no-thing (for further discussion, see Donnellan 1974). From a Russellian point of view, the house I did not build is the same "thing" as the tree I did not plant. Similarly, all legal fictions would refer to "the same" thing, the empty set. Ejectment, legal personhood and becoming steward of the Chiltern Hundreds all become "the same" thing—that is nothing. A theory of legal fictions, or a history of them, becomes impossible.

We therefore face a dilemma: because our ontology of legal fictions is parasitic on our legal ontology simpliciter, any attempt to determine legal fictions is in danger of collapsing them into either "normal" legal objects; or they are seen as cognitive mistakes or lies, and with that no objects at all. Yet neither route is appropriate to explain the semantic role legal fictions actually play when used in legal reasoning.

To find a way out of this dilemma, we need to circumvent the ontological question at least temporarily, and find some data that is independent from a discussion of general legal ontology. The discussion of literary fictions in copyright law and philosophy hopes to achieve just that. The first thing we can learn from it is to separate the "ontological" question of whether fictions exist from a discussion of their "metaphysical nature"—that is, an attempt to determine what characteristics they have to have *if* they exist (see Thomasson 1999). The way to determine their nature in turn is to analyse what contribution they make to the sentences in which they appear. A systematic analysis of copyright decisions would therefore be highly desirable. We cannot offer such a detailed analysis in this paper, however, as it would require a discussion of the underlying legal framework, something that must be left to future work. Instead, we will discuss the three most promising philosophical theories on fictional objects and will highlight, through a few examples, where the connection between copyright law, analytical philosophy of fiction and jurisprudential discussions of legal fictions are the most interesting or promising.

9.3 Law's Fictions: Adjudicating Creativity, Creatively

We have mentioned above three examples from copyright law where courts have had to establish identity criteria for fictional objects or the narratives within which they appear. Even though only a few jurisdictions, most notably the US, grant an independent copyright in fictional "characters", while most focus on the entire storyline, we argue that cognitively, judging two storylines to be the same or nearly the same necessarily also requires us to come to a reasoned conclusion about the identity relation between fictional objects. Is Tanya Grotter the same person as "Harry Potter" (possibly because the story gives them similar experiences)? How do the Sherlock Holmes and Doctor Watson, whose characteristics and character traits are identified only in the later Conan Doyle novels, differ from the Holmes and Watson of the earlier novels? Since Disney's Mickey Mouse would never use obscenities, can another cartoon mouse that looks like him and has the same name but swears a lot really be "him"?[5]

We also argue, using examples from literary fiction, that we pose this type of question about fictional characters all the time, with very strong underlying intuitions. Our ability to reason about fictional objects is far from trivial. The most important systems of classical logic, which lie at the very heart of our ability to reason, cope badly with them. In classical logic with identity, names of fictional objects denote the empty set. In these systems, it can be proven that Potter is indeed strictly "identical to" Tanya Grotter. Unfortunately, we can also "prove" that he is identical to Sherlock Holmes, Zeus and the largest prime number. Every fiction writer could sue any other writer. To express a more reasonable idea about identity requires us to use a much more expressive logic. A candidate could be second order logic. In this system, we can express Leibniz's identity principle: two objects are the same if and only if they share *all* their properties. But now we face the opposite problem: even the smallest change in the way a character is described makes him a new and different object.

Obviously, neither analysis is convincing. The first is overly wide—all fictional entities become the same. The second is overly narrow—almost no two fictional entities will ever be the same, provided there is even the smallest of differences. Yet, classical first- and second-order logic are at the heart of our capacity for reasoning. For physical objects, either approach would work, though with some minor modifications in the second case. If my car is stolen, it is possible to compare the physical properties of the car the defendant has to determine if it is mine. Identity criteria for physical objects are comparatively easy to establish. When an idea of

[5] The opportunity to address this question was missed in the *Walt Disney Productions v Air Pirates* case itself. In that case, the court held that copying a comic book character's visual image constituted copying to an extent sufficient to justify a finding of infringement and this was not contested, the court proceeding directly to consider (and reject) the defendant's plea of a parody-based 'fair use' defence: 581 F.2d 751 (9th Cir. 1978), p. 756. There was no argument about infringement of any rights in the wider 'characters' of the copied cartoon creatures. See further Nevins (1991–1992).

mine is stolen, the situation is considerably more complex, and we need to go beyond classical logic and amend it appropriately. In copyright law, we do this almost unthinkingly. In the jurisprudential discussion on legal fiction, the difficulties in developing a satisfying theory may be due to intuitions that are shaped by our reasoning about physical objects and the classical logic that describes them. In analytical philosophy, interest in our ability to reason with fictions has resulted in several new "metaphysical" theories of fiction, each of them typically coming with proposals to extend classical logic.[6] Several of these theories can be given a rigorous formal treatment. Ultimately, our aim is such a formal account of reasoning with fictional objects in copyright law. This could assist developing more appropriate technological solutions to the increasing costs in copyright litigation through appropriate software tools. Here we are laying only the ground for such an analysis, focusing on the implications and general soundness of the respective theories.

9.3.1 Possibilism

The emergence of possible world semantics gave a major impetus for the renewed interest by analytical philosophers and logicians in the nature of fictional objects (see for example Currie 1990; Lewis 1978). Originally it was conceived to distinguish necessary truth (truths that hold in all possible worlds) from merely contingent truths—statements that are true in some worlds, but false in others (see Goldblatt 2003, p. 309). Possible world semantics later became a powerful tool to model belief sentences of the form: "Peter believes that X is the case". The "X" within the scope of the belief operator behaves differently from contexts were we talk about the physical world. If I murder Peter, and Peter is also the president, we can infer by substitution of identicals that I also murdered the president. If, in contrast, I only believe I killed Peter, we cannot infer that I also believe I have killed the president, as I may not be aware of the contingent identity of the two. The way this is modelled in possible world semantics is to say that, in addition to the real world, there is a possible world, consistent with everything I believe, where Peter is not the president (Hintikka 1962, for a formal treatment see Kripke 1963). Furthermore, if I believe Peter was killed by a unicorn, then there is another possible world where there are unicorns and one of them killed Peter. The last example shows why it was natural to use possible world semantics and the modal logics that it inspired for reasoning about fictions. If, merely by thinking, we can create possible worlds, then this must be true even more so for the worlds that writers of fiction create for us.[7]

However, possibilism faces a significant problem when used to model fictional characters. The possible objects that it postulates behave like "real" objects in every respect, and differ from objects in the actual world only by the fact that they inhabit

[6] Our account is heavily indebted to the excellent exposition of the discussion by Kroon and Voltiolini (2011).

[7] For a discussion see, for example, Putnam (1973) and the papers in Schwartz (1977), critically Howell (1979) with a reply by Pavel (1979).

alternative realities. In these alternative worlds, Sherlock Holmes really *is* a famous detective, and Dumbledore really *is* a famous wizard. This means in particular that any statement about them has a definitive truth value—Holmes, by virtue of being a human, has blood, and therefore also a blood group. But which one? The canonical Holmes stories leave it open. Do we now have at least four different Holmes' in four different possible worlds, each with a different blood group? Which of these is *the* Holmes? (for this line of argument, see Kaplan 1973, pp. 505–506; Kripke 1979, pp. 156–158).

This is obviously also a problem for copyright law—which one of these is the Holmes that is the subject of the property claims made in court? We have seen above that recently, a US court distinguished attributes which Holmes and Watson had "acquired" in novels written after a certain point in time.[8] While we can make intuitive sense of this decision,[9] it does pose problems for a possible world account where characters are treated as "real". Like real humans, the possible world Sherlock acquires new properties and characteristics over time. However, he acquires these whenever changes happen according to the timeline of the narrative and not according the publishing schedule. We learn, for instance, that Sherlock has an older brother, Mycroft, only in "The adventure of the Greek interpreter", published in 1893. This story itself is set in 1888. However, since Holmes was born in 1854 (and is therefore 5 years older than his creator), and Mycroft is Holmes' older brother, the alternative "possible Holmes" always has had a brother since the day of his birth. The distinction that the US District Court made in the Sherlock Holmes case is perfectly intelligible in terms of fiction writing: fictional characters acquire properties the moment their creator writes about them, not when they would have acquired the property according to the timeline of the novel. The decision is also entirely understandable in copyright policy terms.[10] But if we analyse the creative writing process as a creation of entities in possible worlds, this distinction becomes problematic.

There is another problem with probabilism and possible world realism when it is used to analyse fictional contexts. So far, we tried to account for our intuition

[8] Such attributes included character traits such as Dr Watson's athletic background (first described in a 1924 short story) and personal storylines, such as Sherlock Holme's retirement (first described in a 1926 short story): *Leslie S Klinger v Conan Doyle Estates Ltd* (US District Court Northern District of Illinois Eastern Division) 23 December 2013 (available at: http://freesherlock.files.wordpress.com/2013/12/klinger-order-on-motion-for-summary-judgment-c.pdf, accessed 3 April 2014), p. 15.

[9] The US court had no difficulty with the fact that, as Conan Doyle Estates put it, its ruling would in effect 'dismantle' each character into two versions, a public domain version and a copyright-protected version: *Leslie S Klinger v Conan Doyle Estates Ltd* (US District Court Northern District of Illinois Eastern Division) 23 December 2013 (available at: http://freesherlock.files.wordpress.com/2013/12/klinger-order-on-motion-for-summary-judgment-c.pdf, accessed 3 April 2014), pp. 13–14.

[10] See in particular *Leslie S Klinger v Conan Doyle Estates Ltd* (US District Court Northern District of Illinois Eastern Division) 23 December 2013 (available at: http://freesherlock.files.wordpress.com/2013/12/klinger-order-on-motion-for-summary-judgment-c.pdf, accessed 3 April 2014), p. 14. The decision follows existing US case law precedent on this issue, in particular Silverman v CBS, Inc. 870 F.2d 40 (2d Cir. 1989).

that the sentence "Sherlock Holmes is a detective in London" is true by stating that there is a possible world where there really is a Sherlock Holmes in London who is a detective. However, what about the following sentence: "Conan Doyle could have set the Sherlock stories in Edinburgh"? Intuitively, this sentence is true as well. In the standard account in modal logic, this means that there are other possible worlds where Doyle did actually set the Sherlock stories in Edinburgh. It seems we now have two types of possible worlds, and two types of fictional Sherlocks—the ones that exist relative to our actual world (in which he is a real detective in London) and those where he exists relative to the possible world where Doyle varied the Holmes stories and wrote him as a fictional detective in Edinburgh.

How does the situation look when we try to represent *legal* fictions through counterparts in possible worlds? Here too, some of the expressions and the reasoning with them can be expressed in a straightforward manner. We mentioned above the fiction of *Ejectment*, a fictitious story told by the plaintiff in a procedure to avoid trial by combat and get a jury trial instead (see Mellinkoff 1964 and the contribution by Sparkes 2014 (Chap. 13) in this book). In this fiction,—from which came the name "John Doe" for a person unknown—the plaintiff claimed that a certain John Doe leased land under dispute from him. Even though the plaintiff, the defendant and the judge knew that John Doe never existed, the defendant was barred from raising this objection. In this case, it is straightforward to represent the argument using possible world semantics. Since it is easily conceivable that, counterfactually, a real Mr John Doe entered a lease with the plaintiff, making Doe the inhabitant of a possible world is straightforward. The situation is, however, much more problematic with a fiction such as the personhood of the company. Here, our analysis would lead us to argue that there are some possible worlds in which companies "really" are persons—and it is unclear what this is even supposed to mean. This first result might indicate also that a uniform treatment of legal fictions is impossible—different fictions have a very different logic, and contribute to the sentences in which they are used in very different ways. While it seems to be the case that a theory of reasoning with legal fictions needs to go beyond classical logic, plausible extensions might work well with some fictions but less well with others.

Legal fictions, analysed with possible world semantics, faces furthermore the same problems as the "possible Holmes" who lives in Edinburgh. While possible world counterparts might enable us to express what we mean when we say that ""legal persons can sue" is true in Scots law", and ""legal persons can marry" is false for Scots law", we now face problems if we want to express in addition true counterfactual ideas such as "the legislator could have denied legal persons the right to sue". To represent the first two sentences in the language of possible worlds, we would say that there are possible worlds consistent with Scots law where companies "really" are persons and can sue, and none where they can marry. To render the third sentence true, there would, however, have to be alternative worlds where the legislator has denied them the right to sue, contradicting the first statement. Statements about possible actions a legislator might have taken but intentionally avoided play an important role in statutory interpretation. We need therefore a way to maintain an ability to express alternative courses of actions which a legislator could have taken.

All these objections affect different forms of possible world semantics to different degrees, and some of them might be able to handle these problems. However, treating fictional objects just like physical objects, except in other worlds, seems to miss something crucial about their nature. These problems are avoided by the other two theories that we will now look at.

9.3.2 Meinongian Theories

The first theory which we will investigate more closely is historically the oldest attempt to deal adequately with fictional objects, developed by the German philosopher Meinong (1904). Central to his approach is the idea that there are three categories of things: concrete objects (existing in space and time); abstract object, like numbers (existing outside space and time); and, finally, fictional objects (see for this and the following also Kroon and Voltolini). These fictional objects are a sui generis category with similarities to both concrete and abstract objects. Fictional objects, such as the Fountain of Youth, which do not exist but people nevertheless search for, are the paradigmatic case. Rather than "existing", Meinong argues that fictional objects merely "subsist" ("Bestehen"). Crucially, subsisting is, he argues, enough for them to have properties. This allows him to separate the question of what "such and such" an object is (its "So-sein") from the question of whether it exists. The properties that make a fictional object a "such and such" are those properties with which objects of that type are described (Meinong 1904, p. 82). This notion has recently been given a precise formal treatment by Routley under the term *Characterization Principle* (Routley 1980, p. 46): Fictional objects have those and only those properties with which they are characterized, that is, those that they have in the stories that feature them. The "Fountain of Youth" does not exist, yet we can intelligibly say that it is a fountain and that, as described, it grants eternal youth. Sherlock Holmes, then, really *is* a famous detective. However, fictional entities so conceived are not completely determined with respect to their properties. Because Conan Doyle's stories do not say what blood group Holmes is, in the Meinongian approach he is *neither* blood group A, B or 0. And yet he is nevertheless a human being with human blood.

This is important to model adequately the reasoning in copyright law about derivative works. Fan fiction in particular will often take the basic character from the original novel and then expand on those aspects that the original author neglected or omitted. The author of fan fiction therefore balances continuity—there must not be a direct inconsistency with the canonical work—with creativity by adding new features to the character. If we think of fictional characters as real persons in other possible worlds, this idea is difficult to represent. But if we accept that fictional characters are different from ordinary objects by being essentially "incomplete" to some degree, that is there are certain characteristics which are unspecified in respect of them so that they neither have nor have not that characteristic, this aspect of the derivate creation becomes unproblematic. For legal fictions, this explains why, for example, legal persons can be sued, but it makes no sense to ask if they can or cannot marry. As described by the courts, they have the first property, and by being silent about the second, the court created an object that, like all fictional objects but unlike all physical objects, allows for the possibility that it neither has, nor does not have, a certain given property.

As with possible world semantics, there are several modern restatements of Meinong's theory that differ in their technical details (see e.g. Parsons 1980; Jacquette 1996) and in the degree in which they give rise to a fully formal logic (as, for example, in Zalta 1983). Zalta's version is of particular interest for us. He popularised it under the name "abstract object theory", which for him forms an essential part of his wider research project of a "computational metaphysics".[11] In addition to Meinong, Zalta's philosophical position is influenced mainly by the work of another Austrian philosopher, Ernst Mally. It was Mally who suggested distinguishing ordinary concrete objects such as houses, trees or continents which "exemplify" properties, from other "abstract" objects that merely "encode" them. In Zalta's own words:

> The theory is based on Ernst Mally's distinction between exemplifying and encoding a property. This is a distinction between two fundamental kinds of predication, and it is formally represented in the theory as the distinction between the atomic formulas '*Fx*' ('*x* exemplifies *F*') and '*xF*' ('*x* encodes *F*'). The formula '*Fx*' represents the classical kind of predication; it is used to logically analyze such simple sentences as 'John is happy', 'Clinton is president', and 'Socks is a cat'. Mally's idea, in essence, was that we should *not* represent sentences about fictional objects, such as 'Sherlock Holmes is a detective', 'Pegasus has wings', 'King Lear had 3 daughters', and 'Zeus lived on Mt. Olympus', in terms of the notation '*Fx*' (only real, concrete objects can exemplify the properties of being a detective, having wings, having daughters, or living on Mt. Olympus). Nevertheless, Mally reasoned in effect that there must be some mode of predication, some sense of the words 'is' and 'has' (German 'ist' and 'hat'), for which it is true to say 'Sherlock Holmes is a detective' and 'Pegasus has wings' (we wouldn't understand the story and myth properly if we didn't imagine objects that, in some sense, were instances of the properties in question).
> So Mally informally introduced the notion '*x encodes F*' (German: *F determiniert x*) as a new mode of predication that is more appropriate for the logical analysis of sentences about fictions and other abstract objects. Whereas the real detective Pinkerton exemplifies detectivehood ('*Dp*'), Sherlock Holmes encodes this property ('*hD*').

Zalta and other "non-orthodox" Meinongians emphasise the non-spatiotemporal mode of existence of fictional objects, which makes them more similar to abstract objects, such as numbers. Fictional objects in this approach become something like generic objects, or roles. Kroon and Voltolini (2011) describe them in analogy to the object referred to as the U.S. President in the following statement:

> The US President faces an election every four years.

Obviously, no specific US president faces election every 4 years, rather it is the role or office of US President. Similarly, San Pedro, a fictional country from the Sherlock Holmes short story "The Adventure of Wisteria Lodge" is not a country in the same way as Brazil. San Pedro is fictional, countries are not. Rather, it is an

[11] http://mally.stanford.edu/cm/.

abstract object that plays a specific narrative role, to provide a backstory for one of the villains, who before coming to England was Dictator of this fictional country.

Unsurprisingly, because this approach gives us semantics for legal institutions such as "the US President", it also works well for legal fictions. If the court cases on ejectment were theatre plays, then John Doe would be a small role with just one line—his "job" is to create a lease, so that the story can move on and the jury can enter the stage. The role that he plays fully determines his identity.

Finally, we have argued above that a comprehensive theory of legal reasoning about fictions (in copyright law) and reasoning about legal fictions needs to account for two very different types of statement. Some are "internal" to the fiction, and have the form:

A) "Sherlock Holmes is a detective."
B) "Legal persons can enter into contracts."

Others are "external" to these fictional entities, such as:

C) "Sherlock Holmes made Conan Doyle famous."
D) "Legal persons are controversial examples of legal fiction."
E) "It is permissible in copyright law to write new Sherlock Holmes novels."

Meinongians can account for this difference either by distinguishing two types of properties, (which in the literature are called nuclear and extra-nuclear properties), or, as indicated above, by two different ways in which predicates can apply to fictional objects, namely by "encoding" and or "exemplifying" a property. In the first case, being a detective is a core property of Holmes, while making Doyle famous is an extra-nuclear property (see, for example Parsons 1980; Jacquette 1996). On the second account, Holmes encodes the property of being a detective, while he exemplifies the property of "making Doyle famous" (Zalta 1983). Similarly, legal persons encode the property of "being able to enter into contracts" while exemplifying the property of "being a legal fiction".

There is a problem with this account, however. If we accept that fictional objects necessarily have all and only those core properties that are mentioned in the relevant stories that introduce them, a very simple identity criterion follows. If x encodes the same properties as y, then $x=y$. Kroon and Voltolini (2011) use an example from literature to argue that this is problematic and, as we shall see, copyright law comes to the same conclusion. Their example is Jorge Luis Borges's story of Pierre Menard, who writes a text that is word-for-word identical with Miguel Cervantes's *Don Quixote*. Menard and Cervantes have never read each other's works. However, since the stories are word-for-word-identical, the character of Don Quixote is described in an identical way in both books. This in turn means that one and the same set of properties corresponds to two different fictional objects: Cervantes' Don Quixote and Menard's Don Quixote. Are they the same Don Quixote, or do we have two different fictional objects that simply look very similar indeed? Meinongians have to argue the former—the identity of the properties determines the identity of the fictional object, making them more akin to separate scientific discoveries. Most logicians have, however, argued that this is an unsatisfactory outcome.[12] Copyright law agrees: if Menard did not copy from Cervantes's work, they each hold copyright in their own creation, and this should entail that there are indeed two different Quixotes, neither infringing the other. To the extent that the law has to differentiate the two, it would take recourse to non-nuclear properties, e.g., "Quixote 1 was created in 1605 by Cervantes, Quixote 2 was created 1606 by Menard." Meinongians take the idea that fictional characters are determined by the story in which they appear more seriously than possibilism, but maybe not yet seriously enough.

9.3.3 Creationism

Creationism builds on Meinong, but addresses this problem. For Meinongians, abstract objects exist timelessly (we cannot meaningfully ask when the number 4 first came into existence). For them, fictional objects also pre-date the story-telling activities that, at least intuitively, create them. Neither the author nor the audience have a role to play in this account. For *legal* fictions, this might be an advantage. Here, the identity of the author arguably matters considerably less than in literary contexts; it is at best "the court", rather than the judge as a natural person, that matters. The idea that fictions exist as a-temporal, abstract objects fits well into the common law notion that judges "discover" rather than invent the law–legal fictions then exist as abstract plans which "fall into place" when needed by a given legal situation. This again also means, however, that the difference between legal fictions and any other type of legal object gets blurred.

As a position in the analytical philosophy of fiction, creationism tries to address this issue and to take the role of the creator seriously (see, for example, Searle 1979; Salmon 1998; Thomasson 1999; or Voltolini 2006). Fictional objects are still understood as a type of abstract object. They are also, however, essentially artefacts, that is creations of an author. They come into being at the moment in time when their author creates them, which sets them apart from timeless platonic entities such as numbers. Similarly, unlike abstract platonic numbers, they are *dependent* entities—they could not exist but for other objects—the author and the story(s) in which they appear (see, for example, Thomasson 1999). This also means that if an author dies, and if all his works are destroyed and forgotten, the fictional object disappears too—an idea that was recently used to great effect in Jasper Forde's "meta-novels". Being able to speak of the age of a fictional object in this way matters both for literary and for legal fiction. In a copyright case, it may be essential if a character was created under an old versus a more recent copyright regime; or in a commercial law case it may be essential if the parties conducted their transaction before or after the courts introduced a new legal fiction.

[12] As Kroon and Voltolini (2011) note, the Menard thought experiment was introduced by Lewis (1978, p. 39) and then further developed by Fine (1982, p. 107); see also Thomasson (1999, pp. 7 and 56).

Do we gain any insights from this fairly obvious and, one might even say, trivial statement that fictional characters are the creation of their authors?[13] Its solution brings the philosophical analysis in line with the intuitions underpinning copyright law in the case of independent creation of identically described objects. Since there were two independent acts of creation, by two different creators, Menard's and Cervantes' Don Quixote are indeed two different entities (see Voltolini 2006, p. 32 ff). Similarly, identity conditions within one and the same opus do not raise any problem. *X* and *Y* are the same fictional object *F*, if X and *Y* are described by the author as being such (Thomasson 1999, p. 3).

More problematic, but also more interesting for our purposes, is the question of whether we can determine if the same object appears in different works by different authors. Thomasson suggests as a necessary condition that two sets of descriptions *X* and *Y* by different authors refer to the same fictional object only if the author of the second work is competently acquainted with the character *Y* in the earlier work, and intends to import *X* into his work as *Y* (Thomasson 1999, p. 67). This aligns closely with our intuitions from copyright law, where the central issue is of course that of copying. It explains why the translation of a work into another language is still about the same fictional characters, even if they are given new names. It also allows us to model the concept of "derivative works." Fan fiction in particular, such as for example a short story in which Harry Potter has an affair with Hermione, satisfies the condition that the copier is fully acquainted with the original, canonical, work and explicitly intends to incorporate the characters into their own story.

For legal fictions, this approach allows us to model situations where countries harmonise their laws by adopting "the same" legal fiction—different terminology and subtly different characteristics in the various jurisdictions notwithstanding. It also allows us to explain how it can be said that subsequent courts use or talk about the "same" fiction that another court had first created, while developing it further. This was one of the desiderata we identified in the first part, and, while it may seem trivial, it is something jurisprudential theories of legal fiction struggle to account for.

However, the inherently more fuzzy identity criteria in creationist accounts also raise problems. In many novels, the majority of characters are nothing more than background or part of the scenery. For example, in Tolkien's Lord of the Rings thousands of Orcs go into battle at Isengard. Introduced in just a few sentences, these are "indiscriminable"—they are all described by the same set of properties, namely that they are Orcs and have fought at Isengard. Did Tolkien create thousands of Orcs? In copyright law, this can matter. A common form of derivative work is to take a minor character from a novel and tell the story from their perspective. The Orc in Terry Pratchett's *Unseen Academicals* is of this nature. It remains ontologically dependent on another author's work. We understand Pratchett because we know Tolkien. But which one of the many nameless Orcs from Tolkien did Pratchett "pick" to become his hero? Voltolini argues that such "generic" characters are not fictional objects

[13] Those who are sceptical about the explanatory value of such a proposition are, for example, Brock (2010).

at all (Voltolini 2006, pp. 234–235). Intellectual property law seems to reflect this intuition. For example, in US law the principal test on entitlement to protection in copyright for fictional characters is the so-called 'distinct delineation' test.[14] The test stems from the following comments made by Judge Learned Hand in *Nichols v Universal Pictures Corporation*:[15]

> [W]e do not doubt that two plays may correspond in plot closely enough for infringement. How far that correspondence must go is another matter. Nor need we hold that the same may not be true as to the characters, quite independently of the "plot" proper, though, as far as we know, such a case has never arisen. If Twelfth Night were copyrighted, it is quite possible that a second comer might so closely imitate Sir Toby Belch or Malvolio as to infringe, but it would not be enough that for one of his characters he cast a riotous knight who kept wassail to the discomfort of the household, or a vain and foppish steward who became amorous of his mistress....[16]

In *Sunbank Trust v Mifflin,* a case concerning the alleged infringement of copyright in characters from the novel 'Gone With The Wind', the US Eleventh Circuit also noted:[17]

> At one end of the spectrum, *scenes a faire*—the stock scenes and hackneyed character types that "naturally flow from a common theme"—are considered "ideas," and therefore are not copyrightable.... But as plots become more intricately detailed and characters become more idiosyncratic, they at some point cross the line into "expression" and are protected by copyright.[18]

Voltolini's approach accounts for this reasoning. He argues that a proper understanding of the creative process must inform any theory of fiction, and that in particular we must distinguish between intentional objects, that is, objects we think about, and fictional objects proper (see also Thomasson 1999, p. 89). But what turns an intentional object, that is, an object that exists in another possible world, into a fictional object? One potential explanation discussed by Kroon and Voltolini is its ability to be 'shared' amongst readers by appearing in a text. Another possible addition would be to include a readership that joins into a game of pretence (Schiffer 1996, 2003; Thomasson 2003). This fits into the way in which legal fictions are conceived—they only "truly" exist when expressed in a court decision, and in addition,

[14] Although the most used, it should be noted that the 'distinct delineation' test is not the only test which has been used by the US courts on the issue of entitlement to copyright protection for fictional characters. Other tests have included the so-called 'story being told' test, which looks at the relative importance of character over plot in the work in which the relevant character appears: see, in particular, *Warner Bros. Pictures Inc. v Columbia Broadcasting System, Inc.* 216 F.2d 945 (9th Cir. 1954). However, it is thought that US law is now converging on the 'character delineation' test: Kurtz (2012–2013), at p. 447. On the different tests and their application in US law and for commentary on how the 'distinct delineation' test has been applied in practice, see further: Kurtz (1990); Schienke (2005); Karjala (2006); Katyal (2006); Lai Chung (2007–2008); Foley (2008–2009); Coe (2011).

[15] *Nichols v Universal Pictures Corporation* et al 45 F.2d 119 (2d Cir. 1930).

[16] *Nichols v Universal Pictures Corporation* et al 45 F.2d 119 (2d Cir. 1930), p. 121.

[17] *Sunbank Trust v Houghton Mifflin Company* 268 F.3d 1257 (11th Cir. 2001).

[18] *Sunbank Trust v Houghton Mifflin Company* 268 F.3d 1257 (11th Cir. 2001), at p. 1266.

other courts, lawyers and parties accept it so that it becomes an established "game of pretence".

This further refinement of the creationist approach to fictional objects again matches key ideas from copyright law. Merely thinking about a story or a character creates only an "idea"; for protection to arise, however, copyright requires a sufficiently developed expression of the idea in an external medium. It is that expression, not the idea, which is protected. Similarly, when analysing legal reasoning with fictions, it seems highly plausible to argue that they are not created when a judge first thinks about them, but only if and when they are made "concrete" in a public text, such as a court judgement and the relevant community (at the very least other judges, but arguably also the wider legal community or even the general population) join in the game of pretence.

We have seen that the three most popular philosophical theories of fictional objects all avoid the "collapse" of fictions as separate objects of study that bedevilled the discussion in jurisprudence. They all manage to establish fictions as sui generis objects, different from both non-fictional objects and from mere nothingness. All three also matched, to varying degrees, the core intuitions that underpin legal reasoning about fictions in copyright law. We conclude therefore that all three have something to offer when analysing legal fictions proper. However, none of them fully reconciles our traditional philosophical intuitions with those of the lawyer. Rather, they all account for different aspects of the way in which we reason with fictions in law. If it should prove possible to combine these philosophical theories, as was recently tried by Zalta (2000) and Voltolini (2006), a feasible and comprehensive theory of legal fiction may well be the result.

Acknowledgment Work on this paper was supported by the RCUK CREATE network grant. We are particularlygrateful for the help provided by our RA Laurence Diver.

References

Bentham, J. 1838–1843. *The works of Jeremy Bentham*. 11 vols, vol. 5. Edinburgh: William Tait (published under the Superintendence of his Executor, John Bowring).

Boella, G., and L. van der Torre .2006. An architecture of a normative system: counts-as conditionals, obligations and permissions. Proceedings of the fifth international joint conference on autonomous agents and multiagent systems. Association for Computing Machinery.

Brock, S. 2010. The creationist fiction: The case against creationism about fictional characters. *Philosophical Review* 119:337–364.

Coe, S. 2011. The story of a character: Establishing the limits of independent copyright protection for literary characters. *Chicago-Kent Law Review* 86:1305.

Campbell, K. 1983. Fuller on legal fictions. *Law and Philosophy* 2 (3): 339–370.

Currie, G. 1990. *The nature of fiction*. Cambridge: Cambridge University Press.

Donnellan, K. S. 1974. Speaking of nothing. *Philosophical Review* 83:3–32.

Esser, J. 1969. Wert und Bedeutung der Rechtsfiktionen: Kritisches zur Technik der Gesetzgebung und zur bisherigen Dogmatik des Privatrechts. Vittorio Klostermann.

Fine, K. 1982. The problem of non-existents. I. Internalism, Topoi, 1: 97–140.

Foley, K. 2008–2009. Protecting fictional characters: Defining the elusive trademark-copyright divide. *Connecticut Law Review* 41:921.

Fuller, L. L. 1930. Legal fictions. *Illinois Law Review* 25:363–399.
Goldblatt, R. 2003. Mathematical modal logic: A view of its evolution. *Journal of Applied Logic* 1 (5): 309–392.
Hage, J. 2012. The deontic furniture of the world: An analysis of the basic concepts that embody normativity. Maastricht European private law institute working paper 2012/7.
Hintikka, J. 1962. *Knowledge and belief.* Ithaca: Cornell University Press.
Howell, R. 1979. Fictional objects: How they are and how they aren't. *Poetics* 8:129–177.
Jacquette, D. 1996. Meinongian logic: the semantics of existence and nonexistence, Berlin and New York: de Gruyter.
Kaplan, D. 1973. Bob and Carol and Ted and Alice. In *Approaches to Natural Language*, ed. K. J. I. Hintikka, J. M. E. Moravcsik & P. Suppes, 490–518. Dordrecht: Reidel.
Karjala, Dennis S. 2006. Harry Potter, Tanya Grotter, and the copyright derivative work. *Arizona State Law Journal* 38:17–40.
Katyal, S. 2006. Performance, property and the slashing of gender in fan fiction. *Journal of Gender, Social Policy and the Law* 14 (3): 461–472.
Kripke, S. 1963. Semantical analysis of modal logic. *Zeitschrift für Mathematische Logik und Grundlagen der Mathematik* 9:67–96.
Kripke, S. 1979. A puzzle about belief. In *Meaning and use,* ed. A. Margalit, 239–283. Dordrecht: D. Reidel.
Kroon, F., and Voltolini, A. 2011. Fiction. The Stanford encyclopedia of philosophy, ed. Edward N. Zalta. http://plato.stanford.edu/archives/fall2011/entries/fiction/. Accessed 15 Aug 2014.
Kurtz, L. 1990. The rocky road to character protection. *Entertainment Law Review* 1 (2): 62–67.
Kurtz, L. 2012–2013. Fictional characters and real people. *University of Louisville Law Review* 51: 435.
Lai Chung, J. 2007–2008. Drawing idea from expression: Creating a legal space for culturally appropriated literary characters. *William & Mary Law Review* 49:903.
Lewis, D. 1978. Truth in fiction. *American Philosophical Quarterly* 15:37–46. (Reprinted in Lewis, D. 1983. Philosophical papers, vol 1, 261–275. Oxford: Oxford University Press)
Meinong, A. 1904. Über gegenstandtheorie. In *Untersuchungen zur gegenstandtheorie und psychologie*, ed. A. Meinong. Leipzig: Barth. (Reprinted in 1971 *Gesammelte Abhandlungen* (Gesamtausgabe bd. II). 481–535. Graz: Akademische Druck- und Verlagsanstalt.)
Mellinkoff, D. 1964. Who is John Doe? *UCLA Law Review* 12:79.
Meurer, D. 1976. *Die Fiktion als Gegenstand der Gesetzgebungslehre. Studien zu einer Theorie der Gesetzgebung,* 281-295. Berlin: Springer.
Nevins, F. 1991–1992. Copyright + character = catastrophe. *Journal of Copyright Society USA* 39:303.
Parsons, T. 1980. *Nonexistent objects*. New Haven: Yale University Press.
Pavel, T. G. 1979 Fiction and the causal theory of names. *Poetics* 8 (1–2): 179–191.
Putnam, H. 1973. Meaning and reference. *The Journal of Philosophy* 70:699–711.
Quine W. v O. 1969. Ontological relativity and other essays. New York: Columbia University Press.
Routley, R. 1980. Exploring meinong's jungle and beyond, Canberra: Australian National University.
Russell, B. 1905. On denoting. *Mind* 56 (14): 479–493.
Salmon, N. 1998. Nonexistence. *Noûs* 32:277–319.
Schienke, G. 2005. The spawn of learned hand—a reexamination of copyright protection and fictional characters: How distinctly delineated must the story be told? *Marquette Intellectual Property Law Review* 9:63.
Schiffer, S. 1996. Language-created language-independent entities. *Philosophical Topics* 24:149–166.
Schiffer, S. 2003. The things we mean, Oxford: Clarendon Press.
Schwartz, P., ed. 1977. *Naming, necessity and natural kinds*. Ithaca: Cornell University Press.
Searle, J. R. 1979. The logical status of fictional discourse. In *Contemporary perspectives in the philosophy of language,* ed. P.A. French, et al., 233–243. Minneapolis: University of Minneapolis Press.

Sparkes, Peter. 2014. Ejectment: Three births and a funeral. In *Legal fictions in theory and practice*, ed. Maksymilian Del Mar and William Twining. Dordrecht: Springer.
Thomasson, A. L. 1999. *Fiction and metaphysics*. Cambridge: Cambridge University Press.
Thomasson, A. L 2003. Fictional characters and literary practices. *British Journal of Aesthetics* 43:138–157.
Voltolini, A. 2006. *How ficta follow fiction: A syncretistic account of fictional entities*. Dordrecht: Springer.
Zalta, E.N. 1983. *Abstract objects: An introduction to axiomatic metaphysics*. Dordrecht: D. Reidel.
Zalta, E. N. 2000. The road between pretense theory and abstract object theory. In *Empty names, fiction, and the puzzles of non-existence,* eds. Everett A. and Hofweber T, 117–147. Stanford: Center for the Study of Language and Information.

Part III
Change and the Common Law

Chapter 10
Legal Fictions before the Age of Reform

Michael Lobban

Abstract Before the era of reform, the common law was replete with fictions. The procedure by which litigation commenced in the common law courts was premised on fictions, while litigants also used fictions to enable themselves to avail themselves of convenient remedies. In allowing litigants to make false statements of facts, the courts allowed the law to develop in new directions, while disguising the fact that it was changing. However, there were also other kinds of fictions, which operated more like rules of law. They included 'metaphysical' fictions (as where something which no longer existed was deemed still to be in existence) as well as 'fictions' which were in effect metaphors or analogies. This chapter explores the operation of these fictions, as well as the criticisms and defences made of fictions before their nineteenth century reform.

10.1 Introduction

> [T]hese fictions of law, though at first they may startle the student, he will find upon farther consideration to be highly beneficial and useful: especially as this maxim is ever invariably observed, that no fiction shall extend to work an injury; its proper operation being to prevent a mischief, or remedy an inconvenience, that might result from the general rule of law.[1]
> William Blackstone

> Fiction of use to justice? Exactly as swindling is to trade.[2]
> Jeremy Bentham

In the era before the nineteenth-century reforms, fictions abounded in the common law. Very few indeed were those litigants whose case did not rest, in one form or another, on a legal fiction. Fictions came in various kinds. The most

[1] Blackstone (1765–1769), vol. 3, p. 43.

[2] Bentham (1838–1843), vol. 7, p. 283.

M. Lobban (✉)
Law Department, London School of Economics, Houghton Street,
London WC2A 2AE, UK
e-mail: M.J.Lobban@lse.ac.uk

M. Del Mar, W. Twining (eds.), *Legal Fictions in Theory and Practice*,
Law and Philosophy Library 110, DOI 10.1007/978-3-319-09232-4_10

obvious, perhaps, were the procedural fictions, which allowed litigants to use an historically-established form of procedure for purposes for which it was not originally designed. The common law itself, as S.F.C. Milsom has shown, developed in the later middle ages through the use by opportunist litigants and their lawyers of writs in ways which had not been envisaged by the Chancery clerks who had issued them.[3] As judges allowed one form of action to be used for novel purposes, so new areas of law could develop in the royal courts. In this way, the medieval action of trespass *vi et armis*, which was a remedy for forcible wrongs done *contra pacem regis* could give birth over time to a general action for torts (trespass on the case), a contractual action (*assumpsit*) and an action to recover property (ejectment). By pretending the novel case was a variant of the old established one, lawyers could obtain better and cheaper remedies for their clients.

The language of pleading often carried anachronistic hallmarks of the action's heredity: thus, the declaration in the famous case of *Scott* v. *Shepherd*—where the defendant had thrown a lighted squib into a covered market, which had blinded the plaintiff in one eye—began with the words that he had 'with force and arms, (to wit) with sticks, staves, clubs and fists, made an assault upon the plaintiff'.[4] Such words in pleading were mere matters of form: historical hangovers in pleading, which did not need to be proven in court.[5] As Maine saw, fictions allowed the law to develop, while disguising the fact that it was changing. They maintained a sense of stability in law, at the same time that the law moulded itself to the needs of its community.[6] The drawback of this method of change was that it made the orderly arrangement of the law extremely difficult.

As shall be seen in what follows, there was other kinds of fictions as well, which were not devices to allow for change. These included more 'metaphysical' fictions, as where courts treated something which had happened at one time as having occurred at another, or where something which no longer appeared to exist was deemed to have a continued existence. Finally, some things were described as 'fictions', which were in reality metaphors or analogies used to explain and describe legal effects, but where no one pretended that the fiction was true. In what follows, we will examine these different kinds of fictions which were used in the common law, how they were used, and how contemporaries regarded them.

---

[3] Milsom (1981). For the uses of legal fictions in English legal history, see J. H. Baker (2001), chap. 2.

[4] *Scott* v. *Shepherd* (1773) 3 Wils KB 403.

[5] Hawles (1680, p. 19): 'there is a wide difference to be made between words of course, raised by implication of law, and essential words, that either make, or really aggravate, the crime charged. The law does suppose and imply every trespass, breach of the peace, every felony, murder or treason, to be done VI ET ARMIS'.

[6] Maine (1861, p. 26).

10.2 'Factual' Fictions

The common law was replete with procedural fictions, which allowed one form to be used for a novel purpose. In a number of areas, the procedure rested on a fiction that the parties had taken certain steps in the case. The steps in question were ones which litigants had in fact taken in past cases, but which were no longer required, so much so that the court forbade any challenge to the formal assertion that these steps had been taken. Such 'factual' fictions had allowed all three common law courts to expand their business in the later middle ages. A fiction of this kind lay behind the Bill of Middlesex and *latitat* procedure which was used to commence most litigation in the King's Bench, which rested on a fiction that the defendant had committed a trespass in the county of Middlesex, for which he could be arrested and brought into the custody of the marshal of the Marshalsea prison. The King's Bench had an actual jurisdiction over those in the custody of its prison, and the procedure had its origin from a time when litigants used this procedure against adversaries who had in fact been detained; but by the eighteenth century, it had lost all connection with the real fact situations which had given birth to it.[7] Reality had given way to fiction as the King's Bench sought to attract more litigants, and the other common law courts responded in turn with fictions of their own to get parties into court more quickly than they could by using the older procedure by original writ.[8]

Equally familiar were the ruses used by litigants in exploiting existing forms of action which they adapted by pretence to the needs of their case. Among these was the action of ejectment, the action most commonly used to settle questions of title to property. This action—which was, in form, a tort—rested on a fictitious lease by the real claimant to a fictitious nominal plaintiff in the case, John Doe. The declaration claimed that Doe had entered into the lands in question 'and was thereof possessed', until one Richard Roe—another fictitious person, known as the 'casual ejector'—entered 'with force and arms' and ejected him. The declaration also contained a letter written by Roe to the real defendant, advising him to appear in court and be substituted as defendant, 'otherwise I shall suffer judgment to go against me, and you will be turned out of possession.'[9] The remedy had its origin in late medieval cases where real lessees had been ousted from their land, and were unable to use the action for novel disseisin, since as lessees they did not have seisin of the land. Since this remedy was more efficient than the older real actions, landowners began to use it, by going through the motions of leasing the land and having their lessee ejected. 'Doe' and 'Roe' might then have been real people, friends of the real claimant. But by the middle of the seventeenth century, the superior courts had begun to allow

[7] Although the *latitat* in theory depended on the defendant not having been found in Middlesex after the issue of a bill of Middlesex, there was no need to obtain such a bill first: *Carrett v. Smallpage* (1808) 9 East 330 at 337.

[8] On the Bill of Middlesex, see Blatcher (1978), chap. 7.

[9] See Wentworth (1799), vol. 10, pp. 41–42.

parties to use this form without going through the process of granting actual leases: at the same time, they only allowed defendants to defend the case if they did not deny the lease, entry and ouster.[10] The courts were clearly aware that the facts on which the claim rested were not true, and had clear rules preventing the defendant from denying them.[11]

In other areas, forms of action which had evolved to address one problem were adapted to other uses through the use of fictions. They included the action of trover, developed in the later middle ages to give a remedy for the recovery of personal property.[12] The notion of finding was first used to extend the reach of the action of detinue, which was originally only available against bailees, rather than third parties; and it was soon also used in trespass actions. Parties continued to allege that the goods had been lost and found, but the allegations that the plaintiff had 'casually lost' the goods and that the defendant had found them were not traversable.[13] The gist of the action was the defendant's refusal to hand them over.[14] The action had expanded, like many others, because of its procedural advantages over the alternative.[15] The contractual action of *assumpsit* also expanded through the strategic use of fictions. Originally used as a ('tortious') alternative to the inconvenient action of covenant, with plaintiffs claiming the misperformance of an undertaking, it expanded in the fifteenth century to provide in addition a remedy for nonfeasance, for which a 'tortious' justification could be found by adding an allegation that the defendant intended to defraud the plaintiff. By the early seventeenth century, *assumpsit* could also be used in lieu of debt, for the payment of money contractually owed.[16] In the action of *indebitatus assumpsit*, the plaintiff declared that a promise had been made—that 'being so indebted, he undertook'—but the promise itself was fictitious, and could not be challenged, since it was implied by the existing debt. When parties pleaded '*non assumspit*' they consequently did not put in issue

---

[10] See Simpson (1961, pp. 135–141), and Peter Sparkes's chapter in this volume (Chap. 13), for a detailed discussion of the development of this fiction.

[11] The defendant had to enter into a rule to confess lease, entry and ouster, and submit to a fresh declaration drawn against him. See the evidence of John Griffith in the First Report made to His Majesty by the Commissioners Appointed to inquire into the Practice and Proceedings of the Superior Courts of Common Law, Parliamentary Papers 1829 (46) IX. 1, p. 360. See Blackstone (1765–9), vol. 3, pp. 201–207.

[12] See Ames (1909), vol. 3. Note his comment (at p. 417) that 'it is generally true that averments in pleading, however inaccurate, superfluous or fictitious they may be at a given time, were once accurate and full of legal significance'.

[13] By the mid-sixteenth century, the allegation of a finding could not be traversed: Baker (2002, p. 398). As Sir James Mansfield CJCP explained in *Mills v. Graham* (1804) 1 B & P NR 140 at 145–6, 'In trover, the Plaintiff always alleges a finding, but never proves it; and from the very nature of the thing, it is often incapable of proof. A wrongful conversion, or a wrongful detainer after demand, is considered as evidence of finding'.

[14] As Lord Mansfield described it, '[i]n form it is a fiction: in substance a remedy to recover the value of personal chattels wrongfully converted by another to his own use': *Cooper v. Chitty* (1756) 1 Burr 20 at 31.

[15] Until 1833 (3 & 4 W. 4 c. 42), the action of detinue still allowed wager of law.

[16] *Slade's Case* (1602) 4 Co. Rep. 91a.

the promise, but rather the underlying debt.[17] The action of *assumpsit* could itself also be used 'fictitiously' to raise questions on a feigned issue or wager. Where this was done, a question of right to be settled between the parties would be framed as the subject of a bet contracted between them, and the matter would be referred to a jury to determine.[18] This device was used by courts (notably the Chancery) to allow disputed matters to be tried by a jury at the assizes.

Besides such devices to allow parties to use one form to get a more convenient remedy, fictions had evolved in the middle ages to allow parties to transfer property or resettle estates. Like the procedural fictions, these originated in procedures which had once actually taken place. One example was the common recovery, a device perfected in the fourteenth century to bar the perpetual entails which had been permitted by the statute *De Donis* (1285).[19] It involved a collusive real action, in which the tenant in tail would grant the land to another in fee simple. That grantee would then bring a real action claiming title to the land against the tenant, who would vouch a third party to warrant his title. This 'vouchee', who was bound to the tenant to give equivalent land to him if he lost the case, would request a delay but then not appear to defend the case. The collusive plaintiff would consequently gain the land; and the heirs in tail would have to look to the vouchee who had guaranteed their title. However, since the vouchee was a man of straw, they would get nothing. Although in reality this was a fraudulent device to deny the heirs in tail of their inheritance, in its early history it involved real parties using a legitimate procedure recognised in law. There was nothing on the record to show that the heirs were being defrauded by virtue of the fact that the vouchee had no assets in land to be recovered. The real procedure soon turned into a fiction, and by the nineteenth century,

---

[17] See *Lampleigh* v. *Braithwait* (1615) Hob 105 at 106. See the comment of James Manning: "The action of *indebitatus assumpsit* I consider objectionable, as involving a legal fiction, by which term I understand a state of the law resulting from an alteration introduced without the sanction of the proper authorities, and disguised under previously existing forms for the purpose of concealing the encroachment which has been made upon the functions of the Legislature. The object of the innovation in question, appears to have been to get rid of the wager of law, a mode of defence which I submit should either be recognized and protected, or be abolished altogether" (Second Report made to his Majesty by the Commissioners appointed to inquire into the Practice and Proceedings of the Superior Courts of Common Law, Parliamentary Papers 1830 (123) XI. 547, Appendix A, pp. 36–37).

[18] See, e.g., the form of a feigned issue to try a right of common given in Wentworth (1799), vol. 1, p. 120. In the declaration in question, the fictions included not only the contract between the parties, but the fact that one of them was in the custody of the marshal of the marsahlsea, and that there were pledges to prosecute from John Doe and Richard Roe.

[19] According to Daines Barrington, the perpetuities allowed by this statute contributed so much 'to the increase of power in the barons, that, about two centuries afterwards, it was in a great measure evaded, by the invention of what is called a common recovery: it was impossible for the crown to procure a repeal of this law in the House of Lords, and therefore the judges had probably an intimation, that they must by *astutia*, as it is called, render a statute of no effect, which the king could not extort an alteration of, from one part of the legislature': Barrington (1775, p. 131). On its history, see Joseph Biancalana (2001), Chap. 5.

instead of using a man of straw, the deputy *custos brevium* served as the common vouchee, obtaining a fee for the work.[20]

Entails could also be barred, and estates conveyed, by means of a fine, which was a judgement on record arising from a collusive suit. Here, the prospective grantee of land brought a writ of covenant against the prospective grantor. Once the action had commenced, these parties applied to the court to compromise the action in a final concord. The court registered the concord, which acknowledged the right of the grantee—keeping the 'foot of the fine' in court. This method of 'levying a fine' was often used when parties sought to resettle land: the party wishing to resettle would grant the land to the grantee—called the 'conusee'[21] —who would then grant it back. According to Blackstone, this device was first used in real suits commenced at law for the possession of land, but it was soon found so useful that 'fictitious actions were, and continue to be, every day commenced, for the sake of obtaining the same security.'[22]

10.3 'Metaphysical' Fictions

The examples discussed so far suggest the use of fictions as a merely formal device, to bring a case to court, with the courts pretending that something had taken place—which conceivably could have taken place, or which as a matter of fact had taken place in similar cases in the past—even though they knew it had not occurred in the case before them. At the same time, there was also much discussion in the literature of more abstract fictions, which were very different in their nature and operation. These 'fictions' were rules created by the law, rather than the parties, to solve particular conceptual or doctrinal problems. Such fictions might be described as 'metaphysical' fictions, insofar as they deemed things to have happened or to exist when in fact they did not. There were also 'explanatory' fictions, which were used as tools to explain, justify or make sense of law. These could take the form of metaphors which helped describe a rule of law, the 'fiction' in effect taking the form of an analogy. They could also take the form of historical fictions, which served no other purpose than to justify a rule which was fixed.

The more 'metaphysical' fictions can be seen in a list of five kinds of fiction found 'in our law' described by Dodderidge J in 1625: 'abeyance, relation, representation, remitter, & presumption'.[23] The fiction of *representation*, Dodderidge explained, could be seen in the notion that 'parliament is the whole realm', that the 'jury before the justices of oyer and terminer are the whole county' and that 'the executors of a

[20] First Report made to His Majesty by the Commissioners Appointed to inquire into the Law of England respecting Real Property, PP 1829 (263) X 1 at p. 645.

[21] The one whose right had been made cognisance of by the 'conusor'.

[22] Blackstone (1765–1769), vol. 2, p. 349.

[23] *Sheffeild v. Ratcliffe* (1625) 2 Rolle 501 at 502. Dodderidge's list continued to be referred to in the eighteenth century. Eg Cunningham (1783), vol. 2, tit. Fiction of Law.

testator, [or] a husband and wife, are one person by representation'. The notion that a husband and wife were one person could of course never be literally true: it was a metaphysical fiction allowed for the purposes of the law.[24] Dodderidge did not explain the others, assuming that his auditors were familiar with the doctrines he had in mind; but it is evident that they were rules of law developed by the judges, which often also had metaphysical overtones. When a title to property was in '*abeyance*', it was said to be 'in the clouds'.[25] This was Coke's description of the position of the freehold in a parsonage, where the fee was in 'abeyance' between the death of one incumbent and the nomination of his successor.[26] The freehold continued to exist, though it was not vested in any person. With this in mind, Charles Viner defined property in abeyance as being '*in Expectation,* in *Remembrance, Intendment, Consideration* or *Understanding of Law*'.[27] The doctrine of *relation* deemed things which had occurred at one moment to have had effect from some earlier moment.[28] Thus, if a man committed an act of bankruptcy, and some time later a bankruptcy commission was issued against him, vesting his property in the commissioners, they were held to have rights over the property from the moment of the first act of bankruptcy; so that if he had disposed of the goods in the meantime to *bona fide* purchasers, they could still recover them. Similarly, the rights of an administrator of an estate 'related back' to the moment of the death of the person whose estate was being administered, and he could recover any goods removed in the interim. The doctrine of *remitter* allowed a person who had both an ancient and a more recent title to property, but who had entered by the recent title which turned out defective, to be taken to hold it by virtue of the older and surer right. According to Coke, 'the ancient right is restored and set up againe, and the new defeasible estate ceased and vanished away'.[29]

Despite the metaphysical problems raised by the these doctrines, it was not always entirely clear to writers that they were properly described as fictions, rather than as rules of law.[30] Thus, according to Giles Jacob, remitter was an 'Invention of

[24] See also Ayliffe (1734, p. 397): 'all Representation is a kind of fiction, which the law makes use of, by feigning the person of the son to be that of the father[…] yet this fiction is founded upon the presumptive will and mind of the father'.

[25] Originally from Aeneid, Book 4: 173–197, where the goddess Fama ('Rumour') walks on the ground, but hides her head in the clouds.

[26] Coke (1794), 343a [henceforth cited as *Coke upon Littleton* (1794)]: he gave as another example the time between the death of a tenant pur terme d'auter vie, and the entry of the subsequent occupant.

[27] Viner (1742–1751), tit. Abeyance, pp. 104–105.

[28] Finch (1759, p. 69): 'Things relating to a time long before, as if they were done immediately from that time'. Cf *Butler and Baker's Case* (1591) 3 Co Rep 25a at 28b: 'relation is a fiction of law to make a nullity of a thing ab initio, (to a certain intent) which in rei veritate had essence, and the rather for necessity, ut res magis valeat quam pereat [that the thing may rather have effect than be destroyed]'.

[29] *Coke upon Littleton* (1794), 347 b.

[30] In *Garland v. Carlisle* (1837) 4 Clark and Finnelly 693 at 709–710. Coleridge J asked, 'is this doctrine of relation [in bankruptcy] a mere fiction of law?… In what sense is there any fiction here? No fact is supposed to exist contrary to the truth: the assignees have no possession supposed to be in them at a time when it was actually in the bankrupt, but the law, making his title defeasible

the Law […] in Favour of Right.'[31] Equally, presumptions (Dodderidge's fifth example) were often not regarded as fictions, but as beliefs which were so strong that something had occurred that they were taken to amount to proof.[32] These fictions might consequently be regarded as the kind of fiction Hobart had in mind when he observed, 'those things are properly fictions in law that have no real essence in their own body, but are so acknowledged and accepted in law, for some special purpose.'[33]

There was also another set of conceptual 'fictions' much discussed in the literature, which operated more as explanatory analogies than as the kind of 'metaphysical' fictions described above. This was the case, for instance, with the 'fiction' that a corporation was a 'body politic', whereby an aggregate of different individuals were made into one person by a 'Policy or Fiction of Law.'[34] Strictly speaking, a corporation was not a fictitious person; rather it was a creature of the law, which gave it a 'personality' analogous to that of a human.[35] While it was 'said to be invisible, immortal, and to exist only in supposition and intendment of law,'[36] Stewart Kyd pointed out that no one was deceived by these notions:

> That a body framed by the policy of man, a body whose parts and members are mortal, should in its own nature be immortal, or that a body composed of many bulky, visible bodies, should be invisible, in the common acceptation of the words, seems beyond the reach of common understandings. A corporation is as visible a body as an army… When, therefore, a corporation is said to be invisible, that expression must be understood, of the *right* in many persons, collectively, to act as a corporation, and then it is as visible in the eye of the law, as any other right whatever.[37]

A number of fictions acting as explanatory analogies were also used to describe the legal position of the king. Both parliament and king were corporations 'in virtue of their political character, by the universal assent of the community, from the most remote period to which their existence can be traced'.[38] The king was consequently

---

from a certain moment, avoids, in favour of the assignees, the title of all those who claim under him by any intermediate acts.'

[31] Jacob (1736), tit. Remitter.

[32] For instance, the presumption in prescriptive rights that there had been an original grant of the right which had been lost. According to W. M. Best, '[t]he essential distinction between [fictions] and praesumptiones juris et de jure consists in this; that the latter are arbitrary inferences, which may or may not be true, whilst, in the case of fictions, the falsehood of the fact is assumed and avowed' Best (1844, p. 24).

[33] *Needler v. Bishop of Winchester* (1615) Hobart 220 at 222.

[34] Anon (1702, p. 2).

[35] Anon (1702, pp. 2–3). Cf Wood (1720, p. 181): 'A Corporation is a Person in a Political Capacity created by the Law, and is a Body Politick founded by Policy or Fiction of Law to "endure in perpetual Succession with Capacity to take and grant, to sue and be sued"'.

[36] *The Case of Sutton's Hospital* (1613) 10 Coke Report 23a at 32b; Bacon (1736), vol. I, p. 506.

[37] Kyd (1793, pp. 15–16).

[38] Kyd (1793, p. 39). All other corporations were created by the crown or by statute (or by prescription which supposed an original grant from those sources): *Coke upon Littleton* (1794) 250 a.

said to have two bodies: he was not only a natural person, but also an artificial 'body politic' with the status of a corporation sole. This legal status gave the king certain capacities denied to other natural persons, such as the power of being able to make binding grants while under age.[39] It also generated the apparent fiction that 'the king never dies'. This fiction connoted the fact that his heir's reign commenced at the moment of his death, without the title to the crown ever being in abeyance. The maxim was neither literally true, nor legally comprehensive: for (as Maitland pointed out), when kings died much of the legal machinery of the state was disrupted, as officers appointed by one king lost their positions on his demise and had to be reappointed.[40] The fiction was a metaphor: in fact, kings did die, both naturally and legally.

A number of other fictitious qualities attributed to the king were means to sum up and explain rules of law about kingship. The commonly recited maxim that 'the king could do no wrong' summed up the constitutional rule that only the king's ministers, but not the king himself, could be held legally accountable in court. Similarly, the system of tenures was premised on the assumption that all land was held mediately or immediately of the crown. Although some seventeenth century historians had contended that the king had acquired title to all land by conquest in 1066, eighteenth century jurists such as Sir Martin Wright pointed out that it was rather a 'fundamental necessary Maxim, Principle or Fiction of our *English* Law of *Tenures*' which did not reflect historical reality.[41] Like the fiction surrounding other corporations, the fictions surrounding the king were largely ways of summarising certain legal rules respecting his powers, by way of analogy.

Historical fictions were also used to explain other settled rules of law. For instance, under the common law of tenures, a collateral relative could only inherit land from the last person seised of it if he was 'of the whole blood'. This was a settled rule of law in the eighteenth and early nineteenth centuries. The fiction used to explain it was that all land tenures derived from an original feudal grant in exchange for personal military service. In the feudal world, the original grantor would accept the grantee's heir as a substitute—since he could rely on his loyalty—but not the sons (or heirs) of those who might be his enemy. Since one could not be sure of the progeny of the 'half-blood', they were excluded. The same rules applied to modern grants of land in fee simple, which were fictitiously held to derive from an ancient ancestor who had been given the feudal grant.[42]

Edward Wynne also resorted to history to explain the anomalous rule that a person who entered another's land, cut his corn, and took it away, was only guilty of a bare trespass, whereas a person who took away corn which had already been cut

---

[39] *Calvin's Case* (1608) 7 Coke Report 1a at 12a.

[40] Maitland pointed out that on the demise of the king, when many public offices were vacated, a[ll] litigation not only came to a stop but had to start again' Maitland (1911), vol. 3, p. 253.

[41] Wright (1768, pp. 58–60).

[42] Blackstone defended the rule, on the basis that under the feudal rules, it was only by a fiction that collaterals were allowed to inherit in any case. See Blackstone (1765–1769), vol. 2, p. 229 and Blackstone (1762), vol. 1, pp. 207–224.

was guilty of a felony. Wynne's explanation for a rule which seemed to impose a severer penalty on the lesser offence rested on a historical explanation of the reason behind the rule. It was, he argued, assumed in the language of the law that every man's property was fully fenced, and that it was more difficult to get onto enclosed land to cut the corn, than simply to take it when unattached. This justified imposing a severer penalty on an offence which was easier to commit. In the past, Wynne argued, it was probably true that all land was securely fenced; and indeed 'the very supposition is not, even at this day, a bare fiction'. Nonetheless, it was a legal supposition in trespass pleadings that the defendant had broken the owner's close.[43] What was a fiction of pleading was held to explain a substantive rule, which (like the exclusion of the half-blood) looked anomalous. Such conjectures and fictions might be used to rationalise a settled rule; but they could also make the rule vulnerable to reform.

10.4 The Working of Fictions

Writers on fictions frequently invoked maxims to show how they were to be used. Invoking the civilian maxim 'fictio juris est legis adversus veritatem ex rei possibili justa [causa dispositio]' in 1625,[44] Dodderidge J set out three rules about the working of fictions. Firstly, they had to be possible, 'for law imitates nature'; secondly, they had to be 'for the preservation of a ground of the law', and introduced from necessity; and thirdly, they could not be used to the prejudice of any man, since the law would not do a wrong. Later writers added other maxims, such as that fictions 'must be framed according to the rules of law, and there ought to be equity and possibility in every legal fiction.'[45] The fact that the use of fictions was limited by law was often mentioned. Thus, '[a]ll fictions of law are to certain respects and purposes and extend only to certain persons.'[46] In particular, '[t]he king is not to be answered, bound or defeated by fictions.'[47] More broadly, the civilian maxim that 'in fictione juris semper subsistit aequitas' was frequently invoked.[48] This maxim was interpreted to mean that '[n]o fiction shall extend to work an injury' and that 'the law will never make any fiction, but for necessity, and in avoidance of a mischief.'[49]

[43] Wynne (1765, pp. 118–119).

[44] *Sheffeild v. Ratcliffe* (1625) 2 Rolle 501 at 502. The printed report has a blank space for the omitted words. For the maxim, see Westenberg (1754) lib. 22, tit. 3, s. 28 (p. 573). Westenberg spoke of three kinds of fiction: affirmative, negative and translative (whereby 'what is in one thing is transferred to another').

[45] Burn (1792), tit. Fiction, vol. 1, p. 362; Cunningham (1783), tit. Fiction of law.

[46] *Butler and Baker's Case* (1591) 3 Coke Report 25a at 29b.

[47] *Lord Sheffeild v. Ratcliffe* (1615) Hobart 334 at 339.

[48] E.g. *Coke upon Littleton* (1794), 150a; 3 *Comm*. 43. Best invoked the idea, taken from Voet, that fictions were invented 'ad conciliandam aequitatem, cum ratione et subtilitate juris' Best (1844, p. 25).

[49] *Butler and Baker's Case* (1591) 3 Co Rep 25a at 30b; cf. Impey (1796, p. 6).

These maxims were generally invoked in discussion of the 'abstract' fictions, rather than the more routine procedural ones. Nonetheless, some fictions which looked 'procedural' did raise abstract issues, which opened the way for a consideration of how far they should be used. For instance, the use of fines to resettle property involved a 'conceptual' fiction as well as the 'factual' fiction that there was a dispute to be litigated. As Blackstone explained, a fine was 'an acknowledgement of a feoffment on record':[50] in such cases, the livery of seisin was fictitious, but since it was recognised in court, it obtained 'an equal notoriety' as a feoffment. As John Lilly explained, in a phrase often quoted, '[t]he Seisin of the Conusee in a Fine is but a meer Fiction in Law, and an invented Form of Conveyance only'.[51] What this somewhat allusive phrase meant was that the conusee, who was granted the land to reconvey, was recognised as having only 'seisin in an instant to make this render back, but to no other purpose to the prejudice of the conusor'. This meant that it did not entitle his wife to any dower rights, nor did it give his heirs or creditors any rights.[52] It was the law which determined the extent to which the fiction would operate.

Courts were also left to explore the meaning of other procedural fictions. For instance, parties were able to sue at Westminster on contracts made overseas, but they had to allege as a matter of form that they had been made in England, to bring them within the jurisdiction of the court. This involved claiming that the overseas territory was in fact in the metropolis: as where one alleged that a contract was made 'at Fort St. David in the East Indies, to wit at London in the parish of St Mary le Bow in the ward of Cheap'.[53] How far such fictions could be used was considered in *Mostyn* v. *Fabrigas*, where the King's Bench had to consider whether it could entertain an action of tort committed on the island of Minorca (then under British rule). As Lord Mansfield explained, the fiction that a foreign location was situated in London deceived no one into thinking that it was really so: 'it is a fiction of form; every country has its forms, which are invented for the furtherance of justice; and it is a certain rule, that a fiction of law shall never be contradicted so as to defeat the end for which it was invented, but for every other purpose it may be contradicted.'[54] In this case, the fiction was invented to permit a trial to take place in London. However, as elsewhere, there were limits to the use of this fiction: it was only to be used in 'transitory' actions, rather than those where the matter in question was 'local', involving matter (such as issues of property rights) which could only be determined by a local jury.[55]

---

50 Coke described it as a feoffment of record: *Coke upon Littleton* 50a.

51 Lilly (1735), vol. 1, p. 823. Little's comment was repeated without amplification in a number of eighteenth century references: see Cunningham (1783), tit. Fiction of law; Jacob (1772), tit. Of Fictions, Intendments, and Presumptions, p. 130.

52 See *Roe d. Wrangham v. Hersey* (1771) 3 Wilson King's Bench 274.

53 *Robert v. Harnage* (1704) 2 Ld Raym 1043; *Parker v. Crook* (1714) 10 Mod. 255.

54 *Mostyn v. Fabrigas* (1774) 1 Cowp. 161 at 177.

55 Although Lord Mansfield noted that the courts in Westminster had heard cases involving property torts arising overseas, he noted (*Mostyn v. Fabrigas* (1774) 1 Cowp. 161 at p. 176) that 'the

The most extensive discussions of the 'equitable' use of fictions were to be found in the discussion of the abstract fictions described by Dodderidge. One case often mentioned as illustrating the working of fictions was *Richard Liford's case*. According to Coke's report of the case, if a man in possession of land was dispossessed by another, who cut down the trees, grass or corn, he could, on recovering possession of the land, sue the disseisor in an action of trespass vi et armis, for the law accepted the fiction that the plaintiff had been in possession of the land all along. However, if the disseisor granted the land to a third party, the plaintiff could not 'have trespass vi et armis against those who came in by title; for this fiction of the law, that the freehold continued always in me, shall not have relation to make him, who comes in by title, a wrong doer *vi et armis*, for *in fictione juris semper æquitas existit.*'[56] Since it would be inequitable to charge the person who came in by a title, the plaintiff had to recover all the mesne profits from the original disseisor.[57] As Justice Coleridge put it (commenting on the case in 1837), '[h]ere is a fiction of law and therefore moulded by law to meet the ends of justice.'[58]

The idea that third parties should not be adversely affected by fictions was seen particularly in the discussions of the doctrine of relation in land cases.[59] The sixteenth century case of *Butler* v. *Baker* had laid down a rule that the doctrine should 'extend only between the same parties; and never be strained to the prejudice of third persons, who are no parties or privies to the act.'[60] In this case, a widow's waiver of an estate entailed to her husband and herself and their children (in order to have her dower) was held to render her estate void *ab initio* by relation; but her waiver was not held to have relation to the grant of the reversion, for 'in destruction of a lawful estate vested, the law will never make any fiction.'[61] The court accepted that, by relation, her husband could be held to have been seised alone of the estate, but it did not accept that other heirs could be devested of their estates by relation;

substantial distinction is, where the proceeding is in rem, and where the effect of the judgment cannot be had, if it is laid in a wrong place. That is the case of all ejectments, where possession is to be delivered by the sheriff of the county; and as trials in England are in particular counties, the officers are county officers; therefore the judgment could not have effect, if the action was not laid in the proper county'.

[56] *Richard Liford's case* (1614) 11 Co Rep 46b at 51a. In another case, Coke commented that 'the law will never make such a construction to advance a wrong, which the law abhorreth, or to defeat collateral acts which are lawful, and principally if they do concern strangers' *Menvil's case* (1585) 13 Co Rep 19 at 21. Coke notes here that after a reversal of judgment, the plaintiff in error could recover mesne profits from the time of the original judgment reversed; but only the defendant-in-error could not bring an action of trespass for any stranger who had taken the profits in the meantime.

[57] See Broom (1848, pp. 90–91).

[58] *Garland v. Carlisle* (1837) 4 Cl & F 693 at 710.

[59] Eighteenth century writers often commented that the doctrine of relation was used 'most commonly to help acts in Law, and make a thing take effect' and that it was to 'relate to the same thing, the same intent, and between the same parties only; and it shall never do a wrong, or lay a charge upon a person that is no party'. Jacob (1736), tit. Relation.

[60] *Hawkins v. Kemp* (1803) 3 East 410 at 431.

[61] *Butler and Baker's Case* (1591) 3 Co Rep 25a at 28b.

for 'no relation shall make that tortious which was lawful for, as it hath been said, relations are fictions in law, which will never do wrong'.[62] The case illustrates the principle that fictions were not to be used to work a wrong, and it reveals how the court in that case used the doctrine of relation in a qualified manner. Nonetheless, it should be noted that third party rights were sometimes adversely affected by the doctrine of relation (as in bankruptcy cases); and indeed, a later reporter felt it necessary to make the point that '[i]t is true that there is sometimes loss and damage to third persons consequent upon them [relations], but then it is what the law calls damnum absque injuria, which is a known and stated difference in the law'.[63]

The principle that when fictions 'are urged to an intent and purpose not within the reason and policy of the fiction, the other party may shew the truth' was regularly applied in litigation involving legal fictions concerning the date on which legal processes had taken place.[64] When the defendant in *Morris* v. *Pugh and Harwood* claimed that the plaintiff's action must fail, since the cause of action had arisen after the first day of term, on which (by a fiction of relation) the suit was said to have commenced, the King's Bench allowed the plaintiff to submit evidence of when his writ had actually been issued to counter the fiction.[65] In other cases where legal fictions determined the timing of legal actions, the courts ignored the fiction where substantial justice required it. As Abbott CJ put it, '[i]t is a general rule, that where it is for the interest of the party pleading to shew that a proceeding did not take place at the precise time when by fiction of law it is supposed to have happened, it is competent for him to do so.'[66] Similarly, the fiction that there was no fraction in a day could be dislodged: thus, where a claimant stated that his ancestor had died at five in the morning, and that he had granted a lease to 'Richard Roe' on the same day, the court overruled an objection that the lessor's title could not accrue until the following day.[67] Parties using ejectment had to take care, however, to ensure that they got the date of the fictitious lease correct: if the lessor claimed to have demised land to John Doe to hold '*from* 24 June' and alleged that Doe had entered the land on that day and been ejected, this would be fatal, since Doe's right to enter only commenced on 25 June.[68]

---

[62] *Butler and Baker's Case* (1591) 3 Co Rep 25a at 29b.

[63] See *Thompson v. Leach* (1600) 2 Ventris 198 at 200. See as an example *Balme v. Hutton* (1833) 9 Bing 471.

[64] *Morris v. Pugh and Harwood* (1761) 3 Burr 1241 at 1243.

[65] Cf. Mansfield's comment in another case regarding the timing of commencement of actions: 'the Court would not endure that a mere form or fiction of law, introduced for the sake of justice, should work a wrong, contrary to the real truth and substance of the thing': *Johnson v. Smith* (1760) 2 Burrow 950 at 962.

[66] *Lyttleton v. Cross* (1824) 3 B & C 317 at 324. These rules were also modified by statute: see Sugden (1805, p. 347). See also *Bilton v. Johnson* (1667) T Raym 161, *Roe d. Wrangham v. Hersey* (1771) 3 Wils KB 274.

[67] *Roe d. Wrangham v. Hersey* (1771) 3 Wils KB 274: 'It is said there is no fraction in a day, but this is a fiction in law, fictio juris neminem lædere debet, but aid much it may, and this is seen in all matters where the law operates by relation, and division of an instant, which are fictions in law.'

[68] *Macdonnel v. Welder* (1723) 1 Stra 550, 8 Mod 54, discussed in Espinasse (1798), vol. 2, p. 357.

What these cases and comments revealed was that the courts were flexible in their use of fictions in order to promote justice. Fictions could be used expansively, to promote justice for a litigant, as well as restrictively, to prevent a third party being harmed. Moreover, the categories of fiction were not fixed, and sometimes courts attempted to juggle more than one fiction. For instance, in *Cage* v *Acton* in 1704, the King's Bench had to decide on the validity of a bond given by a man to his wife before their marriage that he would leave her £1000 in case she survived him. It was settled law that all contracts or debts due between husband and wife were released by the marriage: after all, as Gould J put it, 'a husband's owing a thing to his wife is owing a thing to himself, which is absurd.' However, this judge felt that there should be a remedy for the wife after her husband's death: 'the law very often makes a fiction for the preservation of a right; and a suspension of a personal duty is not always an extinguishment.... The rule is, that *modus et conventio vincunt legem*. The law, by its own operation, will do no wrong; and surely it would be a great wrong to defeat the wife of her provision.'[69] Chief Justice Holt dissented; but at the end of the century Lord Kenyon endorsed the approach of the majority, in a judgement which lamented the fact that his predecessor 'had recourse to such flimsy and technical reasonings to enforce a case so directly against law and conscience.'[70]

The use of fictions building on fictions can also be seen in *Billon* v. *Hyde and Michell* in 1749. John David Billon was a merchant who had extensive dealings with John Francis Michell, over a long period of time, with long standing running accounts being kept between them. Michell traded extensively in Italy and France, and Billon 'did very frequently assist [him] with large sums of money on [his] drafts on foreign houses'.[71] Michell committed a secret act of bankruptcy on 18 April 1743, but no commission of bankruptcy was issued against him until 13 November. In the intervening period, he had paid over £3018–2-2 to Billon, while Billon's accounts showed that he in turn had paid Michell £712 –2–0. Michell's assignees had sued Billon at common law in an action for money had and received, recovering the full amount that had been paid to Billon, but without setting off the sums due to him on the balance of the accounts.[72] Billon then turned to the Court of Chancery for help. Here, Lord Hardwicke LC was minded to give the claimant relief—not least because a statute had recently passed which would have given him relief, but which was passed too late to benefit him. As he perceived, the common law case

[69] *Cage v. Acton* (1704) 12 Mod 288 at 290; cf 1 Ld. Raym. 515 at 516–17. Gould's argument that the law supported right by inventing 'notions and fictions, as abeyance, &c.' referred to Coke's discussion of the parson's freehold being in abeyance after his death: *Coke upon Littleton* (1794), 343 a.

[70] *Milbourn v. Ewart* (1793) 5 TR 381 at 384. By this time, the common law judges were satisfied that equity would regard the husband in such a case as trustee for his wife, a proposition doubted in the earlier case.

[71] T[he] N[ational]A[rchives] C 12/1926/10.

[72] Billon claimed that he was ready to prove the sums he had paid at the common law trial, but had been told that it was unnecessary to enter a proof of the payments since the commissioners would settle the account between him and the bankrupt. The jury had not set off the sum (he claimed) since they had also believed that it would be settled later: TNA C 11/2108/7.

had rested on two fictions. The first was the fiction of relation, which vested the bankrupt's property in his assignees from the time of the first act of bankruptcy. Commenting on this doctrine, Lord Hardwicke noted that it was the rule that fictions should not prejudice anyone, but added that 'this case is taken out of another general rule, which has been adhered to for the sake of publick utility; *viz.* that it is better a private mischief should issue, than a general inconvenience.'[73] The second fiction was the contractual fiction found in the action for money had and received.[74]

Lord Hardwicke puzzled over the use of this contractual action. 'There is no foundation to raise an *assumpsit*,' he argued, 'which must be founded on contract either in fact or in law'. He was clear that 'there was no contract in fact; for a contract must be with somebody'. Despite his doubts, however, he found a contractual path to give a remedy to Billon, which was to treat the bankrupt as a factor or agent for the assignees from the moment of his bankruptcy. In his judgement, the assignees could not affirm that he had paid over their money, while disaffirming that he had received money from Billon on their behalf.[75] While the Lord Chancellor's reasoning was not always entirely clear—and in the end the parties were encouraged to come to a settlement—it is evident that he (in contrast to some contemporary common lawyers) treated *indebitatus assumpsit* as being founded on a proper contractual relationship which had to be identified.[76] However, the contractual relationship he found was itself a fictitious one—that the bankrupt was to be regarded as a factor for his commissioners—and this fiction was used in this case as a device to evade the fiction of relation. Hardwicke's doubts about the use of *indebitatus assumpsit* for such cases were soon resolved, and later common law courts in such cases were far less concerned with the problem of finding real contracts underlying the action for money had and received.[77] What Hardwicke's musings show is that courts were prepared to use and adapt fictions to further a notion of substantive justice which was not otherwise provided for by the forms of law.

This was demonstrated more clearly in the wider history of the expansion of the action for money had and received in the eighteenth century. Although *indebitatus*

[73] *Billon v. Hyde* (1749) 1 Atk. 126 at 127, 1 Ves Sr. 326 at 328. See also Anon (1761), vol. 1, pp. 163–166.

[74] Hardwicke was bemused by the fact that the King's Bench had allowed an action for money had and received to be used, contending that the better form of action should have been trover, for the wrongful conversion of the money. He cited *Rider v Fowle* (1682) 1 Keb 58 for the notion that trover could be used to recover money. See also *Anon* (1719) 1 Stra 142.

[75] On the issue of affirmation, he cited *Wilson v. Poulter* (1730) 2 Str 859, where the commissioners of bankruptcy were held to have affirmed the defendant's act (in buying stock with the bankrupt's money) by taking possession of some of the stock; and so were unable to sue (in trover) for the money with which he had bought the rest of it.

[76] *Billon v. Hyde* (1749) 1 Ves Sr 326 at 330: 'this action upon contrast cannot be maintained but by contract on one side or the other'.

[77] See *Kitchen v. Campbell* (1772) 2 Wils KB 304 at 307–308: 'whoever has received the money for the bankrupt's goods is supposed, in justice, to have received the same for the use of the assignees, in whom the property of those goods by law was vested, and to have promised to pay the same to the assignees; there is a supposed privity of contract between the persons whose money it lawfully is, and the person who has got or received it.'

assumpsit was devised largely as a remedy for breaches of contract—with the fictitious formal promise to pay the debt being a corollary of a real contract between the parties—the action could soon came to be used where no express contract had been concluded, where the defendant had a non-contractual debt, or where money had been paid by mistake.[78] In such cases, there was no kind of real promise lying behind the fictitious formal one. This was notably the case with counts in *indebitatus assumpsit* for money paid or for money had and received. In neither case did the court look for a real promise, or even a request by the defendant, which might suggest a contractual relationship.[79] In this action, *assumpsit* was merely the legal form through which a different kind of obligation could be enforced by the court.[80] It was a fictitious vehicle to provide a remedy for a class of cases where justice demanded a remedy, but which did not sit happily into the theoretical frameworks hitherto developed by the lawyers.[81]

10.5 Defences and Criticisms of Fictions

There were many defenders of fiction. Some simply accepted fictions as part of the landscape. As Lord Kenyon put it in 1796, if the court were considering for the first time whether to adopt legal fictions, it would 'sift most minutely the foundations on which they could be supported; but it is now too late for us sitting in a court of law at the close of the eighteenth century to consider whether or not that which has at all times been considered as law should continue to be law now.'[82] Others were more enthusiastic in their defence of fictions. Richard Burn defended the fictions in ejectment 'because, the form of the proceeding being entirely fictitious, it is wholly in the power of the court to direct the application of that fiction so as to prevent fraud and chicane, and to discover the real truth of the title.' This remedy, he added, was 'invented, under the control and power of the court, for the advancement of justice in many respects; and to force the parties to go to trial on the merits, without being entangled in the nicety of pleadings on either side.'[83] Edward Wynne compared legal fictions with the 'approximations' made by mathematicians and

[78] In denying the promise by pleading 'non assumpsit', the defendant was not putting in issue that he had made the promise, but was challenging the facts on which the promise was implied by the law. See the comments of Tindal CJCP, explaining the import of the Hilary Rules of 1834, in *Martin v. Smith* (1838) 4 Bing NC 436 at 439.

[79] In the count for money paid, it was necessary to aver a request, but the request could be implied by law; while in money had and received, it was not necessary to aver a request. See W. Cornish et al. (2010), vol. 12, p. 564.

[80] George Spence treated it as an example of those 'presumptive undertakings or *assumpsits*, which though never perhaps actually made, yet constantly arise from this general intendment of courts of judicature, that every man has engaged to perform what his duty and justice require' Spence (1846–1849), vol. 1, p. 245.

[81] See further Lobban (2014, pp. 46–58).

[82] *Bragner v. Langmead* (1796) 7 TR 20 at 23–24.

[83] Burn (1792), tit. Ejectment. See also Gentleman of the Inner Temple (1779, pp. 1–2).

geometricians, which, although 'not strictly true, are so near the truth, that they answer the same purpose'.[84]

The defence of fictions continued into the nineteenth century. In his *Methods of Observation and Reasoning in Matters of Politics,* published in 1852, Sir George Cornewall Lewis spoke of fictions as 'legal inferences founded on imaginary facts, but intended to forward the substantial ends of justice'.[85] In many cases, they served as short cuts: 'Instead of saying that acts done under certain circumstances entail certain consequences, and enumerating these consequences at length, it is found easier to refer this set of acts to a well known legal class, by giving it a name which does not properly belong to it, but which will at once suggest its legal consequences, and obviate the necessity of stating them.'[86] In 1851, George Long commented that the 'modern writers who have made themselves merry over legal fictions, have been more merry than wise.' There was no harm in judges developing the law through fictions: '[h]e who, by virtue of his office, is able to become the interpreter of the common understanding of the people, takes from the people, whose activity is the real generator of law, a material to which his skill gives the proper form, and his office the due authority.' He admitted that there was a time when the legislator should turn the fictions into reality; but it was evident that Long felt that the judge might be in advance of the legislator in recognising social needs and wants.[87] W. D Lewis told the Juridical Society in 1855 that fictions had always been 'directed to the public good, and have always had in view the remedying and supplying of acknowledged defects in the actual law'.[88] In his view, fictions could both be a vehicle for law reform, and also 'expedients for casting out technicality by the aid of technicality itself'.[89] They were, in his view, like the scaffolding used to build a house, which was often left in place thereafter under the mistaken assumption that it was necessary to maintain the building. At the same time, he argued that there was 'an actual *necessity,* in some classes of cases that occur, of resorting to the use of fictions as a mode of enunciating principles.'[90] These included the 'metaphysical' fictions of relation.

---

[84] Wynne (1791, pp. 70–71). Compare the 'Letters to an Attorney's Clerk' by A. C. Buckland and W. H. Buckland (completed in 1824): 'Are the 'swords, staves, and knives' of the lawyer more visionary than the lions, bears, and bulls of the astronomer; or his fanciful representations half so ridiculous as the hieroglyphics and whimsical associations which have been recently pressed into the service of mnemonics?' Buckland and Buckland (1860) pp. 12–13.

[85] Lewis (1852), vol. 1, p. 421.

[86] Lewis (1852), vol. 1, p. 423. This had occurred with 'quasi-contracts'. Where express contracts existed, the legal rights and duties entailed were well defined: '[h]ence, in cases where it is wished that similar legal consequences should be drawn, which come within the spirit of the rules applicable to a contract, though they do not themselves involve any contract, the lawyer cuts the knot by saying that a contract is presumed, that there is a contract by intendment of law'.

[87] Cicero and Long (1851) p. 161.

[88] Lewis (1855, pp. 360–384 at p. 366).

[89] Lewis (1855, p. 372).

[90] Lewis (1855, p. 381). The metaphor of scaffolding is also used by Peter Sparkes in his essay on ejectment in this volume.

At the same time, in an age of Enlightenment, the criticisms of fictions grew, particularly of the 'procedural' fictions. Jeremy Bentham may have been the most famous critic of fictions in the late eighteenth and early nineteenth centuries, but he was not the only one. Daines Barrington condemned the fictions which underlay most property transfers. He had two particular objections to the common recovery: first, 'that it is directly in opposition to the express words of a subsisting law, and let the inconveniences of a statute be what they may, no judge, or bench of judges, can constitutionally dispense with them; their office is *jus dicere*, not *jus dare*'. In his view, there was no reason why the legislature should not intervene to reform the law. Second, he condemned the 'unintelligible trumpery' of the fiction:

> Most men of fortune and rank in this country never enter a court of justice, but to go through this most ridiculous ceremony: can the serjeants who mutter the jargon, or the judges who preside, explain to such a person what is going forward? What an impression must this leave with regard to other legal proceedings![91]

In 1793, Edward Randall wrote that 'Fiction in poetry and in works of imagination is highly beautiful, but in a subject so serious as the composition and administration of laws, ought never to be admitted.' Complex and illogical fictions had no place in a country which held to the maxim that ignorance of the law was no excuse.[92] Like Barrington, he felt that what the common law performed through the medium of fiction could be better done by legislation.

The chorus of criticism grew in the early nineteenth century, particularly of the procedural fictions. In 1826, James Humphreys argued 'that, instead of vainly seeking, by equitable interference, to adapt the crude and scanty institutions of early ages to the complicated relations of cultivated society, one uniform system of laws [should] regulate the whole;—and that no act be done, nor right conferred, by circuitous means, whether of legal fiction, or nominal interest, where the object may be effected *directly*, with its real name and character.'[93] The pleader Edward Lawes also advocated pruning fictions. 'It is desirable to confine forms of law to facts and realities,' he said, 'instead of making them depend on legal fiction, which is nothing else than the fancy of lawyers.'[94] He was particularly critical of a number of the fictitious forms of action, which hid the real nature of the dispute between parties, forcing them to make use of additional forms in order to obtain the real particulars of the demand. He favoured abolishing the action of trover, as well as the action of *assumpsit* 'where it proceeds on fiction, and there is no actual promise made by the party'.[95]

---

[91] Barrington (1775, pp. 132–133).

[92] Randall (1793, p. 48). He added that 'Fiction and absurdity disgust rational minds, and prevent them from turning their attention to the laws of their country'.

[93] Humphreys (1826, pp. 3–4).

[94] Third Report made to His Majesty by the Commissioners appointed to inquire into the Practice and Proceedings of the Superior Courts of Common Law, Parliamentary Papers 1831 (92) X 375 at p. 234.

[95] In such cases, he wanted the plaintiff to sue in debt.

In 1829, the Common Law Commissioners repeated the criticism that 'they tend to bring the law itself into suspicion with the public, as an unsound and delusive system'.[96] It was not merely that the complexity of fictions was putting the law into disrepute. Fictions left gaps, which kept the older, imperfect modes of procedure alive for some unlucky litigants.[97] For instance, the Bill of Middlesex or *latitat*, which was premised on a fictitious arrest, could only be used against parties who could actually be arrested: they could consequently not be used against peers or corporations (so that plaintiffs would need to use the expensive form of the original writs). Similarly, the writ of ejectment was not an adequate means to try the title of all estates, for it could only be used where there could have been an entry on to the land. It was not, consequently, available for disputes about advowsons, rents, common rights or other incorporeal hereditaments: in these cases, claimants still had to make use of the slow and costly real actions.[98] In the case of 'procedural' fictions, the fictions only went so far; the 'underlying reality' might prove a constraint on parties who might wish to use it. Equally, the fictitious forms rested on a multiplicity of procedures, which generated fees for various officers in the court, and which continued to provide opportunities for vexatious defendants to raise objections.[99] In response to such criticisms, the procedural fictions were duly reformed in the first tranche of reforms brought in the aftermath of the report of the Common Law Commissioners: a simple writ of summons was introduced in 1832.[100] The majority of real actions were also abolished, and the device of the common recovery rendered redundant by legislation.[101] Finally, in 1852, the fictitious allegations in ejectment and trover were dispensed with.[102]

Conclusion

For jurists like Maine, and perhaps also Austin, fictions were a passing phase in the history of legal development, a method used by lawyers who wanted to reform the law, without offending those who wished to see the old law preserved.[103] For men like them, the reforms effected in the first half of the nineteenth century, which

[96] First Report made to His Majesty by the Commissioners appointed to inquire into the Practice and Proceedings of the Superior Courts of Common Law, PP 1829 (46) IX.1, p. 88.

[97] In Lon L. Fuller's phrase, fictions were like an awkward patch applied to torn fabric: Fuller (1967), introduction.

[98] Sutton (1803). An exception was made by statute for tithes: 32 Hen. VIII c. 7; Humphreys (1826, p. 123). On the need for a right of entry, see also Woodfall (1804, pp. 437 ff.). Actions in ejectment also had to be brought within the limitation period allowed for rights of entry.

[99] See First Report made to His Majesty by the Commissioners appointed to inquire into the Practice and Proceedings of the Superior Courts of Common Law, PP 1829 (46) IX.1, p. 88.

[100] Uniformity of Process Act 1832 (2 & 3 Wm IV c. 39). See Cornish et al. (2010, pp. 570–571).

[101] 3 & 4 Wm. 4 c 74 s 2.

[102] 15 & 16 Vict. c. 76 Sch. A. See further Peter Sparkes's chapter (Chap. 13) in this volume.

[103] Austin (1873, pp. 629–630).

transformed civil procedure and ultimately abolished the forms of action, seemed to have consigned the very notion of fiction to a bygone age of jurisprudence. Courts of course continued to apply the 'metaphysical' doctrines such as relation, but now tended to speak of them as the creatures of law, rather than of fiction.[104] The fictions which had so exercised the mind of jurists in the eighteenth century and before now seemed to have been consigned to history.

Nevertheless, jurists at the end of the century, and into the twentieth century, continued to argue that the common law was still replete with fictions, and that new ones were regularly being invented. Frederick Pollock challenged Maine's view that the rise of legislation had left no room for fictions, pointing to the mid-century development of '[o]ne of the most brilliant and successful fictions of the Common Law,' the implied warranty of authority which attached to the acts of a professed agent,[105] which was introduced in the case of *Collen v. Wright*.[106] Other jurists identified a large range of fictions found in the substantive law. Discussing 'surviving fictions' in 1917, for instance, Jeremiah Smith included in his list of fictions not only conclusive presumptions (such as 'malice' in criminal law), but also 'constructive' trusts or fraud. Lon Fuller later gave other illustrations where legal doctrines rested on fictions: they included 'constructive notice', vicarious liability, the doctrine that children lured by 'attractive nuisances' had been 'invited' onto the land by occupiers, or the notion that implied conditions in contracts rested on the agreement of the parties.

It may be noted that such 'fictions'—what J.C. Gray, following Jhering, dubbed 'dogmatic' fictions[107]—were not identified as such by writers before the age of reform. In some instances, which were familiar to the pre-reform legal mind, the

---

[104] In *Barnett v. The Earl of Guildford* (1855) 11 Exch. 19 at 31–3, Parke B (where the question whether a party could sue for trespasses before his entry to the land by relation) observed that 'the law undoubtedly establishes a relation for the purposes of justice', to prevent a wrong from being 'dispunishable', which was 'the same principle on which the law has given it in other cases'. He also noted, significantly, that 'it is not by means of the fiction of an ejectment, but by virtue of the relation back at common law, that they are recoverable'. Speaking of the fictions of time in law suits, Maule J observed in *Whitaker v. Wisbey* (1852) 12 CB 44 at 57, 'The relation to the first day of term is in most cases [a] matter of direct operation of law, and not of fiction.'

[105] Pollock (1904, p. 136).

[106] *Collen v. Wright* (1857) 8 E. & B. 647. While Cockburn CJ protested against 'resorting to the fiction of an implied contract hitherto unknown to our law' (at p. 663), Willes J expressed the majority opinion at 657–8, without mentioning 'fiction': 'The obligation arising in such a case is well expressed by saying that a person, professing to contract as agent for another, impliedly, if not expressly, undertakes to or promises the person who enters into such contract, upon the faith of the professed agent being duly authorized, that the authority which he professes to have does in point of fact exist. The fact of entering into the transaction with the professed agent, as such, is good consideration for the promise.' The consequent rule was explained by William Bowstead that 'every person who professes to contract as an agent is *deemed* by his conduct to represent that he is duly authorised'. Emphasis added. Bowstead (1907, p. 382).

[107] Gray (1921, pp. 36–37): 'They should never be used, as the historic fictions were used, to change the Law, but only for the purpose of classifying established rules, and one should always be ready to recognize that the fictions are fictions, and be able to state the real doctrine for which they stand'.

'fictions' were described simply as presumptions, which reflected obligations imposed by law on parties in the defendant's position. For instance, where a party was said to have 'constructive' notice, it was clear that he did not have actual notice; but the law held him accountable as if he had, because he was in a position in which he should have been aware of the facts in question, and was somehow at fault if he was not. Rather than being a fiction, the doctrine of constructive notice rested on a presumption of evidence of notice that was so strong that the party was not allowed to rebut it.[108] Similarly, the notion that an occupier of land had 'invited' children to play on his dangerous land was a means of explaining why an occupier who was aware of dangers which might foreseeably harm children should be liable if they were harmed: that is, because he should have been aware that children would be attracted onto the land, he was presumed to have permitted them to enter.[109] In other instances, where doctrines were newly evolving, the fiction was an intellectual device created by jurists to attempt to explain or justify a rule which did not require or rest on a fiction. Jurists discussing the doctrine of vicarious liability might have been troubled by the notion that a servant's negligent acts were to be taken to be the negligent acts of the master, or by the presumption that a master who had chosen a negligent servant had somehow been negligent himself when making the choice; but the maxim *qui facit per alium facit per se* could equally be explained on simpler policy grounds.[110] It was the jurists' desire to conceptualise liability in tort in terms of personal fault which created these conundrums. Equally, the notion that the implied terms in a contract were somehow the product of the parties' wills was the product of an attempt to explain contractual obligations in terms of the meeting of the minds.

Such 'fictions' were products of the theory used to make sense of the law. It is little surprising that they often proved troubling and constraining. Thus, the notion that the parties had implicitly agreed on what was to be done if the subject matter of the contract were destroyed may have been a useful tool in helping the evolving doctrine of frustration to emerge; but it ultimately proved a constraining explanatory 'fiction'. More striking still was the early twentieth view that 'quasi-contractual' remedies could only be used when the parties could have made a real contract, where an explanatory model based on a fiction hindered the development of better models. Theoretical fictions which might be vehicles with which to explain doctrinal developments could easily turn into roadblocks.

---

[108] *Plumb v Fluitt* (1791) 2 Anst. 432.

[109] The notion that occupiers of land were liable for 'attractive nuisances' developed as judges sought to develop a rule to protect children from certain forseeable harms: see Cornish et al. (2010), vol. 12, pp. 980–984.

[110] See Cornish et al. (2010), vol. 12, pp. 894–895.

References

Reports

First Report made to His Majesty by the Commissioners Appointed to inquire into the Law of England respecting Real Property, PP 1829 (263) X 1
First Report made to His Majesty by the Commissioners appointed to inquire into the Practice and Proceedings of the Superior Courts of Common Law, PP 1829 (46) IX.1
Second Report made to his Majesty by the Commissioners appointed to inquire into the Practice and Proceedings of the Superior Courts of Common Law, Parliamentary Papers 1830 (123) XI. 547
Third Report made to His Majesty by the Commissioners appointed to inquire into the Practice and Proceedings of the Superior Courts of Common Law, Parliamentary Papers 1831 (92) X 375

Statutes

Uniformity of Process Act 1832 (2 & 3 Wm IV c. 39)
3 & 4 W. 4 c. 42
3 & 4 Wm. 4 c 74 s 2
15 & 16 Vict. c. 76

Cases

Anon (1719) 1 Stra 142
Balme v. Hutton (1833) 9 Bing 471.
Barnett v. The Earl of Guildford (1855) 11 Exch. 19
Billon v. Hyde (1749) 1 Atk. 126; TNA C 11/2108/7; TNA C 12/1926/10
Bilton v. Johnson (1667) T Raym 161
Bragner v. Langmead (1796) 7 TR 20
Butler and Baker's Case (1591) 3 Co Rep 25a
Cage v. Acton (1704) 12 Mod 288
Calvin's Case (1608) 7 Coke Report 1a
Carrett v. Smallpage (1808) 9 East 330
Collen v. Wright (1857) 8 E. & B. 647
Cooper v Chitty (1756) 1 Burr 20
Garland v. Carlisle (1837) 4 Clark and Finnelly 693
Hawkins v. Kemp (1803) 3 East 410
Johnson v. Smith (1760) 2 Burrow 950
Kitchen v. Campbell (1772) 2 Wils KB 304
Lampleigh v. Braithwait (1615) Hob 105
Lord Sheffeild v. Ratcliffe (1615) Hobart 334
Lyttleton v. Cross (1824) 3 B & C 317
Macdonnel v Welder (1723) 1 Stra 550, 8 Mod 54
Martin v. Smith (1838) 4 Bing NC 436
Menvil's case (1585) 13 Co Rep 19
Milbourn v. Ewart (1793) 5 TR 381
Mills v. Graham (1804) 1 B & P NR 140
Morris v. Pugh and Harwood (1761) 3 Burr 1241

Mostyn v. Fabrigas (1774) 1 Cowp. 161
Needler v. Bishop of Winchester (1615) Hobart 220
Parker v. Crook (1714) 10 Mod. 255
Plumb v. Fluitt (1791) 2 Anst. 432
Richard Liford's case (1614) 11 Co Rep 46b
Rider v. Fowle (1682) 1 Keb 58
Robert v. Harnage (1704) 2 Ld Raym 1043
Roe d. Wrangham v. *Hersey* (1771) 3 Wilson King's Bench 274
Scott v. Shepherd (1773) 3 Wils KB 403
Sheffeild v. Ratcliffe (1625) 2 Rolle 501
Slade's Case (1602) 4 Co. Rep. 91a
The Case of Sutton's Hospital (1613) 10 Coke Report 23a
Thompson v. Leach (1600) 2 Ventris 198
Whitaker v. Wisbey (1852) 12 CB 44
Wilson v. Poulter (1730) 2 Str 859

Books and Articles

Ames, James Barr. 1909. The history of trover. *Select essays in Anglo-American legal history.* Boston: Little, Brown & Co.
Anon. 1702. *The law of corporations.* London: Isaac Cleeve.
Anon. 1761. *A general system of the laws concerning bankrupts.* 2 vols. London: J. Coote.
Austin, John. 1873. In *Lectures on jurisprudence or the philosophy of positive law.* 4th ed., ed. R. Campbell. London: John Murray.
Ayliffe, John. 1734. *A new pandect of Roman civil law.* London: Thomas Osborne.
Bacon, M. 1736. *A new abridgment of the law.* 5 vols. London: E. & R. Nutt and R. Gosling for D. Lintot.
Baker, J. H. 2001. *The law's two bodies: Some evidential problems in English legal history.* Oxford: Oxford University Press
Baker, J. H. 2002. *An introduction to English legal history.* 4th ed. London: Butterworths.
Barrington, Daines. 1775. *Observations on the more ancient statutes from Magna Charta to the twenty first of James I, cap XXVII.* 4th ed. London: S. Baker and G. Leigh and B. White.
Bentham, Jeremy. 1838–43. Rationale of judicial evidence. In *The works of Jeremy Bentham.* 11 vols, ed. J. Bowring. Edinburgh: William Tait.
Best, William Mawdesley. 1844. *A treatise on presumptions of law and fact, with the theory and rules of presumptive or circumstantial proof in criminal cases.* London: S. Sweet.
Biancalana, Joseph. 2001. *The fee tail and common recovery in medieval England, 1176–1502.* Cambridge: Cambridge University Press.
Blackstone, William. 1762. *Law tracts.* 2 vols. Oxford: Clarendon Press.
Blackstone, William. 1765–1769. *Commentaries on the laws of England.* 4 vols. Oxford: Clarendon Press.
Blatcher, Marjorie. 1978. *The court of king's bench 1450–1550: A study in self-help.* London: Athlone Press.
Bowstead, William. 1907. *A digest of the law of agency.* 3rd ed. London: Sweet & Maxwell.
Broom, Herbert. 1848. *A selection of legal maxims.* 2nd ed. London: A. Maxwell Publishing.
Buckland, A. C., and W. H. Buckland. 1860. Letters to an attorney's clerk (completed in 1824). In *Directions for the study of the law by Buckland, Phillips and North, with notes by the editor of the 'Law Chronicle'.* London: T.F.A. Day.
Burn, Richard. 1792. *A new law dictionary: Intended for general use, as well as for gentlemen of the profession.* 2 vols. London: T. Cadell.

Cicero, Marcus Tullius, and George Long. 1851. *M. Tullii Ciceronis Orationes, with a commentary by George Long, vol. 1. Verrinarum libri septem.* London: Whittaker and Co and George Bell.
Coke, Edward. 1794. *The first part of the institutes of the laws of England, or, a commentary upon Littleton.* 15th ed., 3 vols. London: E. & R. Brooke.
Cornish, W., et al. 2010. *The Oxford history of the laws of England.* Oxford: Oxford University Press.
Cunningham, Timothy. 1783. *A new and complete law dictionary: Or, general abridgment of the law.* 3rd ed., 2 vols. London: J. F. and C. Rivington.
Espinasse, Isaac. 1798. *Digest of the law of actions and trials at Nisi Prius.* 3rd ed., 2 vols. London: J. Butterworth, T. Cadell and W. Davies.
Finch, H. 1759. *Law, or a discourse thereof.* London: D. Browne and J. Shuckburgh.
Fuller, L. 1967. *Legal fictions.* Stanford: Stanford University Press.
Gentleman of the Inner Temple. 1779. *The law and modern practice of ejectments: with the latest determinations both in K.B. and C.B.* London: E. Brooke.
Gray, John Chipman. 1921. *The nature and sources of the law.* 2nd ed. New York: Macmillan. (from the author's notes by Roland Gray).
Hawles, Sir John. 1778. *The juryman's adviser; or Englishman's right.* 1st ed. 1680. London: J. Bew and G. Corrall.
Humphreys, James. 1826. *Observations on the actual state of the English laws of real property, with the outlines of a code.* London: J. Murray.
Impey, John. 1796. *The new instructor clericalis.* 6th ed. London: J. Butterworth.
Jacob, Giles. 1736. *A new law dictionary.* London: J.J. & P. Knapton.
Jacob, Giles. 1772. *A law grammar, or rudiments of the law.* 5th ed. Dublin: Elizabeth Lynch.
Kyd, Stewart. 1793. *A treatise on the law of corporations.* London: J. Butterworth.
Lewis, G. C. 1852. *On the methods of observation and reasoning in politics.* 2 vols. London: John W. Parker and Son.
Lewis, W. D. 1855. The origin and use of legal fictions. *Papers read before the juridical society.* vol. 1. London: V. & R. Stevens and G.S. Norton.
Lilly, John. 1735. *The practical register.* 2 vols. London: E. Ward.
Lobban, M. 2014. Mapping the law: Some lessons from history. *New Zealand Law Review* 2014 (1): 21–67
Maine, Henry. 1861. *Ancient law: Its connection with the early history of society and its relation to modern ideas.* 1st ed. London: John Murray.
Maitland, F. W. 1911. The crown as corporation. In *The collected papers of Frederic William Maitland,* ed. H. A. L. Fisher. Cambridge: Cambridge University Press.
Milsom, S. F. C. 1981. *Historical foundations of the common law.* 2nd ed. London: Butterworths.
Pollock, Frederick. 1904. *The expansion of the common law.* London: Stevens & Son.
Randall, Edward. 1793. *Juridical essays: Being remarks in the laws of England.* London: J. Deighton.
Simpson, A. W. B. 1961. *An introduction to the history of the land law.* Oxford: Oxford University Press.
Sparkes, Peter. 2014. Ejectment: Three births and a funeral. In *Legal fictions in theory and practice,* ed. Maksymilian Del Mar and William Twining. Dordrecht: Springer.
Spence, George. 1846–1849. *The equitable jurisdiction of the court of chancery.* 2 vols. London: Stevens.
Sugden, E. B. 1805. *Practical treatise of the law of vendors and purchasers of estates.* London: Brooke and Clarke and J. Butterworth.
Sutton, Robert. 1803. *A complete guide to landlords, tenants and lodgers: Being a methodical arrangement of the whole law as it now stands.* 4th ed. London: J. Stratford.
Viner, Charles. 1742–1751. *A general abridgment of law and equity.* 23 vols. Aldershot.
Wentworth, John. 1799. *A complete system of pleading.* 10 vols. Dublin: J. Moore.

Westenberg, Johann Ortwin. 1754. *Principia iuris, secundum ordinem digestorum seu pandectarum.* Leipzig: Paul Kraus.
Wood, T. 1720. *An institute of the laws of England.* 2 vols. London: Richard Sare.
Woodfall, William. 1804. *Law of landlord and tenant: Including leases, assignments, tenants in fee.* London: J. Butterworth.
Wright, Sir Martin. 1768. *Introduction to the law of tenures.* 3rd ed. London: J. Nourse.
Wynne, Edward. 1765. *A miscellany, containing several law tracts.* London: no publisher.
Wynne, Edward. 1791. *Eunomus: Or dialogues concerning the law and constitution of England.* Dublin: James Moore.

Chapter 11
Legal Fictions and Legal Change in the Common Law Tradition

Maksymilian Del Mar

Abstract This chapter offers a definition of legal fictions and an evaluation of the role of legal fictions in legal practice, especially insofar as they enable legal change. The first part of the chapter defines legal fictions as any suspension of one or more of the required operative facts leading to the imposition of an associated normative consequence, whether this suspension is introduced because of (1) the absence of proof of some previously required fact; or (2) the presence of proof to the contrary. The second part argues that legal fictions have an unjustifiably bad reputation as enablers of legal change. This chapter makes a plea for seeing legal fictions as forms of tentative cognition that enable courts to communicate with each other, exploring whether a certain change in the law (i.e. precisely a suspension of a required operative fact in the imposition of a certain normative consequence) ought to be introduced at a more explicit level. Under the guise of this relational reading of legal reasoning, legal fictions become an instrument of careful experimentation—a way of testing the extent to which the potential introduction of a rule will be beneficial. Seen in this light, legal fictions are by no means signs of the immaturity of the system; they are, instead, dynamic resources that allow courts, over time, to balance flexibility and responsiveness with stability and predictability.

11.1 Introduction

Any thorough discussion of legal fictions must tackle two fundamental difficulties: first, definitional—circumscribing the object of analysis, and rationally reconstructing it vis-à-vis nearby concepts, such as presumptions and deemings; and second,

A version of this chapter was previously published as: 'Legal Fictions and Legal Change' (2013) 4 *International Journal of Law in Context* 442–465.

M. Del Mar (✉)
Department of Law, Queen Mary, University of London, Mile End Road, London E1 4NS, UK
e-mail: m.delmar@qmul.ac.uk

M. Del Mar, W. Twining (eds.), *Legal Fictions in Theory and Practice*, Law and Philosophy Library 110, DOI 10.1007/978-3-319-09232-4_11

evaluative—understanding and judging the function played by legal fictions in legal practice. This chapter tackles these two issues in two parts: the definitional issue in the first part, and the evaluative issue in the second.

Legal fictions are here defined as any suspension of one or more of the required operative facts leading to the imposition of an associated normative consequence, whether this suspension is introduced because of (1) the absence of proof of some required fact; or (2) the presence of proof to the contrary. This is a broader definition than is commonly found in the literature, because the common trend is to understand fictions as requiring consciousness of falsity, whereas the first reason noted above only requires absence of proof. This definition is employed in this chapter because it helps us better to understand and evaluate the function of legal fictions in legal practice. It helps because it relates the use of the device to the ever-present practical issues of the availability of evidence. Presumptions are closely related to legal fictions so defined, but they operate differently: they do not so much suspend a required operative fact, as they take a stance on the likelihood of an operative fact being present, thereafter either shifting the burden of proof of the operative fact to a party that needs to prove otherwise (and thus rebut the presumption), or simply not allowing proof on the matter, and thus not allowing rebuttal (as in conclusive presumptions).[1] Legal fictions do not take a stance on likelihoods of operative facts being present. Instead, they simply make the operative fact (momentarily) irrelevant or unnecessary to the imposition of the associated normative consequence. As will be seen below, in the first part, this suspension of a required operative fact typically arises in contexts where a certain intention or a certain causal link needs to be proved, but cannot be. Legal fictions, then, are often employed to soften the evidentiary burden of intentionality or causation that a rule or principle otherwise requires. The first part of the chapter illustrates this definition with examples, and also situates it in the literature on legal fictions.

The second part of the chapter then turns to evaluating the role of legal fictions in legal practice. In doing so, it presupposes the first part's definition, but also adds to it. As is often the case, evaluating something pushes us to understand it better. In looking to evaluate the use of fictions, it is observed—as is readily apparent to any reader of the literature—that legal fictions have a lacklustre reputation. They are sometimes begrudgingly recognised as helpful modes of legal change, but then quickly denigrated as signs of an immature legal system—one that has not yet achieved the explicitness and coherence of principle that characterises a fully-grown legal order. This chapter pleads for us to be more patient with legal fictions, and to dwell a little on the potential justifications for suspending a required operative fact as opposed to introducing a new rule that associates a new set of operative facts with a normative consequence. The argument of the chapter is that if we shift our focus away from the individual, isolated decision (in which the legal fiction is

[1] According to Gama, this volume, Chap. 16, this might be the case for some, but certainly not all presumptions. Gama's careful, historically-contextualised, account of the similarities and differences—but especially the similarities—between the functioning of presumptions and legal fictions deserves much more careful attention than can be bestowed upon it here.

employed) to an understanding of legal reasoning as a relational affair across time, i.e. as a matter of present courts paying heed to past decisions but also relating to future decisions, then we will see that the use of legal fictions is one of the ways in which a tentative (rather than assertive) cognition[2] can be exercised. In other words, suspending a required operative fact allows future courts to test the potential boundaries of a potential new rule. It allows them to consider whether the fiction should be articulated as a new rule, or whether they and future courts should continue testing, case by case, the utility of the fiction, or indeed whether the case in which the fiction was employed should be quarantined as an exception (or even a mistake). In this way, when a court employs a fiction—especially for the first time—it invites subsequent courts to consider whether, on the facts before them, the required operative fact ought again to be suspended, and if so, whether the time is now ripe for a rule to be introduced.

Combined together, it is hoped that the two parts of this chapter—the definitional and the evaluative—both place legal fictions in a better light. More broadly, it is hoped that understanding legal fictions this way can reveal to legal theorists the importance of seeing how the modes and devices of legal reasoning operate diachronically, i.e. precisely as relational resources, and thus as ways in which participants in the system collaborate across time.[3] Legal fictions have been hard done by because they have been evaluated from the perspective of a single use—but, as with other modes and devices of legal reasoning, they come into their own only when seen from the perspective of multiple uses. It is too harsh to say of legal fictions that they are a 'syphilis' with 'pestilential breath,'[4] as Jeremy Bentham remarked in his typically acerbic no-nonsense style; rather, they are more like blocks made of plasticine in a world made of blocks with varying degrees of hardness, i.e. building blocks whose shape is particularly pliable, eventually either discarded or used as moulds to produce more stable fixtures on the landscape. Legal fictions, in short, when used wisely, are inherently dynamic resources that allow courts, over time, to balance flexibility and responsiveness with stability and predictability.

---

[2] See also Rescher (2006), who has used the optic of tentative cognition to understand and showcase the utility of presumptions. It is unfortunate that he does not discuss fictions. More broadly, this chapter endorses his plea for more interest in 'lesser degrees of cognitive warrant' (pp. xi–xii), and the relevance of that kind of warrant to legal epistemology.

[3] Methodologically, then, this chapter is part of a plea, which I have also made in other work (see, e.g. Del Mar 2011), for more collaboration between legal theorists and legal historians, but also between philosophers of law and philosophers of history. For another recent attempt at developing a multi-temporal, relational account of legal reasoning, though this time via the concept of narrative, see Del Mar (2013). More generally, see Del Mar and Lobban (2014).

[4] The quotes are: '… the pestilential breath of Fiction poisons the sense of every instrument it comes near' (Bentham and Bowring 1962, vol. 1, p. 235) and '… in English law, fiction is a syphilis, which runs in every vein, and carries into every part of the system the principle of rottenness' (Bentham and Bowring 1962, vol. 5, p. 92). To note disagreement here is of course not to engage in the proper, detailed critique that a justified disagreement would warrant. For an appropriately detailed discussion of Bentham's various attitudes to fictions, see Quinn, this volume Chap. 4, and also Stolzenberg (1999), which lists some more helpful references.

11.1.1 Defining Fictions

Arguably, legal fictions are present in most, if not all, legal systems in which a professional body of persons (judges) decide disputes on the basis of an authoritative corpus of past materials, either laid-down rules or decisions. This is because the legal fiction is a device that is created out of a need—indeed, often a duty—to render one's resolution of the dispute in a manner that respects coherence (and thus some level of predictability and stability), while at the same time attempting to be responsive and efficient in one's dispensation of justice. Legal fictions, if you like, are created in the coal-face of legal change, which serves two masters: the conservative pressure of the system and the call of the injured pleading for a remedy.

It should immediately be noted that legal fictions are understood, in this chapter, as devices used in the process of adjudication. Those theorists who have sought to classify different kinds of legal fictions—e.g. Fuller (1930–1931) and Olivier (1975)—have also made reference to, for instance, legislative fictions,[5] jurisprudential fictions,[6] fictions of legal technique,[7] and the fictional use of legal instruments by citizens.[8] Both Fuller and Olivier also refer to fictions used in adjudication, and in that respect—as we shall see in more detail in a moment—their work is directly relevant here.[9]

[5] I.e. the adoption or creation of fictions by the legislature, see, e.g. Olivier (1975, pp. 130–131).

[6] Such as, for example, the fiction that judges never make law or the unity of law: see Fuller (1930–1931, p. 903). Bentham thought of these as theoretical 'fallacies', and was particularly critical of them: for a discussion, and a taxonomy of types of fictions Bentham identified, see Quinn, this volume, Chap. 4. For more on theoretical fictions in this volume, see Kelsen (Chap. 1), Kletzer (Chap. 2), Samuel (Chap. 3) and Schauer (Chap. 6).

[7] For example, the very concepts of legal right and duty, legal powers and liabilities, legal personality. Of these, Fuller says that they 'represent devices essentially similar to the concepts of the physical sciences', e.g. energy, matter and the force of gravity: see Fuller (1930–1931, p. 905).

[8] As when, for instance, one completes three fictitious sales in order to be free of one's father's rule in Roman law (see Mitchell 1893, pp. 253–254). It is pertinent to add here that Mitchell defines a legal fiction as a 'device for attaining a desired legal consequence, or avoiding an undesired legal consequence', dividing such devices further into three kinds: '(1) the use of one or more of the existing laws in a way unforeseen and unintended at the outset,' this being precisely the above example of three fictitious sales; '(2) the assertion that certain facts do or do not exist, contrary to the truth of the matter' (here Mitchell has in mind jurisdictional fictions, such as one when one treats Minorca as a suburb of London); and '(3) fictions of relation,' which he further subdivides into four categories, but the essence of which is attribution (e.g. of liability from master to servant) (see Mitchell 1893, pp. 253–255). The fictional use of legal instruments by citizens is also familiar in Jewish law (given its dense regulation of everyday life) and in Islamic law (where they are called 'hiyal', which have sometimes been negatively characterised as 'bogus transactions', and more recently defended as creative solutions needed to offer remedies for those who sought them: see Horii 2002). On legal fictions in Jewish law generally, see Hayes (2004) and Moscovitz (2003)—and in this volume Chap. 15.

[9] Smith (2007) has recently attempted to add to this another category which he calls 'new legal fictions,' but these—e.g. the reliability of eyewitness testimony, the ability of jurors to disregard testimony, and predictions of future dangerousness—seem, and are treated by Smith, as more like

When it comes to offering a general definition, Fuller and Olivier differ considerably. Fuller's well-known general definition is that a fiction is '(1) a statement propounded with a complete or partial consciousness of its falsity; or (2) a false statement recognised as having utility' (Fuller 1930–1931, p. 369). To call a fiction a 'statement'[10] seems artificial, especially in the adjudicatory context where it is surely more usefully understood as a device of reasoning.[11] Olivier's general definition is arguably more disciplined, and also more in keeping with the approach taken in this chapter:

> Under legal fiction, I understand an assumption of fact deliberately, lawfully and irrebuttably made contrary to the facts proven or probable in a particular case, with the object of bringing a particular legal rule into operation or explaining a legal rule, the assumption being permitted by law or employed in legal science. (Olivier 1975, p. 81)[12]

Nevertheless, there are some differences between Olivier's definition and the one adopted here. It seems more accurate to say that a legal fiction is a 'suspension' of an operative fact rather than an 'assumption' of fact made—if one knows there is

---

biases, unjustified historical relics or weaknesses of the system. See also the discussion of Smith by Knauer (2010).

[10] Fuller was not the first to do so. He probably took the approach from Vaihinger. Frank also reminds us that, like Vaihinger, Tourtoulon, an important French jurist, defined a fiction as the statement of an erroneous fact with knowledge of its falsity (see Frank, 2009 [1930], p. 339; and see Tourtoulon 1922). Referring to fictions as 'statements' is by no means a feature of past theories—most recently, for instance, Riles (2010, pp. 15–16) has defined a legal fiction as 'a legal conclusion—an act of judgement—that takes the form of a factual statement: it is a theory presented as if it were a fact,' though this seems an improvement, for on this view the 'statement' is understood to be nothing more than the form of 'an act of judgement.'

[11] Though perhaps Fuller was attempting as broad a definition as possible, so as to encompass the other kinds of fictions he includes (as noted above). For a discussion on the extent to which fictions ought to be thought of as propositions, see Petroski (2014, this volume, Chap. 7) of this volume. It is certainly important, as Petroski illustrates so well, to pay attention to the rhetorical and communicative functions of fictions, not only as between members of the legal community, but as between those versed in legal discourse and those not. My focus here—which I think is compatible with Petroski's—is on one particular communicative function of legal fictions, which seems to me to have been underestimated, if not wholly neglected, namely the manner in which they facilitate communication between courts across time.

[12] At another moment, drawing on the work of German jurist Bernhoft, Olivier offers another definition that seems yet more accurate: a 'fiction is a legal rule by which the same legal results are ascribed to a specific fact (the fiction base) as those attached to another fact (the feigned fact). One first imagines the set of facts B, i.e. the imaginary facts and considers what legal consequences these would have had. These legal consequences are then transferred to the set of facts, A, i.e. those to which the fiction will apply' (Olivier 1975, p. 21). Nevertheless, to call this a 'rule' is misleading—this chapter argues that a fiction is often employed precisely in order to avoid creating a rule. In other words, one suspends the operative fact of the rule containing normative consequences one thinks should nevertheless follow. This may help answer the question Olivier raises, namely: 'why are the rules pertaining to the feigned situation applied to the fiction basis? By what process of logic and law is such a transference authorised or allowed?' (Olivier 1975, p. 21). The short answer is: there is no transference—there is just temporary suspension. The justification for a more stable suspension, and thus potentially the introduction of a new rule, might be the normative impetus created by a string of cases in support.

evidence to the contrary of what an operative fact requires, one does not 'assume' it to be otherwise; instead, one knows it is otherwise, but one proceeds anyway to allow the normative consequences to follow. Further, 'suspension' arguably better captures the temporary nature of the fiction. Finally, reference to facts 'probable' in a particular case is arguably unnecessary: for a fiction, all one needs is that one either has evidence to the contrary of the operative fact, or that one does not have evidence of the operative fact—one does not need to pass judgement on the standard (though it is true that sometimes when fictions are employed for lack of evidence of an operative fact, this is done because the judge feels that were evidence to be available it would uncover the otherwise hidden fact).

Olivier's general definition—especially the reference to assumptions[13] made contrary to probable facts—brings him dangerously close to not recognising a distinction between fictions on the one hand, and presumptions and deemings on the other hand. This is a little surprising, for Olivier is otherwise careful to distinguish his notion of a fiction from, for instance, 'analogous application of norms, e.g. if fact A is present apply the rules applicable to fact B' on the basis that there is 'no false factual assumption'; or 'metaphors and symbolic expressions which endeavour to describe legal institutions or concepts but which do not require a false actual assumption, e.g. prescription "runs"'; or 'abstract notions concerning the law or legal institutions, e.g. the concept of subjective rights' (Olivier 1975, pp. 81–82).

Considering the examples Olivier provides, though, we can read him generously and ignore the reference to 'probable facts' in the general definition. For instance, looking at Roman-Dutch law, Olivier says that it is a fiction 'that an illegitimate child has no father and does not succeed on intestacy to his father or father's relations' (Olivier 1975, p. 133)—clearly there is no question of it being probable that a child has no father; or that 'an illegitimate child is legitimated by the subsequent marriage of his parents, based on the fiction that the parents had married before the birth of the child' (Olivier 1975, p. 133)—again, the need for the fiction would not arise unless it was known that the parents did not marry before the birth (or it could not be known whether they did);[14] or that 'that subsequent ratification of the contract of a minor by the guardian validates the contract, based on the fiction of retroactivity' (Olivier 1975, p. 133)—once more, there is no question of the probability of validation (for a minor could not legally validate a contract, let alone physically

[13] Again, Olivier is not the first to make reference to assumptions. Ubaldis, a fourteenth century Italian jurist, referred to legal fictions as 'false assumption[s] known to be contrary to the truth' (see Jones 1940, p. 170). Interestingly, Maine, who we will return to in the second part of the chapter, referred to fictions in a broader sense than 'fictio' in Roman law (i.e. as a false averment) 'to signify any assumption which conceals or affects to conceal, the fact that a rule of law has undergone alteration, its letter remaining unchanged, its operation being modified' (Maine 1931 [1861], p. 22)—it is noteworthy that this definition includes what is often seen to be the most negative feature of fictions, i.e. concealment.

[14] This fiction is also a good example of the preservation of the general principle, i.e. in this case, a normative endorsement of the importance of marriage before birth in the community. To be absolutely clear: the operative fact of 'marriage before birth' is suspended in this case, but no general principle is articulated, thereby avoiding endorsing that practice.

if they are a baby), this also being a good example of where evidence of intention is required by the operative facts and where, in order to achieve what is seen as the just result in the particular case, that requirement is suspended.[15]

Similarly, when Olivier provides an example from the common law—in the case of *Des Salles D'Epinoix v Royal Borough of Kensington and Chelsea* (1970)—it is an example that works in a context where the facts are known to be otherwise. As Olivier summarises it:

> In *Des Salles D'Epinoix v Royal Borough of Kensington and Chelsea*[16] … the appellant, a married man, appeared as the rate-paying occupier of the matrimonial home on the rating authority's valuation list. In 1966 he left his home after marital differences. His wife and children continued to live there. He was called upon to pay the assessed rates but refused to do so. The court, in the person of Lord Parker CJ, suggested that even if in a particular case physical occupation had ceased, a person might still be in 'beneficial occupation' of the property. The notion of 'beneficial occupation' is a fiction, legal shorthand for saying that, although there is no real occupation by him, the husband is liable in law for payment of assessed rates because this liability forms part of his legal obligation to maintain his wife and children. (Olivier 1975, pp. 147–148)

This case is a good example of the approach taken to fictions in this chapter:[17] the normative consequences attaching to the concept of 'occupation' (in this case, liability for the rates) require the operative fact of dwelling physically in the particular abode. This operative fact, however, is suspended—and signalled by the inclusion of the qualification 'beneficial'—in order to reach what is thought to be a just result in the case. Olivier, it should be added, criticises this case, asserting that it should have been decided on the basis of an explicit principle:

> The judge endeavoured to formulate a legal relationship in terms of the occupation. Instead of applying the correct legal principle to the facts, he sought to alter those facts. The correct decision would have been: because the husband is in law compelled, by virtue of his duty of support, to provide accommodation for his wife and children, he is liable for taxes on the abode he so provides. However, the judge over-emphasised the physical facts and could only achieve the intended result by employing a fiction: the husband is deemed to be in occupation of the dwelling and therefore is liable for payment of the tax. (Olivier 1975, p. 149)

From the perspective of this chapter, this is too quick—Olivier may be underestimating the importance—at the time—that was attached to limiting the liability of a divorced husband, or, put differently, the importance—in part because of its unpredictable effects—of not creating a general liability to pay taxes on an abode lived in by the estranged wife and children. But to make this point is to leap ahead to issues we will be considering in more detail in the second part.

---

[15] Sometimes Olivier uses the language of deemings in his examples—as when he says that it is a fiction 'that in the case of prevention of performance it is deemed that performance had been rendered' (Olivier 1975, p. 134). One could read this generously, but even then this is distinguishable from the way fictions are approached in this chapter, i.e. it seems more conclusive and statutory in character than the tentative judicial use made of fictions. More is said about deemings below.

[16] (1970) 1 All ER 18.

[17] Though with the qualification added that to be properly understood and evaluated, this fiction cannot be looked at in isolation in just this one case, but must be traced across time.

In the case of Fuller, although his classification of fictions is somewhat mixed in with his typology of motives for deploying them,[18] there are aspects of his account that are of great assistance to the approach taken here. In particular, Fuller's discussion of the relationship between fictions, presumptions and estoppel as devices used to enable, but also 'obscure' (Fuller 1930–1931, p. 531), the growth of the law, is particularly noteworthy. Although lengthy, the following passage is worth citing in full:

> Nearly any given reform in the law may be described as a redefinition of the operative facts upon which some legal consequence is predicated. For example, we may suppose that under existing law Legal Consequence X arises from Facts A and B. A and B are the facts which give rise to Legal Consequence X. It may now be found desirable to attribute the same consequence (X) to Facts A and C. For example, where previously liability for misrepresentation existed only in the case of an untruthful statement (Fact A) made with knowledge of its untruth (Fact B), it is now thought desirable to impose liability where there is an untruthful statement (Fact A) made negligently (Fact C). How can this reform be accomplished and yet leave the form of existing rules untouched? How can we preserve the appearance that A and B remain the operative facts? There are at least three distinct ways of doing this: (1) When Facts A and C are present, permit an allegation that B is present even thought it is known that B is actually absent from the case. This is the method of the ordinary fiction. (2) Say that Facts A and C raise a presumption that B is present. (3) State the existence of Facts A and C 'estops' the party to deny that Fact B is present. (Fuller 1930–1931, p. 532)

There are a number of observations to make about this important passage. The first is that it need not be the case that Fact B (to use Fuller's terminology) is replaced by Fact C. Instead, Fact B might simply be suspended. Secondly, it is interesting that the example offered by Fuller, where Fact B is replaced by Fact C, is one that relates to a problem with proving intentionality—negligence, from this perspective, becomes an engine of legal change precisely because it offers a practical way of dealing with the unavailability (or, better, rare availability) of proving the requisite intention. Thirdly, it is not quite accurate to say that the existing rules are 'untouched', but nor is it quite correct to assert that the rule has been changed and done so in an 'obscure' way. Looked at by tracing the role of the device across time, and not its use in a single, isolated decision, a fiction (1) puts normative pressure on a rule by noting circumstances in which it may be appropriate (depending on future cases arising before future courts) to suspend one of the rule's operative facts; and (2) gives some normative impetus (but one which subsequent courts may not take up) to the eventual introduction of a new rule. The fourth point is more positive: Fuller distinguishes, but also notes the relationship between three kinds of devices: fictions, presumptions and estoppel. In that respect, he adds that:

> Which device will be employed depends upon which is most expedient. Where Facts A and C can be said to have any tendency at all to prove Fact B, probably a presumption will be used, although the presumption may involve the disadvantage that, if one is to preserve the notion that it is merely a 'presumption,' rebuttal, to some extent at least, will have to be permitted. If there is any conduct of the party which can form the basis for denying him the privilege of disproving B, estoppel may be used. If all else fails, there is left only the bald pretense of the fiction. (Fuller 1930–1931, pp. 532–533)

[18] See Fuller (1930–1931, pp. 513–546).

Fuller is not very generous to fictions here, but his analysis is nevertheless useful: presumptions are more likely to be used (and more likely to be efficient) in situations where the operative fact is probable (given, perhaps, the other operative facts), in which case it also makes sense to leave room for rebuttal should the other side be able to show that the unlikely is the case; with estoppel, on the other hand, an operative fact may again probable, but this time the rebuttal is itself further constrained by an operative fact (the absence of a certain kind of conduct, e.g. duress); and then there are fictions when, says Fuller, 'all else fails.' Fuller's judgement of fictions, however, is clouded by his isolation of a single decision in which a fiction might occur, pitting fictions against presumptions and estoppel on the same time-wave, so to speak. If, instead, we look across time, we will see that presumptions and estoppels tend to be much more embedded than fictions, i.e. they are established rules, though a little hidden in the evidentiary structure of the law. Fictions, then, are not so much obscurantist as they are tentative. In other words, by isolating a single use of a fiction, Fuller precisely misses its value (at least in this context of comparing them with presumptions and estoppels).

Although Fuller is careful to distinguish fictions from presumptions, he is not as explicit, nor as careful, in distinguishing fictions from deemings. He says, for instance, when giving examples of what he calls 'exploratory fictions'—i.e. fictions in which judges create constructions in which they 'feel their way' toward some principle—that the 'doctrine of vicarious liability for tort began with such notions as that the master should be "deemed negligent" for hiring a careless servant' (Fuller 1930–1931, p. 528). It is true that the line between fictions and deemings is not clear. Nevertheless, Fuller's example does appear to have more of the flavour of a deeming than a fiction; after all, it creates an explicit principle—vicarious liability—the operative fact of which is that if a servant is in the master's employ, then the master is liable for the servant's negligence. Were it to be thought of as a fiction, one would need to identify a rule the operative facts of which were being suspended, and it is not clear that there is such a rule. There is a general concept—liability—but the extension of it via the notion of vicariousness does not resemble fictionalisation—it resembles, instead, a policy stipulation or postulation.

Deemings, then, are more stipulative—more arbitrary in a sense—and do not have a clear relationship to difficulties associated with proof.[19] The line, however, as noted above, is not always clear. For example, consider the following well-known device: 'a person missing for seven years or more is dead.'[20] Rescher refers to this as a presumption, and in a sense that is true for it can be rebutted (whereas a deeming typically cannot). However, there is also something stipulative and arbitrary about it—why seven, and not six or eight?—and it also need not be thought of as taking

[19] Deemings were in use in Roman law, often again very stipulative in character. Thus, for example, it was the case that 'a captive returning from captivity shall be deemed always to have been in residence in the Roman state' (see MacLean 1999, p. 3). Here, there is no prior rule the operative facts of which are being changed—instead, a rule in the form of a deeming is created in order to attach a familiar normative consequence (i.e. flowing from uninterrupted residency) to a new class of persons (i.e. those who had been in captivity).

[20] The example comes from Rescher (2006, p. 3).

a stance on the probability or likelihood of a person being alive or dead. It is, then, perhaps a quasi-presumption (or a quasi-deeming?). Other difficult examples are (also from Rescher 2006, p. 5): 'that a wife is incompetent to testify against her husband' or 'that a minor is too immature to vote or to enter into a valid contract.' These certainly feel more stipulative, for they cannot be rebutted, but nevertheless they may be thought to be taking a stance as to the reliability of any potential evidence to the contrary, i.e. that no matter what proof of a wife's competence is offered, it may still be the case that the wife would be biased, and no matter how mature a child is shown to be, they are unlikely to have understood the legal consequences of their promise (or acceptance of one).[21]

Looking beyond Fuller and Olivier, definitions of legal fictions that are close to the one adopted in this chapter can also be found, for instance, in Peter Birks's important piece (but one often overlooked in the literature on legal fictions) entitled 'Fictions Ancient and Modern' (Birks (1986). Birks works with a form of action he considers exemplary for understanding legal fictions: action for money paid. At first, this action was restricted to circumstances (the operative facts) in which (1) there was 'a request (to pay a third party)'; and (2) there was 'a promise to repay' (Birks 1986, p. 87). In the course of time, these operative facts were dropped, such that even when there was proof to the contrary (i.e. proof that there was no request and no promise), the same form of action could be used to regain the money. As Birks says:

> The courts fictionalised the request in the action for money paid and thus made the action available to plaintiffs who had had no communication with the defendants on whose behalf they claimed to have paid out money. That is, the fictionalisation of the request made the action reach into the area of non-promissory indebtedness. (Birks 1986, p. 90)

An example is *Exall v Partridge*, a case from 1799:[22]

> The true facts were that the plaintiff had left his carriage on the defendant's property to be repaired. The defendant's landlord had then taken the carriage into his possession in exercise of his right to distrain for arrears of rent. In order to redeem his carriage, the plaintiff had therefore had to pay to the landlord the amount of the rent owed by the defendant … [The plaintiff] had undoubtedly paid out money to the use of the defendant, but not at the latter's 'special instance and request' and not in circumstances supported by any inference of a promise to repay … Nevertheless the court held that the plaintiff's action for money paid was entitled to succeed … the plaintiff could substantiate the allegations of request and promise by proving not only that by his payment out he had benefited the defendant but also that he had not done so voluntarily. And on these facts he could show that he had not

[21] Another related distinction here is that between fictions and hypotheses, though this discussion is more relevant when comparing allegedly fictional devices in law and in science. The distinction is that hypotheses are directed towards reality, i.e. they take a stance (though a defeasible one) on what is the case, whereas a fiction is a device known to misrepresent reality, but useful because of that. Perhaps the most important source for a discussion of this distinction is Vaihinger's (2009 [1925]) *The Philosophy of 'As If,'* and see also: Frank (2009 [1930], p. 339), Samek (1981, e.g. p. 301), Fine (1993, p. 7), and Fuller's (1930–1931, pp. 877–910) third essay on fictions, which is essentially devoted to exploring and evaluating Vaihinger's contribution. More generally, for Kelsen's view of Vaihinger's book, see the translation in this volume by Christoph Kletzer (Chap. 1) and his commentary (Chap. 2).

[22] (1799) 8 TR 308; 3 Esp. 8.

> conferred the benefit voluntarily by pointing to the lawful compulsion brought to bear on him by the landlord. (Birks 1986, p. 90)

The case is an interesting one if only, in the present context, because it shows how the court's suspension of certain operative facts can be made dependent on the proof of other facts, not explicitly noted in the form of action. What makes Birks's discussion valuable is his generalised analysis of how legal fictions work:

> … the plaintiff advances a routine claim which recites A, B, C and D; he is allowed to win on proving only B and C, or perhaps B, C and Z. The substance of the matter is a judicial determination that B and C, or B, C and Z, ought in law to give rise to the same consequences already attributed to A, B, C and D. However, because this determination is reached behind the recitation of A, B, C and D, and because plaintiffs in subsequent cases continue to make the old recitation even when intending to advance the new facts, the form of the development is fictionalisation of A and D. (Birks 1986, p. 86)

Birks's analysis here is somewhat more dynamic than Fuller's or Olivier's. He speaks of the 'fictionalisation' of A and D, which is in part an acknowledgement, or can be read to be so, of an ongoing process, rather than an isolated act. Although it could be clearer, one assumes that by the 'fictionalisation of A and D' Birks does not mean that one can no longer bring an action on the basis of the facts A, B, C and D, but just that there is another way to reach the same normative consequences by way of proving facts B and C, or B, C and Z. In any event, Birks's approach is close to the one adopted here, for he implicitly recognises the ambiguous, flexible or even unstable character of a situation in which the same normative consequences may be applied via a series of alternative operative facts, at least until—in some unforeseen future—a court decides to articulate a more general principle (e.g. the principle of unjust enrichment, and associated rules) that will encompass these various alternative routes.

This sense of fictions being an instrument via which, incrementally, the law gropes its way towards a principle is important. It echoes the point noted above by Fuller with respect to 'exploratory fictions'. It is a term often acknowledged to be in the spirit of the common law. For instance, Hamilton argues that it is through the use of 'exploratory fictions' that 'common law judges often feel their way incrementally toward some new legal principle or theory', providing the example of the 'genealogy of cases giving rise to the "attractive nuisance" doctrine, which involves a fiction that the children were allured or enticed upon the land, and which eventually results in child trespasser law, such that a child being a trespasser becomes "one fact to be taken into account, with others, in determining the defendant's duty, and the care required from him"' (1988–1989, pp. 1465–1466).[23] As Hamilton summarises it: 'the initial fiction which allowed children to recover for injuries sustained while trespassing "pointed the way" toward development of a full-blown theory of premises liability that allowed recovery' (Hamilton 1988–1989, p. 1466). Once again, we see the benefits of taking a long-lens view of the use of the device, which, interestingly, may be enabled by focusing on common law epistemology. More will be said about these benefits in the next part of the chapter.

[23] The internal quotes are from a torts text book.

Before proceeding to that second part, a few further points concerning the bounds of the definition adopted here will need to be made.

Firstly, there has not yet been occasion to observe that it is important to distinguish fictions from 'virtual entities' in the law, such as the concept of 'legal personality'—thinking of them as virtual rather than fictional helps see the distinction.[24] Secondly, but closely related to the first point, it is not clear how helpful it is to think of fictions as part of, or as further illustrating, the metaphorical character of legal language, where the roots of certain legal concepts can be traced back to their distant more concrete beginnings (e.g. concepts like possession, conversion, delivery, estate, etc).[25] Although it is an interesting exercise to trace the genealogy of terms used in the law, it is not clear how including fictions under the canopy of metaphors in legal language assists us to understand them better.[26] Thirdly, fictions have often been associated—especially in the common law tradition—with jurisdictional wars, as devices used precisely in order to acquire jurisdiction at the cost of a competing court. On the one hand, these fictions could be seen more generously as attempts to provide remedies to those who sought them, but it is difficult to ignore the political and economic context, e.g. in the fictional enlargement of the action of ejectment by the King's Bench (in competition with the Court of Common Pleas). By a series of fictions—e.g. 'no actual lease is made, no actual entry by the plaintiff, no actual ouster by the defendant'—the action of ejectment ends up being a means for trying title (see Holdsworth 1937, Vol. 7, p. 12; see also Vol. 1, p. 200, and pp. 218–219).[27] The need for recourse to fictions was the result, of course, of the reliance on rigid (or only apparently rigid!) forms of action.[28] Certainly, this kind of jurisdiction-extension has the effect of changing the law, but such instruments are not fictions in the definition adopted in this chapter—they are, for instance, not adaptations to difficulties associated with proof.[29] This is not to say that certain ways in which the law was developed by mediaeval and early modern common law courts will not be of interest to a student of legal fictions on the definition adopted here—it is just to say that some uses of them have a decidedly impatient tenor about them: they are not an exercise of tentative cognition in relation to future courts; they are examples of cognition exercised most assertively for the purpose of competing with other courts of one's own age.

[24] See Vermeer-Kunzli (2007, p. 43).

[25] The thought is Fuller's: 'a metaphorical element taints all our concepts' (Fuller 1930–1931, p. 894).

[26] More generally, concerning the comparison between legal fictions and metaphors, see Stern, this volume, Chap. 8; and in the broader context of how accounts of legal fictions relate to accounts of the nature of language, see the chapters from Part II of this volume.

[27] For further discussion of the fiction of ejectment, see Sparkes, this volume, Chap. 13. For the historical background, see Lobban, this volume, Chap. 10.

[28] A feature, it ought to be remembered, not only of the older common law, but also, at certain times and in certain places, of Roman law. I say at 'certain times and certain places' for generalities about Roman law are rife with danger—as is shown by Schiavone's (2012) recent masterly portrayal of the changing culture of Roman law.

[29] Fictions used in this way may indeed be said to be dishonest and concealing, and might have indeed been justifiably included in Bentham's uncompromising attack on judicial artifice and corruption.

Fourthly, and following on from the last point, the approach to fictions adopted here is one closely related to the ways in which a court manages or adapts to difficulties of proof in daily legal practice.[30] We must remember that it has not always been the case—in all legal systems—that those in charge of the law were also evaluating submissions on the facts.[31] Arguably, the character of law and legal reasoning changes greatly when the courts become not only forums of the law, but also forums of fact. Others have associated the use of fictions with issues to do with proof, but have not always made clear that fictions are a means of adapting to difficulties that claimants have with proving certain (often the same kind of) elements of particular actions—especially, as noted above, proving kinds of intentionality (e.g. malice, intention to be bound, intention to hold for beneficiary, etc) or causation. Thus, Baker says that:

> The essence of the classic English fiction is that proof of a certain fact asserted in a lawsuit was completely dispensed with by the simple expedient of denying any means of disputing it. The false allegation in such cases was of some fact which had once been required to be proved, in an earlier stage of history, but which was no longer regarded as material. Here no false testimony was needed, nor any ceremonial appearance of proof. In the mildest forms, the device was used to enable writ formulae to encompass cases which fell within the spirit behind the remedy. (Baker 2001, p. 41)

This is a valuable observation, but we have to be careful: we need to see that it is only after a period of time that it becomes (or might become) clear that a certain operative fact can be dispensed with (the initial cases suspend, rather than dispense with, certain operative facts). Baker would probably agree, for he is mindful of the changing character of a legal fiction: it might at first 'slip into practice without challenge, and if repeated often enough could become so rooted that a future challenge would be unlikely to succeed'; then, 'when they became familiar in practice, they might be extended into more contentious situations, provided that they were seen to have a just objective' (Baker 2001, pp. 54–55). Baker here recognises that the law changes by creeping in degrees, pursuing remedies for claimants, and where fictions are one of the devices via which the waters are tested, so to speak. If enough normative momentum is accumulated, and thus enough cases come before courts to warrant it, there might come a time when a court will articulate the principle or rule

---

[30] This approach is probably not broad enough to include the use of fictions to bridge gaps between substantive and procedural requirements. For a discussion of this function in the case of bridging the gap between substantive requirements of 'individualised reliance' and the procedural requirements of 'predominance of common issues' in the context of class actions in private securities litigation see, Gordon (this volume, Chap. 18) of this volume. From the perspective of this chapter, it seems at first blush that one could try to accommodate that example by conceptualising it as using a fiction to manage difficulties encountered with finding proof of reliance. Looking at it more carefully, however, shows that this would be a misreading of the example: the point in that context is less about the difficulties of proving reliance, and more that if one proves individual reliance (as the substantive requirements demand) then one will not be able to satisfy the procedural requirements of bringing a class action. The use of fictions in such a context may very well be less than ideal and necessitate the legislative creation of an explicit rule not requiring proof of individual reliance in class actions under the Securities Exchange Act of 1934.

[31] This is familiar from Roman law where, at one point, there were separate procedures/personnel for framing the legal issue and trying the facts (see, e.g., Schiavone 2012, p. 139). This has some affinity with the early procedures of irrational proof in the common law.

said to cover the factual pattern of that string of cases. Further, we have to be careful not to return to the mere opportunism of jurisdiction-extension, i.e. the idea is that there is a genuine adaptation to difficulties of proof encountered by otherwise worthy claimants, and not the granting of actions for the sake of attaining jurisdictional (and of course revenue) benefits.

The way legal fictions are framed in this chapter, then, is as part of what can be understood to be the study of common law epistemology.[32] This is an epistemology whose style—if one can speak of it in those terms—is resolutely pragmatic.[33] As Postema put it:

> Common law jurisprudence resolutely resists the theoretical pressure to identify law with canonically formulated, discrete rules of law. Law, on this view, is not a set of rules or laws, but a practised framework of practical reasoning … Its rules and norms can be formulated, perhaps, but no such formulation is conclusively authoritative; each is in principle vulnerable to challenge and revision in the course of reasoned argument and dispute in the public forensic context. (Postema 2003, p. 14)

This is a style that keeps close to the particulars (to paraphrase Bacon: see Postema 2003, p. 16), but also keeps 'an eye on how decisions in particular cases would function in future as examples and rules' (Postema 2003, p. 4). It is a style that prides itself on 'the flexibility and opportunity for judicial testing and re-evaluation' (see Postema 2003, p. 13), recognising that 'past cases do not preclude deliberation and reasoning in subsequent cases, but rather they invite and focus that reasoning' (Postema 2003, p. 17). As Last Stone put it, 'common law reasoning is … a reflective process, a form of collective legal reasoning, in which rules and concepts emerge from and are tested against real and hypothetical narrative situations' (2007, p. 127), and where there is a discipline and art of ceaseless 're-reading', 're-writing', 're-describing' (ibid, p. 132), ceaseless transformation and experimentation, with some formulations (of rules or principles, connected to certain constructed factual patterns) taking precedence for a time over others, until they are potentially replaced with the accumulated effect of what is creatively constructed as another string of cases. Both Postema and Last Stone come close to seeing common law legal reasoning as relational in character, and one in which legal fictions play an important role. To further analyse that role, let us turn to part two of this chapter.

---

[32] Having said that, no claim is being made that the approach taken here is inapplicable to other legal cultures. Indeed, to the contrary, there is good reason to think that most, if not all, legal cultures need devices—whether they call them fictions or not—that allow them to incrementally change the law by, let us say, 'playing with the facts', i.e. suspending and eventually dispensing with, or in general changing over time, the operative facts attaching to certain normative consequences. For discussions of Roman law and legal practice that might bear this comparison out, see Yntema (1950, 1966–1967), Riccobono (1929), Ando (2011), Schulz (1946), Schiavone (2012), Watson (1995), and Thomas (2005). Indeed, Last Stone's (2007) paper (as discussed below) focuses on Rabbinic legal reasoning, especially by reference to aggadot, and here, precisely via techniques of narrativisation, there may indeed be many overlaps with common law reasoning; see also, on narrative in Jewish law (Simon-Shoshan 2012). In this volume, on Roman law, see Ando (2011), and on Rabbinic law, see Chap. 15.

[33] This chapter does not make explicit links with the philosophical literature on pragmatism, but see, in this volume, Lind (Chap. 5), for a sympathetic approach to the use of legal fictions from within the classical pragmatist tradition in philosophy.

11.1.2 Evaluating Fictions

The above part has already found it necessary to mention the need for taking a more diachronic, dynamic view of the use of legal fictions. This part seeks to systematise those brief observations, and to do so (1) by reference to the discussion of legal fictions as enablers of legal change in the literature; and (2) by recourse to a contemporary example in the context of personal injuries litigation.

It should immediately be said that it is not always the case that legal fictions are portrayed negatively.[34] Nevertheless, the bulk of the literature is negative in tone.[35] Certainly, legal fictions are recognised as helpful, if not occasionally necessary, for change to take place, but this is typically qualified in various ways, e.g. that legal fictions are in use only initially, in the infancy of a legal system, and that mature systems do not have recourse to such allegedly dishonest means of reforming the law.

An influential proponent of this attitude was Sir Henry Maine. In his *Ancient Law*, Maine (1931 [1861]) recognises legal fictions as one of the three ways in which law can be changed—the other two being equity and legislation.[36] Maine's evaluation of that function, however, is from the beginning qualified and ends up in harsh criticism. He says, initially, that 'at a particular stage of social progress'—already

---

[34] See, for instance, Kerchove and Ost (1992). Vermeer-Kunzli translates them as saying that 'far from representing a dysfunction of the law's discursivity, fictions merely push the limits of the very efficacy of a discourse, in narrative or performance, firmly established in "its" reality. Classical jurists pretend to believe that fictions constitute an underestimated or unnatural reality, and that it is possible to bypass them, without deviations and artificial constructs, in order to grasp reality as it is. But, since reality is necessarily elusive, being nothing more than the product of conventional nomination, the fiction will appear not as a deficiency but rather as the manifestation of the nature of legal discourse' (see Vermeer-Kunzli 2007, p. 42). Though this is perhaps a back-handed compliment, for it suggests that all law is fictional, and unavoidably so. This echoes Kelsen's (1960) criticism of Vaihinger's *The Philosophy of 'As If'*. See also, in this volume, Kelsen (Chap. 1) and Kletzer (Chap. 2).

[35] Though not in this volume—for a particularly balanced evaluation, see Lind, this volume, Chap. 5.

[36] Diamond, in his valuable, if short, discussion of these three modes of change in Maine, adds a fourth (in the same spirit): re-classification (this may be similar to what Ibbetson calls 'conceptual recharactarisation of claims by litigants (or their lawyers)': see Ibbetson 1999, p. 296). He summarises this mode of legal change as involving 'taking a set of facts, a claim for relief, which naturally falls within one class of writs, and reclassifying it so as to bring it within a different form of action in the other class of writs' (Diamond 1991, p. 252). This is in the same spirit because 'the legal rule … [is] not directly altered or repealed. But the consequence of the legal rule … [is] avoided by reclassifying the claim' (ibid.). Diamond is not exactly complimentary, however, calling this mode of change a 'sleight of hand', albeit an important one, 'for the court cannot be seen to attack the legal rule directly' (p. 253). In evaluations of legal fictions one sees the relationship between the courts and legislature being made prominent—it being the latter that is said to have legitimacy to change the law—and positive (rather than competitive) relations between courts are ignored. Another prominent typology of legal change was offered by Weber, identifying three sources of change: legislation, mutation of custom, and judge-made law—for a discussion, together with reference to legal fictions as a further source, see Wilder (2012). Wilder also reminds us that Savigny referred to fictions as 'polite discontinuities' (see Wilder 2012, p. 34). By contrast, this chapter makes a plea for seeing fictions as potential discontinuities, and more experimental or tentative than polite.

a qualification—legal fictions 'are invaluable expedients for overcoming the rigidity of law' (Maine 1931 [1861], p. 22). His example is the 'fiction of adoption, which permits the family tie to be artificially created', and Maine argues that without this fiction 'it is difficult to understand how society would ever have escaped from its swaddling clothes, and taken its first steps towards civilisation' (Maine 1931 [1861], p. 22). Maine criticises Bentham for being un-historical in his evaluation of fictions, thereby neglecting their 'peculiar office in the historical development of law' (Maine 1931 [1861], p. 22). A few lines later, however, Maine insists that legal fictions have had their day. Indeed, he asserts that legal fictions 'are the greatest obstacles to symmetrical classification. The rule of law remains sticking in the system, but it is a mere shell. It has been long ago undermined, and a new rule hides itself under its cover' and he concludes that 'If the English law is ever to assume an orderly distribution, it will be necessary to prune away the legal fictions' (Maine 1931 [1861], p. 23). It is somewhat ironic that Maine chastises Bentham for being un-historical, and yet himself fails, in his evaluation of fictions, to see how they operate over time, i.e. how they enable courts—including contemporary courts in so-called mature systems—to experiment with which operative facts to attach to what normative consequences, and when to sediment in an explicit way some such association that has proven useful. The law—it might said a little colourfully—is never fully ordered, or better, it is only fully ordered when it is dead. For law to be alive—to be used—means that there are parts of it that are more uncertain and stretchable than others, but all are somewhat tentative, for their meaning (and in some instances, their very relevance) in the next case depends precisely on the facts of that case (and of course how they are constructed).[37]

There is no doubt that Maine influenced many a generation of jurisprudes and legal historians. In the *Spirit of the Common Law*, for instance, Pound recognises fictions as 'modes of growth' (1999 [1963], p. 169), but says that they are 'primitive ... closely akin to the "let's play" so and so of our childhood' (ibid.). Later he is even more explicitly critical:

> Law grows subconsciously at first. Afterwards it grows more or less consciously but as it were surreptitiously under the cloak of fictions. Next it grows consciously but shamefacedly through general fictions. Finally it may grow consciously, deliberatively and avowedly through juristic science and legislation tested by judicial empiricism. (Pound 1999 [1963], p. 173)

In his five-volume text book, *Jurisprudence* (1959), Pound devoted more space to understanding and evaluating legal fictions. Here, he was also more thorough in his review of different modes of legal growth. Thus, he makes an initial division between the traditional element of growth and the imperative (or enacted) element. The traditional element contains eight modes of growth: '(1) fictions; (2) interpretation; (3) equity; (4) natural law; (5) juristic science; (6) judicial empiricism;

[37] I cannot resist quoting Holmes here: 'The truth is, that the law is always approaching, and never reaching, consistency. It is forever adopting new principles from life at one end, and it always retains old ones from history at the other, which have not yet been absorbed or sloughed off. It will become entirely consistent only when it ceases to grow' (Holmes 2009 [1880], p. 35).

(7) comparative law; and (8) sociological study' (Pound 1959, p. 449). Fictions, in turn, he divides into three 'classes': first, 'particular fictions,' which are chiefly procedural and are 'employed to meet a particular type of case or to change or avoid a particular rule or effect a particular isolated result' (like Maine, Pound cites the fiction of adoption); second, 'general fictions', which have 'a more sweeping operation to alter or create whole departments of the law, introducing principles and methods rather than isolated rules' (examples include equity and natural law); and thirdly, and most importantly, 'dogmatic fictions', which are 'fictions worked out after the event by juristic thinking in order to give or appear to give a rational explanation of existing precepts', examples of which include 'representation as an explanation of liability for the tort of a servant and constructive trust' (Pound 1959, p. 450), as well as 'implied malice, implied condition, constructive notice … constructive service, constructive fraud, constructive possession' (Pound 1959, p. 455).[38]

Having mapped fictions in this way, Pound further compliments them as 'the solvent of formalism' (Pound 1959, p. 461). In fact, he is even more subtle than that, for he recognises why, in certain circumstances, the preservation of rules (at the expense of using a fiction) can be important, e.g. 'the rule may not have passed out of a religious or semi-religious stage. Or it may be that the rule has a specially solemn form, such as a law of the XII Tables, having been incorporated in a permanent memorial of the settled customs of the community … or a rule … may be protected against change by a widespread fear of return to a condition of justice without law still remembered with dread …' (Pound 1959, p. 449). Pound therefore recognises the way in which a fiction can play an important role in preserving certain rules that are important for the community—but, and this is crucial, he fails to see how fictions are needed as an incremental, experimental, tentative form of legal change. Like many other theorists and historians, he takes a fiction to be the introduction of a new rule, not the (potentially temporary, potentially more stable) suspension of an operative fact attached to an already existing rule's normative consequences. Failure to see this function of fictions over time, results in seeing them—like Maine—as primitive and 'clumsy':

> Fictions … have played an important part in legal history. But while this is true, we must not forget that they are a clumsy device appropriate only to periods of growth in a partially developed political organisation of society in which legislation on any large scale is not possible. They are not suited to later times and developed systems. In a period of growth, when ideas are few and crude, they enable a body of law to be moulded gradually, without

[38] It is worth adding here that Pound notices that a running theme through those examples (of 'dogmatic fictions') is that of moving away from requiring 'actual and direct intention' (Pound 1959, p. 455). This is clear, too, in the case of the constructive trust, which Pound discusses at some length, where originally, the law would only impose a trust on a person if that person had assumed it expressly; slowly, incrementally, courts began to impose trusts if property was acquired as a result of a breach of fiduciary duty, or through fraud or mistake, and increasingly in other circumstances—all the while moving away from the evidentiary anchor of actual and direct intention. What Pound could have been clearer about is the practical context of these expansions, which had to do not only with the granting of remedies to those perceived as worthy claimants, but also with the evidentiary difficulties faced by those claimants (i.e. they simply could not prove any actual and direct intention).

> legislative action, to meet immediate wants as they arise and to conform to the requirements of cases as they arise. They enable legal precepts to be applied so as to give results in accord with ideals of the end of law. Legislative overhauling of the legal system is neither possible nor desirable in such a period. It demands a thorough understanding of the old law, the mischief and the remedy and a stock of systematic legal ideas beyond the archaic legal order. (Pound 1959, pp. 465–466)

Pound's evaluation here clearly echoes Maine's, which is even more obvious when Pound asserts that 'After a certain stage of legal development, on the other hand, fictions retard growth and clog development' (Pound 1959, p. 466). Fictions are in use initially: 'after law has been put in writing'; they are, indeed, 'the first agency through which the traditional element of a legal system is enabled to grow' (Pound 1959, p. 449). A 'rational age,' however, must do without them, for they 'conceal the substance' (Pound 1959, p. 466); resort to them reveals a 'lack of general ideas' (Pound 1959, p. 462).

Similar sentiments are recorded by contemporary commentators on the use of fictions. Jeremiah Smith, for instance, draws explicitly on Maine to come to the following conclusion:

> … fictions tend to prevent investigation as to the fundamental principle underlying a rule of law, and to retard the framing of a statement of the rule in strictly accurate terms. By giving an erroneous reason for the rule, they make it difficult thoroughly to understand and apply the rule. Indeed, the adoption of an erroneous reason for a doctrine inevitably leads to misapplication of the doctrine … We believe that, at the present day, the use of fiction in law should be entirely abandoned. (Smith 1917, pp. 153–154)

The problem, as already noted above, with this view is that it freezes the frame at which it evaluates fictions: it only considers the utility of a fiction from the perspective of sufficient normative accumulation to warrant the articulation of an explicit rule or principle; it does not go back to the first uses (i.e. to the first few suspensions of the relevant operative fact), and thus does not evaluate the role of fictions across time. Olivier, who we encountered in the first part of the chapter, also takes this distinctly temporally-insensitive approach.[39] He acknowledges that fictions have 'played an extremely significant and beneficial role in the development of the law', but he characterises the judges' deployment of fictions as a matter of 'concealing their law-making activities', and one which, ultimately, can cause more harm than good:

> … if the principle underlying a legal rule is neglected and represented by a fiction, the future development of the rule will remain in a morass of uncertainty. True development of the law is only possible by developing and extending its fundamental principles. In the absence of a clear insight into the principles underlying a legal rule, its application and extension cannot proceed in a rational and intelligent manner. (Olivier 1975, p. 136)

[39] Earlier in the book, Olivier reports on both objections made and compliments paid to legal fictions. The objections are: scientific untruthfulness; fictions create uncertainty; fictions conceal judicial creativity; fictions hinder systemisation of the law; fictions undermine respect for the law; fictions can be applied and developed indiscriminately (see Olivier 1975, pp. 88–91). The advantages are: fiction facilitates thought; fictions serve as terminological devices; that fictions are a form of short-hand, allowing for 'economy of speech'; and that fictions make the language of the law 'more evocative and understandable' (see Olivier 1975, pp. 91–92).

Again, like Smith, Olivier focuses his evaluation on the moment at which the fiction is ripe for articulation, and not the period over which the fiction has been used to explore whether articulation is justified and/or useful. Olivier's full evaluation is worth quoting in its entirety. He distinguishes the following three kinds of cases:

1. As far as the adoption by judges of historical fictions is concerned, the judge is obliged to adopt the rule forming part of the common law, but should reject its fictional form or fictional basis. The judge is obliged to formulate the rule in direct, non-fictional terms, and to find and formulate the true principle behind the fiction.
2. Whenever a judge is compelled to apply a statutory fiction, he should determine and formulate the legal rule envisaged by the legislature and the principle on which the rule is based, and should give effect to the rule and its true basis rather than to the fiction.
3. Whenever a judge finds it necessary to create a new fiction, it indicates that the major premise he is applying is wrong. The judge should then determine whether the major premise is the correct one to apply and if there does not exist a better major premise. Frequently an alternative and better major premise exists which, if applied, will lead naturally and logically to the desired result (Olivier 1975, p. 151).

Olivier, here, like many others, overestimates the value of logic and explicit articulation, and underestimates the value of tentative, fact-anchored, exploration of what operative facts should be attached to what normative consequences. In this respect, his third scenario is the most misleading, though one might even wish to argue that in the first two, Olivier misses the benefits to be gained from continuing to tread carefully, i.e. incrementally and pragmatically.[40]

The first step towards a more sympathetic evaluation of legal fictions will need to pay attention to the practical context in which they are used. Unsurprisingly, perhaps, we need to turn to historians rather than theorists for relevant insights in that respect. Thus, Baker has noted that the use of fictions in the early common law was rather secretive (which of course raises a methodological problem for any historian of the common law), for any judicial approval to relieve 'the plaintiff from proof of certain facts which had to be alleged' (in a form of action) was 'given off the record, at the assizes, and the verdict was returned in common form' (Baker 2001, p. 53; see also the discussion on pp. 54–55). The granting of remedies—on broadly equitable grounds (though of course not articulated explicitly that way)—preceded any 'theoretical justification'; the law, in other words, changed incrementally, pragmatically, as a result of remedies creeping in by degrees (Baker 2001, pp. 56–57). In time,

[40] An example that might bear this out is Olivier's criticism of the common law's resort, in contract law, to implied terms, as opposed to the introduction of the concept—as in the civil law—of good faith (see Olivier 1975, p. 125). But there is a marked difference between the incremental, fact-heavy, case-by-case implication of terms, and the introduction of a general principle of good faith, which, when introduced without the accumulation of case law behind it, is likely to give little guidance to claimants and their lawyers, and which may create more uncertainty than the continual use of a fiction.

the normative accumulation of cases in which such remedies have been granted might result in the articulation of certain coherent theoretical principles, though this may be driven by academic rational reconstruction of the cases (as with, arguably, unjust enrichment: see the discussion in Baker 2001, p. 57; see also Ibbetson 1999, Chap. 14).

Another contemporary historian of the common law, who has also paid attention to the practical context in which fictions were deployed, is Milsom. Indeed, Milsom uses the practical context to dispel the myth that fictions were 'packs of lies', as Bentham would say, used by judges who were surreptitiously 'stealing legislative power' (Milsom 2003, p. 27). He does this by downplaying the active role of the judges in creating fictions. For Milsom, authorship of fictions should lie more with those 'countless individual lawyers through the centuries, each concerned not with "the law" as such but with a small immediate predicament of his client' (Milsom 2003, p. 27; Milsom also recognises the role of jurors), and not with the judges. The role of the judges, according to Milsom, 'was essentially passive. They might facilitate the later stages of a fictional development, but in the important early stages they just accepted results reached by others' (this is perhaps especially so in cases where jurors, 'shut up by themselves', returned 'blank verdicts' that 'enabled them to do their own justice': see Milsom 2003, p. 27). While not wishing to challenge Milsom's (2003, p. 45) thesis (concerning the authorship of fictions in fifteenth century common law), and thus not wishing to question the vital role of the pursuit of remedies for their clients by their lawyers, nor the critical role of the 'dialogue between judges and jurors', it is not inconsistent to add that insofar as judges were involved (even in the act of 'formalising' some result reached by others), and thus played their part, they did so not necessarily or exclusively for political reasons (wanting to preserve legitimacy), but also, or more so, out of fear of the unforeseen and unforeseeable consequences of introducing a new rule or principle, preferring the more incremental, pragmatic, slow change of the law. Fictions, one might say, are a way of slowing down change—of treading carefully—creating resources for future courts, but ones which they are not compelled to respect. Again, attention to the practical context is clearly important—but that should include not only relations between claimant's lawyers and judges, and between judges and jurors, in instant cases, but also dialogues between courts across time.

That pragmatic incrementalism is the spirit of change in the common law is itself widely recognised in the theoretical as well as the historical literature. The first part above has already mentioned Postema's and Last Stone's characterisations of common law reasoning. More specifically on the theme of change in the common law, historians have shown that:

> Legal change occurs through filling in gaps between rules in the way that seems most convenient or most just at the time; through twisting existing rules, or rediscovering old ones, to give the impression that a change in the law is no more than the application of the law that was already in place; through reformulating claims into a different conceptual category, normally one less encumbered by restrictive rules; through inventing new rules that get tacked onto the existing ones; through borrowing rules from outside the Common law; through injecting shifting ideas of fairness or justice; and, very occasionally, through adopting wholesale procrustean theoretical frameworks into which the existing law can be squeezed. (Ibbetson 1999, p. 294)

Leaving aside the question of appearances, Ibbetson is recognising here that legal change occurs via the 'initiative' of the 'litigants' (see Ibbetson 1999, p. 299), and thus, in a bric-a-brac fashion, adding a little bit here, taking away a little bit there—in a sense, precisely playing with the resources one has, re-shaping them as the need arises, but also revising them (re-constructing the alleged pattern of past cases) so as to fit with the justification for the remedy in the instant case. Explicit articulation and overall coherence may occasionally be attempted, but even then essentially for pragmatic reasons: where there are, for instance, practical advantages to be gained (e.g. clarity for litigants) in generalising from what is (at that point) perceived to be the overall normative pattern of a certain string of cases.

Fictions are, of course, not the only mode or device of reasoning used by judges to enable the incremental change that is characteristic of the common law.[41] Allan Hutchinson, in his *Evolution and the Common Law* (2005), takes note, for instance, of techniques for avoiding or loosening the binding force of precedent, including reversing, overruling, distinguishing, not following, asserting the precedent was given per incuriam, characterising subsequent cases as ones that have been doubted in other cases, arguing the precedent was based on a faulty interpretation of earlier cases, claiming the scope of the precedent is unclear, and arguing the precedent has been criticised by academic commentators (see Hutchinson 2005, p. 7).[42] Hutchinson's overall view is sometimes very radical—he applies an evolutionary model he understands as 'blind, contingent, haphazard and entirely opportunistic' (2005, p. 36), going on to characterise law as a 'work-in-progress' that is 'always situated inside and among ... the ideological forces at work in society' (2005, p. 18).[43] However, when Hutchinson says, for instance, law is 'never complete or finished' (2005, p. 18), and that it is 'a rutted and rough road that has innumerable twists and turns and no particular destination', such that 'any particular route taken has been chosen from among the countless and constantly proliferating possibilities for change' (2005, p. 15), he offers some helpful metaphors for understanding the common law, as well as discarding unhelpful ones (such as inevitable progress, natural harmony, universal telos etc).

The common law, then, can only ever be artificially frozen at any point in time: it is better understood as a dynamic domain of possibilities, with each rule or principle

[41] Though not only in the common law: e.g. Glenn (2007), looks at how incremental change comes 'about in the expression of the law and in its avoidance' (p. 241) in Islamic law. Thus, 'parties can set up transactions which might be seen as shams, evasions, fictions or just plain tricks ... so as to remain formally outside the range of prohibited conduct. Riba is prohibited between you and me, but if you need a loan and I have money you can sell me your watch, and agree at the same time to buy it back at a later date, for a higher price (the double sale)' (p. 202). Glenn notes the similarity between fictions in Islamic law and in the common law: e.g. 'There were many tricks and fictions, in the Islamic manner. To avoid the (then) prohibition of interest, living security (le gage vivant) was used (the lender kept the land used as security, and the profit from it). The dead security (mortgage) came later, with the allowance of interest, such that borrowers could just pay the interest and keep the fruits of the land for themselves. Fictions were many ...' (p. 241). See also footnote 8, above.

[42] See also, Duxbury (2008, Chap. 4).

[43] What needs to be avoided here, if Hutchinson's view is to avoid being self-contradictory, is determinism about the role of ideological forces.

better conceived as requiring an understanding of how it might and might not be stretched by way of a re-description[44] of the supporting facts of past cases, and thus a re-construction of the relevant factual pattern.[45] This does not mean, as Hutchinson also recognises (2005, p. 10), that 'anything goes'—for there are many pressures for continuity and stability. Indeed, the techniques—fictions and precedential techniques among them, but including also analogical reasoning and perspectival reasoning[46]—are better thought of as enabling the striking of a balance between flexibility and stability. There is, if you like, a dynamics of relevance at the heart of the common law—one driven by solving particular problems,[47] but always with a view both to the past and the future—and the devices, of which fiction is one, are ways of managing relevance: making sure it is not too unpredictable, but also not too static. As Hutchinson says, 'the common law is a messy, episodic and experimental effort to respect and adapt to the contingent demands that the political and social milieu places upon it' (2005, p. 270); its success has been 'this ability to be flexible, open, experimental and adaptable' (2005, p. 268).[48] 'The best that can be hoped for', adds Hutchinson, is that 'the common law remains supple, experimental and pragmatic' (2005, p. 236).

Are fictions—in the broad sense conceived in this chapter—a thing of the past? Has the common law reached the kind of maturity that some critics of fictions think is attainable, and indeed, according to some, has been attained? This chapter would argue that the contrary is the case: fictions continue to be used, and rightly so. Without them, the common law would lose one of its most treasured instruments for creating potential change; for exploring and experimenting with the extent to which the law might or should be changed; for drawing up dynamic resources for future courts in deciding unforeseen and unforeseeable factual scenarios.[49]

Take, as just one brief contemporary example, the decision of the House of Lords in *McGhee v National Coal Board* (1972),[50] and the string of cases since then.[51] A

[44] For more discussion on the importance of 're-description' in legal reasoning, see Amaya (2011).

[45] For an example of the opposite view, namely that the common law is driven by transcendent, unchanging principles, see Epstein (1980).

[46] Reasoning by reference to an imaginary perspective, such as the officious bystander in contract law, or the reasonable person in many areas of the law.

[47] As Hutchinson (2005, p. 270) notes, 'there are no permanent solutions to life's problems because life is problematic, and any effort to resist that conclusion is itself a problem.' What needs to be added here is that what we understand to be a problem changes over time.

[48] For example, 'the fault standard in Anglo-Canadian negligence law has had such a relatively long and successful life because … it has been malleable enough to adapt itself to a host of changing demands and expectations … from injurious acts to misleading statements, from physical damage to economic losses, and from novices to experts' (see Hutchinson 2005, p. 265).

[49] For an argument that not all fictions used in the common law were about enabling change—and for valuable insights on the role of fictions before the nineteenth century reforms—see Lobban, this volume, Chap. 10.

[50] (1972) 3 All ER 1008.

[51] For a related and sympathetic analysis of the use of fictions in this line of cases, see also Lee, this volume, Chap. 12.

neat overview of the significance of the case[52] is provided by Lord Hope of Craighead in the 2002 Personal Injuries Bar Association Lecture (Hope 2003). The facts of the case—described in such loving detail by Lord Hope—were, briefly, that Mr McGhee was employed by the National Coal Board (NCB) to clean out brick kilns. Mr McGhee was exposed to clouds of abrasive brick dust, which, as a result of the NCB not providing adequate washing facilities, he only washed off once he got home after cycling home 'caked with sweat and grime' (to use Lord Reid's own description, at *McGhee*, p. 1010). After 5 days, Mr. McGhee developed dermatitis and stopped work. There was medical evidence that the dermatitis was caused by the working conditions in the brick kilns, but the evidence also showed that cycling back home after work added materially to the risk. In the Court of Session, Mr McGhee failed because he could not show that the breach of duty (i.e. failing to provide adequate washing facilities) caused his injury. There was, in short, no positive evidence that it was more probable than not that he would have avoided contracting dermatitis if those facilities had been provided.

The House of Lords allowed the appeal and found for Mr McGhee. There were five separate opinions and, as Lord Hope notes, 'an examination of their reasoning will show that it was far from uniform' (Hope 2003, p. 588).[53] Mr McGhee's problem, as will be evident from the above description, was causation—he could not discharge his onus that on the balance of probabilities the NCB's breach of duty caused or materially contributed to his injury.[54] The Lords, then, were faced with a rule that attached a certain normative consequence (satisfaction of the requirement of causation for the purposes of establishing liability) to certain operative facts (including the onus), namely material contribution to injury. Counsel for Mr McGhee argued that the NCB's failure to provide adequate washing facilities 'materially increased the risk' of his contracting dermatitis (Hope 2003, p. 592)—in essence, they argued for suspending, at least in this case, the operative fact of 'material contribution'.[55] The House, in order to reach a conclusion they had thought justifiable—namely, that Mr McGhee was a worthy recipient of a remedy, and that the NCB ought to be found liable—had to re-frame the facts (and who had to prove what) vis-à-vis the law, and it could do so precisely by suspending the required operative fact. In the broad sense, then, one might argue that a fiction was deployed:

---

[52] It bears noting that this is never quite settled, for whether a case is treated as significant (leading etc.) or not is a contingent matter, and itself a sign of how the law changes.

[53] This, incidentally, is another important institutional feature of the common law that helps keep it dynamic: the fact that there are separate opinions creates a fuller and more alive set of resources than would otherwise be available if all judges had to agree on a single formulation and a single description of the present facts and the facts of past cases (either relied on or distinguished).

[54] As was required by *Wardlaw v Bonnington Castings Ltd* (1956) AC 613; see also Hope (2003, p. 592).

[55] One could say, more strongly, that the House replaced that operative fact with another one, viz. 'materially increasing the risk', the onus then shifting to the NCB to show that they did not materially increase the risk (it is important to add here that the mechanics of onus are another very important device used to change the law in subtle ways). But to say this feels too strong, and smacks of wisdom in hindsight (given how subsequent cases have gone on to interpret *McGhee*). One sees here how difficult it is to offer an appropriately temporally-sensitive reading.

because of the absence of proof, a required operative fact was suspended, such that, as a result, the NCB could be treated as if they caused the injury ('as if' because, on the required operative fact, they would not have 'caused' it). Further, one of the Lords—Lord Wilberforce—himself characterised that the inference 'from the fact that the negligence increased the risk that it had materially contributed to the disease was something of a fiction' (Hope 2003, p. 601). It is useful to quote Lord Wilberforce's own words (the concluding paragraph of his speech):

> And I must say that, at least in the present case, to bridge the evidential gap by inference seems to me something of a fiction, since it was precisely this inference which the medical expert declined to make. But I find in the cases quoted an analogy which suggests the conclusion that, in the absence of proof that the culpable condition had, in the result, no effect, the employers should be liable for an injury, squarely within the risk which they created and that they, not the pursuer, should suffer the consequence of the impossibility, foreseeably inherent in the nature of his injury, of segregating the precise consequence of their default. (Lord Wilberforce, *McGhee* 1972, p. 1013)

This quote is instructive, for there is explicit recognition of the intimate link between the use of fictions and the difficulties encountered concerning proof (causation being one of the commonly recurring contexts in which such difficulties are encountered, intention being the other). There is also explicit reference to the re-description of past cases, via the mode of analogy—indicating, also, the link between the use of the device of fictions and the use of the mode of analogy.[56] The suspension of a required operative fact is assisted by the analogical extension of a string of cases now asserted to be relevant to the present problem. Facts extended by analogy are like the bricks in the bridge of the fiction.

As has been repeated throughout this chapter, it is not sufficient—both in order to understand but also in order to properly evaluate the use of fictions—to focus on just one instance, on just the single use of it in a particular case. If we did that in the present case we might think that the Lords took on powers that properly belong to the legislature, and that they tried to hide their law-making by concealing it under the cloak of a fiction.[57] What subsequent cases have brought out—in a way that could not have been foreseen—is that the decision in *McGhee* has provided a fertile though also controversial resource that has allowed the law to adapt and remain responsive to the claims of plaintiffs in personal injury litigation. Some subsequent judges have refused to treat *McGhee* as a relevant resource—e.g. Lord Bridge of Harwich in *Wilsher v Essex Area Health Authority* (1988)[58] said that McGhee:

> … laid down no principle of law whatever … to attempt to extract from it some esoteric principle which in some way modifies, as a matter of law, the nature of the burden of proof of causation which a plaintiff or pursuer must discharge once he has established a relevant breach of duty is a fruitless one. (*Wilsher*, p. 1090)

[56] For an insightful statement concerning the difference between using fictions and deploying analogy, see Stern, this volume, Chap. 8.

[57] Though it needs to be said that this case is hardly a good example of concealment, for the Lordships were relatively open and transparent about their struggle with the requirement of material contribution; and, as indicated, Lord Wilberforce was also explicit in stating he was employing a fiction.

[58] (1988) AC 1074.

This effectively ignores the invitation offered by the fiction in *McGhee*, i.e. to suspend the operative fact, and to potentially systematise and make explicit that suspension, and re-introduces the operative fact of the rule, i.e. it treats material contribution as continuing to be the necessary operative fact (rather than materially enhancing the risk of injury).

Other judges, however, have taken up the invitation, and indeed attempted to formulate a principle so as to unify both the facts of *McGhee* and the facts of the case being dealt with, e.g. in *Fairchild v Glenhavon Funeral Services Ltd and Others* (2002).[59] It is interesting that in that case Lord Rodger observed that (in Lord Hope's summary) 'the House [in *McGhee*] could have proclaimed more clearly and more openly that they were stating a new principle' (Hope 2003, p. 598; see *Fairchild* 2002, para. 144). This already is a taking up of the invitation, for it presents *McGhee* as a principled decision. However, from the perspective of this chapter, it is not a drawback of the decision in *McGhee* that it was not (allegedly) clearer about the effect of its judgement: that was precisely for later courts to either take up or not. The point is that the House in *McGhee* was proceeding tentatively, creating potential resources, but keeping principled articulation at a minimum,[60] for this enables future experimentation and exploration of the benefits—including testing impact on other nearby rules and principles—of adopting a rule or principle. Lord Reid in *Fairchild*, as Lord Hope notes, says on the back of a reading of *McGhee* that 'in a case like this we must take a broader view of causation' (Hope 2003, p. 599; see *Fairchild* 2002, para. 21). What becomes visible here is how the fiction is taken up, transformed into what might not yet be a principle, but at least articulates the need for a different attitude—in this case, 'a broader view of causation'. In doing that, it also reads back, establishing a factual pattern—'in a case *like this*'—which further sediments the relevance of *McGhee*, but also creates resources for future analogical extension.

The debate over the relevance of *McGhee* is by no means over. Nor has the adventure of 'the principle' ceased—it being the point that there is not one formulation, for it is continually being re-formulated in light of future cases. For instance, in *Sienkiewicz v Grief (UK) Ltd* (2011)[61] and *Willmore v Knowsley Metropolitan Borough Council* (2011),[62] the Supreme Court gave further normative impetus to the operative fact of materially increasing risk (potentially displacing the operative fact of material contribution),[63] and thus arguably extending the legacy of *McGhee*, via *Fairchild*.[64] It remains to be seen whether future courts will, in their turn, continue endorsing that normative impetus, or will instead seek to retrospectively narrow the significance of

---

[59] (2002) 3 WLR 89.

[60] On minimalism in legal reasoning in general, see Sunstein (2001). The virtue of minimalism as a technique of communication between courts is recognised, for instance, by Krisch (2011).

[61] (2011) UKSC 10.

[62] (2011) 2 WLR 53.

[63] To assert they amount to the same thing might be another way—a less controversial way—of replacing the former with the latter, for arguably the former is the broader test.

[64] For an instructive discussion of *Sienkiewicz* and *Willmore*, see Laleng (2011).

McGhee and/ or *Fairchild*, turning them into exceptions or *sui generis* outcasts.[65] For the moment, it certainly looks as if—as a result of subsequent courts largely taking up the invitation offered by *McGhee*—the fiction first entertained in *McGhee* will not die a quiet death, and indeed may very well blossom, past a change in attitude to causation in personal injury cases, to a more general principle of causation (or at least the proof of causation) in tort law (or indeed other areas of the law). We do not know—that is part of the magic and utility of fictions, and, simultaneously, the magic and utility of the common law.

Conclusion

Fictions are born in the coalface of legal change. They are one of the devices via which the law—via the creative efforts of its officials—manages to balance flexibility and responsiveness with stability and predictability. In that respect, they are not to be scoffed at, as if they were but an immature stage in some inevitable progress. Legal fictions—understood broadly, as the suspension of a required operative fact, while retaining the associated normative consequence—are a form of tentative cognition, justifiably utilised by courts. They are a way of probing—a form of trial-and-error—across time, enabling communication—and the sharing of dynamic resources—between past, present and future courts. They are a way in which courts solve particular problems—especially problems to do with what claimants need to prove, and especially in the contexts of causation and intention—but always with a view to what has been before and what is to come. Legal fictions cannot be properly understood, and especially evaluated, without looking at them diachronically, as 'relational capital'. And, it might just be that much, if not all, of legal reasoning ought to be approached in this relational, temporally-sensitive manner, combining attention to detail in particular cases with how the modes and devices used in them live and die as the task of justice carries on.

Acknowledgments This chapter grew out of discussions at the workshop on Legal Fictions, held at the 2011 IVR Congress in Frankfurt. My thanks to all speakers and participants at that workshop. Special thanks for helpful comments and discussion to Randy Gordon, Michael Quinn, Karen Petroski, Simon Stern and William Twining.

[65] In that respect, see the decision of the Supreme Court in what is known as the 'EL Trigger Litigation': *BAI (Run Off) Limited (In Scheme of Arrangement) and others v Durham and others* (2012) UKSC 14.

References

Cases

BAI (Run Off) Limited (In Scheme of Arrangement) and others v Durham and others [2012] UKSC 14
Des Salles D'Epinoix v Royal Borough of Kensington and Chelsea [1970] 1 All ER 18
Exall v Partridge (1799) 8 TR 308; 3 Esp. 8
Fairchild v Glenhavon Funeral Services Ltd and Others [2002] 3 WLR 89
McGhee v National Coal Board [1972] 3 All ER 1008
Sienkiewicz v Grief (UK) Ltd [2011] UKSC 10
Wardlaw v Bonnington Castings Ltd [1956] AC 613
Willmore v Knowsley Metropolitan Borough Council [2011] 2 WLR 53
Wilsher v Assex Area Health Authority [1988] AC 1074

Books/Articles

Amaya, Amalia. 2011. Virtue and reason in law. In *New waves in philosophy of law*, ed. M. Del Mar, 123–143. Houndmills: Palgrave Macmillan.

Ando, Clifford. 2011. *Law, language, and empire in the Roman tradition*. Philadelphia: University of Pennsylvania Press.

Ando, Clifford. 2014. Fact, fiction, and social reality in roman law. In *Legal fictions in theory and practice*, ed. Maksymilian Del Mar and William Twining. Dordrecht: Springer.

Baker, John. 2001. *The law's two bodies: Some evidential problems in English legal history*. Oxford: Oxford University Press.

Bentham, Jeremy, and J. Bowring. 1962. *The works of Jeremy Bentham*. 1–5 vols. New York: Russell & Russell.

Birks, Peter. 1986. Fictions ancient and modern. In *The legal mind: Essays for Tony Honoré*, eds. N. MacCormick and P. Birks, 83–101. Oxford: Clarendon Press.

Del Mar, Maksymilian. 2011. What does history matter to legal epistemology? *Journal of the Philosophy of History* 5:383–405.

Del Mar, Maksymilian. 2013. Exemplarity and narrativity in the common law tradition. *Law & Literature* 25 (3): 390–427.

Del Mar, Maksymilian, and Michael Lobban, eds. 2014. *Legal theory and legal history*. Surrey: Ashgate.

Diamond, Alan. 1991. Fictions, equity and legislation: Maine's three agencies of legal change. In *The victorian achievement of Sir Henry Maine: A centennial reappraisal*, ed. A. Diamond, 242–255. Cambridge: Cambridge University Press.

Duxbury, Neil. 2008. *The nature and authority of precedent*. Cambridge: Cambridge University Press.

Epstein, Richard. 1980. The static conception of the common law. *The Journal of Legal Studies* 9 (2): 253–275.

Fine, Arthur. 1993. Fictionalism. *Midwest Studies in Philosophy* 18:1–18.

Frank, Jerome. 2009 [1930]. *Law and the modern mind*. New Brunswick: Transaction Publishers.

Fuller, Lon 1930–1931. Legal fictions. *Illinois Law Review* 25:363–399; 513–546; 877–910.

Gama, Raymundo. 2014. Presumptions and fictions: A Collingwoodian approach. In *Legal fictions in theory and practice*, ed. Maksymilian Del Mar and William Twining. Dordrecht: Springer.

Glenn, Patrick. 2007. *Legal traditions of the world*. 3rd ed. Oxford: Oxford University Press.

Gordon, Randy D. 2014. Fictitious Fraud: Economics and the presumption of reliance. In *Legal fictions in theory and practice*, ed. Maksymilian Del Mar and William Twining. Dordrecht: Springer.

Hans Kelsen. 2014. On the theory of juridic fictions. With special consideration of Vaihinger's Philosophy of the as-if. In *Legal fictions in theory and practice*, ed. Maksymilian Del Mar and William Twining. Dordrecht: Springer.

Hamilton, K. Scott. 1988–1989. Prolegomenon to myth and fiction in legal reasoning, common law adjudication and critical legal studies. *Wayne Law Review* 35:1449–1480.
Hayes, Christine. 2004. Authority and anxiety in the Talmuds: From legal fiction to legal fact. In *Jewish religious leadership: image and reality*, ed. J. Wertheimer, 1127–1154. New York: Jewish Theological Seminary.
Holdsworth, William. 1937. *A history of english law*. London: Metheun & Co Ltd.
Holmes, Oliver W Jr. 2009 [1880]. *The common law*. Cambridge, Mass: The Belknap Press.
Hope, Lord of Craighead. 2003. James McGhee: a second Mrs Donoghue? *Cambridge Law Journal* 62 (3): 587–604.
Horii, Satoe. 2002. Reconsideration of legal devices (Hiyal) in Islamic jurisprudence: The Hanafis and their "Exits" (Makharij). *Islamic Law and Society* 9 (3): 312–357.
Hutchinson, Allan. 2005. *Evolution and the common law*. Cambridge: Cambridge University Press.
Ibbetson, David. 1999. *A historical introduction to the law of obligations*. Oxford: Oxford University Press.
Jones, John W. 1940. *A historical introduction to the theory of law*. Oxford: Clarendon Press.
Kelsen, Hans. 1960. *Reine Rechstlehre*. Vienna: Franz Deuticke.
Kerchove, Michel van de, and Francois Ost. 1992. *Le droit ou les paradoxes du jeu*. Paris: PUF.
Kletzer, Christoph. 2014. Kelsen on Vaihinger. In *Legal fictions in theory and practice*, ed. Maksymilian Del Mar and William Twining. Dordrecht: Springer.
Knauer, Nancy. 2010. Legal fictions and juristic truth. *St. Thomas Law Review* 23:1–51.
Krisch, Nico. 2011. *Beyond constitutionalism: The pluralist structure of postnational law*. Oxford: Oxford University Press.
Laleng, Per. 2011. Sienkiewicz v Grief (UK) Ltd and Willmore v Knowsley Metropolitan Borough Council: A material contribution to uncertainty? *Modern Law Review* 74 (5): 767–793.
Last Stone, Suzanne. 2007. On the interplay of rules, "cases," and concepts in rabbinic legal literature: another look at the Aggadot on Honi the circle-drawer. *Dine Israel* 24:125–155.
Lee, James. 2014. Fictions in tort. In *Legal fictions in theory and practice*, ed. Maksymilian Del Mar and William Twining. Dordrecht: Springer.
Lind, Douglas. 2014. The pragmatic value of legal fictions. In *Legal fictions in theory and practice*, ed. Maksymilian Del Mar and William Twining. Dordrecht: Springer.
Lobban, Michael. 2014. Legal fictions before the age of reform. In *Legal fictions in theory and practice*, ed. Maksymilian Del Mar and William Twining. Dordrecht: Springer.
Maclean, Ian. 1999. Legal fictions and fictional entities in renaissance jurisprudence. *Legal History* 20 (3): 1–24.
Maine, Sir Henry. 1931 [1861]. *Ancient law*. London: Oxford University Press.
Milsom, S. F. C. 2003. *A natural history of the common law*. New York: Columbia University Press.
Mitchell, Oliver. 1893. The fictions of the law: Have they proved useful or detrimental to its growth? *Harvard Law Review* 7 (5): 249–265.
Moscovitz, Leib. 2003. Legal fictions in rabbinic law and Roman law: some comparative observations. In *Rabbinic law in its Roman and near eastern context*, ed. C. Hezser, 105–132. Tubingen: Mohr.
Moscovitz, Leib. 2014. Rabbinic legal fictions. In *Legal fictions in theory and practice*, ed. Maksymilian Del Mar and William Twining. Dordrecht: Springer.
Olivier, Pierre. 1975. *Legal fictions in practice and legal science*. Rotterdam: Rotterdam University Press.
Petroski, Karen. 2014. Legal fictions and the limits of legal language. In *Legal fictions in theory and practice*, ed. Maksymilian Del Mar and William Twining. Dordrecht: Springer.
Postema, Gerald. 2003. Classical common law jurisprudence (Part II). *Oxford University Commonwealth Law Journal* 3 (1): 1–28.
Pound, Roscoe. 1959. *Jurisprudence*. St. Paul: West Publishing Co.
Pound, Roscoe. 1999 [1963]. *The spirit of the common law*. New Brunswick: Transaction Publishers.

Quinn, Michael. 2014. Fuller on legal fictions: A benthamic perspective. In *Legal fictions in theory and practice*, ed. Maksymilian Del Mar and William Twining. Dordrecht: Springer.

Rescher, Nicholas. 2006. *Presumption and the practices of tentative cognition*. Cambridge: Cambridge University Press.

Riccobono, S. 1929. 'Formulae ficticiae: a norms means of creating new law'. *Tijdschrift voor Techtsgeschiedenis* 9:1–61.

Riles, Annelise. 2010. Is the law hopeful? Cornell Law Faculty Working Papers, Paper 68; http://scholarship.law.cornell.edu/clsops_papers/68. Accessed 25 Oct 2012.

Samek, R. A. 1981. Fictions and the law. *University of Toronto Law Journal* 31:290–317.

Samuel, Geoffrey. 2014. Is law a fiction? In *Legal fictions in theory and practice,* ed. Maksymilian Del Mar and William Twining. Dordrecht: Springer.

Schauer, Frederick. 2014. Legal fictions revisited. In *Legal fictions in theory and practice,* ed. Maksymilian Del Mar and William Twining. Dordrecht: Springer.

Schiavone, Aldo. 2012. *The invention of law in the west,*. trans. by J. Carden and A. Shugaar. Cambridge: Belknap Press.

Schulz, Fritz. 1946. *History of Roman legal science*. Oxford: Clarendon Press.

Simon-Shoshan, M. 2012. *Stories of the law: Narrative discourse and the construction of authority in the Mishnah*. Oxford: Oxford University Press.

Smith, Jeremiah. 1917. Surviving fictions I and II. *Yale Law Journal* 27:147–66, 317–29.

Smith, Peter. 2007. 'New legal fictions'. *Georgetown Law Journal* 95:1435–1495.

Sparkes, Peter. 2014. Ejectment: Three births and a funeral. In *Legal fictions in theory and practice*, ed. Maksymilian Del Mar and William Twining. Dordrecht: Springer.

Stern, Simon. 2014. Legal fictions and exclusionary rules. In *Legal fictions in theory and practice*, ed. Maksymilian Del Mar and William Twining. Dordrecht: Springer.

Stolzenberg, Nomi Maya. 1999. Bentham's theory of fictions—a 'curious double language'. *Cardozo Studies in Law and Literature* 11:223–49.

Sunstein, Cass. 2001. *One case at a time: Judicial minimalism on the supreme court*. Cambridge, Mass: Harvard University Press.

Thomas, Yan. 2005. Les artifice de la vérité en droit commun médiéval. *L'Homme* 175–176:113–130.

Tourtoulon, Pierre de. 1922. *Philosophy in the development of law*. Trans. by M. McRead. New York: Macmillan.

Vaihinger, Hans. 2009 [1925]. *The philosophy of 'As If': a system of the theoretical, practical and religious fictions of mankind. Trans. C. K. Ogden*. Mansfield: Martino Publishing. (first published in German in 1911)

Vermeer-Kunzli, Annemarieke. 2007. As If: The legal fiction in diplomatic protection. *The European Journal of International Law* 18 (1): 37–68.

Watson, Alan. 1995. *The spirit of Roman law*. Athens: The University of Georgia Press.

Wilder, Colin. 2012. Teaching old dogs new tricks: Four motifs of legal change from early modern Europe. *History and Theory* 51:18–41.

Yntema, Hessel. 1950. Roman law and its influence on western civilisation. *Cornell Law Quarterly* 35:77–88.

Yntema, Hessel. 1966–1967. Equity in the civil law and the common law. *American Journal of Comparative Law* 15:60–86.

Chapter 12
Fictions in Tort

James Lee

Abstract This essay examines the use of fictions in the reasoning of the House of Lords and United Kingdom Supreme Court in the context of two recent lines of authority on English tort law. First, the essay explores the relevance of counter-factual scenarios to liability in the tort of false imprisonment, in the light of the Supreme Court decisions in *Lumba* and *Kambadzi*. The second series of decisions is on causation in negligence claims arising from asbestos exposure (beginning with *Fairchild v Glenhaven Funeral Services* and considered most recently in *The 'Trigger' Litigation*). These cases have revealed fundamental, ongoing judicial disagreement about the nature and extent of the exceptions made to general principles. The cases are also shown to lend force to Del Mar's argument about the diachronicity of legal fictions. Overall, it is argued that such fictions play an important role in common law reasoning.

12.1 Introduction

Stark examples of fictions in modern English tort law are to be found in recent cases on causation. In Part 2 of the paper, we shall consider the relevance of counter-factual inquiries to the ingredients in the tort of false imprisonment, in *R (Lumba) v Secretary of State for the Home Department*[1] and *Kambadzi*.[2] The other line of

A version of this paper was presented as the Inaugural Public Lecture of the Private Law Discussion Group at Trinity College Dublin, funded by the generosity of the Trinity College's Visiting Professorships and Fellowships Benefaction Fund. I thank all those who attended the lecture, and I am very grateful to Dr Niamh Connelly, Dr Maksymillian Del Mar, Sarah Fulham-McQuillan, Professor Simon Lee, Dr Margaret Martin, Dr Eoin O'Dell, Dr Desmond Ryan and Professor William Twining for helpful comments. Any errors are my own.

[1] [2011] UKSC 12.
[2] [2011] UKSC 23.

J. Lee (✉)
King's College London, Dickson Poon School of Law Somerset House East Wing,
London WC2R 2LS, UK
e-mail: j.s.f.lee@bham.ac.uk

M. Del Mar, W. Twining (eds.), *Legal Fictions in Theory and Practice*,
Law and Philosophy Library 110, DOI 10.1007/978-3-319-09232-4_12

authorities, to which the majority of the paper is devoted, concerns causation in negligence, and the reasoning in *Sienkiewicz v Greif (UK) Ltd*[3] and *Durham v BAI (Run Off) Ltd (Employer's Liability 'Trigger' Litigation)*[4] will be examined in Parts 3 and 4. The area has proven to be one of the 'most intractable and recurrent problem[s] in the recent history of the common law of torts' (Stevens 2009, p. 645). We shall see that the arguments in the causation cases map on to the controversies which run through this collection, relating to the essence of what a fiction is.

There are many other aspects of the law of tort which one might choose for an essay on legal fictions. Much work, for example, has been undertaken on the contingent relationship between the now abolished forms of action[5] and the operation of fictions, notably in the field of conversion and other torts relating to the interference with property.[6] Several other contributions to the collection consider this historical theme, especially those of Professors Lobban[7] and Sparkes.[8] Instead, therefore, I propose to consider contexts where the 'fictiveness' is not derived from the forms of action, but rather directed at an element (or putative element) of a claim, as considered by our highest court.[9]

There often seems to be a tendency for 'fiction' to be used as a term of disparagement in legal argument (Del Mar 2013; Chap. 7, p. 498), indicating that the user of the fiction is guilty of the supposedly 'diabolic tendency' to manipulate language (Birks 1986, p. 83). In 2007, Lord Nicholls of Birkenhead took aim at the device[10]: 'I would like to think that, as a mature legal system, English law has outgrown the need for legal fictions' (*OBG v Allan* 2007, para 229), because such 'fictions, of their nature, conceal what is going on. They are a pretence' (*OBG v Allan* 2007, para 228). And in some contexts, fictions can be properly criticised if they involve distortions of existing concepts, or if they are used solely for teleological justifications in certain decisions (Lee 2014).

But, as Del Mar argues in this volume, 'legal fictions… when used wisely, are inherently dynamic resources that allow courts, over time, to balance flexibility and responsiveness with stability and predictability' (Chap. 11, p. 227). It is hoped that this essay provides some support for that proposition, especially in the context of

---

[3] [2011] UKSC 10.

[4] [2012] UKSC 14 (*'"Trigger" Litigation'* hereafter).

[5] Ss3 and 49, Common Law Procedure Act 1852. The title of s 49 refers to 'Fictitious and needless averments [which are] not to be made' (Baker 2002, pp. 90–92).

[6] See inter alia Green and Randall (2009); Douglas (2009); and Hickey (2011). On fictions more generally, see Leeming 2013, Part VII; and Birks (1986).

[7] Chap. 10.

[8] Chap. 13.

[9] In 2009, Professor Stevens remarked that, in contrast to other areas of private law, the 'modern law of torts is dominated by the House of Lords' (Stevens 2009, p. 629). As will be seen, that trend has continued with the transition to the United Kingdom Supreme Court. Given the constitutional change, I shall refer collectively to Law Lords and Supreme Court Justices as 'judges', without meaning any disrespect, but then to Law Lords or Justices as appropriate in any given case. Throughout, 'Supreme Court' refers to the UK Supreme Court rather than any other.

[10] In his dissent in *OBG v Allan* [2007] UKHL 21; [2008] 1 AC 1, speaking in the context of the tort of conversion (see in footnote 2 above).

causation, and for Del Mar's plea for patience with fictions. In what follows, we shall also consider the extent to which fictions in this area are a characteristic legal device (Fuller 1930–1931, p. 363). For the selected cases are notable not only for judicial creativity, but also for the debate between the judges about whether fictions are indeed being used, and if so, what it means to deploy them.

I shall demonstrate that the regularity of fictions (and of accusations of the use of fictions) suggest that we can understand them to be a crucial aspect of common law reasoning. And it is perhaps fundamental to the assessment of compensation in tort: in asking what the claimant has lost, we are necessarily asking what would have happened if the tort had not been committed.[11] The chapter will conclude by arguing that it is crucial to appreciate the utility, and perhaps power, of fictions in facilitating the development of the law, whether judicially or by legislation.

12.2 Counter-factual Imprisonment?

In this section, I wish to examine the approach to a particular counter-factual problem for the tort of false imprisonment, as considered recently the Supreme Court in a pair of decisions from 2011. The tort of false imprisonment, as a species of trespass to the person, is actionable per se: the claimant need not demonstrate that they have suffered any harm. They need only show an intentional, complete restriction of their freedom of movement, and that this detention was without lawful justification.[12] But does it matter in such a case if it is established that the claimant would have been detained even if the defendant had acted lawfully? If it does matter, is the point properly taken into account at the stage of liability or that of damages?[13]

12.2.1 Lumba

R (Lumba) v Secretary of State for the Home Department concerned claims by foreign nationals who were due to be deported upon completion of their prison sentences for various crimes. The men were detained on the authority of the Home Secretary under paragraph 2(2) of Schedule 3 to the Immigration Act 1971 prior to their

[11] Professor Stapleton has recently argued for a clear separation between the requirement for causation and the 'principle of compensatory tort damages': Stapleton 2013, pp. 54–56. There are of course debates in psychological and philosophical literature over the extent which causal and counterfactual reasoning correlate: see eg Spellman and Kincannon (2001); Moore (2003) and Paul (2009).

[12] *R v Governor of Brockhill Prison, Ex p Evans (No 2)* [2001] 2 AC 19.

[13] In the cases, there is consideration of the scope of the enforceable right to compensation in respect of a breach of article 5 of the European Convention on Human Rights and Fundamental Freedoms (art 5(5)): see eg *Kambadzi* 2011, para 59 (Lord Hope); cf. Lord Brown, ibid, paras 94 and 112. However, since my focus is on the use of fictions at common law, and the majority's view is that there *is* a right to recover damages in tort in such situations, we shall not consider this aspect here.

deportation. Mr Lumba, a Congolese national, was convicted of various offences including wounding with intent, and was sentenced to a term of four years' imprisonment. The day before his scheduled release, he was notified that the Secretary of State had authorised his detention pending deportation. Mr Mighty, a Jamaican national, was imprisoned in respect of offences including possession with intent to supply a Class A drug. The Secretary of State had a published policy on the detention of prisoners pending deportation, which referred to a 'presumption' in favour of release. However, it transpired that a very different policy had been applied in the relevant period, which was a 'near blanket ban on release' (*Lumba* 2011, para 5, Lord Dyson JSC, quoting a document from the then Home Secretary). The claimants were detained pursuant to this secret, unlawful policy, and brought claims in false imprisonment. However, it was accepted that, had the Home Secretary applied the published policy, the men would still have been detained: 'each claimant had a very bad criminal record and would undoubtedly have been kept in custody under the Secretary of State's published policies.' (*Lumba* 2011, para 195, Lord Walker).

There were two principal points of relevance[14] for the Court to address. First, given that the inevitability of the men's detention had the published policy been applied to them was accepted, did that mean that their detentions were lawful? This is the 'causation test' question. Second, if they were able to recover in principle, what was the extent (or nature) of the damages to which they were entitled? This is the 'damages' question.[15] The Supreme Court divided 6:3 on each point, but with different majorities.

12.2.1.1 The 'Causation Test' Point

The majority of the Supreme Court held that the claimants did not have to show that they would not have been detained, on the basis that 'all that a claimant has to prove in order to establish false imprisonment is that he was directly and intentionally imprisoned by the defendant' (*Lumba* 2011, para 65, Lord Dyson) and it is then for the defendant to justify it. The importance of the right to liberty, with the attendant need to scrutinise the executive power to detain, requiring that it be exercised lawfully, compelled the conclusion that there be liability in such cases. Lord Dyson gave the leading majority judgment and dismissed the existence of

> any defence of causation so as to render lawful what is in fact an unlawful authority to detain, by reference to how the executive could and *would have* acted if it had acted lawfully, as opposed to how it *did in fact* act. (*Lumba* 2011, para 62)

[14] There are various administrative law points of importance in the case, chiefly the proper approach to the exercise of the Secretary of State's power of detention and the application of the *Hardial Singh* principles, (from *R v Governor of Durham Prison, Ex p Hardial Singh* [1974] 1 WLR 704). But for present purposes we shall proceed on the basis that the Home Secretary was found to have detained the claimants pursuant to an unlawful policy.

[15] The damages point embraces two questions—whether nominal or exemplary/vindicatory damages should be awarded.

The view of the majority on the causation test is therefore focused on the 'counter' in 'counter-factual': the Secretary of State's protestations about what they could or would have done are not relevant, because it did not actually happen. This is not an 'over-determination' case, where there are two sufficient causes of the claimant's detention, counting both the unlawful decision of the Secretary of State and their possible lawful decision, because only one of those decisions was really made. The emphasis is on the 'could' and the conditional in the above quotation:[16] '[detention] cannot be justified on some putative basis, unrelated to the actual reasons for it' (*Lumba* 2011, para 242, Lord Kerr). To allow the Secretary of State's argument would be to ignore what actually happened and instead to admit a fiction: it would involve putting the 'cart before the horse' (*Lumba* 2011, para 197, Lady Hale).

On the other hand, the minority were concerned that the *majority* approach seems somewhat fictive: that it ignores the accepted inevitability—though, as a counter-factual, it cannot be said to be the 'reality'—of what would have happened had the Secretary of State acted lawfully. The necessary result of the application of the published policy would have been the detention of the claimants. The counter-factual has, for the minority, more power than the majority admit.

Lord Brown in particular vehemently dissented. In his Lordship's view, the majority's approach had a 'beguiling simplicity and apparent purity', but would 'seriously devalue the whole concept of false imprisonment' (*Lumba* 2011, para 343). In his Lordship's view, to say that the claimant can sue in false imprisonment even though he would have been detained anyway, but then to 'deny compensation' (*Lumba* 2011, para 344) *because* they would have been detained anyway, is illogical. It is tantamount to saying that the detainee was simultaneously 'both rightly and wrongly imprisoned' (*Lumba* 2011, para 344). Instead, it would be better to refuse liability in the first place: 'the detainees… were rightly detained and it would have been wrong to release them' (*Lumba* 2011, para 361).

12.2.1.2 The Damages Point

On the damages point, a different majority of Justices held that it *was* relevant to take into account the fact that the men would inevitably have been detained in awarding only nominal damages: 'they suffered no loss or damage as a result of the unlawful exercise of the power to detain' (*Lumba* 2011, para 95, Lord Dyson). Although the men were able to claim, the counter-factual problem was relevant to the damages which they received. The majority rejected the contentions either that a separate head of vindicatory damages existed in English law, or that such a head should be created (*Lumba* 2011, para 237, Lord Collins). As Lord Kerr put it, the 'the actual impact on the individual who has been falsely imprisoned … should feature prominently' when assessing damages (*Lumba* 2011, para 253).

The minority of Lady Hale, Lords Hope and Walker accepted that the claimants could not be compensated for loss which they had not suffered. But the dissenting

[16] As is also apparent, for example, in Lord Kerr's judgment: *Lumba* 2011, paras 239 and 240.

Justices desired something more than nominal damages, 'not [to] purport to compensate him for harm or to punish the defendant for wrongdoing but simply to mark the law's recognition that a wrong has been done' (*Lumba* 2011, para 213, Lady Hale). They would have awarded a 'conventional' sum of £1000, on the basis of such vindication.

12.2.1.3 Lumba Overall

In her contribution to this volume, Petroski observes the relationship between judicial disagreement over fictions and the multiplicity of judgments in decisions of the United States Supreme Court (Chap. 7, pp. 496–498). The United Kingdom Supreme Court decision in *Lumba* also speaks to this phenomenon. Across the two main points of the appeal in *Lumba*, the nine Justices of the Supreme Court fall into three groups of three when it comes to the relevance of the counter-factual. In the majority on both points—Lords Dyson, Collins and Kerr—hold that the counter-factual should not be relevant to liability but should mean that the claimant is entitled only to nominal damages. The three of the 'causation test' majority who dissented on the damages point—Lord Hope, Lord Walker and Baroness Hale—would seem to agree that the claimant cannot claim any loss because of the counter-factual, but would argue that in such circumstances a special award is necessary in order to 'vindicate' the claimant's rights which would otherwise be insufficiently protected. The minority on the causation test would have held the counter-factual to be a bar to a claim at all, and in fact have concerns about the award of nominal damages in the case, as it portrays liability in an important tort as established merely on the basis of a technicality (*Lumba* 2011, para 343, Lord Brown). For Lords Phillips, Brown and Rodger, the two stages of analysis are inextricably linked.

12.2.2 Kambadzi

Two months after the decision in *Lumba*, the Supreme Court considered a variation on these themes in *R (Kambadzi) v Secretary of State for the Home Department*. The case had been heard by a five-Justice panel before *Lumba*, but judgment was delayed in *Kambadzi* so that the parties could make submissions on the basis on the reasoning in *Lumba*. The appellant, Mr Kambadzi, had been convicted of common and sexual assault. He was sentenced to a year's imprisonment, and before he became eligible for release a deportation order was made against him. Thereafter, his detention had not been subject to sufficiently regular review as required by rule 9(1) of the Detention Centre Rules 2001 and the Secretary of State's published policy.[17] Without good reason, the necessary reviews were either not carried out at all or not

[17] Lord Hope preferred to focus on the policy rather than the Rules: *Kambadzi* 2011, para 16.

carried out correctly. The appellant sued in false imprisonment, arguing that his detention had been unlawful because of the failure to comply with this procedure.

The Court was divided, along the same lines as in *Lumba*. The majority, Lord Hope DPSC, Baroness Hale and Lord Kerr, had been in the majority on the causation test point in *Lumba*. We may note that, although Lord Hope and Baroness Hale were in the minority on the damages point in *Lumba*, it was accepted that, in the light of that decision, there was no prospect of establishing an entitlement to vindicatory damages in *Kambadzi*. Lords Brown and Rodger again dissented.

For the majority, the review was a prerequisite of the continued authority to detain. 'Unless the authority to detain was renewed under the powers conferred by the statute [the appellant] was entitled to his liberty' (*Kambadzi* 2011, para 54, Lord Hope). Without it, the detention was unlawful. On the other hand, 'the continued detention could at all times have been justified by the Secretary of State had he been faced with an application for judicial review' (*Kambadzi* 2011, para 34, Lord Hope). The position is succinctly summarised by extracting from two paragraphs of Lord Kerr's judgment: 'causation is not a necessary ingredient for liability' but 'is relevant to the question of the recoverability of damages' (*Kambadzi* 2011, paras 88–89). The possible conclusion that only nominal damages should be awarded 'does not affect the issue of principle' (*Kambadzi* 2011, para 56). Furthermore, Lord Hope declined to 'foreclose… the possibility that the appellant [may be] entitled to more than a purely nominal award' (*Kambadzi* 2011, para 55).

Again, for the minority, Lord Brown was almost incredulous in his dissent. His judgment contains a reassertion of his reasons in *Lumba* and his belief that the outcome 'devalue[s] the whole concept of false imprisonment' (*Kambadzi* 2011, para 108). (His Lordship noted that the first 23 paragraphs of his judgment were an expression of his view before the decision in *Lumba*). But Lord Brown was in any event of the view that the majority approach in *Lumba* did not dictate that the claimant must succeed in *Kambadzi*. Mr Kambadzi had been lawfully detained in the first place; the only defect here was a procedural one in relation to the continuing review. As in *Lumba*, the dissent turns on a different view of the status of the counter-factual that, had the reviews been correctly carried out, the claimant would still have been detained. The majority, as we have seen, held that the lawfulness of the claimant's detention needed to be re-established at each review. The dissentients by contrast view the procedural requirement as giving the detainee the opportunity to establish that they should be released. For that reason, Lord Brown viewed it as 'still more undesirable' to find liability in *Kambadzi* than it had been in *Lumba* (*Kambadzi* 2011, para 115). Indeed, the implications of the respective approaches in *Lumba* for a case such as *Kambadzi* were expressly considered as hypothetical examples given by some of the Justices in the former case.[18] And, in the case of the minority, there was the suggestion that the case would be less compelling: Lord Phillips viewed the ability to recover in a case of a failure to review the detention to be an 'extraordinary result' (*Lumba* 2011, para 336).

[18] Eg *Lumba* 2011, para 249 (Lord Kerr); para 357 (Lord Brown).

12.2.3 Reflections on the Counter-Factuals

These two cases demonstrate confusion over how, if at all, 'causation' is relevant to liability in false imprisonment. Our focus tends to be on loss when discussing causation: '[tort] liability in general is standardly thought to require successful application of the "but for" test of causation in fact'.[19] But on the majority view of false imprisonment, causation is only applicable insofar as it is established that the defendant 'caused' the imprisonment in a narrow sense: to quote from *Bird v Jones* (1845, 115 ER 668), 'the acts will amount to imprisonment neither more nor less from their being wrongful or capable of justification.'[20] The counter-factual problem consequently raises questions about the essence of the tort of false imprisonment and a rights-based analysis of the wrong, as it is not clear that we have a counter-factual baseline at all.[21]

If the 'causation test' is not to operate as a control mechanism, we have to reflect on how we attribute responsibility and impose liability in the tort. It must be recognised that there remains some uncertainty as to the degree or nature of public law error that will 'justify resort to the common law remedy' (*Kambadzi* 2011, para 40; Steel 2011, p. 529). Indeed, one of the public errors in *Kambadzi* was deemed insufficient to establish compelled the conclusion that there be liability in such cases for one month in December 2007 the review was 'carried out by an official of the wrong grade' (*Kambadzi* 2011, para 60).

The analysis above has shown that the counter-factual or fictional scenario is central to the cases. Underlying the debate in the *Lumba* and *Kambadzi*, especially in the minority judgments and the majority view on the damages point, are apparent misgivings about seeming to ignore the 'fact' (or 'counter-fact') that the claimant would still have been imprisoned. It is a more substantial concern than the mere feeling that the given appellant 'may not be a very nice person' (*Kambadzi* 2011 para 61, Baroness Hale). And most of the Justices clearly believed that the counter-factual ought to be taken into account in some way.[22] Even the minority on the damages points accept that the claimants could not show that they had suffered any loss: hence the perceived need to identify the special character of the wrong with a novel award of vindicatory damages.[23] The Justices' divergent analyses on the two points are then ultimately based on an acceptance that, at least in some sense, the alternative scenario *is* relevant to the resolution of the case.

---

[19] Moore (2003, p. 1184).

[20] (1845) 115 ER 668.

[21] Kamm (2003, p. 1369).

[22] Cf Steel (2011, pp. 530–531).

[23] For further reflections on the availability of vindicatory damages, see *Welch v Attorney General of Antigua and Barbuda* [2013] UKPC 21, paras 18–23, and Barker (2013). The Supreme Court rejected an award of exemplary damages in *Lumba*.

12.3 Fictional Causation in Negligence? Context

> The liability of employers for deaths caused by mesothelioma has preoccupied courts and legislators over recent years. (*Trigger Litigation* 2012, para 1, Lord Mance).

In this section, we shall turn to examine the more traditional context of causation debates: the tort of negligence. A decade of authorities at the highest level since the decision in *Fairchild v Glenhaven Funeral Services*[24] has seen the Law Lords and now Supreme Court Justices grapple with principles of causation and legal fictions.[25] What is also conspicuous is that the judges have not been in agreement on what the law is, or as to the extent to which they are using fictions at all. Nor is the problem limited to England (Stapleton 2006). Del Mar notes towards the end of his paper that this area is an excellent example of a modern fiction (Chap. 11, pp. 460–462): in this section, I shall explore the case law in further detail,[26] particularly in the light of the Supreme Court's decision in the *Employers' Liability 'Trigger' Litigation*.[27]

First, it is necessary briefly to establish some background. It is axiomatic that, in order to establish a successful claim in the tort of negligence, a claimant must demonstrate that the defendant owed them a duty of care, that the duty was breached, and that that breach caused actionable harm. At the causation stage, the 'but for' test must be satisfied: 'but for' the defendant's breach of duty, would the claimant have suffered their injury or loss (*Barnett v Chelsea and Kensington Hospital Management Committee*)?[28] We are always directing our inquiry towards the question of what would otherwise have happened. In the relevant cases, we shall see that the judges expressly advert to the possible resort to fictions in attempting to solve the problems.

12.3.1 Fairchild

The case law from *Fairchild* onwards has concerned claims by victims of mesothelioma, which is an invariably fatal cancer caused principally by exposure to asbestos. The claimants in *Fairchild* itself had been exposed to asbestos while working for more than one employer and had developed mesothelioma. Scientific knowledge did not enable the determination of the source of the causative asbestos, because the aetiology of mesothelioma is uncertain (and the precise understanding of the uncer-

[24] [2002] UKHL 22; [2003] 1 AC 32.

[25] For a fuller account of the background to the 'Asbestos Saga', see Morgan (2011) and Lee (2011).

[26] Dr Del Mar correctly locates the origin of the fiction in *McGhee v National Coal Board* [1973] 1 WLR 1. I shall begin rather with *Fairchild* because it gave more coherence to the exact operation of the fiction, and because it is the more recent starting point for the latest discussions.

[27] [2012] UKSC 14.

[28] [1969] 1 QB 428.

tainty has itself evolved in parallel with the litigation).[29] Thus, where a claimant had been exposed to asbestos in breach of duty by more than one employer (only one of whom may now be solvent and worth suing), and subsequently developed mesothelioma, it was impossible to identify the source of the particular exposure which had caused the cancer. There was an 'evidentiary gap' and the claimant could not prove causation according to the 'but for' test, because it was possible that the causative asbestos fibres had come from another employer.

Their Lordships unanimously held that in such a case the claimant should be entitled to succeed, on the basis that the defendant had 'materially increased the risk' of the harm eventuating, relying upon *McGhee v National Coal Board*. The traditional test of 'but for' causation was suspended, and causation was held to be satisfied upon proof of something else—that the defendant had materially contributed to the risk of the harm which had in fact occurred. Lord Rodger, following *McGhee*, held

> that, by proving that the defendants individually materially increased the risk that the men would develop mesothelioma due to inhaling asbestos fibres, the claimants are taken in law to have proved that the defendants materially contributed to their illness. (*Fairchild* 2002, para 168)

Although their Lordships were unanimous, they were not univocal in their reasoning as to the basis of the exception. Lord Hutton for example viewed it as the drawing of a factual and legal inference (*Fairchild* 2002, para 109). Their Lordships were however clear that, although there would inevitably be the possibility of future development of the principle, it was intended to be limited in its application (*Fairchild* 2002, para 34, Lord Bingham).[30] Lord Nicholls stated that the principle was 'emphatically not intended to lead to such a relaxation whenever a plaintiff has difficulty, perhaps understandable difficulty, in discharging the burden of proof' (*Fairchild* 2002, para 43). For the answer to the 'but for' question in an evidentiary gap case is neither 'yes' nor 'no': it is 'we do not know'. Subsequent cases have sought to engage with the nature of this exception and the extent to which it is a fiction.

12.3.2 Barker and the Compensation Act 2006

In *Fairchild*, the extent of liability was not expressly considered (*Fairchild*, para 117, Lord Hutton). The assumption was that the liability of a defendant held liable under the principle was *in solidum* (i.e., for the full extent of the harm caused). That was challenged in *Barker v Corus*,[31] in which the claimant had been partly responsible for his exposure to asbestos, during periods of self-employment. A majority of the House of Lords, led by Lord Hoffmann, took the view that, because the *Fairchild* principle focused upon increasing the risk, the creation of the risk was the gist

[29] And the scientific understanding of mesothelioma has evolved even during the course of the asbestos litigation: see paras 19–20 of Lord Phillips' judgment in *Sienkiewicz*, 2011 and the Annex to it. See also Stapleton 2012, pp. 224–225.

[30] See Oliphant (2010).

[31] [2006] UKHL 20.

of the action (*Barker* 2006, para 31). It would therefore 'smooth the roughness of the justice' of the *Fairchild* exception (*Barker* 2006, para 43) for liability to be attributed to each defendant proportionately, on the basis of their respective contribution to the risk. Furthermore, Lord Hoffmann rejected the idea that *Fairchild* relied on a fiction of deeming causation to be satisfied (*Barker* 2006, paras 31 and 61).

Lord Rodger, who had also sat in *Fairchild*, dissented as to the outcome of the appeal, emphasising that the defendant was liable 'for causing the mesothelioma, not for causing the risk of developing mesothelioma' (*Barker* 2006, para 68). Baroness Hale agreed that liability should be proportionate, but concurred with Lord Rodger's analysis on the gist of the action (*Barker* 2006, para 120). Pointedly, Lord Rodger argued that the problem was not with the *Fairchild* fiction, but with a fiction of Lord Hoffmann's own making:

> a fiction that the members of the House did not link proof that the defenders had materially increased the risk of injury to the pursuer with proof that the defenders had materially contributed to his injury. I would respectfully prefer not to resort to such legal fictions but to recognise what their Lordships actually said and did in *McGhee*. (Barker 2006, para 78)

But Lord Rodger's powerful dissent[32] was nevertheless a minority view and liability under the *Fairchild* principle was established to be proportionate to the contribution to risk.

The consequence of this decision was that claimants would receive only a proportion of the damages to which they would otherwise be entitled. Parliament responded swiftly[33] to reverse this effect of the *Barker* decision for asbestos-related mesothelioma claims with s 3 of the Compensation Act. The section provides that where a responsible person is liable under the *Fairchild* principle for such claims, they are jointly and severally liable for all of the damage. It thus rests on the same common law fiction.

12.3.3 Sienkiewwicz

In 2011, the Supreme Court had the opportunity to revisit the *Fairchild* principle in the light of the Compensation Act in *Sienkiewicz v Greif (UK) Ltd.*[34] The two appeals raised issues as to the relevance of environmental exposure, and how 'material' a 'material contribution to risk' must be. Both claims succeeded. The decision must now be understood in the light of the *'Trigger' Litigation* to be considered in the next section, and so we shall merely advert to it here.

A noticeable feature of the Justices' opinions is that they are generally characterised by a weariness over the consequences of the *Fairchild* fiction, or over perhaps any exception to causal requirements. For example, whilst accepting that

[32] See also Lee 2008a, p. 12. Lord Dyson has commented that Lord Rodger's dissent was based on 'the need to maintain a clear, coherent, and consistent set of rules to deal with the particular problems of causation generated by mesothelioma': Dyson 2013, p. 42.

[33] For more detail see Lee 2011, pp. 79–86.

[34] [2011] UKSC 10.

the claimants in the present appeals must succeed, Lord Brown insisted on recording 'just how unsatisfactory I for my part regard this [state of the law] to be and how quixotic the path by which it has been arrived at' (*Sienkiewicz* 2011, para 174). Lord Mance believed that the asbestos saga should stand as 'a lesson of caution' in respect of other possible departures from 'conventional principles of causation' (*Sienkiewicz* 2011, para 190). And the principle does need to be explained: Broadbent has characterised the *Fairchild* exception as 'either a pretence or a very odd kind of liability' (Broadbent 2011, p. 251).

The judgments in *Sienkiewicz* also urge caution in respect of the use of epidemiological evidence: these comments are clearly open to criticism, as subsequent comment has ably demonstrated.[35] It is not necessary to rehearse that debate here, but we may note that the deployment of a causal fiction may permit either the masking, or compounding, of statistical difficulties: 'in legal writing, we can see [the] intersection of discourses most dramatically in the treatment of scientific information for purposes of dispute resolution' (Petroski, this volume, Chap. 7, p. 143).

12.4 The Trigger Litigation

> Rules regarding causation are created by the courts for the purpose of determining when liability arises in particular contexts. Normally, they reflect a common sense understanding of what is ordinarily understood when we speak of a cause in a particular context. (*'Trigger' Litigation* 2012, para 55, Lord Mance)

The story so far had been 'brought to a head in *Sienkiewicz*' (Steel and Ibbetson 2011, p. 451): and yet it was not the end, because the series continued with the decision in the *'Trigger' Litigation*.[36] In *Sienkiewicz*, the intervention of the Compensation Act had the effect of distracting from the more fundamental questions about the nature of the *Fairchild* fiction. The *'Trigger' Litigation* forced the Supreme Court to confront these questions directly. After the lukewarm treatment of the *Fairchild* principle in *Sienkiewicz*, the majority judgments in the *'Trigger' Litigation* represent a reaffirmation of it.

As between a claimant and any given employer, the *Fairchild* exception, as developed, may be relatively straightforward to apply. However, the position becomes more (or yet more) complicated when determining liability as between various insurers. Liability will depend upon when the injury has occurred, but if liability is based only upon a period of exposure, how are we to work out when exactly the liability is 'triggered' for the purposes of a policy? The insurance policies used various verbs to refer to the occurrence of injury: 'sustained', 'suffered' and 'contracted', and some were used in the active or passive voice. The claimants and employers argued that the policies should respond to the exposure of the claimant to the asbestos. It was on this basis that the insurers had paid out on such policies

[35] See e.g. Fulham-McQuillan (2014), McIvor (2013), Stapleton (2012) and Miller (2012).

[36] See generally Merkin and Steele (2013, chap. 12).

until *Bolton Metropolitan Borough Council v Municipal Mutual Insurance Ltd*,[37] which concerned public liability insurance contracts. In the *'Trigger' Litigation*, the insurers[38] argued that the policies could only respond when an injury had actually occurred. The latency period for mesothelioma is such that it may rarely be the case that the insurance liability would be triggered, because the cancer would only manifest decades after exposure. The Supreme Court had to consider how insurance policies would respond to liability generated on the fictional *Fairchild* basis, and whether employers could avail themselves of those policies.

On the construction of the contracts, the Court, led by Lord Mance, unanimously preferred the argument of the victims and employers. The language of the insurance contracts pointed to 'an underlying focus on causation' (*'Trigger' Litigation* 2012, para 27). Furthermore, the requirement of the maintenance of insurance imposed by the Employers' Liability (Compulsory Insurance) Act 1969 was held to be relevant (*'Trigger' Litigation* 2012, para 44): 'the conclusion which gives proper effect to the protective purpose of the legislation is that the [Act] requires insurance on a causation basis' (*'Trigger' Litigation* 2012, para 47).

It was then necessary to apply the policies to the nature of liability under *Fairchild*. Lord Mance for the majority held that the policies responded to the exposure. Lord Phillips dissented on this point, and it is convenient to begin by with his judgment, which is heavily influenced by the analysis of Lord Hoffmann, both in *Barker* and extra-judicially (Hoffmann 2011). Thus, Lord Phillips thought it clear that the *Barker* majority's approach 'was not based on the fiction that the defendants had contributed to causing the mesothelioma' (*'Trigger' Litigation* 2012, para 130).[39] To create such a fiction in order to impose liability on the insurers 'would be judicial law-making of a different dimension' (*'Trigger' Litigation* 2012, para 135).

Lord Mance noted that the majority in *Barker* 'were at pains to reject any analysis of *Fairchild* as proceeding upon a fiction' (*'Trigger' Litigation* 2012, para 59). Although this seemed to be a 'bright-line distinction', closer scrutiny of the reasoning suggested that the issue was not clear-cut (*'Trigger' Litigation* 2012, paras 59 and 61). Bundling causation and damage together leads only to muddled thinking (Stapleton 2013, p. 65): an employer was only liable if and when the claimant developed mesothelioma. It would frustrate the purpose of the exception in *Fairchild* were the policies not to respond to liability under it. 'The concept of a disease being "caused" during the policy period must be interpreted sufficiently flexibly to embrace the role assigned to exposure by the rule in *Fairchild* (*'Trigger' Litigation* 2012, para 74).

The majority's analysis in the *'Trigger' Litigation* is to be preferred as a more faithful approach to the reasoning in *Fairchild*, and a vindication of the underlying rationale for the fiction in the first place. McBride and Steel agree, but note that this is not 'to say that the present law is conceptually satisfactory, only that it is as it is'

---

[37] [1973] 1 WLR 1492. The basis upon which the insurers had paid out on policies generally was not unanimous or consistent: *Trigger' Litigation*, [37].

[38] This is an umbrella term, although Zurich Insurance was on the side of the victims/employers.

[39] Hogg 2007, p. 13; and to the same effect but more pithily Weir 2002, p. 519.

(McBride and Steel 2012, p. 290). In my view, the position which we have reached is that the *Fairchild* principle or fiction is a defensible and limited exception to the standard causation requirements, as will be explored below. A final key point is made by Lord Phillips:[40]

> If the law of tort, whether laid down by the courts or by Parliament, resorts to legal or doctrinal fictions, it seems logical that the policies should respond as if the fictions were facts. (*'Trigger' Litigation* 2012, para 109)

With Lord Mance's judgment, it may be tempting to view the *'Trigger' Litigation* as the definitive statement of the law: however, that may not be the case. At the time of writing, we await judgment in yet another case before the Supreme Court.[41] The clock then continues to run, as we shall see in the next section.

12.5 Diachronicity

> Fiction of the English kind is one response to a conviction that an acceptable principle could indeed be spelt out and would prove to be legitimately within interpretative reach, if only time and spare brain-power were available. (Birks 1986, p. 101)

Having traced the development and controversy of the *Fairchild* principle, we shall reflect in this section upon some features of the fiction, most notably its operation over time (its 'diachronicity': Del Mar, this volume, Chap. 11). With the benefit of interpretation over time and the collective brain power of many top judges, have the courts been able to reach an acceptable principle? For, as Lobban notes in his essay, some 'fictions might be used to rationalise a settled rule; but they could also make the rule vulnerable to reform' (this volume, Chap. 10, p. 208). I suggest that the diachronicity of the *Fairchild* principle can be understood in two senses.

12.5.1 Fairchild and Its Development

The first diachronic aspect is the possibility of the future development or revision of the principle, to see whether, as Del Mar suggests, it may 'blossom'[42] into a 'more general principle of causation' (this volume, Chap. 11, p. 250). Although the speeches in *Fairchild* are very cautious on the point, Lord Bingham recognised that 'it would be unrealistic to suppose that the principle here affirmed will not *over time* be the subject of incremental and analogical development' (*Fairchild* 2002,

[40] Lord Phillips of course dissented overall but was speaking here of what he recognised was a valid concession by counsel.

[41] Permission to appeal was granted in the case of International Energy Group v Zurich Insurance [2013] EWCA Civ 39 and argument was heard on 15–16 July 2014: http://www.supremecourt.uk/cases/case_2013_0057.html

[42] Language which Stern also uses: Stern, this volume, Chap. 8.

para 34).[43] And in the *'Trigger' Litigation*, Lord Clarke suggests that the principle is based broadly on fairness, which might seem to offer potential for a broader application of the relaxed causation rules (*'Trigger' Litigation* 2012, para 83), especially given 'the ineluctable pull of analogical reasoning in common-law argumentation' (Chap. 8).

However, in this context, it does not seem that the judges have any real desire for the future extension of the *Fairchild* doctrine, and, in the cases since the 2006 Act, the Justices have indicated that any further changes must be the province of the legislature. The fiction has been preserved by the line of authorities, but, as Lady Hale remarked in a 2013 case, *Fairchild* 'can scarcely be described as the herald of a brave new world in which people may be held liable for harm whether or not they have caused it' (*Re J (Children)* 2013, para 41).[44]

There would seem to have been four options mooted in this litigation (assuming that we are to maintain a causal requirement at all).[45] The first option would be to depart from *McGhee* or its sequels and not to admit any exception whatsoever, leaving it to Parliament to legislate if thought necessary. This was not seriously contemplated in *Fairchild* or *Barker* but has with hindsight been adverted to by some of the Justices since (*Sienkiewicz* 2011, para 167, Lady Hale, and para 183, Lord Brown). And the certain intervention of Parliament, were such a judicial attempt to be made, is viewed to render that course undesirable.

The second option is that pursued by Lord Hoffmann, which presents itself as an attempt to rationalise the principle and explain its operation. This takes a radical view of the response to the fiction: that the invitation for future clarification taken up by the House of Lords from the seed sown in *McGhee* is the attempt to recognise a 'new species of tort, the gist of which is breach of duty leading to the creation of risk of injury, where the injury actually occurs' (Smith 2009, p. 108).[46]

The *Fairchild* principle is 'the product of judicial innovation' (*'Trigger' Litigation* 2012, para 5). Viewing the case over ten years later, we have seen some of the judges exhibiting inventors' remorse. Since his retirement, Lord Hoffmann has even conceded, with perhaps alarming insouciance, that he was indulging in 'some judicious rewriting of history' (Hoffmann 2013, p. 67)[47] in *Barker*.[48] It might be generously viewed as 'pragmatic tactics',[49] but in any event 'Lord Hoffmann's extra-judicial (or judicial) words cannot by themselves alter the true effect of a

---

[43] *Fairchild*, [34].

[44] Lee (2008b).

[45] Although there may be a tendency towards a pro-claimant bias in these causal cases (Hamer 2014, pp. 162–163) there is no suggestion that we should abandon causation entirely, and, indeed, the *Fairchild* fiction can be viewed as evidence of a commitment to the demands of causation.

[46] The idea was also canvassed briefly in argument in the High Court of Australia in *Wallace v Kam* [2013] HCATrans 45 (the *Fairchild* principle has, however, not so far been adopted as a matter of common law in Australia: cf s 5D(2), Civil Liability Act 2002 (NSW)).

[47] But there is apparently 'nothing unusual' about doing so: Hoffmann 2013, p. 67. For further, less dramatic reflections from his Lordship, see Hoffmann 2011, pp. 8–9.

[48] As I argued shortly after the decision: Lee 2008a, pp. 10–13. See also Steele (2007).

[49] Paterson 2014, p. 94.

statute' (*'Trigger' Litigation* 2012, para 62). The Hoffmann approach is problematic as a matter of precedent and principle—why are other forms of risk not actionable, for example?—and has been rejected by the majority in the *'Trigger' Litigation.* The result is that the analysis of three of the majority in *Barker* (Lady Hale excepted) is seen to be an anomaly insofar as their Lordships indicated that the material contribution to the risk is the gist of the action. This is not, with a respect, a 'new' tort.

The final two options would both involve delimiting the extent of the causal fiction, which 'clearly needs to be confined' (Broadbent 2011, p. 248). This seems in line with the approach of Lord Bingham in *Fairchild*, confining the principle to mesothelioma cases but recognising the possibility of future extension (*Fairchild* 2002, para 35). The third option would then be to limit *Fairchild* to (asbestos-related) mesothelioma cases:[50] Lord Brown began his rueful judgment in *Sienkiewicz* by noting that 'Mesothelioma claims are in a category all their own' (*Sienkiewicz* 2011, para 174). But that is only in the light of the subsequent legislative intervention which, as we have seen, solely applies to asbestos-related mesothelioma. And it is difficult to see that this can be correct as a matter of principle. Lord Phillips' observation in *AB v Ministry of Defence*,[51] for example, which involved claims in respect of radiation exposure, was arguing that it was not a case in which *Fairchild* could apply, rather than that the principle only applies to mesothelioma.

The better view, it is submitted, is the fourth option, which is that the refined and consolidated *Fairchild* fiction, as explained, continues to be applicable wherever the factual circumstances identified by Lord Rodger are satisfied (*Fairchild* 2002, para 170).[52] Of course, as seen above, insofar as *Fairchild* applies beyond asbestos-related mesothelioma cases, the Compensation Act 2006 does not speak to the operation of the *Fairchild* principle in other circumstances, and so *Barker* proportionate liability presumably continues to apply as a matter of common law. But it will be open to Supreme Court in a future case either to reconsider *Barker* after the Act, or at least to alert Parliament to the legislative enclave. The value of this view is linked to the next diachronic feature.

12.5.2 *Fairchild and Its Quietus*

The second diachronic aspect of the *Fairchild* fiction is its contingency in any given scenario. It is expressly linked to the limitations of scientific knowledge—whenever (if ever) it may be that it becomes possible to prove the true cause of a claimant's illness, its operation in the mesothelioma context will disappear. Section 3 of the Compensation Act 2006 recognises the built-in obsolescence of the principle.

[50] Swift J in *Jones & Ors v The Secretary of State for Energy And Climate Change & Anor* [2012] EWHC 2936 (QB), para 543: 'It does not appear that there is any appetite in the appellate courts for extending the *Fairchild* exception to cases involving diseases other than mesothelioma.' See McIvor 2013, p. 226.

[51] [2013] UKSC 9, para 157.

[52] Lord Rodger was endorsed on this point subsequently by Lord Hoffmann in *Barker* 2006, paras 18–24.

The section applies where a person has contracted mesothelioma after having been exposed to asbestos in breach of duty, and (in Sect. 3(1)(c))

> because of the nature of mesothelioma and the state of medical science, it is not possible to determine with certainty whether it was the exposure or another exposure which caused the victim to become ill.

The judgments in *Sienkiewicz* are very clear that, should medical science permit causation to be established definitively either way, the courts would '[revert] to the conventional approach' (*Sienkiewicz* 2011, para 70, Lord Phillips) as 'the rationale for the *Fairchild* exception would disappear' (*Sienkiewicz* 2011, para 208, Lord Dyson). Over time, the operation of the *Fairchild* principle in other situations would also have a sunset clause for as long as the evidentiary gap problem endured.

That we are dealing with a fiction rather than some other feature seems to be demonstrated by the fact that the very crux of the problem is a problem of proof—we are not shifting the burden of proof (Del Mar, Chap. 11, p. 226) onto the defendant in any meaningful sense, as the whole point is that scientific knowledge does not enable us to identify which of several similarly-operating causes is responsible for the claimant's mesothelioma. It is perhaps possible that, should there be a dramatic advance in medical science between the date of judgment in the initial case and subsequent contribution proceedings against other tortfeasors, the defendant may be able to identify the extent of their individual responsibility, but that would not affect the fiction as between claimant and defendant. The key point is that it is instructive to view the *Fairchild* fiction across time rather than in terms of its application in any single case. The requisite proof of causation is suspended, but it is an avowedly temporary suspension.

To adopt the scaffolding simile endorsed by Fuller (1930–1931, p. 529),[53] the judges have correctly disavowed the idea that, once the scaffolding is removed, we shall find a new tort concealed. Rather, it is the same tort of negligence, with the same elements, that has been there all along, but with one element suspended. As Lord Clarke noted, 'none of the cases is authority for the proposition that causation is irrelevant' (*'Trigger' Litigation* 2012, para 83). The asbestos cases thus teach us not only about legal epidemiology but also about legal epistemology.

Conclusion

> 'Ultimately, there is no magic about concepts such as causation or causal requirements, wherever they appear. They have the meanings assigned to them and understood in ordinary usage in their context. A logician might disagree with a reference to causation or a causal link in a particular context, but that is not the test of meaning.' (*'Trigger' Litigation* 2012, para 66, Lord Mance)

The aim of this essay has been to engage with, and to understand, two important problems for the law of tort which have been recently addressed by the Supreme Court. The modern deployment of fictions, or fictive arguments, is related

[53] See also Lord Steyn in *Republic of India v India Steamship Co Ltd (No 2)* [1998] AC 878, 913.

to, but distinct from, English tort law's formalist heritage. Fictions hold a notable fascination in the context of tort, with its emphasis on counter-factual reasoning. Their use in tackling the causal challenges above suggests that fictions are a key part of modern legal reasoning, as opposed to an unsophisticated shortcut to a desired result. In these cases, there is no subterfuge in the way in which the fictions are being deployed.[54] The question is often *which* fiction should be adopted rather than whether one should be adopted at all. Our law of civil wrongs remains a dynamic subject, and much of that dynamism comes from the utility of legal fictions.

References

Cases

Barker v Corus UK Ltd [2006] UKHL 20; [2006] 2 AC 572.
Barnett v Chelsea and Kensington Hospital Management Committee [1969] 1 QB 428.
Bird v Jones (1845) 115 ER 668.
Bolton Metropolitan Borough Council v Municipal Mutual Insurance Ltd [2006] 1 WLR 1492.
Durham v BAI (Run Off) Ltd (Employers' Liability Trigger Litigation) [2012] UKSC 14.
Fairchild v Glenhaven Funeral Services Ltd [2002] UKHL 22; [2003] 1 AC 32.
International Energy Group v Zurich Insurance [2013] EWCA Civ 39.
Jones & Ors v The Secretary of State for Energy And Climate Change & Anor [2012] EWHC 2936 (QB).
McGhee v National Coal Board [1973] 1 WLR 1.
OBG v Allan [2007] UKHL 21; [2008] 1 AC 1.
R (Kambadzi) v Secretary of State for the Home Department [2011] UKSC 23.
R (Lumba) v Secretary of State for the Home Department [2011] UKSC 12.
R v Governor of Brockhill Prison, Ex p Evans (No 2) [2001] 2 AC 19.
R v Governor of Durham Prison, Ex p Hardial Singh [1974] 1 WLR 704.
Re J (Children) [2013] UKSC 9.
Republic of India v India Steamship Co Ltd (No 2) [1998] AC 878.
Sienkiewicz v Greif (UK) Ltd [2011] UKSC 10.
Wallace v Kam [2013] HCATrans 45.
Welch v The Attorney General of Antigua and Barbuda [2013] UKPC 21.

Books/Articles

Baker, J. H. 2002. *An introduction to English legal history*. 4th ed. London: LexisNexis Butterworths.
Barker, Kit. 2013. Private and public: The mixed concept of vindication in torts and private law. In *Tort law: Challenging orthodoxy*, eds. J. Neyers, E. Chamberlain, and S. Pitel, 59–93. Oxford: Hart Publishing.

[54] Lord Edmund-Davies once resolved that, as a judge, he would 'be unrepentantly trying to fill the gaps. So confining myself, I shall regard the term "judge-made" law not as an accusation or a sneer, but merely as an epithet which can be accepted with a modest measure of mild self-satisfaction' (Edmund-Davies 1977, p. 18). We might say the same of legal fictions.

Birks, Peter. 1986. Fictions ancient and modern. In *The legal mind: Essays for Tony Honoré,* eds. N. MacCormick and P. Birks, 83–101. Oxford: Clarendon.
Broadbent, Alex. 2011. Epidemiological evidence in proof of specific causation. *Legal Theory* 17 (4): 237–278.
Del Mar, Maksymilian. 2013. Recovering legal fictions: An introduction. *International Journal of Law in Context* 9 (4): 437–441.
Del Mar, Maksymilian. 2014. Legal fictions and legal change in the common law tradition. In *Legal fictions in theory and practice,* ed. Maksymilian Del Mar and William Twining. Dordrecht: Springer.
Douglas, Simon. 2009. The nature of conversion. *Cambridge Law Journal* 68 (1): 198–223.
Dyson, Lord. 2013. Some reflections on Lord Rodger's contribution to the development of the common law. In *Judge and jurist: Essays in memory of Lord Rodger of Earlsferry,* eds. A. Burrows, D. Johnston, and R. Zimmermann, 39–50. Oxford: Oxford University Press.
Edmund-Davies, Lord. 1977. *Ferment in the law: Holdsworth club presidential address.* Birmingham: Holdsworth Club of the University of Birmingham.
Fulham-Mcquillan, Sarah. 2014. Judicial belief in statistics as fact: Loss of chance in Ireland and England. *Professional Negligence* 30 (1): 9–31.
Fuller, Lon. 1930–1931. Legal fictions. *Illinois Law Review* 25:363–399, 513–546, 877–910.
Green, Sarah, and John, Randall. 2009. *The tort of conversion.* Oxford: Hart Publishing.
Hamer, David. 2014. "Factual casuation" and "scope of liability": What's the difference? *Modern Law Review* 77 (2): 155–188.
Hickey, Robin. 2011. Wrongs and the protection of personal property. *Conveyancer and Property Lawyer* 75 (1): 48–57.
Hoffmann, Lord. 2011. Causation. In *Perspectives on causation,* ed. R. Goldberg, 3–9. Oxford: Hart Publishing.
Hoffmann, Lord. 2013. Fairchild and after. In *Judge and jurist: Essays in memory of Lord Rodger of Earlsferry,* eds. A. Burrows, D. Johnston QC, and R. Zimmermann, 63–70. Oxford: Oxford University Press.
Hogg, Martin. 2007. Re-establishing orthodoxy in the realm of causation. *Edinburgh Law Review* 11 (1): 8–30.
Kamm, F. M. 2003. Baselines and compensation. *San Diego Law Review* 40:1367–1386.
Lee, James. 2008a. Fidelity in interpretation: Lord Hoffmann and the adventure of the empty house. *Legal Studies* 28 (1): 1–19.
Lee, James. 2008b. Causation in negligence: Another fine mess. *Professional Negligence* 24 (3): 194–98.
Lee, James. 2011. "Inconsiderate alterations in our laws": Legislative reversal of Supreme Court decisions. In *From House of Lords to Supreme Court: Judges, jurists and the process of judging,* ed. J. Lee, 71–100. Oxford: Hart Publishing.
Lee, James. 2014. Yearworth v North Bristol NHS trust: Instrumentalism and fictions in property law. In *Landmarks in property law,* eds. E. Waring, S. Douglas, and R. Hickey. Oxford: Hart Publishing (forthcoming).
Leeming, Mark. 2013. Theories and principles underlying the development of the common law: The statutory elephant in the room. *University of New South Wales Law Journal* 36 (3): 1002–1029.
Lobban, Michael. 2014. Legal fictions before the age of reform. In *Legal fictions in theory and practice,* ed. Maksymilian Del Mar and William Twining. Dordrecht: Springer.
Mcbride, Nick, and Steel, Sandy. 2012. The "trigger" litigation. *Professional Negligence* 28 (4): 285–290.
McIvor, Claire. 2013 The "Doubles the Risk" test for causation and other related judicial misconceptions about epidemiology. In *Tort law: Challenging orthodoxy,* eds. J. Neyers, E. Chamberlain, and S. Pitel, 215–234. Oxford: Hart Publishing.
Merkin Rob, and Jenny, Steele. 2013. *Insurance and the law of obligations.* Oxford: Oxford University. Press.

Miller, Chris. 2012. Causation in personal injury after (and before) Sienkiewicz. *Legal Studies* 32 (3): 396–420.
Moore, Michael. 2003. For what must we pay? Causation and counterfactual baselines. *San Diego Law Review* 40:1181.
Morgan, Jonathan. 2011. Causation, politics and law: The English—and Scottish—asbestos saga. In *Perspectives on causation,* ed. R. Goldberg, 57–91. Oxford: Hart Publishing.
Oliphant, Ken. 2010. Fairchild v Glenhaven funeral services Ltd (2002). In *Landmark cases in the law of tort,* eds. C. Mitchell and P. Mitchell, 335–358. Oxford: Hart Publishing.
Paterson, Alan. 2014. Decision-making in the UK's top court. *Cambridge Journal of International and Comparative Law* 3 (1): 77–99.
Paul, L. A. 2009. Counterfactual theories. In *The Oxford handbook of causation,* eds. H. Beebee, C. Hitchcock, and P. Menzies. Oxford: Oxford Univ. Press.
Petroski, Karen. 2014. Legal fictions and the limits of legal language. In *Legal fictions in theory and practice,* ed. Maksymilian Del Mar and William Twining. Dordrecht: Springer.
Smith, Janet. 2009. Causation—the search for principle. *Journal of Personal Injury Law* 2:101–13.
Sparkes, Peter. 2014. Ejectment: Three births and a funeral. In *egal fictions in theory and practice,* ed. Maksymilian Del Mar and William Twining. Dordrecht: Springer.
Spellman, Barbara, and Kincannon, Alexandra. 2001. The relation between counterfactual ("But for") and causal reasoning: Experimental findings and implications for jurors' decisions'. *Law and Contemporary Problems* 64 (4): 241–2614.
Stapleton, Jane. 2006. Two causal fictions at the heart of U.S. asbestos doctrine. *Law Quarterly Review* 122 (Apr): 189–195.
Stapleton, Jane. 2012. Factual causation, mesothelioma and statistical validity. *Law Quarterly Review* 128 (Apr): 221–231.
Stapleton, Jane. 2013. Unnecessary causes. *Law Quarterly Review* 129 (Jan): 39–65.
Steele, Jenny. 2007. "Breach of duty causing harm?" Recent encounters between negligence and risk. *Current Legal Problems* 60 (1): 296–337.
Stevens, Robert. 2009. Torts. In *The Judicial House of Lords 1876–2009,* eds. L. Blom-Cooper, B. Dickson, and G. Drewry, 629–652. Oxford: Oxford Univ. Press.
Steel, Sandy. 2011. False imprisonment and the fetch of hypothetical warrant. *Law Quarterly Review* 127 (Oct): 527–531.
Steel, Sandy, and Ibbetson, David. 2011. More grief on uncertain causation in tort. *Cambridge Law Journal* 70 (2): 451–468.
Weir, Tony. 2002. Making it more likely v making it happen. *Cambridge Law Journal* 61 (3): 519–522.

Chapter 13
Ejectment: Three Births and a Funeral

Peter Sparkes

Abstract Fictional ejectment evolved under Elizabeth I and morphed into a completely new form at the beginning of the Commonwealth. At a much later stage openly fictitious names were used. Baker has asserted that the origins of fictions are inherently unknowable, and an attempt is made to explore the origins of these three forms of ejectment to see whether the available evidence supports his view of the genesis of fictions. Attention will then turn to the end of the fictional action in 1852 when it moved to an 'honest' basis of jurisdiction. Fictions can be seen as scaffolding which supports case law development but which becomes obsolete once the building is complete. The procedural mechanism used to mould leasehold ejectment into a form suitable for testing freehold titles represents the scaffolding. If the metaphor holds good, it should be possible to discard this mechanism without affecting the substance of the action. Abolition of the fiction was not wholly successful because removal of the scaffolding left an unfinished building.

Ejectment was perhaps the ultimate legal fiction in the early nineteenth century. An action designed to secure the recovery of a leasehold term, *ejectione firmae*, was modified by a series of procedural innovations so as to become the primary means of recovering freehold land. The general shape of the fictional actions laid down by Blackstone (1765–1769, vol. III, p. 261) and expounded in a detailed essay by Sedgwick and Wait (1909) has scarcely been altered by the work of the succeeding century (e.g. Holdsworth 1925, vol. VII, pp. 4–25; Simpson 1986, Chap. VII; Chap. 10). As the title to this essay suggests, there is something to be added to our knowledge of the beginnings and end of the history, which may possibly help to elucidate deeper truths about the life cycle of fictions. So far as the origin is concerned it takes as its text Baker's (2001, p. 33) statement that

> It is of the essence of a fiction that it leaves no explicit evidence of its existence.

He suggests a process similar to a birth which is proclaimed to the world by a birth certificate but where the actual birth is hidden. An attempt will be made to show that the key steps in the evolution of fictional ejectment were quasi-legislative in

---

P. Sparkes (✉)
Southampton Law School, University of Southampton, Highfield,
Southampton SO17 1BJ, UK
e-mail: P.Sparkes@soton.ac.uk

M. Del Mar, W. Twining (eds.), *Legal Fictions in Theory and Practice*,
Law and Philosophy Library 110, DOI 10.1007/978-3-319-09232-4_13

character, and this is no less the case because some of the documentary evidence has been lost making it difficult to pin down the key steps precisely.

Abolition of the fictional tradition in ejectment in 1852 enables us to consider the moment when a fiction is no longer a white lie, a bit of harmless fun, and it becomes an oppressive reminder of legislative impotence, no longer to be tolerated and subject to an imperative to move to an "honest" basis. There is little doubt that the abolition process is itself public, likened to a funeral rather than a death made official later by a death certificate. The fiction in ejectment can be seen as scaffolding, a metaphor which implies that a fiction is useful when building a new doctrine out of existing case-law only to achieve redundancy as soon as the construction is complete. While a building under construction is clad in scaffolding the external appearance is an imitation of the final shape, even though the scaffolding carries the purely procedural role of facilitating access to the work by the builders. When work is complete the scaffolding is removed to reveal the true shape of the edifice, the substantive doctrine to which the scaffolding provided a path. This is equivalent to the abolition of the fiction. In the course of ejectment this was supposed to leave a pure substantive doctrine underneath, a precise replica of its fictional predecessor.

13.1 Use of a Genuine Lease for Freehold Recovery

Even if fictional origins are obscure, it will always be possible to define some parameters within which a doctrine must have evolved in order to limit the scope of enquiry. Trespass very early on split into its three main variants: to the body; to chattels; and to land—the latter being trespass *quare clausum fregit*. The specific action by a tenant to enforce his lease against a stranger was *ejectione firmae*, at first sounding only in damages, but suddenly in 1499 extended to allow recovery of the term of a lease *in specie* by the tenant (Wonnacott 2011, pp. 329–330; *Games v Smyth* Fitz. N.B. 220). King's Bench warded off the threat to its jurisdiction over leases from Chancery by equipping a leasehold tenant with a modern form of action for the recovery of land from a stranger. This egregious decision, if such it was, was extended by *Solle v Edgare* to the Common Bench in 1526 (Baker 2003–2004, p. 226). There is, therefore, no point in looking for the origin of this before 1499, and if there was any movement to adapt the leasehold action to the trial of freehold titles under Henry VIII, Baker has not detected any (Baker 2003, pp. 636–637).

The switch from trespass-based leasehold recovery to the resolution of freehold titles in trespass succeeded soon after the death of Henry VIII. Freehold ejectment can be located in its origin with a good degree of confidence to the short married life of Mary and the first 3 years of the reign of Elizabeth (that is the second half of the 1550s). The first few reported cases from the joint reign of Philip and Mary involved long leases of tithes (*Ibrave v. Lees* 2 Dyer 116b; *Wrotesley v. Adams* 1 Plowd. 187). The very first surviving report involving freehold title appears to be *Willion v. Berkley* (1 Plowd. 223, c. 1561), 3 years into the reign of Elizabeth, decided, contrary to popular belief, in the Common Bench where real actions were also heard. There was a brief hiatus while the new procedure was digested by the profession, but this was followed by an explosion in the use of *ejectione firmae*, as the action was always called until the Commonwealth, 10 years into the reign of Elizabeth. Very soon it was standard practice to grant a lease of a relatively short duration (5 years allowing time for all the litigation to be completed unless Chancery intervened) in order to try titles. Business was diverted from Common Pleas to King's Bench for, as Dyer C.J. complained, "the speed which is there" (*Anon.* 3 Leon. 51, c. 1573; Chap. 11). The ejectment process was well settled when it was decided, for example, that a lease could be made by an infant if the purpose was the trial of title (*Humphreston's case*, 2 Leon. 216, c. 1574). At the end of Elizabeth's reign, ejectment was viewed as an ancient action. The explosion of business can be seen from the following table collating figures of actions collected by leading reporters of the time:

Reporter	Reign	Ejectment	Real action
	Elizabeth (1558–1603)		
Plowden	1–20 Eliz.	7	3
Popham	26–33 Eliz.	30	7
Popham	34–37 Eliz.	15	1
Coke	Late Eliz.	22	1
Croke Eliz.	32–45 Eliz.	60	2
Croke Jac.	James I (1603–1625)	54	2
Croke Ch.	Charles I (1625–1649)	60	1

Throughout Elizabeth's long reign, ejectment was fictional in the sense that an artificial lease was used to secure leasehold recovery when the underlying issue was determination of freehold title, in the same sense that contract and tort had emerged from fictional adaptation of the action in trespass. References to leases sealed to try titles were common throughout Elizabeth's reign. However, all stages of the procedure in the action were genuine, including the entry on the land, a grant of a real lease,[1] and an ouster from the land.

The problem was legislation which prevented the true character of the action being revealed in open court which beefed up the rules on maintenance by prohibiting also the buying of pretended titles (Statute 32 Henry VIII, 1540, c. 9). In order to avoid the sanctions of the statute it was necessary either to have held possession of the land for the previous year or to have possession at the time of the grant of the lease, though possession for a single hour was sufficient. The sanction was draconian, consisting of the forfeiture of half of the value of the land to the Crown and the award of the other half to the plaintiff bringing the complaint, a penalty sufficient to inhibit avoidance. That a (genuine) lease was caught by this legislation was decided in *Partridge v. Strange* (1 Plowd. 77, c. 1552). The profession must have assumed that actual entry was required for a lease made for the sole purpose of trying title but

[1] A partially fictionalised lease appears early on in *Griffyn v. Leonard* (Baker 1993, p. 129, c. 1566) in which the defendant was the *custos* of the *brevium* of the Bench and was presumably not genuinely interested in the litigation.

this was confirmed in *Gerarde v. Worseley* (3 Dyer 374b, c. 1579) and reconfirmed in *Slywright v. Page* (Moore K.B. 266; Goulds. 101, 1 Leon. 166, c. 1588). Joan Wade had made a lease to her half-brother to try title when not in possession and away from the land, and this was treated as a pretended lease within the mischief of the statute. Apparently a lease to a brother of the whole blood would have been good (1 And. 201) and dicta in the case suggested that the real target was a lease made to a great person with the resources to oppress a poorer possessor. The point remained active 10 years later in *Willis and Jermine's* case (2 Leon. 97) and apparently divided professional opinion in 1615 (West 1615: s. 449, an obscure text for which one must acknowledge the citation by Holdsworth (1925, p. 10, fn. 4)).

Coke (1628, fo. 369a) in his *Commentary on Littleton* used the case law to differentiate the position of commoners and great men and to suggest that commoners were relatively safe in granting leases off the land to try titles (Hawkins 1739, p. 264, nn. d–e) That view was disproved by the subsequent decision of the Star Chamber in *Leach v. Fuljambe* (Gardiner 1886, p. 65, c. 1632) following a riot at the collection of tithes at Chesterfield. Sir Francis Fulliam made a lease to Godfrey Somershill to try the title and, as a baronet, was convicted of champerty and maintenance and fined £ 1000. A common person would have been acquitted of maintenance but convicted of champerty. The whole issue of granting leases out of possession seems to have evaporated under the Commonwealth, presumably as a result of the abolition of the Star Chamber and its jurisdiction (Statute 16 Charles I, 1640, c. 10).

The tabulation set out above of the relative frequency of reported actions reinforces the received wisdom that the invention of ejectment very quickly killed off the real actions. Coke's report of *Alden's case* (5 Co. Rep. 105a, 1601) contains a lengthy lament by the reporter for the real actions, but he protested too much; the reports show what a good living he had made since 1583 arguing numerous ejectment cases, speaking on occasion for 2 days at a time. What he did not explain, and what is not well explained by existing literature, is why a trespass-based action came to triumph. It is conventional to blame the very precise rules of pleading that had to be followed in the real actions, but minute detail was needed to describe the land accurately in ejectment as well (Holdsworth 1925, vol. VII, p. 7). It is more that, at bottom, the real actions were weighted in favour of defendants in terms of delay whereas trespass was favourable to claimants, and it was claimants who chose the form of action.

However, that is not the whole story. This crucial point runs quite counter to received wisdom. It is conventional to think of ejectment as a possessory remedy from which the unsuccessful party could chance his arm on success in a real action. This may have been true later, but it was not the position during the reign of Elizabeth when the use of ejectment actions exploded. The position was the exact reverse. A Statute of Limitation passed in 1540 (32 Henry VIII c. 2) imposed a realistic limitation period in real actions of 50 years for a case based on the possession of an ancestor and even less if based on the plaintiff's own possession. This did not delimit the right of entry which was tested in ejectment, a defect not corrected until 1623 when a limitation period of 20 years was imposed on a right of entry (Statute 21 James I c. 16). Reeve's *History* suggested that limitation was a reason for the switch to ejectment (Reeves 1880, p. 418 n; Baker 2003, pp. 724–725), and if so the triumph of ejectment achieved during the period 1540–1623 arose because it allowed a claimant more scope to exploit long held grievances. This may also explain why *ejectione firmae* won over trespass, even though trespass was the form of action used in the most famous property case reported by Coke, *Shelley's case* (1 Co. Rep. 93b), supposedly ranked by lawyers of the time ahead of *Hamlet* as literature.

Real actions determined the title to land and were conclusive between the parties to the action. Ejectment held a massive advantage for a wealthy *claimant*. An ejectment was litigated between the parties to a fictional lease and between those parties it was conclusive, and as to about the title to possession under the ejectment lease, but the outcome did not bind the rival claimants to the freehold, and a losing claimant could avoid *stare decisis* simply by granting a new fictional lease to a differently named tenant. It was stated quite correctly in *Ferrer's case* that this operated to the infinite vexation of land owners—meaning potential *defendants* in settled possession of land (6 Co. Rep. 7a, 1603). A huge tactical advantage was handed to litigants with deep pockets such as the claimant in *Thrustout d. Parke v. Troublesome* (2 Strange 1099, 1726), who had forced a defendant to attend five different assizes to defend his land. The only solution for a defendant was yet more expense: an application for an injunction after repeated unsuccessful ejectments to Chancery as in *Bath v Sherwin* (4 Bro. P.C. 373, 1709, H.L.) or to the equitable jurisdiction of the Exchequer. Sadly, the lust for fees had prevailed over the interests of litigants.

In summary, it was 60 years after leasehold recovery was first allowed in 1499 that the leaseholder's action was moulded to secure the recovery of freehold land. This development was suggested by the recovery of long leases of tithes and adapted to freehold land by the ingenuity of counsel. The origin is knowable, but is obscured from our understanding because it more or less coincides with the invention of the modern style of reporting. Very soon after the invention of ejectment the course of the pleadings and argument can be followed in great detail in Dyer and Plowden, a pattern of reporting perfected towards the end of the reign of Elizabeth by Sir Edward Coke. The action was convoluted in form because of the need to avoid the Henrician legislation against dealing with pretended titles, a development mirroring the evolution of conveyancing after the legislation against uses, but it was not in essence fictitious.

13.2 Confessing the Lease, Entry and Ouster

The process of evolution was described thus, long after the event, by Lord Blackburn:

> A lease was made by the person wishing to recover the land. At first it was a real lease to a real person. The lessee entered on part of the farm; and, if his lessor had title, that entry put the lessee in possession of the whole farm, and enabled him to maintain an action against anyone who ousted him. Afterwards the person who sought to defend the possession was permitted to do so only on the terms that he should 'confess lease, entry, and ouster, and rely only on title.' After this, the lease, entry, and ouster, never took place in fact. (*Bristow v. Cormican* (1878) L.R. 3 App Cas. 641, 661)

During the Commonwealth *ejectione firmae* gave way to "trespass and ejectment", and later still the recovery of possession in ejectment was separated from the question of mesne profits. An attempt will now be made to attach some dates to Lord Blackburn's chronology.

Fictionalisation of the ouster occurred early in the reign of James I. Many cases suggest genuine parties as shown by a contemporaneous case in which the parties were mistaken. Litigation on the issue was very frequent which suggests that the principles were evolving at the time. An ejectment could occur on the day of the lease, but this was only too likely when entry against an established possession might be fleeting. More serious problems arose if an entry was alleged before the date of the lease pleaded; as such a lease must have been purely fictitious, unless the pleading had been quite extremely slack, and it was inevitable that the ejectment would fail when this defect in pleading emerged (*Llewellyn v. Williams* Cro. Jac. 258). The concentration of case law in the years 1606–1611 must suggest that a battle was underway for the heart of ejectment. Eventually the date of ouster did not have to be stated since it was recognised that this was not a real event (Sedgwick and Wait 1909, pp. 611, 630).

A casual ejector was a person who chanced upon the land after the claimant had entered and granted a lease to the notional plaintiff. Invention of the casual ejector seems to have been stimulated simply by the churn of case law. *Wilson v. Weddell* (Yelv. 144) was decided about 1609. A son who was trying to eject Margery from possession of copyhold land did so by taking action against a servant living with Margery. This choice was available to ensure that the master could not avoid proceedings by absconding.[2] From this it was a short step to develop the idea of the casual ejector, a nominal defendant in an ejectment action whose role is to confess the plaintiff's case and so lead to a default judgment for possession against the casual ejector, leaving the defendant to come in and defend the case on the merits of his own title if he wishes to do so. Moves toward the complete fictionalisation of the casual ejector date from the Commonwealth and are always attributed to Henry Rolle. He had practised in the King's Bench throughout the reign of Charles I and was well versed in ejectment. When he was appointed Lord Chief Justice it was first to the King's Bench in November 1648, but this soon transformed itself into the Upper Bench with the execution of the King in January 1649. He must be admired for the skill with which he avoided complicity in regicide, resigned rather than fall out with Cromwell, and died before facing the new king's wrath. Rolle's judgments can be followed in the reports of Style.

The rapid evolution of the casual ejector can be traced in the practitioner's bible, Style's *Practical Register*.[3] First a notional ejectment was recognised (Easter 1646: Style 1657, p. 110) and then any occupation of land against the claimant (Trinity 1646: Style 1657, p. 108). An ejector could be casual in the extreme, possibly,

[2] During the Parliamentarian period it was indicated that the master was the appropriate defendant when the servant was in possession: Michaelmas 1647 and Easter 1648: Style 1657, pp. 110–111.

[3] I must acknowledge the exceptional help I received from Joy Caisley, law librarian of Southampton Law School, in finding materials for this essay.

> any person who comes upon any part of the Land …, although it be by chance, and with no intent to disturb the Lessee of the possession (Michaelmas 1648; Style 1657, p. 109.)

It was held at this time not to be acceptable to choose an artificial ejector, and also unacceptable for the real parties to agree upon an ejector if any other party would be prejudiced (Michaelmas 1646 and Michaelmas 1648: Style 1657, pp. 109, 111). After the execution of the King, a number of cases in the renamed Upper Bench in 1650 and the succeeding couple of years explicated details of the concept of the casual ejector (Style 1657, pp. 109–112).

Style appended to his discussion the nonsensical observation that "*there is no prejudice to any person by having such an Ejector*". In fact purely fictional Casual Ejectors opened the door to collusive ejectments, as Lord Mansfield recognised long afterwards:

> Ejectment is an ingenious fiction for the trial of titles to the possession of land. In form it is a trick between two to dispossess a third by a sham suit and judgment. The artifice would be criminal, unless the Court converted it into a fair trial between the proper parties. (*Fairclaim v. Shamtitle* (1792) 3 Burr. 1290, 1294; cf the second epigram by Jeremy Bentham cited in Lobban, this volume, Chap. 10, p. 199)

Quite clearly recognition of a purely fictional ejectment and the changed practice allowed by Rolle L.C.J. required to be balanced by protection for those claiming title to the land. Things moved very quickly between 1650 and 1652. First, it was decided that it was unnecessary to give notice of the sealing of the ejectment lease to the person claiming title since "it is sufficient to give notice of the Lease to the Tenant or Under-tenant of the Land in question" (Hilary 1647; Style 1657, pp. 167–168). This ruling follows logically from the fact that the ejectment action is based on entitlement to possession rather than title, "though the Title of the land doth also come into question and is tried collaterally" (Style 1657, pp. 107–108). In other words, the issue is the right to possession. Note how the ejectment lease on the eve of the interregnum is genuine and it continues to be so for the next few years.

If ejectment was designed for the trial of title to land, the corollary was that a person with an arguable title must be heard. Style extracts this point in these words:

> One who hath Title to the Land in question in an *Ejectione firmae*, may upon motion to the Court be made a Defendant in the Action with the Tenant in possession, that he may thereby defend his Title …. (Upper Bench 1649: Style 1657, p. 111)[4]

So, both the tenant in possession and an outsider with title could defend an ejectment. When the claimant entered his declaration, the filing was accompanied by rules, drawn up by the claimant, in a standard form approved by the court, allowing pleading to the ejectment, but only on terms authorised by the court. Throughout the Commonwealth the defendant to an ejectment was required to confess the entry, lease and ouster. If he did not he would face eviction under the default judgment against the casual ejector. Rolle's innovation was to require this confession in order to force the parties to confront their real dispute, opening the way for fictionalisation

[4] This Rule could not be avoided by a collusive release between the claimant and the casual ejector: *Keys v. Brandon Raym*. T. 93 (also referring to *Leicester v. Holborn*).

and, at the same time, a formal separation of the scaffolding from the underlying structure.

The step described above required a potential defendant to raise a motion before the court. The next step was the making a general Rule of the Court, issued on a Wednesday in March 1649,[5] which provided that

> It is ordered that after the ordinary rule of this Court hereafter given to the Defendant to plead in any action of trespass and Ejectment, and the Defendant doth not plead to the Declaration, Judgment may be given and entered for the Plaintiff against the defendant, for want of Plea, as in other Actions … (Cooke 1747: Hillary 1649)

For the sake of clarity hereafter, "Rule" refers to a general Rule of the Court and "rule" refers to a document drafted by a particular party and authenticated by the court office allowing him to plead in a particular action. This was a Rule and still written in Latin. It immediately predates the decision to switch writs and court proceedings to English under legislation passed in November 1650 and confirmed in April 1651, the moment when *ejectionae firmae* transmute into 'trespass and ejectment' and when the King's name was excised from writs and so on. This Rule refers to the usual practice of giving a rule to the defendant in trespass to plead. It therefore provides a quasi-legislative framework for the court registry to create "soft" law by imposing a common form on the rules authorised by it. This is clear from the following description of the refined procedure:

> If the tenant doth not appear at the beginning of the next term, then if upon affidavit made of the delivery of a copy of the declaration …, the court will make a rule for the tenant to appear and plead by a certain day, at which time, if the tenant appears, he must by his attorney file common bail, and draw up a rule to confess lease, entry and, ouster, and leave it at a judge's chamber, and give notice thereof to the plaintiff's attorney to proceed if he thinks fit; but if he doth not appear there after the day appointed by the court for the tenant to appear and plead, judgment will be entered up against the casual ejector by default. (Style 1694, pp. 198–199)[6]

This last exposition makes clear that the "rule" was a document prepared by the defendant wishing to be allowed to defend. If the draft was not in the correct form the clerks would not allow it and the defendant was not let in to defend. So Lord Hale was correct to assert to the Lords after the Restoration that there had never been a general Order made in relation to ejectment (Holdsworth 1925, p. 11). It is little wonder that a "rule" based on the practice of the clerks cannot be traced. Style links the Rule change allowing a defendant in to plead with the requirement in the Upper Bench that the defendant "joyn in the rule to confess the lease, entry and ouster" (Style 1657, p. 111).[7]

The practice requiring this confession must have occurred within a 3 year window. Execution of the King on 30 January 1649 (new style) is a starting point;

---

[5] The chronology is complicated by the retention of the Julian calendar at the time under which the year ended on March 24th; the King was executed in January 1648 (old style) but 1649 (new style).

[6] Capitalisation has been modernised in order to emphasise the Rule/rule dichotomy.

[7] This is dated inconsistently both to Michaelmas 23 Car. (=1647) and to B.S. (= Upper Bench); the latter makes more sense and if so the decision may date from 1649.

the outer point is the clear reference to the rule in the Upper Bench in *Theoball v. Conquest* (Style 343) pleaded in Trinity term 1652 and heard that autumn. It was decided that, if an application was made during the course of proceedings to alter the details of the lease pleaded, the rule did not require confession of the altered lease; the rule was confined to confession of the lease as pleaded. The new rule applied to the Upper Bench and not to the Common Bench. So well were the mechanics of ejectment hidden that the reporter in a case considering the changed rule in 1652 (*Anon.* Style 368) had never heard of the new rule.[8] After the Restoration the obligation to confess lease, entry and ouster was described as a "former rule" (*Okely v. Norton* 2 Keble 699, 1671), so a bonfire of the Protector's vanities is one plausible reason why no such Rule can be traced today, but a more credible explanation is that this was a quasi-legislative initiative contained in "soft" legislation of a kind that is inherently ephemeral.

Henceforth reports of cases are confined to the substantive issue in the case (one example of the new style of report being *Saunders v Ritch* (Style 278) and others occurring throughout volume 2 of Siderfin). It must have been better in troubled times to separate the trial of title from disputes about violent entries.

During the last years of Charles I and the early years of the Commonwealth, real leases were required in ejectments. This all changed sometime between 1650 and 1657 with a decisive step towards total fictionalisation. The obligation on a defendant to confess the lease must naturally have suggested the possibility that the lease could be made up. Now occurs a radical departure in practice, a true fictionalisation, which is very difficult to date. It was no longer necessary to seal a lease but merely to deliver a (false) declaration that a lease had been made. Thus the recognition of the fiction of the casual ejector led to the fictionalisation of the entire ejectment action. Just how radical a change this was can be seen from further reference to Style's *Practical Register*:

> But now by the new way of practice, it is not usual to Seal any Lease of Ejectment at all in an Action of Trespass and Ejectment, but the plaintiff that intends to try the title, delivers a Declaration to an Ejector of his own making, and that Ejector sends or delivers the Declaration to the Tenant in possession, who gives notice therefore to his Lessor, whose title is concerned to defend the title, and if neither the Tenant in possession, nor his Lessor will defend the title, then the Ejector will confess a Judgment to the Plaintiff, and so the Tenant will be stripped out of possession. (1657, p. 108)

This practice applied in King's Bench.[9] The practice of delivery of the declaration only was enshrined in Rules of the Court after the Restoration (Cooke 1747: Michaelmas 33 Charles II, 1685). The concern of the courts in future would be to ensure that all proper parties received a copy of the declaration. Care was taken to make sure that the tenant understood the document delivered:

[8] Sedgwick and Wait 1909, p. 627 give the date as 1625, a most unfortunate typo since it was actually decided in 1652.

[9] In King's Bench costs for the preparation of the lease were disallowed, whereas in Common Pleas the costs of lease were allowed despite the lease being confessed, a situation which for a time threatened to divert the whole business of ejectment to Common Pleas.

> … the Plaintiff … delivers a copy of the Declaration in Ejectment to the Tenant in possession or his wife, … which Declaration must have an Endorsement … in English, acquainting the Tenant what the thing is, which Endorsement … must be read to the Tenant by the Person, Who delivers the same, at the time of the delivery thereof, which Person also must tell the Tenant, that unless he forthwith shall procure an Attorney of the Kings Bench to appear for him and defend his Title, if he hath any, he shall be turned out of possession, or words to that effect.

That was the practice as described slightly later in time (Style 1694, 3rd edn., pp. 198–199).[10]

The day of the Restoration saw William Bartholomew blasting out a sermon at Gloucester on the theme of "The Strong Man Ejected by a Stronger than He". Many of Cromwell's innovations were reversed by this new strong man, but very soon it was decided that the confession of entry, lease and ouster was an innovation destined to survive. This became known as the consent rule or the common rule (Anon 1700, Chaps. 4–5). The early cases can be followed in the Reports of Bridgman, Raymond and Siderfin and appear to involve delivery of a declaration alone. The decision to retain Rolle's procedure was reached in a whole clump of cases within 4 or 5 years of the Restoration, starting with *Anon v. Davies* (1 Keble 28, 242) allowing a defendant to escape costs when he had indicated his intention to defend but failed to appear in order to do so. The same view was taken in *Colingwood v. Pace* (1 Lev. 59) and *Middleton's case* (1 Keble 240) making clear that a defendant would be non-suited if he failed to make the requisite confession of entry, lease and ouster. This continuity was re-emphasised by successive Rules of the Court in the Trinity terms of 1662, 1663 and 1666 (Cooke 1747). The reason the new procedure survived is, it is suggested, that the change had never been made by a formal Rule of the Court but merely by practice of the clerks; the rule was too "soft" to be torn up and too soft to be identified with the Protector. In any event, once the tables were turned, the interests of Royalists were best served by having a simple action to recover lands lost during the Civil War.[11]

Confession of the entry became so entrenched that a lease was considered to be forfeited without the landlord actually needing to re-enter. This nonsensical rule adopted in *Wither v. Gibson* (c. 1674, 3 Keble 218) and again in *Little v. Heaton* (1702, 1 Salk. 259) was eventually entrenched by statute (4 George II c. 28) and survives to this day.

In conclusion, tradition has been right to credit Henry Rolle with invention of fictional ejectment. The chronology set out above proves that the Upper Bench over which he presided invented the "modern" procedure in ejectment in 1649–1652. The origin of the rule requiring confession of lease, entry and ouster was knowable although the birth certificate has been lost.

---

[10] There were four exceptional cases where this "new practice" described in Style's *Register* could not be used and an ejectment lease remained essential, notably when the property was vacant. This was decided in *Harvey v. Mountnet*, (Style 1657, p. 425) and confirmed after the restoration (Cooke 1747: Trinity 1662, 14 Car. II).

[11] Indeed the interests of the King were best served by preserving the lands of the rebels, since their property was forfeited when they were attainted for treason; much of the rebels' property was assigned to the Duke of York, afterwards James II.

13.3 Fictionalisation of the Parties

Evolution of ejectment from pure fiction to farce occurred at a remarkably late stage of the evolution of the action.[12] Elizabethan cases reveal neither fictional names nor fictional leases. John Doe had certainly taken to the stage by 1588, but only as a pledge of suit and not as the main party to the ejectment. There was no evidence throughout the Jacobean monarchy that John Doe would spawn one thousand two hundred reports of ejectments actions (not all separate cases) in the English Reports, nor as yet any mention of Goodtitle, Thrustout or any of the other dodgy plaintiffs who appear immediately after the Glorious Revolution.

When did parties become openly fictitious? Soon after the Restoration in *Addison v Otway* (1 Mod 250, 252) it was argued that the case should lapse when the nominal plaintiff died; showing that a real person had been named as lessee, but the court suggested that the parties were oftentimes wholly imaginary; the name was accepted provided there was someone with the name used alive in the county at the time. Lord Hale told Parliament soon afterwards that fictitious parties were disallowed when known. There is no evidence that fictitious parties had come out of the closet until after James II had been ousted, but almost immediately afterwards fictional names appear in the reports, a development which can be located with some confidence in the early days of William & Mary. *Goodwin v. Blackman* (3 Lev. 334, 1692) was the first of 96 cases brought by a plaintiff of that name and *Goodright* makes an appearance in 1694 (again the first of many). Recognition of purely fictitious parties took place against the backcloth of a battle over liability for costs, the issue which bothered Blackstone so much, especially given the prevalence of repeated ejectments. In c. 1669 solicitors in an ejectment brought in the name of a plaintiff with diplomatic immunity were committed until they found someone able to pay the costs. Battle over costs was really joined in 1705 when costs were awarded against an attorney bringing an action using fictional names in a case reported as *Anon.* (6 Mod. 310). It was said to be a great abuse in ejectment to name as nominal lessees persons who were not *in rerum naturâ* or at least unknown to the defendant, causing the defendant to lose his costs. Another attorney was made to bear costs after, on this occasion, being subjected to interrogatories on the matter. This decision caused only a brief delay in the evolution of the pure fiction.

In 1717 there is the first appearance of the rather vulgar Thrustout—a name which one would have thought best reserved for defendants, but often adopted by plaintiffs eager perhaps to boast about their virility as ejectors (1 Str. 12, 2 Str. 1099). The very next year in Common Pleas in *Thrustout v. Goodright* (1 Lutw. 1219) it was said that a motion to name a better plaintiff was constantly denied. So obviously fictional plaintiffs evolved during the reign of George I and the very last few years of that reign see the first use of the *Doe d.* formula (2 Str. 1121, 1152). Creativity in the naming of parties appears to flower in the first 6 years of George II

[12] According to the definition offered by Del Mar (this volume, Chap. 11) consciousness of falsity is not required for a fiction, and in any event it is clear that after the Restoration, at least, the courts were turning a blind eye to fictitious parties.

(1727–1733)—the period when Barnes was reporting, perhaps stimulated by a statute regulating forfeitures of leases (Statute 4 George II c. 28) which recognised as an aside the naming of nominal defendants and casual ejectors in ejectment. Barnes' collection of cases on ejectment covers twenty two extraordinary pages (Barnes: 171–194) where we find the predecessors of Doe and Roe:

Goodright and Goodtitle;
Holdfast;
Makepeace or Peaceable;
Positive and Negative;
Right against Noright or against Wrong;
Thrustout;
Troublesome, and finally, the ultimate loser,
Vice.

The use of John Doe as a nominal plaintiff emerges during the reign of George II notably in cases brought by the Duchess of Hamilton in 1727/28 (2 Str. 1121, 1152) and again in the House of Lords in error in 1741 (*Doe d. Hamilton v. Atherley* 7 Mod. 420). There are other spasmodic reports of John Doe as a litigant in the reign of George II, but he suddenly pushes to the front of the pack (if a fictitious person can be said to push through a fictitious pack) 10 years or so into the reign of George III, the name becoming common as a plaintiff only after 1771, and then establishing itself as the archetype. A thorough reading of the case law would be required before these changing fashions could be explained. The archetype of *Doe d.* followed by the *claimant v.* the real *defendant* is followed in some 1200 cases in the English Reports (though this includes many duplicates). In the nineteenth century this signified a first ejectment. Fictionalisation led to a renewed battle over costs in the middle of the eighteenth century. In *Goodright d. Roswell v. Vice* (Barnes 182, 1740) a claimant who secured judgment against a casual ejector was barred from proceeding to claim his costs from the real defendant. The issue came to a head in *Orion v. Mee* (Barnes 188, 1752). In this case Stevenson who practised as an attorney in St Ives used the name Jacob Mee as a standard false name in all ejectments, but unfortunately there was a real person of that name living in St Ives. The Chief Justice would have made the real Jacob Mee liable for costs, but the other three justices exonerated him, recognising that he was wholly unconcerned in the matter and that the action had become purely fictitious. Even then the Chief Justice favoured altering the rule.[13]

There was no reason why openly fictitious parties could not have been recognised as soon as Rolle L.C.J. invented the new procedure during the Commonwealth, but the case law shows that the fictional parties came out to the courts half a century later, during the joint reign of William and Mary. The author has not been able to trace any convincing reason for the delay or source for the change. Here at the very last step we may find support for the proposition that the origins of fictions

[13] Recognisances were required before proceeding in error; O Bridgman who reported in the first 6 years of the Restoration has two cases (at 464 and 475) of recongisances of £ 1000 and £ 2000, huge sums at the time.

are unknowable, since here, finally, was a fiction driven by litigants, and not by the judiciary. Further work is required to unravel all the mysteries.

13.4 Defictionlisation

This is a convenient point at which to turn to the second object of our study, the idea that fictional developments of procedure are merely a scaffolding and that this can be removed, leaving a complete edifice beneath. Where Arkansas led, England eventually followed. States in America had three approaches to ejectment. American law depended heavily on Blackstone's *Commentaries* and some states imported the Blackstonian fictional model wholesale, with all its baggage including repeated ejectments. Secondly there were states which adopted a legislative action shorn of the fictions, that is a simple suit between the real litigants by name for land precisely described in the suit. This was the post-fictional action used in England between 1852 and 1875. The Arkansas version was debated by the Supreme Court in *Sturdy v. Jackaway* (71 U.S. 174, 1869). It was held that a prior ejectment between the parties was an absolute bar to a later action involving the identical title. Sturdy sued and lost, and his attempt to relitigate in another court in the state was rejected.

> The action of ejectment was devised for a lessee of a term of years, who was ousted of his term, … It was but an action of trespass in effect, and the remedy was in damages only for the dispossession. But afterward the court determined the lessee should not only recover damages, but also his term, which soon brought the action into general use; and, by the formal scaffolding of a lease, entry, and ouster, the action was converted into a method of trying, collaterally and incidentally, the title of the lessor. (Justice Grier: 175–6)

When the fictitious scaffolding had been removed, the action was a straightforward action for recovery of the land in issue and the decision in the first suit created an estoppel between the parties to the action (176). Finally, there were some states which demolished the scaffolding by statute, but which made express provision for a second trial.

England followed the same model in the Common Law Procedure Act 1852 (15 & 16 Vict. c. 76). Section 3 allowed an action to be brought without naming a cause of action, though of course the causes of action retained a shadowy existence, and this was especially true of ejectment. Later parts of the Act (1852: s. 168 ff) constituted a code of procedure in ejectment. The key provision is section 168 which provided that recovery of possession of land would no longer be based on an ejectment; instead the action was to be commenced by a writ naming the defendants in possession. It was no longer necessary to invent names and dates for a lease, entry and ouster, nor for a defendant to confess events which had never occurred. Land law had become honest.

This leads immediately to the outstanding advantage of statutory ejectment; the action is now based on title to possession and a decision in favour of one party or the other attracts *res judicata*. It is no longer determining entitlement to be restored to a fictional lease. The issue of repeated ejectments had been controlled by common injunctions and by costs orders, and it is by no means clear why the court that had long controlled defendants could not have found a way to control plaintiffs. So here we have a clear benefit of the change. Under the old law one could erect a fictional scaffolding which led to a failure of substance, and dismantle it and erect a slightly different scaffolding and try again. The problem with the fiction was that it did not frame the issue in a manner that was binding on an unsuccessful claimant. Removal of the scaffolding removed this defect. For the future, the substance would be tried once and only once.

Little change was made to other procedural aspects of the recovery of land. The latter parts of the 1852 Act have been said to have created a code of procedure in ejectment. The effect of the Code was considered in *Butler v. Meredith* (11 Ex. 85, 1855). The "new" procedure introduced by Henry Rolle had been designed to ensure that any person with title could come in and defend an ejectment on their title. The statutory procedure introduced almost precisely two centuries later allowed any person showing an interest in possession by himself or by his tenant was entitled to defend (1852: s. 172). When a statutory ejectment was brought for some property in Bermondsey the action was defended by two Spaniards called de Palacio, and the question was whether, as foreign residents, they should be required to provide security for costs. An order to provide security was upheld. As it happens this reproduced the pre-statutory procedure, but this was a mere coincidence; what matters was that the new Act, so provided in words said to be exceedingly plain (Platt B.: 97). The legislators chose to duplicate the old procedure so that "the action of ejectment is placed by that statute on the same footing as when it existed as the mere creature of the court" (Pollock C.B., p. 89).[14] There never was any doubt that Parliament could demolish the scaffolding; it just happened to replace it with an identical set.

It is easy to see why a decision was made to codify rather than to reform. In the Elizabethan and Jacobean periods, ejectments could fail for procedural defects meaning that the substantive issue did not reach court, if, for example, the pleading inadvertently placed the grant of the ejectment lease before the entry. If these pitfalls could be avoided, an Elizabethan jury could bring in a special verdict focusing on the legal dispute in a form not at all dissimilar to a Chancery Division puisne hearing a property dispute under Elizabeth II. Rolle L.C.J. did not abolish the fiction, but he did identify which parts of the whole charade were procedural and which amounted to the substance of the action. That was his brilliance. The only procedural issue which arose was whether a particular defendant should be forced to confess the fictional elements, but once this confession had been required in a particular case it did force the parties to address the substance of their dispute. Actually there is one area of dispute where the requirement to confess the ouster had a huge impact. This was where a right of action to recover land depended upon an ouster, two examples being the action for recovery of a share between tenants in common and a landlord's forfeiture of a lease for breach

[14] A similar view was taken of the Judicature reforms of 1873–1875: *Gledhill v Hunter* (1880) 14 Ch. D. 492, Jessel M.R.

of covenant. Rolle L.C.J. did not intend, when he required a defendant in ejectment to confess to the lease, entry and ouster, to compel a defendant to confess to the very act required to create a cause of action. However, it was decided by Hale C.J., and again by Holt C.J., that the tenant was required to confess the landlord's physical re-entry, the effect being the catastrophic modern law that a forfeiture occurs when the tenant breaks a condition of the lease without any re-entry by the landlord (*Little v. Heaton* Holt K.B. 264, 1703, a point first decided by Hale C.J.). This is best characterised as an erroneous line of authority rather than an inherent flaw in the Rollean confession. At any rate, having identified the two constituent parts of the ejectment action, Rolle L.C.J. could and should have gone on to a straightforward action without any demise at all. That was his reticence. It is quite understandable but it led to a delay of two centuries in the evolution of an honest basis of jurisdiction for possession actions.

When ejectment became the sole action for the recovery of land this became the basis of the common law itself. This remark prompts reflection on the most difficult issue of all, the extent to which modern land law has been scarred by the use of an ejectment-based action for the recovery of land. That the fictional basis of ejectment was limiting can scarcely be doubted. In *Graham v Peat* a lease of a rectory was void and this meant that the tenant could not maintain an ejectment upon such a demise "because it is a fictitious remedy founded upon title" (1801) East 244). This dictum prompts some further reflections:

Reliance by land owners on a possessory remedy sits ill with a property law based on ownership. If a landlord grants a short periodic tenancy of the land to a tenant, it is the tenant, and not the landlord, who is entitled to recover possession from a third party. An action by a mortgagor would fail on proof of an outstanding term in a mortgagee (*Doe d. Oliver v. Powell* (1834) Ad. & E. 532). Ejectment was not a sufficient action in the nineteenth century when it became possible to create interests in land apart from seisin.

As Kerr considered in his elementary text, ejectment was not an adequate means to try the title to all real property nor to remedy every ouster; thus for example because no entry could be made on an incorporeal right then no ejectment could be made (Kerr 1854, p. 65). This all suggests that dismantling the scaffolding will not leave a building of a pure architectural design.

Ejectment relied on title to grant a legal lease, and hence upon a legal freehold title. It is very unfortunate that the chance to create a vindication type action based on a better (legal or equitable) right was lost twice, both on the reform of common law procedure in 1852 and on the fusion of the administration of law and equity in 1875. Two categories of case had to be fought out in equity. First was where the claimant had a strong legal title that lacked an immediate title to possession, so that a declaration of title was required. Second were disputes involving mortgages since a nineteenth century mortgage passed legal title to the lender, disputes about the borrower's title had to be fought out in equity, the remedies being declaration and injunction. Equitable defences based on acquiescence could be considered after 1852, and more general equitable defences after the judicature reforms of 1873–1875. One could scarcely have expected a merger of law and equity under the

Commonwealth, but it is very unfortunate that the tentative moves by Lord Mansfield to a fusion of the actions (or rather to a consideration of equitable defences in a legal ejectment) were overruled by Lord Kenyon (Holdsworth 1925, p. 19).

It is not clear that any of these issues can properly be said to involve fictional aspects of ejectment. In reality if there had been a non-fictional ejectment established during the Commonwealth it would have been limited to recovery of possession by a person showing legal title. The creation of a modern action to assert rights in land is an important task, but it is a task within the province of the legislator and not of the courts.

Conclusion

Some fictions are driven by litigators, and such children are likely to have undiscoverable births, because claimants are unlikely to proclaim the novelty of their action for fear of being nonsuited. Where, on the other hand, a court drives the evolution of a fiction—whether to remedy a defect in the law or to expand its jurisdiction—the origin is likely to be guessable if not actually discoverable. Fictions were a form of quasi-legislation, but also an acknowledgement of legislative impotence; when they are abolished it is likely to be because a fiction has been superseded by formal legislation. One would expect to find a public ceremony akin to a funeral at this stage, consisting of a public proposal for reform, Parliamentary debate and the enactment of legislation.

Ejectment has been scrutinised in terms of the rise and fall of its fictional character. Three stages were identified in its evolution, giving rise to the search for three births. Most innovative was the very first stage in which an action for the recovery of leasehold rectories and tithes was suddenly modified to secure the possession of freehold land. The formal machinery was an entry on the land, the grant of a lease and an ouster from the land. This stage appears to have been driven by claimants, but it can nevertheless be pinned down pretty precisely to the latter part of the 1550s. This involved a diversion of a leasehold action to the use of freeholders, but fictionalisation was prevented by legislation aimed at preventing maintenance. The second and decisive step was fictionalisation of the entry, lease and ouster which took place in the Upper Bench presided over by Rolle L.C.J. during the early stages of the Commonwealth. It was always a puzzle that the clear and persistent attribution of this innovation to Henry Rolle could not be matched by any documentation, but this essay has sought to explain that the search for a Rule of the Court or court decision enshrining this practice is misguided since the innovation in fact took place within the clerks' office. A possible explanation has been provided for why maintenance was no longer a problem. The third stage was the obvious fictionalisation of the notional parties, a birth which must have taken place in court when a case brought by a plaintiff with an obviously dubious name (perhaps Goodright or Thrustout) was first allowed. The decision by the litigant's attorney to try this out is obviously unknowable but the court's decision to allow such a farce is knowable but at present unknown. So much for the three births of ejectment and the new light thrown here on the certification of the births.

The burial of ejectment is much better documented and more straightforward. The US Supreme Court characterised the procedural steps in fictitious ejectment as scaffolding, a vivid image adopted here as a prism through which to consider the process of abolition in England. An attempt has been made to show that Rolle L.C.J. separated the scaffolding so effectively from the substance of an ejectment that statutory abolition in 1852 is best seen as a belated formalisation after two centuries of a death long since announced. Parliament has dismantled the scaffolding but has then chosen to duplicate the substance of the old action, a sad abnegation of legislative responsibility.

References

Anon. (Gilbert C. B.?). 1700. *The law of ejectment*. London: John Deede.

Baker, J. H. 1993. *Dyers reports*. London: Selden Society.

Baker, J. H. 2001. *The law's two bodies: Some evidential problems in legal history*. Oxford: Oxford University Press.

Baker, J. H. 2003. *Oxford history of the laws of England*. Vol. 6, 1483–1558. Oxford: Oxford University Press.

Baker, J. H. 2003–2004. *Reports from the time of Henry VIII*. London: Selden Society.

Blackstone, William. 1765–1769. *Commentaries on the laws of England*. Many subsequent editions, book III, Chap. XI. Oxford: Clarendon.

Coke, Sir Edward. 1628. *The first part of an institute of the laws of England, or a commentarie upon Littleton*. London: Societie of Stationers.

Cooke, G. 1747. *Rules orders and notices in the court of King's Bench from the second of King James I to 1747 inclusive*. London: Stephens, Worrall, Waller and Sandby.

Del Mar, Maksymilian. 2014. Legal fictions and legal change in the common law tradition. In *Legal fictions in theory and practice*, ed. Maksymilian Del Mar and William Twining. Dordrecht: Springer.

Gardiner, S. R. 1886. *Reports of cases in the courts of star chamber and high commission*. London: Camden Society.

Hawkins, W. 1739. *Treatise of the pleas of the crown*. 3rd ed. London: E. Nutt.

Holdsworth, William S. 1925. *History of English law*. Vol. 7. London: Methuen.

Kerr, R. M. 1854. *An action at law being an outline of the jurisdiction of the superior courts of common law with an elementary view of the proceedings in personal actions and in ejectment*. Philadelphia: T. & J.W. Johnson.

Lobban, Michael. 2014. Legal fictions before the age of reform. In *Legal fictions in theory and practice*, ed. Maksymilian Del Mar and William Twining. Dordrecht: Springer.

Reeves, J. 1880. *History of English law from the time of the Saxons to the end of the reign of Edward I*. 1st American ed. Philadelphia, M. Murphy.

Sedgwick, A. G., and F.S. Wait. 1909. *Trial of title to land: Select essays in Anglo-American legal history*. Vol. 3. Boston: Little Brown.

Simpson, A. W. B. 1986. *History of land law*. 2nd ed, Chap. VII. Oxford: Clarendon.

Style, W. 1657. *Style's practical register*. 1st ed. London: Charles Adams.

Style, W. 1694. *Style's practical register*. 3rd ed. London: Dring and Leigh.

West, W. 1615. *Symboleography*. London: The Stationer's Company.

Wonnacott, M. 2011. The history of the law of landlord and tenant in England and Wales. Clark, New Jersey: Lawbook Exchange.

Part IV
Fictions in Practice: Past, Present and Future

Chapter 14
Fact, Fiction, and Social Reality in Roman Law

Clifford Ando

Abstract Roman and civil law fictions were notorious among early modern critics for their variety and scope. The unborn are treated as living; the living are treated as dead; aliens are classified as citizens; clauses in legal instruments are assumed not to have been written. The essay surveys fictions in classical Roman law, both those the Romans themselves labeled fictions and others that functioned through similar linguistic operations. Particular attention is given to the use of fictions in practice, both in statute and surviving legal instruments. Finally, the essay explores the theoretical frameworks within which Romans understood the operation of fictions, especially the distinction between social and legal facts and the natural and the imaginary.

14.1 Introduction

Fictions are ubiquitous in Roman law. Yet for all the ire they have attracted from philosophical skeptics, most notably Bentham, they have received remarkably little attention from Romanists, and almost none to speak of from comparatists, either.[1] Some at least of this neglect can be attributed to the Roman jurists: they flag as fictions only a tiny percentage of the fictional work-arounds that Roman legislation and jurisprudence employ. To recover and assess the full scope of the work performed by fictions in Roman law and jurisprudence, one must first discover the range of linguistic operands by which they were instantiated. Having commenced by exploring Roman analyses of fictions they identify as such, this essay begins this work of recovery by exploring two such operands, to wit, third-person exhortatives,

[1] On Bentham see Stolzenberg (1999) and the essays by Michael Lobban and Michael Quinn (Chaps. 4 and 10) in this volume. Romanists on Roman legal fictions: Richardson (1995), Thomas (1995), Bianchi (1997), Ando (2011b, pp. 1–18, 115–131), and Cornu Thénard (2011). Roman fictions within comparative projects: Maine (1861, pp. 13–25), Gray (1909, pp. 30–38), Fuller (1930/1931, pp. 373, 378, 389–390, 521–523, 545), Knauer (2010), see also Eden (1986, pp. 45–48), Moscovitz (2003).

C. Ando (✉)
Department of Classics, University of Chicago,
1115 E. 58th Street, Chicago, IL 60637, USA
e-mail: clifford.ando@uchicago.edu

M. Del Mar, W. Twining (eds.), *Legal Fictions in Theory and Practice*,
Law and Philosophy Library 110, DOI 10.1007/978-3-319-09232-4_14

used to declare suppositions of fact as well as to effect procedural shortcuts, and the preposition *pro*, one among several lexemes employed to effect substitutions and assert equivalence across taxonomic boundaries. Confronting the range of fictions in public and private law at Rome will then permit a more fine-grained assessment of their utility and importance, in effecting change at law, resolving conflicts and bridging interstices in laws on jurisdiction, negotiating among competing sources of law, and providing a cognitive apparatus to assess the gap between social reality as the Romans perceived it and the world the law at once described and called into being.

14.2 Roman Theory: The Supposition of (Fictional) Facts

Only one extended treatment of fictions as foundational to Roman civil procedure is known to have been written in classical antiquity, namely, that occurring in the fourth book of Gaius's *Institutes*, and, alas, the one manuscript of that text to survive is missing the page and, indeed, the sentence just prior to the apparent introduction of the topic of fictions.[2] Nevertheless, it seems clear that Gaius raised the topic as an afterthought when writing about changes in the law regarding the punishment of those convicted for delinquent payment of tax. At one time, taxes being collected by magistrates, those magistrates had the power to seize real security from delinquent taxpayers, who would have to pay some sum in order to redeem their property. Once the collection of select taxes was handed over to private tax farmers, the question arose as to how to endow the tax farmers as private persons with effective but appropriately limited power over delinquents. A statute gave them the power to seize real security: this was power. The power was limited, according to Gaius, by a fiction: delinquents were to be condemned to redeem the security "for as much money as they would have been condemned formerly [by a magistrate], if real security had been seized, which security ought to be redeemed by the person from whom it was seized."[3]

This seems an exceedingly elaborate solution to a simple problem. Clearly, it is a procedural work-around in response to an unwillingness to amend statute. One

[2] For a description of the constitution of the text of the Institutes, see Schiller (1978, pp. 43–46). The break falls between Chaps. 31 and 32 of book 4: see de Zulueta (1946, pp. 244–246). The only other extended treatment directed to fictions as a general topic rather than the operation of a particular fiction occurs in a rhetorical handbook of the first century CE. There, the author is concerned with suppositions made by parties to the dispute in pleading: "It seems appropriate to add that arguments may be developed not only on the basis of agreed upon facts but also from fictitious supposition, which the Greeks call καθ' ὑπόθεσιν (*kath'hypothesin*), 'hypothetical.' This is true of all the types of argument listed above, since there as many species based on fiction as on truth. To suppose a fiction means, in this context, either to put forward something that, if true, would either destroy or strengthen the point raised or to make the matter under dispute appear similar to one's fiction" (Quintilian, *Institutio Oratoria* 5.10.95-96 = Russell (2001, pp. 414–415)).

[3] Gaius *Institutes* 4.32 = de Zulueta (1946, p. 246).

might either have altered the law granting power to magistrates to set contracts for tax farming or, possibly, simply altered those contracts, the bulk of which were tralatician in character.[4] It is therefore worth remarking that, insofar as the condition of the text permits such inference, the legal action for seizure of security by private tax collectors that contains the fiction was granted by the Praetor. That is to say, it was not created by statute but announced as a permitted legal action by the magistrate who exercised supervisory jurisdiction over the city of Rome. The details to one side, the enactment of statute and the creation of new legal actions by the Praetor were two among several sources of law at Rome. Statutes being troublesome to pass, Roman jurists understood it to be the responsibility of the Praetor "to aid, supplement or correct" statute law in light of evolving social, material and economic realities.[5] A modern legal theorist judging the particular fiction employed to grant but also limit the power of tax-collectors might add that, in this case at least, the Praetor did so in a fashion that respected the legitimacy of earlier law and, more importantly, of alternative sources of law.[6] The power of private tax collectors was thus situated in typological relation to, and indeed made parasitic upon, the unquestionably legitimate power of magistrates, albeit in a domain from which those magistrates were now excluded by exactly the institutionalization of private power that the fiction invoked them to justify.

Evidently prompted by these remarks, Gaius embarks on what are clearly unsystematic remarks on "fictions of another kind" (*alterius generis fictiones*), where the singular "kind" suggests, if no more than that, that Gaius understands the five fictions that he then treats as being of a single type. That said, he makes no gesture whatsoever toward describing what that other "kind" is. In the terms of ancient philosophical handbooks, Gaius provides at best an ostensive definition. The fictions that he discusses are: (i) a purchaser or would-be possessor of the goods of a deceased had no action in statute law against those who held the decedent's property or owed the decedent money, and so was allowed by the Praetor to sue as if he were heir to the property in question (the so-called *actio Serviana*); (ii) similarly, such a purchaser or possessor might be allowed to sue in the name of the decedent for recovery of goods or payment of debts, but the defendants would be condemned in the name of the purchaser, and so upon victory the goods or debt would be delivered

---

[4] The text of the Roman law governing the farming of customs duties in the Roman province of Asia was discovered in 1976 and fully published in 1989; Cottier et al. (2008) presents an updated edition of the Greek text and an English translation. The text dates from 62 CE but the form of the text reveals that much of its content was tralatician, passed down, despite periodic revision, all the way from its first enactment late in the second or early in the first century BCE. On this aspect of its character see Ando, *Roman Social Imaginaries*, Chap. 3.

[5] In one problematic but classic formulation, the Praetor created new legal actions "by imitating proper law" (Gaius *Institutes* 4.111 = de Zulueata (1946, pp. 276–277): Gaius here describes a special case but the particularities do not merit discussion in this context). On the development of Praetorian law see Frier (1985); for an old-fashioned, formalist account see Jolowicz and Nicholas (1972, pp. 191–199). Maine likewise characterizes the use of fictions in England as effecting the "extension, modification and improvement of law" (1865, p. 18).

[6] For an account of legal legitimacy at Rome along these lines see Ando (2011b, pp. 4–11).

to him (the so-called *actio Rutiliana*); (iii) a person who had acquired possession lawfully but not yet completed the time period for usucapion could not, upon losing possession, sue for the item in statute law, and so a Praetor allowed such persons to employ the fiction that they had in fact completed the period of usucapion and might sue as owners (the *actio Publiciana*); (iv) aliens being largely excluded from Roman courts, at least at Rome, but nonetheless deeply embedded in Roman society, citizenship could be fictively attributed to an alien, "provided," writes Gaius, "that it is just that the action in question be extended to an alien"; and (v), if one's opponent in a lawsuit had suffered a penalty entailing a diminishment in legal rank and concomitant inability to appear in a Roman court, Praetorian law permitted the fiction that the diminution of status had not occurred.[7]

What ties these fictions together? In one perspective, the third fiction, concerning usucapion, exhibits a structural resemblance to the fiction concerning real security and tax delinquency: One legal institution, the office of the Praetor (which had the power both to create and to apply law), had to close a gap that yawned between contemporary practice and statute law, created by another law-creating body, that notionally governed that practice. In both cases, the Praetor did so through a fiction that assimilated current practice to the normative horizons of earlier statute: the gap was closed, and the legitimacy of statute and statute-law more generally was preserved. The first two fictions, by contrast, concern individuals whose possession fell short of Roman doctrines of ownership in one or more ways (not least because succession to obligations was a matter of Praetorian rather than civil law), and one additional consequence of the procedure envisioned by Gaius, beyond mere recovery of property, would be a court decision affirming title to the property in question.

That said, the ambition that unites Gaius's fictions "of another kind" seems rather narrower than affirming the legitimacy of sources of law and less specific—and less substantivist—than a concern for title. The problem in each case concerns justiciability: the case coming before the court fell short of some threshold. What was at stake, therefore, was the transfer of an individual, action or thing across some taxonomic divide: from purchaser to heir; from possessor to owner; from alien to citizen. It is a matter of some interest that the Roman jurists often felt the need to construct or construe the fiction as a plausible extension of the legal life history of the party in question—thus, one does not imagine the possessor as owner, but as having completed the period of usucapion, and so as having become owner in plausible continuance of present arrangements. I will take up this topic at greater length below (Sect. 14.5).

A particularly colorful rather than elaborate instance of negotiating such a threshold, indeed, one involving a supposition, concerns the procedure to be applied when a soldier or magistrate is accused of adultery. Normally cases of adultery had to be resolved within 60 days of the charges being made. A regular exception was made for persons in state employ who could be expected to be away from Rome on state business. Those persons as a class could not be indicted on a charge of adultery, triggering the 60-day window, so long as they were absent without intent of

[7] Gaius *Institutes* 4.34–38 = de Zulueta (1946, pp. 246–249).

evasion.[8] But what about soldiers serving in the night guard of the city of Rome or the city's own military unit?

> But if someone who is present is nevertheless treated in the place of the absent person [imagined by judicial norms] (*vice tamen absentis habetur*)—as, for example, someone serving in the *vigiles* or the urban cohorts [to wit, a soldier serving in the city of Rome]—, it should be stated that he can be accused, for he does not have to take any pains to put in an appearance.[9]

To paraphrase: if a person was in fact present who would otherwise be presumed absent, he could be accused—though the status of the normative presumption would normally require that in such cases he be treated *as if* absent. The fact of actual presence is allowed, mirabile dictu, to trump the presumption of a legal fact of absence.

How might one assess whether such procedural fictions were controversial in their Roman context, apart from the anxieties they have aroused in later periods? One index might be this: I am aware of no case in which the use of such a fiction was contested.[10] One must of course be cautious about an argument from silence, particularly given the paucity of extant evidence for actual pleadings at Rome. That said, we do know that people argued about the degree of analogical resemblance in the adducing of precedent.[11] What is more, in the case of procedural fictions, it was only at the moment of their first devising that they might truly have been contested. Thereafter, like all formulae, they became part of the repertoire of available actions, to be imposed by the magistrate holding jurisdiction when the facts, whether true or contrived, fit the model.[12] In classical procedure, the moment for pleading came later, before the lay judge charged with adjudicating the dispute in light of the model the Praetor had applied.[13]

14.2.1 The Language and Epistemics of Supposition

In *The Nature and Sources of the Law*, John Chipman Gray paid some attention to the language of Roman legal fictions, which remarks inspired a response but also criticism from Lon Fuller. Gray relied nearly wholly on the account provided by Gaius, neglecting both jurisprudential literature and, much more consequentially,

[8] Cf. Hermogenianus bk. 2 *Iuris Epitomarum* fr. 54 Lenel = *Dig*. 27.1.41. On this text see further Ando, *Roman Social Imaginaries*, Chap. 2.

[9] Ulpian *[Ad legem Iuliam] de adulteriis* bk. 2 fr. 1949 Lenel = *Dig*. 48.5.16.3.

[10] Here one might make a cautious and limited comparison to the apparently non-controversial nature of fictions in Rabbinic law, on which see Leib Moscovitz's Chap. 15 in this volume.

[11] Ando (2014a).

[12] Of course, it was possible in theory for a later praetor to remove formulae from the published list of available legal actions, just as he might add ones, but it seems quite clear that the vast bulk of the content of the Praetor's edict (as the list of formulae was known) was tralatician. Far the best guide to this material remains Lenel (1927).

[13] On the distinction between issues of fact and issues of law supposed by this scheme see Cornu Thénard 2012.

the linguistic operands by which fictions were enacted in statute. Though we shall turn presently to those bodies of evidence, this seems an appropriate moment to consider a point of convergence between Gray and Fuller, to wit, their agreement that Roman fictions "contained a grammatical acknowledgment of [their] falsity."[14] However, where Gray urges that Roman "assumptive" fictions (to use Fuller's term) might be construed as less violent than English fictions, the court only saying "that it is dealing with A as if it were B," and thus "stating nothing contrary to the fact," Fuller dissents quite strongly from this position. Fuller does not deny, of course, that the fictions described by Gaius worked so as to expand the scope of the law, to embrace persons, things and actions excluded by statutory language. Rather, in his view they nevertheless stated a falsehood, and the act was all the more pernicious insofar as it was precisely by this means that Roman fictions "appease[d] a longing for an appearance of conservatism."

> The Roman praetor apparently felt that by framing his innovations in terms of older rules he had secured some justification for them, even though the pretenses involved carried on their face the acknowledgement of their falsity.[15]

This seems to me to involve a mischaracterization of the language involved in Praetorian formulae, a problem arising from Gray's mistranslation or misrepresentation of the Latin text and Fuller's reliance on Gray. Gray explicitly represents the fiction of citizenship as instantiated in the form of a contrafactual: "If, in case Aulus *had been* a Roman citizen" (Fuller reprints Gray's paraphrase and adds the emphasis on the past contrafactual). But the linguistic form employed by Gaius, whose text Gray quotes but which he only paraphrases, employs an imperfect subjunctive for both protasis and apodosis. Two features of so-called "should/would" conditionals are of relevance here. First, the conditional is (in modern terms) implicative. It asserts only that the one thing being true, the other would follow. Second, Latin conditionals of this type imagine something as possible but not yet fulfilled, nor do they make any claim as to the likelihood of future fulfillment.[16] Thus Gray's transformation of the clause into a declarative past contrafactual radically distorts both the rhetorical status of the conditional and also the ontological security it attributes to the world that it imagines.

One might go further. Insofar as the apodoses of the conditionals that instantiate these fictions apply only to the conditions of judgment, they might well be said to do no more than require the construal of the situation at hand on analogy with another. To use the language of Peter Birks, the fictions do no more and no less than require a symmetry of consequence between two situations, the one fact identified

---

[14] Fuller (1930/1931, p. 390), following Gray (1909, p. 31). As my engagement here is with Gray and Fuller over their characterization of Roman evidence, I do not entertain the broader question whether their characterization of fictions (whether via Vaihinger or Ross or some other theorist) is sufficient: on that topic see Kelsen (Chap. 1) and Stern (Chap. 8) in this volume.

[15] Fuller (1930/1931), pp. 390–391.

[16] We are thus in the vicinity of a fact "posed but not affirmed," on which see Ross (1969, p. 231), with the reading of him in Stern, this volume, Chap. 8.

as variable.[17] Consider a more precise translation of the sort of fiction paraphrased by Gray: "If it appears that a golden cup has been stolen from Lucius Titius by Dio the son of Hermaeus or by his aid and counsel, on which account, if he were a Roman citizen, he would be bound to compound for the wrong as a thief, and so on."[18] It is easy to imagine the appropriate juridical Latin with which to produce the same outcome via analogy: "An action for theft in which the thief is an alien should be handled on analogy with (*ad exemplum*) the action for theft in which the thief is a citizen, the alien thief serving in the place of (*vice, vicem* or *loco*) the citizen one."[19] What is more, what Gaius elides with his "and so on" is the command, framed as an imperative, that instructed the judge as to what penalty to impose. The elision was possible for him because he was interested in the fiction; the rest of the formula was the same as it would have been without the fiction. That of course is telling, but so, for us, is the imperative that is elided. The sequence "conditional subjunctive + imperative" is the classic form of the implicative rule.

It might be helpful to examine a fictitious supposition in operation. It just so happens that a fiction is employed in the one so-called formula to survive from practice in the Roman Republic, to wit, the instructions prepared by a Roman praetor in Spain in delivering a dispute between two peoples (the Sosinestani and Salluienses) to a third party for judgment.[20] The translation is keyed to the line numbers of the text as it appears on the bronze tablet on which it was inscribed:

1. Let those of the Senate of Contrebia who shall be present at the time be judges. If it appears, with regard to the land that the Salluienses
2. purchased from the Sosinestani for the purpose of making a canal or channeling water, which matter is the subject of the dispute, that the Sosinestani

[17] Birks (1986, esp. pp. 94–99); compare Fuller on what he calls "Fictitious Legal Relations," perhaps the weakest part of his essays (1930/1931, pp. 383–384). In his chapter in this volume, Stern urges that legal fictions can be distinguished from metaphors as a matter of both form and intent, fictions being *employed* in such a way that all parties understand the limited purpose and effect of the operation; but he also suggests that further study is needed in order to assess how the audiences of legal fictions understood and elaborated upon the fictitious facts in question. I have made a limited gesture in this direction regarding the regular employment of fictions assimilating aliens to Romans (2011b, pp. 10–11).

[18] Gaius *Institutes* 4.37, translation in de Zulueta (1946, p. 249).

[19] Compare *RS* text no. 63, the *Lex Quinctia* on aqueducts. An initial clause concerns the punishment to be imposed for "holing or fracturing" an underground conduit. A later clause treats disregard for the boundary stones that demarcate the materials and right-of-way of the water system, and concludes: "Whoever shall have done anything contrary to these rules, against him statute, law and position in all matters and for all <---> are to be exactly the same as it would be or it would be appropriate for it to be, if he contrary to this statute had fractured or holed an underground conduit" (see esp. lines 30–31: *siremps lex ius causaque omnium rerum omnibusque <---> esto atque uti esset essve oporteret* ...).

[20] The bronze tablet from Contrebia received a magnificent first edition from John Richardson, which was followed immediately by an exemplary exploration by Birks, Rodger and Richardson of the legal issues that it raises: Richardson (1983); Birks et al. (1984). My esteem for those publications notwithstanding, I dissent from the interpretation of the fiction on which they settle (Birks et al. (1984, pp. 52–54)). The details are irrelevant to the status of the fiction in argument and so I set them aside here.

3. were within their rights to sell it, although the Allavonenses were unwilling, then, if it so appears, let the judges judge
4. with regard to the land which is the subject of the dispute that the Sosinestani were within their rights to sell it to the Salluienses; if it does not so appear, let them judge
5. that they were not within their rights to have sold it.
6. Let the same persons who are written above be judges. If there were a Sosinestan *civitas*, then, in the place
7–8. where the Salluienses recently and officially put in stakes, which matter is the subject of this action, if it would be permissible for the Salluienses within their rights to lead a canal within those stakes through the public land of the Sosinestani;
8–11. or if it would be permissible for the Salluienses within their rights to make a canal through the private land of the Sosinestani, in the place where a canal ought to be made, so long as the Salluienses pay the sum for which the land would be assessed, where the canal would be led; then, if it so appears, let the judges judge that it is permissible for the Salluienses within their rights to make the canal; if it does not so appear, let them judge that it is not permissible for them within their rights so to do.
12–14. If they judge that it is permissible for the Salluienses to make the canal, then let the Salluienses pay from public funds money for the private lands where the canal shall be led, on the arbitration of five men whom a magistrate of Contrebia shall appoint from his/their Senate.
14. Gaius Valerius Flaccus, son of Gaius, *imperator*, assigned jurisdiction.
15. They pronounced the opinion: Whereas right of judgment is ours, in the matter that is under dispute we judge in favor of the Salluienses.

The key conditional occurs in line 6. I translate it literally, but the phrase might also be elaborated in English of quite different form: "On the assumption that there is a Sosinestan *civitas*," which is to say, "On the assumption that the Sosinestani are an autonomous polity ..." The messy historical details of the case notwithstanding, it should be clear that the Praetor himself makes no claim in respect to the status of the Sosinestani. In this sense, the episteme of the Roman legal fiction harmonizes closely with the security that such formulae attribute even to the facts that lead to judgment. Observe that the lay judges here (as at Rome) are not charged with rendering judgment on the basis of what is true, but only on what appears to be so (lines 3–4, lines 8–11: "if it appears" (*sei parret*), "if it does not appear" (*sei non parret*)).

14.3 Jurisdictional Rules[21]

The absence from extant sources of any controversy in regard to the fiction of citizenship might still surprise, if only because Romans often discussed, and strongly disapproved, aliens in respect to Rome conducting themselves as if they were Roman citizens, a behavior nearly universally described using the phrase *pro cive gerere*, which one might translate variously as "to conduct oneself in the place of," "to conduct oneself as," or "to conduct oneself as if one were" a citizen.[22] Indeed,

[21] The exposition here partly adapts and compresses Ando (2011a, b, 2014b, Chap. 2, Sect. 14.3). On the use of fictions in Roman jurisdictional rules see also Thomas 1996.

[22] I will explore this use of *pro* further below. For its range of meaning see *OLD* s.v. *pro* 6, 8 and 9. On Roman terminology for, and conceptualizations of, the usurpation of citizenship see the Conclusion to Ando, *Roman Social Imaginaries*.

around the turn of the millennium, the emperor Augustus (reigned 31 BCE—14 CE) himself sponsored a statute on jurisdiction that restricted the use of Roman legal forms to the city of Rome and the first milestone beyond it, and likewise required that, even at Rome, Roman legal forms be employed only in disputes the parties to which were all Roman citizens.[23]

The so-called *Lex Iulia Iudiciaria* was something of an exception to Roman jurisdictional rules in the extent to which it allowed ideological interests, in particular regarding the position of the metropole and the status of metropolitan citizenship, to shape its contents. But it was an outlier only to a certain extent, for Roman legislation seems always to have been committed to a cohomology of territoriality, jurisdiction, choice of law, and rights of citizenship. Extant evidence for Roman jurisdictional rules derives largely from one of two sources: the orator Cicero provides a summary of the law governing jurisdiction in Sicily in the early first century BCE; and we possess a number of fragments of actual jurisdictional laws as these were inscribed on bronze tablets from contexts on the Italian peninsula and in Spain in the first centuries BCE/CE.

Cicero claims that in Sicily, cases between persons of the same citizenship were tried in courts of their polity, using their own laws. In cases involving Sicilians of discrepant citizenship, the Roman governor appointed a judge by lot from a roster of third-party judges. In cases in which a Roman citizen sued a Sicilian, a Sicilian was assigned to adjudicate; contrariwise, when a Sicilian sued a Roman, a Roman adjudicated. Cases between Roman citizens were heard by a Roman tribunal.[24] Cicero's summary suggests that Rome generally preferred to assign cases to fora based on the citizenship of the parties to the dispute, and his statement in this regard accords with other Roman evidence suggesting a strong preference for the use of indigenous law among indigenes.[25] At the same time, Cicero's summary is clearly inadequate: among other things, it provides no specification as to choice of law in cases involving persons with discrepant citizenship and third-party judges.

The law summarized by Cicero comes from a political and temporal context somewhat distinct from the fragments of actual statute law that we possess.[26] These derive from a variety of contexts outside of Rome and treat a range of problems in procedure and private law. None of the relevant statutes survives complete. Nonetheless, it is possible provide a schema of a typical clause of the following form:

> (1) In communities of types A, B, and C, in area D,[27] (2) in which jurisdiction rests with magistrates of types G or H,[28] (3) legal actions of type K shall be handled locally, using

[23] Gaius *Institutes* 4.103-105 = de Zulueta (1946, pp. 274–277).

[24] Cicero *In Verrem* 2.2.32; for a text and facing translation see Greenwood (1928, pp. 326–327).

[25] See Ando (2014b, Sect. 14.3) and idem, Legal Pluralism.

[26] Relevant at least are *RS* texts no. 6, 15, 16, 17, 24, 28 and 29.

[27] See *RS* no. 16, ll. 4–5; *RS* no. 17, ll. 3; *RS* no. 18, l. 7; *RS* no. 24, l.83; *RS* no. 28, col. 2, ll. 54–55.

[28] *RS* no. 16, l. 11; *RS* no. 17, l. 15; *RS* no. 24, l.83; *RS* no. 28, col. 2, ll. 54–55.

> procedure M, if conditions P and Q are met,[29] or (4a), if condition P and Q are not met, procedure R should be used locally, or (4b) the case shall be sent to Rome.[30]

In these statutes, the principal condition that selects a case to be judged locally or sent to Rome is the value of the dispute in monetary terms and not, I stress, the juridical status of the parties to the dispute. That said, even when disputes were to be treated locally, these laws occasionally required the use of Roman procedure or even Roman substantive law, in one of two ways. In the law on jurisdiction in the lands of Italy north of the Po, for example, one chapter supposes that the framework for adjudication is the edict of the praetor at Rome who held jurisdiction over foreigners in the city; and yet it also specifies that the judge should set the punishment according to the decree of the magistrate holding jurisdiction in the locality in question.[31] (The details, which are messy, are happily irrelevant to this context.) In contrast, in another chapter, concerning suits in respect of debt, *after* specifying that the following procedure applies to low-value cases, the text runs:

> the law, the issue, the right of action, and the suit shall be exactly the same for all persons in every respect as they would be, or as it would be appropriate for them to be if that person … had confessed concerning these matters before the praetor at Rome or before the person who in Rome had jurisdiction over these matters ….[32]

Here, the law and procedure to be used locally, in a case avowedly below the statutory threshold that would require transfer to a Roman court, are explicitly assimilated to Roman law and procedure. What is more, this occurs through a contrafactual, flagged as such through the lexeme *siremps … atque utei … sei* + pluperfect subjunctive, "exactly the same as if *x* had done *y*." That said, the fiction is not employed so as to assert that the defendant had done something he had not, to wit, that he had in fact confessed before a Roman magistrate holding jurisdiction at Rome. Rather, it is specified that he is to be treated locally as he (or another) would be in a similar case, were that case to be heard before such a magistrate in a court in the city of Rome.

To summarize, jurisdictional rules of the Republican period distinguish explicitly between Rome and everywhere else. In line with other legislation of their era, they reserve the power and capacity of judgment in matters of import to the metropole. Late Republican jurisdictional clauses also cleave the empire socially, for it is not all disputes, nor even all disputes between citizens, that are removed to Rome for adjudication, but only those in which the matter in dispute, converted to monetary terms, was worthy of Roman attention. That said, for reasons unspecified, they also occasionally require that local practice adhere to Roman norms and, while this might be accomplished through the imposition of Roman positive law, it was

---

[29] *RS* no. 16, line 6.

[30] *RS* no. 17, ll. 16–17 (the text is defective, but the sense seems clear).

[31] *RS* no. 28, Chap. 20, Col. I, ll. 21–31.

[32] *RS* no. 28, Chap. XXII, ll. 40–43 (see also ll. 45–40): *siremps lex res ius caussaque omnibus omnium rerum esto, atque utei esset esseve oporteret sei is … de ieis rebus Romae apud praetorem eumve quei de ieis rebus Romae iure deicundo praeesset in iure confessus esset ….*

apparently less controversial to accomplish this through fiction because proceeding in this way left the principle of the exclusivity of Roman law undisturbed.[33]

This is the context in which the emperor Augustus intervened with his law on jurisdiction, which appears to have been an effort to draw traditional distinctions more radically than ever before. Its effects remain visible nearly a century later in a municipal charter discovered in Spain. Such charters derived from a template written at Rome, which was then very minimally adapted, also at Rome, to suit the particular locality to which they were sent. In the 91st chapter of that text, specification is made as to details of civil procedure:

> Rubric. According to what law notice for the third day may be served, the day may be postponed or have been postponed, a matter may be judged, a case may be at the peril of the iudex, a matter may cease to be under trial:
> … if judgment has not taken place within the time laid down in Chap. XII of the *lex Iulia* that was recently passed concerning *iudicia privata* and in the decrees of the senate that relate to that chapter of the statute, so that the matter be no longer under trial; the statute and law and pleading is to be as it would be if (*siremps lex ius causaque esto adque uti esset si*) a praetor of the Roman people had ordered the matter to be judged in the city of Rome between Roman citizens …[34]

Please note that the Flavian municipal law does not revise the Augustan law on jurisdiction that it cites. On the contrary, it genuflects before its principles: Roman justice is best administered by a Roman praetor, judging a case between Roman citizens in the city of Rome. It would be more accurate to say that the Flavian municipal law preserves the distinction between Rome and elsewhere only to upend it, by means of a fiction that operates on two levels, geographic and social. For it dissolves both distance in space and distinctions in the legal status of persons: disputes between potentially alien citizens of the municipality are to be resolved "as if a praetor of the Roman people had ordered the matter to be judged in the city of Rome between Roman citizens." Provinces and provincials are thereby assimilated to Rome and Romans. To the politics of this act, I will return in closing.

14.4 Let there be Legal Facts

14.4.1 3rd Person Imperatives and Public Law Procedure

We have several times seen equivalences made, and their consequences asserted, through third-person imperatives, especially *esto*, "Let X be …; X is to be …" Such was the foremost operation by which Roman law brought new legal facts into being

---

[33] Roman jurisdictional fictions thus blur the distinction drawn by Michael Lobban in his Chap. 10 (this volume) between procedural and metaphysical fictions, in the sense that they rendered matters justiciable by Roman courts using Roman procedure, but they also accomplished this by taking as fact things that had not happened or did not exist as supposed.

[34] *Lex Flavia municipalis* Chap. 91 = González (1986, p. 179 [Latin], p. 198 [English]).

and so shaped the world that it regulated. What were the limits of the power of this language? And how was its operation understood? In one notable case, we have both a representation of relevant language in a statute (albeit one that did not pass) and an interpretation of its functioning, in which its operation is likened to a fiction. This case can then be situated in hermeneutic relation to other uses of such imperatives in legal texts of the period.[35]

The instance in question concerns an agrarian law proposed by one Publius Servilius Rullus in the year 63 BCE, the year of Cicero's consulate. In order to carry out its terms, the law enjoined the creation of a board of ten officials with power of command, but that power of command could not be created by the legislative act alone, or so Rullus feared. Election to offices that carried *imperium*, strictly speaking, the power to command Roman citizens, was actually a two-stage process. One had first to be elected by the citizen assembly and subsequently invested with power of command. This latter act was apparently accomplished through the passage of a *lex de imperio*, a statue concerning *imperium*, by the *comitia curiata*, a sort of vestigial assembly of the People in which citizens at large had long since ceased directly to participate. Rather, they were represented in the curiate assembly by 30 lictors representing the 30 *curiae*—in this context the term means something like "voting units"—into which the people had once been classified.[36] Normally, the passage of a curiate *lex de imperio* followed immediately and unproblematically upon election, as votes in the American electoral college follow the results of a purely numerical count at the state level. As it seems, however, there was nothing automatic about its passage.

Rullus sought to circumvent the potential failure of the *lex de imperio* by a procedural shortcut, instantiated in a third-person exhortative. According to Cicero, he simply wrote into his bill that the officers created by it and charged with carrying out its terms should possess the same legal standing as those created according to strict procedure even if the curiate law did not pass. In Cicero's speech in opposition, he claims first to quote the text of Rullus's bill and then explicates its operation:

> What then, if the [curiate] law is not passed? Note his ingenuity! "Then let the decemvirs be of the same legal standing as those created according to strict procedure" (*eodem iure sint quo …*). If this is indeed possible, that in this polity, which excels all other polities by far in the rights of liberty, someone should be able to obtain command over citizens or administrative authority without the authorization of any electoral body! What is the point of ordering the passage of a curiate law in the third chapter, when in the fourth you permit that these officials should have the same legal status without a curiate law as they would have had if they had been created by the people according to strict procedure?[37]

Cicero confronts statutory language that ordered the voting of a curiate law immediately upon the passage of Rullus's plebiscite. What is more, the first law declared

[35] Thus, although Roman jurists did employ fictions in explantory roles of the sort described by Michael Lobban in this volume, Chap. 10, I treat many of these as heuristic, to wit, as revealing the operation of fictions in the statutes under study.

[36] For a summary of views on the so-called curiate law see Gizewski (2003).

[37] Cicero, *Contra Rullum* 2.29 = Clark (1909, p. 139), on which see Ando (2011b, pp. 7–8).

through a third-person exhortative that officials created under its clauses shall possess the power conferred by the second law, regardless whether it passed or not. Cicero explains this legal chicanery by redescribing it as operating through the use of fiction, one instantiated with a past contrafactual: "they shall have the same legal status without a curiate law *as they would have had if* they had been created by the people according to strict procedure."[38]

With Cicero's gloss on Rullus's bill as a guide, we can more readily identify the fictions at work in other public law texts of the Roman republic. For example, an inscription from Furfo preserves the regulations established there in 58 BCE to govern the practice of ritual and control of sacred properties at the cult of Jupiter. A number of clauses treat properties given to the temple (whether goods or money), which things become sacred once dedicated to the god; others concern the status of goods purchased by temple officials. Two of those clauses contain fictions, one explicit, the other implicit. As in the bill of Rullus, both clauses in the law of Furfo operate through third-person imperatives and both effect procedural shortcuts.

> (7–10) If something shall be given, donated or dedicated as a gift at this temple, that it be permitted to use or sell [that thing]; when it shall have been sold, let it be profane (*id profanum esto*). The sale or leasing shall be up to the aedile, whomsoever the village of Furfo shall create, so far as they feel that they are willing, without impiety or guilt; no one else shall be able to.
> (12–14) What shall have been bought with bronze or silver, for that money which money shall have been given to this temple, what will have been bought, to those things the same regulation is to apply as if they had been dedicated (*eis rebus eadem lex esto quasei sei dedicatum sit*).[39]

Objects given to or dedicated at a temple became sacred and were henceforth the property of the god to whom the temple was dedicated. As a matter of law, they were placed beyond human ownership and outside the possibility of economic exchange, nor could they be released or sold unless subjected to a rite of desacralization and hence rendered profane. Reading these clauses against that background, we may say that in the first clause, a legal religious fact is asserted to follow even upon the non-performance of the rite of desacralization, though the non-performance of the ritual is itself not cited. Rather, the effect of the rite is created through the operation of legal language alone: *id profanum esto*, "let it be profane." The second clause focuses on goods purchased by the temple and addresses the question of whether they are sacred, like those that are dedicated. Are objects purchased with sacred money themselves sacred? In this case, an imperative attaches to the objects the status consequent upon an explicitly fictional rite of sacralization.

The power of such language to create new legal facts through authoritative utterance alone, in contravention of the realities—the truth?—of the context of utterance,

---

[38] In constitutional terms, what Rullus envisaged, which Cicero elsewhere approved, was the dismantling of constitutional procedures-*cum*-safeguards through the implicit ascription of power to the popular assembly or, if you will, to the People as sovereign to create new constitutional realities by legislative enactment, regardless of earlier practice or even of earlier constraints the People had voted upon itself. For a reading of this text along these lines see Ando (2013).

[39] I adapt the edition and translation of Adamik (2003).

is perhaps most nakedly revealed by another public law text of the Republican period, a vow taken by the Roman people in 217 BCE. The text of the vow is quoted by Livy, an historian writing some 200 years later. I quote only the first few sentences:

> Let him who performs the sacrifice do so whenever he wants, by whatever rite; however he shall do it, let it be considered to have been done properly (*quo modo faxit, probe factum esto*). If something intended for sacrifice should die, let it be held profane and let it be understood that no crime has taken place (*Si id moritur quod fieri oportebit, profanum esto, neque scelus esto*). If someone should steal <something intended for sacrifice>, let no blame attach to the people nor to the person from whom it was stolen. If he should unwittingly perform the sacrifice on an inappropriate day, let the sacrifice be considered to have been done properly (*Si atro die faxit insciens, probe factum esto*). If by night or day, if slave or free should perform the sacrifice, let it be held to have been done properly. If the sacrifice shall be performed on the day before the Senate and People order it to be performed, let the people be held free and absolved from it.[40]

The vow is unusual in respect to other legal texts that employ such performatives only in nakedly stating the reality that it supersedes. The protases systematically enumerate conditions that would normally vitiate the performance; the third-person imperatives just as systematically declare in advance the performance to be successful, in potential contrafaction of the reality of that performance.

14.4.2 Prorogation[41]

The word prorogation, like its Latin ancestor *prorogatio*, is often defined as a prolonging or extension of a term of office, nor are such definitions wholly inaccurate.[42] But the term does not mean prolongation or extension: through considerable compression, it means something like, "investiture with the powers of a magistracy that one has already held, without the mechanics of election," or, in brief, "in place of an election."[43] In other words, the modern notion of the word's meaning is that which it acquired at the end of a long period of development, during which time a fiction of investiture was naturalized and its status as fiction lost. As with Cicero's reading of Rullus's bill, we possess in this case a record (in this case, a fragile one) of public denouncement of prorogation precisely for its reliance on fiction, which

[40] Livy 22.10.2-6 = Walters and Conway (1929, ad loc.). This text was the object of an extraordinary article by the historian of religion Arthur Darby Nock (1939), which is reprinted with introduction and translations of all Greek and Latin texts in Ando (2003, pp. 84–97).

[41] The material below adapts arguments first made in Ando (2013, pp. 922–924). Those pages were in turn inspired by Richardson (1995, pp. 122–123).

[42] *OLD* s.v.; Lewis and Short (1879, s.v.).

[43] As a related matter, grants of honorific titles or honorary membership in corporate bodies usually declare only the fact of the grant, but occasionally the logic is spelled out. See, e.g., a decree of the city council of Veii from 26 CE: Gaius Julius Gelon "should be considered [to be] among the number of the Augustales exactly as if he had held that honor …" (Dessau (1906, pp. 624–625), text no. 6579). On such grants see Melchor Gil and Rodríguez Neila (2012).

helps to cast light both on its status and provokes the search for evidence of what we might term, on analogy with metaphor, its naturalization.

According to Roman sources of the age of Augustus, the first prorogation of a magistracy took place in 327 BCE. According to Livy's narrative, the consul of that year, Quintus Publilius Philo, was on the cusp of a military victory when his term of office expired. Livy describes a tribune bringing a bill before the people to the effect that "when Quintus Publilius Philo should depart the consulate, he should conduct matters as if he were consul (*pro consule*) until the war with the Greeks should be successfully ended."[44] And not unexpectedly, the historian Livy's Augustan narrative finds confirmation in the Augustan *Fasti triumphales*, a chronological list of the award of triumphal parades to successful commanders, compiled (and almost certainly in part invented) during the reign of Augustus.[45]

I translate the Latin phrase *pro consule* with the English phrase "as if he were consul," rather than with some such language as "in the place of a consul," in order to highlight the operation of fiction in the constitutional manoeuvre.[46] But in other contexts, a translation that draws out the use of *pro* to indicate substitution or equivalence or both would do nearly as well. Indeed, some dictionaries written later in antiquity explain the term *proconsul* as a person who operates *vice/vicem consulis*, "in lieu of a consul." (*Vice/vicem* becomes a term of art in analogical modeling in jurisprudential argument, used to indicate the variable amidst a structure that otherwise transfers from one domain to another.[47])

To justify the claim that fiction is essential to the invention and institutionalization of prorogation, and hence to justify the translation "as if he were consul," one might cite two kinds of evidence. First, according to Livy, it remained possible as late as 187 BCE for newly elected magistrates to complain that they were being assigned duties in impoverished and unimportant areas while others (i.e., those operating *pro consule*), exercising power as though they were magistrates, conducted affairs in the eastern Mediterranean as private individuals.[48] The term *privati*, which I translate as private individuals, was intended to highlight the "truth" of the matter, at least as the dissent saw it, which was that the legislation that authorized prorogation was not sufficient to grant those individuals magisterial power. We are returned to the world of Cicero and Rullus.

---

[44] Livy 8.23.10-12 = Walters and Conway (1919, p. 180), on which passage see Oakley (1998, pp. 658–661). See also Livy 10.22.9 = Walters and Conway (1919, p. 340).

[45] *Fasti triumphales capitolini* year 326 B.C.E. = A.U.C. 428 = Degrassi (1947, pp. 70–71).

[46] For another case in which ancient sources draw an equivalence between the use of *pro* to strike an equivalence and a more explicitly fictional operand see n. 69.

[47] Cf. Isidore, *Etymologiae* 9.3.8 = Lindsay (1911, p. 363): *Proconsules suffecti erant consulibus, et dicti proconsules eo quod vicem consulis fungerentur, sicut procurator curatori, id est actori*, which is translated in Barney et al. (2006, p. 200) as follows: "Proconsuls were substitutes for consuls, and were called proconsuls because they would function in the place of consuls, as a procurator does in the place of curator, that is, an agent."

[48] Livy 38.42.8-10 = Walsh (1999, p. 184); the crucial contrast is drawn in the last sentence: *Si exercitus in his terris esse placeat, consules iis potius quam priuatos praeesse oportere.*

The second body of evidence that we might cite to justify a translation that highlights the operation of fiction behind *pro*-rogation is as follows. On current evidence the term *proconsul* doesn't replace the legally precise *pro consule* ("in the place of a consul") until the fall of the Republic.[49] Details to one side, the first incontrovertible instance known to me at present is the decree of an Augustan legate of 27 BCE.[50]

In other words, if we take the formation of a noun *proconsul* from the phrase *pro consule* as an index for the effacement of the fiction that the latter expresses, the naturalization or routinization of prorogation—of the investing of private individuals with the power of magistracy without the formality of an election—took almost exactly 300 years, and it finally occurred in precisely the year in which the emperor Augustus first attempted to formalize and stabilize the holding of monarchic power *qua* aggregation of magisterial powers in a notionally democratic republic.

14.4.3 Analogy, Equivalence and Substitution

Prorogation served to create individuals with the powers of magistrates although they were not such, who then served alongside individuals who had actually been elected and invested with magisterial power through proper procedure. In this way, prorogation proved an enormously useful instrument in the reduplication of institutional structures across an ever-expanding empire, without the necessity of constitutional innovation.[51] The same linguistic operation was employed regularly outside the law of magistracies to extend the reach of the law to persons, things and actions outside some normative taxonomy: it thus urged that extraneous things be treated in the same way as properly recognized ones. It might also be invoked to justify the substitution of some non-regulation item for a proper one. In a number of cases it is clear that substitution was useful because it allowed legislation drafted at Rome to give normative description to social, material and ecological realities in a vast and heterogeneous empire.

For example, the second-oldest Roman statute for which we have access to a significant portion of its actual wording is a law regulating lands owned by the Roman people in Italy and in varied provincial contexts. In its clauses dealing with Italy, it employs a third-person imperative to establish an absolute equivalence in procedure between aliens and Roman citizens: the magistrate hearing the case is to grant trial and appoint a judge in a case involving aliens "just as it were appropriate to grant trial ... if anyone were demanding trial concerning that matter who was a Roman citizen ..." (*ita utei ... sei*).[52] It likewise offers a taxonomy of civic settlements

[49] *TLL* s.v. "proconsul" = vol. 10, fasc. 2 (1998), p. 1542 line 17—p. 1545 line 58 (Hadjú).

[50] Sherk (1969), document no. 61, line 12, a governor's edict from 27 BCE inscribed at Cyme: *Vinicius proconsul salutem dat magistratibus Cumas.* Regarding the late Republican evidence that I here set aside see Ando (2013, pp. 922–924).

[51] For a study of Roman institutions along these lines see Ando, *Roman Social Imaginaries*, Chap. 2.

[52] *Lex agraria* (*RS* 2) ll. 29–31, on which see Ando (2011b, pp. 119–120).

that includes "colonies and municipalities and any equivalents of municipalities or colonies" (*seive quae pro moinicipieis colon[ieisve*) and, in regard to provincial contexts, it refers to "each colonist and each person who was enrolled among the number of colonists" (*quoi colono eive quei in colonei numero scriptus est*).[53] It remains entirely mysterious what settlements these were that were not colonies or municipalities but were to be treated as if they were, or who might have resided officially among the number of colonists in Roman colonies in North Africa and yet not been a colonist. This is of course merely an index of the fiction's success, intended as it was to erase the non-normative particularity of the objects in question and instead assimilate them to justiciable categories within some overall taxonomy. It is worth observing, too, that three quite distinct linguistic operations are used to establish the relation of analogy or extend the reach of the normative taxonomy, despite their shared status as fictions.[54]

A similar move is made by Gaius in his remarks on the religious status of provincial land in Roman public law. The language and framework are wholly transparent. The example is interesting because it involved two principles that the Romans desired to uphold but which the situation brought into tension: a desire to respect the particularities of their own law, which distinguished between the status of land in Italy and land elsewhere; and an equally principled desire to display piety before all forms of the divine. The passage in Gaius runs as follows:

> That alone is thought to be sacred, which is consecrated on the authority of the Roman people, either by law or by decree of the Senate. We make things religious in private actions by bearing our dead to particular sites .... But on provincial soil it is generally agreed that the soil cannot be religious, since there ownership rests with the Roman people or with Caesar, while we seem to have only possession or use. Nevertheless, even if it is not religious, it is treated as though it were [or, perhaps, "even if it were not religious, it is treated as religious"] (*utique tamen, etiamsi non sit religiosum, pro religioso habetur*). Similarly, whatever in the provinces is not consecrated on authority of the Roman people is properly not sacred, but it is nevertheless treated *pro sacro*, as if it were (*item quod in prouinciis non ex auctoritate populi Romani consecratum est, proprie sacrum non est, tamen pro sacro habetur*).[55]

---

[53] *Lex agraria* (*RS* 2), ll. 31 and 66.

[54] One might clarify the stakes in such assimilations by examining a case of fraud, to explain which the extant record employs a similar assimilation. According to Valerius Maximus, Gaius Visellius Varro was having an affair with Otacilia, a married woman. Falling ill and fearing death, Varro recorded a false loan to himself from Otacilia in the amount of 300,000. According to the explanation of Valerius Maximus, his was plan was that if he should die, she could claim the sum from his heirs, which he wanted to be *legati genus*, "a kind of legacy" (Valerius Maximus 8.2.2 = Briscoe (1998, pp. 508–509)). Compare the language used by Paul to assimilate a good-faith possessor of land to its owner in respect of their ownership of its fruit, against the specificities of statute: "in all things that pertain to its fruit, [the good-faith possessor] is practically in the place of its owner" (*quia quod ad fructus attinet, loco domini paene est*) (Paulus *Ad Plautium* bk. 7 frag. 1140 = *Dig.* 41.1.48.*pr.*). Many uses of *quasi* should be understood along these lines, on which see Ando, *Roman Social Imaginaries*, Chap. 2.

[55] Gaius *Inst.* 2.5-7a = de Zulueta (1949, pp. 66–67).

At one level, the recourse to fiction is clearly conservative in form. Gaius cites the long-standing distinction in Roman public law between Italian and provincial soil, which requires that provincial land can be neither sacred nor religious. Nor does the text revise or challenge that principle. Rather, it simply assimilates exactly and precisely the efficacy of ritual action on provincial soil to that of ritual action on Italian soil. Nevertheless, it is hard to escape the sense that the principle is being subverted.

That such manoeuvres involved fictions is reiterated in a late text very similar to Gaius, but concerning a substitution rather than equivalence. The remark arises in a late Latin commentary on Vergil's Aeneid, compiled, as it seems, in the first decade of the fifth century CE. It is prompted by an aside in Vergil's text that the unwary reader might interpret as a reference to human sacrifice. The commentator, one Servius, is keen that readers should not think this. He insists that the girl was not truly killed; rather, it only seemed that she had died. He then elaborates:

> THE MAIDEN KILLED: not truly, but in seeming. Indeed, one should know that in rites the pretend (*simulata*) is taken for the true (*pro veris*): whence, when it is necessary to sacrifice an animal but they are hard to find, the sacrifice is made from bread or wax and these are accepted in the place of the true (*pro veris*).[56]

Servius attests a recognition, if not an anxiety, that the cognitive work of assimilation, and the material work of substitution, are nominalist fantasy: you can call it an animal, and you can pretend it's an animal, but that doesn't make a wax figurine of a cow, a cow. Whence derived the power, and how did one justify, treating the simulated as true?

14.4.4 Legal Facts and Social Reality

The language used by Servius echoes a famous obiter dictum of the jurist Ulpian (d. 223 CE), preserved in the final chapter of the Digest, which serves as a dumping ground for famous such expressions, gathered under the title "Diverse rules of ancient law":

> *Res iudicata pro veritate accipitur.*
> A legal judgment is accepted in the place of truth.[57]

Taken on its own, the "rule" appears to take the performative or constructivist power of legal language to an ideological extreme. But thanks to the work of Otto Lenel, who attempted to reconstitute the works from which the Digest was excerpted, it is possible to read this sentence in something very much like the context in which it appeared. Ulpian wrote the dictum while considering the possibility of an erroneous legal judgment in a suit for freedom. What if a slave or freedman sues for the status of a freeborn person and, for whatever reason, he is judged freeborn although he was not? And what if this occurred through the suborning of false testimony? Ulpian appears immediately to have moved on to a related problem, to wit, the

[56] Servius *ad Aen.* 2.116 = Thilo and Hagen (1881, p. 238).

[57] *Dig.* 50.17.207.

ramifications of such a change in status, amounting as it did to a re-writing of one's life history. What if a freedman, having legally obtained the status of a freeborn person, wants nevertheless to advertise his patronal relationship to his former master?

> We must accept as freeborn someone concerning whom there is a judgment to that effect, even if he was born a freedman: for legal decisions are accepted in the place of truth.
> If a freedman has through collusion been pronounced of free birth and the collusion is discovered, from that time he begins to be a quasi freedman in all respects (*quasi libertinus incipit esse*). Nonetheless, in the intervening time after the judgment for free birth and before discovery of the collusion, he is certainly taken as quasi freeborn (*quasi ingenuus accipitur*). If a freedman has sought and obtained the right to rings, although he has acquired the rights of free birth—his patron's rights being protected—nonetheless he is understood as a freeborn person (*intelligitur*): so the divine Hadrian ruled by rescript.[58]

Read in context, Ulpian's rule emerges as the solution to an epistemic and ontological conundrum. It was always possible for courts to issue decisions based on error or fraudulent information. In the case in question, a court might well create someone in a new legal status when it believed it was doing no more than restoring him to the status he should have held. A discrepancy would then yawn between the new legal fact created by the decision and the reality on which it had rendered judgment and about which its knowledge had been imperfect. Sudden revelations in a given case notwithstanding, the possibility of such a discrepancy cannot ever be eliminated, nor doubts about how wide it might yawn from case to case be wholly allayed. That being the case, and given the possibility that a court could correct the error, Ulpian urges that social order can only be sustained by honoring the knowledge produced by those institutions empowered to adjudicate its facts.

That said, the same conundrum leads Ulpian in the second paragraph to shy from the ontological implications of his constructivism. *Of course* after the suborning of false testimony is discovered, the individual's status as free-born is ontologically problematic, but prior to a court decision affirming his new (old) status, he must remain as he was first said by the court to be: free-born. But Ulpian's indignation will not permit this, nor will his rectitude allow him to pre-empt the court. *Quasi libertinus* is the best he can do. More curious is Ulpian's second conclusion regarding this case ("in the intervening time …"): surely it would be in keeping with the dictum *res iudicata ... accipitur* that the man begin to be free-born, which is to say, conduct himself and be taken in society to have been free-born, immediately upon a judgment to that effect. How not so, before the false testimony is even discovered? Forced to choose between legal judgment and truth, and committed to a set of terms that would render that choice naked, Ulpian attempts to split the difference: the man exists as *quasi ingenuus*.

Ulpian leaves unresolved and indeed unarticulated a further and more complicated problem. Do *res iudicatae*, matters adjudged, possess their own truth, or do they acquire truth through the power of legal institutions to shape the world in which they intervene? In extant Roman literature, the question what is the power of law as a system of language to make social facts out of legal ones is taken up most

[58] Ulpian *Lex Iulia et Papia* bk. 1 frag. 1978 Lenel = *Dig.* 1.5.25 (also, in part, 50.17.207) & *Dig.* 40.16.4 & *Dig.* 40.10.6.

explicitly by Gaius, in a passage not on fiction but theft. Roman law recognized multiple degrees of theft. (There was in fact disagreement among jurists just how many degrees there were.) A statute established that refusing to allow one's property to be searched for stolen goods rendered one liable for the action against manifest theft, the most serious degree. Such refusal was taken very seriously: merely being caught with stolen goods made one liable for a lesser degree of theft. According to Gaius, the fact that one could be made liable for a charge of manifest theft on grounds other than having committed such theft caused some writers to say that a given act of theft could be manifest *aut lege aut natura*, "either by statute or in reality."[59] But was this in fact true? Was manifest theft a particular form of theft, or could any act of theft be not merely classified as, but in fact transformed into manifest theft through statutory language? Gaius denounced the question:

> The truer answer is that manifest theft is understood as such in reality. For statute can no more bring it about that a non-manifest thief is a manifest one than it can make someone who is altogether not a thief into a thief, or someone who is not an adulterer or a homicide into an adulterer or a homicide. Rather, what law can do is simply this, it can make someone liable to punishment exactly as if he had committed theft or adultery or homicide (*proinde ... atque si*), although he had committed none of those things.[60]

Gaius frames the choice more starkly than does Ulpian in his musings on the would-be free-born freedman: the manifest thief created by the law is not a *quasi* manifest thief, indeed, he is possibly not a thief at all. Where Ulpian's *quasi* operates to flag doubt about the fit between his language and the world it describes, Gaius openly employs a contrafactual ("as if he had"). Again, unlike Ulpian's example, wherein an error at law might 1 day be corrected, Gaius, and indeed Ulpian, at least in his dictum, seem to know that the gap between *res iudicatae* and "truth," even truth in *natura*, is not constant. In bringing it about that the untrue bears the same consequence as the true, the law's descriptions bring a new world into being and so re-write even the past. After all, "free-born" and "freed" are not simply legal statuses. They are perfective participles, and in applying one or another to a specific situation, the past that created the present is likewise rewritten. A freeborn ex-slave was no slave at all, his patron was never his master, his slave parents were perforce free.

14.5 Life Histories[61]

The distinct interests shown by Ulpian and Gaius into the varied lives that Romans lived in the law and in the world the law sought both to describe and regulate returns us to a problem raised earlier in this chapter, concerning the tendency of Roman jurists to explore and explain the operation of legal fictions by constructing fictional narratives that turn on the choice presented by the legal operation and the reality

[59] The use of the term *natura*, "nature," to mean "reality" or even "social reality" is the subject of an extraordinary essay by Yan Thomas (1991), closely related to his work on fiction.

[60] Gaius *Inst.* 3.194 = de Zulueta (1946, pp. 216–217).

[61] This section reproduces with some alteration material in Ando (2011b, pp. 11–14).

that it calqued. Let me summarize two networks of fictions in which seemingly rigid distinctions in the juridical status of persons were regularly and systematically reimagined before the law.[62]

Bracketing the granting of citizenship to freeborn aliens, there were two common circumstances in which individuals passed in and out of the Roman citizen body: slaves appropriately freed by Roman citizen owners themselves became citizens, and Roman citizens lost their citizenship when captured in war. Each of these acts had legal consequences for the social and economic relationships the parties had had with others in the Roman community prior to the change in status. Controlling, and in some cases subverting or denying, those changes motivated bravura acts of imagination on the part of the jurists. In order to make clear the stakes in those acts, it will be necessary to lay out some background information on slavery and testamentary succession in the Roman world.

Rome was a slave society, but in many respects a peculiar one. Among other things, manumission was extremely common, and *liberti*, freedmen, who were manumitted by one of several formal processes received Roman citizenship. Their citizen rights were, however, prejudiced in several respects. Most importantly for my purpose here, they continued to owe various duties to their former owners, now styled their "patrons." Among those were *obsequium*, respect; *operae*, "works," meaning regular or periodic labor; and their savings. For freedmen could not have heirs; they had to leave their estates to their patrons *manumissionis iure*, by law of manumission.[63] (Patronal rights were passed along the patron's agnatic line, but the duties on the part of the freedman were not so passed to his descendants.)

Slaves freed informally did not receive citizenship, or any civil law rights. Indeed, at civil law such freedmen remained slaves. But in a gesture typical of praetorian law's role "to aid, supplement or correct *ius civile*,"[64] and typical also of the respect accorded each other by the different sources of law, it became regular in the late Republic for informally-manumitted freedman "to be protected in a framework of freedom by the aid of the praetor."[65] (Given the acknowledgment that such freedmen remained slaves at law, the notion of a framework of freedom, *forma libertatis*, is obviously itself a kind of fiction.)

The emperor Augustus seems to have thought the rate of manumission at Rome too high—or, rather, he seems to have felt too great a percentage of the free population to be of servile extraction—and his reign saw the passage of two statutes regulating manumission, the more important of which, the *lex Aelia Sentia* of 4 C.E., imposed very substantial restrictions on manumission, of many kinds.[66] But his reign (or that of his adopted son, Tiberius [reigned 14–37 CE]) also saw the formalization

---

[62] These acts of imagination should be read in light of Simon Stern's Chap. 8: (this volume) they should perhaps be taken as a riposte to any easy assumption that legal fictions always foreclose the generative effects that analogy or simile promote (to paraphrase Stern).

[63] Gaius *Inst.* 3.56, 3.58 =de Zulueta (1946, pp. 166–169). On Roman law of slavery see Buckland (1908).

[64] Papinian *Definitiones* bk. 2 frag. 46 Lenel = *Dig.* 1.1.7.1.

[65] Gaius *Inst.* 3.56.

[66] For extra-legal evidence for Augustus's worries regarding the purity of the citizen body see Cassius Dio 56.33.1-3 = Cary (1924, pp. 72–75), on which see Swan (2004, pp. 316–317), though

of the protection that the praetor had previously extended on an informal basis to improperly freed slaves. For by a *lex Iunia* it was provided that henceforth informally manumitted slaves (except those known to have committed violent crimes) should become "Latin." What does that mean, and what consequences did it have?

In this context, "Latin" was a legal status named for a confederation of cities located near Rome and united by ethnicity and language (the region was Latium; their language was Latin), with which Rome maintained an alliance and which Rome ultimately brought to heel in the late fourth century B.C.E. After that date, according to the treaty that settled the war, the citizens of any one of those cities were forbidden to forge certain types of social and commercial bonds with citizens of any other, but they were permitted to forge such ties with Romans. They therefore existed in a special relationship with the Roman state, and their status came to be regarded in complex ways as intermediate between citizen and alien. In point of fact, it only becomes clear that the composite of rights and obligations created by the treaty of 338 BCE *was* a status, as opposed to a purely contingent agglomeration of rights and obligations, when the Romans began to assign the so-called *ius Latinum* ("Latin right" or "Latin status") to people who were neither ethnically nor juridically Latin. That is to say, the term Latin once had a referent whose ontological status was prior to any grant of *ius Latinum*, but the operation of law wrenched that term from a realist to a nominalist usage, even as it created people as Latin through the actions of government.[67]

Though the text of the *lex Iunia* does not survive, the analysis of it provided by Gaius reveals it to have operated by a double fiction. The first operated to effect the change in status:

> We proceed to consider the estates of [Junian] Latin freedman. In order to make this branch of law clearer, we must call to mind that, as we have said elsewhere, those who are now termed Junian Latins were in earlier times slaves by Quiritary law (i.e., civil law in the strict sense), but that they were maintained in a framework of freedom by the aid of the praetor; and therefore their property used to go to their patrons by law of *peculium*; later, owing to the *lex Iunia*, all who used to be protected in a state of freedom by the praetor came to be free and to be styled Junian Latins: Latins because the law made them free *exactly as if* they were free-born Roman citizens who, by migrating from the city of Rome to Latin colonies, had become colonial Latins; Junian because it was by the *lex Iunia* that they were made free, though not Roman citizens.[68]

The author of the *lex Iunia* seems thus to have declined to emend civil law doctrine on manumission. (He may also be declining to correct the *lex Aelia Sentia*, if, in fact, the *lex Iunia* postdates that law.) That is to say, the *lex Iunia* did not imagine a new, statutory form of manumission to citizen status, nor did he codify in statute the "framework of freedom" previously guaranteed by the praetor. Rather, the law posited a new life history to informally-manumitted slaves: they were *ingenui*, freeborn, and had voluntarily surrendered their citizenship in order to enroll in a Latin

---

I am not so pessimistic about the reliability of this passage as some of those whose views are summarized by Swan.

[67] On Latin as a legal status see Oakley (1998, pp. 538–542, 567–568) and Kremer (2006).

[68] Gaius *Inst.* 3.55-56 = de Zulueta (1946, pp. 166–169).

colony. The legitimacy of the legal system seems to have trumped any concern over the ideological consequences of thus redescribing the prior life of slaves.

Beyond the operation of this fiction lay a further problem. Previously, the property of informally-manumitted freedmen passed upon their death "to their patrons *peculii iure*, by law of *peculium*." A *peculium* was the personal property of a slave, who possessed but did not own it. (The same term embraced the property of children while they remained "in the power" of their father.) The "framework of freedom" by which the praetor protected such freedmen evidently permitted the description and control of their property according to the rules of civil law, by which those freedmen were, in fact, still slaves; and thus owners who manumitted informally did not have to forego the material rewards available to those who manumitted properly.

But Junian Latins were not understood to be ex-slaves, or to have *ever* been slaves, and so did not have *peculium*. As Gaius observes, the author of the law foresaw this difficulty.

> Realizing that as a result of this fiction the estates of deceased Latins would no longer go to their patrons, because of course they would die neither as slaves, whose property would go to their patrons *iure peculii*, nor as freedmen, whose estates would go to their patrons (*manumissionis iure*), the author of the *lex Iunia* therefore deemed it necessary, in order to prevent the benefit given to them from being turned to the injury of their patrons, to provide that their estates should go to their manumitters *exactly as if* the *lex* had not been passed (*proinde ... ac si lex lata non esset*). Hence under the *lex* the estates of Latins go to their manumitters in some fashion by the law of *peculium*.[69]

Here, then, is the second fiction. In order to create an obligation exactly parallel to the law of *peculium*, the *lex Iunia* requires conduct in its aftermath to be carried out in one crucial respect as if it had not passed. The fiction of the law is of its own non-existence.[70] Gaius shies from calling the resulting obligation an operation of *ius peculii*: it occurs, rather, *iure quodammodo peculii*, "in some fashion by the law of *peculium*."[71]

Next, prisoners of war. By long-standing tradition, Roman citizens captured in war lost their citizenship status. (If they returned to Roman territory, they could recover their citizenship by right of *postliminium*, a word whose etymology suggests a meaning like "beyond the threshold.") But the loss of citizenship left the civil law status of their wills, their property and their heirs in question, for non-citizens could not write a valid will. This situation was remedied by a *lex Cornelia* of the late

[69] Gaius 3.56 = de Zulueta (1946, pp. 166–167).

[70] One might compare the arguments elaborated by jurists about invalid or impossible conditions in wills and testaments: these must be regarded as never have been written–*pro non scripto*–for the will to possess validity (see, *exempli gratia*, *Dig.* 28.7.20 or 29.7.2.1). The language of scholarship consolidates elsewhere around fiction: for a codicil to function as a testament, for example, their contents must be regarded *perinde ac si*, exactly as if they had been written in a will (again, *exempli gratia*, see *Dig.* 29.7.2.2; 29.7.14).

[71] Further problems arose when a Junian Latin received Roman citizenship, which he might do by one of several procedures. On this contingency see Gaius *Inst.* 3.72-73 = de Zulueta (1946, pp. 172–175). Note the contortions that produce, and are produced by, the case where "a Roman citizen freedman dies a Latin …".

Republic, perhaps c. 80 B.C.E. That statute provided that the testamentary dispositions of prisoners of war should be treated *perinde ... atque si in civitate decessissent*, "exactly as if they had died in citizenship." (Note that all accounts of the "fiction of the Cornelian Law" do employ past contrafactuals.) *Propter quam fictionem*, "because of that fiction," all civil law enactments regarding testation were held to apply to the wills of those captured in war.[72]

In the case of the *lex Cornelia*, then, live non-citizens are imagined as citizens, albeit dead ones.

Of course, not everyone who died on campaign was *sui iuris*, an independent legal actor. Some were "sons in power," males who remained under the control of their father, who therefore had no right of ownership of property but, like slaves, had a *peculium*, property they controlled only. The jurist Paul, writing in the first decades of the third century C.E., imagined a complex situation regarding just such a son-in-power, who left a codicil behind, with a *fideicommissum*, a trust, asking his father to give the savings of his military pay (his *peculium castrense*) to one Titius:

> A son in power who died while serving in the military charged his father by means of a codicil with a trust, to deliver to Titius his *peculium castrense* after death. It is asked whether the heir (namely, the father) could deduct a quarter. I said that the *lex Falcidia* had been extended by the Divine Pius in respect to trusts even to cases of intestate succession. That said, in the case before us, there was no inheritance, although I would have agreed that, had someone outside the family been named heir, his acceptance would have created an inheritance. As the son in our case remained in the power of his father, the erstwhile legal framework obtained and the property was *peculium*. Nor is this contrary to the fact that the lex Falcidia governs the wills of those who die as prisoners of war, for the fiction of the *lex Cornelia* creates both an inheritance and an heir.[73]

Paul asks the question whether his father can deduct from his son's military savings, left in trust to Titius, "the Falcidian quarter." (A *lex Falcidia* of 40 B.C.E. required that testators leave at least one quarter of their estate to their heirs, and this rule was extended to trusts in the second century C.E.) The answer is simple, according to Paul: in the hypothetical situation, there is no inheritance. The property is *peculium*. That is to say, the son, being a son-in-power, did not as a matter of law own the property, and could therefore not dispose of it.

But Paul is not content with that answer. As he sees it, had the son-in-power instituted an heir outside his family, acceptance by that nominal heir would have created an inheritance. Then, indeed, his father could have withheld the Falcidian quarter, but likewise the son's wish that his property should pass to Titius would have been respected. No matter, says Paul, that the *lex Falcidia* here regulates the will of someone who died as a prisoner of war: "for the *fictio legis Corneliae*, the fiction of the *lex Cornelia* creates both an inheritance and an heir."

Given that, by what justification can we understand the situation to create an obligation upon the father? That is to say, how might we understand the situation—

---

[72] Paul *Ad legem Falcidiam* frag. 921 Lenel = *Dig.* 35.2.1.1. Compare Julian *Digest* bk. 62 frag. 759 Lenel = *Dig.* 28.6.28.

[73] Paul *Quaestiones* bk. 11 frag. 1373 Lenel = *Dig.* 35.2.18.*pr*.

how might it be redescribed using the operations of law and legal language—to permit the son to bequeath, and to require the father to respect the bequest? Paul continues:

> But I also said that I did not doubt but that the charity of the law should also be satisfied, if the father were required to transfer the assets *as if* those of a *paterfamilias* and, being instituted as heir but declining acceptance under the will, he were then sued in respect of legacies on the pattern of the edict.[74]

Paul's answer is to carry the fiction of the son's emancipation to its natural conclusion: if the son is imagined to be *sui iuris* and the father is recipient of his *fideicommissum*, then the father can be imagined as his heir, indeed, most simply as his son. The obligation upon the father to honor his son's *fideicommissum* is thus understood by Paul to be entailed by the fiction of the Cornelian law, and not as a consequence of this peculiar family's peculiar egalitarianism.

The power Paul grants the fiction is remarkable. The desire to respect what he terms *legis beneficium*, the spirit or charity of the law, permits the fiction to trump civil law twice: for the son-in-power died an alien, and absent the fiction could not write a will; and had he died *in civitate*, in citizenship, he had no civil law status to write a will in the first place.

The Junian and Cornelian laws thus transferred individuals across status boundaries of many kinds, and imagined them embedded in networks of legal relations across prior and future life histories whose operations were made to depend on the susceptibility of citizenship, the civil law, and the Roman state itself, to the transgressive work of fiction.

Conclusion

Fictions performed heroic labor in Roman law. In part this came about because of historic change of two kinds. The first change was the creation of a new source of law in the early second century BCE, to wit, the granting to the praetor of not merely the power to hear cases but to create new legal actions. This power was rapidly understood as sufficient to create work-arounds to statute law. Friction of various kinds at the level of procedure and substance between statute and praetorian law was often negotiated by means of operations the Romans deemed fictions but which can to a point be described as analogical: two situations were construed as similar, and a symmetry of consequence was ordered to exist between the two.

The second change driving the use of fictions was the expansion of the empire. The rapid embrasure of new territories demanded the reduplication of institutions of governance, including both magistracy and jurisdiction. Often (though not always), this need was met by fiction: private individuals were invested with magisterial power without the formality of an election, and cases between aliens before

[74] Paul *Quaestiones* bk. 11 frag. 1373 Lenel = *Dig.* 35.2.18.*pr*.

local magistrates on alien soil were conditionally imagined as being lodged between Roman citizens and heard by a Roman magistrate, presiding over the case in the city of Rome.

The fictional nature of these operations is not always superficially apparent. Substitutions were made, equivalences struck and third-person imperatives deployed without being flagged as fictional or marked by contrafactuals. Often enough, however, they can be detected because an ancient commentator provides an interpretive gloss on the lexical apparatus that unpacks the fiction at work in its operation.

These fictions thus constitute a special case of legal change, of the sort so ably described by Maks Del Mar in this volume (see Chap. 11). For one thing, the form of social change that drove legal change was specific to empire. It was not simply expansion of the state, but the ever present need to account for social, economic and ecological realities scarcely imagined in the heyday of Roman legislation and conducted in languages other than its own. And for another, Roman fictions went nearly wholly uncontested. This may have occurred because they were felt to be conservative in intent (as Maine, Fuller and others suggest, which position I have to a point endorsed). It may also have occurred because of some wider endorsement of the constructivist power of legal language, of which the early use of third-person imperatives in the vow of the Sacred Spring and the late reflection of Ulpian on *res iudicatae* are but tips of an iceberg.[75] It is nonetheless tempting to observe that the assimilation of things outside some normative taxonomy to items inside (as Gaius did in respect to sacred and religious land) is conservative in the same way that gay marriage is conservative: the hitherto illicit is hereafter recognized only at the expense of its assimilation to preexisting standards of (hetero)normativity. Understood in these terms, many Roman fictions were acts of power, that governed indigenous realities by re-imagining them in Roman garb.

However intended, fictions also threatened the stability of existing social ontologies. This power is certainly latent in those operations of law whereby social facts of considerable ideological importance, like servile status or descent from slaves, were bracketed or betimes rewritten. And it was occasionally (re)marked, as when Ulpian felt and flagged the insufficiency of some cohomology between legal principle, social principle and normative language, caused not least by an epistemic weakness in the conditions of judgment whose status as structural haunted the Roman (legal) imagination.

That said, the abiding impression left by Roman texts is of a constructivism, or nominalism, if you will, of surpassing power. Consider in closing Cicero's claim in regard to people sentenced to exile who do not leave the city and, in remaining resident, might seem to violate a principle material condition of the ontology of exile: "All criminal and imperious people whom the laws want to be punished with exile are exiles, even if they do not exchange [Roman for alien] soil."[76]

[75] For an argument along these lines see Ando, *Roman Social Imaginaries*, Chap. 3.

[76] Cicero, *Paradoxa Stoicorum* 31 = Rackham (1942, pp. 282–283).

Acknowledgements My thanks to Maksymilian Del Mar and William Twining for the invitation to participate in this project.

Note *Dig.* = Alan Watson, ed., *The Digest of Justinian*, 4 volumes (Philadelphia: University of Pennsylvania Press, 1985). The Digest will be cited by book, chapter, and paragraph number. Lenel = Otto Lenel, *Palingenesia Iuris Civilis* (Leipzig: Tauchnitz, 1889). Fragments from Lenel will be cited by author, book title, and fragment number.

References

Adamik, Tamás. 2003. Temple regulations from Furfo (CIL I² 756). In *Latin vulgaire—latin tardif VI,* eds. Heikki Solin, Martti Leiwo, and Hilla Halla-aho, 77–82. Hildesheim: Olms-Weidmann.

Ando, Clifford, ed. 2003. *Roman religion*. Edinburgh: Edinburgh University Press.

Ando, Clifford. 2011a. Law and the landscape of empire. In *Figures d'empire, fragments de mémoire: Pouvoirs (pratiques et discours, images et représentations), et identités (sociales et religeuses) dans le monde romain impérial (Ier s. av. J.-C.—Ve s. ap. J.C.),* eds. Stéphane Benoist, Anne Daguey-Gagey, and Christine Hoët-van Cauwenberghe, 25–47. Paris: Presses Universitaires de Septentrion.

Ando, Clifford. 2011b. *Law, language and empire in the Roman tradition*. Philadelphia: University of Pennsylvania Press.

Ando, Clifford. 2013. The origins and import of republican constitutionalism. *Cardozo Law Review* 34:917–935.

Ando, Clifford. 2014a. *Exemplum*, analogy and precedent in Roman law. In *Between exemplarity and singularity: Literature, philosophy, law,* eds. Michèle Lowrie and Susanne Lüdemann. New York: Routledge.

Ando, Clifford. 2014b. Pluralism and empire, from Rome to Robert cover. *Critical Analysis of Law* 1:1–22.

Ando, Clifford. In progress. Legal pluralism in practice. In *The Oxford handbook of Roman law and society*, ed. Clifford Ando, Paul du Plessis and Kaius Tuori. Oxford: Oxford University Press.

Ando, Clifford. Forthcoming. *Roman social imaginaries*. Toronto: University of Toronto Press.

Barney, Stephen A., W. J. Lewis, J. A. Beach, and Oliver Berghof. 2006. *The etymologies of Isidore of Seville*. Cambridge: Cambridge University Press. (trans.)

Back-Walter = Hans Beck, and Uwe Walter, eds. 2004. *Die Frühen Römischen Historiker*. 2 vols. Darmstadt: Wissenschaftliche Buchgesellschaft.

Bianchi, Ernesto. 1997. *Fictio iuris: ricerche sulla finzione in diritto romano dal periodo arcaico all'epoca augustea*. Padova: CEDAM.

Birks, Peter. 1986. Fictions ancient and modern. In *The legal mind: Essays for Tony Honoré,* eds. Neil MacCormick and Peter Birks, 83–101. Oxford: Clarendon Press.

Birks, P., A. Rodger, and J. S. Richardson. 1984. Further aspects of the Tabula Contrebiensis. *Journal of Roman Studies* 74:45–73.

Briscoe, John. 1998. *Valeri Maximi Facta et Dicta Memorabilia, Volume II: Libri VII–IX*. Stuttgart: Teubner.

Buckland, W. W. 1908. *The Roman law of slavery. The condition of the slave in private law from Augustus to Justinian*. Cambridge: The University Press.

Cary, Earnest. 1924. *Dio's Roman history. Volume 7: Books LVI–LX*. Cambridge: Harvard University Press.

Clark, Albert. 1909. *M. Tulli Ciceronis Orationes, Volume IV: Pro P. Quinctio ....* Oxford: Clarendon Press.

Cornu Thénard, Nicolas. 2011. *La notion de fait dans la jurisprudence classique. Étude sur les principes de la distinction entre fait et droit*. PhD. thesis, Université de Paris 2. A monographic version of this text will be published in 2014 by Editions de Boccard, Paris.

Cornu Thénard, Nicolas. 2012. Le duel entre fait et droit chez les juristes classiques. In *Carmina iuris. Mélanges en l'honneur de Michel Humbert,* eds. E. Chevreau, D. Kremer, and A. Laquerrière-Lacroix, 191–205. Paris: De Boccard.

Cottier, M., M. H. Crawford, C. V. Crowther, J.-L. Ferrary, B. M. Levick, O. Salomies, and M. Wörrle, eds. 2008. *The customs law of Asia*. Oxford: Oxford University Press.

Degrassi, Attilio, ed. 1947. *Inscriptiones Italiae*. 13 vol. fasc. 1. Rome: La Libreria dello Stato.

Dessau, Hermann. 1906. *Inscriptiones Latinae Selectae*. 2 vol, part 1. Berlin: Weidmann.

Eden, Kathy. 1986. *Poetic and legal fiction in the Aristotelian tradition*. Princeton: Princeton University Press.

Frier, Bruce W. 1985. *The rise of the Roman jurists*. Princeton: Princeton University Press.

Fuller, L. L. 1930/1931. Legal fictions. *Illinois Law Review* 25:363–99, 513–546, 877–910.

Gizewski, Christian. 2003. Curiata lex. In *Brill's new pauly,* eds. Hubert Cancik and Helmuth Schneider, 1014. 3 vols. Leiden: Brill.

González, Julián. 1986. The *lex irnitana*: a new Flavian municipal law. *Journal of Roman Studies* 76:147–243.

Gray, John Chipman. 1909. *The nature and sources of the law*. New York: Columbia University Press.

Greenwood, L. H. G. 1928. *Cicero VII. The verrine orations I.* Cambridge: Harvard University Press.

Hans Kelsen. 2014. On the theory of juridic fictions. With special consideration of Vaihinger's Philosophy of the as-if. In *Legal fictions in theory and practice*, ed. Maksymilian Del Mar and William Twining. Dordrecht: Springer.

Jolowicz, H. F., and Barry Nicholas. 1972. *Historical introduction to the study of Roman Law*. 3rd ed. Cambrige: Cambridge University Press.

Knauer, Nancy J. 2010. Legal fictions and juristic truth. *St. Thomas Law Review* 23:1–51.

Kremer, David. 2006. *Ius Latinum. Le concept de droit latin sous la République et l'Empire. Romanité et modernité du droit*. Paris: de Boccard; Rome: École française de Rome.

Lenel, Otto. 1927. *Das Edictum Perpetuum. Ein Versuch seiner Wiederhestellung*. 3rd ed. Leipzig: Tauchnitz.

Lewis, Charlton T., and Charles Short. 1879. *A new latin dictionary, founded on the translation of Freund's Latin-German Lexikcon edited by E. A. Andrews, LL.D.* New York: Harper & Brothers.

Lindsay, W. M. 1911. *Isidori hispalensis episcopi etymologiarum sive originum libri XX. Tomus I Libros I-X continens*. Oxford: Clarendon Press.

Lobban, Michael. 2014. Legal fictions before the age of reform. In *Legal fictions in theory and practice*, ed. Maksymilian Del Mar and William Twining. Dordrecht: Springer.

Maine, Henry Sumner. 1861. *Ancient law*. London: J.M. Dent & Sons.

Melchor Gil, Enrique, and Juan Francisco, Rodríguez Neila. 2012. La integración real o ficticia en los *ordines decurionum: lecti, cooptati, adlecti* y *ornamentarii*. *Epigraphica* 74:109–171.

Moscovitz, Leib. 2003. Legal fictions in rabbinic law and Roman law: Some comparative observations. In *Rabbinic law and its near eastern context,* ed. Catherine Hezser, 105–132. Tübingen: Mohr Siebeck.

Moscovitz, Leib. 2014. Rabbinic legal fictions. In *Legal fictions in theory and practice*, ed. Maksymilian Del Mar and William Twining. Dordrecht: Springer.

Nock, A. D. 1939. A feature of Roman religion. *Harvard Theological Review* 32:83–96.

Oakley, S. P. 1998. *A commentary on livy books VI–X. Volume II: Books VII and VIII*. Oxford: Clarendon Press.

OLD = Glare, P. G. W., ed. 1982. *Oxford latin dictionary*. Oxford: Clarendon Press.

Quinn, Michael. 2014. Fuller on legal fictions: A benthamic perspective. In *Legal fictions in theory and practice*, ed. Maksymilian Del Mar and William Twining. Dordrecht: Springer.

Rackham, H. 1942. Cicero De Oratore Book III. De Fato. Paradoxa Stoicorum. De Partitione Oratoria. Cambridge: Harvard University Press.
Richardson, J. S. 1983. The Tabula contrebiensis: Roman law in Spain in the early first century B.C. *Journal of Roman Studies* 73:33–41.
Richardson, J. S. 1995. The Roman mind and the power of fiction. In *The passionate intellect: Essays on the transformation of classical traditions presented to Professor I.G. Kidd*, ed. L. Ayres, 117–130. Rutgers University Studies in Classical Humanities 7. New Brunswick: Transaction.
Ross, Alf. 1969. Legal fictions. In *Law, reason, and justice,* ed. Graham Hughes, 217–234. New York: New York University Press.
RS = Crawford, Michael. ed. 1996. *Roman statutes*. 2 vols. London: Institute of Classical Studies.
Russell, Donald A. 2001. *Quintilian: The orator's education*. 2 vol. Books 3–5. Cambridge: Harvard University Press.
Schiller, A. Arthur. 1978. *Roman law. Mechanisms of development*. New York: Mouton.
Sherk, R. K., ed. 1969. *Roman documents from the Greek east: Senatus consulta and Epistulae to the death of Augustus*. Baltimore: John Hopkins.
Stern, Simon. 2014. Legal fictions and exclusionary rules. In *Legal fictions in theory and practice*, ed. Maksymilian Del Mar and William Twining. Dordrecht: Springer.
Stolzenberg, Nomi Maya. 1999. Bentham's theory of fictions. A "Curious double language." *Cardozo Studies in Law and Literature* 11:223–261.
Swan, Peter Michael. 2004. *The Augustan succession. An historical commentary on Cassius Dio's Roman history books 55–56 (9 BC—AD 14)*. Oxford: Oxford University Press.
Thilo, Georg, and Hermann Hagen, eds. 1881. *Servii Grammatici qui feruntur in Vergilii carmina commentarii, Volume 1: Aeneidos Librorum I-V commentarii*. Leipzig: Teubner.
Thomas, Yan. 1991. Imago naturae. L'institution de la nature. In *Théologie et droit dans la formation de l'Etat moderne*, 241–278. Rome: École Française de Rome.
Thomas, Yan. 1995. *Fictio legis. L'empire de la fiction romaine*, 17–63. 21 vol. *Droits: revue française de théorie juridique*.
Thomas, Yan. 1996. *"Origine" et "commune patrie." Étude de droit public romain (89 av. J.-C.—212 ap. J.C.)*. Rome: École Française de Rome.
TLL = *Thesaurus Linguae Latinae*. 1904. Leipzig: Teubner.
Walsh, P. G. 1999. *Titi Livi Ab Urbe Condita. Tomus VI. Libri XXXVI–XL*. Oxford: Clarendon Press.
Walters, Charles Flamstead, and Robert Seymour, Conway, eds. 1919. *Titi Livi Ab Urbe Condite*, Volume 2: *Libri VI–X*. Oxford: Clarendon Press.
Walters, Charles Flamstead, and Robert Seymour, Conway, eds. 1929. *Titi Livi Ab Urbe Condita, Volume 3: Libri XXI–XXV*. Oxford: Clarendon Press.
de Zulueta, Francis. 1946. *The Institutes of Gaius*. 2 vols. Oxford: Clarendon Press.

Chapter 15
Rabbinic Legal Fictions

Leib Moscovitz

Abstract Rabbinic literature, the product of the great centers of Jewish learning in Palestine and Babylonia during the first centuries of the common era, contains numerous legal fictions. These fictions are attested in all periods and geographical centers of rabbinic literature, and they address issues of both ritual and civil law, although ritual fictions seem to dominate. In this chapter, I describe the principal characteristics of rabbinic legal fictions, analyze their legal significance, and attempt to account for their origins and development—why they were utilized in the first place, and how later fictions differ from their predecessors. One of the most prominent characteristics of rabbinic legal fictions discussed in this chapter is their frequently scholastic character, which contrasts with the practical use of fictions in other legal systems. Thus, rabbinic fictions often facilitate the theoretical analysis and explanation of the law, rather than aiming to make the law conform with desired legal outcomes. Likewise, rabbinic fictions usually do not account for exceptions to clear-cut, explicit laws of universal applicability. Rather, they emerge in the course of consolidating and generating general rules which are assumed to underlie the law.

15.1 Introduction

15.1.1 Rabbinic Literature—Preliminary Remarks

Rabbinic literature, the product of the great centers of Jewish learning in Palestine and Babylonia during the first centuries of the common era,[1] contains numerous legal fictions.[2] However, before we can analyze these fictions from a legal perspective,

[1] Legal fictions also appear in Jewish legal literature from later periods, but such fictions will not be discussed in this chapter.

[2] The most comprehensive and systematic discussions of legal fictions in rabbinic literature are Atlas (1978), pp. 224–237, 265–294 (which, however, suffers from significant methodological problems, discussed inter alia in the literature cited below); Moscovitz (2002), pp. 163–199;

L. Moscovitz (✉)
Department of Talmud, Bar-Ilan University, Ramat-Gan 52900, Israel
e-mail: leib.moscovitz@gmail.com

M. Del Mar, W. Twining (eds.), *Legal Fictions in Theory and Practice*,
Law and Philosophy Library 110, DOI 10.1007/978-3-319-09232-4_15

a few words are in order about the principal literary works which comprise rabbinic literature, their chronological framework and literary character. As we shall see below, the legal character of rabbinic legal fictions and the way in which they are deployed depend in no small measure on the literary sources in which they appear, and hence some basic familiarity with these sources is necessary before we can analyze these fictions from a legal perspective.

The principal works of rabbinic legal literature derive from two chronological periods. The first period, which is called the tannaitic period, extends over approximately the first two centuries of the common era. During this period a number of legal compendia were produced[3] (in Hebrew). Two especially important works from this period should be noted: the central work of tannaitic law, the Mishnah, and an important but ultimately secondary and less authoritative work, the Tosefta. These compositions contain a wide variety of rulings pertaining to both civil and ritual law (usually extensions or interpretations of biblical law dealing with issues such as the festivals, sacrificial law, or the laws of ritual purity). For the most part the tannaitic compositions cite rulings about particular cases, without giving the reasons for these rulings. Legal analysis and argumentation are thus relatively uncommon in these works, although they are by no means wholly absent from them. And while some of the rulings in these compositions are clearly judge- or court-based decisions regarding particular cases,[4] there is no clear evidence that this is the case with regard to most of the rulings in these works.

The second period of rabbinic law, called the amoraic period,[5] is marked by the production of two massive quasi-commentaries on the Mishnah. These works, which were composed in a mixture of Hebrew and Aramaic, were produced in ancient Palestine, during approximately the third and late fourth centuries CE, and Babylonia, from the third to sixth centuries and apparently later; they are called the Palestinian and Babylonian Talmuds respectively. In contrast to the tannaitic compendia, the amoraic compositions are discursive in nature, with dialectical analysis of the law their principal component. While these works discuss the Mishnah at length—inter alia, they explicate the reasons for Mishnaic rulings (reasons which

Moscovitz (2003); and see also Moscovitz (2013) for a detailed discussion of one particular type of rabbinic fiction. Additional literature dealing with specific rabbinic fictions or aspects of rabbinic fiction is cited below as necessary.

[3] Scholars disagree as to precisely how authoritative and widely accepted these works were, and as to whether and to what extent they were intended as actual legal codes, as opposed to study books (note for example the existence of conflicting opinions and unresolved contradictions in these works). However, these issues are of minimal importance for purposes of the present discussion, which focuses on those aspects of these works which are relevant to the analysis of rabbinic fictions from a legal perspective, rather than a literary or historical perspective.

[4] Many such rulings are explicitly identified as such, usually using the term *ma'aseh* ("an incident/ a case"), followed by the ruling of the rabbi who ruled on the case in question.

[5] Numerous scholars of rabbinic literature add a third period, that of the anonymous stratum of the Babylonian Talmud (*stam* in Hebrew), which in their view postdates the amoraic period. However, for purposes of the present discussion, which focuses, as indicated, on legal aspects of fiction in rabbinic literature, this distinction between amoraic and anonymous material is of limited importance, so I do not give it greater consideration here.

the Mishnah itself is generally silent about)—they also contain a good deal of material unrelated to the Mishnah. Indeed, the Talmuds often seem to engage in legal discussion for its own sake, with minimal if any attempt to determine the actual legal "bottom line." Thus, these works take an essentially academic and scholastic approach to legal analysis rather than a practical approach, and the importance of this point for a proper understanding of rabbinic legal fictions will become clear below.

Two important corollaries of the preceding remarks should be noted here. First, since this chapter discusses a legal system whose literary sources are more than a thousand years old, the orientation of this chapter is descriptive: we seek to describe how and why legal fictions were used in rabbinic law, but not to draw any practical or ideological conclusions therefrom. Second, the fictions in rabbinic literature are almost invariably not judge-based fictions (legislative fictions). And while it is not fully clear what legal or historical significance this point has, if any, it should certainly be noted, in light of the fact that rabbinic fictions differ in this respect from the fictions in many other legal systems.

15.1.2 Definition of Legal Fictions

For purposes of the present discussion, we define legal fiction as the assertion[6] for legal purposes of "facts" which are clearly untrue.[7] This definition accordingly excludes legal presumptions,[8] since the facts which they presume are not clearly or necessarily untrue, as well as legal loopholes or subterfuges ("dodges"), since these are not assertions, but rather techniques for circumventing existing laws.[9] And while phenomena of this sort do occur in rabbinic literature, they will not be discussed here, since they do not qualify as legal fictions according to our definition.[10]

[6] For the possibility of implicit fictions, viz., rulings which were based, albeit not explicitly, on the adoption of a fictional perspective, see below, Sect. 2.4. One interesting and somewhat borderline case ought to be briefly mentioned here: the notion that "there is retrospective determination of reality" (*yesh bererah*; see Moscovitz (2002), pp. 171–172). This principle is somewhat reminiscent of the common law doctrine of relation, on which see Lobban, this volume, Chap. 10, p. 205. However, it is difficult to conclusively define either of these notions as a fiction; see the discussions of Moscovitz and Lobban, ibid.

[7] This definition excludes what I have elsewhere termed referential classification, and what other scholars of legal fiction have termed analogous application/extension of legal rules or Gleichsetzung. For a more detailed discussion of such phenomena in rabbinic law, with (somewhat complex) examples, see Moscovitz (2002), pp. 164–167.

[8] See especially Schauer, this volume, Chap. 6. To be sure, such phenomena are sometimes deemed legal fictions by scholars of rabbinics; see e.g. Hayes (2004), pp. 135–137, 143–147, and Novick (2009), especially pp. 11–12. (Precisely how problematic classifying presumptions as fictions can be emerges from formulations such as Novick (2010), p. 48, who discusses "legal presumptions … that, in their improbability, *border on the fictional*" [emphasis added].)

[9] Such phenomena, too, are sometimes deemed legal fictions by scholars of rabbinics; see e.g. Ancselovits (2011) and the literature cited there, p. 3 n. 2.

[10] While an analysis of such phenomena as legal presumptions, dodges and the like in rabbinic literature is unquestionably a worthy endeavor, such discussion would distract us from investigation

15.1.3 The Principal Questions

Various questions arise in connection with legal fictions in rabbinic literature. How are fictional statements formulated in rabbinic literature, and what functions do these statements serve? Are fictions used with greater frequency in connection with particular areas of rabbinic law? When fictions are used to explain legal rulings, how tenable (or necessary) are these fictional explanations, hermeneutically speaking? What justification was there, according to the rabbinic sources, for claiming that the facts should be treated for legal purposes in a manner different from reality? Finally, to what extent are fictions used as a tool for legal or historical change and/or for furthering desired legal results, which presumably could not be achieved without outright alteration or reformulation of the law?[11]

15.2 Tannaitic Fictions

15.2.1 Introduction

Scores of legal fictions are found in tannaitic literature. These fictions are generally used in the course of formulating the law—frequently, laws regarding issues which are not discussed in other sources. Thus, such fictions, unlike those in many other legal systems, are not used to justify deviation from existing laws and they presumably do not reflect historical development. Nevertheless, we sometimes find tannaitic fictions which are used to explain existing rulings rather than to formulate new ones, or which reflect deviation (not necessarily historical development) from apparent "base laws."

Tannaitic fictions usually deal with specific cases, and thus are not formulated as general rules.[12] Such fictions generally address ritual matters rather than issues of civil law.[13] Accordingly, the fictions adduced below derive primarily from the realm of ritual law, and hence may seem somewhat esoteric.

---

of the "hard core" fictions which form the focus of this chapter, and indeed would add relatively little of substance to such an analysis.

[11] As indicated above, the focus of this chapter is essentially descriptive. Accordingly, comparisons with fictions from other legal systems have been kept to a minimum, and such comparisons have generally only been adduced where important for a proper understanding of rabbinic fictions per se.

[12] This may account for the fact that tannaitic fictions are ordinarily not applied to multiple cases, in contrast to certain post-tannaitic fictions; see below, Sect. 3.6.

[13] Why this is the case is not fully clear, but see below, n. 36.

15.2.2 Terminology

Tannaitic fictions are usually introduced by the expression "we view [or: treat, consider] X ... as if ..." and minor variants; note that similar expressions are used to formulate fictions in Roman law.[14] Indeed, this expression seems to be used exclusively in tannaitic literature for introducing legal fictions, and later we shall consider the significance of this usage at greater length.[15]

15.2.3 Types of Tannaitic Fictions

Several main types of fictions are found in tannaitic literature. The first of these is what might be termed assessive fiction. For example, M. Zevahim 8:6:[16]

> (a) If [sacrificial] blood was mixed with water and [the mixture] looks like blood, it is acceptable [for sprinkling on the altar]. (b) If [sacrificial blood] was mixed with [red] wine [which looks like blood], *we consider [the wine] as if it were water.*

According to (a), diluted sacrificial blood is acceptable for ritual sprinkling provided that the mixture looks like blood—presumably, because the blood in the mixture is not nullified by the water there. However, this "visibility criterion" for defining what constitutes legally acceptable sacrificial blood is not applicable if the blood was mixed with another red liquid, such as wine. Hence the Mishnah prescribes a fiction—"we consider the wine as if it were water"—to determine whether or not the blood in this mixture is nullified by the wine.

Several observations are in order about this fiction (and other tannaitic fictions like it).[17] The justification for this ruling is obvious: since the visibility criterion is not relevant here, an alternative criterion (based on the relative quantities of the components of the mixture) had to be used. Note that this fiction clarifies the relevant legal requirement *ab initio*, but it does not reflect deviation from any known and presumably universally applicable base law. Thus, the use of fictional formulation here serves as a technique for clearly and concisely formulating the relevant law, but it does not reflect the adoption of an innovative legal perspective about reality or the need to achieve a desired legal outcome.

Other tannaitic fictions are *neglective*, as they instruct us to disregard particular facts or objects as irrelevant or treat them as nonexistent for legal purposes. For example, T. Menahot 11:14:

---

[14] See Moscovitz (2003 p. 115), with references to additional literature.

[15] See below, Sect. 3.2.

[16] All translations of rabbinic sources in this chapter are mine, and they are based on the text of these sources according to the standard critical editions or manuscripts. Due to the frequently laconic style of the rabbinic writings, I have supplied additional explanatory material in square brackets where necessary. The following abbreviations are used below to cite rabbinic sources: M. = Mishnah, T. = Tosefta, B. = Babylonian Talmud, P. = Palestinian Talmud.

[17] See e.g. M. Shevi'it 1:3; T. Terumot 9:2; T. Mikva'ot 7:4.

> (a) The [Temple] showbread is arranged by setting six loaves in [the first] row and six loaves in the [second] row … (b) If one arranged two rows of fourteen [loaves], Rabbi says: *We consider the upper [loaves] as if they do not exist,* and the lower ones are acceptable.

The fictional formulation here—Rabbi's statement in (b)—instructs us to disregard the upper loaves and treat them as nonexistent. As in the previous example, the use of a fiction here was presumably not motivated by the need to achieve a desired legal goal. Rather, this seems to be a felicitous way to formulate the relevant legal requirement *ab initio*, viz., that at least two rows of six loaves of showbread are necessary, but not exactly two rows of six loaves. As with the previous example, this fiction entails no deviation from any existing base law, and the fiction does not seem to reflect an innovative legal perspective on the relevant facts in light of unique attributes which these facts might possess; it simply instructs us to disregard certain aspects of reality as irrelevant for legal purposes.[18] Indeed, Rabbi's ruling in (b) could just as well have been formulated without a fiction: "If there were two rows of fourteen loaves, the bottom ones are acceptable." Here too, then, the use of a fictional formulation (as opposed to simply presenting the relevant legal "bottom line," viz., that the lower loaves are acceptable) presumably reflects stylistic rather than legal or conceptual considerations.

Other tannaitic fictions, however, do seem to reflect legal considerations, rather than serving as an elegant way to formulate the law in question. Indeed, some of these fictions instruct us to alter reality for legal purposes, and not just to disregard particular aspects of reality. For example, T. Eruvin 1:1, 5:

> (a) If an alley was more than 20 cubits high, one must … put a beam on top of it [to permit carrying there on the Sabbath]… (b) If one [beam] was on top and another below, R. Jose b. Judah says: We consider the bottom [beam] as if it rises and the top [beam] as if it descends, [so they join fictionally to form a single beam].

The beginning of this passage (a) states that a beam over an alley permits carrying there on the Sabbath. Judging from how this ruling is formulated, however, it would seem that it would not apply to a pair of noncontiguous beams, since this statement speaks solely of "a beam," without mentioning the acceptability of other, similar structures. Hence a fiction was invoked in (b) to enable a pair of noncontiguous beams to join, thereby forming a single, legally acceptable but ultimately fictional beam.

What legal justification is there for this fiction? We cannot say for certain, although it stands to reason that the law here was conceived of from the outset in geometrical terms rather than physical terms: for legal purposes, a "beam" need not be a single, solid, contiguous object. Rather, even a combination of beams whose joint projection outlines a single beam is acceptable. Such reasoning makes particularly good sense if the rationale behind the beam requirement was to erect a visibly distinctive structure over the alley (so according to at least one view in the Talmud; see B. Eruvin 12b), for even a geometrically constructed beam could serve this purpose.

---

[18] For additional examples of tannaitic fictions of this sort (sometimes formulated "we consider … as if it does not exist"), see e.g. M. Kilayim 5:2; M. Ahilot 12:3; T. Ahilot 16:2.

In the examples considered above fictions appear in the course of formulating a law *ab initio*. However, on rare occasions tannaitic fictions are used to explain existing laws. For example, T. Ahilot 11:10:

1. If there is an opening between the lower story and the upper story [of a house], and [the opening] is not a handbreadth wide … and there is something impure in the upper story, utensils in the lower story are pure,
2. *because I consider the beams [of the roof of the upper story] as if they had descended and sealed off [the opening].*
3. *Another explanation*: Impurity cannot enter or exit a tent [a horizontal overhanging structure] less than a handbreadth wide.

This passage discusses a case where a corpse was located under the roof of the upper story of a house, and the floor of the upper story has a hole which opens to the lower story. According to rabbinic law, objects under a horizontal overhanging structure (a "tent") become impure if a corpse (or certain parts thereof) was located under this tent, even if these objects did not come into contact with the corpse. Accordingly, one might expect items in the lower story to become impure, since they are located under the "tent" formed by the roof of the upper story. (The floor of the upper story presumably would not interpose between the upper and lower stories, thereby protecting items beneath it from the impurity in the upper story, since this floor contains a hole.)[19] Nevertheless, the Tosefta rules that objects in the lower story are pure (1), and it provides two explanations for this ruling (2 and 3), the first fictional and the second non-fictional. According to the fictional explanation, we imagine the beams on top of the upper story descending to the floor of the upper story and sealing off the hole, whereas the non-fictional explanation asserts that the opening is too small to let corpse impurity enter.

This fiction resembles those in the previous examples in numerous respects. As in the previous examples, this fiction deals with a case of ritual law. The idea that an object fictionally descends, thereby legally restructuring a partition (here, sealing off the hole in the floor of the upper story)—in effect, the mathematical concept of a projection given legal force—is attested in other tannaitic passages as well (e.g. the previous example).[20] Thus, the justification for adopting this fiction might be a unique rabbinic take on legal space, which was defined in geometrical terms rather than physical terms.[21]

Why was a fiction used here, particularly seeing that the relevant legal "bottom line" (viz. that the objects in the lower story are pure) can be justified without resort to a fiction, as we see from the nonfictional explanation in 3? Presumably,

[19] The suggestion advanced here is based essentially on common sense about how tent impurity should operate, since we do not find clear and explicit tannaitic rules about how such impurity spreads; such rules emerge from "between the lines" analysis of the cases treated by these sources.

[20] See also T. Ahilot 9:3–4, and perhaps also M. Ahilot 12:5 and 14:5 (implicit).

[21] Interestingly, a fair number of rabbinic fictions, both tannaitic and post-tannaitic, deal with issues such as legal space, partitions, and the like, perhaps because such issues are readily conceived of in terms of formalistic, legal definitions (and hence geometric or mathematical definitions), rather than literal, physical definitions. Cf. Moscovitz (2002): 172 n. 37 (and see examples throughout the discussion of legal fictions in this work).

the need for such a fiction arose because the ruling in 1 seems to deviate from a common-sense understanding of tent impurity: as indicated above, we might well expect objects in the lower story to become impure, due to the hole in the roof above them. That said, it should be stressed that this ruling entails no clear-cut deviation from any explicit or near-explicit tannaitic base law, and in this respect the fiction discussed here resembles most other tannaitic fictions.

15.2.4 Implicit Fictions

Might some tannaitic rulings which were not formulated or explained fictionally have been based on the implicit adoption of a legal fiction? This possibility emerges in light of the fact that numerous tannaitic rulings which are not explained in the relevant tannaitic sources (fictionally or otherwise) are explained on fictional grounds by the Talmuds. The question accordingly arises: do the fictional explanations offered by the Talmuds in such cases correctly reflect the implicit reasoning underlying the tannaitic rulings?

Due to the complexity of potentially relevant passages, I cannot consider any specific examples here. Suffice it to say, though, that many and perhaps most rulings of this sort can be plausibly explained without resorting to fictions, and thus there is generally no need to assume that tannaitic rulings were based on implicit fictions.[22]

15.2.5 Chronology of Tannaitic Fictions

Many tannaitic fictions cannot be dated with any degree of certainty, since they are not attributed to named scholars.[23] However, those fictions which are attributed to named and hence datable figures stem from all parts of the tannaitic period. Accordingly, the development and use of tannaitic legal fiction cannot convincingly be attributed to any particular part of the tannaitic period, rabbinic figure or circle.

Legal fictions do not seem to be attested in Jewish legal texts before the tannaitic period,[24] even though a fair amount of texts of this nature have survived (the Qumran texts). This might stem from the essentially "realistic" character of the Qumran material, which perceived reality as it was, in contrast to the frequently more abstract and legalistic character of the rabbinic material, which was accordingly

[22] To be sure, there may be some exceptions; see e.g. M. Ahilot 10:3 (R. Jose); ibid. 15:8 (end); M. Mikva'ot 10:5 (see below, text near n. 44).

[23] Tannaitic literature (and similarly its post-tannaitic counterpart) is a collective endeavor which contains the rulings of numerous scholars. Many of these are identified by name, although much of this material is anonymous.

[24] Indeed, even the Hebrew term for "as if" (*ke-illu*), which is frequently used to introduce legal fictions in both tannaitic and post-tannaitic sources, is unattested in pre-rabbinic sources.

more open to adopting legal definitions and conceptions which were not necessarily based on physical reality. Ultimately, though, the precise origins of the rabbis' use of fiction remain unclear.[25]

15.2.6 Relationship with Roman Fictions

The tannaitic period overlaps in large part with the classical period of Roman law,[26] where legal fictions occur frequently.[27] Accordingly, the question arises as to whether there is any connection between the use of fictions in the two systems—and, more specifically, whether the tannaitic use of fictions was in any way influenced by parallel phenomena in Roman law. In fact, however, this seems extremely unlikely.[28] Thus, the two systems hardly share any fictions,[29] and none of the more-or-less common fictions appear in tannaitic sources. Indeed, the possibility of (direct) Roman legal influence on tannaitic law in general seems highly questionable.[30]

15.3 Post-tannaitic Fictions

15.3.1 Introduction

Legal fictions occur frequently in post-tannaitic literature. Such fictions resemble tannaitic fictions in certain respects and differ from them in others, as we shall see in greater detail below.

---

[25] For the possibility that the rabbis' the use of fictions was influenced by Roman law see the next section.

[26] While some Roman fictions are attested well before the tannaitic period, others are contemporary with the tannaitic period.

[27] See most recently Ando (this volume, Chap. 14), with references to earlier literature (n. 1).

[28] That said, the fact that legal fictions in the ancient world seem to be first attested among the Romans and the Jews—"the two most legally minded peoples of antiquity," in Boaz Cohen's famous words (Cohen 1966 vol. 1, p. 124)—might not be coincidental; see further Moscovitz (2003, pp. 131–132) (although the considerations suggested there may apply more to the post-tannaitic period than to the tannaitic period).

[29] This is not surprising, in light of the fact that most rabbinic fictions stem from the realm of ritual law, and the rabbinic rituals were obviously not shared by the Romans. In fact, I am aware of only two more-or-less shared (and, obviously, non-ritual) fictions: the *condicio pro impleta* fiction, according to which a condition whose fulfillment was forcibly prevented by external factors is regarded as if it had been fulfilled, and the fiction that conditions which are physically impossible should be treated as if they had not been written and hence are not binding. See further Moscovitz (2003, pp. 122–125).

[30] The most comprehensive study of this is Jackson (1981), with extensive references to earlier literature, and see also Katzoff (1989).

15.3.2 Stylistic Aspects

The amoraic sources use new terminology, unattested in the tannaitic sources, to formulate fictions. One of these terms, which appears exclusively in the Palestinian Talmud, closely resembles the parallel tannaitic expression: "*you* consider [lit. see]… as if" (Palestinian Talmud), rather than "*we* consider [lit. see]… as if" (tannaitic sources). Indeed, this talmudic phrase, like its tannaitic counterpart, is apparently used exclusively to introduce fictions.

However, two new modes of formulating fictions are found in the Talmuds.[31] The first mode entails the use of various types of comparative terminology. These new terms, in both Hebrew and Aramaic, include such expressions as "it is considered as if," "[the authority cited] treats [case X] as if," "it is as if one had done …," etc. Nevertheless, this new terminology seems to be essentially a stylistic phenomenon, and as such it is presumably devoid of any legal significance.

However, in the Babylonian Talmud we sometimes find fictions which are formulated without comparative terminology, as metaphors rather than similes. These statements do not speak of how we consider, treat, or "see" matters, but (as it were) of how matters really are. Such fictions may be expressed using imperatives, e.g. "extend the partitions upward," "beat and throw down"[32] (describing the fictional extension of a partition or other structure of inadequate size), or indicative verbs in the present tense, with the relevant assertions formulated as ordinary declarative statements (e.g. "its quantity is crushed"[33] [and hence deemed nonexistent], "we hollow out to complete [a space]").[34] The use of these formulations, too, might just be a stylistic phenomenon. However, this new mode of formulating fictions might have legal significance, as it might indicate the adoption of a new perception of reality, and later we shall consider the implications of this possibility at greater length.[35]

15.3.3 Functionalist Fictions

Fictions in other legal systems often seek to advance socioeconomic and other types of functionalist goals (e.g. equity). However, the vast majority of legal fictions in

[31] Perhaps the explanatory function served by most post-tannaitic fictions, in contrast to their generally prescriptive tannaitic counterparts, played some role in the evolution of new terminology. In any event, I tend to doubt that there is any connection between the fact that the tannaitic terminology closely parallels that found in Roman legal sources, which are in large measure contemporaneous with the tannaitic material. This similar phraseology is most likely attributable to coincidence and not to any sort of direct contact or influence between rabbinic law and Roman law.

[32] See B. Eruvin 89a and B. Sukkah 4b for the first fiction and B. Sukkah 22a–b for the second.

[33] See B. Eruvin 80b and parallels. Interestingly, a similar principle is formulated elsewhere using ordinary fictional terminology: "It is as if it had been crushed" (B. Yevamot 103b).

[34] See B. Shabbat 7b and parallels.

[35] This possibility might account (at least in part) for the application of particular fictions to multiple cases from different legal domains; see below, text at n. 59.

rabbinic literature do not seek to further moral, legal or utilitarian goals,[36] or to amend unsatisfactory existing law. Indeed, I can only think of one fairly clearcut (and post-tannaitic) exception[37]—apparently, the exception which proves the rule—and as such it is worth considering this fiction at greater length here. P. Yevamot 10:5, 11a:[38]

> Rav said, If a woman was married [on the testimony] of two [witnesses], even if [the husband] comes, we say: It is not him.[39]

According to rabbinic law, a woman who has relations with a man other than her husband is guilty of adultery, and the children of such a relationship are illegitimate. This applies even if the woman married the second husband because she mistakenly assumed that the first husband had died: since the first husband is still alive, the original marriage remains in effect.[40]

Our passage deals with a case where two witnesses testified that the first husband had died, after which he appeared, thereby decisively disproving their testimony. Presumably, such a woman should be deemed an (unwitting) adulteress and her children from the second relationship illegitimate, since her marriage to the first husband is still in effect. Nevertheless, the Talmud states that when the original husband appears, we deny his identity ("we say: It is not him"), thereby maintaining the legitimacy of the woman's relationship with her second husband and of any offspring of that marriage. And it goes without saying that such a claim is a legal fiction *par excellence*.

---

[36] This might account for the fact that so many rabbinic fictions stem from the realm of ritual law rather than civil or criminal law, although this suggestion remains conjectural. In any event, it is noteworthy that rabbinic fictions are sometimes used to justify stringent rulings (e.g. the fictional explanations of R. Aqiba's ruling in M. Shabbat 11:1, discussed below, in the text after n. 44), whereas functionalist considerations would presumably prompt the adoption of an approach marked by greater leniency.

[37] Theoretically, it might be argued that some rulings which were explained in fictional fashion by post-tannaitic sources were actually based on functionalist considerations. For example, tannaitic rulings which permit building ritual booths for the festival of Tabernacles (see Leviticus 23:42) with defective partitions, which the Talmud fictionally validates on grounds such as "extend the partitions upwards," might be attributed to such considerations as the need to deal with a dearth of building materials. Yet while such a possibility cannot be dismissed out of hand, it ultimately remains unproven (and, to my mind, unlikely). Moreover, even if laws explained fictionally were initially motivated by functionalist considerations, the sages who explained them in fictional fashion might well have considered these fictions to be the correct explanations of the relevant rulings, since there is nothing intrinsically implausible about such explanations (at least from a rabbinic perspective; see also below, Sect. 3.7).

[38] Cf. also the parallel ibid., 15:5, 15a (and see below, n. 41).

[39] A similar ruling, attributed to the same sage, is found in the Babylonian Talmud (B. Yevamot 88a), although there this ruling appears without any explanation (but see the Talmud's discussion further on) and without use of a fiction: "Rav said, This only applies where [the woman] was married with one witness, but with two witnesses she need not leave [the husband]." See further Friedman (1977): pp. 331–333; Hayes (2004): pp. 137–143; Hayes (2006): pp. 134–137.

[40] In rabbinic law marriages cannot be terminated by the disappearance of a husband, regardless of how long he was missing, but only by his actual death.

The motivation behind this fiction seems clear: the sages wanted to save the woman and her children from the tragic consequences of adultery, especially since the adultery here had been committed unwittingly. However, the actual legal justification for this ruling remains unclear,[41] and it seems extremely problematic. (Indeed, both the Palestinian and Babylonian Talmuds record objections to this ruling, to the point where the Babylonian Talmud actually reformulates this statement in toto, thereby reconstructing it out of existence![42]) To be sure, it might be argued that a court decision based on the testimony of two witnesses is legally constitutive, so the woman's status after reappearance of the original husband is a function of the law (viz., was the court's ruling based on legally valid testimony) rather than the facts (viz., whether or not the original husband is still alive).[43] But in the final analysis this suggestion remains speculative, and our initial uncertainty about the legal basis of the fictional ruling here remains.

15.3.4 Hermeneutic Character

Post-tannaitic fictions are generally used to explain earlier rulings—often, tannaitic rulings. These fictions are usually invoked to account for rulings which seem to deviate from existing legal rules or other accepted legal notions.

Two sets of questions arise here. First, in what sources, literary or otherwise, do we find the "base laws" from which fictionally explained rulings seem to deviate? Second, are post-tannaitic explanatory fictions hermeneutically or logically justifiable (or necessary), or might other, non-fictional explanations of rulings explained fictionally be possible or preferable? And if fictional explanations could have been avoided, why did the rabbis sometimes prefer them to non-fictional explanations?

Beginning with the first question, only on rare occasions are the relevant base laws articulated explicitly in relevant literary sources. However, most such laws are fairly obvious, and even where they are not spelled out explicitly in earlier sources they can often be inferred without too much difficulty from such sources. For example, M. Mikva'ot 10:5 rules that a utensil whose handle will eventually be cut off need only be immersed to the joint between the utensil and the handle. This ruling is

---

[41] From the partial parallel in P. Yevamot 15:4, 15a (see the statement of R. Jose b. R. Bun there) it might appear that denial of the newly appeared husband's identity reflects at least some degree of uncertainty as to whether this man is the original husband. However, this claim seems extremely disingenuous. Moreover, the plain sense of the talmudic text suggests that the Talmud realizes full well that the man who just appeared is the woman's original husband ("if he comes, we say …").

[42] See the discussions of Friedman and Hayes cited above, n. 39.

[43] For a similar suggestion see Edrei (1998–2000, pp. 15–16). Prima facie, such an approach might seem to have a Roman parallel (the idea that *res iudicata pro veritate accipitur* with regard to certain issues of personal status; see Chap. 14). However, two significant reservations should be noted here. First, rabbinic law does not adopt such an approach as a general principle (see e.g. T. Horayot 1:6). Second, the Roman approach seems to have been motivated by the need to sustain the social order (cf. Ando, ibid.), whereas such a line of reasoning would presumably be irrelevant to a case which, from a rabbinic perspective, ultimately dealt with a ritual issue (=the laws of adultery).

explained by the Talmud on the grounds that "whatever will [eventually] be cut off is considered as if had already been cut off" (B. Hullin, pp. 72b–73a). Clearly, the assumed base law here, deviation from which had to be explained by using a fiction, is that a utensil must ordinarily be immersed in its entirety. Nowhere is such a law explicitly formulated in tannaitic sources, although it can be readily inferred from a number of specific rulings in these sources.[44]

This observation, in turn, may help shed light on our question about the hermeneutic character of post-tannaitic fictions. To illustrate, we consider M. Shabbat 11:1:

1. If one threw [something on the Sabbath] from a private domain into a public domain or from a public domain into a private domain, one is liable [for carrying on the Sabbath, which is forbidden].
2. If one threw [something] from a private domain into another private domain, and there is a public domain between them—
   a. R. Aqiba rules that he is liable
   b. but the Sages exempt him.

According to 1, one who throws something from a public domain into a private domain or vice-versa violates the Sabbath. Presumably, this is the only way to violate this prohibition, since no other way is mentioned here. In light of this assumption, the ruling of the Sages in 2b is readily understandable: one who threw something in a different fashion has not violated the Sabbath. Why then does R. Aqiba (in 2a) disagree? The answer, according to both Talmuds, is that the object which was thrown makes a fictional landing in the intermediate domain—"an [object] intercepted [by the air] is considered as if it had been set down" (B. Shabbat 4a and parallels), "R. Aqiba treats the empty space of a public domain like solid material" (P. Shabbat 1:1, 2c).[45] According to this explanation, R. Aqiba agrees in principle with the Sages that one is only liable for throwing something from a private domain into a public domain or vice-versa. However, R. Aqiba holds that the person described in 2 has in fact thrown something from a private domain into a public domain (here, the public domain in the middle), since the object which passed though this intermediate domain is considered as if it had landed there, by virtue of the legal fiction proposed by the Talmuds.

Now, we could dispense with this fictional explanation if we assumed that R. Aqiba holds that types of throwing other than those mentioned in 1 are forbidden—for example, throwing from one private domain to another one via an intervening public domain.[46] Indeed, such an interpretation seems to be found elsewhere in the

[44] See e.g. M. Mikva'ot 10: 1–4. The base law here can also be inferred from the ruling which was fictionally explained: by implication, if the handle of the utensil will not be cut off later, this handle must also be immersed.

[45] The statements in both Talmuds seem to mean the same thing, despite the difference in formulation (as is the case with many parallel statements in these works).

[46] To better comprehend the difference between the two explanations of R. Aqiba's ruling suggested here, consider what would happen if the object thrown was destroyed in the air of the intermediate domain before it landed in the second private domain. According to the fictional explanation, one would be liable under such circumstances for Sabbath violation, since the object

Palestinian Talmud.[47] Thus, the fictional explanation cited here is not exegetically necessary. Accordingly, use of a fiction here seems to stem from the assumption that the ruling in 1 is all-inclusive, and hence one is only liable for Sabbath violation under the circumstances described there. Thus, the only way to account for R. Aqiba's view was to assume that the object described in 2 makes a fictional landing in the intermediate domain.

A more extreme example of how fictional explanations were necessitated by the assumption of absolute, all-encompassing and universally accepted "base laws" is provided by the Talmudic discussions of M. Sotah 4:2. That Mishnah states:

> If husbands died before [their wives] drank [the bitter waters mentioned in Numbers 5:12–28], Beit Shammai say: [The women] receive marriage settlement, but do not drink [the bitter waters]. But Beit Hillel say that they either drink or do not receive the marriage settlement. [And since they cannot drink, they do not receive the marriage settlement.]

This Mishnah deals with a suspected adulteress who is unable to drink the bitter waters because her husband predeceased her (this ritual is only practiced if the husband is alive). The Mishnah does not explain why Beit Shammai hold that the suspected adulteress is awarded the marriage settlement. However, P. Sanhedrin 8:6, 26b explains: "[Since the woman can say]: Bring me my husband and I will drink." In other words, since it is not the wife's fault that she could not drink the bitter waters, she should not be penalized by loss of her marriage settlement. Such reasoning is clearly based on considerations of equity, and thus no fiction was necessary to justify Beit Shammai's ruling.

However, a fictional explanation of this Mishnah is suggested in B. Sotah 25a–b:

> Beit Shammai hold that a deed due to be collected is considered as if it had [already] been collected, and Beit Hillel hold that a deed which is due to be collected is not considered as if it had been collected.

The explanation of Beit Shammai's view here is clearly based on a fiction. Presumably, this explanation was proposed because Beit Shammai's ruling ostensibly deviates from a common and widely accepted tannaitic (and post-tannaitic) legal principle, according to which the burden of proof in cases of disputed property rests with the party who is not currently in possession of the property.[48] Specifically, the suspected adulteress here seeks to take property (= the marriage settlement) away from her husband's heirs. Why then does Beit Shammai allow her to collect such money, which is not currently in her possession? The answer, according to the Talmud, is that a "deed due to be collected" (the wife's marriage contract) is fictionally considered as if it had already been collected, and hence the wife is deemed the legal possessor of the marriage settlement, even though the real possessors of this property are clearly the heirs of the late husband. Here too, the relevant "base law" about the burden of proof in property disputes was conceived of not just as a

had fictionally landed in the intermediate domain. According to the non-fictional explanation, however, one would be exempt, since this object never landed anywhere.

[47] See P. Shabbat 11:1, 12d–13a.

[48] See M. Bikkurim 2:10 and parallels.

notion accepted by all sages, including Beit Shammai,[49] but as a law so inflexible and universally binding that no deviation from it can be brooked on the basis of functionalist considerations[50] (such as those suggested in the Palestinian Talmud), obvious and convincing as such considerations might seem to be.[51]

Summarizing, then, we see that post-tannaitic fictions frequently do not deal with undisputed exceptions to clear-cut laws of incontrovertibly universal applicability, but (often) to inferred generalizations whose universal applicability is merely assumed. However, once the relevant base laws were so construed, seemingly anomalous rulings had to be accounted for by resorting to fictions.

These observations have important implications about the possible adoption of implicit fictions during tannaitic times. As indicated earlier, numerous tannaitic rulings are explained fictionally in post-tannaitic sources, but no such explanations are found in the tannaitic sources (although these sources generally do not offer non-fictional explanations either). In most such cases the fictionally explained rulings could be explained without recourse to fiction if we assume that the relevant base laws were disputed or that they were not applied universally and inflexibly. Accordingly, it is usually difficult to prove that tannaitic rulings were based on implicit fictions, and it follows that the fictional explanations found in post-tannaitic sources might not necessarily provide historically accurate explanations of the relevant tannaitic rulings.

15.3.5 Types of Post-tannaitic Fictions

Providing a precise and comprehensive typology of post-tannaitic fictions is difficult, although several significant categories of post-tannaitic fictions should be noted. Many post-tannaitic fictions instruct us to disregard a particular object or event or treat it as nonexistent.[52] Other post-tannaitic fictions assert that time, space, or various physical objects should be extended or contracted for legal purposes. Such fictions accordingly treat cases which are relatively similar to the relevant classifying categories as if they were members of those categories. Such fictions include the fictional extension of defective partitions, thereby validating them for legal purposes ("extend (them) upward/downward," "the edge of the roof descends and closes off"), as well as other types of spatial extension, e.g., "a house is considered

---

[49] Indeed, despite the fact that the base law here is very widely accepted in rabbinic literature, it is not universally accepted; see Kehat (2010).

[50] Fictions of this sort might also reflect the predilection of the post-tannaitic sources and especially the Babylonian Talmud for conceptualist explanations; see Moscovitz (2002, pp. 27–29).

[51] For another potentially illuminating example of this sort, see B. Eruvin 87a, where a particular law is explained based on a fiction, while similar (though admittedly not identical) rulings are explained elsewhere on the basis of discretionary leniency (see B. Eruvin 12a and parallels: "The [rabbis] were lenient about partitions suspended above water").

[52] See e.g. B. Eruvin 3a; B. Zevahim 18b; B. Hullin 58b=B. Bekhorot 40a.

as if it is full."[53] Likewise, fictions may assert that time should be contracted for legal purposes, generally when a legally significant action has not yet occurred, but is mandatory or inevitable ("what stands to be cut off is considered as if it had been cut off," "a deed which is due to be collected is considered as if it had been collected").[54]

Why are post-tannaitic fictions frequently extensional? As indicated, most post-tannaitic fictions stem from the need to account for apparent deviation from assumed base laws. Now, such deviation is frequently not too marked, and the seemingly deviant cases come fairly close to fulfilling the legal requirements assumed by the base laws. Under such circumstances, it was only natural that these deviations were smoothed out by fictionally stretching matters somewhat—for example, by fictionally extending defective partitions to reach the required dimensions—instead of explicitly admitting that the base laws should not be applied in totally rigid fashion.

15.3.6 Multiple Application of Post-tannaitic Fictions

Sometimes legal fictions are applied to one case or group of cases, but not to another case or group of cases to which they are ostensibly applicable. Such passages are not very common and are usually rather complex,[55] and hence we do not consider examples of this sort here. In any event, such inconsistent application of post-tannaitic fictions should come as no surprise, since fictions are frequently utilized inconsistently in other legal systems as well.[56]

Nevertheless, some post-tannaitic fictions are invoked in connection with different cases from different legal domains,[57] in much the same way as we find in other legal systems.[58] (I have not found any criteria to determine which fictions were subjected to multiple application; indeed, this may be due largely to chance.) The question accordingly arises: why were fictions applied to different cases from different legal domains? A priori, several possibilities obtain here, and it is usually impossible to determine with certainty which of them is correct. Sometimes the cases to which a particular fiction was applied were similar enough to warrant multiple application

[53] For the first fiction see B. Shabbat 101a and parallels and B. Eruvin 89a=B. Sukkah 4b; for the second see B. Eruvin 25a (and cf. P. Eruvin 1:1, 18b and parallels); for the third see B. Shabbat 5a and parallels (and cf. P. Shabbat 1:1, 2c and 2d).

[54] For the first fiction see B. Ketubbot 51a and B. Hullin 72b–73a; for the second see B. Yevamot 38b and parallels.

[55] See e.g. Moscovitz (2002): 189 n. 102.

[56] See e.g. Fuller (1967): x. This inconsistent use of legal fictions might be attributable to a variety of factors, e.g. the fact that the relevant legal requirement or "bottom line" was formulated in figurative, fictional style without reconceptualizing the facts for legal purposes, or that fictions were deemed inapplicable to cases which are governed by special, individual requirements.

[57] The same applies to other types of post-tannaitic rabbinic rules as well; see Moscovitz (2002, pp. 327–337).

[58] For similar phenomena in Roman law see Moscovitz (2003, pp. 128–129), and cf. Olivier (1975, pp. 163–165), and see now Stern, this volume, Chap. 8, pp. 168–70 (including discussion of possible distinctions between fictions and deeming provisions).

of the fiction. Elsewhere, the authors of the fictions (or later scholars who deployed them) might have actually reconceptualized reality for legal purposes, rather than merely altering local legal requirements.[59] In still other passages, the multiple application of legal fictions might stem from literary considerations, since rabbinic statements (including fictions) were often subjected to literary transfer from one context to another. Finally, the multiple application of legal fictions might be rooted in analogical reasoning of sorts, whereby the similarity between cases prompted the application of similar modes of (fictional) interpretation, even if these cases cannot all be subsumed under a common legal category or conceptual rubric.[60]

Post-tannaitic fictions can be applied to different cases in different ways. Sometimes a fiction is applied to different cases in different passages, although the fiction is not directly extended from one case to another. Consider, for example, the talmudic treatment of the principle of "fictional hollowing," which appears in various Talmudic passages, two of which we consider here:[61]

I. B. Shabbat 7b = ibid. 100a

Rabbi Hiyya said: If one throws [something] higher than ten [handbreadths] and it goes and lands in a tiny hole [in a wall], we arrive at a dispute of R. Meir and the Rabbis—

1. According to R. Meir, who holds: We [fictionally] hollow out [an object] to complete [a space of a specified size], he is liable [for Sabbath violation].
2. According to the Rabbis, who hold: We do not hollow out to complete, he is not liable.

Ordinarily, one who throws something on the Sabbath from a public domain is only liable for Sabbath violation if the object landed in a closed space at least ten handbreadths high and four handbreadths wide.[62] And since the hole mentioned here is less than four handbreadths wide, one is only liable for Sabbath violation if the dimensions of the hole are fictionally extended, as proposed in 1 according to R. Meir.

II. B. Eruvin 11b = B. Yoma 11b

1. We have learned: "R. Meir said: An arched doorway requires a *mezuzah*,[63] but the Sages exempt" [such a doorway from a *mezuzah*]…
2. [R. Meir and the Sages] disagree where the lower part [of the doorway, below the arch] was three handbreadths high, its total height was ten cubits, and the width [of the arch]

[59] This possibility might gain added plausibility from the fact that many post-tannaitic fictions are formulated using ordinary verbs rather than comparative terminology (see above, text at n. 32–34), perhaps suggesting that this is how reality was actually conceived for legal purposes. At the same time, it should be stressed that some of the post-tannaitic fictions subjected to multiple application are formulated using comparative terminology (e.g. the fiction discussed above at n. 45, that "an [object] intercepted is as if it had been set down"/"R. Aqiba treats the empty space of a public domain like solid material"; these notions are invoked in both Talmuds in connection with both the Sabbath laws and the laws pertaining to delivery of a bill of divorce).

[60] Analogical reasoning of this sort seems to be extremely widespread in rabbinic literature; see Moscovitz (2002, pp. 228–273), passim, especially pp. 260–271.

[61] I omit the other passages, which are quite complex and add little to the discussion here.

[62] See T. Shabbat 1:1 and parallels.

[63] A parchment containing certain biblical passages which must be affixed to the doorpost of a house; see Deuteronomy 6:9.

was less than four handbreadths, but [the sides of the arch] can be hollowed out to a width of four handbreadths [the minimum width for a doorway to require a *mezuzah*]—

a. R. Meir holds that we hollow out [the top of the arch] to complete [the requisite four handbreadths].
b. But the Sages hold that we do not hollow out to complete [the four handbreadths].

Both of these passages invoke the principle of fictional hollowing, albeit in different contexts and in connection with different laws. The first passage applies this principle to the laws of carrying on the Sabbath, and the second to the laws of *mezuzah*. The extent of the fictional hollowing and the conditions under which it occurs also differ in the two cases. In the first case fictional hollowing occurs above a height of ten handbreadths, whereas in the second case it occurs at a lower height. Indeed, the legal basis of the rulings of R. Meir in these passages might differ: these laws might be based on distinct, local requirements and not on a single, all-encompassing principle. Accordingly, acceptance of the notion of fictional hollowing in connection with the Sabbath laws does not logically necessitate adoption of this principle with regard to the laws of *mezuzah* (and similarly vice-versa). And while the multiple application of the fiction here might stem from an assumption that the scope of this fiction is exceptionally broad and that it applies to as many cases as possible, this is by no means certain. Rather, the fiction cited in these passages might have been applied to different cases for literary reasons: since the wording of the fiction is equally appropriate regarding both of the relevant cases, it was applied to both of them, even though the precise legal basis for each ruling might differ.[64]

Elsewhere legal fictions are applied to different cases within a single literary context, and the fiction is directly extended from one case to another. Here we illustrate with B. Sukkah 22a–b, which deals with the case of a ritual booth[65] (*sukkah*) covered with reeds at different heights. Ordinarily such a structure is only acceptable if the difference in height between the reeds is less than three handbreadths, but there are exceptions:

1. Rava said, (a) If the upper reed is a handbreadth wide, [the *sukkah*] is valid (b) because we say "Beat and throw down." [The upper reeds are fictionally considered as if they had been "beaten and thrown down" to form a single layer with the lower reeds.]
2. Rava said, Whence do I say that if the upper reed is a handbreadth wide, we invoke [the principle of] "Beat and throw down"?... From what we have learned [in M. Ahilot 2:5]: "... If the upper roofbeams [of a house] were opposite the gaps between the lower beams and an unclean object lay beneath one of the beams, the space beneath them all is unclean [because they fictionally combine to form a single covering]... And regarding this it was taught: "When does this apply? When the beams are each a handbreadth [wide]..."
3. Rav Kahana was sitting and stated this teaching. Rav Ashi said to Rav Kahana, Do we not say "Beat and throw down" where an object is not a handbreadth wide? Why, it has been taught: "... If there were two parallel beams, neither of which can support a half-brick ... we consider the upper [beam] as if it were lower and the lower one as if it

[64] In both cases the fiction is invoked to account for a ruling of the same scholar, Rabbi Meir. However, while it is obvious that both rulings of this sage can be explained in light of a common principle, there is clearly no logical necessity to do so.

[65] See above, n. 37.

were higher ...," [so they combine to form a single beam, which permits carrying on the Sabbath] even though neither of them is a handbreadth [wide]!...

The notion of "beat and throw down" is clearly a legal fiction, and it resembles certain tannaitic fictions.[66] The idea that reeds of varying heights combine if the reeds are a handbreadth wide is invoked in this passage in connection with three different legal domains, albeit in different fashions and with different functions (see below): regarding the laws of ritual booths (1), the ritual impurity conferred by an overhanging structure (2), and the laws of beams which permit carrying on the Sabbath (3). The first time the fiction is used to explain and justify a legal ruling, that of Rava in 1a. The second time a source for the original fiction is adduced from use of this fiction in a different context (2), while the third time an objection is raised to the previous discussion based on the assumption that our fiction should apply, but apparently does not, to a third legal domain. Significantly, none of the scholars cited here attempts to distinguish between the different cases by denying the universal applicability of the fiction, and even when such an objection is raised (in 3), it was not solved by rejecting this assumption, but rather by reinterpreting and apparently emending the problematic source cited there![67] Thus, multiple application of the fiction here led to the forced interpretation of a literary source, which had to be forcibly harmonized with the fiction, rather than to rejection of the otherwise unproven assumption that our fiction is equally applicable to multiple cases from different legal domains.

15.3.7 Rabbinic Attitudes toward Fictions

In contrast to modern legal scholarship, where the desirability of legal fictions has been the subject of considerable discussion, rabbinic sources are almost completely devoid of any reflection about such matters.[68] This might be due to the fact that

---

[66] Such as the ones in T. Eruvin 1:5 (see above, text after n. 18) and T. Ahilot 11:10 (see above, text after n. 19). However, there is an important difference between the tannaitic and post-tannaitic fictions: the former are formulated casuistically, as they deal with specific items (beams, roofs), while the latter is formulated in more general terms (="beat and throw down," without specifying what). Indeed, this more general formulation might well have facilitated the multiple application of the fiction presented here; cf. above.

[67] See the next part of our passage, not cited here because of its complexity.

[68] Hayes (2004) (passim, and see especially the Conclusion, pp. 152–154) argues that there is evidence of rabbinic discomfort with certain bold legal fictions, and that some fictions of this sort were eliminated or defused by later authorities who found them objectionable. However, of the five examples Hayes cites to support this claim, only one would qualify as a fiction under our definition (=Hayes' third example, on which see below), and as noted below, this case seems to be the exception which proves the rule. And while post-tannaitic sages sometimes disagreed as to whether a particular fiction or fictional explanation should be accepted (see e.g. the Talmud's analysis of the dispute between Abbaye and Rava in B. Eruvin 95a), it is highly questionable whether those scholars who rejected fictions in these cases opposed legal fiction per se. Such scholars generally seem to have preferred non-fictional approaches on localized grounds or in particular cases, without rejecting or objecting to the use of fictions as a matter of principle.

rabbinic sources generally engage in little reflection about the modes of legal reasoning they contain. Moreover, most post-tannaitic fictions[69] serve to explain existing laws rather than to formulate new ones. And since such fictions are generally devoid of any practical ramifications—the laws in question retain their binding character regardless of whether or not we accept the fictional explanations of these rulings—it was only natural that such theoretical legal analysis should not have aroused too much opposition.[70] To be sure, one rabbinic fiction was criticized, and quite sharply so, by some of the Talmudic rabbis, namely, the fiction denying the identity of a returning husband who had hitherto been presumed dead.[71] However, this case is basically the exception which proves the rule.[72] Indeed, the reason for the objection to this fiction is obvious: the claim that the man who just appeared is not the original husband is clearly an out-and-out lie. Moreover, the law regarding this case presumably depends on the actual facts—is the original husband dead or not—and not on some sort of legal conception or definition. By contrast, most rabbinic fictions deal with issues which are not necessarily predicated on the actual physical facts, but on how such facts are defined or conceived from a legal perspective, and in such cases there is ample room for defining legal truth in a fashion which differs from truth *simpliciter*.[73]

Conclusions

As indicated above, post-tannaitic fictions generally function in an explanatory capacity. Most such fictions seek to ensure the conceptual consistency of problematic rulings with assumed base laws; they facilitate the theoretical analysis and explanation of the law, rather than attempting to make it conform with desired goals or legal outcomes. Such fictions generally do not seem to be the product of historical development or the desire to amend existing law.

This use of fictions in post-tannaitic sources reflects the adoption of a highly formalistic and rigid approach to law. For it demonstrates how relevant base laws, generally inferable from though frequently not articulated explicitly in earlier literary sources, were endowed with rule-like character and treated as universally binding, in a fashion which brooked no exceptions.

[69] While tannaitic fictions frequently are prescriptive, and hence their adoption does have practical import, one could hardly expect to find reflection about legal fictions in tannaitic sources, since these works are basically just collections of rulings, with very limited theoretical analysis and no real legal rumination.

[70] Note too that far-fetched explanations of various sorts occur frequently in the Talmuds, and only on rare occasions do such explanations arouse opposition.

[71] See Hayes (2004, pp. 140–142), and Hayes (2006, pp. 136–137).

[72] Note too that this particular fiction is used in a prescriptive capacity (even if it also has somewhat of an explanatory element); cf. the text above near n. 69.

[73] Cf. further Schauer, this volume, Chap. 6.

Earlier we noted most of the principal differences between tannaitic and post-tannaitic: the former are usually prescriptive and not explanatory. Moreover, tannaitic fiction often seems to be more of a stylistic phenomenon than a conceptual phenomenon—a figurative way to formulate the relevant legal requirements. Likewise, we noted that tannaitic fictions usually do not serve as general rules, but address specific cases, and hence, in contrast to their post-tannaitic counterparts, are not subject to or capable of multiple application. Yet despite these differences between tannaitic and post-tannaitic fictions, the relationship between these two is better described as evolution than revolution: the use of legal fictions in tannaitic literature certainly prefigures the use of such notions in post-tannaitic sources, despite the differences between fictions from the two periods.

Finally, it is worth noting that post-tannaitic fictions share important characteristics with other types of rabbinic legal rules, such as the frequently explanatory character of such statements, the abstract and "legalistic" approach to reality which they reflect, and the fact that they are frequently subjected to multiple application. Thus, post-tannaitic legal fictions should not be considered an utterly unique phenomenon in the world of rabbinic law, but rather (at least to a certain extent) as a particular instance of the broader phenomenon of legal rules in post-tannaitic literature.[74]

References

Ancselovits, Elisha. 2011. The prosbul—a legal fiction? *Jewish Law Annual* 19:3–16.

Ando, Clifford. 2014. Fact, fiction, and social reality in roman law. In *Legal fictions in theory and practice*, ed. Maksymilian Del Mar and William Twining. Dordrecht: Springer.

Atlas, Samuel. 1978. *Pathways in Jewish law* [In Hebrew.]. New York: American Academy for Jewish Research.

Cohen, Boaz. 1966. *Jewish and Roman law*. 2 vols. New York: Jewish Theological Seminary.

Edrei, Aryeh. 1998–2000. The beit din's prerogatives in marital law [In Hebrew.] *Annual of the Institute for Research in Jewish Law* [In Hebrew.] 21:1–35.

Friedman, Shamma. 1977. A critical study of Yevamot X with a methodological introduction [In Hebrew.]. In *Texts and studies: Analecta Judaica*, [In Hebrew.], ed. H. Z. Dimitrovsky, vol. 1, 275–441. New York: Jewish Theological Seminary.

Fuller, Lon L. 1967. *Legal fictions*. Stanford: Stanford University Press.

Hayes, Christine. 2004. Authority and anxiety in the Talmuds: From legal fiction to fact. In *Jewish religious leadership: Image and reality*, ed. Jack Wertheimer, 127–154. New York: Jewish Theological Seminary.

Hayes, Christine. 2006. Rabbinic contestations of authority. *Cardozo Law Review* 28: 123–141.

Jackson, Bernard S. 1981. On the problem of Roman influence on the halakah and normative self-definition in judaism. In *Jewish and Christian self-definition: Aspects of Judaism in the Graeco-Roman period*, ed. E. P. Sanders, A. I. Baumgarten, and Alan Mendelson, vol. 2, 157–203. Philadelphia: SCM.

Katzoff, Ranon. 1989. Sperber's dictionary of Greek and Latin legal terms in rabbinic literature—a review essay. *Journal for the Study of Judaism* 29:195–206.

Kehat, Barukh. 2010. The claimant must produce evidence in rabbinic literature [In Hebrew.] PhD Thesis, Bar-Ilan University.

[74] The use of legal rules in rabbinic literature has been discussed at length in Moscovitz (2002), passim.

Lobban, Michael. 2014. Legal fictions before the age of reform. In *Legal fictions in theory and practice*, ed. Maksymilian Del Mar and William Twining. Dordrecht: Springer.
Moscovitz, Leib. 2002. *Talmudic reasoning*. Tübingen: Mohr Siebeck.
Moscovitz, Leib. 2003. Legal fictions in rabbinic law and Roman law: Some comparative observations. In *Rabbinic law and its near eastern context,* ed. Catherine Hezser, 105–132. Tübingen: Mohr Siebeck.
Moscovitz, Leib. 2013. It is as if he had said (Na'aseh keomer). [In Hebrew.]. In *Ke-tavor be-harim: Studies in rabbinic literature presented to Joseph Tabory,* ed. Arnon Atzmon and Tzur Shafir, 193–214 [In Hebrew.] Alon Shvut: Tevunot.
Novick, Tzvi. 2009. They come against them with the power of the torah: Rabbinic reflections on legal fiction and legal agency. *Studies in Law, Politics, and Society* 50:1–17.
Novick, Tzvi. 2010. The 'for I say' presumption: A study in early rabbinic legal rhetoric. *Journal of Jewish Studies* 61:48–61.
Olivier, Pierre J. J. 1975. *Legal fictions in practice and legal science*. Rotterdam: Rotterdam University Press.
Schauer, Frederick. 2014. Legal fictions revisited. In *Legal fictions in theory and practice*, ed. Maksymilian Del Mar and William Twining. Dordrecht: Springer.
Stern, Simon. 2014. Legal fictions and exclusionary rules. In *Legal fictions in theory and practice*, ed. Maksymilian Del Mar and William Twining. Dordrecht: Springer.

Chapter 16
Presumptions and Fictions: A Collingwoodian Approach

Raymundo Gama

Abstract This essay examines the explanatory power of the traditional distinction between presumptions and fictions in the light of two problems. First, the relationship between these concepts is usually presented in isolation of the context in which it was elaborated. A careful examination of this subject requires devoting a space to try to put in context the intellectual tradition to which this distinction belongs. The essay surveys the intellectual origins of the distinction and shows that the common conception of presumptions and legal fictions in both the Continental and the Anglo-American legal cultures descends from Medieval Law in an unbroken tradition. Secondly, the analysis of the relationship between presumptions and legal fictions is largely problematic because of the ambiguity of these expressions. Particular attention is given to a specific and perhaps more persistent ambiguity in the analysis of these concepts: the distinction between the theoretical (cognitive) and practical (normative) dimension of presumptions and legal fictions.

16.1 Introduction

A recurrent theme in the literature of legal fictions is the analysis of the similarities and differences between fictions and other related concepts. For centuries, legal scholars have relied on this practice for the purpose of acquiring a better understanding of this concept.[1] The question "What is a legal fiction?" is expected to be clarified by making explicit what legal fictions are not, and how they differ from other concepts. Following this path, several authors have explored the difference between fictions and lies, deceptions, errors and false hypotheses (Frank 2009 [1930], pp. 338–340 and Fuller 1967, p. 5). Historically, particular attention has been devoted to explore the relationship between legal fictions and other related

[1] As Franco Todescan (1979), observes, the relationship between *fictio* and the concepts of *extensio* (analogy) and *preasumptio* (presumption) was a recurrent practice in the literature of the fifteenth and sixteenth centuries.

R. Gama (✉)
Instituto Tecnológico Autónomo de México, Río Hondo 1, ProgresoTizapan,
Álvaro Obregón, Ciudad de México, Distrito Federal 01080, México
e-mail: raymundo.gama@itam.com

M. Del Mar, W. Twining (eds.), *Legal Fictions in Theory and Practice*,
Law and Philosophy Library 110, DOI 10.1007/978-3-319-09232-4_16

legal instruments. Among all the potential candidates for having a family resemblance with legal fictions, the literature emphasizes the concept of presumption.

The relationship between presumptions and legal fictions is traditionally presented in terms of two different types of assumptions. A legal fiction is characterized as a "consciously false assumption" (Ross 1969, p. 223), or as "an assumed fact, notoriously false, upon which one reasons as if it were true" (Bentham 1840, p. 91). In presumptions, in contrast, a fact is also assumed to be true, but in this case the assumed fact may be true, and in some cases is probably true. As expressed by Fuller "a presumption (whether conclusive or rebuttable) assumes something that may possibly be true" (Fuller 1967, p. 40).

In both cases, there would be a common element of assumption, since a proposition is assumed to be true. The main difference between these concepts would consist in the contingent conformity with truth in the case of presumptions and in the necessary deviation from reality in the case of legal fictions.[2] In legal fictions a proposition is known to be false, and from this knowledge we reason as if it were true. Presumptions operate instead in situations of uncertainty in which we do not know whether a proposition is true or false. Despite this uncertainty, the presumption assumes beforehand that something is true. [3]

The aforementioned distinction is repeated time and time again both in the literature of presumptions and legal fictions.

In his classical work on legal fictions, Fuller proposed to examine the explanatory power of the traditional distinction by asking: "How valid is this distinction?" and "how significant is it?" (Fuller 1967, p. 40). He advanced interesting ideas about these topics. One of them is his thesis that presumptions and legal fictions are instruments that obscure the growth of the law by redefining the operative facts to which legal consequences are attached (Fuller 1967, pp. 72–77).[4] Fuller was fully aware of the close relationship between these concepts. As he observed:

> [Th]e mental process involved in the invention of the ordinary fiction is at least a close relation to that involved in the establishment of a presumption, and suggests the possibility that there may be a primitive, undifferentiated form of thought that includes both (Fuller 1967, p. 48).[5]

[2] For a discussion and criticism of the reconstruction of legal fictions as counterfactual propositions see Karen Petroski's essay in Chap. 7 of this volume.

[3] As observed in Lewis and Short's *Latin dictionary*, the term "presumption" derives from the Latin *praesumptio*, which means "taking before hand", "using or enjoying in advance" and has a sense of "anticipation". This expression was used in the realm of rhetoric in the sense of "an anticipation of possible or suspected objections". On the other hand, "fiction" derives from "*fictio*", which is equivalent to "fashioning", "forming", "modelling", "manufacturing" "feigning", "counterfeiting" and "disguising". In rhetoric, this expression was used to refer to "an assumed or fictitious case, a supposition" (Lewis and Short 1998 [1879]; regarding the concept of *fictio* see additionally Pugliatti 1968, p. 659).

[4] This thesis is discussed in Del Mar, this volume, Chap. 1. 2014. Another suggestive idea is Fuller's thesis of presumption as "a lens held before the facts of reality", producing either (i) a clear image of what we see, (ii) a distortion of reality (a fictitious representation) or, when the lens is used as a corrective device to cure a defect of our vision, (iii) a corrected image (Fuller 1967, p. 45).

[5] He also detects the proximity between these concepts in the way they are usually formulated: "The close kinship of the ordinary fiction and the presumption is shown by the fact that the two

On balance, one should acknowledge his contribution to the literature of legal fictions.[6] However, at some points it seems that he was more worried about exploring which requirements a presumption should meet to avoid the charge of "fiction", than in questioning the validity of the distinction between these concepts.[7] Besides, his definition of legal fictions as statements and his insistence on the parallelism between fictions of science and legal fictions[8] are symptomatic of a persistent ambiguity in the analysis of these concepts.

In the light of these observations, this essay examines the explanatory power of the traditional distinction between presumptions and legal fictions in two parts.

First, the relationship between presumptions and legal fictions is usually presented in isolation of the context in which it was elaborated. A careful examination of this subject requires devoting some space to put in context the intellectual tradition to which this distinction belongs.

Secondly, the traditional distinction attempts to offer a clarification of the relationship between presumptions and legal fictions in general. However, both terms are used in legal discourse to refer to a variety of phenomena. The second part of the essay addresses the problem of the ambiguity in the use of these expressions. In particular, it explores the distinction between the theoretical (cognitive) and practical (normative) dimensions of presumptions and legal fictions as a preliminary step for clarifying the relationship between these concepts at the level of rules.

As expressed in the title, this essay adopts a Collingwoodian approach to the topic of the relationship between presumptions and legal fictions. This requires some explanation. First, this paper takes Robert G. Collingwood's thesis of understanding ideas in historical terms.[9] When applied to the topic of this essay, this thesis implies that the problem of the explanatory power of the traditional distinction could not be analyzed *in vacuo*; it should be examined in connection with the context in which this distinction emerged. Secondly, it takes Collingwood's thesis of clarifying ideas through the formulation of questions.[10] This thesis supposes that before asking: Is

---

meet upon a grammatical field in such expressions as 'deemed' and 'regarded as'" (Fuller 1967, p. 47).

[6] As Kenneth Campbell points out in a critical analysis of Fuller's contribution to the theory of legal fictions, there are at least two aspects of his account that deserve to be acknowledged and emphasised still today. First, "the extremely wide range of his legal examples". Secondly, "his knowledge of the continental literature of his period and of the preceding generation is of an order which one would expect nowadays to find in few Anglo-American writers on jurisprudence" (Campbell 1983, p. 340).

[7] Fuller argued that in order to escape the charge of fiction a presumption should meet the three following requirements. "(1) be based on an inference justified by common experience, (2) be freely rebuttable, and (3) be phrased in realistic terms; order, not an 'inference' but a disposition of the case in a certain contingency". (Fuller 1967, p. 45). From these requirements it follows that for Fuller conclusive presumptions are fictions.

[8] The similarity between fictions of science and legal fictions is discussed in Fuller 1967, p. 124. For a discussion of this thesis see Karen Petroski's essay in Chap. 7 of this volume.

[9] For his thesis that "all history is the history of thought" see Collingwood 1961 [1946], pp. 315–320.

[10] This thesis is related with Robert G. Collingwood's "logic of question and answer". See Collingwood 2002 [1939], p. 29. For a characterisation of a Collingwoodian approach in legal theory see Twining 1998.

this distinction valid? One should ask: To what problem does this distinction purport to answer? Is this distinction applicable to all the different phenomena identified with the names "presumption" and "legal fiction"?

16.2 The Distinction in Context

In order to examine critically the explanatory power of the traditional distinction between presumptions and legal fictions it might be useful to take a step back and consider, although briefly, the context in which this distinction was originally elaborated. This implies going back to Medieval Law, where civilians elaborated most of the notions, definitions and classifications of presumptions and legal fictions, which, to a greater or lesser extent, we still use today.

For this purpose, it is relevant to point out that the doctrines of presumptions and legal fictions elaborated in the *ius commune* were not the product of one individual or a single work elaborated at a single time. On the contrary, they were the result of a combined contribution by different scholars over a period of five centuries.[11]

As observed in Franco Todescan's book on the doctrinal history of legal fictions, the first attempts to clarify the relationship between the concepts of *praesumptio* and *fictio* are found as early as the twelfth century in the work of the glossators and canonists (Todescan 1979, p. 88). But it was mainly through the works of Cinus of Pistoia, Bartolo, Baldo and the rest of the commentators that a new methodology based on the influence of Aristotelian epistemology and the use of dialectical methods were applied to elaborate the concepts of presumption and fiction as well as their relationship. In the sixteenth century, the tendency to examine the relationship between the concept of *fictio* and other related concepts, such as the concept of *praesumptio* and *extensio* (analogy) became consolidated in the treatises of presumptions of Alciato and Menochio and the rest of the humanists, who applied philological and historical methods in the analysis of these subjects.[12]

The continental jurists applied their efforts to adapt the Roman law to the conditions of their time. They tried to conciliate the tension between a static system that was considered as valid, on the one hand, and an emergent reality with new and unregulated situations, on the other. To this end, the civilians found in presumptions and legal fictions two powerful instruments for transforming legal reality: in the case of presumptions, by approximating as far as possible legal reality to natural reality, and in the case of legal fictions, in contrast, as an instrument that constructs legal reality by deviation from natural reality (Todescan 1979, pp. 177–178).

The civilians turned to Roman law in an effort to systematize and identify the rationale of each concept. These subjects were dealt with in a series of passages dispersed throughout the different parts of the Compilation of Justinian. The Roman

[11] For the history of presumptions in these periods see Ramponi 1890; Hedemann 1931; Reggi 1986 and Giuliani 2009. For the history of legal fictions the fundamental text is Todescan 1979.

[12] On the different methods used in the late Middle Ages see Todescan 1979, Chap. 1 and Errera 2007.

jurists achieved a masterful application of these concepts, but they did not elaborate a theory. Regarding the concept of *praesumptio* in Roman law, it was mainly understood as a method for reaching decisions in situations of uncertainty, irrespective of whether the decision was based on considerations of probability and common opinion, or on reasons of convenience or justice (*aequitas*).[13] The concept of *fictio iuris* was understood as a powerful instrument for the transformation and adaptation of the *Ius Civile* to new situations, either through the creation of legislative fictions (as in the famous *fictio legis Corneliae*) or through the *formulae ficticiae* introduced by the praetor.[14]

In examining the concepts of *praesumptio* and *fictio* in Roman law the civilians managed to reduce a mass of particular cases into a more limited number of general principles with the intention of capturing the essential notes of each concept through a series of definitions, classifications and distinctions. These efforts could be synthesized as follows.

The notion of presumption characteristic of the *ius commune* is condensed in a definition elaborated by the canonist Tancredi in the twelfth century that was subsequently repeated in the works of the following centuries: "*Praesumptio est argumentum ad credendum unum factum surgens ex probatione ulterior facti*" (Decottignies 1950, p. 33; Giuliani 1971, p. 166).

According to this definition, presumption consists in an indirect and conjectural type of reasoning that operates in situations in which direct evidence is missing. A fact is thus established as a result of a process of reasoning that goes from the ascertainment of one fact or group of facts, to the assumption of the existence of another fact (Campitelli 1986, p. 261; Giuliani 2009, p. 24).

This way of understanding the concept of presumption reveals a strong influence of rhetoric in the elaboration of the doctrine of presumptions. As Cujas, a French legal humanist of the sixteenth century expressed:

> Presumptions are only conjectures, arguments (…) the burden of proof shifts to the person against whom the presumption is made. Presumptions prevail unless there is counter proof (…). Little has come to us about presumptions. However, whatever can be said about presumptions should be said by the 'rhetores', not by the jurists: for they are factual in nature.[15]

In fact, the medieval concept of presumption was the equivalent to the rhetorical notion of argument (*argumenta*), one of the species of the rhetorical category of artificial proofs. As characterized in Quintilian's *Institutio Oratoria*, an argument is a process of reasoning affording a proof, by which one doubtful thing is established by reference to another thing that is certain.[16]

---

[13] On the concept of presumption in Roman law see Ferrini 1929; Donatuti 1976a [1931]; Donatuti 1976b [1933]; Reggi 1986; Thomas 1995; Hohmann (2001) and Franklin (2002, p. 6).

[14] For an analysis of fictions in Roman law see Clifford Ando's Chap. 14 in this volume. See additionally Todescan 1979; Pugliatti 1968, pp. 662–664, and Birks 1986.

[15] The translation is taken from Shain 1944, p. 95.

[16] See Quintilian, *Institutio Oratoria*, 5. 10. 9=Russell (2001, pp. 367–368). On the influence of rhetoric in the doctrine of presumptions see Donatuti (1933); Todescan 1979, pp. 168 ff. and Giuliani 2009, pp. 39 ff.

On the other hand, the rhetorical theory of signs provided the grounds for the well-known classification of presumptions. *Praesumptiones iuris et de iure* (conclusive presumptions) were associated with the necessary sign (*tekmerion*). In this case, the connection between a known fact and an unknown fact was believed to be so strong that the presence of the former is a conclusive proof of the existence of the latter, excluding any possibility of rebuttal. *Praesumptiones iuris tantum* (rebuttable presumptions) were associated with the probable sign (*eikos*). In this case, the presumption was also legally established, but since the connection between two facts was only probable it was open to rebuttal. Finally, presumptions of fact or human presumptions (*praesumptiones facti vel hominis*) were also based on a probable connection between a known fact and an unknown fact, but they were not legally established.

As for the concept of fiction, the main elements are condensed in a definition by Cinus of Pistoia (1270–1336) that was subsequently adopted by the jurists of the next generations as a starting point for the elaboration of the doctrine of *fictio iuris*. In examining the relationship between *praesumptio* and *fictio*, Cinus of Pistoia defined the latter as follows: "*fictio est in re certa contrariae veritatis, pro veritate assumptio*".

Following the method of Aristotelian classification by *genus* and *species*, Cinus of Pistoia puts the element of assumption at the centre of the concept of fiction, which is later specified as an assumption as true of a fact that is known to be contrary to the truth (*in re certa contrariae veritatis*) (Todescan 1979, p. 106; Thomas 1995, p. 17).

Cinus of Pistoia's definition was criticized for being too broad, encompassing all kinds of falsehoods. Bartolo and Baldo managed to narrow down this concept to the realm of law by adding that it is an assumption made by the law for having certain legal consequences (*a iure facta assumptio*), but they also added the requirement that the legal fiction should refer to possible hypotheses (*fictio est in re certa, eius quod est possibile contra veritatem a iure fact assumptio*). All the subsequent definitions of the commentators of the following generations attempted to achieve a complete characterization of the concept of *fictio*, and yet the main elements of the concept of fiction identified in Cinus of Pistoia's definition remain.

Thus, in the fiction established in the *fictio legis Cornelia*, the truth is that a Roman citizen had been captured by the enemy and later returned; by virtue of a fiction, the law assumed that this person had never been absent for the purpose of maintaining the validity of his will.

The commentators observed a close relationship between the concepts of *praesumptio* and *fictio*. In both cases a fact is assumed to be true, and from that assumption certain legal consequences are attached. This affinity seems even stronger in *praesumptiones iuris et de iure*, the term used by the civilians to refer to what is called today conclusive presumptions, since in these cases a fact is assumed to be true, and no evidence to the contrary is admitted (Todescan 1979, p. 175).

But the civilians observed a basic difference between these concepts. In fictions, something that is known to be false is feigned as true, while in presumptions there is no evidence about the truth or falsehood of a fact. Presumptions operate in situations of doubt.[17] They are probable conjectures that are founded on truth and on what generally happens, while fictions are legal declarations adverse to truth. The concept of presumption is associated with doubtful and uncertain hypotheses, while legal fictions are based on certainties (Thomas 1995, p. 17). The degree of doubt that is always present in presumption may vary in decreasing order, from *praesumptiones hominis* to *praesumptiones iuris et de iure*. But even *praesumptiones iuris et de iure* were conceived as legal declarations about doubtful matters, while legal fictions were described as falsities.[18]

However, it should be observed that despite the proximity in the elaboration of the doctrines of both presumptions and legal fictions during this period, the history of these concepts follows different paths. The concept of presumption has been related historically to truth and conjectural reasoning about questions of fact.[19] The concept of legal fiction, in contrast, has been related to questions of law and has been historically conceived as an instrument for the creation, modification and adaptation of law.[20] The gap between questions of law and questions of fact would indicate two different modes of investigation, the former as eminently uncertain, while the latter as requiring certainty.[21]

At this point someone might object that this is all part of history, since these conceptions are not reflected in the common understanding of both the concepts of presumptions and fiction. So, to what extent does this intellectual tradition still survive in the common understanding of the concepts of both presumptions and fictions? This question deserves at least a schematic response.

The traditional conception of presumptions of the *ius commune* still survives in both the Continental and the Anglo-American traditions.

In the Continental tradition presumptions are characterized as inferences, mental operations and logical procedures by which an unknown fact is inferred from a known fact. These inferences may be established by a rule of law, or may be left to the discretion of the judge. In the former case, the presumption is called "legal", which is further subdivided into "relative legal presumptions" that could be defeated by evidence to the contrary or they could be "absolute legal presumptions", which do not admit any evidence to the contrary.[22]

---

[17] See Ramponi 1890, p. 51, where he cites the classical definitions of Menochio and Cuyacio. According to Menochio: "*Fictio fingit vera esse ea quae vera non sunt. Praesumptio vero praesumit super re dubia, quae ita esse aut non esse potest. Unde fictio nunquam convenit cum veritate, praesumptio vero saepe*". According to Cuyacio: "*Fingimus ea quae non esse scimus; praesumimus ea quae vera esse arbitramur ducti probabilibus argumentis.*"

[18] See Todescan 1979, p. 172, where he cites the following definition of Baldo: "*praesumptio iuris et de iure est declaratoria rei dubiae, quia praesumptio est verorum; fictio est falsorum*".

[19] For the use of the term "presumption" ("Chazaka") in the Talmud, see Edna Ullmann-Margalit 1983b, p. 467, where she provides an account of some categories of presumptions. Further references to the use of presumptions in the ancient law of proof can be found in Franklin 2002, p. 9.

[20] For an account of the use of fictions in the ancient oriental law see Boyer 1954, pp. 73–100, and Pugliatti 1968, pp. 660–662.

[21] Cf. Giuliani 2009, pp. 25–37.

[22] This conception is a true common place in the literature of presumptions in the Continental tradition. Among of the most representative works of this conception see Ramponi (1890) and

In the Anglo-American tradition, the British treatises written in the nineteenth century were strongly influenced by the continental doctrine of presumptions.[23] The term "presumption" was understood as a synonym of "inference" almost in the same terms as the civilians did.[24] As regards to the common understanding of presumptions in the modern law of presumptions, it is worth mentioning that legal writers have constantly warned against the use of "presumption" as a synonym of inference. But despite the efforts of Thayer, Wigmore, Morgan and scholars of the following generations, the term "presumption" is still used to refer to a rule that requires the drawing of an inference from the existence of one fact to the existence of other facts and legal operators hold that presumptions almost carry an inferential relationship.[25]

Regarding legal fictions, the concept of fiction characterized so far still survives both in the Common Law and the Continental tradition, as exemplified in the accounts of this concept by such eminent jurists and philosophers as Bentham,[26] Best,[27] Vaihinger, [28] Tourtoulon,[29] Olivier[30] and Fuller.[31]

Serra (1963). For a critique of this conception in the Continental legal tradition see Andrioli (1966); Taruffo (1991) and Gama (2015).

[23] For a historical survey of these works see Twining (2006 Chap. 2). See additionally Thayer [1898], p. 545; Shain 1944.

[24] The definition of presumptions as inferences that goes from the existence of one fact to the existence to another fact is reproduced in the treatises of Gilbert, Philipps, Starkie, Wills and Best. According to Best: "Presumptions or, as they are sometimes called, intendments of law, and by the civilians *praesumptiones seu positiones iuris*, are inferences or positions established for the most part by the common but occasionally by statute law, and are obligatory alike on judges and juries". He then went on to argue that legal presumptions differ from presumptions in fact in that "the law peremptorily requires a certain inference to be made" (Best [1845], p. 33).

[25] As observed in Mason Ladd's meticulous article: "Courts and legislators often carelessly use the term 'presumption,' however, to describe factual assumptions which are not subject to a rule of law which requires a finding of the presumed fact in the absence of rebuttal testimony" (Ladd 1977, p. 277). The distinction between presumptions as rules, on the one hand, and presumptions as inferences was one of the main contributions of James Bradley Thayer in his famous essay on the subject.

[26] See Bentham [1838–1843], vol. 9, p. 77: "By fiction, in the sense in which it is used by lawyers, I understand a false assertion which, though acknowledged to be false, is at the same time argued from, and acted upon, as if true." For an account of a Benthamic perspective on legal fictions see Quinn's essay in Chap. 4 of this volume.

[27] See Best (1845, p. 36): "The essential distinction between these [legal fictions] and *praesumptiones juris et de jure* consists in this: that the latter are arbitrary inferences, which may or may not be true, whilst, in the case of fictions, the falsehood of the fact assumed is understood and avowed."

[28] Vaihinger's theory of fictions is discussed in different chapters of this volume. See additionally Marí 2002, Chap. 12.

[29] For an account of Tourtoulon's concept of fiction see Frank 2009 [1930], p. 339.

[30] See Olivier 1975, p. 59 where he observes: "the civilian school is the only one which enables us to form a clear and correct understanding of the fiction structure."

[31] See Fuller 1967, p. 9.

16.3 The Theoretical and Practical Dimensions of Presumptions and Legal Fictions

The analysis of the concepts of presumption and legal fiction is largely problematic because of the ambiguity of these expressions. These terms are used in a variety of meanings and for a variety of purposes by courts, legislators, commentators and legal philosophers. Several confusions and disagreements are due to the unawareness of the fact that these expressions are used to refer to a variety of phenomena.

As observed by Riccardo Guastini (1992), the term "legal fiction" is applied to a variety of different situations: (i) It is used to refer to statutory or legislative fictions, such as the famous *fictio legis Cornelia* or the statutory fiction of the unborn child. (ii) It is also used to describe historical, creative or jurisprudential legal fictions, i.e. a judicial technique conceived to modify an existing rule in order to make it applicable to new situations, while leaving the same wording, as when "the English court pretended that the Island of Minorca was a part of the city of London".[32] (iii) The same expression is also used to refer to fictitious entities, i. e. mental constructs of the legal science upon which we speak as if they exist, as in the Kelsenian analysis of the concepts of persons, state and organ.[33] (iv) Furthermore, the term "legal fiction" is used in the sense of a false representation, in relation to an ideology, as the fiction that judges do not make the law.

A similar situation occurs in respect of the use of the term "presumption". Among the principal meanings in which this expression is used in legal language it is possible to identify the following: (i) "Presumption" sometimes designates a general principle or a maxim of legal reasoning.[34] (ii) "Presumption" sometimes describes a statement about the usual connection between two facts, according to which the assertion of the existence of one of these facts entitles one to presume the existence of another fact.[35] (iii) Additionally, "presumption" sometimes denotes a rule of substantive law formulated in presumptive terms, as in conclusive presumptions.[36]

---

[32] Fuller 1967, p. 18. For a conceptual analysis of jurisprudential fictions and the fiction created in the Minorca case see Chiassoni 2001, p. 71. See additionally a discussion of this fiction in Frederick Schauer's essay published in Chap. 6 of this volume.

[33] See Kelsen's essay on legal fictions now translated and published in English in Chap. 1 of this volume. For a comment on Kelsen's essay see Kletzer, this volume, Chap. 2.

[34] E.g. the presumption that individuals act honestly, the presumption of sanity or the presumption that everybody knows the law. See Thayer [1898], p. 335.

[35] In Continental law the terms that are usually applied are "judicial presumptions" or "simple presumptions". In English law, these presumptions are labelled as "provisional presumption". In Anglo-American law these presumptions are called "permissible inferences". See Denning 1945, p. 379; Dennis 2002, pp. 420–421 and Allen and Callen 2003, p. 3.

[36] The legal effect of these rules consists of establishing a full equivalence between the basic fact and the presumed fact. See this argument in Morgan 1943, 245 and Taruffo 1991. An interesting example of a conclusive presumption is discussed in Allen, et al. 2011, p. 715: the Federal Coal Mine Health and Safety Act of 1969 indicates that once that it is established that a miner has complicated pneumoconiosis, the law conclusively presumes that the miner is totally disabled.

(iv) "Presumption" is also used to describe a rule that changes the burden of proof to the opponent.[37]

The very fact that the same expression is used to refer to such a variety of different situations is sufficient to generate doubts on the explanatory power of the traditional distinction between presumptions and fictions (i.e. legal fictions as consciously false assumptions or false statements, and presumptions as assumptions that may be true).

However, there is a particular ambiguity that is possibly more basic and perhaps more persistent that affects both the concepts of presumption and fiction and in consequence the relationship between them. This ambiguity is produced by the confusion between the role of presumptions and legal fictions in theoretical and practical discourse, i.e. for not discriminating the use of these concepts for theoretical and cognitive purposes, from their use for practical and normative purposes.[38]

The traditional distinction overlooks this ambiguity when it defines presumptions and legal fictions in general as assumptions, irrespective of whether this assumption is established in a rule of law or is the result of a mental operation.

In fact, the traditional approach to these concepts not only disregards this ambiguity but has also contributed to deepen the confusion between the role of these concepts in theoretical and practical discourse by putting an excessive emphasis on epistemological considerations.[39] On the one hand, the traditional approach holds that the central features of a fiction are: (i) its deviation from reality, (ii) the negation of truth, (iii) the consciousness of its falsity, and (iv) its nature of false assertions. On the other hand, the traditional approach holds that the basic features of a presumption are: (i) its relation to truth, (ii) the approximation to reality, and (iii) its nature of statements that establish an inferential relationship between two facts, a fact that gives rise to the presumption and a presumed fact.

The following paragraphs are intended to clarify the distinction between the role of presumptions and legal fictions in theoretical and practical discourse by making reference to the opinions of some eminent authors.

16.3.1 The Role of Presumptions in Theoretical and Practical Reasoning

In one sense, the literature on presumptions could be read as a struggle to differentiate between the use of presumptions as a synonym of inferences, from the use of

[37] On this respect, since there are two types of burdens of proof in the Anglo-American law of presumptions (the burden of producing evidence—or evidential burden—and the burden of persuasion—or persuasive burden), some presumptions shift the burden of production to the opponent (e.g. the presumption that a letter properly addressed, stamped and mailed has been duly delivered), while others shift the burden of persuasion (e.g. the presumption of paternity). For a survey of this discussion see Ladd 1977, p. 281; Allen (1994) and Allen and Callen (2003).

[38] For an account of this ambiguity in the literature of presumptions see Aguiló 2006.

[39] See this argument in Varga and Szàjer 1988, p. 170.

presumptions as rules that apply legal consequences when certain conditions are verified.

As a matter of fact, it has been in the field of evidence, not in the field of legal theory, where this ambiguity has been mainly detected. For more than a century, legal scholars have warned us against the confusion between the use of presumptions as rules and the use of presumptions as inferences. As observed by John Henry Wigmore:

> The distinction between 'presumption' in the sense of a mere circumstantial inference and in the sense of a rule of procedure affecting the duty of proof has in modern times led to confusion. The term is often met with in the sense of 'inference', as applied to the probative value of ordinary circumstantial evidence (Wigmore 1937 Sect. 6 n. 1.)[40]

In making this observation Wigmore was following one of the main contributions of his former professor James Bradley Thayer, who in response to James F. Stephen's definition of presumptions as rules that require one to draw an inference, argued that "it involves the misconception that the law has any rules at all for conducting the process of reasoning". In stating this, Thayer urged legal scholars and authorities to discriminate the use of presumptions as statements about what is probable from the use of presumptions as a rule of law that attaches legal consequences:

> A rule of presumption does not merely say that such and such a thing is a permissible and usual inference from other facts, but it goes on to say that this significance shall always, in the absence of other circumstances, be imputed to them. (Thayer 1898, p. 317)

In the light of these considerations, Wigmore, Morgan and several evidence scholars of the following generations argued in favor of a redefinition of the concept of presumption, reserving this expression for the rules that require the trier of facts to hold a fact as true, and using the term "inference" to refer to the process of proof.[41]

The aforementioned ambiguity may be further clarified if we move from the discourse of legal scholars to the more abstract discourse of philosophers. There are two philosophers in particular who have contributed extensively to unraveling the nature of presumption in the cognitive and practical terrains: Nicholas Rescher and the late Edna Ullmann-Margalit.[42] Both authors observe that the concept of

---

[40] See additionally Wigmore 1923, §2487 where he observes: "The particular ambiguity which we need here to guard against is the confusion between the inference itself—i. e. the propriety of making the inference from the evidence to the '*factum probandum*'— and the effect of the inference in the hands of the judge."

[41] Despite the efforts for redefining the concept of presumption, courts and legislators often carelessly use this expression as a synonym of inferences as well as for many other purposes. See Ladd 1977, p. 277. In the last years Ronald Allen has favoured a realistic approach to the subject of presumptions, arguing that the efforts to reconcile the different uses of the term "presumption" are misdirected: "[I]t is the failure to recognize that the word 'presumption' is simply a label applied to a range of evidentiary decisions that has caused essentially all the confusion and controversy surrounding presumptions" (Allen 1980, p. 845). See additionally Allen (2003), for an account of his argument of presumptions as isomorphs of other evidentiary devices.

[42] Richard Gaskins's *Burden of proof in modern discourse* (1993) is also relevant for the analysis of presumptions and burden of proof, but his study is primarily oriented toward the use of these instruments in the sphere of public discourse.

presumption is a wonderful, pragmatic resource that could be used for both cognitive and practical purposes. Rescher and Ullmann-Margalit are fully aware that the most prominent role of this concept is in the law, but they argue that its potential goes further than the realm of law and legal reasoning.

On the first page of her illuminating essay Edna Ullmann-Margalit points out two main directions in which the analysis of the concept of presumption could be undertaken: practical deliberation and theoretical inquiry. In doing so she provides a succinct clarification of the use of the concept of presumption in each field in the following terms:

> The clarification of the epistemic claims that presumptions have on us—or rather on our set of beliefs—is undoubtedly part of any adequate account of the notion of presumption. But this will not be the orientation of the explanation I shall offer. I shall look, rather, to the role that the notion of presumption can be made to play within the theory of action. That is to say: rather than treat a presumption as an assumption in advance of some theoretical venture, I shall treat it as an assumption made in advance of practical deliberation. Furthermore, rather than view presumption as a logical prerequisite for the launching of a theoretical inquiry I shall view it as a rational prerequisite for arrival at a variety of decisions about action. (Ullmann-Margalit 1983a, p. 143)

For Ullmann-Margalit, presumption rules play an important role in practical reasoning in situations in which a (practical) solution depends on the factual issue of whether a proposition is true of false. In these situations, presumption rules operate as a "method of extrication" by providing an agent with "a baseline for action which is to be abandoned just in case some counter indication is more or less thrust upon him". She holds that in practical discourse the presumption rule neither requires nor entitles one to believe in the truth of a presumed proposition, as may occur in the use of presumptions as inferences that provide inferential support for the belief that a certain fact is true. The whole instruction of presumption rules is this: to hold certain propositions as true for the purpose of a decision related with action.[43]

The distinction between the role of presumptions in theoretical and practical discourse has also been fully appreciated by Nicholas Rescher, who introduces the distinction between "cognitive presumptions" and "practical presumptions" to differentiate the different role they display. Rescher is mainly interested in clarifying "cognitive presumptions", the presumptions that are established for helping us to do what we can in situations of incomplete information. These presumptions operate as default assumptions that are made to fill the gaps in our information for the lack of anything better and until there is evidence to the contrary. In contrast, "practical presumptions" are made for guiding our decisions about action, as legal presumptions do to facilitate the resolution of cases (Rescher 2006, p. 27).[44]

---

[43] See Ullmann-Margalit 1983a, pp. 149–151.

[44] It should be noted however that it is not possible to maintain an absolute separation between theoretical and practical discourse, as Rescher himself observes in considering Edna Ullmann-Margalit's (2006, p. 11) approach: "Some writers see presumption as merely an action-guiding device. But this does not do full justice to the matter, for while a practice is indeed at issue with presumption, this can also include the practice of information management—of epistemic or cognitive procedure". This observation is not an obstacle for distinguishing the use of presumption for cognitive or practical purposes.

16.3.2 Fictions of Legal Theory and Fictions of Legal Practice

In an essay originally published in 1919 that appears now translated in English in Chap. 1 of this volume, Hans Kelsen discusses the potential of Vaihinger's concept of fiction for the analysis of legal fictions.[45] His main argument is that many of the legal fictions that Vaihinger's takes as paradigmatic examples of his concept of fiction are not authentic fictions in Vaihinger's sense.

In the present context, Kelsen's analysis is relevant because he took Vaihinger's concept of fiction as a starting point for establishing an interesting distinction between fictions of legal theory and fictions of legal practice.

Kelsen accepts that fictions of legal theory are similar to Vaihinger's concept of fictions of the theory of knowledge. They are mental constructs designed to obtain a better understanding of reality, a reality that in the case of the legal science is a legal reality. The objective of these fictions, then, is the knowledge of legal reality, i.e. the knowledge of the "legal ought". Fictions obtain such knowledge by introducing a contradiction with natural or legal reality. His characterization of fictions, including the fictions of the legal theory, is described in the following passage:

> [W]e have to speak of a fiction as soon as cognition (and especially juridic cognition) takes a detour in knowing its object (and in juridic knowledge this object is the law, the legal order, the legal ought) a detour in which it consciously sets itself in contradiction to this object; and be it only in order to better grasp it: just like a rock-climber, in order to avoid an obstacle and reach his goal more easily, is sometimes forced to temporarily climb downwards, i.e. in a direction opposed to his goal, the peak. (Kelsen 2014 [1919])

Fictions of legal theory are different from the fictions of legal practice, i. e. the fictions of the legislator and fictions in the application of the law. The so-called fictions of the legislator are not mental constructs, but legal norms that result from an act of will. With them, the legislator does not pretend to obtain knowledge of legal reality, but to regulate conduct. In establishing such a rule, there is no fiction, Kelsen argues, since the rule of the legislator involves no contradiction with reality (nor natural, nor legal reality). The whole function of the legislator consists in attaching legal consequences to certain situations and in this function the legislator is "almighty". Thus, the so-called fictions of the legislator are not fictions at all, since they involve no contradiction with the legal order (within the discourse of the legislator). He then goes on to say that the grammatical form in which these rules are traditionally formulated ("A shall be treated as if B") is only an abbreviated form for saying that the legal consequences foreseen by a certain rule of law in one case are to be applied to another case. [46] As Kelsen observes:

> [T]he grammatical form of the "As-if" thus is not in any way essential, it can be replaced by a mere 'just as'. If the law subsumes two cases under the same norm, it by no means claims that both cases are alike—in the sense of *naturally* alike. Or otherwise every general norm would be a 'fiction' since there are not two men, two facts which are alike. (Kelsen 2014 [1919])

---

[45] See Kletzer, 2014, for a comment on Kelsen's essay on legal fictions in this volume, Chap. 2.

[46] This thesis is also discussed in Kletzer, this volume, Chap. 2.

Although Kelsen condemns the creation of fictions by the judge, his reconstruction of this practice is basically the same. In these fictions, he argues that the judge (unjustifiably) extends the application of an existing rule to a situation that is different to what was originally foreseen by a previously existing rule of the legislator. In Kelsen's example, a legal fiction in the application of the law occurs when a judge extends the sanction established by the law to the damages on a public telegraph to the damage on telephones. As in the fictions of the legislator, "the judge here does not proceed *as if* the telegraph were a telephone" but maintains that the sanction established for damaging telegraphs is to be applied to the damage of telephones.[47]

In sum for Kelsen, the use of legal fictions could be used either for cognitive purposes or for normative purposes. When legal fictions are placed at the level of rules, they work by establishing a full legal equivalence between two cases, subsuming them under the same rule. This may result in a legitimate operation when these rules are established by the legislator, or in an illegitimate modification of the existing rules.

Conclusion

In the previous two sections I have presented three points. First, the necessity to put into context the analysis of the relationship between presumptions and fictions. The conceptions of legal fictions as consciously false assumptions and of presumptions as assumptions that may be true belong to an intellectual tradition in which glossators, canonists, commentators and humanists elaborated the notions, classifications and definitions that we continue using today.

Secondly, despite the long history of the traditional approach to this subject, it is unsatisfactory. As we have seen, both the terms "presumption" and "legal fiction" have been used to refer to a variety of different phenomena. An examination of all the different situations in which these expressions are used in legal discourse show that they hardly belong to a same *genus*, as Hart cogently argued in his criticisms of the traditional Aristotelian method *per genus* and *differentiam* (1983 [1953]).

Thirdly, the traditional approach to the relationship between presumptions and fictions is problematic since it does not distinguish clearly between the use of these concepts for theoretical (cognitive) and practical (normative) purposes. In the

[47] Kelsen's repudiation of judicial fictions should be understood in connection with his conception of both the creation and the application of the law. He argues that the fictions in the application of the law are "completely inadmissible" since the judge "cannot arbitrarily extend and restrict legal norms". For Kelsen, jurisprudential fictions are genuine fictions since they involve a rule that is fully or partially inconsistent with the legal system. For an analysis of Kelsen's position regarding judicial fictions, see Chiassoni 2001, pp. 87–88, where he provides an account of the "apparently paradoxical" thesis that it makes sense to speak of a jurisprudential fiction in those legal systems in which the law has no power to make law. Kelsen's thesis of fictions in the application of the law is also discussed in Kletzer's essay included in this volume (Chap. 2).

second section I intended to clarify this ambiguity by examining the opinions of some leading authorities. As a result of this clarification the distinction between the theoretical and practical use of both presumptions and fictions could be restated as follows.

In theoretical discourse, presumptions are statements of the form "If A then presumably B", as in the statement "A letter properly addressed, stamped and mailed has presumably been duly delivered". These statements work as generalizations that establish a correlation between two facts: a fact that gives rise to the presumption (A) and a presumed fact (B). The proof of fact A licenses one to infer the existence of a second group of facts. These statements are founded upon the observation of a regular association between two facts. Additionally, the function of these statements is to approximate to truth. Last, the force of these statements depends on the strength of the inductive argument from which they are obtained.[48]

In practical discourse, presumptions are not factual statements but rules. In the case of legal presumptions, presumption rules indicate the legal consequences that follow from the verification of the facts specified in the *protasis* of the rule. These rules may be grounded in (i) inductive-probabilistic considerations, (ii) in considerations of policy, or (iii) in considerations of justice.[49] The function of presumption rules is dependent on the type of considerations in which they are based. As observed by Professors Morgan (1931) and Ladd (1977), the function of presumption rules may vary between one or more of the following reasons: (a) To expedite trials on issues not likely to be litigated (e.g. "an employee is presumed to be acting in the course of his employment while he is using his employer's property, unless contrary evidence is introduced"), (b) To avoid a procedural impasse and an undesirable result because of the lack of evidence (e.g. the presumptions related with the survivorship of persons who died in the same accident), (c) To weigh certain inferences more heavily because they accord with what usually happens (e.g. the presumption that a letter properly addressed, stamped and mailed has been duly delivered), (d) To correct an imbalance resulting from one party's superior access to the proof (e.g. the presumption of negligence in medical malpractice), and (e) To recognize the social desirability of the legal consequences of a presumed fact (e.g. the presumption of paternity). Finally, the force of presumption rules derives from their normative force, which derives from the specific grounds in which they are based.

In theoretical discourse fictions are, roughly, mental constructs, false assumptions or false assertions. The objective of these constructions is epistemological: the cognition of reality (sensitive or an ideal reality made by norms). Theoretical

[48] I take this conceptual scheme from González (2013), who distinguishes the notions of grounds, purpose and force for two basic types of warrants (epistemic or legal) in inferences of facts. On generalizations see Anderson et al. (2005, Chap. 10), as well as Schauer (2006).

[49] This characterization of presumptions contrasts with Frederick Schauer's view of rules as presumptions presented in Chap. 6 of this volume. The thesis advanced in this essay is that not all presumption rules are based on probabilistic considerations, and not all the rules based on probabilistic considerations are presumptions. On the different grounds of presumptions see McCormick 1978 pp. 343 and Ullmann-Margalit 1983, p. 157.

fictions operate through a negation of reality, through a contradiction with its object. Finally, these fictions are founded primarily on epistemological grounds.[50]

In practical-normative discourse, legal fictions are neither statements, nor assertions. It is odd to characterize legislative fictions as belonging to the assertive discourse since the legislator does not pretend to assert anything (the fact that the proposition expressed in the rule is false is irrelevant).[51]

For the same reasons it is odd to define the fictions of the judge as consciously false assertions or as statements formulated with consciousness of their falsity. In other words, fiction rules created in the application of the law are not assertions that pretend to express an empirical truth. They are operations at the level of rules by which, irrespective of their legitimacy or illegitimacy, a judge extends the application of an existing rule to a situation of fact that cannot be subsumed under that rule, and in doing so he creates a new rule.

In light of the ambiguity in the use of the terms "presumption" and "fiction" it may be convenient to avoid talking about the relationship between presumptions and legal fictions in general. Rather, the relationship between these concepts should be focused at the level of rules, that is, the distinction between presumption rules and legal fiction rules. From this perspective, the traditional distinction between these rules would clarify at best the mental process involved in the creation of such rules, but it does not provide an adequate account of their differences as two different types of rules.

If this is the case, we may then ask what sort of rules are presumption rules and fiction rules. It is widely accepted that presumption rules are mandatory rules that instruct the trier of facts to assume a fact as true. But what sort of instruction is this? Since rules deal with legal consequences, "to assume for the time that one fact is, in legal effect, the same as a certain other" means that "the rule fixes the legal effect of a fact, its legal equivalence with another" (Thayer 1898, p. 317).[52]

From this perspective, presumption rules would not differ much from fiction rules. As Alf Ross observes:

> To 'pretend' that A is B is merely an odd way of expressing the thought that, for purposes of law, A is to be treated as subject to the same rules as apply to (Ross 1960, p. 223).

Ross was aware that this operation is not exclusive of legal fictions. He argues that the same result could be achieved by the use of presumptions, with the difference that if considered as a descriptive statement, the presumption would be generally

[50] I am aware that this reconstruction does not do justice to this complex subject. A careful analysis would require entering, for instance, into considerations of ontology, language and debates about scientific realism.

[51] See Guastini 1992, p. 353 and Chiassoni 2001, p. 73 ff., where he discusses the problem of the nature of jurisprudential fictions as assertions or rules.

[52] I cannot enter in detail into this point, but it seems to me that both presumption rules and fiction rules have a characteristic feature of constitutive rules, in the sense that they establish that "A counts as B in the context C". For an account of this thesis regarding legal fiction rules see Hernández 1986; Guastini 1992, p. 355; Chiassoni 2001, p. 78 ff.; Mendonca 2003. Regarding presumption rules see Aguiló 2006 and Gama 2015.

true. But in both cases the legal operation is the same: subsuming two cases under the same rule.

This suggests that presumption rules and legal fictions rules are not too different from the perspective of their content. The linguistic formulations "A is to be presumed as B" or "A is to be considered as B" would only be grammatical forms with no special significance from the point of view of the content of the rule, since the instruction is the same: to attach to A the same legal consequences which are attached to B.[53]

From this perspective, both presumption and fictions rules established by the legislator are normative shortcuts that result from an operation of language. The legislator does not presume nor pretend that A is B. What the legislator indicates is that the legal consequences established by a certain existent rule for B are to be attached to the class of operative facts A.[54]

The creation of presumptions and fiction rules as a result of the activity of the judge is a more complex phenomenon. It is commonly accepted that judges have created presumption rules and fiction rules with the purpose of introducing substantive innovations in the law, while apparently maintaining the existing law. However, the implications of these innovations may vary in each case. Presumption rules operate as an evidentiary device designed to manage factual uncertainty through the assignment of the burden of proof. The effect of a fiction rule introduced by the judge supposes a tacit abrogation of an existing law, which is substituted with a new rule that is considered as morally acceptable by the same judge. This suggests the necessity to focus on the relationship between presumption and fiction rules created by courts.

References

Aguiló, Josep. 2006. Presunciones, verdad y normas procesales. *Isegoría* 35:9–31.

Allen, Ronald. 1980. Presumptions in civil actions reconsidered. *Iowa Law Review* 66:843–867.

Allen, Ronald. 1994. How presumptions should be allocated. *Harvard Journal of Law and Public Policy* 17:627–645.

Allen, Ronald J., and Craig R. Callen. 2003. The juridical management of factual uncertainty. *International Journal of Evidence & Proof* 7:1–30.

[53] In chap. 11 of this volume, Maksymilian Del Mar defines legal fictions as rules that suspend a required operative fact, and he sees a difference with presumptions in the fact that the latter "take a stance on the likelihood of an operative fact being present". As we have seen, not all presumptions are based on probability considerations and in any case this is a question for the grounds of presumptions, not a question about how they operate. The thesis advanced in this essay is that presumption and fiction rules operate almost in the same way. Rebuttable presumptions differ from fiction rules and from conclusive presumptions in the procedural consequences that follow from the application of the presumption in terms of the burden of proof.

[54] A different question is what procedural consequences follow in terms of the burden of proof, which in the case of statutory presumptions may affect either the burden of production or the burden of persuasion.

Allen, Ronald, et al. 2011. *Evidence: Text, problems and cases*. New York: Aspen.
Anderson T., et al. 2005. *Analysis of evidence*. 2nd ed. New York: Cambridge University Press.
Andrioli, Virgilio. 1966. Presunzioni (Diritto civile e Diritto processuale civile). In *Novissimo Digesto Italiano*, vol. XIII, 766–772. Torino: Editrice Torinese.
Bentham, Jeremy. [1838–1843]. *The works of Jeremy Bentham now first collected under the superintendence of his Executor, John Bowring*. vol. ix. Edinburgh: Tait.
Bentham, Jeremy. 1840. *Theory of legislation*. Etienne Dumont, trans, vol. 1. Boston: Weeks, Jordan.
Best, William. M. 1845. *A treatise on presumptions of law and fact, with the theory and rules of presumptive or circumstantial proof in criminal cases*. Philadelphia: T. & J. W. Johnson.
Birks, Peter. 1986. Fictions ancient and modern. In *The legal Mind: Essays for Tony Honoré,* ed. N. MacCormick and P. Birks, 83–101. Oxford: Clarendon.
Boyer, Georges. 1954. Sur quelques emplois de la fiction dans l'ancien droit oriental. *Revue International des Droits de l'Antiquité* 1:73–100.
Campbell, Kenneth. 1983. Fuller on legal fictions. *Law and Philosophy* 2 (3): 339–370.
Campitelli, Adriana. 1986. Presunzione (Dir. intermedio). In *Enciclopedia del Diritto*, vol. 31, 260–264. Torino: Giuffrè Editore.
Chiassoni, Pierluigi. 2001. Finzioni giudiziali. *Analisi e diritto* 71–94.
Collingwood, R. G. 1961 [1946]. *The idea of history*. Oxford: Oxford University Press.
Collingwood, R. G. 2002 [1939]. *An autobiography*. Oxford: Oxford University Press.
Decottignies, Roger. 1950. *Les présomptions en droit privé*. Paris: Librairie Générale de Droit et de Jurisprudence.
Del Mar, Maksymilian. 2014. Legal fictions and legal change in the common law tradition. In *Legal fictions in theory and practice,* ed. Maksymilian Del Mar and William Twining. Dordrecht: Springer.
Denning, A. T. 1945. Presumptions and burdens. *Law Quarterly Review* 61:379–383.
Dennis, Ian. H. 2002. *The law of evidence*. 2nd ed. London: Sweet & Maxwell.
Donatuti, Guido. 1976a [1931]. Le "praesumptiones iuris" come mezzi di svolgimento del diritto sostanziale romano. In *Studi di Diritto Romano*, vol. 1, 421–486. Milan: Giuffré.
Donatuti, Guido. 1976b [1933]. Le *praesumptione iuris* in diritto romano (loro origine). In *Studi di diritto romano,* vol. 1, 487–532. Milan: Giuffrè.
Errera, Andrea. 2007. The role of logic in the legal science of the glossators and commentators. Distinction, dialectical syllogism, and apodictic syllogism: An investigation into the epistemological roots of legal science in the late middle ages. In *The Jurists' philosophy of law from Rome to the seventeenth century,* ed. Andrea Padovani and Peter Stein, vol. 7 , 79–156. Dordrecht: Springer.
Ferrini, Contardo. 1929 [1892]. Le presunzioni in diritto romano. In *Opere di Contardo Ferrini,* vol. 3, 417–451. Milan: Ulrico Hoepli.
Frank, Jerome. 2009 [1930]. *Law and the modern mind.* New Brunswick: Transaction.
Franklin, James. 2002. *The science of conjecture: evidence and probability before Pascal.* Baltimore: John Hopkins University Press.
Fuller, Lon L. 1967. *Legal fictions*. Stanford: Stanford University Press.
Gama, Raymundo. 2015. *Las presunciones en el Derecho. Entre la perplejidad y la fascinación de los juristas* (forthcoming).
Gambaro, Antonio. 1992. Finzione giuridica nel diritto positivo. In *Digesto*, vol. 8, Civile, 342–353. Torino: Utet.
Gaskins, Richard. 1993. *Burden of proof in modern discourse*. New Haven: Yale University Press.
Giuliani, Adolfo. 1971. *Il concetto di prova: contributo alla logica giuridica*. Milan: Giuffrè.
Giuliani, Alessandro. 2009. Civilian treatises on presumptions (1580–1620). In *The law of presumptions: Essays in comparative legal history,* ed. R. H. Helmholz and W. D. H. Sellar, 21–71. Berlin: Duncker & Humboldt.
González, Daniel. 2013 [2007]. Hechos y conceptos. In *Quaestio facti. Ensayos sobre prueba causalidad y acción*, 75–85. Mexico D.F.: Fontamara.

Guastini, Riccardo. 1992. Finzione giuridica nella teoria generale. In *Digesto*, vol. 8, Civile, 354–356. Torino: Utet.

Hans Kelsen. 2014. On the theory of juridic fictions. With special consideration of Vaihinger's Philosophy of the as-if. In *Legal fictions in theory and practice,* ed. Maksymilian Del Mar and William Twining. Dordrecht: Springer.

Hart, H. L. A. 1983 [1953]. Definition and theory in Jurisprudence. In *Essays in jurisprudence and philosophy,* 21–48. Oxford: Oxford University Press.

Hedemann, J. W. 1931 [1904]. Die Vermutung nach dem Recht des Deutschen Reiches. Trans. esp. Las presunciones en el derecho. Madrid: Revista de Derecho Privado.

Hernández, Rafael. 1986. Ficciones Jurídicas. *Doxa. Cuadernos de Teoría y Filosofía del Derecho,* 141–147.

Hohmann, Hans. 2001. Presumptions in Roman legal argumentation. In *Argumentation and its applications, Proceedings of the Fourth OSSA Conference,* ed. Hansen, Hans et al. University of Windsor (May 2001). CD Room.

Kelsen, Hans. (1919). Zur Theorie der juristischen Fiktionen. Mit besonderer Berücksichtigung von Vaihingers Philosophie des Als-Ob, tr. Eng. by Christoph Kletzer, In *On the Theory of Juridic Fictions. With special consideration of Vaihinger's Philosophy of the As-If in Legal fictions in Theory of Practice*, ed. Maksymilian del Mar and William Twining, 630–658. Springer.

Kletzer, Christoph. 2014. Kelsen on Vaihinger. In *Legal fictions in theory and practice,* ed. Maksymilian Del Mar and William Twining. Dordrecht: Springer.

Ladd, Mason. 1977. Presumptions in civil actions. *Arizona State Law Journal* 275–294.

Lewis, C. T., and C. Short. [1879] 1998. *A Latin dictionary founded on Andrews' edition of Freund's Latin dictionary*. Oxford: Clarendon.

Marí, Enrique. 2002. *La teoría de las ficciones*. Buenos Aires: Eudeba.

McCormick, C. T. 1978. *McCormick's handbook of the law of evidence*. Minnesota: West.

Mendonca, Daniel. 2003. Estudio preliminar. In *Ficciones jurídicas,* Hans Kelsen, ed. Lon, L. ,y. Fuller, and Alf Ross, 7–22. Mexico: Fontamara.

Morgan, Edmund. 1931. Some observations concerning presumptions. *Harvard Law Review* 44 (6): 906–934.

Morgan, Edmund. 1943. Further observations on presumptions. *Southern California Law Review* 16 (4): 245–265.

Olivier, Pierre. 1975. *Legal fictions in practice and legal science*. Rotterdam: Rotterdam University Press.

Pugliatti, Salvatore. 1968. Finzione. In *Enciclopedia del Diritto,* vol. 17, 658–673. Milan: Giuffrè.

Ramponi, Lamberto. 1890. *La Teoria Generale delle Presunzione*. Torino: Fratelli Bocca.

Reggi, Roberto.1986. Presunzione a) Diritto romano. In *Enciclopedia del Diritto,* vol. 35, 255–260. Torino: Giuffrè Editore.

Rescher, Nicholas. 2006. *Presumption and the practices of tentative cognition.* Cambridge: Cambridge University Press.

Ross, Alf. 1969. Legal fictions. In *Law, reason and justice: Essays in legal philosophy.* ed. G. Hughes, 217–231. New York: New York University.

Russell, Donald A. 2001. *Quintilian: The Orator's education.* Vol. 2, Books 3–5. Cambridge: Harvard University Press.

Serra, Manuel. 1963. *Normas de presunción en el Código Civil y ley de arrendamientos urbanos.* Barcelona: Nauta.

Schauer, Frederick. 2006. *Profiles, probabilities, and stereotypes*. London: Belknap Press of Harvard University Press.

Schauer, Frederick. 2014. Legal fictions revisited. In *Legal fictions in theory and practice,* ed. Maksymilian Del Mar and William Twining. Dordrecht: Springer.

Shain, Mark. 1944. Presumptions under the common and the civil law. *Southern California Law Review* 18 (2): 91–109.

Taruffo, Michele. 1991. Presunzioni (Diritto Processuale Civile). In *Enciclopedia Giuridica Trecanni* vol. 24: 1–5. Roma: Instituto della Enciclopedia Italiana.

Thayer, J. B. [1898]. *A preliminary treatise on evidence at the common law.* Boston: Little, Brown.

Thomas, Yan. 1995. Fictio legis. L' empire de la fiction romaine et ses limites médievales. *Droits. Revue française de théorie juridique* 21: 17–63.
Todescan, Franco. 1979. *Diritto e realtà. Storia e teoria della fictio juris*. Padua: Cedam.
Twining, W. L. 1998. R.G. Collingwood's autobiography: One reader's response. *Journal of Law and Society* 25 (4): 603–620.
Twining, W. L. 2006. *Rethinking evidence: Exploratory essays* 2nd ed. New York: Cambridge University Press.
Ullman-Margalit, Edna. 1983a. On presumption. *Journal of Philosophy* 80 (3): 143–163
Ullman-Margalit, Edna. 1983b. Some presumptions. In *How many questions? Essays in honor of Sidney Morgenbesser*, ed. L. S. Cauman, et al., 451–473. Indianapolis: Hacket.
Varga, Csaba, and József Szájer. 1988. Presumption and fiction: Means of legal technique. *Archiv für rechts-und Sozialphilosophie* 74 (2): 168–184.
Wigmore, J. H. 1923. *A treatise on the Anglo-American system of evidence in trials at common law, including the statutes and judicial decisions of all jurisdictions of the United States and Canada,* 2nd ed. Boston: Little, Brown and Company.
Wigmore, J. H. 1937. *The science of judicial proof as given by logic, psychology, and general experience, and illustrated in judicial trials,* 3rd ed. Boston: Little, Brown and Company.

Chapter 17
Some Uses of Legal Fictions in Criminal Law

Peter Alldridge

Abstract The essay considers fictions in four areas of criminal law. The area of jury nullification fits most easily into a narrative of fictions as a mechanism for gentle amelioration of undesirable laws (in particular, undesirable penalties). The value of fictions in this narrative depends upon acceptance of the reactivity of the jury as the finger on the contemporary moral pulse. The construction of facts as a bargaining process is easier to accept in the civil field, but can also operate successfully in the criminal law, in which to fail altogether to recognise the possibility of fact construction would be to commit to a worse fiction. The essay contrasts these two against two other uses of fiction in criminal law which ought to be treated with greater scepticism. One is the use of forfeiture deriving its justification from the medieval fiction to the effect that the thing is guilty. This is impossible to justify and the recent growth of forfeiture is to be regretted. Finally, by way of contrast, the essay looks at the use of deeming provisions in criminal proscriptions. Whatever their value elsewhere, they ought not to be countenanced in substantive criminal law.

17.1 Introduction

The criminal law in England arose from the fiction that particular incidents between subjects violate the King's Peace. It embodies a number of pretences, some necessary (individual agency), some contingent (the defensibility of jury decision-making), some unnecessary (corporate personality), some (perhaps) a consequence

P. Alldridge (✉)
Department of Law, Queen Mary University of London,
Mile End Rd, London E1 4NS, UK
e-mail: p.w.alldridge@qmul.ac.uk

M. Del Mar, W. Twining (eds.), *Legal Fictions in Theory and Practice*,
Law and Philosophy Library 110, DOI 10.1007/978-3-319-09232-4_17

of needing fixed numerical limits in various areas,[1] and some just plain appalling.[2] Particularly since the advent of the human rights jurisdiction,[3] the relationship of the criminal law to fictions in a more precise sense has never been quite the symbiotic one which can be claimed for it in other areas.

> The essence of every legal fiction and presumtio juris et de jure, even the presumption of innocence […], is the prevalence of purpose and policy over truth.[4]

In consequence the sorts of metaphor that spring to mind are (if from construction) not so much scaffolding[5] as *ad hoc* repairs or patches.[6] This essay will explore areas in which fictions are used in or (in the case of forfeiture) adjacent to the criminal law. The first, jury nullification, covers a range of findings of fact, usually by juries, to avoid either liability or particular penal consequences. Broadly speaking, it fits into the narrative of fictions as means of testing out possible moves towards a better legal structure. If contested criminal litigation is to be ended by a verdict, publicly labelling the offender, and sentence follows from an unreviewable jury verdict, the jury itself is empowered to acquit in the face of the evidence, indicating, perhaps, its disapproval of the rule. Those who like juries will like this. The second, plea bargaining, puts the fact/fiction dichotomy itself very clearly in issue. Here the litigation will not, in general, be contested. The verdict will not be brought on a basis that is demonstrably untrue, but one that is taken as an appropriate public statement of the upper limit of the defendant's criminality. The third (forfeiture), seizure by the state of property because of its connection to crime, is a practice that might have been expected to disappear, but instead is being multiplied. The original rationale for forfeiture was the fiction that the thing was guilty, and that has attracted withering criticism at least since the eighteenth century. The range of cases to which forfeiture now applies cannot be justified by appeal to a single principle, but is probably a curious legacy of the old fiction. The use of forfeiture needs to be considered critically. The fourth case, by way of a contrast, is not a fiction properly so called, but a deeming expression, that has moved from the law of theft to that of proceeds of crime. The essay will trace the use of the expression "pecuniary advantage" in deeming provisions of the criminal law of property and proceeds of crime. It will show that they have not and could not have worked well, and will suggest that there is no place in criminal law for such out-and-out deeming.

[1] *Doli incapax*, as to which see the saga from *C. v. D.P.P.* [1996] A.C. 1, via Crime and Disorder Act 1998s 34, to *R. v. J.T.B.* [2009] UKHL 20, [2010] 1 A.C. 1310.

[2] The fiction of consent as the basis of the marital rape immunity was only finally laid to rest in *R. v. R.* [1992] 1 A.C. 599, [1991] 4 All E.R. 481.

[3] "[T]hose infelicitous legal fictions a court of human rights can well do without." *Al-Skeini v United Kingdom* (55721/07) European Court of Human Rights (Grand Chamber) (2011) 53 E.H.R.R. 18; 30 B.H.R.C. 561.

[4] *Zupančič* (1983), p. 21.

[5] *Sturdy v. Jackaway* (71 U.S. 174, 1869) and Sparkes, this volume, Chap. 13.

[6] Lon Fuller (1967), introduction.

17.2 Jury Nullification

In jury trials in England and Wales we know, where there is a record, what the judge told the jury and what the jury decided. We do not know[7] whether the jury decided what it decided because it followed and applied what the judge told them. We can normally assume that *if* the judge told the jury that where facts a, b, c, d and e were proved beyond reasonable doubt, they should convict, then, if they do convict, that those facts were proved. Where the jury acquits, it will usually be for the absence of one or more of a, b, c, d or e, but might, rarely, be for some other reason. Even if the trial is structured, admissions made and the issue between the parties refined to the point where there is only one issue of fact between them, this can still be the case.

The jury nullification[8] power—the power of juries to find facts so as to acquit in the face of the evidence—implies power to install a fiction in any area of substantive, procedural or evidential law. It stands in the way of judges directing guilty verdicts.[9] Where successive juries refuse to convict in similar cases, then that might be a reason to legislate. An example that can be given is the unwillingness of juries (qualified by property ownership) in the 1950s to convict of the "barbarous-sounding"[10] crime of manslaughter by driving a car. Acquittals led in due course to the instantiation of the offence of causing death by driving dangerously,[11] which, for many years, put in place a culture of greater tolerance of killing people with cars than otherwise which has yet fully to be displaced. The same kinds of approaches took place to workplace deaths, where more euphemistically named offences, if any, are prosecuted so as to avoid manslaughter charges.[12]

The most significant area in which judges and jurors, sometimes with prosecutors and with the active involvement of the legislature, acted together so as to relax a harsh law, was in relation to the death penalty. Fictions were deployed so as to avoid capital punishment. These included benefit of clergy,[13] pleading the belly,[14] and the

---

[7] Because of Contempt of Court Act 1981 s.8. See also the critique by Lord Steyn, dissenting in *R v. Connor, R v. Mirza* [2004] UKHL 2.

[8] The authority usually cited is *R v. Penn* (1670) 6 How.St. Trials 951. More modern examples are *R v Ponting* (Central Criminal Court, 1985, and see Ponting 1987) and *R v Randle &. Pottle* (1991, Alliott J.) acquittals said to have been " … quite as much welcomed as resented by the public, which over many centuries has adhered tenaciously to its historic choice that decisions on the guilt of defendants charged with serious crime should rest with a jury of lay people, randomly selected, and not with professional judges." *R v. Wang* [2005] UKHL 9 para 16, citing famous passages from Devlin 1956, pp. 160, 162. Compare *R. v Smith (Patrick) R. v Mercieca* [2005] UKHL 12; [2005] 2 Cr. App. R. 10.

[9] *D.P.P. v Stonehouse* [1978] A.C. 55; *R v. Wang* [2005] UKHL 9, [2005] 1 All E.R. 782.

[10] D.W. Elliott and H. Street (1968), p. 20, cited in Law Commission (1996).

[11] First appeared in Road Traffic Act 1956. And see Horder, 2008 and Cunningham 2008.

[12] And see Clarkson and Cunningham 2008.

[13] See Radzinowicz 1948, pp. 268 and 333–337. Langbein 1983 at 37–43.

[14] And see Kesselring 2003, Appendix 2 pp. 46, 78, 212–214 (benefit of the belly), 46–48, 57, 62, 63, (benefit of clergy).

insanity defence.[15] To some extent they were used by prosecutors and, from the time that they became available,[16] defence lawyers, but they were deployed largely by judges and jurors.

17.2.1 Benefit of Clergy[17]

As part of the Concordat of Avranches (1172), Henry II was purged of any guilt in Becket's murder, but agreed that the secular courts, with few exceptions (high treason being one of them), had no jurisdiction over the clergy. Proof of clergy-hood quite soon was by a literacy test: defendants demonstrated their clerical status by reading from the Bible. This led to literate lay defendants also claiming the benefit of clergy. In 1351, under Edward III, this loophole was formalised in statute,[18] and benefit of clergy was officially extended to all who could read. In 1512, Henry VIII further restricted the benefit of clergy by making certain offences "felonies without benefit of clergy".[19] A statute of 1575 radically changed the effect of the benefit of clergy. It was no longer a bar to jurisdiction, but was pleaded after conviction but before sentencing, and it did not nullify the conviction. It could only be invoked once.[20] Defendants who availed themselves of the benefit once were branded on the thumb and not allowed to use it again.[21] The benefit was eventually extended to women in 1624,[22] although it was not until 1691 that they were given equal privileges with men in this matter. Before 1691, women could plead the benefit of clergy if convicted of theft of goods valued less than 10 shillings, while men could plead clergy for thefts up to 40 shillings.[23] In 1706, the reading test was abolished, and the benefit became available to all first-time offenders of lesser felonies.[24] An increasing number of seemingly minor property crimes became exempt from the benefit of clergy. Eventually, housebreaking, shoplifting of goods worth more than 5 shillings, and the theft of sheep and cattle all became felonies without benefit of clergy and earned their perpetrators automatic death sentences. Benefit of clergy was finally abolished for commoners in England in 1827.[25] In 1841, as a result of a duel, it was shown that peers retained the privilege and then it was removed.[26]

[15] This list is by no means exhaustive. A range of decisions at the border of murder and (both voluntary and involuntary) manslaughter could be considered in the same light, as could valuations of property so as to avoid grand larceny.

[16] Langbein 2003.

[17] Baker 1927; White 1912.

[18] 25 Edw.III, c.4.

[19] 4 Henry VIII. c. 2.

[20] Blackstone IV *Commentaries* 360.

[21] 18 Eliz.I c.7.

[22] .Blackstone IV *Commentaries* 362.

[23] 3&4 W. & M. c. 9, 4&5 W. & M. c. 24.

[24] 6 Anne, c. 9.

[25] 7&8 Geo VI c 28.

[26] 4&5 Vic c.22.

17.2.2 Fiction of Pregnancy

Less significant, but appealing to popular culture,[27] was the rule that pregnant women should not be executed, which led to the fiction that a particular woman defendant was pregnant when she was not. The "jury of matrons" was empanelled to determine whether or not she was pregnant. There appears to have been a common understanding that some women granted the privilege were not, in fact, pregnant. Women granted such reprieves were often subsequently granted pardons or had their sentences commuted to transportation. Even when the original sentences were carried out, women were often executed behind schedule.[28] This privilege was finally abolished in 1931, from when pregnant women convicted of capital offences were given life imprisonment.[29]

17.2.3 Fiction of Insanity

In the years before the Homicide Act 1957 introduced other defences to murder, the only defence available to many defendants who admitted having killed intentionally was that of insanity. Judges and jurors found reasons to treat the defendant as insane within the (narrow) definition in the M'Naghten rules.[30] As a result of the nullification power, juries had power to hold a defendant to be guilty but insane, and thus, on a capital charge, not liable to be sentenced to death. Jury findings of this sort did not disappear until capital punishment went.[31] During the years 1900–1949, of 3130 people committed for trial for murder, 49 were certified insane before trial, 428 were found insane on arraignment, 798 were found guilty but insane, and of the 1210 convicted and sentenced to death, a further 48 were certified insane after medical enquiry and yet a further 77 were respited and commuted.[32] Because we do not know, and might not even be able to tell from the directions to juries, whether these juries held that the defendant was insane within the definition or simply should not

[27] Mention appears in Daniel Defoe, *Moll Flanders* (1722) Chap. 9: see Lacey 2008, and John Gay, *The Beggar's Opera* (1728) I, ii. See Gallacher 2006.

[28] Oldham 1985.

[29] Sentence of Death (Expectant Mothers) Act 1931.

[30] *M'Naghten Rules* (1843) 10 C & F 200. A striking example is *R v Eric Brown* (Essex Assizes, 1943, The Times, November 5, 1943) (the 'Rayleigh bath chair murder'). The defendant killed his father with an anti-tank mine during an air-raid, hoping that the outcome would be mistaken for injuries caused by bombing. He gave a confession that presented his actions as a response to his father's abusive attitude both to him and to his mother. The jury nonetheless held him to be insane within the *M'Naghten Rules*. I have been unable to trace the direction to the jury. The verdict can be read as a statement by the jury that taking the lives of people with disabilities does not "count".

[31] The Homicide Act 1957 differentiated capital from non-capital murders. The Murder (Abolition of Death Penalty) Act 1965 ended capital punishment for murder in the U.K.

[32] Gowers 1953 p. 77 and Appendix 3 table 8, p. 311.

be hanged, it is very difficult to generate data beyond the anecdotal,[33] but there is a sentiment that accomplices and young defendants were generally more appropriately held to be insane than were perpetrators, and that defendants who used guns, poison, or killed policemen should not be found insane.[34] It did not help to be foreign.[35] It can be suggested that the findings of jurors in murder trials that defendants were guilty but insane were a means of exerting the pressure that led eventually to the establishment of the Royal Commission on Capital Punishment,[36] the defence of diminished responsibility,[37] the categories of capital and non-capital murder[38] and perhaps even to the abolition of capital punishment itself. After 1965 the outcome of a successful insanity plea was worse than a conviction and the rate of insanity pleas went down almost to zero.[39] Of course, the fiction of insanity was not a wholly satisfactory expedient. It presented difficult choices for defendants who were innocent. One could not plausibly run defences of insanity and alibi.

The general response in the literature to these fictions is that they are a good thing, giving the courts a flexibility they wanted but Parliament would not supply.[40] As Langbein put it:

> The sanction-specific quality of the substantive criminal law is what permitted the jury to exercise a de facto sentencing discretion, since the jury had the power to choose among different offenses for the conduct charged. Suppose, for example, that the defendant were accused of burglary—:- the indictment alleged that he broke into a house at night and stole five pounds worth of goods. Although the indictment charged burglary, for which the sanction was death, the jury had the power to convict the defendant of a lesser offense. It might (and it often did) return a verdict of "not guilty of burglary, but guilty of the theft." The effect of this formulation was to spare the defendant from the death penalty, and to consign him to transportation (later imprisonment) for grand larceny. If the jury were extraordinarily concerned to be lenient, it could (but seldom did in such a case) find the defendant guilty of a theft to the value of ten pence, hence mere petty larceny, for which the main sanction was whipping. Thus, the jury in this example could choose among three sentences- death, transportation, or whipping-by manipulating the offense. This mitigation practice was widespread and immensely important. In a famous phrase, Blackstone called it "pious perjury,"[41] by which he meant that the jury knowingly returned a false verdict (in our example, theft rather than burglary) in order to reduce the sanction.[42]

[33] The Commission received some unspecific anecdotal evidence of cases where the rules are ignored (Gowers at page 82).

[34] Ruth Ellis (*R v Ellis* [2003] EWCA Crim 3556), Derek Bentley (*R v Bentley (Deceased)* [1998] EWCA Crim 2516, [2001] 1 Cr. App. R. 21) and Guenther Podola (*R v. Podola* (1959) 43 Cr. App. Rep. 220) are examples. Podola shot a police officer. Bentley was complicit in killing one.

[35] *R v. Pod*ola (1959) 43 Cr App Rep 220.

[36] Gowers 1953.

[37] Homicide Act 1957 s. 2.

[38] Homicide Act 1957 s. 5. Murder of police and prison officers, murder in the course of theft, murder by shooting or explosion (but see *Brown*, above footnote 30) remained capital.

[39] White 1985.

[40] Oldfield 1901, Chap. 9,"The Fiction"; Tonry 2009.

[41] The reference is to Blackstone IV *Commentaries* 239, 359 *et seq* (my footnote).

[42] Langbein 1987, p. 37.

It is difficult to criticise any actions by juries that reduce the incidence of the death penalty. There is, of course, the argument that failure to impose the death penalty where it was mandated was what kept it in force for so long, but we should be sceptical about that. The reasons for the abolition of the death penalty for murder in England and Wales at the time it was abolished have little to do with juries and more to individual agency.[43]

Hay famously argued that the discretion that is exercised in the death penalty cases is one of the ways in which the exercise of brute power by the ruling class is legitimated.[44] Where might jury nullification fall into such an account, or one derived from the account of the Rule of Law in E.P.Thompson's celebrated passage about the Rule of Law towards the end of *Whigs and Hunters*,[45] and his other writings in the 1970s and 1980s on the jury?[46] The answer is that it would be critically important.

> Jurors have found, again and again, and at critical moments, according to what is their sense of the rational and just. If their sense of justice has gone one way, and the case another, they have found "against the evidence,"... the English common law rests upon a bargain between the Law and the people: The jury box is where the people come into the court: The judge watches them and the people watch back. A jury is the place where the bargain is struck. The jury attends in judgment, not only upon the accused, but also upon the justice and the humanity of the Law.[47]

One might be cynical about the composition, competence and commitment of the usual eighteenth (or twenty-first century) jury, and consider Thompson's view a romanticised one.[48] Only recently a jury appeared to be asking permission of a judge to acquit in the face of the evidence and were roundly denounced.[49] The advent of the European Convention of Human Rights, which does not insist upon a jury as an element of a fair criminal trial,[50] has taken some of the force from the debates of the 1980s about the jury.

17.3 Plea Bargains

Jury nullification fictions require, and were often instigated by, juries. There are other ways of introducing fictions into the criminal justice process. All systems of criminal justice have arrangements for dealing with cases in which some kind of

[43] Radzinowicz 1999.

[44] Hay 1975, and see Langbein 1983b and Hay 2011.

[45] Thompson 1975, pp. 258–269.

[46] Thompson 1980, 1986.

[47] Thompson 1980, p. 108, cited by Lord Justice Auld in his Criminal Courts Review report 2001 Chap. 5 para 99 page 173–174.

[48] Thompson also has many defenders—e.g. Cole 2001.

[49] Sweeney J. in *R. v. Vicky Pryce* (2013). "Vicky Pryce faces retrial after jury 'fails to grasp basics'", *The Guardian,* 20 February 2013.

[50] And see Roberts 2011.

agreement has been made between the prosecutor and the accused.[51] There does appear to have been something recognisable as a plea bargain in England even in the eighteenth century,[52] yet for many years the courts roundly denied its existence.[53] In one of the ground-breaking socio-legal studies in England,[54] Baldwin and McConville showed that events around Crown Court trials were only explicable by the inference that some kind of covert deals were being struck. Save in the most exceptional circumstances, *R v Turner*,[55] as underlined and applied in subsequent cases, prohibited the judge from giving any indication of sentence in advance of a guilty plea by the defendant. The Royal Commission on Criminal Justice noted wistfully that:

> A significant number of those who now plead guilty at the last minute would be more ready to declare their hand at an earlier stage if they were given a reliable early indication of the maximum sentence that they would face if found guilty.[56]

Sir Robin Auld's review of the criminal courts discussed advance indications of sentence. It concluded that subject to a number of specified safeguards, a defendant, through his advocate, should be able to request to be informed of and the judge should be entitled formally to indicate the maximum sentence in the event of a plea of guilty at that stage and the possible sentence on conviction following a trial.[57] Auld believed that the ability of the judge to give an indication to a defendant who wished to know the maximum sentence s/he faced would "enable the guilty defendant and those advising him to evaluate the judge's indication and assess the advantage or otherwise of proceeding with a plea."[58] It would clearly be in the interests of all that s/he be able to undertake a comparison between the sentence on a plea of guilty and a possible sentence on conviction:

> He knows and will in any event, be advised by his lawyer that a plea of guilty can attract a lesser sentence and broadly what the possible outcomes are, depending on his plea. So what possible additional pressure, unacceptable or otherwise, can there be in the judge, whom he has requested to tell him where he stands, indicating more precisely the alternatives?[59]

As noted by Auld, one aspect of the criminal justice system in England and Wales that has always been inconsistent with the idea that pleas should be uninfluenced

---

[51] *Pace* Alschuler 1979. See Baldwin and McConville 1977; Brants 2007; Boll 2009.

[52] Smith 2005.

[53] E.g. *R. v. Wise* [1979] R.T.R. 57: "If a judge enters into a blatant plea-bargain, his fitness to sit as a judge on the criminal law Bench is called into question." (Lord Widgery C.J. at 59C–D); *R. v. Grice*(1978) 66 Cr. App. R. 167 "We find it quite astonishing that any recorder should characterise what he is doing as 'plea bargaining.' But even more so when it clearly was 'plea bargaining'" (Roskill L.J. at 308).

[54] Baldwin and McConville 1977. See Thomas 1978; McConville et al. 1994, pp. 189–198.

[55] *R. v. Turner* [1970] 2 Q.B. 321.

[56] Runciman 1993, paragraphs 41–58. And see McConville 1998.

[57] Auld 2001, pp. 434–444.

[58] Ib.

[59] And see Ashworth 2010, p. 172. Sentencing Advisory Panel (Now Council) *Reduction in Sentence for a Guilty Plea: Definitive Guideline* (2007).

by considerations as to what their outcome might be is the sentencing discount. Judicial precedent created the one-third discount for guilty-pleas, which was incorporated into criminal statute later.[60]

Following the guidance published by the Sentencing Guidelines Council in December 2004 on the Reduction in Sentence for Guilty Plea,[61] in *Goodyear*,[62] adopting the procedure in *Attorney General's Reference (No. 1 of 2004)* and *Simpson*,[63] a five-judge Court of Appeal, presided over by the Lord Chief Justice, was convened to consider whether the *Turner* rule of practice should be modified, and if so, to what extent. It laid down new guidelines[64] which state that normally speaking an indication of sentence should not be given until the basis of the plea has been agreed or the judge has concluded that he or she can properly deal with the case without the need for a trial of the issue. The plea and case management hearing in the Crown Court now specifically requires the judge to seek and be given information first, on whether the defendant has in fact been advised about the credit to be obtained for a guilty plea, and second, what steps had been taken to see whether the case might be resolved without a trial.[65]

Within this framework there are several techniques of "negotiated diversion." The idea is obvious: to avoid costly and time-consuming opportunity for adversarial conflict. This recommendation and subsequent legislation[66] placed it on a more formal footing. Subject to those imposed by the judges[67] the main constraints upon the prosecutor in making deals with defendants are set out in the *Attorney-General's Guidelines on the acceptance of pleas.*[68] This requires, amongst other things, attention to transparency, the basis of plea, attention to the interests of victims and to mitigating factors.

Plea bargains and other techniques of diversion are usually arrived at by a process of negotiation, in effect, to agree the facts to be approved by a court and avoid contested litigation. They may result in the reduction of punishment, or the reclassification of the offence. Typically English Law has broad offences with wide sentencing discretions, rather than narrow ones with more closely confined sentencing ranges, so it is more usual for the agreement to bear upon punishment. There are nonetheless some scales of graduated offences. Charges might be reduced, for example, from murder to one or another form of manslaughter, from Section 18 to Section 20 of the Offences against the Person Act 1861, from burglaries or robberies

---

[60] Criminal Justice and Public Order Act 1994 s. 48, Criminal Justice Act 2003 s. 144.

[61] Sentencing Guidelines Council on the Reduction in Sentence for Guilty Plea (December 2004).

[62] *R. v. Goodyear* [2005] EWCA Crim 888.

[63] *Attorney General's Reference (No. 1 of 2004)*[2004] 1 W.L.R. 2111, *R v Simpson*[2004] Q.B. 118.

[64] Auld 2001, above footnote 57, paras 55–80.

[65] *Goodyear* at para 46.

[66] Criminal Justice and Public Order Act 1994s.48.

[67] Below, pp. 376–378.

[68] http://www.attorneygeneral.gov.uk/Publications/Pages/AttorneyGeneral'sguidelinesontheacceptanceofpleas(revised2009).aspx.

to simple thefts, from car thefts to taking and driving away, from possession of drugs with intent to supply to simple possession and so on.

There is in plea bargains no pre-existing truth against which to oppose a fiction, because there never will be evidence otherwise. The outcome will be negotiated and constructed in the process of the discussions.[69] The facts are created, neither fictitious nor abounding in historical verisimilitude. The fiction, if any, will generally be that the facts and the charge presented properly represent the *gravitas* of the defendant's wrongdoing in the respect in question. When the defendant is relatively powerless and the adjustment of the facts is, or seems, an act of mercy, that is one sort of fiction, and one with which we may sympathise. When the defendant, or an overseas prosecutor is exerting economic muscle to fix the facts in its favour that is quite another, and it is not so satisfactory. Could Bean J. in *BAE Systems* have refused to endorse the agreement? In theory, yes, but there were factors of international relations in play.

When, therefore, a judge is asked to approve the outcome of a negotiation the effect of which is to generate a given outcome, on a guilty plea and without a hearing of the evidence, the pressures of caseload, time, public expenditure and even (in the cases to be considered) international relations will affect the outcome. In *R v BAE Systems*[70] the defendants pleaded guilty to a charge under Section 221 of the Companies Act 2005, that the company had failed to maintain the required accounting records. What had happened was this. On February 5 2010, it was announced on the Serious Fraud Office (SFO) website that in 2010 BAE had reached settlements with U.K. and U.S. authorities and agreed to pay fines totalling $ 400 million to settle the long-running corruption allegations concerning the Tanzanian air traffic control system. BAE Systems Plc admitting it had failed to keep adequate accounting records in relation to a defence contract for the supply of an air traffic control system to the Government of Tanzania.[71] So far as concerned proceedings in England, BAE agreed to make an *ex gratia* payment for the benefit of the people of Tanzania of £ 30 million less any fine imposed by the Crown Court. Additionally, BAE was to be ordered to pay £ 225,000 costs to the SFO. All this was announced before the case came before the court. When it did, in sentencing BAE, Bean J. took the view that BAE had concealed from the auditor and ultimately the public the fact that they were making payments to a particular individual, the overwhelming preponderance via offshore companies, and that they were giving him wide powers to make such payments to such people as he thought fit in order to secure the radar contract for BAE but in such circumstances that BAE did not need and did not want to know the details. The judge therefore questioned whether the charge under section 221 of the Companies Act 2005—and not bribery—was an appropriate one. The danger of this charge, which did not, for example, carry debarment from procurement tendering,[72]

---

[69] Bennett and Feldman (1981).

[70] *R. v. BAE Systems Plc* [2010] *EW* Misc 16.

[71] *Companies* Act *1985* s. 221.

[72] Under EU *Directive* 2004/18/EC Article 45.

was that it may have appeared to have understated the extent of the defendant's culpability.

In *Innospec*,[73] Thomas L.J. made his disapproval or this sort of arrangement even clearer. In this case the plea was to a crime of turpitude, not one that might be dismissed as a technical accounting infringement. As was the case in *BAE*, however, there was pressure from a US Department of Justice prosecutor. Innospec, a UK company, a wholly owned subsidiary of Innospec Inc., manufactured TEL, a fuel additive which was being phased out in many countries because of environmental and health concerns. By 2000 Indonesia was of one of the four remaining principal customers for TEL. Although Innospec Inc was a Delaware company "its executive offices were in Cheshire and the corruption in Indonesia was organised by the directing minds of Innospec Ltd based in the UK". Following investigation by the US Government and the SFO, Innospec pleaded guilty to conspiracy to make corrupt payments to Indonesian public officials. The "best estimate" of the total amount of bribes was approximately $ 8 million. In addition, Innospec was implicated in $ 5.8 million worth of bribes in relation to the UN's Oil for Food Programme in Iraq. The company's independent directors admitted the criminal offences and began discussions with the US prosecutors, to which the SFO became party, as to the fines and other penalties: both the SFO and the DOJ agreed that in the light of Innospec's full admission and full co-operation, they should not seek to impose a penalty which would drive the company out of business."[74]

An unprecedented global settlement was agreed between the US and UK authorities in respect of concurrent criminal proceedings. Innospec's offer to pay approximately $ 40 million over the next 3 years was accepted subject to the approval of the US and UK courts. The UK portion was to be a third of this. Innospec Ltd and the SFO asked the court to approve an agreement in which there would be a confiscation penalty of $ 6.7 million and a civil recovery order of $ 6 million but no criminal fine as such. The concurrent US plea agreement was made under the Federal Rules of Criminal Procedure. In England and Wales the Consolidated Criminal Practice Direction envisages that the prosecution may indicate acceptance of a plea and discuss the basis of it, but emphasises, as did Thomas L.J., that it is for the court to consider whether evidence should be called in order to consider the basis on which to sentence. In this case the court agreed with the choice of charge, conspiracy to make corrupt payments. In addition, in cases of serious fraud the prosecutor may enter a plea agreement, indicate the range of penalty, and include an assessment of the defendant's financial means. What is clear is that "the SFO cannot enter into an agreement under the laws of England and Wales with an offender as to the penalty in respect of the offence charged".[75] The agreement that the court had been asked to approve preferred confiscation and civil recovery to the payment of a fine. Thomas L.J. agreed, albeit reluctantly, to keep within the agreed

[73] *R. v. Innospec Plc* [2010] EW Misc 7 (EWCC); [2010] Lloyd's Rep. F.C. 462, [2010] Crim. LR 665.

[74] Para 7.

[75] *Para* 26.

$ 12.7 million but did impose it as a fine, making it clear that it will "rarely be appropriate for criminal conduct by a company to be dealt with by means of a civil recovery order." Such was the level of his disapproval, however, that since *Innospec* no *"global plea agreement"* has been brought before the courts for endorsement, ratification or approval.[76]

Instead, legislation allowing "Deferred Prosecution Agreements" has been put in place.[77] As Director of the Serious Fraud Office from 2008 till 2012, Richard Alderman was inclined to settle with alleged criminals—even inviting self-reports. His successor, David Green, has stated that he is more disposed to prosecute than to make deals. Irrespective of Green's position, this issue will not go away, and as the range of crimes grows that are prosecuted in more than one jurisdiction, we do need a clearer and more easily applied set of principles to govern the creation of facts for presentation to courts.

17.4 Forfeiture

Forfeiture is a venerable legal mechanism, which appeared to be obsolescent 30 years ago, but has undergone a revival in more recent years. It is action by the state to seize permanently a person's property because of some connection to crime, other than its being the proceeds of crime (in which case proceedings are possible either for confiscation orders or civil recovery orders) or as a punishment (a fine). It has acquired increased significance in recent years, as a consequence of the extended jurisdictions under the Proceeds of Crime Act 2002, increased use of cash and customs forfeitures, attempts to deal with 'terrorist property' and other *ad hoc* deployments. Provision for forfeiture has become standard in the growing range of international instruments dealing with criminal law.

The ancient fiction[78] underlying forfeiture, 'about as irrational and unjust a proposition as a sober mind can concoct',[79] is that there is something criminal about the thing itself.[80] This fiction was associated by Blackstone with the 'blind days of popery'.[81] It is the reason for the amusing case names.[82] Forfeiture, in addition to criminal sanctions is not, on this account, double punishment.[83] Because the thing, rather than a person, is guilty, the State can seize it and arguments from double jeopardy can be side-stepped. It is now used in an increasingly wide range of cases.

---

[76] And see para 47.

[77] Crime and Courts Act 2013 s. 45.

[78] Luna 1997.

[79] Finkelstein 1973 at 257.

[80] Berman 1999.

[81] 1 Blackstone, Commentaries, 300.

[82] *U.S. v Sixty* Pipes *of Brandy* (1825) 23 U.S. (10 Wheat) 421; *R v Forty-Nine Casks of Brandy* (1836), 3 Hag. Adm. 257, 166 E.R. 401 (H.C. Adm.)

[83] *United States v Ursery* (1996) 518 U.S. 267; 116 S. Ct. 2135.

This change has been achieved without a proper analysis being conducted of its rationale. This is to be regretted.

Briefly, forfeiture is acceptable as a fine *in specie*, where a fine would be acceptable.[84] It is acceptable in the prevention of crime to the extent that it is justified by the end. It is justified when an item must be forfeit to make the law make sense (where possession of the item is criminal). It is also justified to enforce customs prohibitions. Any extension of forfeiture beyond these narrow categories should be subject to close scrutiny. At the moment, it seems to be being extended without any such consideration.

The uses of forfeiture that are most difficult to justify, and yet are central both to cash forfeiture[85] and the extended forfeiture jurisdiction in respect of terrorism, are those where the property is "intended for criminal use". The "intended for criminal use" justification asserts that the fact that the possessor of property has decided to use it in the commission of a criminal offence provides sufficient grounds without more for the State to seize the property. While the formation of an intent to use the property illegally may be evidence of a likelihood that it will be so used, this rationale differs from, and goes beyond the 'prevention of crime' rationale in that mere intention that the property be deployed for criminal purposes, without necessarily creating a risk of crime is considered enough. Whilst there are statutory provisions to that effect,[86] the underlying justification is not explicit and remains unclear.

The analogous area of the substantive criminal law—the law of inchoate crime and in particular the law of attempts—has developed on the basis that in order to give fair warning, protect the Rule of Law and prevent abuse of State power it is inappropriate to impose criminal liability without some action from the defendant that goes beyond thinking about the crime.[87] To penalise mere intention conjures up images of 'thoughtcrimes' in the intrusive surveillance society of Orwell's *Nineteen Eighty-Four*. In substantive criminal law, the defendant must engage in ascribable behaviour,[88] even if it is only making a suggestion or entering into an agreement, or doing nothing when there is a duty to act.[89] It required an exception to be created dealing with the case of terrorism, so that the limits of the law of attempts could be stretched earlier in time than the performance of an act 'more than merely preparatory' to the commission of the consummated crime, but even then there must

---

[84] Powers of Criminal Courts (Sentencing) Act 2000 s. 143.

[85] Proceeds of Crime Act 2002 s. 294 et sEq.

[86] Terrorism Act 2000 *s*. 23 and 23A.

[87] '[T]he imagination of the mind to do wrong, without an act done, is not punishable in our law.' *Hales v Petit* (1562) 1.Plow. 253, 259, 75 E.R. 387, 397; Hitchler 1934, p. 97; 4 Blackstone, *Commentaries* 21 ('[A]s no temporal tribunal can search the heart, or fathom the intentions of the mind, otherwise than as they are demonstrated by outward actions, it therefore cannot punish for what it cannot know.'); Perkins 1939, p. 907, all cited in Goldstein 1959, fn. 1. Even the Terrorism Act 2000 s 5 requires 'preparation'. See, *e.g.*, A.P. Simester et al. 2010 and Chan and Simester 2011.

[88] 'Compassing the sovereign's death' in treason does not just mean thinking about it. See, e.g., Barrell 2000.

[89] Which is *what* would be required respectively for incitement or conspiracy or the general law on criminal liability for omissions.

be acts.[90] In other areas the idea that the State should seek to control what people think, even in circumstances when they do nothing to put the thought into action, is regarded as *anathema.* It is not clear why it should become acceptable simply because the adverse consequence is not a criminal conviction. If forfeiture is to operate simply on the basis that property that is intended for criminal use, without any act to give effect to the intention, then the threshold for liability to forfeiture is crossed significantly before that for criminal liability. It is therefore suggested that forfeiture cannot be justified on the basis of the intention with which property is held, and the use of metaphors of attaint is, in this context, unhelpful.

17.5 Pecuniary Advantages

Use in criminal law of deeming provisions ("x shall be treated as y or as not-x") is relatively rare. The generally received reason is that it is desirable and should be possible to set out the limits of serious crimes in plain language and in such a way as to guide behaviour, and that this is inconsistent with the use of "deeming provisions" which are a concession that may be tolerated in other areas of law, taxation, for example. Criminal law is in this respect distinct. Hence the reference in the 1966 Practice Statement to the "especial need for certainty", [91] and the particular treatment given to criminal law by Article 7 of the European Convention on Human Rights. In criminal law, if deeming is the only way to achieve whatever it is that the draftsperson wants to achieve, alarm bells should sound. If the metaphor is to be taken from mathematics the appropriate one is not approximations[92] but imaginary numbers.[93]

"Pecuniary advantage" was an expression, used with its natural meaning in contractual and fatal accident damages,[94] rules on succession and so on. The draftspeople of the Theft 1968 wanted an expression to cover[95] three cases in which there was a dishonest obtaining of something but what was obtained was not "property" within the (extended) meaning of section 15 of the Act. There had been doubt, for example, whether, where income was obtained in an employment, that employment having been obtained by false pretences, the income was obtained by false pretences. In these three cases the defendant was deemed by Section 16 to have obtained a "pecuniary advantage". The expression and the use of "deeming" (the precise expression was "shall be regarded") were not well chosen because in each case the

---

[90] Terrorism Act 2006 s 3: compare Criminal Attempts Act 1981 s 1.

[91] Practice Statement (Judicial Precedent) [1966] 1 W.L.R. 1234.

[92] Lobban, *supra* ch 10 citing Edward Wynne, *Eunomus: or Dialogues concerning the Law and Constitution of England* (Dublin: James Moore 1791), pp. 70–71.

[93] An imaginary number is a number that can be written as a real number multiplied by the imaginary unit i, which is defined by its property $i^2 = -1$.

[94] *Taff Vale Railway Co. v. Jenkins* [1913] A.C. 1, *Barnett v. Cohen* [1921] 2 K.B. 461.

[95] Criminal Law Revision Committee 1966.

governing hypothesis was that a pecuniary advantage had not been obtained. It soon gave rise to difficulties,[96] was described as a "judicial nightmare",[97] and had to be referred back to the Criminal Law Revision Committee.[98] First of all, the provision that gave rise to most of the trouble—Section 16(2)(a)of the Theft Act 1968—was repealed.[99] A further *lacuna* was revealed,[100]and after a brief consideration by the Law Commission[101] the Theft (Amendment) Act 1996 introducing a new offence of obtaining a money transfer by deception.[102] The Fraud Act 2006[103] finally replaced Section 16 Theft Act 1968 altogether.

In spite of the inauspicious history, when provision was put in place for confiscation orders to deal not just with property that had been obtained, but to more widely defined benefits, the expression "pecuniary advantage" was again used, but this time the expression was not defined. Rather, the statute[104] said:

> s.76(4) A person benefits from conduct if he obtains property as a result of or in connection with the conduct.
> (5) If a person obtains a pecuniary advantage as a result of or in connection with conduct, he is to be taken to obtain as a result of or in connection with the conduct a sum of money equal to the value of the pecuniary advantage.

In the area of the proceeds of crime, the expression is giving rise to its own difficulties. There is no definition of the expression "pecuniary advantage" in the Proceeds of Crime Act 2002 or the preceding legislation. In *Smith*[105] Lord Rodger held that there was no need to look at the Theft Act meanings of "pecuniary advantage" but that the expression had a natural meaning that included the deferment of debt.[106] Where a debt is deferred, it is still owed, so if the statute is read properly, the value of the advantage will usually be small. The expression has contributed to the unnecessarily extensive confiscation orders, especially in tax cases, usually involving either carousel or tobacco smuggling.[107] At the time of writing a further appeal is pending before the Supreme Court.[108]

Difficult though it is when dealing with confiscation orders (where it is used to quantify the order), the "deeming use" of the expression "pecuniary" is also used in

---

[96] It had to be considered by the House of Lords in *DPP v Turner* [1974] A.C. 357, *DPP v Ray* [1974] A.C. 370, *MPC v Charles* [1977] A.C. 177 and *R v Lambie* [1982] A.C. 449.

[97] *R v Royle* [1971] 1 W.L.R. 1764 per Edmund-Davies L.J.

[98] Criminal Law Revision Committee (1977).

[99] Theft Act 1978.

[100] *R v Preddy* [1996] A.C. 815, [1996] 2 Cr. App. R. 524.

[101] Law Commission 1996.

[102] Theft Act 1968 Section 15A.

[103] Introduced after Law Commission 2002.

[104] First in the Criminal Justice Act 1988, now the Proceeds of Crime Act 2002 s. 76.

[105] *R. v. Smith (David Cadman)* [2001] UKHL 61; [2002] 1 All E.R. 366.

[106] Para 20.

[107] *R. v. Dimsey* [2001] UKHL 46; [2002] 1 A.C. 509; *R. v. Allen* [2001] UKHL 45; [2002] 1 A.C. 509.

[108] On appeal from *Shakeel Ahmad, Syed Mubarak Ahmed v. R.* [2012] EWCA Crim 391.

an identical subsection[109] defining "criminal property" for the purposes of the laundering offences under sections 327–329 of the Proceeds of Crime Act 2002. Since a mental element (knowledge or suspicion) must be held in respect of the property that is deemed to exist, at the time that it is laundered, the metaphysics become tortured. Nonetheless the Court of Appeal held that where a taxpayer cheated the Revenue by falsely representing the turnover of a business, the "criminal property", as defined by the Proceeds of Crime Act 2002 s. 340, was the entirety of the undeclared turnover, not merely the tax due.[110] This is the logical conclusion of the previous decisions, and it is that anyone who under-declares for the purposes of taxation so as to cheat the revenue will be liable for laundering. Since almost all acquisitive crime is, in principle taxable, analogous laundering charges could supplement almost any other charge.

This is the easiest area of the four with which to deal. Lord Mildew was right: 'there is too much of this damned deeming'.[111] In principle, deeming provisions have no place where the liberty of the subject is in issue. They offend the principle of fair notice, and to the extent that they do, they are objectionable. They also unnecessarily complicate the law. If someone is to face a serious penalty it should be on the basis of a clear and comprehensibly defined prohibition. These provisions, both so far as concerns confiscation and criminal laundering, should go.

Conclusion

The jury equity cases will be popular with people with whom the jury is popular. They are the closest to the Maine/Fuller idea of the constructive fiction. The plea bargaining cases are more problematic. They involve not so much fictions but fact creations. As such they do represent, in criminal law, something of a threat, because the requirements of transparent and open justice should imply that decisions by prosecutors as to the facts of a case and a proposed determination should coincide as closely as possible, so far as it is possible to establish, to the history. Forfeiture is based no less on superstition now than it was in the eighteenth century. Save where there is a clear and sufficient justification, it should be abolished. That justification can never arise from the thing itself. Deeming provisions ought never to be permitted in that part of criminal law that is intended to provide a guide to conduct.

[109] S.340(6).

[110] And see Mumford and Alldridge 2005, making a series of points ignored in *R. v. K* [2007] EWCA Crim 491; [2007] 1 W.L.R. 2262; [2008] S.T.C. 1270; *R. v. Anwoir* [2008] EWCA Crim 1354; [2009] 1 W.L.R. 980 and *R. v. William et al.* [2013] EWCA Crim 1262.

[111] *Travers v. Travers*, noted in Herbert 1982, 80 wrongly ascribed to Churchill, by Lord Lloyd of Berwick, HL Debates, 29 Jan 2003: Column GC168—this pointed out in Morgan 2006.

References

Alschuler, A. W. 1979. Plea bargaining and its history. *Columbia Law Review* 79:1.

Ashworth, Andrew. 2010. *Sentencing and criminal justice*. 5th ed. Cambridge: Cambridge University Press.

Auld, R. (Chair). 2001. *Review of the criminal courts of England and Wales*, September.

Baker, Newman F. 1927. Benefit of clergy—A legal anomaly. *Kentucky Law Journal* 15:85–115.

Baldwin, John and Michael McConville. 1977. *Negotiated justice*. Oxford: Oxford University Press.

Barrell, J. 2000. *Imagining the king's death: Figurative treason, fantasies of regicide 1793–1796*. Oxford: Oxford University Press.

Bennett, W. Lance, and Martha S. Feldman. 1981. *Reconstructing reality in the courtroom—Justice and judgment in American culture*. Camden: Rutgers.

Berman, Paul Schiff. 1999. An anthropological approach to modern forfeiture law: The symbolic function of legal actions against objects. *Yale Journal Law & Humanities* 11:1.

Boll, Matthias. 2009. *Plea bargaining and agreement in the criminal process*. Hamburg: Diplomica Verlag.

Brants, Chrisje. 2007. Consensual criminal procedures: Plea and confession bargaining and abbreviated procedures to simplify criminal procedure vol.11.1. *Electronic Journal of Comparative Law* (May). http://www.ejcl.org/111/article111-6.pdf.

Chan, Winnie, and Andrew Simester. 2011. Four functions of mens rea. *Cambridge Law Journal* 70:381.

Clarkson, C. M. V., and Sally Cunningham. 2008. *Criminal liability for non-aggressive death*. Aldershot: Ashgate.

Cole, Daniel H. 2001. 'An unqualified human good': EP Thompson and the rule of law. *Journal of Law and Society* 28:177–203.

Criminal Law Revision Committee. 1966. Eighth report: Theft and related offences (Cmnd 2977).

Criminal Law Revision Committee. 1977. Thirteenth report: Section 16 of the Theft Act 1968 (Cmnd 6733).

Cunningham, Sally. 2008. *Vehicular homicide: Need for a special offence?* In ed. Clarkson and Cunningham, 97.

Devlin, P. 1956. *Trial by jury*. London: Stevens.

Elliott, D. W., and H. Street. 1968. *Road accidents*. London: Allen Lane.

Finkelstein, J. 1973. The goring ox: Some historical perspectives on deodands, forfeitures, wrongful death and the western notion of sovereignty. *Temple Law Quarterly* 46:169.

Fuller, L. 1967. *Legal fictions*. Stanford: Stanford University Press.

Gallacher, Ian. 2006. The beggar's opera and its criminal law context. In *John Gay's the beggar's opera 1728–2004: Adaptations and re-writings*, eds. Uwe Boeker, Ines Detmers, and Anna-Christina Giovanopoulos, 103–125. Amsterdam: Rodopi.

Goldstein, A. 1959. Conspiracy to defraud the United States. *Yale Law Journal* 68:405.

Gowers, E. (chair). 1953. Royal Commission on Capital Punishment 1949–1953 (Cmd. 8932).

Hay, Douglas. 1975. *Property, authority and the criminal law. In Albion's fatal tree*, ed. Douglas Hay et al., 1. Harmondsworth: Penguin.

Hay, Douglas. 2011. Writing about the death penalty. *Legal History* 10:1.

Herbert, A. P. 1982. *More uncommon law*. London: Mandarin.

Hitchler, W. H. 1934. The physical element of crime. *Dickinson Law Review* 39:95.

Horder, Jeremy. 2008. Homicide reform and the changing character of legal thought. In ed. Clarkson and Cunningham, 11.

Kesselring, K. J. 2003. *Mercy and authority in the Tudor state*. Cambridge: Cambridge University Press.

Lacey, Nicola. 2008. *Women, crime, and character: From Moll Flanders to Tess of the D'Urbervilles*. Oxford: Oxford University Press.

Langbein, John H. 1983a. Albion's fatal flaws. *Past & Present* 98:96–120.

Langbein, John. 1983b. Shaping the eighteenth-century criminal trial: A view from the Ryder sources. *University of Chicago Law Review* 50 (1): 37–43.
Langbein, John H. 1987. The English criminal trial jury on the eve of the French revolution. In *The trial jury in England, France, Germany 1700–1900,* ed. Padoa Schioppa, 34 et sEq. Berlin: Duncker & Humblot.
Langbein, John H. 2003. *Origins of the adversarial criminal trial.* Oxford: Oxford University Press.
Law Commission No 237. 1996a. Legislating the criminal code: Involuntary manslaughter.
Law Commission No 243. 1996b. Offences of dishonesty: Money transfers.
Law Commission No 276. 2002. Fraud.
Luna, Erik Grant. 1997. Fiction trumps innocence: The Bennis court's constitutional house of cards. *Stanford Law Review* 49:409.
McConville, M. 1998. Plea bargaining: Ethics and politics. *Journal of Law and Society* 25:562.
McConville, M., et al. 1994. *Standing accused.* Oxford: Oxford University Press.
Morgan, J. 2006. The rise and fall of the general duty of care. *Professional Negligence* 4:206–224.
Mumford, A., and P. Alldridge. 2005. Tax evasion and the proceeds of Crime Act 2002. *Legal Studies* 25:353.
Oldfield, Josiah. 1901. *Penalty of death or the problem of capital punishment.* Bell Ch. 9, The fiction.
Oldham, James. 1985. On pleading the belly. *Criminal Justice History* 6:1–64.
Perkins, R. 1939. A rationale of mens rea. *Harvard Law Review* 52:905.
Ponting, C. 1987. R v Ponting. *Journal of Law and Society* 14:366.
Radzinowicz, Leon. 1948. *A history of English criminal law and its administration*, 2. Oxford: Oxford University Press.
Radzinowicz, Leon. 1999. The awkward question of capital punishment. In *Adventures in criminology*, 245 et sEq. London: Routledge.
Roberts, Paul. 2011. Does Article 6 of the European convention on human rights require reasoned verdicts in criminal trials? *Human Rights Law Review* 11:213.
Runciman, W. (chair). 1993. Royal Commission on Criminal Justice (Cm.2263).
Simester, A. P., et al. 2010. *Criminal law theory and doctrine*. 4th ed. Oxford: Hart Publishing.
Smith, Bruce P. 2005. Plea bargaining and the eclipse of the jury. *Annual Review of Law and Social Science* 1:131.
Sparkes, Peter. 2014. Ejectment: Three births and a funeral. In *Legal fictions in theory and practice*, ed. Maksymilian Del Mar and William Twining. Dordrecht: Springer.
Thomas, Philip A. 1978. Plea bargaining in England and Wales. *Journal of Criminal Law and Criminology* 69:170.
Thompson, E. P. 1975. *Whigs and hunters*. Harmondsworth: Penguin.
Thompson, E. P. 1980. The state versus its enemies. In *Writing by candlelight,* 99. London: Merlin Press.
Thompson, E. P. 1986. Subduing the jury. *London Review of Books*, Dec 4.
Tonry, Michael. 2009. The mostly unintended effects f mandatory penalties: Two centuries of consistent findings. *Crime and Justice* 38:65.
White, Edward J. 1912. Benefit of clergy. *American Law Review* 46:78.
White, Stephen. 1985. The insanity defense in England and Wales since 1843. *Annals of the American Academy of Political and Social Science* 45:477.
Zupančič, Boštjan M. 1983. *Criminal law: Its nature and its function*. New York: B. M. Zupanclicl.

Chapter 18
Fictitious Fraud: Economics and the Presumption of Reliance

Randy D. Gordon

Abstract In the popular imagination, legal proceedings and their rules of law are thought of as paths to unalloyed truth. Both practitioners and scholars know this is often not the case because the law is, as are other domains, riddled with fictions. Indeed, the law sometimes borrows fictions from other domains to help it achieve results that would otherwise be unobtainable. One such place is securities law, in which courts in the United States have borrowed the concept of the 'efficient market' from economics to make fraud class actions possible. But that concept is—if not wholly—at least in good measure fictional.

18.1 Introduction: Fiction as a Mode of Justice

Lon Fuller (1930–1931, p. 516) once suggested that 'a fiction is intended to escape the consequences of an existing, specific rule of law'.[1] I think that's right, but in this paper I hope to show that the matter can be even more complicated. Specifically, I posit that courts often resort to multiple, nested fictions in deciding cases and, moreover, that those fictions may themselves be the result of or required by pre-existing fictions. Put in more common parlance, one falsehood may father a thousand others. To explore this concept, I propose that we adopt a loose, literary definition of 'fiction' (i.e. under this construct, a fiction need not be wholly false)[2] to examine private securities litigation in the US. But first, let me take a brief detour born of personal experience, one that at some level of generality should resonate with most all practising lawyers.

[1] For the purposes of this paper, it may be helpful to keep in mind a particular type of fiction: viz. a fiction devised to circumvent a procedural difficulty (Del Mar, this volume, Chap. 11, pp. 240–1) (discussing Roscoe Pound's theory positing that law's growth comes via distinct modes, one of which is 'fictions').

[2] I have in mind things like historical or 'true crime' novels, which are classified as 'fiction' despite being more or less grounded in fact. For example, in 1959, Dick Hickock and Perry Smith murdered Herb Clutter and his family in rural western Kansas. That is a fact. Yet many incidents in Truman Capote's 1966 telling of that story in In Cold Blood are pure fancy.

R. D. Gordon (✉)
Gardere Wynne Sewell LLP, 1601 Elm Street, Suite 3000, Dallas, TX 75201, USA
e-mail: rgordon@gardere.com

M. Del Mar, W. Twining (eds.), *Legal Fictions in Theory and Practice*,
Law and Philosophy Library 110, DOI 10.1007/978-3-319-09232-4_18

Many years ago, when I practised law in Oklahoma, I was asked to represent an out-of-state defendant in a lawsuit.[3] He had never been to Oklahoma, other than to have testified several years earlier in an unrelated proceeding involving his divorce (setting aside minor things like being aboard a plane that stopped for fuel). Initially, he asked the family lawyer who had represented him in the divorce proceeding to again represent him and she agreed. At the time, there was a procedural rule that allowed an attorney to file an entry-of-appearance and thereby automatically receive a 20-day extension of time to respond to the petition. She filed such an appearance and also subsequently lodged an objection to the forum, based on the fact that the client had no contacts with Oklahoma sufficient to subject him to the jurisdiction of an Oklahoma court. But the entry-of-appearance rule clearly stated that its automatic-extension provision came at a price: a waiver of all objections to personal jurisdiction. The Court held a hearing and found that it had personal jurisdiction, both because of the waiver and because of the previous appearance in the divorce proceeding. At this point, the client decided to retain new counsel, and the file landed on my desk, presumably because I was a fairly new lawyer and the matter looked like the sort of sure loser that a more senior lawyer in our firm would not like to add to his résumé.

I duly investigated the toxic file, researched the substance, filed a motion to reconsider the decision with the district court, and set it for hearing. Back then, the district judges set aside Friday mornings for motion dockets (which resembled nothing so much as cattle calls), at which each judge would hear cases seriatim. Lawyer after lawyer would approach the bench when called and make his or her argument. I sat for 2 h and was finally called at the heel of the docket, which I took to mean that the judge planned to dress me down but spare me an audience. When my opponent and I arrived at the well, the judge looked at me and said, 'So, you think I got this wrong?' I shuffled uncomfortably and offered that 'Your Honour didn't have all the law before him when the matter was heard'. He peered down from the bench and said, 'I've read your brief and the case you cite. It's not that old and it clearly holds that appearance in a prior proceeding is jurisdictionally irrelevant. But what do I do with the appearance she entered?' I had no good answer, and all I could really offer was a non sequitur: 'Well, she tried to do the right thing by objecting to personal jurisdiction.' The judge leaned back in his chair and thought for a few moments. Finally, he said, 'I had no jurisdiction at the time she entered her appearance, so I'm going to grant your motion. Case dismissed. Please prepare an order in which you cite the cases in your brief.'

He was wrong as a matter of law, of course, and he knew it. The moment that the previous counsel signed her name to the entry of appearance, filed it, and thereby claimed the statutory extension of time, she waived her client's—my client's—right to object to personal jurisdiction. That was conclusive. But the judge was wise and saw that it was unfair to drag my client all the way from Florida to defend a claim that had no connection with Oklahoma, just because of a ministerial error

[3] Given the passage of time, some of what I am about to say may be fictional, though unintentionally so.

committed by a lawyer unfamiliar with general civil practice. So he re-narrated the facts and thereby created an as-if fiction, one in which the jurisdictional objection was filed first and the entry of appearance was merely a motion for extension of time. On the way out of the courthouse, my opposing counsel shook my hand and said, 'That was the right result', which goes to show that a good fiction is one that everyone can enjoy. Now, on to matters of greater import.

18.2 Securities Laws and Their Fictions

During the early days of the Roosevelt New Deal era, Congress enacted two landmark statutes aimed at the regulation of securities, the Securities Act of 1933 and the Securities Exchange Act of 1934. The 1933 Act was intended to 'provide full and fair disclosure of the character of securities sold in interstate and foreign commerce and through the mails, and to prevent frauds in the sale thereof, and for other purposes'.[4] The 1934 Act similarly sought 'to provide for the regulation of securities exchanges and of over-the-counter markets operating in interstate and foreign commerce and through the mails, to prevent inequitable and unfair practices on such exchanges and markets, and for other purposes' (p. 728). To this day, Section 10 of the 1934 Act makes it

> unlawful for any person ... (b) [t]o use or employ, in connection with the purchase or sale of any security registered on a national securities exchange or any security not so registered, any manipulative or deceptive device or contrivance in contravention of such rules and regulations as the [Securities and Exchange] Commission may prescribe as necessary or appropriate in the public interest or for the protection of investors.

In 1942, acting under the authority granted to it by § 10(b) of the 1934 Act, the Securities and Exchange Commission promulgated Rule 10b-5, which provides that:

> It shall be unlawful for any person, directly or indirectly, by the use of any means or instrumentality of interstate commerce, or of the mails or of any facility of any national securities exchange,
>
> a. To employ any device, scheme, or artifice to defraud,
> b. To make any untrue statement of a material fact or to omit to state a material fact necessary in order to make the statements made, in the light of the circumstances under which they were made, not misleading, or
> c. To engage in any act, practice, or course of business which operates or would operate as a fraud or deceit upon any person,

in connection with the purchase or sale of any security.

As the Supreme Court noted in *Blue Chip Stamps v. Manor Drug Stores,* Section 10(b) does not expressly provide a civil remedy for its violation, nor does its legislative history indicate that Congress considered the issue of private suits under it (p. 729). Similarly, that Court also registered 'the contrast between the provisions of Rule 10b-5 and the numerous carefully drawn express civil remedies provided in

[4] *Blue Chip Stamps v. Manor Drug Stores,* 421 U.S. 723, 727 (1975).

the Acts of both 1933 and 1934'.[5] So, looking solely at the text of the statute and the rule, one would conclude that there is no private right of action under either. Nonetheless, the Court acknowledged its previous confirmation 'with virtually no discussion … that such a cause of action did exist' (p. 730). Thus, I would submit that the whole area of private securities litigation has—right down to its roots—more than a whiff of fiction about it. By this I mean only that a court offering essentially no reason for ascribing an unstated intent to the legislature is indulging in a fiction.[6] But this particular indulgence is not our primary object of study here, although it of course looms in the background.

The Supreme Court has repeatedly held that 'the elements of a private securities fraud claim based on violations of 10(b) and Rule 10b-5 are: (1) a material misrepresentation or omission by the defendant; (2) scienter; (3) a connection between the misrepresentation or omission and the purchase or sale of a security; (4) reliance upon the misrepresentation or omission; (5) economic loss; and (6) loss causation.'[7] One of these elements—the fourth, reliance—causes a particular problem in private litigation because it stands as a potential obstacle to proceeding on behalf of *all* defrauded purchasers or sellers of the subject security in a single case (rather than on a plaintiff-by-plaintiff basis). Class actions gain their legitimacy from principles of judicial economy and efficiency, so a class action that doesn't promote economy and efficiency is by definition anathema. These principles animate Rule 23 of the Federal Rules of Civil Procedure,[8] which is loaded with standards that provide at least some guidance as to the desired characteristics for all class actions. Specifically, a court may not certify a class unless it finds that the prerequisites set out in Federal Rule of Civil Procedure 23(a) and at least one subsection of Rule 23(b) have been met.[9] The requirements of Rule 23(a) are commonly referred to as numerosity, commonality, typicality and adequacy. The requirements of 23(b) are not so easily captured in shorthand, but our discussion will be confined to (b)(3), which permits a class action if 'the court finds that the questions of law or fact common to the members of the class *predominate* over any questions affecting only individual members,

[5] See, e.g. §§ 11, 12, 15 of the 1933 Act, 15 U.S.C. §§ 77k, 77l, 77o; §§ 9, 16, 18, 20 of the 1934 Act, 15 U.S.C. §§ 78i, 78p, 78r, 78t. One might also note that both before and after passage of the primary securities acts, Congress has shown an ability clearly to articulate the existence of a private right of action. See, e.g., Section 4 of the Clayton Act, and Section 1964(c) of the RICO statute.

[6] Ultimately, the Court gave up all factual pretences to the issue: 'Judicial interpretation and application, legislative acquiescence, and the passage of time have removed any doubt that a private cause of action exists for a violation of § 10(b) and Rule 10b-5, and constitutes an essential tool for enforcement of the 1934 Act's requirements.' *Basic, Inc. v. Levinson,* 485 U.S. 224, 231 (1988).

[7] *Matrixx Initiatives, Inc. v. Siracusano,* 131 S. Ct. 1309, 1317 (2011).

[8] *Cf. Mace v. Van Ru Credit Corp.,* 109 F.3d 338, 344 (7th Cir. 1997) ('policy at the very core of the class action mechanism' aims to solve 'the problem that small recoveries do not provide the incentive for any individual to bring a solo action …') with *Andrews v. AT&T,* 95 F.3d 1014, 1025 (11th Cir. 1996) (although 'Rule 23 is to be applied flexibly, the manageability problems [here] defeat the Rule's underlying purposes and render these claims inappropriate for class treatment').

[9] *Amchem Prods., Inc. v. Windsor,* 521 U.S. 591, 614 (1997).

and that a class action is superior to other available methods for the fair and efficient adjudication of the controversy'.[10]

This requirement that common issues 'predominate' over individual issues is the sticking point because '[r]equiring proof of individualized reliance from each member of the proposed plaintiff class effectively would [prevent named plaintiffs] from proceeding with a class action, since individual issues then would … overwhelm[] the common ones'.[11] How then to bridge this gap between the substantive requirement of proof of reliance and the procedural requirement of predominance? Cast in Fuller's terms, how is a court in this situation 'to escape the consequences of an existing, specific rule of law' without simply ignoring it?

18.3 *Basic, Inc.* and its Economic Fiction

In *Basic, Inc. v. Levinson,* the US Supreme Court faced this very problem—and solved it with a fiction.[12] The case was based on allegations that Basic had lied three times in denying that it was conducting merger negotiations with a potential suitor, a suitor with which it ultimately struck a deal. The Court found that this situation 'required resolution of several common questions of law and fact concerning the falsity or misleading nature of the three public statements made by Basic, the presence or absence of scienter, and the materiality of the misrepresentations, if any. In their amended complaint, the named plaintiffs alleged that, in reliance on Basic's statements, they sold their shares of Basic stock in the depressed market created by [defendants]' (*Basic,* p. 242). As noted above, requiring proof of individualised reliance from each member of the proposed plaintiff class effectively would have prevented respondents from proceeding with a class action, since individual issues then would have swamped the common ones. To slip this knot, the Supreme Court invoked the fraud-on-the-market theory, which it described thusly:

> The fraud-on-the-market theory is based on the hypothesis that, in an open and developed securities market, the price of a company's stock is determined by the available material information regarding the company and its business … Misleading statements will therefore defraud purchasers of stock even if the purchasers do not directly rely on the misstatements … The causal connection between the defendants' fraud and the plaintiffs' purchase of stock in such a case is no less significant than in a case of direct reliance on misrepresentations. (*Basic,* p. 241)[13]

---

[10] Fed. R. Civ. P. 23 (b) (3) (emphasis added).

[11] *Basic, Inc. v. Levinson,* 485 U.S. 224, 231 (1988).

[12] In fraud cases, reliance is the usual—though not the only—way of showing that a misrepresentation proximately caused a plaintiff harm. When considered this way, the *Basic* fiction that we'll be discussing is just an instantiation of a common judicial move when a court is facing evidentiary gaps or procedural difficulties (see Lee, this volume, Chap. 12).

[13] The US Supreme Court fairly recently confirmed the ongoing viability of the theory and also held that—although a plaintiff must plead and prove loss causation (*Dura Pharmaceuticals, Inc. v. Broudo,* 125 S. Ct. 1627 (2005))—no proof of loss causation is required to invoke the

In adopting the theory, the Supreme Court tacitly agreed with the District Court, which had 'found that the presumption of reliance created by the fraud-on-the-market theory provided "a practical resolution to the problem of balancing the substantive requirement of proof of reliance in securities cases against the procedural requisites of [Federal Rule of Civil Procedure] 23"'. Interestingly, though, the Court seemed to hint that the theory might have no solid foundation: 'Our task, of course, is not to assess the general validity of the theory …' (*Basic,* p. 242).

Ultimately, the Court grounded its holding on the argument that modern fraud is different from historical fraud and that, consequently, the concepts of reliance and causation must change as well: 'The modern securities markets, literally involving millions of shares changing hands daily, differ from the face-to-face transactions contemplated by early fraud cases, and our understanding of Rule 10b-5's reliance requirement must encompass these differences' (*Basic,* pp. 243–244). And how best to do this? By deeming the 'market' the 'agent' of the investor:

> In face-to-face transactions, the inquiry into an investor's reliance upon information is into the subjective pricing of that information by that investor. With the presence of a market, the market is interposed between seller and buyer and, ideally, transmits information to the investor in the processed form of a market price. Thus, the market is performing a substantial part of the valuation process performed by the investor in a face-to-face transaction. The market is acting as the unpaid agent of the investor, informing him that given all the information available to it, the value of the stock is worth the market price. (*Basic,* pp. 243–244)[14]

With the stage thus dressed, the Court set out to justify its resort to this construct. First, it catalogued the salutary uses of presumptions in law: 'Presumptions typically serve to assist courts in managing circumstances in which direct proof, for one reason or another, is rendered difficult' (*Basic,* p. 245). Fuller would probably concede this point, but in his estimation, a 'conclusive presumption attributes to the facts "an arbitrary effect beyond their natural tendency to produce belief." It "attaches to any given possibility a degree of certainty to which it normally has no right. It knowingly gives an insufficient proof the value of a sufficient one"' (Fuller 1930–1931, p. 394). A conclusive presumption is thus fictional, even though its application in any given case may square with truth. With respect to rebuttable presumptions, Fuller observes that '[s]ome rebuttable presumptions have, in the course of time, gathered about them rules declaring what is sufficient to overcome them. So soon as you have begun to limit and classify those things which will rebut a presumption you are importing into the facts "an arbitrary effect" beyond their natural tendency to produce belief.' Accordingly, then, '[n]o presumption can be wholly non-fictitious which is not "freely" rebuttable'.

In *Basic,* the Court identified 'a presumption, created by the fraud-on-the-market theory and subject to rebuttal by petitioners, that persons who had traded Basic

fraud-on-the-market presumption for purposes of class certification. *Erica P. John Fund, Inc. v. Halliburton,* 131 S. Ct. 2179 (2011). But, as I note at the end of this paper, the Court has once again granted a petition for writ of certiorari in Halliburton, this time to consider overruling Basic.

[14] Here, the Court is relying on a lower-court decision, In re LTV Securities Litigation, 88 F.R.D. 134, 143 (N.D. Tex. 1980).

shares had done so in reliance on the integrity of the price set by the market, but because of petitioners' material misrepresentations that price had been fraudulently depressed' (p. 245). As justification, the Court stated that 'requiring a plaintiff to show a speculative state of facts, *i.e.,* how he would have acted if omitted material information had been disclosed, or if the misrepresentation had not been made, would place an unnecessarily unrealistic evidentiary burden on the Rule 10b-5 plaintiff who has traded on an impersonal market' (p. 245). But is this really so? Could not an individual plaintiff testify as to what he would or would not have done and let the jury determine the credibility of that testimony? The answer is 'of course', but it would be unwieldy (probably impossible) to march *every* purchaser or seller into the witness box to tell his or her story.[15]

The Court attempted to buttress this justification with appeals to Congressional policy and intent, as well as 'common sense and probability', including 'recent empirical studies [that] have tended to confirm Congress' premise that the market price of shares traded on well developed markets reflects all publicly available information, and, hence, any material misrepresentations. It has been noted that "it is hard to imagine that there ever is a buyer or seller who does not rely on market integrity. Who would knowingly roll the dice in a crooked crap game?"' (p. 247).

With respect to rebuttal, the Court held that '[a]ny showing that severs the link between the alleged misrepresentation and either the price received (or paid) by the plaintiff or his decision to trade at a fair market price will be sufficient to rebut the presumption of reliance' (*Basic,* p. 248). It listed three 'examples', which included 'market makers' who knew the truth, news leaking into the market, and plaintiffs who disbelieved Basic's false statements but traded for other reasons. As anticipated in Fuller's argument, *Basic*'s rebuttable presumption of reliance soon hardened into something close to a conclusive presumption: 15 years on, no defendant had successfully rebutted the presumption, and no court had allowed a defendant to invoke anything other than the three defences enumerated in *Basic* (Weiss and Beckerman 1995, p. 2077, n. 128). But what of this notion of 'market efficiency' upon which the presumption of reliance depends?

When the Court, as quoted above, stated that 'in an open and developed securities market, the price of a company's stock is determined by the available material information regarding the company and its business', it was wading into an economic swamp many decades in the making. Beginning in the late nineteenth century (seeds can be found even farther back in thinkers as diverse as Thomas Aquinas and Adam Smith), stock market gurus postulated that the value assigned to corporate shares in an open market reflects all information available about them (Fox 2009, p. xiii). This mindset soon crystallised into a theory, the rational market theory, which built from the observation that stock prices move randomly (referred to in finance literature as the 'random walk'), to the claim that one cannot predict stock prices based on public information, and on to the conclusion that stock prices

[15] Raymundo Gama (this volume, Chap. 16) suggests that one of the functional reasons for a court's resort to a presumption is 'to avoid a procedural impasse' (p. 361).

are fundamentally correct (p. xiv). As subsequent research has shown, though, these premises are not exactly right and the conclusion is in any event overstated.

18.4 A Random Walk Through Economic History

The drive to rationalise markets is probably just an instantiation of the larger drive prevalent in the nineteenth and twentieth centuries to make all the humanities and social sciences more 'scientific'. There is good evidence that the early proponents of the rational market theory (and its more legally significant adjunct, the 'efficient-market hypothesis') saw it as a construct—a model—not a complete description of the economic universe. In a landmark 1953 essay, Milton Friedman made a nod in this direction:

> [T]he relevant question to ask about the "assumptions" of a theory is not whether they are descriptively "realistic," for they never are, but whether they are sufficiently good approximations for the purpose in hand. And this question can be answered only by seeing whether the theory works, which means whether it yields sufficiently accurate predictions. (Quoted in Fox 2009, p. 76)

What Friedman is getting at here is the dissatisfaction that comes with purely mathematical descriptions of observed phenomena. This is why scientists build physical models to conceptualise the abstract and thereby offer a surface against which to sharpen their insights. Of course a model is only a representation of reality, but, for scientists, 'a good model is a successful compromise between simplicity and accuracy' (Brescia et al. 1975, p. 17). Accordingly, both pure and applied scientists build models that ignore troublesome, yet marginal, physical realities. Take, for example, the concept of an 'ideal gas', which consists of molecules having mass and velocity, but no volume, and showing no attractive or repulsive forces among themselves or with other matter.[16] The ideal gas disperses when unconfined and bounces off the walls of a container with no loss of energy. Despite these departures from reality, the ideal gas model pretty well describes the behaviour of many common gases at ordinary temperatures. Then too, Newtonian models—though at odds with relativity theory at high speeds and quantum mechanics at very small sizes—are generally good enough to keep planes in the air and buildings standing tall. In short, they're good enough for the workaday world.

In the same way, the rational-market hypothesis has had many salutary uses, including as the inspiration for index funds and the development of risk-management tools. So where did it go wrong? The answer is neither simple nor without qualification, but I would lay down three intersecting threads worth following. First, some economists became so enamoured with mathematics and game theory (facilitated

[16] Thanks to Burkhard Schafer for reminding me of this example. Simon Stern (this volume, Chap. 8) elaborates on the parallels between 'textbook' scientific models and artificial legal concepts to conclude that the value of these approximations resides in their ability to 'explain[] phenomena within [a] field' (p. 162).

by massive advances in computing power) that they gave short shrift to the realities of human behaviour (Morgan 2007, p. 165). For example, Friedman (along with statistician Jimmie Savage) proposed that John von Neuman and Oskar Morgenstern's mathematics-based utility theory could be used as a way to describe how people in *reality* make economic decisions: 'individuals behave *as if* they calculated and compared expected utility and *as if* they knew the odds' (quoted in Fox 2009, p. 75). Friedman famously justified this position with an analogy: billiards players act *as if* they know the underlying laws of physics. But, as with all tropes (we should regard 'as-if' as signalling the presence of a fiction), the analogy's usefulness must be limited by reality: e.g. the analogy cannot be literally true (or an expert billiard player would never miss a carom and would therefore always run out on points) (Vromen 2009, p. 262). The point here is that mathematics-inspired models can be useful as predictors, but they cannot be counted on to perform flawlessly.

Second, there was no agreement as to what was meant by the idea of market 'efficiency'. Three candidates emerged in a taxonomy proposed by Eugene Fama. 'Weak' efficiency implies only that one cannot beat the market using data on how the market has moved in the past. 'Semi-strong' efficiency means that one cannot beat the market using public information. (This is the version underpinning the *Basic* Court's holding.) 'Strong' efficiency describes an ideal market in which one cannot beat it even with access to private information (Fox 2009, p. 101). But by the late 1960s, some evidence began to appear that even weak-form market efficiency was not a given and that strong-form efficiency could not be true because there would be no incentive to develop proprietary information, a condition plainly contrary to fact.

Finally, 'behavioural' economists began to ask questions concerning how people actually make decisions in the face of uncertainty. What scholars like Daniel Kahneman and Amos Tversky found is that people are more heavily invested in the present than in the future (so that they are more frightened by the prospect of a loss today than they are elated by the prospect of a gain tomorrow) and that they evaluate probabilities at the margins different from those in between (Fox 2009, p. 183). And investigators following in this wake learned that people who chose to play the market traded too much, chased stocks that were performing well, and made less money than if they had invested in index funds (Fox 2009, p. 292; Erdlen 2008, p. 891; Ribstein 2006, p. 139–141). In other words, they behaved irrationally and inefficiently.

None of this is to suggest that the efficient-market hypothesis is useless or flat-out wrong.[17] But it is not the only valuable description of how markets work, and experts in the field have not accepted it as a fundamental in the way that would make it anything like a scientific fact. Indeed, after the financial collapse of 2008, the shortcomings of modern economics and finance were starkly revealed. As Princeton economist Paul Krugman opined in the depths of the recession, 'the economics profession went astray because economists, as a group, mistook beauty, clad in

[17] The hypothesis continues to have its defenders, either nearly wholesale (Klock 2010) or in the main (Ribstein 2001).

impressive-looking mathematics, for truth' (quoted in Fox 2009, p. 325). Put in our terms, they resorted to a fiction.

18.5 Fiction at the Crossroads of Law and Economics

Against this background, as many commentators have noted, the *Basic* Court's detour into an economic morass was not inevitable (Langevoort 2009, pp. 157–158). It could have, for instance, held that reliance is not an element of a 10b-5 claim—i.e. causation is key and reliance is but one way to demonstrate causation.[18] That is the tack that the Court has taken with respect to at least some other statutory-fraud claims (like civil RICO).[19] Or it could have adopted an outright fiction and held that a purchaser or seller of a registered security is 'deemed' to have relied on an issuer's statements. Two commentators have recently suggested that the Court actually did something stronger: viz., it created a new tort (Goldberg and Zipursky 2013). In a nutshell, their argument is that three types of recurring situations cause courts to resort to three corresponding types of presumptions. First, there are compliance-enhancing presumptions. These correct evidentiary asymmetries that—in the ordinary course of litigation—would result in false-negative outcomes for plaintiffs. Res ipsa loquitur is the paradigm here: if a plaintiff had to prove, for example, exactly how a barrel came to fall out a window, he would usually lose for want of precise evidence. The presumption corrects this asymmetry by allowing a jury—in the right kind of case—to infer carelessness (because a barrel doesn't typically fall out of a window unless the person with custody of and control over it has been careless). Second, there are substance-morphing presumptions. These go beyond evidentiary issues and effectively change the substance of legal rules. The "tender years" doctrine is a good example: in many states, a child below a certain age is conclusively presumed not to have been careless. This is a policy choice that—as a practical matter—removes an entire category of cases from the reach of ordinary negligence law. Third, there are mixed presumptions. These serve both evidentiary and substance-modifying ends. Two-shooter negligence cases give rise to a classic example: a plaintiff is injured by one of two hunters and the evidence is equivocal as to both. This gives rise to the alternative liability doctrine, which is (1) compliance-enhancing because it avoids early dismissals for want of specific pleading or proof and incentivizes those with superior access to evidence (the defendants) to produce it and (2) substance-morphing because it creates a new rule of tort law in which a defendant may be liable to a plaintiff without proof that he caused the plaintiff's injury.

If we examine the *Basic* presumption through the lens of this scheme, at least at first blush, it appears to be a simple compliance-enhancing maneuver: absent the

[18] For a Benthamite, though, this would amount to trading one fiction for another because the concept of 'causation' is itself a fiction Quinn, this volume, Chap. 4, p. 72).

[19] See, e.g. *Bridge v. Phoenix bond & Indemnity Co.*, 533 U.S. 639, 650–660 (2008).

presumption, class actions would fail and thereby impair an aspect of securities regulation because it would be impracticable to have every member of a class provide evidence that she relied *on the contents of defendants' misrepresentations*. But, as Goldberg and Zipursky go on to opine, the *Basic* presumption doesn't address that question: instead, it holds that every purchaser or seller relied *that the market price was not distorted.* This, they say, marks a change in the substantive rules, one constituting 'a new statutory tort' (1799).

We needn't decide whether this new tort description is exactly right. For our purposes, it's enough to note that the Court did not explicitly adopt this approach (or one of the others that I suggested above as possibilities) and chose to cloak a fictional kernel within a presumptive shell. The fiction here is that its version of the fraud-on-the-market theory pivots on the Court's belief that the efficient-market hypothesis not only reflects reality but that there was general agreement at the time that this was so. But as we just noted, and as Justice White noted in dissent, the majority's insistence that purchasers and sellers rely on the 'integrity' of market prices as reflection of 'value' was at odds with both some prior case-law and some then-current economic studies (*Basic,* pp. 255–256).[20]

At the end of the day, the Court created what many have considered a 'muddle', and its 'obfuscation about the role of efficiency sent the [lower] courts off on a long journey without a particularly good compass' (Langevoort 2009, p. 167). So why did the Court base its holding on a theory that was undeveloped, untested and at least partially fictive? I would offer two answers, one pragmatic, the other rhetorical. The pragmatic answer, as I already suggested, is that the efficient-market hypothesis solved a procedural problem: 'Without the … hypothesis, there appeared to be a loophole in using the class action remedy for securities fraud' because defendants could credibly argue that individual issues of reliance would require separate trials on a class member by class member basis (Dunbar and Heller 2006, p. 457). And this would defeat one of the animating forces behind the class-action device—namely, that the most compelling reason for a class action is the 'negative value' suit (i.e. a suit in which the damages for each plaintiff are so small that no reasonable person would bother to sue).[21] As a consequence, in the case of a widely held security, a fraud that causes a relatively small injury on an individual basis—yet massive in the aggregate—could go unremedied and thereby thwart Section 10b. So the Court made a *policy* decision to shore up the class device with an economic theory that came with an associated cost to the legal rules involved. Thus, '*Basic* cannot be understood except by appreciating that the Court's response is far more a lesson in civil procedure than financial economics' (Langevoort 2009, p. 158).

As a matter of rhetoric, Justice White was probably on to something when he posited that what the majority found alluring was that it could hide behind a shield

---

[20] See also Dunbar and Heller (2006, p. 523): 'While there were doubts about the theory at the time, and even the different measures of market efficiency were not necessarily clear, the efficient market hypothesis seemed to have been the right theory at the right time for the purposes that the Court was attempting to address'.

[21] See *Castano v. American Tobacco Co.,* 84 F.3d 734 (5th Cir. 1996).

of 'scientific' authenticity: 'For while the economists' theories which underpin the fraud-on-the-market presumption may have the appeal of mathematical exactitude and scientific certainty, they are—in the end—nothing more than theories which may or may not prove accurate upon further consideration' (*Basic,* p. 253). His central point here is that the majority was wrapping itself in a scientific cloak for a *rhetorical* reason—namely, to borrow the authority of science and thereby give strength to its own, (After all, the methods of science are offered as objective and neutral, cardinal virtues of any system of justice).

Fuller might have branded this move a 'creative' fiction either (1) born of 'the motive of policy', which may uncharitably be described as a deceit contrived to disguise a usurpation of legislative authority or, more generously, as an obscurity 'serv[ing] to create the impression that the change is no greater than that involved in the ordinary case'; or (2) born of the 'motive of convenience', 'which brings the reform within the linguistic cover of existing law' (Fuller 1930–1931, pp. 519–520). In *Basic,* as we've already noted, the majority stressed that the complexities of the modern world compelled it to act (*Basic,* p. 244). In taking this turn, the Court confirmed Robert Ferguson's (1990, p. 213) observation that the various writing strategies that an appellate court employs tend to cohere in what he calls a 'rhetoric of inevitability'. In any event, Justice White saw another 'inevitability': 'Confusion and contradiction in court rulings are inevitable when traditional legal analysis is replaced with economic theorisation by the federal courts.' His point was essentially twofold, both prudential and jurisdictional. First, 'with no staff economists, no experts schooled in the efficient market hypothesis, no ability to test the validity of empirical market studies, [federal courts] are not well equipped to embrace novel constructions of a statute based on contemporary microeconomic theory' (*Basic,* p. 253). Second, even if securities markets have undergone radical transformations because of technology and other advancements, Justice White

> … prefer[red] that such changes come from Congress in amending 10(b). The Congress, with its superior resources and expertise, is far better equipped than the federal courts for the task of determining how modern economic theory and global financial markets require that established legal notions of fraud be modified. In choosing to make these decisions itself, the Court, I fear, embarks on a course that it does not genuinely understand, giving rise to consequences it cannot foresee. (*Basic,* p. 254)

18.6 Law and the Allure of Science

Why the turn to science in *Basic*? The key may be found, I think, in law's claims to legitimacy, which hinge, at least in significant part, on what Gerald Postema has identified as 'the objectivity of characteristic modes of reasoning and the normative judgments they produce' (2001, p. 101)—namely, the popular belief that 'scientific' evidence is evidence of truth.[22] 'The idea that scientific inquiry is objective

[22] For a discussion of these notions of objectivity and law and economics in the context of narrative theory, see Gordon (2011, pp. 160–164, 194–195).

is unquestionably among the ruling ideas of our epoch, and it represents science as not serving the interests of a particular class, but a purely general interest in the understanding of nature. Indeed, the idea of scientific objectivity has often been invoked on behalf of the claim that the attitude of modern science is "the only rational, universally valid" one' (Railton 1991, p. 763).[23] And, even in law, science has brought certainty to many questions that heretofore could only be answered with unreliable means and with an uncomfortable degree of inaccuracy.[24] Think, for example, of the famous and comical paternity trial of Charlie Chaplin, who was found to be the father of Carol Ann Berry based on 'what the butler said' and what the child looked like, even though undisputed and impartial blood-typing evidence showed that Chaplin could not have been the father.[25] Or, more recently, consider the dozens of individuals cleared by DNA evidence, even though they had been convicted years before with seemingly objective things like eye-witness testimony. In sum, objectivity-believers lodge their faith in the Enlightenment position that, as Peter Railton puts it, 'objectivity follows automatically once we proceed rationally' (p. 764). Not surprisingly, then, lawyers and judges often invoke concepts of objectivity in support of their arguments and judgments (Postema 2001, p. 115).[26]

Now we may ask a narrower question: Why economics? Although few today would argue that law itself is a 'science' in the way that David Dudley Field and Christopher Columbus Langdell argued in the nineteenth century, standards of scientific objectivity as the gold standard still hold sway. Oliver Wendell Holmes was perhaps never more prescient than when he said in 1897 that '[f]or the rational study of the law the blackletter man may be the man of the present, but the man of the future is the man of statistics and the master of economics'. This fits hand-in-glove with Holmes's 'predictive' theory of law, which valorised above all tools that would allow legal observers to predict how judges would rule in particular cases. Science, of course, offers an attractive model for the very reason that it has shown itself adept at explaining (at least in controlled conditions and across a limited range of inquiry) what happened in the past and what is likely to happen in the future. But it remains true that economics has far fewer 'laws' at its disposal than do the hard sciences and that scientists do not use hypotheses to generate 'facts', even though a hypothesis is often a useful way of positing what may prove to be the case once experimental techniques catch up (e.g. as I am writing this, maybe the existence of the Higgs boson was confirmed). But it seems to me that that when the law is using a *hypothesis* to settle a *fact*, that may be one indication that we are in the presence of a fiction.

At any rate, Holmes's anticipation of the ultimate rise of economics in law has proven more or less true in many ways—e.g. the Law and Economics movement

[23] Of course, some have argued that science cannot rid itself of the human dimension through which it is practised and so bias inevitably creeps in. For a neat summary of this issue see, Grinnell (2008, pp. 10–18).

[24] For this reason (and others) legal language has for some time been under pressure to conform to—or at least accommodate—scientific vocabulary (Petroski, this volume, Chap. 7, p. 149).

[25] *Berry v. Chaplin,* 169 P.2d 442 (Cal. App. 1946).

[26] Postema cites *Whitney v. California,* 274 U.S. 357, 372 (1927) (Brandeis concurring) (we want our society to be one in which 'deliberative forces prevail over the arbitrary').

has proven influential inside both the academy and courthouses. I'm thinking here foremost of Judge Richard Posner's reflections on the subject; his thoughts are of special importance because he was an early and certainly the most visible proponent of economic legal analysis.[27] Plainly, Posner once hoped that economics held the interdisciplinary key that would unlock the secret to a perfectly functioning legal system (and explain the breakdowns in less than perfectly functioning legal systems). Thus, in 1975, he was able to opine that an

> … important finding emerging from the recent law and economics research is that the legal system itself—its doctrines, procedures and institutions—has been strongly influenced by a concern (more often implicit than explicit) with promoting economic efficiency … The idea that the logic of the law is really economics is, of course, repulsive to many academic lawyers, who see in it an attempt by practitioners of an alien discipline to wrest their field from them. Yet the positive economic analysis of legal institutions is one of the most promising as well as most controversial branches of the new law and economics. It seeks to define and illuminate the basic character of the legal system, and it has made at least some progress toward that ambitious goal. (Posner 1975, pp. 763—764)

More recently, however, Posner has retreated from the notion of an all-embracing theory of law formed by yoking the precepts of a unified normative system (like utilitarianism) to the teachings of economics: 'It has been many years since I flirted with such an approach' (2003, p. 78).[28]

But that does not mean that economics does not inform legal analysis in deep and significant ways. For good or ill, economic concepts have swamped all others in my primary practice area (anti-trust). In most federal courts, an anti-trust plaintiff cannot state a claim in most types of cases brought under the Sherman Act unless he can plead—in his initial complaint—that competition has been injured in a market defined in precise *economic* terms.[29] And this is so no matter how ruthlessly anti-competitive the conduct at issue is alleged to be. As a consequence, it is impossible to practise, teach or write about anti-trust law without having a solid working knowledge of economic concepts, and the influence of economics does not end there. As Posner aptly observes, '[o]ne by-product of [law and economics] research that has considerable pedagogical importance has been the assignment of precise economic explanations to a number of fundamental legal concepts that had previously puzzled students and their professors, such as "assumption of risk," pain and suffering as a category of tort damages, contract damages for loss of expectation, plea bargaining, and the choice between damages and injunctive relief' (1975, p. 764).

[27] Posner's (1971, 1975) most influential work in the law and economics vein began to appear in the early 1970s. The seminal work in what we now think of as law-and-economics analysis traces to a decade earlier, especially with the work of (now Judge) Guido Calabresi and Ronald Coase; see Calabresi 1961; Coase 1960.

[28] Even more recently, Posner (2010, p. 278) has suggested that the current economic crisis has undermined the efficient-market hypothesis.

[29] See, e.g. *Apani Southwest, Inc. v. Coca-Cola Enters.*, 300 F. 3d 620, 628 (5th Cir. 2002) ('Where the plaintiff fails to define its proposed relevant market with reference to the rule of reasonable interchangeability and cross-elasticity of demand, or alleges a proposed relevant market that clearly does not encompass all interchangeable substitute products even when all factual inferences are granted in plaintiff's favor, the relevant market is legally insufficient, and a motion to dismiss may be granted').

None of this general 'helpfulness' means that economics avoids the pitfalls that are spread throughout all the social sciences. Indeed, over a century ago, John Ruskin decried the scientific pretensions of economics that—in his view—ignored the social realities of human experience:

> Among the delusions which at different periods have possessed themselves of the minds of large masses of the human race, perhaps the most curious—certainly the least creditable—is the modern *soi-disant* science of political economy, based on the idea that an advantageous code of social action may be determined irrespectively of the influence of social affection. (1881, p. 17)

Ruskin's point is that—even though it *looks* like science from a lay perspective because it brims with formulas and numbers—a maths-oriented mode of economic analysis will always be incomplete because it is aimed at *social* phenomena (as opposed to or in addition to *natural* phenomena). Ultimately, I can only register that whether economics is or is not a science is a debate that continues to this day and is one that I cannot hope to resolve here. But suffice it to say that even Posner early on conceded that 'economics is an incomplete and imperfect science' (1975, p. 772). Nonetheless, economics is alluring as a haven from contingency and powerful as a rhetorical mode. This is so, I think, because it can be made to appear as if it were not a human artefact, which it to say that it can be dressed up to appear objective, neutral and independent of human whim and bias. Here's how.

Legal and moral rules depend on human agency and social context (polygamy is illegal and wrong, except where it is not), whereas physical laws do not (the Second Law of Thermodynamics holds no matter what we think about it). Economics facially seems closer to the second category than the first (again, because it uses equations and such), and its predictive failures can be ascribed to its relative immaturity as a discipline or the fact that its inputs are currently too complex and numerous for us to process (which may not always be the case, of course). By some lights, then, this puts economics in the objective-and-neutral camp, which means that its results are superior to those generated by legal rules as interpreted and applied by human agents because they are dictated by 'real' laws. In other words, economics can produce a fact of the matter in cases that would otherwise generate sharp divisions of opinion amongst legal observers (for example cases that present difficult or novel problems of classification or categorisation).

18.7 Conclusion: Law, Narrative, Economics (and a Dollop of Irony)

What is at work here is probably nothing more than the human desire for coherence, to make sense of it all. Because humans process, store and retrieve information in narrative form, it is not all that surprising that we have created explanatory narratives to make sense of economic phenomena that we cannot directly or completely observe. And, as with many other instances of socially constructed narratives, 'myth' and 'fiction' are words that capture at least some of the underpinnings of our economic narratives. So just as our ancestors spun stories about Thor's hammer or

Apollo's chariot to explain natural phenomena as diverse as the sound of thunder and the movement of the sun, we rely on the narratives of social science to bring sense to things like currency fluctuations and the gyrations of the stock market (Ruskin quipped that, 'as in the instances of alchemy, astrology, witchcraft, and other such popular creeds, political economy has a plausible idea at the root of it' (1881, p. 17)). At bottom, then, one way to explain the economic turn in law is to think of it as a double engraftment: the narrative of scientific progress engrafted onto economics followed by the engraftment of economics onto law itself. And as with all hybrids, we will have to see what fruit this new creation finally bears.

In any event, given the ascendancy of law-and-economics thought in the early 1980s, it is not surprising that it began to infect the way that lawyers and judges thought about securities markets. And it is even less surprising that the impetus for efficient-market thinking came from Judge Posner's University of Chicago colleagues, specifically Daniel Fischel and Frank Easterbrook (who is now Posner's colleague on the Seventh Circuit). But what is surprising is that, as Donald Langevoort demonstrates, the *Basic* Court essentially misinterpreted Fischel and Easterbrook's work, which found reliance 'trivial in the context of market efficiency'. Their approach requires causation only and their theory is focused on 'assessing materiality and measuring damages' (Langevoort 2009, p. 165). And in one of the law's little ironies, their essentially conservative and scientific approach under which markets are efficient and hard to fool (so genuine fraud cases are rare)—'staying close to the scientific method thus checks unnecessary litigation'—was hijacked in a way that led to an explosion of litigation (p. 189). In any event, '[d]oubts about the strength and pervasiveness of market efficiency are much greater today than they were in the mid-1980s' (p. 175), and, accordingly, an inevitable backlash set it.

Although the *Basic* Court intended its question 'Who would knowingly roll the dice in a crooked crap game?' to be rhetorical, it turns out that the answer is 'lots of people'.[30] This sort of uneasiness about the economic soundness of the fraud-on-the-market presumption, coupled with a widespread dismay at the number of post-*Basic* securities-fraud 'strike suits', led courts and Congress to take action. For example, some courts have found that particular securities do not trade on efficient markets (Mustokoff 2008, pp. 227–228) and almost all courts have declined to extend the *Basic* presumption to non-securities cases.[31] Congress, for its part, passed the Public Securities Litigation Reform Act in 1995, which—although leaving the fraud-on-the-market presumption intact—sharply curtailed a range of abusive litigation practices.[32] And just last year, in *Amgen, Inc. v. Connecticut Retirement*

[30] See Dunbar and Heller (2006, p. 521) (listing as reasons, among others, that even rational investors might trade without believing in the validity of the market price if (1) they are reacting to cash flows, (2) there are no close substitutes, (3) they believe that a bubble will continue, (4) they are herding because they weigh the decisions of others more than information about fundamentals, or (5) they use simple strategies like momentum trading).

[31] See, e.g., *McLaughlin v. American Tobacco Co.*, 522 F.3d 215 (2nd Cir. 2008) (cigarette market); *Sikes v. Teleline, Inc.*, 281 F.3d 1350 (11th Cir. 2002) (certain telephone services).

[32] See Oldham (2002), discussing, among other things, the legislative history of the PSLRA.

Plans & Trust Funds,[33] four Supreme Court Justices called *Basic* into question and suggested that it was time to revisit its holding. Justice Alito went so far as to state that 'reconsideration of the Basic presumption may be appropriate' because 'more recent evidence suggests that that the presumption may rest of a faulty economic premise.' Even more recently, the Supreme Court granted a petition for writ of certiorari in *Halliburton v. Erica P. John Fund*; the petition requested the Court to overrule (or at least significantly modify the presumption of reliance endorsed by) *Basic*, so that specific issue is currently slated for decision.

Not unexpectedly, the petitioners in *Halliburton* have drawn the Court's attention to the literature and arguments that we reviewed above. They do so in two ways: first, they object to the way that the *Basic* Court allowed an *economic* theory to infect the answer to a *legal* question; second, they maintain that the situational use of a fiction in the securities context has warped the otherwise consistent standards that the Court has devised for evaluating the propriety of class actions:

> The *Basic* majority erred by substituting economic theory for law—and bad economic theory at that. In the years since *Basic*, scholars have roundly rejected its approach to market efficiency. Meanwhile, *Basic*'s legal framework has proven unworkable in the lower courts and inconsonant with this Court's recent decisions. Relying on an acknowledged fiction, *Basic* allows certification of internally disparate classes that would not be tolerated outside of the securities-fraud context. As a judge-made rule that generates no societal reliance interests, *Basic*'s presumption is ripe for reconsideration.[34]

The *Halliburton* respondent of course tells a different story, one gauged to fit within notions of common tradition and settled expectations: '[t]he fraud-on-the-market presumption, adopted by this Court in *Basic*, has been repeatedly endorsed by this Court, Congress, the SEC, and the DOJ and enjoys widespread support among economists.'[35] This argument tacitly posits that a fiction—once sufficiently institutionalized—becomes a fact and cannot be undone without doing violence to *stare decisis* and, thereby, the Rule of Law.

After these latest turns of the screw, we are left with a fiction that is still viable, but under a degree of assault that has probably—and fairly quickly!—put it on one of the two evolutionary paths that Fuller identified. Will it be rejected? Or will it be redefined? It is hard to say. But we can be certain that, as Fuller (1930–1931, p. 366) said more generally of fictions, we should continue to 'take this skeleton in the family of the law … from its closet and examine[] [it] thoroughly. After that examination we may decide what we ought to do with it'. And *that* task is one that the US Supreme Court has set for itself in *Halliburton.*

Acknowledgments This chapter has its genesis in a paper presented at a seminar on 'Legal Fictions' at the IVR 2011. World Congress. Thanks to Maks Del Mar for organising the seminar and for many helpful suggestions along the way. A version of this chapter was previously published as 'Fictitious Fraud: Economics and the Presumption of Reliance' (2013) 4 *International Journal of Law in Context* 506–519.

[33] 133 S. Ct. 1184 (2013).

[34] Petition for a Writ of Certiorari, *Halliburton v. Erica P. John Fund,* No. 13–317 at 11.

[35] Brief in Opposition *Halliburton v. Erica P. John Fund,* No. 13–317 at 30.

References

Brescia, Frank, John, Arents, Herbert, Meisclich, and Amos Turk. 1975. *Fundamentals of chemistry*. 3rd ed. New York: Academic Press.

Calabresi, Guido. 1961. Some thoughts on risk distribution and the law of torts. *Yale Law Journal* 70:499–553.

Coase, Ronald. 1960. The problem of social cost. *Journal of Law & Economics* 3:1–69.

Del Mar, Maksymilian. 2014. Legal fictions and legal change in the common law tradition. In *Legal fictions in theory and practice,* ed. Maksymilian Del Mar and William Twining. Dordrecht: Springer.

Dunbar, Frederick C., and Dana Heller. 2006. Fraud on the market meets behavioral finance. *Delaware Journal of Corporate Law* 31:455–532.

Erdlen, Andrew. 2008. Timing is everything: Markets, loss, and proof of causation in fraud on the market actions. *Fordham Law Review* 80:877–922.

Ferguson, Robert A. 1990. The judicial opinion as literary genre. *Yale Journal of Law & Humanities* 2:201–219.

Fox, Justin. 2009. *The myth of the rational market*. New York: HarperCollins.

Fuller, L. L. 1930–1931. Legal fictions. *Illinois Law Review* 25:363–399, 513–546, 877–910.

Gama, Raymundo. 2014. Presumptions and fictions: A Collingwoodian approach. In *Legal fictions in theory and practice,* ed. Maksymilian Del Mar and William Twining. Dordrecht: Springer.

Goldberg, John C. P. and Benjamin C. Zipursky. 2013. The fraud-on-the-market tort. *Vanderbilt Law Review* 66:1755–1806.

Gordon, Randy. 2011. *Rehumanizing law: A theory of law and democracy*. Toronto: University of Toronto Press.

Grinnell, Frederick. 2008. *Everyday practice of science: Where intuition and passion meet objectivity and logic*. New York: Oxford University Press.

Holmes, Oliver Wendell. 1897. The path of the law. *Harvard Law Review* 10:457–478.

Klock, Mark. 2010. Contrasting the art of economic science with pseudo-economic nonsense: The distinction between reasonable assumptions and ridiculous assumptions. *Pepperdine Law Review* 37:153–203.

Langevoort, Donald C. 2009. Basic at twenty: Rethinking fraud on the market. *Wisconsin Law Review* 2009:151–198.

Lee, James. 2014. Fictions in tort. In *Legal fictions in theory and practice,* ed. Maksymilian Del Mar and William Twining. Dordrecht: Springer.

Morgan, Mary. 2007. The curious case of the prisoner's dilemma: Model situation? Exemplary narrative? In *Science without laws: Model systems, cases, exemplary narratives,* eds. Angela N. H. Creager, et al., 157–185. Durham: Duke University Press.

Mustokoff, Mathew L. 2008. Fraud not on the market: Rebutting the presumption of reliance twenty years after Basic, Inc. v. Levinson. *Hastings Business Law Journal* 4 (2): 225–250.

Oldham, Jeffrey L. 2002. Taking "efficient markets" out of the fraud-on-the-market doctrine after the private securities litigation reform act. *Northwestern University Law Review* 97 (2): 995–1044.

Petroski, Karen. 2014. Legal fictions and the limits of legal language. In *Legal fictions in theory and practice,* ed. Maksymilian Del Mar and William Twining. Dordrecht: Springer.

Posner, Richard A. 1971. Killing or wounding to protect a property interest. *Journal of Law and Economics* 14:201–232.

Posner, Richard A. 1975. The economic approach to law. *Texas Law Review* 53:757–782.

Posner, Richard A. 2003. *Law, pragmatism and democracy*. Cambridge: Harvard University Press.

Posner, Richard A. 2010. On the receipt of the Ronald H. Coase Medal: Uncertainty, the economic crisis, and the future of law and economics. *American Law and Economics Review* 12 (2): 265–279.

Postema, Gerald. 2001. Objectivity fit for law. In *Objectivity in law and morals,* ed. Brian Leiter, 99–143. New York: Cambridge University Press.

Railton, Peter. 1991. Marx and the objectivity of science. In *The philosophy of science,* eds. Richard Boyd et al., 763–773. Cambridge: MIT Press.
Ribstein, Mark. 2001. Rational markets: Yes or no? The affirmative case. *Financial Analysts Journal* 57:15–29.
Ribstein, Mark. 2006. Fraud on a noisy market. *Lewis and Clark Law Review* 10:137–168.
Ruskin, John. 1881. *Unto this last.* New York: Wiley.
Stern, Simon. 2014. Legal fictions and exclusionary rules. In *Legal fictions in theory and practice,* ed. Maksymilian Del Mar and William Twining. Dordrecht: Springer.
Vromen, Jack. 2009. Friedman's selection argument revisited. In *The methods of positive economics,* ed. Uskali Maki, 257–284. Cambridge: Cambridge University Press.
Weiss, Elliott and John Beckerman. 1995. Let the money do the monitoring: How institutional investors can reduce agency costs in securities class actions. *Yale Law Journal* 104:2053–2127.

Index

M. Del Mar, W. Twining (eds.), *Legal Fictions in Theory and Practice*,
Law and Philosophy Library 110, DOI 10.1007/978-3-319-09232-4

9783319092317